P9-DFI-705

Leonard J. Arrington

Brigham Young: American Moses

University of Illinois Press Urbana and Chicago

Illini Books edition, 1986

Published by arrangement with Alfred A. Knopf, Inc.
Copyright © 1985 by Leonard J. Arrington
Manufactured in the United States of America
P   5   4   3   2   1

LIBRARY OF CONGRESS CATALOGING IN PUBLICATION DATA
Arrington, Leonard J.
  Brigham Young: American Moses.
  Bibliography: p.
  Includes index.
  1. Young, Brigham, 1801-1877.   2. Church of
Jesus Christ of Latter-day Saints—Presidents—
Biography.   3. Mormon Church—Presidents—Biography.
I. Title.
[BX8695.Y7A85 1986] 289.3'32'0924 [B] 85-24533
ISBN 0-252-01296-8

LINCOLN CHRISTIAN COLLEGE

Brigham
Young:
American
Moses

TO MY ASSOCIATES IN CAMELOT

75944

CONTENTS

LIST OF ILLUSTRATIONS

Illustrations were provided courtesy of the following organizations:
The Church of Jesus Christ of Latter-day Saints Graphics Library (LDS)
Utah State Historical Society Photograph Collection (USHS)
University of Illinois and Huntington Library (UI)

ACKNOWLEDGMENTS

I owe the greatest debt to two colleagues. The first is Davis Bitton, my close associate in the Historical Department of the Church of Jesus Christ of Latter-day Saints for ten years and professor of history at the University of Utah. He has given me almost daily counsel on Mormon history, made cogent comments on my manuscript, chapter by chapter, and helped me to interpret Brigham Young's doctrinal pronouncements. I am indebted, secondly, to Ronald K. Esplin, Research Historian with the Joseph Fielding Smith Institute for Church History at Brigham Young University, whose primary assignment, from 1973 to 1980, was to assist with the organization and identification of the enormous mass of Brigham Young papers in the LDS Church Archives, Salt Lake City. Dr. Esplin's acquaintance with these papers and his willingness to share his expertise have made it possible for me to use these masses of materials with the greatest effectiveness. He also supervised the preparation of typescripts of much of this material.

Nearly all of the transcribing was done by Edyth Jenkins Romney, surely one of the most cheerful, dependable, and intelligent of typists. Now in her late seventies, she is still directing her labor to the continuation of this effort.

I acknowledge also the help of several research assistants who have combed through the abundant materials in the LDS Archives for useful information. Richard Jensen has helped with the research on Brigham's direction of immigration; William G. Hartley, on the work of the bishops and priesthood quorums; Rebecca Cornwall, on Young's family and religious background and his meetings with literary figures; Lawrence Coates, on Indian affairs; and Linda Wilcox on Brigham as an administrator and correspondent. JoAnn Jolley followed Brigham across the plains; Ronald W. Walker furnished autobiographical statements; and Dr. Walker and Lavina Fielding Anderson helped improve my writing style. Maureen Beecher, Carol Madsen, Jill Mulvay Derr, and Jeffrey Johnson have provided information on the women in Brigham's life—his wives, his daughters, and his associates in administering church programs. Dean Jessee has answered innumerable questions about Mormon history and generously shared material in his files. Elder G. Homer Durham has lent support to the project, as did Elder Joseph Anderson and Presidents Harold B. Lee and Spencer W. Kimball. Earl Olson and Donald T. Schmidt gave permission for the extensive use of materials in the Church Archives. I am grateful as well to the LDS Archives and the Utah State Historical Society for permission to use photographs in their collections. None of these, however, is to be held responsible for the material included, or for any errors in fact and interpretation.

I should also make it clear that this book was written entirely on my own time, and the research assistants who have helped me plow through the vast amount of manuscript material have done so at no expense to the Mormon church. Moreover, Latter-day Saint authorities have not screened this volume for its suitability for Mormon readers. In short, this has been a private, not a church project.

I am grateful to Ron Watt, archivist; Gordon Irving, oral historian; Glen Leonard, museum director; James B. Allen and Dean Martin Hickman of Brigham Young University; L. Dwight Israelsen of Utah State University; and my secretaries, Chris Waters, Nedra Pace, Kathy Stephens, Mary Miller, and Kathleen Anderson. Many colleagues and associates in the Mormon History Association have shared their knowledge of various localities in which Brigham Young lived and events in which he participated. I have tried to give them credit in the bibliography and reference notes. This has not been a "one man" project; I owe a deep debt to many scholars.

My son James Arrington, who as an actor and playwright has studied Brigham Young's character and personality for several years, has been generous with his help, as has my son Carl Arrington, a writer and editor in New York City and Los Angeles. My daughter, Susan Madsen, has listened to many sketches that have gone into this book. I have benefited from her suggestions as well as those of my late wife, Grace Arrington, who, until her unfortunate death, enthusiastically encouraged me in this long and demanding project. To my present wife, Harriet Ann, I express gratitude for unrestrained and loving support.

Finally, I am grateful to the family of the late David W. and Beatrice Cannon Evans, who generously established the Evans Award for the best unpublished or recently published biography of a person who has played a significant role in Mormon country during the past 150 years. The awards committee, which consisted of Howard Lamar of Yale University, Merlo Pusey of the Washington *Post*, and Ray West, Jr., a distinguished literary critic, was very kind in declaring this book the winner for 1984, the first year the prize was awarded. I express to them my profound thanks.

LEONARD J. ARRINGTON
Salt Lake City
June 1984

PREFACE

Brigham Young was a kingdom builder with dreams as grandiose as those of Sam Houston or John C. Frémont. Unlike them, he was successful. Yet when he is mentioned by historians and biographers, he usually appears as an anomaly, a freak, rather than as an expression of some of the most deeply held characteristics included in the word "American."

The reason is not hard to find. Brigham Young's kingdom was religious rather than secular, a theocracy, in his mind a kingdom of God. Americans are always uneasy with such causes except when they are melded with the national or civil religion. And Mormonism, however American in some respects, repelled and frightened many who observed it. Young's success might have been forgiven; his otherworldliness, never.

He was a hard-headed Yankee businessman, as shrewdly aware of the West's exploitable properties as were the men who put together Wells Fargo, the pony express, the transcontinental railway. But he exerted every ounce of his personal and ecclesiastical influence to keep his people out of the California gold fields; he poured the surplus of the church into bringing emigrants to his mountain Zion; and when the United States Army threatened the Mormons, he stood ready to abandon and burn all that they had accumulated. The businessmen who might have been comfortable negotiating with him as a partner in the rape of the West's resources suspected—and the suspicion made them uneasy—that his bottom line was not cash but the souls of men.

Brigham Young was the supreme American paradox, not because he contained elements foreign to American soil but because he united them—the business genius of a Rockefeller with the spiritual sensitivities of an Emerson, the lusty enjoyment of the pleasures of good living with the tenderness of a Florence Nightingale. He was not merely an entrepreneur with a shared vision of America as the Promised Land; he was a prophet with visions of his own and he built beyond himself.

Small wonder, then, that the popular image of Brigham Young in his own lifetime was usually simplified to two manageable stereotypes: Brigham the Lecher, presiding over the comic opera of his many-wived household; or Brigham the Tyrant, stark against the background of the Mountain Meadows Massacre with a bloodthirsty cloud of Danites hovering in anticipation of his commands. He was too complex for minds that could respect either power or piety but had not seen them, in the American system, combined so insistently before.

Attempts to portray Brigham Young accurately have had to wait until now, more than a century after his death, both for the glamour of the image to fade and also for some important manuscript sources to become available. Like many flamboyantly public men, Brigham Young was also intensely private in important ways. Identified closely as he was with the Church of Jesus Christ of Latter-day Saints, which combines the publicity of a vigorous proselyting program with a recognition of the bedrock importance of private spiritual experience, Brigham has also had to wait for the church itself to come of age, so that both he and it can be appraised objectively.

Previous attempts have suffered most frequently from inadequate documentation and the author's preformed bias—either for or against the Mormon leader. A kind of "official" biography appeared as the "History of Brigham Young" serially in two Mormon newspapers, the *Deseret News* of Salt Lake City in 1858 and the *Latter-day Saints' Millennial Star* of Liverpool in 1863–64. Written by personnel in the Mormon Church Historian's Office, it was based on Young's holograph diaries, 1832–44, and consists mainly of brief chronological accounts of Young's experiences in the church, without much commentary. It was recently reissued by Elden Watson, a Salt Lake bibliophile.

While Young was still alive, Mormon Edward W. Tullidge published *Life of Brigham Young; or, Utah and Her Founders* (New York, 1876). Admiringly written, this expanded eulogy was not based upon careful study of the documents related to Brigham Young's history.

Edward H. Anderson, who had access to some materials in the Church Archives in Salt Lake City, published a brief biography in 1893 under the title *The Life of Brigham Young.* In many respects it is a rewriting and expansion of both the Tullidge volume and the "History of Brigham Young" published by the *Deseret News* in 1858.

As a part of an anti-Mormon crusade, Frank J. Cannon and George L. Knapp wrote *Brigham Young and His Mormon Empire* (New York, 1913). This work also is without systematic documentation.

The next volume to appear was M. R. Werner's *Brigham Young* (New York, 1925). A New York sportswriter, Werner based his book upon published Mormon and non-Mormon sources, but made no effort to use manuscript materials. Although he resisted few opportunities to poke fun at Brigham Young and the Mormons, he attempted to recognize some good qualities in his subject. For many years it was the single best biography of Brigham Young.

Next followed a work by one of Young's daughters, Susa Young Gates, in collaboration with her daughter, Leah D. Widtsoe, *The Life Story of Brigham Young*, published in London and New York in 1930. This is a good biography, but, again, it did not make extensive use of the large Brigham Young Collection in the LDS Church Archives.

In 1935–36 Preston Nibley, an official church historian, wrote a series of articles for the *Deseret News* that were then combined to form *Brigham Young, the Man and His Work* (Salt Lake City, 1936). This is a compilation from sources in the Journal History of the Church in the LDS Church Archives, with occasional commentary. Controversial topics, such as polygamy, are avoided. A charming look at Young's home and family life is given in Clarissa Young Spencer's *One Who Was Valiant*, published in 1940. Other biographical studies were by Leah D. Widtsoe, a granddaughter, *Brigham Young, the Man of the Hour* (1947); and by S. Dilworth Young, "*Here Is Brigham . . .*" (1964), taking his life up to 1844. All such studies have been valuable, but they were written before the extensive Young manuscript collection was catalogued.

The most recent biography, Stanley P. Hirshson's *The Lion of the Lord* (New York, 1969), was written essentially from articles published in New York newspapers during Brigham Young's life, which the author seldom checked against documentary sources. As Fawn M. Brodie has pointed out (*New York Times Book Review*, 9 November, 1969), Hirshson, misled by an improper reliance on these biased newspaper reports, portrayed Brigham Young as a liar and scoundrel, while ignoring his genuine accomplishments as a leader.

The first studies based upon the enormous collection of documentary materials available in the LDS Church Archives began to appear in the 1970s. These include articles in *Utah Historical Quarterly*, *Brigham Young University Studies (BYU Studies)*, and *Western Historical Quarterly*. They also include *Letters of Brigham Young to His Sons*, edited by Dean C. Jessee (Salt Lake City, 1974); Eugene England's *Brother Brigham* (Salt Lake City, 1980), well-written essays covering seven aspects of Young's life; and Francis Gibbons's *Brigham Young, Modern Moses/Prophet of God* (Salt Lake City, 1981), all written for Latter-day Saint readers. A valuable recent work that makes use of hitherto unused primary sources in New York is Richard F. Palmer and Karl D. Butler, *Brigham Young: The New York Years* (Provo, Utah, 1982), a short volume that has been helpful in filling out the early chapters of *American Moses*.

The massive primary materials for Brigham Young's life have now been catalogued; the register alone, prepared in 1980, requires seventy single-spaced pages. These rich documentary sources, which are described more fully in the bibliography at the end of this book and which, by and large, have not been previously used, include three holograph diaries covering the years 1832 to 1844 and ten office journals kept by his private secretary from 1844 to 1863; forty-seven thick, handwritten "histories," representing almost fifty thousand pages, maintained by his clerks and covering the years 1801 to 1877; twenty-one thousand-page volumes of letterpress copybooks containing about thirty thousand letters signed by Young; copies of more than a thousand telegrams sent out by Young; and several hundred archival boxes of paper including correspondence, transcripts of his speeches, minutes of meetings, political and Indian affairs papers, business and financial records and office papers, diaries and papers of his close associates, and manuscript histories of the various wards, stakes, and missions of the church. There are also historical records of immigration and colonizing parties, ecclesiastical organizations, and business enterprises he directed, and diaries of about two thousand contemporary Mormons, both male and female, containing entries about his activities and character.

Confronted with this enormous mass of manuscript material, the biographer wishes he could do a several-volume "life and times." One could easily write a volume on Brigham Young as husband and father of one of the most unusual families in American history, another on his thirty years as Church President, still another on his six years as governor, a fourth on his six years as superintendent of Indian affairs, a fifth on his activities in founding more than three hundred settlements in the Great Basin, a sixth on his business interests and economic enterprises, and a final one on his thought—his theological and doctrinal beliefs and assertions. But I have concluded that the proper place to begin is with a one-volume survey. Since the full story cannot possibly be told, how does one decide what to include and what to omit? Every reader of the finished work may be disappointed that I did not devote more attention to matters he or she would like to see more fully discussed.

Part of the problem of preparing this single volume lay in a classic dilemma of the biographer—how to steer between the extremes of, on the one hand, telling the Mormon story with Young as merely a leading personality and, on the other, recounting the life of Young without placing it sufficiently in its proper historical setting. There is also the necessity for candor. Can one really present Brigham, as his daughter Susa tried to do, without seeing him in his confrontations with contrary humans? Latter-day Saint biographers have avoided conflicts in their subjects' lives as being too "controversial." The reader is left assuming that "anointed ones" have not been plagued with the frustrations and ambiguities that have afflicted the rest of humanity. Yet here was a demanding leader, a harsh disciplinarian, ruthless in his requirements, whose people were yet unbelievably loyal to him. Indeed, they felt so warmly toward him that in their diaries, letters, and reminiscences they almost invariably refer to him not as President Young nor as Governor Young nor even as Brother Young, but as "Brother Brigham." Obviously, although he was sometimes arbitrary in the exercise of power, he was seen as a leader who could also be tender and considerate of the feelings of others.

Brigham Young possessed apparent contradictions. His contempt for government officials was seldom tempered by political expediency, and his attitude toward the Civil War was one of near-satisfaction; yet he insisted that his people were loyal Americans. He shared with most public men the subtleties of policy that give every appearance of duplicity, yet he acted again and again in ways that could have been fueled only by deep sincerity. He sometimes put people down with sarcasm, but he also showed understanding and sympathy, occasionally using sarcasm deliberately to motivate people to do "right" as he understood it. He could be quick to judge, but he was also sensitive and warmhearted, especially toward the poor and helpless. He was eminently practical; he was also an idealist. In short, he was a complex person—neither a saint nor a devil. One cannot romanticize him, as his family has tended to do. One must show the loyalty, goodness, and spirituality exhibited in Mormon writings, but one must also cite examples of willfulness, selfishness, and violations of current standards of proper deportment. As Carl Van Doren suggested of Benjamin Franklin, like most people of real stature Brigham contained within himself a "harmonious human multitude."

This complexity of characteristics helps to explain how Young was able to function on many different levels of leadership and in many different fields of human activity and how he was able to retain the loyalty of the wide variety of persons who made up the Mormon community. He could be logical; he could also be mystical. He was both a romantic and a pragmatist. These qualities force the biographer to acknowledge a certain inconsistency of conduct, contradictoriness in policy, and diversity of reactions to the various situations in which he was placed. Such a portrait is frustrating to those who like their heroes and villains clearly labeled. But it is true to the evidence, true to the life as it was lived.

The statue of Justice, symbol of the law, as she holds aloft her balance scale, is blindfolded. Justice is blind to race, creed, and color—and to personal eccentricity. If there were a comparable statue of Clio, the Muse of history, she would have to be presented with the blindfold lying at her feet, because the balance of her scales must be preserved with a conscious awareness of the facts and interpretations she must weigh. Of course, Brigham Young, like other deeply religious people, did not expect absolute justice at the hands of men. "I care nothing about my character in this world," he said. "I do not care what men say about me. I want my character to stand fair in the eyes of my Heavenly Father." But if we humans cannot achieve the absolute justice that we attribute to divine omniscience, we can try to be fair, to seek balance in our understanding, and to exert the kind of empathy that we ourselves would hope for if our own lives were being examined by someone who has not lived in our skin. This is what I have tried to do in *Brigham Young: American Moses.*

Brigham
Young:
American
Moses

Prologue ✦

"A Portly, Frank, Good-natured . . . Man"

I T was the summer of 1859, and tensions in Mormon settlements throughout North America's Great Basin were high. The Utah War of 1857– 58 had ended in an uneasy compromise as a result of which some five thousand United States troops, teamsters, and suppliers monitored Mormon activities from headquarters only forty miles southeast of Great Salt Lake City. Their presence was not lightly feared by a body of people who had experienced ruinous encounters with militias in Ohio, Missouri, and Illinois.

The Eastern establishment had seldom been kind to the Latter-day Saints. Now one of its eminent leaders, New York editor and reformer Horace Greeley, announced his intention of making a journey to California by way of the heart of Mormon country. He wanted, he told his readers, "to learn what I can of that country [the West] with my own eyes, and to study men in their cabins and at their work instead of reading about them in books." He would travel by rail and steamboat, stagecoach and pack horse, and he would come alone.

In 1859 the forty-eight-year-old Greeley was at least as famous as, and probably more admired than, President James Buchanan. His Abolitionist and Republican sentiments, widely read in the New York *Daily Tribune*, had already made him a potential political candidate, though he would not run for national office until 1872.

Brigham Young, now fifty-eight, was one of the Westerners the New Yorker was eager to study. Greeley had become familiar with the Mormons even before the mob killing of Joseph Smith in 1844. From his editorial desk he had watched Young take command and unite Smith's followers after the martyrdom. Since then Young had led his people through the American wilderness to their present mountain and desert home where Greeley's own correspondent, during the Gold Rush, had stopped to write admiringly of their "noble, daring, stern, and democratic spirit." Greeley must have seen the reports of such United States Army engineers as Howard Stansbury and John W. Gunnison, which alluded favorably to the Mormons. He may even have read some of the antipolygamy "memoirs" in the spirit of *Uncle Tom's Cabin* written in the 1850s for women readers. But as yet no adequate report on the Great Basin settlement was available.

Arriving in Salt Lake City on July 10, the journalist immediately arranged through John M. Bernhisel, former Utah territorial delegate to Congress, to call upon the Mormon prophet. July 13 was the date set for a meeting of the leading American reformer and the most controversial religious leader of the age.

On the appointed afternoon, a hot, dry Wednesday, Greeley entered Brigham's office promptly at two o'clock. He astounded the clerks, one of whom wrote, "Mr. Hah'-riss Gree'-lih [as it translates from the phonetic code] has the appearance of anything but a smart man or an editor." Another of Young's associates described the eastern visitor as "middling well dressed [in] white but bald headed—his head very dirty, looked as though he had not washed his head since he came off the plains. He had quite a feminine soft green appearance." Indeed, the spectator concluded, "Neither his head, phisiogomy [sic], looks, acts, or speech indicated in the least a man of knowledge, refinement, talent, influence, or ability sufficient to edit a Tribune."[1]

Greeley was received graciously by Young and a handful of other high churchmen. After being shown to an upper-floor sitting room of Brigham's Mansion House, the journalist requested permission to ask "a few questions." Young politely assented, though, as it turned out, Greeley asked many questions, and the result was the historic dispatch "Two Hours with Brigham Young," which the Librarian of Congress has called "the first full-fledged modern interview with a well-known public figure" to be published in an American newspaper.[2]

And what did the great crusader find in the Mormon patriarch? "A portly, frank, good-natured, rather thickset man of fifty-five [actually fifty-eight]." Far from emitting a pompous or sanctimonious air, Young was "plainly dressed in thin summer clothing" and seemed "to enjoy life, and to be in no particular hurry to get to heaven." Besides his modest appearance, Young "spoke readily, not always with grammatical accuracy, but with no appearance of hesitation or reserve, and with no apparent desire to conceal anything." Moreover, Greeley could find in none of the Mormon leaders the "cant or snuffle" he had expected, but concluded that they looked "as little like crafty hypocrites or swindlers as any body of men I ever met." Observation of Mormon physiognomy, he later added, with a more generous judgment than theirs of him, revealed none of the ignorance, superstition, or brutality of which he had read: "Very few rural congregations would exhibit more heads evincing decided ability."

Young later recalled that Greeley's questions "touched on the grand point of difference between us and other denominations, the order of the Priesthood, the wealth of the Church, the disposition made of the tithing, the number of wives I had, etc." The dispatch itself bears this out, attending, to Greeley's credit, as much to substantive matters of theology as to more sensational questions of finances, slavery, polygamy, and myths about the Destroying Angels. As reported by Greeley, Young's responses had directness, clarity, and a certain modest eloquence.[3]

H.G.—Am I to regard Mormonism (so-called) as a new religion, or as simply a new development of Christianity?

B.Y.—We hold that there can be no true Christian Church without a priesthood directly commissioned by, and in immediate communication with, the Son of God and Saviour of Mankind. Such a church is that of the Latter-day Saints, called by their enemies Mormons; we know no other that even pretends to have present and direct revelations of God's will.

. . .

H.G.—Do you make removal to these valleys obligatory on your converts?

B.Y.—They would consider themselves greatly aggrieved if they were not invited hither. . . .

. . .

H.G.—Am I to infer that Utah, if admitted as a member of the Federal Union, will be a slave state?

B.Y.—No; she will be a free state. Slavery here would prove useless and unprofitable. I regard it generally as a curse to the masters. . . .

. . .

H.G.—How, then, do your ministers live?

B.Y.—By the labor of their own hands, like the first apostles. . . . We think a man who cannot make his living aside from the ministry of Christ unsuited to that office. . . . I am called rich, and consider myself worth two hundred and fifty thousand dollars; but no dollar of it was ever paid me by the church. . . .

. . .

H.G.—Can you give me any rational explanation of the aversion and hatred with which your people are generally regarded . . . ?

B.Y.—No other explanation than is afforded by the crucifixion of Christ and the kindred treatment of God's ministers, prophets and saints, in all ages.

. . .

H.G.—What do you say of the so-called Danites, or Destroying Angels, belonging to your church?

B.Y.—What do *you* say? I know of no such band, no such persons or organization. I hear of them only in the slanders of our enemies.

. . .

H.G.—Does not the Apostle Paul say that a bishop should be "the husband of one wife"?

B.Y.—So we hold. We do not regard any but a married man as fitted for the office of bishop. But the apostle does not forbid a bishop having more wives than one.

These are representative excerpts of the meeting. Greeley omitted much of the discussion on polygamy because, in his words, it "assumed somewhat the character of a disputation."

The interview over, Greeley returned to his Main Street hotel to file his report. Its reception in New York was phenomenal; the *Tribune* of August 20 possibly sold more copies than any previous issue. Of course, Greeley considered Mormonism "a delusion and a blight." But his fair-minded estimation of its head and guiding agent set off renewed controversy over the Mormons, and Brigham in particular, that would inspire through ensuing decades many more first-person evaluations as well as scores of secondhand and fictional portraits of the Mormon leader. These varied from Fitz Hugh Ludlow's exaggerated assertion that Brigham was "more shrewd than a Talleyrand and richer than the Rothschilds" to the speculation of Justin McCarthy that Young was the most evil man in the world.[4] Indeed, as we shall see, so much was said about Brigham, and with so many contradictions, that he himself might have wondered what sort of man he really was.

Brigham was fully cognizant that some editors regarded him, as he expressed it in his usual hyperbole, "guilty of the death of every man, woman, and child that has died between the Missouri River and the California gold mines." Once he introduced himself by saying, "I am the notorious Brigham Young." But when one of his followers expressed concern about his reputation, Brigham responded, "Don't fret your gizzard over that." And about the time of Greeley's visit Brigham remarked to his replacement as governor: "I care nothing about my character in this world. I do not care what men say about me. I want my character to stand fair in the eyes of my Heavenly Father."[5]

What, indeed, are the beginnings and early history of the pleasant, courteous, yet enigmatic figure encountered by Horace Greeley in 1859, a man who was at the height of his creative powers when the interview took place in the heart of Mormon country just two years before the outbreak of civil war?

1 ✤

Boyhood in Vermont
and New York

In my youthful days, instead of going to school, I had to chop
logs, to sow and plant, to plow in the midst of roots bare-
footed, and if I had on a pair of pants that would cover me
I did pretty well.[1]

T H E small Vermont village of Whitingham lies along the Deer-
field River, just a few miles north of the Massachusetts border. Here on the
eastern side of the southern extension of the Green Mountains, the mountains
have been rounded off by thousands of years of erosion. Still, it is a country
of rocky fields, ravines, and ridges, for the Haystack Mountains rise out of the
Green range to 3,462 feet above sea level a few miles from Whitingham. The
fir, maple, and birch forests boast several glacial lakes and many ponds, with
rabbit and deer abounding. If the land has long winters with heavy snow and
a short growing season, the summers are mild, offering beautiful panoramas
from the hilltops and glimpses into lovely waterfall canyons.

In the year 1797 there occurred a mild land rush to southern Vermont, as
disputing parties settled a fifty-year-old controversy involving absentee land-
lords who were holding patents obtained before the Revolutionary War and
settlers who had simply drifted in to cultivate the land and organize towns.
When the land was clearly open to settlement, several families moved into the
area from central Massachusetts. Among them were the Wheelers, Fullers,
Faulkners, Sayers, and Youngs.

John and Abigail (Nabby) Young brought seven of their eight children
to Whitingham from Hopkinton, Massachusetts, a farming community about
twenty-five miles southwest of Boston where, with the exception of a brief
interlude across the border from Massachusetts in the Platauva District of east
central New York, they had lived for sixteen years. John, a Revolutionary War
veteran born in 1763, was the third of six children born to Joseph Young and
Betsy Hayden Treadway. When John was only six years old, his father, a

medical practitioner in Hopkinton and nearby Framingham, was killed, apparently by a falling tree, and within a year or two the family's farm and possessions were sold to pay debts. The town selectmen dutifully found places for most of the children and "bound them out."[2] John was bound out to Colonel John Jones, a well-to-do Hopkinton landowner. After ten years of this servitude, punctuated by frequent whippings at the hands of the colonel's wife, John ran away and joined the Continental Army (1780), serving in three campaigns under General George Washington. At war's end he returned to work for Colonel Jones, this time on a paying basis. During this period John, described as a "small, nimble, wiry man," met and began courting Nabby Howe.[3]

Abigail Howe, one of five daughters of Phineas and Susanna Goddard Howe, was born in 1766 in Shrewsbury, Massachusetts, not far from Hopkinton. With "blue eyes, yellowish brown hair folded in natural waves and ringlets," Nabby was thought foolish by her parents to want to marry "the little orphan" whose past was undistinguished and future uncertain.[4] Nevertheless, Nabby and John married and in 1785 started life together on a farm in Hopkinton.

That life was hard. Probably tenants on overworked land, John and Nabby found it difficult to keep up with the needs of their growing family, which by 1801 numbered ten: John, age thirty-seven; Abigail, age thirty-four; Nancy, age fourteen; Fanny, age thirteen; Rhoda, age eleven; John, Jr., age nine; Nabby, age seven; Susannah, age five; Joseph, age three; and Phinehas Howe, age one. They finally yielded to the desire to "try again" in Vermont. For some reason, perhaps to console Nabby's parents, Rhoda was left behind in Hopkinton.[5] In November 1800 John purchased fifty acres in Lot 21 of "Fitches Land Grant" in Whitingham. For this land John had paid his sister's wealthy husband, Joseph Mosely, $50—a seeming bargain.[6]

The Youngs' decision to migrate in January has been explained by S. Dilworth Young, a family descendant well acquainted with New England: most of the traces that passed for roads in the area were impassable during the spring and fall because of the mud, and during the dry summer because of dust. Heavily laden wagons cut into the soft soil until the roads became a succession of deep chucks. As a result, wheels sank into ruts until the wagon bed rested on the mud. In winter there was neither dust nor mud, and bobsleds moved easily over the frozen surface.[7]

This does not mean that there were not dangers and difficulties. The 100-mile journey would have required at least ten days; the migrants might have encountered blizzards, deep drifts of snow, heavy rain turning to ice, and streams that were only partly frozen. Whether the family camped out each night or stayed at inns we cannot know, and what they subsisted on during the journey can only be surmised: perhaps corn cakes, salt pork, jerky, and an occasional hapless animal—a cottontail or fox—that they saw on the trail. In making the journey the Youngs apparently used two bobsleds, wagon boxes mounted on runners. One sled, pulled by horses, carried Nabby and the children. The other, pulled by oxen, contained the transportable family possessions.

Upon their arrival in Whitingham the Youngs arranged to stay in the cabin of an earlier migrant until they could build their own dwelling. The building of the one-room shelter about sixteen feet square required perhaps sixty poles, eighteen to twenty feet in length. Fortunately, winter was a good time for oxen to drag large logs to the treeless clearing chosen as the best location. When John had completed getting out the logs and stacking them on the intended lot, if tradition were followed, men in the village joined in the "log raising." With this help, the walls were up in one day, and the roof, the chinking with mud clay, and other finishings were completed in the next few days. At the end of the cabin was a stick chimney to carry out the smoke from fires usually made from dry maple wood, beech, or birch. Inside the cabin were bunk beds for the children, usually two-deckers, on which lay corn shuck mattresses or balsam fir boughs.[8]

Until the harvest, the family's food came from available corn, wild berries, nuts, squirrels, pigeons, rabbits, turkeys, partridges, quail, deer, and bear. The most valuable plant on the Young plot was the sugar maple. Having arrived in January, the Youngs were ready to begin the "sugaring off" in late March and April. John and John, Jr., made several wooden troughs to serve as sap basins, and the tree was tapped with hollow tubes from the sumac. When full, the troughs were emptied into wooden buckets and carried to a large iron kettle under which a fire was kept burning day and night until the liquid thickened. By the end of the operation the family had many pounds of solid maple sugar, which the family consumed during the year or traded for other needed commodities. Maple syrup was delicious on corn bread or "dodgers"— cornmeal fried or baked into a hard breadstick.[9]

On the first day of June, when the trees had broken forth in pastels of green, corn planted between the tree stumps had sent forth green shoots, and patches of wild strawberries were beginning to show their color, Nabby gave birth to her ninth child and fourth son—a child she had conceived in Hopkinton and had carried, four months pregnant, on the journey to Whitingham. Whether he was delivered by his father, by a doctor in the vicinity, or by a midwife we cannot be sure, but almost certainly the birth took place in the newly built Young cabin. After the surname of Nabby's maternal grandparents, John and Nabby named him Brigham.

Nabby's health was not good. She had suffered from spells of coughing and consumption and was so weak that she could not properly care for the baby, let alone the remainder of the family. We recognize today the signs of tuberculosis, a not uncommon disease at the time. Because of her illness Brigham, who was probably referred to as Briggie, was bottle-fed by his thirteen-year-old sister Fanny, to whom he became so attached that she had to carry him on her hip while she milked the cow.[10]

T H E family's lot was a hard one. Occupying the time and energy of those members old enough to work were spinning and weaving, sewing cloth, churning butter, securing food, preparing meals, and caring for livestock. It is not surprising that the oldest girl, Nancy, on whom had devolved much of the task of supervising the younger children, left home to marry Daniel Kent when Briggie was two. In 1803, when Briggie was two and a half, Fanny also departed, to marry Robert Carr.

The ever-present task of clearing the land was the most difficult. Whitingham was not an area of good agricultural potential; there were few level acres fit for cultivation, and most of the land was stony. The winters were long and hard on Nabby, and the labor of John and the boys was backbreaking. After three years the Youngs decided to make another move, this time west of the Alleghenies to Sherburne, Chenango County, in central New York, where the land was reported to be better than in Vermont.[11]

The move took place in the spring of 1804, just after the completion of sugar-making.[12] The family traveled to Bennington, then to the Hudson River, crossing it on a ferry at Troy. From Troy they went west by way of an old Indian trace up the gently sloping, still heavily timbered Mohawk Valley to Utica, then southwest to Sherburne. The 160-mile journey required two wagons, a team of horses, and a yoke of oxen, and probably took two or three weeks.

More primitive than Whitingham, Sherburne was located at a junction of the Chenango and Susquehanna rivers. The area was rich in wild berries, nuts, and wild animals, large and small. During that first year John cleared and planted enough acres of corn to hold them through the next winter. Meanwhile, work proceeded on the construction of a log cabin, and a baby girl, Louisa, was born soon after the family's arrival. Three years later the eleventh and last child of John and Nabby Young was born, and named Lorenzo Dow after the great exhorter who had made an impression on the family at a camp meeting in nearby Smyrna. The excitement of the new addition, however, was subdued by the family's sadness when Brigham's sister Nabby, then eleven, died of tuberculosis, a disease she had doubtless acquired from her mother. Apparently that same year the family moved a short distance away to "Dark Hollow," near Cold Brook, about three miles southwest of Smyrna (the portion of Sherburne where the Youngs had settled in 1804). Once more, they lived in a log cabin.[13]

As a boy in Sherburne–Smyrna–Cold Brook, living there from his third to his thirteenth year, Brigham joined his father and brothers in clearing their own land for farming and, in exchange for needed products and supplies, the land of others in the region as well. Brigham later described his experience: he had the privilege, he said, of cutting down the hemlock, beech, and maple trees and then rolling them together, burning the logs, splitting the rails, and fencing the little fields. He went on to describe the tasks "of picking up brush, chopping down trees, rolling logs, and working amongst the roots, and of getting our shins, feet and toes bruised."[14] He used to work in the woods, he said, "logging and driving a team, summer and winter, not half clad, and with insufficient food until my stomach would ache. . . ."[15]

He must have learned how to use and care for a flintlock; how to trap for muskrat, fox, beaver, marten, fisher, lynx, wolves, mink, and otter; how to catch fish; how to plant, cultivate, and harvest crops; how to make Indian webs or snowshoes; how to gee and haw at oxen; how to construct a root cellar; and how to work with neighbors in building homes. In short, while deprived of formal education (Brigham stated later that he had only eleven days of schooling), he learned the skills of home and shop and field—enough, as he expressed it, to enable him to be independent.

Unquestionably, the family was poor and lacked compensating amenities. By a fortunate set of circumstances, Brigham recalled, he came to own a pair of shoes. Unaccustomed to wearing them, he used them only for church meetings and even then carried them in his hands until he reached the church lot, taking them off again after the service before he walked home.[16] In the winter he would wear a "Jo Johnson" hat knitted by his sisters, and in the summer a straw hat he braided for himself. "I learned," said Brigham, "how to make bread, milk the cows and make butter . . . how to economize."[17]

The family remained in the Sherburne area for nine years. One happy event during this period was the return of Brigham's sister Rhoda in 1809, after an absence of eight years. She was now eighteen. Joseph's moving account of the reunion suggests the family's closeness:

> . . . in September of this year she arrived at our humble home on Cold Brook with old deacon Abner Morton, our mother's uncle. The whole family were much overcome by the arrival of sister Rhoda, whom we had not seen for 8 years. It was like one rising from the dead! Never did a child seem to appreciate a father's home more—humble as it was, than did sister Rhoda; this was fully reciprocated by the whole family. It seemed as though an Angel had visited our house, and to add to our happiness she had come to abide with us.[18]

In 1813, when Rhoda married John P. Greene, a Methodist preacher, and John, Jr., married Theodosia Kimball, John and Nabby decided to move to Aurelius, Cayuga County, some six miles from the upper end of Cayuga Lake. This is where John and Rhoda Greene "kept house," and perhaps John and Nabby Young thought the Greenes would be helpful in looking after Nabby and the little children. Or John Greene's enticing description of Aurelius and its potential may have attracted John to take the remainder of the family there. One year after the move, Susannah married James Little, a local builder and horticulturist.

The Youngs had been in Aurelius for two years when Mother Nabby, in June 1815, finally lost her extended and painful battle against consumption. Though she had long since relinquished her share of household burdens, her death at the age of forty-nine seems to have been a significant disruption to the family. Restless as usual, and perhaps thinking himself unable to properly care for his younger children, John took leave of the farm and its many improvements. With his boys (Joseph, eighteen, Phinehas, sixteen, Brigham, fourteen), he moved some thirty-five miles west to the "Sugar Hill" district of Steuben County near Tyrone, along the Tioga River. Fanny, who had separated from her unfaithful husband and returned to look after Nabby in her final illness, oversaw the household for a brief period, but soon Louisa and Lorenzo were sent to Rhoda and John Greene in Aurelius, also spending time with Susannah, who lived in the vicinity of Auburn in the Aurelius township. When Rhoda and John moved to Tyrone in the fall of 1815, Lorenzo, at least, was reunited with his father and brothers, but only temporarily.

Tyrone was then regarded as the Far West. It was unsettled frontier, eighteen miles from the Indian and trading establishment at Painted Post, where land could be had cheaply. From a General Wordsworth, John Young purchased 100 acres in the midst of "a dense forest fifteen miles from any settlement where there were any supplies to be gotten."[19] Close by were John's eldest daughter Nancy and her husband, Daniel Kent—the only neighbors near enough this time to help John and his boys build a small cabin. With a grove of maple trees on the farm, the Youngs once again sugared off the trees, also planting corn in the area cleared off, burning trees for potash, hunting and trapping, and working for farmers in the region to earn needed goods.

One surmises that Brigham's father was not always a good manager. Once when Joseph and Phinehas had hired out to others in the area, John left fourteen-year-old Brigham and eight-year-old Lorenzo Dow at home while he went to Painted Post to trade his sixty pounds of maple sugar for flour. He was to be gone two full days and he left behind an empty flour barrel. Hungry as they returned to the cabin after a day of burning and clearing, the boys noticed a robin. Brigham hurriedly fetched the musket, probably the old muzzle-loader his father had carried during the Revolutionary War. Brigham returned, took careful aim, and killed the bird, then skinned and cleaned it and, back at the cabin, put it to boil. He and Lorenzo held the flour barrel upside down and thumped it until they obtained enough flour to make a kind of roux, adding it to the stew. That and maple syrup were all they ate until their father's return the following evening.[20]

"I have seen the time that I had not food to satisfy the craving of my nature," said Brigham later of the Tyrone experience. "I know what it is to be in poverty, and to be destitute of the raiment necessary to keep my body warm." If he was "very close and economical," it was because he learned how to economize, "for my father had to do it."[21]

By 1817, the family was doing reasonably well. Then one day John Young came home with a bride, the widow Hannah Brown, and her several children. (She later bore three children to John; two died shortly after birth, while a son named Edward, born in 1823, lived to maturity.) In a short time John and his own remaining brood separated. Brigham's older brother Phinehas got married. Joseph and Lorenzo were taken in by their sister Susannah Little. As for Brigham:

> When I was sixteen years of age, my father said to me, "You now have your time; go and provide for yourself"; and a year had not passed away before I stopped running, jumping, wrestling and laying out my strength for naught. . . .[22]

Actually he, too, resided temporarily with the Littles, who had settled at "Half Acre," near the village of Cayuga in the township of Aurelius about four miles from Auburn. Susannah's husband James carried on farming and gardening with some ingenuity. The Irishman is said to have been the first person in New York State to sell packaged seeds, and he is also credited with introducing tomatoes for table use in this area.[23]

But the Littles too, or perhaps their circumstances, must have required that Brigham provide his own support, for he did as his father advised and found a job. Auburn in 1817 was a rapidly growing county seat of perhaps a thousand people. Along Genesee Street, the main thoroughfare, was the wood-working shop of John C. Jeffries, who advertised "Chair Making, Sign Painting and Gilding." "When I was seventeen years of age," Brigham later recalled, "I laid my strength in planing a board. . . ."[24] In other words, he apprenticed himself to Jeffries to learn the trades of carpenter, painter, and glazier. He later described his initiation:

> The first job my boss gave me was to make a bedstead out of an old log that had been on the beach of the Lake for years, waterlogged and water soaked. Said he—"There are tools; you cut that log into right lengths for a bedstead. Hew out the side rails and the posts; get a board for a headboard, and go to work and make a bedstead." And I went to work and cut up the log, split it up to the best of my ability, and made a bedstead that, I suppose, they used for many years. I would go to work and learn to make a washboard, and make a bench to put the washtub on, and to make a chair.[25]

Over the next five years Brigham helped build the first marketplace in Auburn, the prison, the theological seminary, and the home of "Squire" William Brown (later occupied by William H. Seward, who served as Governor of New York and Lincoln's secretary of state). In addition, he built door fittings, louvered attic windows, and carved ornate mantelpieces for many homes in the region at a time when open fireplaces were almost universal as sources of heat, and decorative mantels were prized as enhancing the beauty of the internal decor. Today, the occupants of virtually every old house in Auburn boast of a Brigham Young mantelpiece, staircase, or semielliptical fanlight doorway. A number of these homes also have desks and chairs reputedly made by Brigham. Architectural historians who have examined these report them to be chaste and beautiful, with exquisite and sturdy workmanship. But they were typical of Federal-style architecture, and probably only in retrospect were most of them attributed to Brigham Young.[26]

There was little in the young Brigham that foreshadowed the man of controversy of later decades. Certainly he did nothing to arouse the ire or jealousy of the townspeople. His versatility appeared early, for at seventeen, besides carpentry and glazing, he also began "cultivating the ground to raise something from it to benefit myself."[27] Auburn folklore has it that he helped landscape homes and plant gardens and orchards about the town. As a laborer, townspeople would remember him as "an energetic, active and capable young man," and his services were in demand for as long as he remained in Auburn.[28]

With the ill luck that seemed to follow the Youngs and keep them poor, James Little was killed in November 1822 when his one-horse wagon overturned while returning home from a trip to town. Brigham by then was twenty-one, a man according to law and the judgment of his associates, for he was named executor of Little's estate along with his older brother Joseph and a neighbor of the Littles. These estate papers contain his earliest known signature.[29]

In the spring of 1823, Brigham left Auburn, probably to avail himself of better-paying work opportunities. He moved eight miles north to Bucksville, later called Port Byron, an important stop on the Erie Canal. There he served several employers as a furniture repairman and maker and painter of canal boats. Eventually he settled in with Charles Parks, manufacturer of furniture, pails, and buckets, whose shop was located a mile and a half south at Bucksville. Parks, who paid Brigham $2.50 per week, appreciated his craftsmanship and gave him plenty of responsibility.[30]

A painter's most difficult and time-consuming task, Brigham had discovered, was mixing—that is, pulverizing the pigment powder to mix with the oil and lead. So he invented a water-powered pigment crusher that used a cannonball obtained from his father, who had saved it from his Revolutionary War experience, as a pestle to an iron pot mortar. Parks was reported to be fascinated with the invention, as were other villagers, some of whom brought to Brigham their dreams of a perpetual motion machine. On one occasion, Brigham is said to have pointed to a large basket nearby, and declared: "When one of you will get into that and carry himself up that flight of stairs I will believe it possible to carry out your [perpetual motion] ideas."[31] Still impressed, Parks promoted him from painter to carpenter, whereupon Brigham began turning out chairs, tables, settees, cupboards, and doors.

Old-time residents later told of another Bucksville episode in which Brigham proved himself. Lightning had struck the chimney of the furniture shop, sparks from which fell into the wood shavings. According to the story, Brigham grabbed a bucket of water and organized the shop to fight the fire. In a few moments the flames were doused and the place was saved.[32]

Soon Brigham was put in charge of constructing an addition to the "factory." This work was interrupted one day by the screams of a woman who had lost her baby. Fearful it might have fallen in the mill race, Brigham stopped the mill wheel, dove into the flume, felt the bottom, and clutched and pulled the child out. But when he started to administer artificial respiration, the distraught mother grabbed the child and ran home with her, thus preventing the action that might have saved the infant's life.[33]

Other stories contradict Brigham's own recollection of himself as a reluctant and clumsy speaker in his young manhood. He is said to have helped organize the Bucksville Forensic and Oratorical Society and participated actively in its meetings. According to William Hayden's account, on Brigham's first visit to the debating society he intended to be a listener only but was drawn in as a participant. In the course of his argument he did so well at drawing a satirical verbal portrait of "a would-be smart young man" that someone in the audience took it personally, removed his coat, and vowed to whip Brigham then and there. Brigham reportedly took it calmly, saying that, although he was not a fighting man, he would defend himself and leave it to observers to determine who received the whipping. He was not attacked.[34]

It is hard to assess the reliability of these anecdotes, but they depict an appealing young man who was hardworking, conscientious, clever, and not above a bit of fun, as Hayden remembered:

> He [Brigham] was a great favorite with the small boys then quite numerous in the pail factory neighborhood. Having on this occasion collected a pack of kids of which I was one, he took them onto the bridge and arranged them in a row and after making them a short speech on good manners for boys, he ordered all to take their hats in their hands and do as he did, and to bellow as loudly as possible. "Now, all at once, swing your hats and hurrah for Andrew Jackson."[35]

S O O N after starting work for Parks, Brigham met eighteen-year-old Miriam Angeline Works, whose family lived near the pail factory and were said to be friends of Charles Parks. The second child of Asa and Abigail Works, born at Aurelius on June 6 (or June 7), 1806, Miriam (sometimes referred to as Angeline) was "a beautiful blonde with blue eyes and wavy hair; gentle and lovable."[36] Her father, like Brigham's, was a Revolutionary War veteran. He had moved to western New York from Worcester, Massachusetts, not far from Hopkinton where John Young had lived. Brigham and Miriam became acquainted, he walked her home, they sang together and discussed life. At the age of twenty-three Brigham borrowed a horse and carriage from William Hayden's father, rented a house up the road, and married Miriam.

The marriage was performed on October 5 (some sources say October 8), 1824, by Gilbert Weed, Aurelius Justice of the Peace, at the tavern of James Pine between Auburn and Bucksville.[37] Perhaps by prearrangement, Weed presided at the marriage of Brigham's sister Louisa to Joel Sanford the next day. William Hayden later declared that Brigham and Miriam spent their honeymoon in a modest log dwelling at the rear of the Hayden farm, across from the pail factory where Brigham worked. The home they established in Aurelius township was approximately sixteen by twenty-four feet, with a fireplace, two bedrooms, kitchen, dining room, and living room. They kept this home for four years, until 1828. They joined the Methodist church the year of their marriage. Their first child, Elizabeth, was born on September 26, 1825.

As at Aurora, Brigham left a favorable impression on Bucksville citizens, who regarded him as honest, industrious, and a good craftsman. One proprietor later declared that Brigham "would do more work in a given time and secure more and better work from his help without trouble than any man they have ever employed."[38]

I N 1827 or 1828 Brigham, Miriam, and their daughter Elizabeth moved from Bucksville to Oswego, a busy port on Lake Ontario forty miles north of Auburn. In his history Brigham simply stated that there he helped build a large tannery, perhaps having been employed by an Auburn or Bucksville entrepreneur for that specific purpose. Though remaining in Oswego only a few months, Brigham and Miriam apparently participated in the village social and religious life. One associate there, Hiram McKee, who later became an evangelical preacher, recalled that Brigham had been exemplary in his conduct and conversation, "humble and contrite," had demonstrated "deep piety and faith in God," and had joined in "fervent prayers and enlivening songs."[39]

Near the end of 1828, Brigham took his family to Mendon, forty miles from Bucksville, where his father had moved from Tyrone in 1827 and where several brothers and sisters lived. It seems likely that Brigham and Miriam lived with his father for a brief period until Brigham built a house and shop for himself on John's land. The 1830 census lists Brigham and Miriam Young, John and Hannah Young, Susannah Little, Louisa and Joel Sanford, and Rhoda and John Greene as residents of Mendon. Fanny was also there, living with the Heber C. Kimball family; Phinehas was in nearby Victor; and John, Jr., in nearby Hector. Joseph was living with his father, and Lorenzo was there part of the time.[40]

In the Mendon-Canandaigua area the Youngs had finally found a region with excellent agricultural potential. A contemporary called it "one of the finest farming districts I have yet seen in the State of New York."[41]

Although numerous, the Youngs did not cut an impressive figure in socioeconomic terms. Heber C. Kimball, a longtime resident and soon to become Brigham's closest and lifelong friend, said that they "were in low circumstances and seemed to be an afflicted people in consequence of having a great deal of sickness and sorrow to pass through; and of course were looked down upon by the flourishing church where we lived."[42]

In Mendon, Miriam gave birth to a second daughter, Vilate, on Brigham's birthday, June 1, 1830. When Miriam was able, they moved into a small house at "Number Nine," a rural area a few miles west of Canandaigua, while Brigham helped Jonathan Mack, a respected local farmer, build a new house. They moved back to Mendon in 1832.

Miriam contracted chronic tuberculosis and became a semi-invalid. A familiar way of life during the illness of Brigham's mother was now repeated in his own household: his work often had to be on a part-time basis, for he had to get breakfast for himself, Miriam, and the girls; dress the children; clean up the house; and carry Miriam to the rocking chair by the fireplace before he could leave. When he returned, he cooked the evening meal, cleaned up, read to Miriam from the Bible, and carried her back to bed.[43] A Canandaigua resident later recalled in a letter to the Ontario *Republican Times*:

> . . . there could scarcely be a more kind and affectionate husband and father than he [Brigham] was, and few men in his circumstances would have provided better for their families. Mrs. Young was sick, most of the time unable to do any kind of work, but she was a worthy woman, and an exemplary Christian; she was well deserving his care and attention, and she had it while she lived in Canandaigua. . . . We never thought him fanatical, . . . he was looked upon by his neighbors generally to be a consistent Christian.[44]

Apparently, Brigham did a variety of "custom work" in the Mendon-Canandaigua area. This included building homes; making and repairing furniture (chairs, tables, desks, chests, baby cribs); putting in windowpanes, doorways, staircases, and fireplace mantels; and other "handyman" types of work. Heber Kimball later recalled:

> Brother Brigham and myself used to work hard, side by side, for fifty cents a day and board ourselves; we had seventy-five cents a day when we worked in the hayfield; we would work from sunrise to sunset, and until nine o'clock at night if there was sign of rain. We would rake and bind after a cradler for a bushel of wheat a day, and chop wood, with snow to our waist for eighteen cents a cord, and take our pay in corn at seventy-five cents a bushel.[45]

Farmers for whom Brigham worked remembered him years later as handy with tools and industrious at his trade.[46] George Hickox, whose descendants still live in the area, declared that Brigham once approached him about borrowing a dollar. "Chop wood with me and earn it," was Hickox's reply. On another occasion Brigham owed Hickox a bill and made a dozen chairs to satisfy the account.[47] A fine splint-bottomed chair made by him is now on display in the Ontario County Historical Society Museum in Canandaigua.

The archives of the Rush Rhees Library of the University of Rochester, New York, contain a promissory note signed by Brigham on March 16, 1830, in favor of Milton Sheldon, owner of a Mendon general store, for the sum of $18.50 "in good Kitchen Chairs at Fifty Cents apiece, well done off painted and Bottomed according to the usual mode of doing off such chairs." On the back the note is endorsed to indicate that Brigham, on the request of the owner of the note, had made a picket fence and worked "on A. Parks Barn." The Sheldon General Store account book, still in existence, shows Brigham taking out $4.36 of merchandise in June 1829 and $2.34 in August 1829. The merchandise included cloth, tobacco, tea, indigo, cups and saucers, a comb, a broom, sugar, and brandy.[48]

J. Sheldon Fisher, a local historian, archaeologist, and owner of a museum that exhibits artifacts connected with the history of the region, has a lathe that he is certain Brigham used in making turnings for chairs, furniture, and spinning wheels. Fisher has found bits and pieces of furniture, broken crockery and dishes, and even bricks with the letter "B" engraved on them at the site of Brigham Young's woodworking shop or mill on Trout Creek where he built a sizable undershot waterwheel to power the machinery.[49]

Somewhat to the surprise of the Young family and the students of Brigham's life, Fisher discovered evidence that Brigham also worked in metal in his Mendon shop. He apparently had a forge near the first-floor fireplace of the shop, and a precision lathe for metalwork, together with a variety of steel-cutting tools, chisels, jackknives, drills, reamers, screwdrivers, hammers, axes, punches, awls, files, and screws. The litter of the place, abandoned when Young left Mendon in 1832, also included antlers of elk, moose, deer, and ram used as bushings for spindles or shafts, and various leather products—washers, bushings, hinges. A forge hammer found near the fireplace, together with a number of horse and oxen shoes, suggests that he shod his own beasts of burden. There were a fireplace shovel and tongs, door latches, locks and keys, iron hinges for doors, and many sizes of hand-wrought nails. Fisher also found a flint and steel, called a Strike-o-light, used before the invention of sulphur matches, and an ancient type of garden hoe, complete with handle, preserved in the mud.[50]

The archaeological dig suggests that, while life was undoubtedly hard, it surely had its pleasant aspects. There were fragments of handmade toys and some marbles, a crushed Easter egg with a painted design, and pits of cherries, peaches, apricots, and wild plums; seeds of apple, pumpkin, melon, squash, and charred corn; chestnuts, butternuts, hickory nuts, pig nuts, black walnuts, and beechnuts. Bones from roast beef and beef steak were plentiful, as well as pork bones, lamb and mutton, passenger pigeon, various game birds, chicken, duck, and goose bones. Brigham's family also ate turtle, fish, and freshwater clams.[51]

Late in his life, reflecting on his boyhood, Brigham Young emphasized the poverty. "I grew up in a country," he said, "where it often was impossible to hire to do a day's work, and when the labor was performed, it was frequently worth twice the amount to get the pay, which would generally be only three or four bits [37½ to 50 cents]."[52] It is clear that, while missing a formal education, Brigham had become an expert farmer, gardener, carpenter, glazier, mason, cabinetmaker, painter, and boatbuilder. He had learned the necessity of being both practical and economical.

2 ✤

Conversion and Commitment

> "Hold on," says I.... "Wait a little while; what is the doctrine
> of the book, and of the revelations the Lord has given? Let
> me apply my heart to them"; and after I had done this, I
> considered it to be my right to know for myself.... I wished
> time sufficient to prove all things for myself.[1]

E A R L Y in April 1830 an unschooled twenty-two-year-old preacher
passing through Mendon village stopped to eat at Tomlinson's Inn. There he
encountered Brigham's oldest brother, Phinehas Young, himself an itinerant
Methodist exhorter, who was interested in the text Samuel Smith was peddling,
a purported new work of scripture he called the Book of Mormon. Smith
described its 600 pages as a "translation" of ancient golden plates prepared by
his brother Joseph Smith, Jr., and printed in Palmyra, New York, fifteen miles
from Mendon. It was, he declared, a supplement to the Holy Bible, being the
record of people who had left the Middle East and established a civilization
in the Western Hemisphere. "I know the book to be a revelation from God,"
said Samuel, "translated by the gift and power of the Holy Ghost, and that
my brother Joseph Smith, Jun., is a Prophet, Seer and Revelator."[2]

The Youngs had heard rumors of Joseph Smith's golden treasure and "knew
something of the doings of the Saints."* (9:1; 15:135; 5:55; 15:35) But this hearsay
had prompted no further investigation until Phinehas met Samuel Smith.

Even now Phinehas's immediate thought was that the book must have
been gotten up "to lead people astray," so he determined, "as a teacher in
Israel," to read it in order to expose its errors and "save the people from the
delusion." He studied it for a week, could not find the errors he had expected,
and even began to believe that the book was authentic. Phinehas lent his copy
to his father, who, after reading it, declared it to be "the greatest work . . .

---

* Because the most definitive and reliable source on Brigham's encounter with religion and
Mormonism is his own recollections, as contained in his sermons published in the *Journal of
Discourses*, I have given, in this chapter, the volume and page after each quotation from that
source and have not resorted to footnote documentation in those instances.

he had ever seen." Phinehas next passed it on to his sister Fanny. She examined it and reported the book to be "a revelation." Fanny gave it to Brigham.

Brigham later claimed to have been slower and more methodical in his convincement than others of his family. His reaction was this: "Says I, 'Wait a little while; what is the doctrine of the book,' . . . I considered it to be my right to know for myself, as much as any man on earth."[3] He then studied not only the book but the character of those who were distributing it or professed to believe in it:

> I watched to see whether good common sense was manifest; and if they had that, I wanted them to present it in accordance with the Scriptures. . . . When I had ripened everything in my mind, I drank it in, and not till then.[4]

In the end, he was converted and baptized at the same time as his father, brothers, and sisters.

It is a remarkable fact that all of Brigham Young's immediate family became Mormons, and all remained loyal, practicing Mormons throughout their lives. In the single month of April 1832, John Young and his wife, Hannah, Fanny and her new husband, Roswell Murray, Rhoda and John Greene, Joseph, Phinehas and his wife, Clarissa, Brigham and Miriam, and Lorenzo and Persis were all baptized. The remaining members of the family were not far behind. Susannah, married to William Stilson in 1829, was baptized in June, and Louisa and Joel Sanford joined later the same year. Nancy and Daniel Kent joined in Tyrone in 1833, while John, Jr., after a thorough investigation of the church and its tenets, was baptized in October 1833. Eleven of the Youngs proved to be "valiant" in the faith.[5]

What was the family's early religious training and experience, and how had these prepared Brigham and his parents and brothers and sisters to receive positively this new "restoration of Bible religion," as one of them called it? In what ways did the existing churches fail them, and what were the special attractions of the new Church of Christ (not until 1838 did the name become the presently used Church of Jesus Christ of Latter-day Saints)? What were the Youngs reacting against, and why should they have been drawn toward Mormonism? In short, what set Brigham on the path that eventually led him to become the chief Mormon—the leader of more than one hundred thousand disciples by the time of his death?

B R I G H A M Young had a great deal to say about the poverty and rigor of his early life. Part of it was the Puritan harshness of the country. "I have never found, in all my travels through these [Utah] mountains," he said later in life, "so rough a country as where I was born." (4:328) The winters were frigid, the summers hot and humid, the soil rocky and uneven, and everywhere there were trees to be cleared off. Social conditions were just as stark—the Young family seldom had enough to eat, enough clothes to wear, or comfortable living quarters. (Brigham recalled his grandmother's "company" dress—the dress in which she had been married and the one fine garment of her lifetime.) (5:97; 12:287; 19:74) Because he and his brothers and sisters could not go to school, their education came from their parents and neighbors. The family could not cultivate the social graces, social recreation was unthinkable, and the only improvement of the mind came from reading the Bible.

The ways of his parents were as exacting as those of the countryside. The mature Brigham described John and Nabby as "some of the most strict religionists that lived upon the earth," people who forbade in their home the playing of cards and such expressions as "Darn it" or "the Devil."[6] "I don't say that we children did not say such things when out of the sight of father and mother," Brigham confessed, but "if it came to their ears, we were sure to be chastized." (6:290) Moreover, he recalled:

> When I was young I was kept within very strict bounds, and was not allowed to walk more than half-an-hour on Sunday for exercise. . . . I had not a chance to dance when I was young, and never heard the enchanting tones of the violin, until I was eleven years of age; and then I thought I was on the highway to hell, if I suffered myself to linger and listen to it. (2:94)

His father was the stricter of the parents—with John it was "a word and a blow . . . but the blow came first." (4:112) Yet he was "very circumspect, exemplary and religious," never demanding of his children behavior he himself did not display.[7] Brigham said he never heard his father swear, "not so much as a darn it or curse it or the devil." (16:73; 6:290) Though the family remembered Mother Nabby as tempering the sternness of her husband,[8] she was just as fervent in her beliefs, not tolerating in her children "the least act that was wrong according to her traditions." Said Brigham:

> My mother, while she lived, taught her children all the time to honour the name of the Father and the Son, and to reverence the holy Book . . . do everything that is good; do nothing that is evil; and if you see any persons in distress, administer to their wants. . . . Never did my mother or my father countenance any of their children in anything to wrong their neighbour or fellow-being, even if they were injured by them. (6:290)

Perhaps Nabby's most frequent admonition was in regard to the Bible: "Read it," she told the children from her bed, "observe its precepts, and apply them to your lives as far as you can."[9] The young Brigham gained respect for both the Book and the promulgator. "I can say no better woman ever lived in the world than she was."

The austerity of life was formalized in frontier religion. The Youngs had a predilection for Methodism, first affiliating with this sect in Hopkinton, Massachusetts. Perhaps they were attracted to the circuit riders, who were often struggling commonfolk like themselves. Less pretentious than the Congregationalist graduates of Harvard and Yale, proud of having obtained an education instead at "Brush College," Methodist preachers emphasized free grace and free will, "the witness of the Spirit" over form and ceremony, works and "Christian perfection" over election. But eventually Methodism, founded in reaction to the established churches, came to spawn its own dissenters. In Vermont John and Nabby joined such a group—Reformed Methodists who believed that Episcopal or "high church" Methodism had itself strayed from the biblical doctrines of baptism by immersion and faith healing.[10]

In most matters, however, Methodism differed little from other Protestant religions. After the family moved to New York, they could fairly comfortably have supported, like other communicants in "this transplanted New England community," the Sherburne "Calvinistick Congregationalist Society." In 1808, when Brigham was seven, the annual meeting of this group included an unusual catechizing of small children and baptized youth "with regard to their views and feelings on religious subjects." Brigham may well have gone through this searing experience. The records of the group during the years the Youngs were there show disciplinary action taken against members who had violated the Christian Sabbath, gone to dances and "vain amusements," used "spiritous liquors," neglected family prayers, acted dishonestly in a business transaction, and not attended to public worship.[11]

With such a religious background, it is not surprising that several of the Young boys later became exhorters. John, the oldest, joined the Methodist church at fourteen or fifteen and remained "devotedly attached to that religion" until he became a Mormon.[12] Joseph, the next son, "was very moral and devoted," becoming "attached to religion" at an early age.[13] For many years he was a Methodist preacher, but he was also a seeker of sorts, once saying to Brigham, "There is not a Bible Christian in the world; what will become of the people?" (12:95) Phinehas, just a bit older than Brigham, was also partial to Methodism but for several years was unable to find a spiritual identity. Failing to "get religion" after his marriage in 1818, he continued to waver between religious and worldly values until the fall of 1823, just before his twenty-fourth birthday, when he joined the Methodist Reformed Church and received a "license to speak in public." After moving to Mendon in 1828, Phinehas took the lead in "opening a house for preaching." "We soon had a good society organized," he later wrote, "and the Lord blessed our labors."[14] He was a Methodist circuit rider at the time he was introduced to Mormonism.[15]

The last son, Lorenzo, was considered to be one of the meekest and most saintly of the brothers and very prayerful, but his "guardian spirit," he declared afterward, counseled him against joining any religious denomination. It was Lorenzo, according to his later testimony, who first intimated that he and the members of his immediate family would play a significant part in an important religious movement. In 1816, barely nine years old, Lorenzo had this startling dream:

I thought I stood in an open space of ground and saw a good, well defined road leading, at an angle of forty-five degrees, into the air as far as I could see. I heard a noise similar to that of a carriage in rapid motion, at what seemed the upper end of the road. In a moment it came into sight, drawn by a pair of beautiful white horses. The carriage and harness appeared brilliant with gold, and the horses traveled with the speed of the wind. It was manifested to me that the Savior was in the carriage, and that it was driven by His servant. It stopped near me and the Savior inquired, "Where is your Brother Brigham?" After answering His question He inquired about my other brothers, and concerning my father. His queries being answered satisfactorily, He stated that He wanted us all, but especially my brother Brigham. The team then turned about and returned the way it came. . . . Subsequent events proved that it foreshadowed our future. It was evidently fulfilled, when my father and all of his family entered into the new and everlasting Covenant [Mormonism].[16]

Brigham was "one with his brothers" in the seriousness with which he considered religion. Not being a ready reader, however, his study was mostly limited to private meditation that tended to be practical in outlook. This made him from boyhood "a person of observation," as he once characterized himself, noting, for instance, "When you see a person at a distance you can, at times . . . discern his spirit by the appearance of his countenance. This has been my experience from my younger days." (4:21) He would, as a boy, converse with himself about eternal things, "things which the frivolous, the vain, and those who are engaged only with the things of this world, never think of." (19:6–7)

Brigham was even more circumspect than his father in personal conduct, considering it his duty to control all passions, and, though he came to use tobacco, he abstained from liquor.

Young men would say to me, "Take a glass." "No, thank you, it is not good for me!" "Why, yes, it is good for you." "Thank you, I think I know myself better than you know me." . . . I recollect my father urged me [to sign the temperance pledge]. "No sir," said I, "if I sign the temperance pledge I feel that I am bound, and I wish to do just right, without being bound to do it: I want my liberty"; and I have conceived from my youth up that I could have my liberty and independence just as much in doing right as I could in doing wrong. (14:225)

Even in later life he confessed to an inclination to contend, when opposed, or "if a sharp word is spoken to me to give a sharp word back," though by then he gave in to this tendency "but rarely." (14:149) In younger years his temper was even more "indomitable and unyielding" (11:290); he became pugnacious when "crowded" or forced to do a thing. (9:248) Once, Brigham recalled, when eating at a boardinghouse, a fellow boarder made light of his, Brigham's, youthful vegetarianism, claiming he could throw "any man that don't eat meat."

Brigham angrily retorted: " 'Mr. Pratt, if you will step here into the middle of the floor I will show you how to dirty coats.' But he dared not try it." (16:17) Apparently such incidents were rare. His brother Joseph said he could remember Brigham getting angry only once, though "on this occasion he was violent, I thought."[17] Brigham learned early that a man may "overcome his passion if he will struggle earnestly to do so." (11:290)

Thus Brigham, with his brothers and sisters, endured and came to accept parental standards. "I do not know that I had ever committed any crime, except it were in giving way to anger, and that I had not done more than two or three times. I never stole, lied, gambled, got drunk, or disobeyed my parents." (8:37–38)

In one respect young Brigham was considered an "infidel": he would not swallow some of the prevailing religious doctrines, and he would not join a church. (15:165) "The priests were after me from the time I was eight years of age. . . . I used to think to myself, 'Some one of you may be right, but hold on, wait awhile! when I reach the years of judgment and discretion I can judge for myself; and in the meanwhile [I will] take no course either with one party or the other.' " (19:65; 14:112) Nevertheless, he spent "many anxious hours" searching for a religion that would satisfy his needs. (5:127) "In my youth . . . I would have freely given all the gold and silver I ever could possess, to have met with one individual who could show me anything about God, heaven, or the plan of salvation, so that I could pursue the path that leads to the kingdom of heaven." (9:248) In his search for religious truth he became "well acquainted with the Episcopalians, Presbyterians, New Lights, Baptists, Freewill Baptists, Wesleyan and Reformed Methodists."

But the practical and thoughtful youth was left unmoved, even by the noted Methodist revivalist Lorenzo Dow. Years later, from a Utah pulpit, Brigham gave a burlesque of one of Dow's sermons. "He stood up some of the time, and he sat down some of the time; he was in this position and in that position, and talked two or three hours, and when he got through I asked myself, 'What have you learned from Lorenzo Dow?' and my answer was, 'Nothing, nothing but morals.' He could tell the people they could not work on the Sabbath day; they should not lie, swear, steal, commit adultery, &c., but when he came to teaching the things of God he was as dark as midnight." (14:197)

Though it was a time of emotional extremes, of "those flaming, fiery revivals so customary" on the western New York frontier, Brigham was not a partaker. "I have seen them from my youth up, working on the passions of the people, making them crazy. About what? Nothing at all. I have seen them lie, when under their religious excitement, from ten minutes to probably an hour without the least sign of life in their systems; not a pulse about them, and lay the slightest feather . . . to their nose and not the least sign of breathing could be discerned there. . . . After lying awhile they would get up all right. 'What have you seen, sister or brother? What have you to tell us that you have learned while in this vision?' 'Nothing at all.' It always wound up like the old song, 'All about nothing at all.' " (8:37; 14:90)

Actually, the young Brigham was timid in such conclusions. As a youth, he deferred to the thinking of others, including his older brother Joseph. "I had more confidence in his judgment and discretion, and in the manifestations of God to him, than I had in myself." (8:37) Probably only in retrospect did he dare pronounce "one of the finest speakers America has ever produced" as having "no more sense in his discourse than in the bleating of a sheep or the grunting of a pig." At the time he "palliated the facts" by attributing incomprehension to his own ignorance. (14:198)

But at last, at age twenty-three, Brigham committed himself to Methodism. "I thought to myself," he said later, that "I would try to break off my sins and lead a better life and be as moral as I possibly could." What were his sins and where he was going after this life he did not know, but he thought he would like to be "as good as I know how while here." (14:197) At his express request he was baptized by immersion, local Methodist church elders consenting to do so only because he "absolutely required it." (14:197; 13:267) Brigham may have stretched the point a little in later declaring that one of his purposes in joining the Methodists was to prevent being pestered about his unbelief. "I joined the Methodists," he said, "to get rid of them and all the sects—same as the girl married the man to get rid of him."[18]

Once in the church Brigham was not content. He continued to believe that it lacked more profound yet explicit teachings about God and man.

> As I became acquainted with smart, intelligent, literary priests . . . I thought, Now I can obtain some intelligence from this or from that man; and I would begin to ask questions on certain texts of Scripture; but they would always leave me as they found me, in the dark. (5:73)

On the one hand, he had inherited a religious intensity unusual even for that era in the "Burned-Over District" of western New York, so called because of the prevalence of emotion-laden preaching by fiery-tongued evangelists and fervent emotionalism. On the other hand, he became increasingly cynical about professors of religion, an attitude he maintained throughout his life. "I would as lief go into a swamp at midnight to learn how to paint a picture," he said, "as to go to the religious world to learn about God, heaven, hell or the faith of a Christian." (14:198)

His cynicism came to extend to many of the frontier characters who peopled his world. He told of once overhearing a minister's wife comment to her sisters in the church: "Do you suppose that we shall be under the necessity of eating with our hired help when we get into heaven? We do not do it here, and I have an idea that there will be two tables in heaven." (14:100) Similarly critical of many men who were considered "good, clever, honest," he added:

I have seen deacons, Baptists, Presbyterians, members of the Methodist church, with long, solid, sturdy faces and a poor brother would come along and say to one of them, "Brother, such-a-one, I have come to see if I could get a bushel of wheat, rye or corn of you. I have no money, but I will come and work for you in harvest," and their faces would be drawn down so mournful, and they would say, "I have none to spare." "Well, deacon, if you can let me have one bushel, I understand you have considerable, I will come and work for you just as long as you say, until you are satisfied, in your harvest field, or haying or anything you want done."

After much talk this longfaced character would get it out, "If you will come and work for me two days in harvest, I do not know but I will spare you a bushel of rye."

When the harvest time comes the man could have got two bushels of rye for one day's work; but the deacon sticks him to his bargain, and makes him work two days for a bushel of wheat or rye. . . . I could not swallow such things . . . if they had been greased over with fresh butter. I did not read the Bible as they read it . . . said I, "Just go your own way, I want none of it." I wanted no religion that produced such morals. (15:164–65)

Then what was he looking for? Religion that conformed with the Bible and appealed to his mind.

I understood from the Bible that when the Lord had a church upon the earth it was a system of ordinances, of laws and regulations to be obeyed, a society presided over and regulated by officers and ministers peculiar to itself to answer such and such purposes, and to bring to pass such and such results. . . . (11:254)

Yet when he asked the ministers "how the kingdom of God should be built up; if that which is laid down in the New Testament is not the pattern," their reply was: "You know, my dear friend, that these things are done away." Brigham's conclusion was that "Jesus Christ had no true Church upon the earth." (11:254) As for the existing sects, he said, "I . . . found I could put all their doctrines, when simmered down to truth, into a snuffbox of the smallest class, put it into my vest pocket and go on my way."[19]

Thus Brigham Young's inner life was quite different from the cheerful, busy exterior remembered by neighbors. He often felt "cast down, gloomy, and despondent . . . lonesome and bad," he himself recalled; life seemed to be veiled with "a dark shade, like the shade of the valley of death." (3:320–21) Besides fear for Miriam's health he was plagued with a vague, continuing sense of guilt.

The Evil One would whisper to me that I had done this, that, or some other thing wrong, and inquire whether that looked like a Christian act, and remark, "You have missed it; you have not done right, and you know it; you did not do as well in such a thing as you might; and are you not ashamed of yourself in saying you are a Christian?" (7:6)

His observations had made him "sick, tired, and disgusted with the world"; to his mind society had produced only "sorrow, wretchedness, death, misery, disappointment, anguish, pain of heart . . . crushed spirits prevail over the earth." (6:39)

This, then, was the Brigham Young that Mormonism found: industrious, practical, respected, yet trusting few men and suffering from acute religious sensitivity. "He had reached the beginning years of his prime," Walker and Esplin have remarked, "without discovering the key for unloosing the torrent which lay within him."[20]

T H E steps that led Brigham and his parents, brothers, and sisters to become Mormons are described in their autobiographical recollections. In late August 1830, after reading the Book of Mormon, Phinehas and Joseph left New York on a preaching mission. Calling on an old acquaintance by the name of Solomon Chamberlain, they were surprised when he burst into an impromptu sermon on Mormonism. He told them that a church had been organized, ten or more had been baptized into it, and "everyone must believe the Book of Mormon or be lost." "This was the first I had heard of the necessity of another church," wrote Phinehas, "or of the importance of re-baptism; but after hearing the old gentleman's arguments, . . . I began to inquire seriously into the matter, and soon became convinced that such an order of things was necessary for the salvation of the world."[21]

Able to think of "but little except the Book of Mormon and what I had heard of Mormonism," Phinehas now found his own preaching ineffective and returned home. "I still continued to preach," he wrote, "trying to tie Mormonism to Methodistism [sic], for more than a year, when I found they had no connection and could not be united, and that I must leave the one and cleave to the other. . . ." It was at about this time that Brigham told him he was convinced there was something to Mormonism. Phinehas replied that he "had long been satisfied of that."[22]

What impressed the Youngs about the Book of Mormon was the plain, biblical style they recognized in it; its answers to questions of life and afterlife that had vexed them; its clarification of obscure passages in Isaiah, Revelation, and other books in the Old and New Testaments. Brigham was most attracted to the Restored Gospel's universality, its willingness to embrace truth wherever found. "When I undertook to sound the doctrine of 'Mormonism,' " Brigham explained, "I supposed I could handle it as I could the Methodist, Presbyterian, and other creeds of Christendom." Instead he discovered something new he could not quickly master. "I found it impossible to take hold of either end of it; I found it was from eternity, passed through time, and into eternity again.

When I discovered this, I said, 'It is worthy of the notice of man.' " (2:123–24) Further investigation, instead of causing him disillusion, increased his enthusiasm.

> Were you to ask me how it was that I embraced "Mormonism," I should answer, for the simple reason that it embraces all truth in heaven and on earth, in the earth, under the earth, and in hell, if there be any truth there. There is no truth outside of it; there is nothing holy and honorable outside of it; for, wherever these principles are found among all the creations of God, the Gospel of Jesus Christ, and his order and Priesthood, embrace them. (11:213)

After thoroughly examining the Book of Mormon, and coming to view it as of "priceless value," Brigham would have liked to study, as was his wont, the people who believed in it. But for a year and a half he had no opportunity of contact with the new sect. During this period his reading and pondering were interspersed only with religious conversations with members of his family and his friend Heber Kimball. Not until the fall of 1831 did Mormon elders again visit Mendon, apparently hying from Columbia, Bradford County, Pennsylvania, where there was a small Mormon branch. On their way to Kirtland, Ohio, since February 1831 the seat of the church and Joseph Smith's residence, they passed through the township, perhaps calling on the Youngs. This time Brigham himself heard them say that "the angel had visited Joseph with the fulness of the gospel," all men should repent, and "the signs and gifts of the Spirit would follow those that believed."[23]

Gifts of the spirit were indeed manifested by the Mormons. Heber Kimball was stirred, "for they spoke in tongues and interpreted, which tended to strengthen [our] faith."[24] Brigham, more cautious by nature, must have said to himself again, "Watch and see." But he too could not help but compare such a display to doings of the early Christians he was so familiar with from the Holy Book.

The missionaries returned to Mendon several months later. By now Brigham had mentally accepted their religion but was mulling over in his soul the costs of associating with it.

> I had this trial when I embraced this Gospel, "Can you forsake your friends and your father's house?" This was in the vision of my mind, and I had just as much of a trial as though I had actually been called to experience all that some really have. I felt, yes, I can leave my father, my brothers and sisters, and my wife and children, if they will not serve the Lord and go with me. . . .
>
> I did not know, when I was baptized, whether my wife believed the Gospel or not; I did not know that my father's house would go with me. I believed that some of them would [some already had], but I was brought to the test, "Can I forsake all for the Gospel's sake?" I can, was the reply within me. "Would you like to?" "Yes, if they will not embrace the Gospel." "Will not these earthly, natural ties be continually in your bosom?" "No; I know no other family but the family

of God gathered together, or about to be, in this my day; I have no other connection on the face of the earth that I claim." (4:281)

After hearing the missionaries preach, Brigham hurried home to his room to pray: "If this religion is true, send the missionaries to my home, that they might pray for my sick wife and also explain the gospel to her." Next evening, according to a statement of one of the elders, they happened to pass by Brigham's property. The thought came to them that the tidiness of the yard bespoke a person worth visiting. From the window Brigham saw them approach his door; he hurriedly welcomed them in and invited them to give Miriam a blessing. They were, he assured them, the answer to his prayer.[25]

These experiences kindled something in Brigham. "The brethren who came to preach the Gospel to me," he would later declare, "I could easily outtalk . . . though I had never preached; but their testimony was like fire in my bones; I understood the spirit of their preaching; I received that spirit; it was light, intelligence, power, and truth." (9:141) They called for obedience to the moral demands of the old Christian covenant, as a church should. They promised remission of sins and eternal salvation, the balm to the soul that religion should be. And the still, small voice of the Holy Spirit accompanied them and set their teachings apart.

Three weeks after the elders' visit, Brigham, Phinehas, their wives, and Heber Kimball traveled by horse and sleigh to Bradford County, Pennsylvania, to observe a Mormon meeting.[26] It was January 1832, and so eager were they, Brigham recalled, that "we traveled amid snow, fording rivers and sometimes crossing on the ice." On the way they visited Brigham's sister Nancy Kent in Steuben County. Once in Columbia,

We stayed with the church the[re] about six days, attended their meetings, heard them speak in tongues, interpret and prophecy: these things truly caused us to rejoice and praise the Lord. We returned home being convinced of the truth of these things . . . and bore testimony to the truth of those things which we had seen and heard to our friends and neighbors.[27]

A few days after their return, Brigham took another journey, this time to Kingston, Ontario—250 miles away—"to tell the glad tidings to our brother Joseph, who was there preaching Methodistism [sic], and to try to get him to come home with us." Joseph was easily persuaded. Deeply moved by the message Brigham brought, hailing it as his "spiritual jubilee—a deliverance from a long night of darkness and bondage," Joseph returned to Mendon with his brother, arriving in March.[28]

Other Youngs now made the pilgrimage to Bradford County. In April father John, Phinehas, and Joseph were baptized there. A friend said later that, while he had never seen Joseph Young laugh during the several years he was a Methodist, he now "laughed for six months" because he was "so overjoyed to think he had found out the truth."[29]

Either John brought the missionaries back to Mendon with him or they swiftly followed his trail, for ten days after the baptisms in Pennsylvania—on a cold, snowy Sunday, April 15—they baptized Brigham in the icy waters of his own mill pond. Eleazer Miller, only a four-month convert to Mormonism himself, performed the ordinance. "Before my clothes were dry on my back," Brigham later recalled, "he laid his hands on me and ordained me an Elder, at which I marvelled."[30]

The next day Brigham's friend Heber Kimball submitted to baptism. Feeling unworthy, he would not allow his ordination as an elder until a few days later. Within two weeks Vilate Kimball followed her husband, and in another week, as soon as the water was warm enough to more nearly favor her diseased condition, Miriam Young was baptized. Brigham needn't have worried over having to forsake his loved ones. A crucial corps of Mormonism's most devoted followers had cast their lot with the new faith.

O N C E his experience with the new believers had satisfied him, once he became fully and completely persuaded that the Mormon gospel "would save all the human family that would obey it, and it would make them righteous," Brigham then was proud to be identified with it. "When Mormonism came along," he said, "I fathomed it as far as I could and then I embraced it for all day long." (9:364; 8:15–16) After his baptism he could say that "religion has been a continual feast to me . . . it is Glory! Hallelujah! Praise God!" Now he hoped always to be found "walking in the light of eternal truth." (8:119, 129–30)

3 ✛

Ardent Disciple, 1832–1834

[After I was baptized into the Restored Church] I wanted to
thunder and roar out the Gospel to the nations. It burned in
my bones like fire pent up, so I [commenced] to preach the
Gospel of life to the people. . . . Nothing would satisfy me
but to cry abroad in the world, what the Lord was doing in
the latter days. . . . I had to go out and preach, lest my bones
should consume within me.[1]

O N E week after his baptism, Brigham Young gave his first
sermon. He was so carried away by the spirit that he spoke for more than one
hour. As with every sermon he gave in his lifetime, more than eight hundred
of which we have record, it was delivered without a prepared text or notes.
"I opened my mouth," he said, "and the Lord filled it."[2]

Brigham's own impression of his early attempts at public speaking was
that they were pitifully inadequate:

When I began to speak in public, I was about as destitute of language as a
man could well be. . . . How I have had the headache, when I had ideas to lay
before the people, and not words to express them; but I was so gritty that I always
tried my best.[3]

"When I first commenced speaking," he said on another occasion,

I made up my mind to declare the things that I understood, fearless of friends
and threats, and regardless of caresses. They were nothing to me, for if it was my
duty to rise before a congregation of strangers and say that the Lord lives, that
He has revealed Himself in this our day, that He has given to us a Prophet, and
brought forth the new and everlasting covenant for the restoration of Israel, and
if that was all I could say, I must be just as satisfied as though I could get up
and talk for hours. . . . Had it not been for this feeling, nothing could have
induced me to have become a public speaker.[4]

Despite his feelings of inferiority, there must have been, in his youth, some impulses toward preaching. His older brothers Joseph and Phinehas and his brother-in-law John P. Greene had done some itinerant preaching, and there is even family lore that his father had done some as well. Brigham was following in a family tradition. None of the family friends would have been surprised by this first vigorous and colorful discourse.

The sermon was delivered to other members of the new church. In April 1832, the Mendon branch consisted of fifteen families, eight of them Youngs. One member, Rachel Flummerfelt, had been baptized by Brigham himself. Nathan Tomlinson, owner of the inn where Phinehas had met Samuel Smith, had joined. Closest to Brigham was Heber C. Kimball, who, until his death in 1868, shared nearly all of Brigham's experiences in Mormonism. Shortly before their baptisms, Brigham's widowed sister Fanny married Roswell Murray, brother of Heber's wife Vilate, thus binding the families even closer together. Tall and lanky, with dark eyes that broke quickly into a twinkle when he thought of something humorous, Heber, like Brigham, lacked formal education but possessed a rich vocabulary of "homey" expressions that delighted audiences.

One morning, happening upon the Kimballs as they knelt in family prayer, Brigham silently joined them. Serving as voice was Alpheus Gifford, the Pennsylvania missionary who had done most to convert the Youngs and Kimballs. Gifford suddenly began to speak in an unknown tongue. "At the same instant," said Brigham, "the spirit came on me like an electric shock to speak in an unknown tongue, and though I was kneeling in an opposite direction, the same moment I turned round on my knees towards him and spoke in tongues also."[5] Those present were awed by this rare phenomenon in Mormonism.[6]

Such experiences helped the little branch survive the vicissitudes of unorthodoxy that soon presented themselves. On one occasion, when the Mendon branch was meeting in a barn in the neighboring town of Victor, nearby residents attacked the assemblage until they dispersed.[7] Brigham later gave a rueful description of the contemporary reaction to Mormonism:

> In the Branch where I lived, we had not met together three times before our beloved, kind, anti-Godlike Baptists, priests, and people declared that we had made a practice of meeting together, stripping stark naked, and there having the "holy roll." . . .
>
> You cannot mention any crime that this people called Latter-day Saints [a name preferred by Mormons, particularly after 1834] have not been accused of committing by their so-called Christian neighbors; and these stories would generally commence by the priests [ministers] whispering to some sister—"Did you hear of such and such a thing?" That was enough, all that was wanted, it became a solemn fact by the time it passed the third mouth.[8]

It is difficult now to comprehend the intensity with which these early Mormon converts grasped the new gospel. It became their vocation and avocation, Brigham feeling its power so strongly that he abandoned his shop and trade to devote himself wholeheartedly to the "Kingdom of God":

> I commenced to contract my business operations and dealings, and laid away my ledger, and notebooks, saying, "I shall never want you anymore." . . . I expected we should be one family, each seeking to do his neighbor good, and all be engaged to do all the good possible.[9]

Sheldon Fisher's investigations of Brigham Young's home and shop at Mendon suggest that this is indeed what happened.[10] Brigham simply left them—and they were apparently not used by anyone afterward. As for personal possessions, "I had not a coat in the world, for previous to this I had given away everything I possessed, that I might be free to go forth and proclaim the plan of salvation." He added: "I . . . had not a single doubt but what my wants would be supplied."[11]

Brigham placed Miriam, by now in weakened consumptive condition, under the care of Vilate Kimball and spent the summer of 1832 traveling and preaching with Heber. They canvassed Hector, Henrietta, Reading, Hornby, Patten, Avon, and Warsaw—all townships in western New York not far from Mendon. Like the early Christian apostles, they traveled "without purse or scrip," meaning they had no money or wayfarer's bag but depended on Providence (or those they encountered) for food and shelter. That they met with a degree of success can be learned from Brigham's advice many years later to missionaries sent out from Utah: he had gotten into homes, he said, and then tactfully become acquainted with the family before preaching to them. In this way he and Heber usually found a room and meal. Thus they "preacht as opertunity prezented," Brigham recorded in his diary, baptizing at least seven persons before returning home.[12]

He returned to Mendon to find Miriam dying. Still in the Kimball house, he nursed her through the final weeks. At last, on September 8, 1832, clapping her hands and praising the Lord, she drew her last breath. Brigham buried her in the town cemetery not far from his shop and accepted the Kimballs' offer to keep his daughters Elizabeth, seven, and Vilate, two. There was now nothing to prevent him from devoting himself fully to the church.

Miriam's death occurred at a critical point in Brigham's life. He had already been troubled by much in his social environment, even though he was learning to be a productive member of society and assume responsibility. He carried some psychological scars from his youth: his previously unexpressed grief over his mother's death when he was changing from a boy to a young man and the suppressed frustration and hurt fostered by his terse-spoken, demanding father. Miriam's death forced a catharsis, marking a dividing point he would never forget. Later he referred to his young manhood and first marriage as seeming so long ago and far away that it was as if they had been part of the life of a different person.

It was no accident that about the same time as her death—actually starting somewhat earlier—he was drawing close to the new religion. It gave him a new loyalty, a new commitment. It provided meaning in his life that he had not experienced before. In some ways the intense personal attachment to the prophet Joseph Smith took the place of his marriage. His willingness to overlook Joseph's flaws was not unlike the way in which partners in a marriage subordinate such things in the interest of a powerful loyalty. He was turning away from what he afterward called his "dark" background to his new life in "the light."

D U R I N G the summer of 1832, Brigham's sister Rhoda and her husband John Greene had moved to Kirtland to be with the body of Latter-day Saints. At the end of September, Brigham, his brother Joseph, and Heber Kimball decided it was time to go themselves to Ohio to meet the twenty-six-year-old prophet Joseph Smith. Taking Heber's wagon, they visited many friends and branches of the church along the 325-mile journey. "We exhorted them and prayed with them, and I spoke in tongues," Brigham wrote. "Some pronounced it genuine and from the Lord, and others pronounced it of the Devil."[13]

Once in Kirtland, they stayed with the Greenes. This, by Brigham's account, is how they first met the Prophet:

We went to his [Joseph Smith's] father's house, and learned that he [Joseph] was in the woods, chopping. We immediately repaired to the woods, where we found the Prophet, and two or three of his brothers, chopping and hauling wood. Here my joy was full at the privilege of shaking the hand of the Prophet of God, and received the sure testimony, by the Spirit of prophecy, that he was all that any man could believe him to be, as a true Prophet. He was happy to see us, and bid us welcome. We soon returned to his house, he accompanying us.[14]

Joseph Young recalled that, after welcoming them, Joseph Smith, tall, flaxen-haired, blue-eyed, and robust, "threw down his ax, and . . . we went with him to his house. He introduced us to his wife Emma; who was in bed with the infant, Joseph, her first born."[15]

Still with the Prophet that evening at prayers, Brigham again spoke in tongues. "As soon as we arose from our knees the brethren flocked around him [Joseph Smith] and asked him his opinion concerning the gift of tongues that was upon me." Joseph told them, "It is of God."[16] During the course of the evening the Prophet, who had never before heard speaking in tongues, received the gift himself. Those present remembered this event as a modern replication of "the day of Pentecost," when the early apostles were "filled with the Holy Spirit, and began to speak with other tongues, as the Spirit gave them utterance."[17] That Brigham, a seemingly practical, rather staid person, should have been one of the few who exercised this "gift" is extraordinary.[18] Only rarely did he speak in tongues after 1832.[19]

Brigham and his companions remained in Kirtland approximately a week and then, as Joseph Young wrote, "took leave of the man that could reveal the hidden things and the mysteries of the kingdom of God, as no other man ever did before."[20]

A F T E R their return from Kirtland, Brigham and Heber apparently abandoned their business and properties and once more resumed their free-lance missionary efforts in the region around Mendon. Brigham later summarized the labors of the summer and early fall of 1832 in western New York: "We went preaching into the North, East, West and South and started the work. . . . Seven months had scarce passed away when there was a dozen branches raised up."[21] In December he and his brother Joseph started out on foot for Kingston, Ontario, which Joseph had previously visited as a Methodist preacher. Brigham reported that they walked "most of the way through snow and mud from one to two feet deep."[22] They held about forty meetings and baptized fourteen persons. In February they returned to Mendon by crossing Lake Ontario from Kingston on the ice.

After a few weeks at Heber's home, even this stay punctuated by frequent forays into the western New York countryside "preaching and witnessing," Brigham left alone for Canada, again on foot. On the way he preached at Lyonstown, Aurelius, Clarksville, Indian River Falls, Shantyville, and Ogdensburg. The Canadian destination was "Loburro" (Loughborough), where he found seventeen persons had been baptized since he and Joseph had left them four months earlier. During this mission to upper New York and Canada in April and May of 1833, Brigham summarized each day's religious activities in his diary:

April 30. Started for Canaday, went to Palmiria, took a bote, went to Lyonds.

May 1. Spent the day with the brotherin.

May 2. Preached at Brother Drowns and the Lord pord out his spiret upon the people and I had good liberty in speaking.

May 3. Baptized six, held a prair meting in the evening and then preached to them.

May 4. Went to Sodas and the next morning, a Sunday, baptized two. The same day returned to Lyonds, held meting at Brother Drowns, had a good time. . . .

May 12. Preached at 9 o'clock at the new schoolhouse and at 3 p.m. north schoolhouse. Put up at Brother William Drapers. The presence of the Lord was with me. . . .

May 22. Took the steamboat *Great Britton*, landed at Kingston and from their to Brother James Lakes. Found them all well and in good sperits. . . .

May 27.   Monday. Went to Loburro, had a prair meting in the evning, found
the brotherin in good helth and in good sperits.

A busy time for Brigham, it was nevertheless an introspective period,
partly because he did not have the constant companionship of his brother
Joseph or his friend Heber. It may have been during this mission that "I made
up my mind . . . that I would be governed by certain principles and among
them I decreed that women should not govern me neither should my passions of lust or anger, but I would be boss over myself my passions and
appetites. . . ."[23]

Brigham remained in Canada until July 1, 1833, when he decided to accompany James Lake and family and Daniel and Abraham Wood to Kirtland. He remained there a week, helping the Lake family get settled.[24] He also took advantage of the opportunity to get better acquainted with Joseph Smith. At a meeting
of twenty or thirty elders, Smith, in the words of Brigham, "gave us the word of
the Lord"—advice that, because it widened the breach between Mormons and
non-Mormons in his mind, profoundly influenced Brigham's future.

> It was simply this: Never do another day's work to build up a Gentile [non-
> Mormon] city; never lay out another dollar while you live, to advance the world
> in its present state. . . . It is the word and commandment of the Lord to his
> servants that they shall never do another day's work, nor spend another dollar to
> build up a Gentile city or nation.[25]

What did the Prophet declare to be the responsibility of the Saints? Said
Brigham: "To sustain the Kingdom of God to your uttermost."[26] Brigham
determined to move to Kirtland, informing Heber and others after his return
to Mendon that they should do the same. Brigham's father had already made
the move, selling his land in May 1833 (apparently this included the property
on which Brigham's mill and home had been located) and leaving Mendon in
June without his wife Hannah, who refused to accompany him and instead
went to live with one of her sons at Tyrone. Two years later, she wrote John
that she wished to live with him again if he would come to get her. So Lorenzo
drove his father to Tyrone and moved Hannah to Kirtland, where she lived
until most of the Saints left it in 1838.[27]

Brigham, his brother Joseph, and Heber, meanwhile, continued their
proselyting in Lyonstown, Avon, Canandaigua, and Mendon. On September
4, according to his diary, Brigham performed his first marriage as "an Elder
in the Church of Christ." Later in the month Brigham and Heber, with their
"little families," including, of course, Brigham's girls, "gathered up to Kirtland."[28] They sent their household goods by boat and traveled by land in
Heber's wagon.

KIRTLAND, in the fall of 1833, was a village of about thirteen hundred
people. Situated on the Chagrin River some twenty miles northeast of Cleve-

land and eleven miles south of Fairport, it was a trading and milling village of rolling green hills, densely wooded areas, and fertile farming land. After some notable conversions there in the summer and fall of 1830, Joseph Smith had moved his New York membership of about two hundred into the Kirtland area in January and February of 1831, with new converts migrating there from Maine, Vermont, New Hampshire, New York, and Pennsylvania at the rate of several hundred per year.

In 1831, anxious to build a Zion or "City of God," Joseph Smith had appointed a "central" gathering place for the Saints in Jackson County, in western Missouri. About twelve hundred Saints, including most of his followers who had originally gathered at Kirtland, had gone there by the fall of 1833, but Kirtland remained the residence of Joseph Smith and more than a thousand Saints until 1838.[29]

Heber Kimball rented a small house where the Kimballs and Youngs crowded together until Brigham was able to build Heber his own home, completed in April 1834. In the meantime, for pay, Brigham also built homes for Andrew Cahoon and John Smith (uncle of Joseph Smith).

Among those who heard Brigham preach was Mary Ann Angell, a native of Seneca, Ontario County, New York, not far from Mendon. She had been working in Providence, Rhode Island, in 1830 when first introduced to Mormonism. Wishing to learn more, she returned to Ontario County in 1832, to be "on the scene" where Mormonism originated. There she met Joseph, Phinehas, and Lorenzo Young, all of whom encouraged her in the new faith, and she was finally baptized, along with her parents, by John P. Greene. She then "gathered" to Kirtland in the spring of 1833 and was there when Brigham and Heber arrived.

When Brigham heard her "bear testimony," he was impressed, as she had been when she heard him preach. They were married on February 18, 1834, when Brigham was thirty-two and she, born June 8, 1803, was thirty.[30] Whether Brigham had built his own house by then or had rented one is not clear; Brigham recorded only that Mary Ann "took charge of my children, kept my house, and labored faithfully for the interest of my family and the kingdom."[31]

T H E R E were two principal problems for Mormon leaders in Kirtland: first, acquiring land and establishing industries that would provide the means of a livelihood for incoming settlers; second, counteracting the opposition of old settlers who feared the Mormon migrants would eventually take over. Joseph Smith sought to provide the land by asking all converts to "consecrate" their "surplus" to the bishop of the church, who would then use it to purchase land and implements and support the building and publishing programs of the church. The second goal was to be achieved primarily by missionary work and the preparation and distribution of publications. At the same time, Smith announced plans to erect a "temple" for worship and the performance of religious ordinances, and the establishment of an adult education program called "School of the Elders."

As for "consecrating his surplus," Brigham, of course, had none to consecrate:

> When we arrived in Kirtland, if any man that ever did gather with the Saints was any poorer than I was—it was because he had nothing. I had something and I had nothing; if he had less than I had, I do not know what it could be. I had two children to take care of—that was all. I was a widower. "Brother Brigham, had you any shoes?" No; not a shoe to my foot, except a pair of borrowed boots. I had no winter clothing, except a homemade coat that I had had three or four years. "Any pantaloons?" No. "What did you do? Go without?" No. I borrowed a pair to wear till I could get another pair. I had travelled and preached and given away every dollar of my property. I was worth a little property when I started to preach; but I was something like Bunyan—it was "life, life, eternal life," with me, everything else was secondary.[32]

Though Brigham's skills as a craftsman were in heavy demand in Kirtland, a growing community, it would be some time before he could consider himself in comfortable circumstances.[33]

In the meantime, Mormon difficulties intensified in Ohio and Missouri.[34] In Kirtland, Smith was subjected to continuous legal harassment, was once tarred and feathered, and endured many threats to his life. In Independence, Missouri, a mob destroyed the Mormon store and printing establishment, tarred and feathered the bishop, and in November 1833 drove the Mormons from their homes with whippings and plunder. Many houses were burned, livestock killed, and furniture and other domestic property seized and carted away. The Saints complained to Governor Daniel Dunklin, who promised to restore their homes to them if they would provide him with a posse of assistance.

Joseph Smith decided to take the governor's offer in earnest and began recruiting an "army" of at least a hundred loyal Mormons to "help their brethren in Missouri." Among the first to volunteer were Brigham and Heber. Joseph Young, out preaching when the matter was first discussed, was later invited by Brigham to go with them.

> [Joseph] hesitated; but while walking together a few days afterwards we met the Prophet, who said to him, "Brother Joseph, I want you to go with us up to Missouri." I informed the Prophet that my brother was doubtful as to his duty about going, to which the Prophet replied, "Brother Brigham and brother Joseph, if you will go with me in the camp to Missouri and keep my counsel, I promise you, in the name of the Almighty, that I will lead you there and back again, and not a hair of your heads shall be harmed," at which my brother Joseph presented his hand to the Prophet, as well as myself, to confirm the covenant.[35]

With the departure of Zion's Camp two months away, Brigham and other volunteers each acquired a gun, bayonet, dirk, powder, and shot. They had also to take axes, saws, chisels, spades, hoes, and other tools for the Missouri Saints to use when restored to their homes, as well as food, bedding, clothing, teams, and wagons for themselves. The 2,000-mile round trip would require at least forty-five days each way.

Brigham had the added responsibility of providing for Mary Ann, now pregnant. Her brother Solomon Angell, who might have cared for her, wanted to go with Zion's Camp, as did Solomon's friend Lorenzo Booth. So they left their families with Mary Ann.[36]

About twenty men and four baggage wagons left Kirtland on May 1. Brigham was in a larger party of 135 recruits that joined the advance group four days later at Portage, Ohio. At that point Smith appointed general officers, announced that their monies would be pooled, and divided the band into companies of twelve, each electing a captain from its own ranks. Brigham and Heber were chosen captain of their companies, and, following standard camp procedure, organized their men as follows:

> . . . two to attend to cooking, two to see that fires were made, two to pitch the tent at night and prepare the bedding and also to strike the tent each morning, two to fetch and provide water, one to do the running, two to see to the horses and wagon, and have every thing prepared for starting. [The captain's] business was to see that the company was provided for, and that all things were done in order.[37]

Additional recruits were added along the trail. By the time they reached Missouri, there were 205 men, 11 women (wives of the recruits, taken along as cooks and washerwomen), and 7 children.[38] Their twenty-five baggage wagons were loaded with arms, supplies, and relief provisions for the embattled Saints in Missouri. With no room to ride, they all walked.

BRIGHAM'S recollections, and the remembrances of those with him, provide a visual image of the march in the summer of 1834. One memory that stood out was the hardship:

> The longest journey on foot that ever I took at one time was in the year 1834, when a company of the brethren went up to Missouri, the next season after the Saints were driven out of Jackson county. . . . We performed a journey of two thousand miles on foot; we started on the 5th day of May, and accomplished that journey inside of three months, carrying our guns on our shoulders, doing our own cooking, etc. And instead of walking along without having to labor, much of the way we had to draw our baggage wagons through mud holes and over sections of bad road. Twenty or thirty men would take hold and draw a wagon up a hill, or through a mud hole; and it was seldom that I ever laid down to rest until eleven or twelve o'clock at night, and we always rose very early in the

morning. I think the horn was blown at three o'clock to arouse us, to prepare breakfast, etc., and get an early start; and we averaged in the outward trip upwards of forty miles a day. . . .[39]

We laid on the ground every night, and there was scarcely a night that we could sleep, for the air rose from the ground hot enough to suffocate us, and they supplied musketos in that country, as they did eggs, by the bushel. . . .[40]

It was anything but a pleasure trip. Brigham's brother Joseph, reflecting upon the march at a Zion's Camp reunion in 1865, testified that

I never went through a more severe trial of my faith; it was as much as we all could bear. We performed 100 miles in three days, in the hottest weather, some of us at times carrying our muskets and knapsacks weighing some 20 or 30 pounds on our backs, traveling until the blood could be heard in our boots and shoes.[41]

At the start, wrote Heber Kimball, "Our living generally was very good, being able to buy bread from the bakers or inhabitants on the way through the settled part of the country [presumably Ohio and Indiana]." Farther along the trail, "we purchased flour and had to bake our own bread. We sometimes had to live mostly on johnny cake and corndodger, and sometimes our living was scant."[42] (Johnnycake was baked or fried bread made from cornmeal, eggs, and milk. Corn dodgers were made by cooling cornmeal mush and shaping it into oblong cakes that were then fried.)[43]

George A. Smith, at sixteen one of the youngest travelers, recorded the following for May 26: "The day was exceedingly hot and we suffered much from thirst, and were compelled to drink water which was filled with living creatures. Here I learned to strain wigglers with my teeth."[44] Young Smith also recounted a buttermilk incident worth reproducing:

Sat. May 17. We camped in the Township of Wayne, Indiana. Myself and many others were much fatigued and sore-footed and our stockings wet with blood for we had travelled 40 miles. I called at a house and drank the first buttermilk I ever drank in my life. I told the company what I had been drinking when they produced a bucket and desired me to get them some. I got them a bucketfull. All drank heartily except Roger Orton, who complained because it was the horses' drinking bucket. I told him that if he had seen the churn he would not complain of the bucket. They all laughed and sent for more.[45]

In the evenings there was singing and prayer. Brigham and his brother Joseph had learned, during their missions, to sing as a duet, and their "musical voices cheered many a drooping heart, and encouraged their flagging energies while performing that memorable journey." Levi Hancock added that "the songs of Brigham and Joseph were the sweetest I ever heard in the Camps of Zion."[46] A favorite anthem of the camp often sung by the Young duo and others contained a statement of purpose and a call to heroism.[47]

> *Hark! listen to the trumpeters!*
> *They sound for volunteers;*
> *On Zion's bright and flowery mount*
> *Behold the officers.*
>
> *Their horses white, their armor bright,*
> *With courage bold they stand,*
> *Enlisting soldiers for their king,*
> *To march to Zion's land. . . .*
>
> *We want no cowards in our bands,*
> *Who will our colors fly:*
> *We call for valiant-hearted men,*
> *Who're not afraid to die!*

This was often sung to the accompaniment of a fife made by Levi Hancock from the joint of a sweet elder tree. "That fife," George A. Smith remembered, "may be considered almost the introduction of martial music among the 'Mormons.' "[48]

It was to the interest of the Mormons to keep their mission secret. When local inhabitants asked Brigham Young where they were from, he cannily replied: "From every place but this, and we will soon be from this." "Where are you going?" "To the West."[49]

When they stopped to hold religious services each Sabbath, the camp was a curiosity. Such a service was held June 1 near Jacksonville, Illinois, with two or three hundred visitors present. George A. Smith reported as follows, illustrating the way in which they disguised their true identity and purpose.

> When Squire Cook (Joseph Smith) took standing professing to be a liberal free thinker he spoke to the people very freely about one hour on his particular views. . . . He was listened to with great attention and those present remarked that he was one of the greatest reasoners they ever heard. The free thinker was followed by Elder John S. Carter, who delivered a very eloquent address on "Practical Piety." Elder Joseph Young spoke on the principles of free salvation, followed by Elder Brigham Young, who set forth baptism as necessary for salvation. . . . The congregation was also addressed by Elder Orson Hyde on baptism for the remission of sins.
>
> After the services of the day were closed many of the people made remarks on the preaching they had heard. They thought Joseph Young was a Methodist, and were anxious he should stay in the country and preach. They supposed Brigham Young was a close Communion Baptist, Orson Hyde a Campbellite or Reformed Baptist, Lyman E. Johnson a Presbyterian, Amasa Lyman a Restorationer and Orson Pratt a Unionist.[50]

Heber C. Kimball wrote that the observers then "inquired if we all belonged to one denomination." The answer was "We *were* some of us Baptists, some Methodists, some Presbyterians, some Campbellites, some Restorationers."[51]

The march proved a training mission for Brigham along with every other member of Zion's Camp. Unlike most armies, its members knelt in solemn prayer every evening; like them, it saw plenty of "bitching" during the daytime. Brigham was both shocked and angry at this, expecting Joseph Smith to call down the wrath of heaven upon the malcontents. Instead the young Prophet taught him some lessons in the handling of refractory human nature. George A. Smith wrote:

> The Prophet . . . never uttered a murmur or complaint, while most of the men in the camp complained to him of sore toes, blistered feet, long drives, scanty supply of provisions, poor quality of bread, bad corn dodger, "frouzey" butter, strong honey, maggoty bacon and cheese, etc. Even a dog could not bark at some men without their murmuring at Joseph. If they had to camp with bad water, it would nearly cause rebellion. *Yet we were the Camp of Zion*, and many of us were careless, thoughtless, heedless, foolish or devilish, and yet we did not know it. Joseph had to bear with us and tutor us like children.[52]

Under such tutoring Brigham's instinctive anger at "uneasy, unruly, and discontented spirits" was bent to more nearly resemble Joseph's patient and forgiving nature. Afterward Brigham would refer to the culprits as "Zion's Scamps."[53]

In early June, Joseph Smith appointed Orson Hyde and Parley P. Pratt to hurry ahead to Jefferson City, Missouri, to obtain confirmation from Governor Dunklin of his pledge to assist the Saints. The two envoys returned on June 15 with the distressing news that Dunklin had changed his mind: faced with the prospect of a nasty civil war over the matter, he had simply withdrawn his support. On June 16, the matter came to fiery debate at a crowded courthouse in Liberty, Clay County, Missouri; anti-Mormon sentiment was at the boiling point, and the meeting adjourned in a stalemate just short of bloodshed. Clearly, the Saints were going to have trouble regaining their lands in Jackson County.[54]

A S Zion's Camp approached Jackson County, threats of mob violence lowered on every hand. The evening of June 19 found the camp established on a rise between two branches of Fishing River not far east of the Clay County line. It was to be a night of terror and deliverance.

"Just as we halted and were making preparations for the night," wrote Heber Kimball,

> five men rode into the camp and told us we should see hell before morning, and such horrible oaths as came from their lips I never heard before. They told us that sixty men were coming from Richmond, who had sworn to destroy us; also seventy more were coming from Clay county, to assist in our destruction. These men were black with passion, and armed with guns; the whole country was in a rage against us, and nothing but the power of God could save us.[55]

The "power of God" was manifest within minutes of the visitors' departure. The sky became "overcast with densely dark and angry clouds," and "the rain began to fall in torrents, accompanied with terribly fierce wind."[56] Brigham and most of the others were sheltered in a nearby log meetinghouse. Huddled together, they watched the awesome spectacle, as described by Levi Hancock:

> I have witnessed rain storms in various portions of the earth, but nothing I have ever experienced has equaled that storm . . . missiles of hail . . . were hurled in vast quantities by the currents of wind that rushed and roared through the woods . . . causing the sound of falling trees and massive limbs to add additional terrors to the general clang of the storm.
>
> The heavens above us were so completely lit up by the electric display that the dense and sombrous clouds appeared as ponderous masses floating through luminous areas of glowing light. . . . Amazement filled our minds as we contemplated the inimitable wonders of the God of nature.[57]

Another member of Zion's Camp remembered:

> The lightning flashed and thunder roared one continual sound and flash so connected one could hardly hear any interval between the flash and the peal of thunder, as if all the Marshal [martial] bands of drummers of the whole earth had assembled and was beating the bounds of war.[58]

The terror and wonderment gave way to a realization that the storm would prevent the mob from reaching them.[59] "It was evident," reflected Heber, "the Almighty fought in our defence."[60] Later they learned that the mob had come within two miles of them before encountering impassable, swollen waters. "The hail fell so heavy upon them," Heber was told, "that it beat holes in their hats, and in some instances even broke the stocks off their guns; their horses being frightened fled leaving the riders on the ground."[61]

Next day came another heaven-sent visitation in the person of Colonel John Sconce, who, with two other representatives from Ray County, wished to ascertain the camp's "intentions."[62] Smith explained the sufferings and persecutions of his people, indicated that the camp's purpose was to assist the Saints in Missouri in whatever ways they could, and assured Sconce that the group "had no intentions to molest or injure any people, but only to administer to the wants of our afflicted brethren."[63] The colonel and his companions were moved by Smith's eloquent discourse:

> They arose and offered him their hands, and said they would use their influence to allay the excitement which every where prevailed against us. They accordingly went forth and rode day and night to pacify the people; and they wept because they saw we were a poor, afflicted people, and our intentions were pure.[64]

For the moment, at least, Zion's Camp could breathe a little easier.

The sense of well-being would be short-lived. On the very day of Sconce's visit three of the Mormon band fell sick with cholera. Within the week it would scourge the camp, but before then other difficulties had to be faced. One was what to do with the camp now that its mission was null. Smith answered this problem by simply dissolving it, advising those free to do so to remain in Missouri, and those with families in Kirtland or elsewhere to return home. They would have to wait before Zion could be redeemed.[65]

Most men, Brigham and Heber among them, stayed temporarily with the camp, for a substantial supply of clothing, bedding, and other relief provisions had yet to be delivered to the exiled Saints in Clay County. Hence, on June 23, the march toward Liberty, Clay County, resumed. Only five or six miles short of their goal, they were met by a small military contingent headed by General Clyde B. Atchison, "who desired us not to go to Liberty because the feelings of the people were so much enraged against us."[66] Heeding Atchison's advice, Joseph Smith turned his company upon a different course, at length situating them about two and a half miles from Liberty, "on the bank of Rush Creek, in Brother Burket's field."[67]

There at Rush Creek, late in the evening of June 24, the nightmare of cholera descended. "About 12 o'clock at night," wrote Heber, "we began to hear the cries of those who were seized. Even those on guard fell with their guns in their hands to the ground."[68] Joseph B. Noble wrote a graphic description of his own struggles:

. . . just at the time when we were dismissed to make our own arrangements to get back, Behold, the Colerry came on us with mighty power and forteen of our best men fell, and I my-self verry narely ascaped with my life. . . . I . . . was violently seased with the Collery, puking and purging powerfully then cramping from head to foot in the most powerful manner. With a burning fever in my bowels, in this situation I lay forty hours. My voice and my hearing had nearly left me. While in this situation Brothers Brigham Young, Joseph Young, Heber C. Kimball, Orson Hide and Peter Whitmeer, with some three or fore more, prayed for me. I was laying on the floor, and they formed a ring around me. While in this situation, the vail became verry thin between me and my God.[69]

"It was truly affecting," wrote Heber C. Kimball,

to see the love manifested among the brethren for each other during this affliction; Brother Joseph [Smith], seeing the sufferings of his brethren, stepped forward to rebuke the destroyer, but was immediately seized with the disease himself; and I assisted him a short distance from the place, when it was with difficulty he could walk.[70]

For four days the cholera raged; of the sixty-eight stricken, fourteen died. "We felt to sit and weep over our brethren," wrote Kimball, "and so great was our sorrow that we could have washed them with our tears."[71] Several of the victims were wrapped for burial in blankets only, as no lumber for coffins was available. Interment was by night, under guard, on a small rise near Rush Creek.

Brigham and Joseph Young were among the most active in caring for the sick and burying the dead. "Their presence gave us much consolation," Heber Kimball recalled. At one point,

> While brother Luke Johnson was digging, the cholera attacked him with cramping and blindness; brother Brigham laid hold of him and pulled him out of the grave, and shook him about, talked to and prayed for him, and exhorted him to jump about and exercise himself; when it would leave him for a few moments, then it would attack him again; and thus we had the greatest difficulty to keep the destroyer from laying us low.[72]

Heber himself was among the afflicted. He fought as violently as if it were a human opponent "to extricate myself from the grasp of death."[73]

Brigham, who with his brother Joseph was spared, related the circumstances under which the epidemic was finally checked:

> President Joseph Smith called the members of the camp of Zion together, and told them if they would humble themselves before the Lord, and covenant that they would from that time forth obey his counsel, that the plague should be stopped from that very hour, and there would not be another case in camp, whereupon the brethren with uplifted hands covenanted that they would from that very hour hearken to his counsel and obey his word, and the plague was stayed according to the words of the Lord through his servant.[74]

On July 3, 1834, all the members of Zion's Camp were officially discharged. The next day, Brigham and his brother, "in company with several of the brethren, started for home, and walked all the way, arriving in Kirtland in August."[75]

H O W E V E R disappointing Zion's Camp had been, it is clear that to Brigham Young it was well worth every foot-sore, mosquito-ridden, mob-threatened mile. From among the faithful of Zion's Camp were to be chosen many of the prophets, apostles, and other responsible leaders who would stand at the head of the church for decades to come. Brigham never questioned its immense value to himself. Perhaps his most significant statement on the matter was made many years after that journey:

> I have travelled with Joseph a thousand miles, as he has led the Camp of Israel. I have watched him and observed every thing he said or did . . . for the town of Kirtland I would not give the knowledge I got from Joseph from this Journey; and then you may take the State of Ohio and the United States, and I would not

give that knowledge for them. It has done me good and you good and *this was the starting point of my knowing how to lead Israel.* I watched every word and summed it up, and I knew just as well how to lead this kingdom as I know the way to my own house. It is God within me, and God upon me; God by day and by night, and it is for His Kingdom on the earth.[76]

On another occasion he commented on what he had learned about the complexities of organizational behavior:

> My measure was filled to overflowing with the knowledge that I had received by travelling with the Prophet. When companies are led across the plains by inexperienced persons, especially independent companies, they are very apt to break into pieces, to divide up into fragments, become weakened, and thus expose themselves to the influences of death and destruction.[77]

From what many termed the "failure" of Zion's Camp, Brigham had reached his own conclusion:

> When I returned from that mission to Kirtland, a brother said to me, "Brother Brigham, what have you gained by this journey?" I replied, "Just what we went for; but I would not exchange the knowledge I have received this season for the whole of Geauga County; for property and mines of wealth are not to be compared to the worth of knowledge."[78]

For Brigham Young, in 1834 energetic but inexperienced as a leader, Zion's Camp had been a momentous beginning.

4 ✤

Apostle

> Some of the knowing ones marvelled when we [Heber Kim-
> ball and I] were called to the Apostleship. It was indeed a
> mystery to me; but when I considered what consummate
> blockheads they were, I did not deem it so great a wonder.
> When they would meet brother Kimball and myself, their
> looks expressed, "What a pity!" Then I would think, You may,
> perhaps, make tolerably good men after a while; but I guess
> that you will tumble out by-and-by, just as they did: they
> could not stay in the Gospel net, they were so big and grew
> so fast; they became larger than the ship and slid overboard.[1]

W H E N Brigham returned to Kirtland, he worked periodically
for wages at his carpentry, painting, and glazing trade. But his major effort
through the fall and winter of 1834 was devoted to "public" construction—
"quarrying rock, working on the Temple and finishing off the printing office
and school room."[2] He attended a grammar school that was held for a few
weeks. In October, Mary Ann was delivered of her first child (and Brigham's
third), Joseph Angell.

Brigham had several personal experiences with Joseph Smith during these
months. Denis Lake, a Zion's Camp participant, disillusioned by his experience
and supported by several witnesses, sued Smith for breach of contract; that
is, for failing to provide him the lot of Missouri land allegedly promised those
who made the march. As a principal witness for the defense, Brigham acknowledged that everything had not gone as had been wished and that the
impatient and critical would suppose many instances of failure. But "not one
word will fail," he assured the court. When asked how much he understood
a "lot" of land to mean, Brigham replied, "In the cemetery it generally means
six feet." The plaintiffs lost the suit.[3]

At a Sunday worship service, Smith listened to Brigham and Joseph Young
sing and preach and then invited them to his home to sing for him, as they
had done during Zion's Camp. He reminisced about Zion's Camp, grieved

over those who had died from the cholera, and talked about his plans for the church "until he had exhausted much of his feelings." He told both Brigham and Joseph that they would soon be called as special witnesses to the truth of Mormonism.[4]

BACK in June 1829, Joseph Smith had stated that he had received divine instruction to appoint twelve special disciples to "go into all the world to preach my gospel unto every creature." Just as Jesus had chosen apostles to direct the mission of the church in his day, these latter-day Twelve would testify to the divinity of Christ, see that the Christian message was carried, and perform "a marvelous work among the children of men." The Twelve were to be selected by the three individuals who had seen the plates of gold from which the Book of Mormon had been translated: Oliver Cowdery, David Whitmer, and Martin Harris.[5]

On Saturday, February 14, 1835, a few months after the return of Zion's Camp and almost five years from the time the church had been organized, Joseph Smith called together the veterans of the camp and other leading church officials for a "conference." Smith set the tone for the meeting by reading from Christ's instructions to his apostles in John 15 of the New Testament. He had seen in vision, Smith said, the calling and order of the quorums of Apostles and Seventies. He knew by the Spirit that "it was the will of God" for those who had gone to Zion at the risk of their lives to be the ones to "be ordained to the ministry and go forth to prune the vineyard for the last time."[6]

After prayer and ordination, the Three Witnesses, as they were called, proceeded to choose twelve men "as apostles, to go to all the nations, kindreds, tongues, and people." Brigham was the second to be selected, Heber the third. Listed in order of age, the twelve were: Thomas B. Marsh, David W. Patten, Brigham Young, Heber C. Kimball, Orson Hyde, William E. McLellin, Parley P. Pratt, Luke S. Johnson, William Smith, Orson Pratt, John F. Boynton, and Lyman E. Johnson. Only three of these (Marsh, McLellin, and Boynton) had not been members of Zion's Camp.[7]

In his ordination Brigham Young was promised a strong body and long life, "that he might go forth and gather the elect, preparatory to the great day of the coming of the Lord." Besides recognizing his desire to preach and his power as a messenger of truth, the speaker ordained him to grow in his office, "that he may add ten talents: that he may come to Zion with many sheaves." The blessing predicted that he would travel abroad, "behold heavenly messengers going forth," and "do wonders in the name of Jesus" by the power of his priesthood. Finally, possibly in reference to the American Indians, Brigham was promised that he would have influence among "heathen nations" and would take pleasure in "declaring the tidings to nations that know not God."[8]

One week later, on February 21, when those not present at the initial meeting were ordained, the Twelve were given an "apostolic charge" by Oliver Cowdery, assistant president of the church—a charge that Brigham "treasured up" in his heart.[9] "You have enlisted in a cause that requires your whole attention," Cowdery said. "The greatness of your commission consists in this: you are to hold the keys of this ministry: you are to go to the nations afar off—nations that sit in darkness." While the sacrifice would be great, the apostles would be blessed:

> You will see what you never expected to see; you will need the mind of Enoch or Elijah, and the faith of the brother of Jared [in the Book of Mormon]; you must be prepared to walk by faith, however appalling the prospect to human view.

With all of this there was also a promise: "Your lives shall be in great jeopardy; but the promise of God is, that you shall be delivered."[10]

Cowdery enjoined the Twelve to be unified: "You are as one; you are equal in bearing the keys of the Kingdom to all nations. . . . This appointment is calculated to create for you an affection for each other stronger than death."

Joseph Smith gave further instructions to the Twelve on February 27. When the Twelve assembled, he said, they should appoint one of them to preside over the meeting and another to keep a record of their proceedings and decisions. Obviously, he intended for them to function as a separate quorum, at least on occasion, with their own secretaries, minutes, and presiding officer. Although their assignments would take them far afield, they should, to the extent possible, function as a group. "They are . . . to preside over all the churches of the Saints among the Gentiles [non-Mormons], where there is no presidency established; and they are to travel and preach among the Gentiles, until the Lord shall command them to go to the Jews. They are to hold the keys of this ministry to unlock the door of the kingdom of heaven unto all nations, and to preach the Gospel to every creature."[11]

From the very beginning, then, the Twelve Apostles were to be "witnesses for Christ" throughout the world and preside over areas of the church away from the center. They were to be, as Joseph Smith told them, "equal in authority and power" to the presiding officers of the church.[12]

B Y late March, the Twelve had completed plans for a series of proselyting missions and meetings to organize the branches of the church in New York, New England, and Ontario. They would also collect monies to buy land for "gathering the Saints."

Their departures were set for May 4. On May 2, Joseph held "a grand Council of all the church authorities in Kirtland" in which he organized the Twelve according to age and provided a structure of leadership.[13] Thirty-four-year-old Brigham, the second called, now sat number three, behind Thomas B. Marsh and David W. Patten, both less than two years his senior. Heber, just fourteen days Brigham's junior, was seated fourth. After this first arrangement of seniority, any new replacements were to be seated in the order of their ordinations.

Brigham capsulated his activities of the next two days, May 3 and 4, in his diary:

> This day held a meting with my Brotherin the Twelve. In the evening we met at the house of President Joseph Smith Jr. At two oclock in the morning of the 4th wee the Twelve started on our mishon to the East, acompened by two other Brotherin.

Apparently they started in the night in order to meet a steamer in Fairport, on Lake Erie, at 6:00 A.M.

This mission was to last five months. The Twelve traveled individually and in pairs to preassigned towns and villages for a week or two, after which, by prior agreement, they would meet at a central location for a two-day preaching "conference." Brigham's diary indicates that he usually spent each morning walking to a given village. In the afternoon he contacted known local members and arranged for a meeting place. In the evening he "preacht" to the people. Staying overnight with some willing family, he would start out by foot the following morning for the next village.

One of Brigham's first encounters was with a relative at Dunkirk, on Lake Erie. He and his companion preached the gospel to the man, but he was "not inclined" to receive it, and, Brigham coolly notes, "to avoid calling on me to ask a blessing at table, he asked the blessing himself, probably for the first time in his life."[14] During the last week of May, Brigham, now with his brother-in-law, John P. Greene, visited with an Indian group, of which, Brigham notes, one chief was a Presbyterian and one a pagan.

By midsummer Brigham was seeing members and branches in his former mission field of Ontario, where the brethren now had limited success. One problem was hecklers—Brigham and William E. McLellin "preached to an attentive congregation" on July 5 until one Daniel Perry "made som distirbance and tride to brake up the meting but was stoped by the oner of the house." On July 23, after Brigham's companion had given a sermon,

> . . . a woman got up and . . . sed that we ware prud decevers and ahoering [awhoring] after the wiming [women] and monney. A number of them spoke and after they had got thruw I arose and spoke. I testifide against the Sperit they had, then went to my apointment which was at 5 p.m. and I preached to the congrtion.

But the major problem was skepticism and rejection, which occasionally moved Brigham to invoke a New Testament curse on the people:

> At intermision we cald upon the charity of the people to help ous on our jurney. Old Mr. Snider gave a York shillen [shilling] and a black man gave ten or eleven

cents. When I was a preachin the Sperit came upon me to shake my garments in their presence and declare myself clar from their blood. We then left the naborhood.

This symbolic gesture of shaking the dust off their garments (and subsequently washing their feet in the first stream they crossed) was to witness to God the stubborn refusal of the townspeople to listen to the message of repentance.[15]

Some of the groups Brigham preached to were not small. On Sunday, July 19, for instance, he faced a conference composed primarily of members:

> . . . the barn and yard were crowded. It was thought their ware between two and three thousand people. Their was 144 cariges that was counted by the Brotherin. Here we found fathers and mothers, brothers and sisters. Here we had our wants administered to more than eney other church.

Though the crowds were usually more modest, the Twelve nevertheless found many ready and willing to abandon family, property, and livelihood to follow the new church.

After preaching in the Boston area during August and early September, Brigham and a companion traveled twenty miles southwest to Hopkinton to visit his Howe relatives. He found his grandmother Howe "alive and comforttible weel for heir. She exsprest grate joy for the privileg of seeing one of mother's children once more."

The mission ended with his return to Kirtland on September 26. "This season," as he called it, he had traveled by wagon, canal boat, and on foot, a total of 3,264 miles, or an average of almost 20 miles a day. Arriving home, "we found our fameules well, and [likewise] all the Brothering."

A L T H O U G H Brigham took some time to provide for the needs of his family, he was soon asked to superintend the painting and finishing of the temple. He possibly designed and quite certainly glazed the windows—both the dramatic Federal-style arched windows that framed the triple-tiered pulpits at each end of the temple, and the unusual Gothic but sectioned side windows with their intricate panes. He worked closely with his early Canadian convert, Artemus Millett, who was supervising the exterior masonry work. Millett had invented for the exterior of the temple a remarkably hard and beautiful plaster that shone in the sun because of the china dishes donated by the Mormon women to be broken up in it.[16]

Once work on the temple resumed, Brigham had little time to support his family. This second winter in Kirtland was a season of poverty for the Youngs. Smith had told the Twelve that they had "a right by virtue of their offices to call upon the churches to assist them" and their families.[17] But Brigham would not call for church help except in the direst emergency. "Who supported my family?" he asked rhetorically. "God and I. Who found clothing? The Lord and myself."[18] He also borrowed. Jonathan Crosby remembered that Brigham Young, Heber Kimball, and Parley Pratt were "very poor" in January 1836. Brigham stood in the door of the printing office, a building he had helped construct, "thinking of his condition & he felt so bad the swet rold off . . . him. Soon P P Pratt [a fellow apostle] came along, & he said to him, What shall we do? I have nothing to eat & dont know whare to get it. . . ." Parley knew that Crosby, who had just arrived, had some money and at his suggestion Brigham, Heber, and Pratt went to Crosby and each borrowed $25 to feed his family.[19]

There were other church responsibilities in addition to the work on the temple. Brigham and his colleagues assisted in the ministry in the Kirtland region. Later they were assigned to oversee all missionary labors in outlying areas.[20] Then Joseph Smith invited the Twelve and other leading elders of the church to form what he called the School of the Prophets, where instruction would be given in theology, philosophy, history, and languages. Here, too, sacred ordinances were performed, such as the washing of feet,[21] which were calculated "to unite our hearts, that we may be one in feeling and in sentiment and that our faith may be strong, so that Satan cannot overthrow us, nor have any power over us."[22]

Mormonism would need such bonds. For, while the Kirtland church produced many signs of unity and Christian love, some of the Twelve, having basked in the importance of presiding over eastern branches, felt slighted when they sometimes appeared to play second fiddle to the Kirtland High Council, a group of twelve men who had the responsibility of governing the Kirtland Stake (diocese). They had "borne the burden in the heat of the day [i.e., Zion's Camp], and passed through many trials," and they expected the church presidency to show more confidence in them. The day came when these things were expressed to the Prophet "in a verry forcible and explicit manner, yet cool and deliberate."[23] Brigham was not among the complainants. Why does Joseph "keep the Twelve so far from him and snob them so much," he later remembered them exclaiming. "We are Apostles; it's an insult for us to be treated so." Brigham's reflection on this was that Joseph "snobed us and when we proved ourselves willing to be everybody's servant for Christ's sake, then we are [became] worthy of power."[24]

Smith's response was characteristically mild. After eliciting a pledge that "they were determined to persevere in the work of the Lord," he assured the Twelve that he had not lost confidence in them and that their authority was "next to the presidency." From that time there seems to have been no question that the Twelve were second in authority; they were seated second and came second in voting after the presidency.[25] With this matter settled, church authorities in Kirtland held a harmonious Sunday meeting wherein "the Lord poured out his Spirit upon us, and the brethren began to confess their faults one to the other and the congregation was soon overwhelmed in tears and some of our hearts were too big for utterance."[26]

As the temple neared completion, Smith apparently felt the time was ripe to begin the ordinance work to be associated with it. On the evening of January 22, 1836, the Twelve and other church authorities met in the temple to receive "the ordinance of holy anointing." Joseph Smith placed his hands on their heads, one at a time, and pronounced blessings that those present considered marvelous. The Twelve then exercised their authority by anointing the Seventy (a group of men appointed especially to do missionary work; Brigham's brother Joseph was the first president of the Seventies). There followed a general "spiritual feast" during which some received visions, spoke in tongues, and were attended by "ministering angels."[27] Brigham sometimes later alluded to these experiences, but in general he followed Joseph Smith's advice, "If God gives you a manifestation, keep it to yourselves."[28]

T H E most important event in Kirtland during the spring of 1836 was the dedication of the Kirtland Temple on March 27. Hundreds of Saints and priesthood officers were present. For the new church, now having fewer than five hundred members in the Kirtland area all struggling for basic survival, the $60,000 three-story building was a remarkable accomplishment.

The evening after the dedicatory prayer, Smith gathered the Twelve and other leaders into the temple to instruct them on the ordinance of washing of feet and also "the spirit of prophecy."[29] Brigham wrote that he and other members of the Twelve received the washing of feet ordinance three days later, adding, "I . . . was privileged to listen to the teachings and administrations of the Prophet of God."[30] The religious enthusiasm included prophesying and speaking or singing in tongues. Some felt the presence of heavenly beings.[31]

After the ordinance, Smith gave instructions while the Twelve prepared the bread and wine. The Twelve, Smith said, "are not to serve tables, but to bear the keys of the kingdom to all nations." Where would they go? "The Twelve are at liberty to go wheresoever they will and if one shall say, I wish to go to such a place, let all the rest say Amen."[32] So spiritually exalted was the experience that for several hours the participants did not wish to leave. They had received their first "divine endowment."[33]

Brigham, profoundly impressed, nevertheless kept a sense of perspective about this "Pentecost." He had always believed in the reality of spiritual manifestations, but that they should not be sought. He later told of an experience he had with the Twelve, probably at this time. The Twelve, he said, "Set Stakes" to see an angel. They were determined to pray until they did so. But they never saw one, "though [we] prayed ourselves into darkness." Understanding what had happened, Young "praid to God with all my heart that I might never again meet with that Quorum with the spirit they possessed and I never did."[34]

A final vicarious experience connected with the temple dedication was impressed indelibly on Brigham's mind. Joseph Smith and Oliver Cowdery reported that, in a sacred moment in the temple, they had seen and received, in turn, Moses, with the keys of the gathering and the return of the Ten Tribes; Elias, with the keys of the dispensation of Abraham; and Elijah, with the keys of redemption and sealing.[35] The Twelve later testified that they received all of these keys from the Prophet, with the instruction to use them to build up the Kingdom of God.[36]

J O S E P H Smith suggested that Brigham and Joseph Young undertake a mission to New England to preach to their family and friends. Although in debt, Brigham did not hesitate. "It has never entered into my heart," he declared when later remembering this time, "from the first day I was called to preach the Gospel to this day, when the Lord said, 'Go and leave your family,' to offer the least objection."[37]

This did not necessarily mean that leaving Mary Ann and the children was easy, nor that his attitude toward their welfare was cavalier. He made arrangements for them as best he could. But he did trust the church (and, more than that, God) to provide for them in his absence, writing Mary Ann:

> What shal I say to you to comfort your hart. I pray for you and I feele that the Lord will bles you and keep you from danger and bare you upon the arms of faith. Tell the children that I remember them in my prares. I pray the Lord to give you strength and wisdom in all things.

Brigham probably knew by then that she was again pregnant, though he could not yet have guessed that she would produce twins.

The two letters that survive from this mission reveal, besides Brigham's deep and particular concern for Mary Ann and the children, his loneliness:

> Let me say to Elizebeth [now eleven], be a good girl and mind your mother and be good to Vilate [now seven] and letle Joseph [only two], and I [k]now you will be. Vilate be a good girl and mind your mother and studdy your book. . . . Mary, kiss that lettle son of ours and tell him to make hast[e] and groe so he can goe with me. . . . If enney [of] the Brethern inquire about me tell them I am doing as well as I can. So Fair Well. The Lord bless you.[38]

In July he wrote:

> Once more I take my pen in hand to right to you. I think this is the fo[u]rth time that I have ritten to you sence I left home, but I have not heard a word from you sence I left. I have som faint hopes that I shall here from you when I get to Boston. . . . I am calculating to return home as so[o]n as posable after the first of September.

He said his first intention on reaching home was to "pay for my house and I want to repare it this fall so that I can feele contented about my famely when I leve them." He concluded: "My Dear Mary, I remember you continuly in my prayrs. My love to all my little children. Be good to your mother and pray for me when I am away. Fairwell. I remane your hosbon and frend."[39]

Brigham's mission would bear much fruit. It would bring a number of firsts—his first train trip (from Providence to Boston); his first visits to Connecticut, Rhode Island, and Maine as well as returns to New York, Vermont, and Massachusetts; and his first eastern journey with his beloved Prophet, who joined him in Massachusetts. Of course, there were some of the old, familiar occurrences, such as a hostile encounter with a Boston minister. But Brigham knew how to handle him: "We bore testmoney of the Book of Mormon and drouned him in his own words and let him goe."[40]

And the mission would bring some noteworthy conversions. In Hopkinton, Brigham and his brother made their way to the home of Joseph and Rhoda Richards, their mother's sister. Here they found a ready audience in the Richards's sons (Brigham's first cousins), Phineas, Levi, and Willard. Willard and Levi would follow Brigham to Kirtland in September to further investigate Mormonism. Within four years Willard would be an apostle, converting many in England and in the Salt Lake Valley, and would serve Brigham as his counselor in the First Presidency, the highest administrative body of the Mormon church, consisting of the prophet and his two counselors.

It took courage to face another relative, John Haven. Uncle John looked Brigham square in the face "to see if he could say he was a Mormon." But, said Haven later:

> . . . I found that he had the courage to say that he was—I wanted to know what they said and then I took the Bible to see if it was true—I found they were the only sect that kept to the Bible in all its purity.[41]

Both the Haven and Richards families eventually came into the church.

On this as on previous proselyting missions Brigham was able to hone his skills in persuasion and improve upon his "grit," which was already considerable. Preaching without purse or scrip was "never hard" for him, by his telling. While he spent some hungry days and cold nights with his companions, he was never refused hospitality when it was his turn to ask.

> Now, you may think that I am going to boast a little . . . brag a little of my own tact and talent. But when I had the privilege of asking, I never was turned away— no, not a single time.

What was his secret? The same manner that would charm illustrious visitors to the Great Basin decades later, the manner that said:

"Come, my friend, sit down; do not be in a hurry," and he would begin and preach the Gospel in a plain, familiar manner, and make his hearers believe everything he said, and make them testify to its truth, whether they believed or not, asking them, "Now ain't that so?" and they would say, "Yes."[42]

His method, Brigham continued, was never to denigrate other religions and to gain the friendship of the people first:

I could make the acquaintance of the family, and sit and sing to them and chat with them, and they would feel friendly towards me; and when they learned I was a "Mormon" Elder, it was after I had gained their good feelings.[43]

It was shortly after Brigham and Joseph's return to Kirtland on September 9, 1836, that their cousins Levi and Willard Richards arrived. Willard stayed at Brigham and Mary Ann's home throughout that fall and winter and was baptized by Brigham in December.[44]

In December, too, Brigham and Mary Ann became the parents of twins— a boy and a girl they named after themselves. Little Mary Ann would die in Nauvoo, Illinois, at the age of six, but Brigham, Jr., would live to be sixty-seven and become an apostle himself.

THE Kirtland to which Brigham returned in the fall of 1836 was markedly different than the one he (and his fellow apostles) had left. In place of the poverty and want of the winter before, they found a village where "the noise and bustle of teams with lumber, brick, stone, lime or merchandise, were heard from the early dawn of morning till the grey twilight of evening." With work for the laborer, a ready market for the farmer, and merchandise easily available, "every countenance was lit up with a smile." Everywhere they found "a firm confidence that our days of pinching adversity had passed by, that the set time of the Lord to favor Zion had come."[45] Wilford Woodruff, who had been gone longer than Brigham, wrote in his diary:

How changed the scene. Now I behold a cheerfulness beaming upon every countenance that indicates Prosperity and the noise of the ax and the hammer and the sight of their walls and dwellings newly erected and their Bank and market and especially [the] house of God speaks in language loud as thunder that the saints will have a City in prosperity in spite of all the fals Prophets . . . because God is with them. . . .[46]

Kirtland was sharing an economic boom that affected other towns in the region, a boom fired by increasing population and attendant optimism.[47] New houses were going up every day. "Carpenters and joiners . . . command any price," wrote Willard Richards to his sister Hepsibah.[48]

Kirtland's expansion was in part a result of Joseph Smith's program of ecclesiastical involvement in temporal affairs to stimulate economic development. Brigham later said that the Prophet took heaven and earth and made them shake hands. For Brigham that meant both making heaven comprehensible to men and trying to raise earth up to a new, more heavenlike society. He came to believe that the merging of the temporal and spiritual under the authority of the priesthood was the essential pattern for building the Kingdom of God on earth. Not all Smith's religious followers agreed, however. Imbued with what Brigham described as "sectarian" notions of the limited role of religion, some of them thought a prophet had no business in temporalities.

Because most of the wealth of Mormon Kirtland was in real estate—the temple and church and individual landholdings—Smith and his associates felt the necessity of a bank, which could make assets more liquid and supply the credit for further expansion. Articles of agreement were prepared in November 1836, and the Kirtland Safety Society began to issue notes in January of 1837. The bank failed to receive a charter from the Ohio legislature, however, and Smith, after consulting legal opinion, organized the Kirtland Safety Society Anti-Banking Association to perform the same functions. (If the establishment of a bank was illegal, the founding of an antibank was not.) Because the antibank's notes were not well received by non-Mormon merchants, it soon failed. Inevitably, Smith was blamed both for the failure of the bank and for the economic deterioration that followed.[49] Some wanted to unseat him as president.[50]

Brigham Young was furious. Speaking to some of the leading missionaries in January, he warned them "not to murmur against Moses [Joseph Smith] or the heads of the Church."[51] Like the covenant children of ancient Israel, he said, the modern Saints were slow to hearken, quick to rebel.

But on the last day of January, the First Presidency went to Monroe, Michigan, in the hope of buying the charter of a bank there under which to operate and save the Kirtland enterprise. While they were away, a group plotted to depose Smith and appoint a leader with less aggressive temporal ambitions. A council was called to meet in the upper room of the temple. Most of those present were opposed to Smith's continuing in office, but Brigham and Heber, the two senior members of the Twelve still in Kirtland, were there as well. Brigham later reported that such occasions left him "pretty well charged with plenty of powder and ball," until he "felt like a thousand lions."[52] On this occasion he "rose up . . . in a plain and forcible manner" and told them

> that Joseph was a Prophet, and I knew it, and that they might rail and slander
> him as much as they pleased; they could not destroy the appointment of the
> Prophet of God, they could only destroy their own authority, cut the thread that
> bound them to the Prophet and to God, and sink themselves to hell.[53]

Some of those present reacted violently. Jacob Bump, with whom Brigham had worked on the temple, fancied himself a pugilist. While several held him back, he twisted and turned, shouting, "How can I keep my hands off that man?" "Lay them on," responded Brigham, "if it will give you any relief!" The meeting broke up with the dissenters unable to unite in their opposition.

Brigham had other occasions to show his loyalty. One midnight he heard a Brother or Mister Hawley running through the Kirtland streets loudly denouncing the Prophet. Brigham went out with cowhide in hand,

> jerked him round, and assured him that if he did not stop his noise, and let the people enjoy their sleep . . . I would cowhide him on the spot, for we had the Lord's Prophet right here, and we did not want the devil's prophet yelling round the streets.[54]

Hearing of a plot to waylay Smith as he returned to Kirtland, Brigham and William Smith (the Prophet's brother) borrowed a horse and buggy and met Joseph's stagecoach. William took Joseph's place in the coach and Joseph finished the trip in the buggy, by a different route.[55] When William Smith was recognized, he was not harmed.

In March, Joseph Smith sent Brigham and his cousin Willard Richards east on a special mission. The nature of their assignment was not disclosed, but Brigham later stated that they "transacted much business." They were gone until late May and traveled several hundred miles, mostly by stage. There was such a sense of urgency that they often moved both by day and by night.[56] A surviving letter from Brigham to Mary Ann during this mission suggests, once again, his style and feelings:

> My companion:
> Having a fue mineuts I atempt to wright a fue lines to you. Brother Willard and myself are now at his father's. Tomorrow we shall start for New York. We found our frends well. They want to com to Kirtland. We had a good journey thou[g]h very much fortuegd [fatigued], riding day and night in the stage. . . .
> I can vue my famely with the eye of the mind and desire to be with them as so[o]n as duty will permit. Yet I [pe]n this to comfort my mind that they are not suffering for food and rament. . . . Tell the girls to be good and pray for me, and as for my wife I [k]now that she pray[s] for me allways. Mary, I remember you allways in my prayrs. . . . My best love to my wife and then to my household. So fair well. I remane yours.

He added the following postscript: "Please read this and keep it to yourself [and] not expose my poore righting and speling."[57]

The crisis of confidence in Joseph's temporal policies continued through the summer of 1837. "When temporal matters were talked of," wrote Brigham, "men were ready to decide at once, that they knew more than the Prophet about such matters; and they did so decide." They did not doubt that Joseph "understood spiritual things," Brigham said, "that he understood the Spirit of the Lord, and how to build up a spiritual kingdom among men." But they thought he simply "did not understand anything about temporal matters."[58]

By the time Brigham Young and Willard Richards had returned from their mission, the dissension had spread to the Twelve, several of whom had signed their names to documents that declared Joseph to be a fallen prophet. It was "a crisis," said Brigham, "when earth and hell seemed leagued to overthrow the Prophet and Church of God. The knees of many of the strongest men in the Church faltered."[59] Brigham finally decided that he must publicly challenge the opposition.

> I said, "Ye Elders of Israel, Father Smith is present, the Prophet is present, and here are his counsellors, there are also High Priests and Elders of Israel, now, will some of you draw the line between the spiritual and the temporal in the Kingdom of God, so that I may understand it?" Not one of them could do it.

It was ludicrous, Brigham said, for a man to think to "point out the path a Prophet of God should walk in, or point out his duty, and just how far he must go, in dictating temporal or spiritual things." For Brigham and others in harmony with Joseph's efforts, "Temporal and spiritual things are inseparably connected, and ever will be."[60] At issue was the shape of the Mormon commonwealth, the role of Mormon leaders, the extent to which the Saints would submit to prophetic direction in their lives.[61]

Brigham Young could sometimes think that "Joseph was not right in his financial management." But he dismissed the thought quickly:

> It gave me sorrow of heart, and I clearly saw and understood, by the spirit of revelation manifested to me, that if I was to harbor a thought in my heart that Joseph could be wrong in anything, I would begin to lose confidence in him, and that feeling would grow . . . until at last I would have the same lack of confidence in his being the mouthpiece for the Almighty.

Then he would be left at the brink of the precipice ready to plunge into the gulf of infidelity, "ready to believe neither in God nor His servants, and to say that there is no God, or, if there is, we do not know anything about Him." He would not allow himself to lose confidence in Joseph.[62] Brigham did not claim that every temporal act of Joseph Smith was inspired. But Joseph's failings were between him and the Lord:

> Though I admitted in my feelings and knew all the time that Joseph was a human being and subject to err, still it was none of my business to look after his faults. . . . It was not for me to question whether Joseph was dictated by the Lord at all times and under all circumstances or not. . . . He was called of God; . . . and if He had a mind to leave him to himself and let him commit an error, that was no business of mine.

Anyway, Brigham added, many of Joseph's problems were exacerbated by his most vocal critics:

Joseph was a first-rate fellow with them all the time, provided he never would ask them to pay him. . . . When he had let many of the brethren and sisters have goods on trust, he could not meet his liabilities, and then they would turn round and say, "What is the matter, brother Joseph, why don't you pay your debts?" "It is quite a curiosity that you don't pay your debts; you must be a bad financier; you don't know how to handle the things of the world."[63]

Brigham did not worship Joseph Smith or consider him perfect, but on balance his appraisal was positive:

I can truly say, that I invariably found him [Joseph Smith] to be all that any people could require a *true prophet* to be, and that a *better* man could not be, though he had his weaknesses; and what man has ever lived upon this earth who had none?[64]

In short, Joseph Smith "was God's servant, and not mine."[65]

A S we have seen, the Twelve had long anticipated preaching missions abroad. Since Thomas Marsh felt it his privilege as president of the quorum to lead such a mission, Heber Kimball was surprised when Joseph Smith announced, on June 1, 1837, that Heber was assigned to go to England to "open the door of salvation to that nation." Overwhelmed, Heber went daily to the attic story of the temple to ask God for the power to fulfill his mission. He was hopeful that Brigham would accompany him to England, but Smith said he needed Brigham at home. If Heber was to establish the church abroad, Brigham was to help preserve and defend it at home.[66] Orson Hyde, another apostle, was later assigned to go with Heber, as were Willard Richards and Joseph Fielding, a Canadian convert with family in England. Brigham accompanied the party the twelve miles to the Lake Erie shore where they boarded a steamer, then returned to a Kirtland troubled not only with dissension but with growing economic problems as well. "I could not sleep those days," he later confessed. "I spent many a night without sleeping at all. I prayed a good deal. My mind was constantly active in those days."[67]

By the end of July a majority of the Twelve had come to accept Joseph Smith again as leader, and he felt confident enough in his own position to send Brigham on another business mission. At the same time, Joseph decided to visit the Saints in Canada. He and Brigham and a few others left Kirtland on July 27 heading east. "Shunning . . . places where we suspected our enemies were laying in wait to annoy Joseph," Brigham wrote, they boarded a steamer for Buffalo. "I gave the Prophet my valize for a pillow, and I took his boots for mine, and we laid down on the deck of the vessel for the night." At Buffalo they parted company.[68]

Brigham arrived home on August 19. When Joseph Smith drove in a week later and found the church still in turmoil, Brigham determined to take decisive action against the malcontents. On Sunday, September 3, a conference was held to remove the disloyals from positions of leadership. Brigham wrote: "Owing to the disaffection existing in the hearts of many, I went to the brethren whose votes could be relied on, early in the morning, and had them occupy the stand and prominent seats."[69] Three apostles were disfellowshipped: Luke and Lyman Johnson and John F. Boynton. Each was given the opportunity "of making their confession if they had any to make." Boynton "partly confessed his sins and partly justified his conduct," but this was not enough for Brigham. According to the conference minutes, "Elder Brigham Young in a plain and energetick manner stat[ed] the various reasons why he could not receive [Elder Boynton] into fellowship untill a hearty repentance was manifested."[70] Later, when all three apologized for their conduct and "gave satisfaction," they were once more received into fellowship.[71] It was a time of reconciliation.

Sometime in November, however, the Kirtland calm was swept away by another wave of strife and contention. Boynton and Luke Johnson and others "united together for the overthrow of the church,"[72] and Roger Orton, a longtime dissenter who did not appear for trial, was cut off from the church "for abusing Elder Brigham Young."[73]

Soon after Joseph Smith and Sidney Rigdon, his counselor, returned from a trip to Missouri in December, the dissenting band publicly renounced the church and claimed themselves to be the Old Standard Church of Christ. The stage was set for a battle between the Old Standard and the Saints, or, as they called each other, the Lick Skillets and the Apostates.[74]

This time Smith was prepared to deal with them. In late December "between forty and fifty" dissenters were removed in a "high and mighty pruning." No doubt Brigham, who had been present in Kirtland throughout the fall, testified against many of these excommunicants. Before the month was out, his life was in jeopardy; on December 22 he fled. "I had to leave [Ohio] to save my life," he stated. "I was going to the west where Joseph told me to go." He described his leave-taking:

> On the morning of December 22, I left Kirtland in consequence of the fury of the mob, and the spirit that prevailed in the apostates, who had threatened to destroy me because I would proclaim, publicly and privately, that I knew by the power of the Holy Ghost, that Joseph Smith was a Prophet of the Most High God, and had not transgressed and fallen as apostates declared.[75]

Joseph Smith and the rest of the "Saints" left Kirtland in January. Meanwhile, until friends took Mary Ann west, she and the children were terrorized by apostates who frequented their property, "pretending to believe" that Brigham was "hid up there." They used "threats and vile language" that undid her emotions until her health became frail. This was, she told her biographer, "undoubtedly the severest trial of my life."[76]

5 ✚

The Missouri Interlude

On motion of Prest Brigham Young it was resolved that we
this day enter into a covenant to stand by and assist each other
to the utmost of our abilities in removing from this state and
that we will never desert the poor who are worthy till they
shall be out of the reach of the exterminating order of Gen.
Clark, acting for and in the name of the state.[1]

W H E N Brigham left Kirtland under cover of night near the end
of December 1837, he went to Dublin, Illinois, where he stayed with his brother
Lorenzo, who was wintering there on the way to Missouri. Joseph Smith and
Sidney Rigdon fled Kirtland in mid-January, arriving at Dublin about a month
after Brigham. Lacking means to continue his journey, Joseph told Brigham,
"You are one of the Twelve who have charge of the kingdom in all the world,
and I believe I shall . . . look to you for counsel in this case." With this charge,
Brigham approached a brother who was trying to sell his property and promised that if he would use some of the proceeds to sustain the Prophet he would
soon have a good offer. Several days later Joseph proceeded on his journey
with $300.[2]

Brigham decided to follow the Prophet, catching up with him at Quincy,
Illinois. They traveled the remaining two hundred miles together, arriving
in Far West, Missouri, on March 14, 1838. There they were welcomed "with
open arms and warm hearts." Long anxious to have their leader live with them,
the Missouri Saints promised to provide for the Prophet's physical needs,
so he would have "nothing to do but attend to . . . the spiritual affairs of the
Church."[3]

Within two weeks of Brigham's arrival in Far West, he had provided a
place for Mary Ann and the children and was ready to break the ground for
seed. As he phrased it, "I . . . expended what little means I had left to purchase
an inheritance [living space] for my family." He began fencing and plowing
a "small improvement" on Mill Creek, a tributary of Shoal Creek, about eight
miles east of Far West. Though close enough to travel to Far West for meetings,

Brigham would not be in the mainstream of the town's activities. Most of his energies would go toward his farm and family.[4]

Mary Ann Young and the children joined Brigham in Missouri sometime in the spring. Only then did Brigham realize how greatly she had suffered from the harassments in Kirtland, her poor health, and fatigue. She appeared nearly in the grave, he thought, and continued so weak and sick "that her life was despaired of for a long time." For the next season, at least, the first priority would be his family. On April 17, 1838, Joseph Smith freed him from heavy church demands with this revelation:

> Verily thus saith the Lord, let my servant Brigham Young go unto the place which he has bought, on Mill Creek, and there provide for his family until an effectual door is opened for the support of his family, until I command him to go hence, and not to leave his family until they are amply provided for.[5]

Aware of the continuing opposition to the Mormons from Missourians, Brigham had what he called "a revelation based upon natural principles." (Indeed, throughout most of his life, Brigham's impressions of the will of God were based on "natural principles.") Brigham recalled:

> I saw upon natural principles, that we would be driven from there [Missouri], but when, I did not know; but still it was plain to me that we would have to leave the State, and that when we did leave it we would not go south, north or west, but east, back to the other states.[6]

The Saints would not go west, he probably surmised, because they were prohibited from intercourse with the Indians on the Missouri frontier. They would not go south because they had already been expelled from there in 1833. East was the most likely possibility.[7] Somewhere there would be a place of refuge where the Saints might be able "to walk by themselves and take care of themselves."[8] In any case, Missouri would not long be that place.

At general conference on April 6, 1838, not long after the arrival of the Youngs and Smiths in Missouri, Thomas B. Marsh, president of the Twelve, was appointed "President pro tempore of the Church in Zion," and David W. Patten and Brigham Young, the next two ranking apostles, were chosen as his assistants. This meant they would direct all branches of the church in Missouri.[9] The Twelve were not immune from the dissent that had flared up in Kirtland, but they were now ready, by radical surgery, to restore unity to their quorum. Within a week, in separate proceedings, Luke and Lyman Johnson were dropped from the Twelve and excommunicated. A month later, William E. McLellin suffered the same fate. John F. Boynton having already been excommunicated in Kirtland in January, there were now openings for four new apostles.

Following the counsel to provide for his family, Brigham did not participate actively in most of the council meetings and conferences in Far West in the late spring and early summer of 1838. But in July Joseph Smith announced additional revelations that would have particular influence on Brigham's future. The first three were on the law of tithing and how it would be administered. This law, as then taught and practiced in the church, specified that each convert should turn over to the bishop one-tenth of his property and from that time forward one-tenth of his "increase" or income.[10] It would later become Brigham's responsibility to administer this program.

A fourth revelation, one that Brigham carefully copied into his diary, specified that the Twelve should be organized once again. Their president, Thomas Marsh, was instructed to direct the printing in Far West; the remaining apostles should again go out and preach. More specifically, "next spring let them depart to go over the great waters" to preach the fullness of "my gospel . . . and to bear record of my name" in Europe, and let them "take leave of my saints in the city [of] Far West on the 26th of April next [1839] on the building spot [of the temple]." They were to depart from the very spot on the very day that an earlier revelation had designated for laying the cornerstone of the temple. Named as new apostles "to supply the place of those who are fallen" were John E. Page, John Taylor, Wilford Woodruff, and Brigham's cousin Willard Richards.[11] Page and Taylor were ordained by Brigham and Heber Kimball in December 1838; Woodruff by the same two the following April. Richards, as we shall see, was ordained by Brigham in England in 1840.

Late in July Brigham had an emotional reunion with Heber, just arrived in Far West after his one-year mission to England. As Brigham had done earlier, Heber now applied his major effort toward establishing a home and caring for his family. Another of the Twelve, Orson Hyde, also arrived. Being sickly, he stayed with Joseph Smith that summer and fall.[12]

T H E Mormons continued to experience difficulty with their Missouri neighbors. Local settlers were apprehensive about their bloc voting, the possibility that they might "take over," and in general their strong group behavior. When the Mormons attempted to vote at Gallatin, Missouri, on August 6, a mob of local citizens sought to prevent it. There was violence. By September armed mobs were openly attacking Mormon settlements, and in October mob forces besieged the one at DeWitt, Carroll County, and set fire to the town. The residents, stripped of their belongings, made their way to other settlements. Depredations continued throughout the month. Brigham found it necessary to move his family into Far West for safety.

Since he had remained on his farm until October, Brigham was not known by the Missourians and thus was permitted to "learn their acts and feelings unsuspected." He said that he personally observed Missouri settlers gather up their families, animals, and belongings, prepare to leave the region, and then burn their own houses. Later he saw their names attached to affidavits stating the Mormons had "burned them out." "This was quite effectual in raising prejudice against us," he declared.[13]

The Mormons were surely guilty of intemperate rhetoric and overzealous claims, and Mormon dissenters and apostates fueled the fire of their opponents. More to the point, a group of Mormons who had experienced the mob action in Jackson County, Missouri, in 1833 refused to "bear it" any longer. Led by Sampson Avard, they secretly organized a paramilitary band of "Danites" to take vengeance on their enemies. Both Brigham and his brother Lorenzo played a role in exposing the Danites. Lorenzo later described how he had been invited to a meeting of the secret organization:

> From the meeting I went directly to Brother Brigham and related the whole history of the affair. He said he had long suspicioned that something wrong was going on but had seen no direct development. He added, "I will go at once to Brother Joseph [Smith], who had suspicioned that some secret wickedness was being carried on by Dr. [Sampson] Avard." Dr. Avard was at once cited before the authorities of the Church and cut off for his wickedness. He turned a bitter enemy of the Saints.[14]

Though their activities were short-lived and their more extreme retaliatory measures unauthorized, the Danites had a profound impact on the image of the Mormons in Missouri.

By October, after months of zealous defense of Joseph Smith and his policies, Thomas Marsh lost confidence in him. There were several factors in his disaffection, but one of them was that he felt that he and the Twelve had not received due honor and recognition. "I became jealous of the Prophet," he later explained; "and then I saw double and overlooked everything that was right, and spent my time looking for evil."[15] Marsh went on to say:

> I got mad and I wanted everybody else to be mad. I talked with Brother Brigham and Brother Heber, and I wanted them to be mad like myself; and I saw they were not mad, and I got madder still because they were not. Brother Brigham, with a cautious look, said "Are you the leader of the Church, brother Thomas?" I answered, "no." "Well then," said he, "Why do you not let that alone?"[16]

Sensing that his time of decision was imminent, Marsh retired to the printing office, his place of labor, and, as Heber reported it, "prayed, and was humble, and God gave him a revelation, and he wrote it." He met Brigham and Heber as he came out of his office and read the message to them. "In it God told him . . . to sustain brother Joseph [Smith] and to believe that what brother Joseph said was true." But, pride and stubbornness in the way, he could not.[17]

Once committed to leaving, Marsh made preparations ostensibly to settle a few miles away, then quietly departed and never returned. Apparently that same night, probably October 18, Orson Hyde, who had suffered from violent fever and was not yet fully recovered, followed Marsh in leaving the Saints. Upon learning of their departure, John Taylor proposed to Heber Kimball that they see if they could not overtake them and persuade them to return. "If you knew him [Marsh] as well as I do," replied Heber, "you would know that if he had made up his mind to go, you could not turn him."[18] It would be nearly two decades before Marsh decided to return to the society of Saints.[19]

With the departure of Marsh from the church, David Patten became the senior apostle in the Twelve. Then, precisely one week after Marsh and Hyde left Far West, Patten received a fatal wound while leading a Mormon charge against an armed mob. Brigham and Heber were now the senior apostles in the church. Thus, before the four new apostles could be ordained to complete the quorum after the defections of the winter and spring, apostasy and death had brought three more vacancies. Now Brigham presided over a decimated quorum. In late October 1838, besides his friend Heber, only Parley and Orson Pratt and the unstable William Smith remained of the original Twelve.

o n October 27, Missouri governor Lilburn W. Boggs issued his "Exterminating Order," which instructed the militia commander:

> The Mormons must be treated as enemies and must be exterminated or driven from the state, if necessary for the public good. Their outrages are beyond all description. If you can increase your force, you are authorized to do so, to any extent you may think necessary.[20]

This legitimized the pillage and burning that began immediately and culminated three days later in the massacre of men, women, and children at the Mormon settlement of Haun's Mill. Brigham's brother Joseph was an eyewitness to that tragic scene.

Brigham was present when the governor's proclamation was later read by the militia commander, General John B. Clark. Standing close to the general, though not recognized, Brigham heard him add the following words: "You [Mormons] are the best and most orderly people in this State, and have done more to improve it in three years than we have in fifteen. You have showed us how to improve, how to raise fruit and wheat, how to make gardens, orchards and so on; and on these accounts we want you. But we have this to say to you, No more bishops, no more high councils, and as for your prophet, . . . you will never see him again. . . . [You should] disperse and become as we are." In other words, as Brigham interpreted it, the Saints must renounce their religion or leave the state.

Brigham's response was characteristic:

I will see you in hell first. . . . Renounce my religion? No, sir, . . . it is my all, all I have on this earth. What is this world worth as it is now? Nothing. It is like a morning shadow; it is like the dew before the sun, like the grass before the scythe, or the flower before the pinching frosts of autumn. No, sir, I do not renounce my religion. I am looking beyond; my hope is beyond this vale of tears, and beyond the present life. I have another life to live, and it is eternal. The organization and intelligence God has given me are not to perish in nonentity; I have to live, and I calculate to take such a course that my life hereafter will be in a higher state of existence than the present.[21]

On the morning of October 28, 150 Mormon men, one of them Brigham, rode out from Far West under a white flag to survey the countryside and learn, if possible, the intentions of the mob-militia. A late-afternoon alarm that troops were approaching from the south prompted the thought that the Latter-day Saint men had returned, until the numbers ("thousands of men") belied that hope. Were they friendly troops sent for protection or a mob to plunder? Near sundown, the 500 Mormon men remaining at Far West went out under a white flag to determine the intentions of the unknown army. The reply was alarming: "they wanted three persons out of the city before they massacred the rest." Impending darkness postponed hostilities. Meanwhile, the 150 were able to return "because of their superior knowledge of the country." Instead of protection and relief, Brigham and his associates watched as the militia struck hands with a mob—some painted as Indians—that had also gathered.[22]

In a statement made less than a year later, Heber Kimball told how he and Brigham were "appointed captains of fifty, in a hurry," as the Mormons rushed to defend themselves. Some men known to be wanted, particularly those of the Caldwell County Mormon militia who had engaged the mob at Crooked River, fled to save their lives. Those remaining spent the night arranging wagons and pulling down houses to use as fortifications. Next morning Joseph Smith counseled the defenders and then ordered Brigham and Heber with their men to take up a position directly in line with the militia's advance. The troops approached within rifle shot to examine the defenses and then withdrew.

Instead of "the awful tragedy of a bloody massacre" that Heber had anticipated as he watched the approaching troops, negotiations began. Colonel George M. Hinkle, representing the Caldwell militia, won a pledge from government officers that Mormon leaders could pass safely into the evening camp for further discussions. Thus, under flag of truce, Joseph Smith, Sidney Rigdon, Parley Pratt, Lyman Wight, and George Robinson crossed lines and were immediately seized. (Hyrum Smith and Amasa Lyman were taken the following day.) When they did not return the next morning as agreed, Brigham and Heber and the others knew they had been betrayed.[23]

Apparently Governor Boggs's exterminating order of the twenty-seventh was not known to the body of Mormons until publicly read by General Clark the evening of the twenty-ninth. Parley Pratt wrote that once they knew the force was authorized by the governor, the Mormons were ready to submit—i.e., meet with militia leaders in their camp under truce to work out terms for surrender. But with Smith and other leaders held hostage, the Mormons dared not offer effective defense. They stood helplessly as the mob-militia, cannons at the ready, disarmed them.

Now whatever discipline there had been within the ranks of the government forces broke.

> They commenced their ravages by plundering the citizens of their bedding, clothing, money, wearing apparel, and every thing of value they could lay their hands upon, and also attempting to violate the chastity of women in sight of their husbands and friends, under the pretence of hunting for prisoners and arms.[24]

Brigham watched as soldiers shot Mormon animals and turned horses loose to trample fields ready for harvest.

Meanwhile, an attempt to have Joseph Smith and several others shot was foiled by the courageous stand of Colonel Alexander Doniphan, a secondary Missouri officer. Instead of court-martial and execution, the prisoners were taken on November 2 to Jackson County (and subsequently elsewhere) for prison and trial.

Desperadoes and looters terrified Far West for several more days. They surrounded the city and attempted to take "every man a prisoner who seemed to have any influence." Kimball afterward felt certain that he would have been imprisoned had they known him. The fact that he had been in Missouri only a few weeks and that Brigham had lived away from the Mormon center preserved them from recognition and arrest. They remained with the Saints to witness the desecration and suffering and administer what comfort they could.[25]

On November 5, General Clark entered Far West, assembled all the Mormon men, ordered them to form a line, and, from a list provided by "our open and avowed enemies" (according to Brigham), called out the names of fifty-six for arrest. Again Heber and Brigham were overlooked. They were both present the next day when Clark returned to deliver a written statement to his captive audience alleging that they and their leaders had entered into a treaty that included the signing over of their property to pay for expenses of the "war" and the surrendering of their leaders. Clark said it was now time to comply with the remaining provisions and leave the state. "Whatever may be your feelings concerning this, or whatever your innocence, it is nothing to me," he told them. He would be merciful and allow those not arrested to gather in some corn, but they must not think of planting again and must soon be gone or they would simply be exterminated.

> I am sorry, gentlemen, to see so great a number of apparently intelligent men found in the situation that you are; and oh! that I could invoke that Great Spirit, the unknown God, to rest upon you, and make you sufficiently intelligent to

break that chain of superstition, and liberate you from those fetters of fanaticism
. . . that you no longer worship a man.

The Mormons had been the aggressors, Clark concluded, and had brought all their troubles upon themselves. The only way to prevent an occurrence of the same wherever they went, he reiterated, was to "become as other citizens." "I would advise you to scatter abroad, and never again organize yourselves . . . lest you excite the jealousies of the people, and subject yourselves to the same calamities."[26]

F R O M prison on January 16, 1839, Joseph Smith, Sidney Rigdon, and Hyrum Smith wrote to Brigham and Heber, the two original Twelve Apostles still in Missouri, pointing out that "the management of the affairs of the Church devolves on you," and telling them to proceed to ordain the new apostles as soon as possible and "regulate the Elders as the Lord may give you wisdom."[27] The Presidency nominated George A. Smith and Lyman Sherman to fill the vacancies in the Twelve created by the apostasy of Marsh and Hyde. (Sherman, however, died before he could be ordained, so he is not listed among the Twelve Apostles of the church.) The Twelve, the Presidency suggested, should still plan to go to England:

> If we live we live, and if we die for the testimony of Jesus we die, but whether we live or die let the work of God go on. . . . Brethren fear not, but be strong in the Lord and in the favor of his might. What is man that the servant of God should fear him, or the son of man that he should tremble at him. . . . The fiery trials with which we are tried [are] but the afflictions by which [men] are perfected.[28]

Actually, concluding that early release of the Presidency was unlikely, Brigham and Heber had already reorganized the Missouri High Council, conducted meetings and conferences, and begun supervising the removal of the Saints from the state. Now they ordained John E. Page and John Taylor to the apostleship and gave missionary and other assignments to various leaders. Privately and publicly they reaffirmed their faith in the Prophet and even made an attempt to visit "their brethren" in jail. They found them chained together in the "dungeon" but were not permitted to talk with them.[29]

S I N C E November, Mormons had been leaving their Missouri homes and communities as fast as they were able. Although militia commanders had promised them the "privilege" of staying through the winter if they seeded no crops, armed men rode through the country threatening death to any Mormons they found after February. By January many of those remaining simply had no means to leave. Teams and wagons had been stolen or destroyed, and they had little left of value to trade for new ones.[30]

At this point Brigham began to discover how fully the leadership of the church had devolved upon Heber and himself. Assisting the poor being the province of the Presiding Bishop, Edward Partridge, Brigham proposed that Partridge see what could be done about evacuating the poor. It is said that the bishop, weary, overburdened, and without means himself, responded that he guessed they'd have to take care of themselves.[31] Brigham had to look elsewhere.

His solution was to call a general meeting of those leading elders who remained in Missouri and present the dilemma to them. It convened on January 26 with doleful tenor. Complying with the Executive Order to leave immediately seemed impossible "in consequence of the extreme poverty of many," they concluded, but thereupon appointed a committee of seven to determine how many families were actually destitute. All three ordained apostles, Brigham, Heber, and John Taylor, were placed on the committee, which was also to prepare an appeal to Missouri citizens for assistance. A second survey was to discover all the means within the church, it being "the duty of those who have to assist those who have not."

Three days later Brigham moved that those present "stand by and assist each other to the utmost of our abilities in removing from this state." The secretary then drew up "an instrument expressive of the sense of the covenant entered into this day," and thirty-three men signed to bind themselves "to the extent of all our available property . . . for providing means for the removing of the poor and destitute . . . till there shall not be one left who desires to remove from the state."[32] Brigham persuaded eighty additional family heads to sign the covenant the first day and three hundred more the second.[33] By using the "committee on removal" and by leapfrogging his own weary teams across the state, Brigham became the head of the Mormon evacuation of Missouri.

If he had escaped arrest in the fall because of his low profile, Brigham was now the "most wanted" Mormon. For a time he continued under disguise, but by mid-February it was necessary for him to leave Missouri. Still less well known, Kimball agreed to remain behind to finish the removal and if possible help the prisoners to escape. (Before leaving in April, Heber, too, would be in hiding by day, counseling with the committee only at night.) On February 14, in the bitter winter cold, with his and Heber's families and several others, Brigham departed Far West.

Mary Ann later remembered the journey from Missouri as dangerous and traumatic. Slowly, by great exertion, and facing frostbite, illness, and threats to their lives, they made their way east. Several times Brigham left his family in camp or at the house of a friendly family and returned with his teams to help others. During one absence their infant daughter was thrown from a wagon and run over. She nevertheless survived. The Youngs finally gained refuge in Atlas, Pike County, Illinois, where they remained for several weeks.

Before arriving at the Mississippi River gathering place in the spring of 1839, Mary Ann "kept house in eleven different places."[34]

All this time Joseph Smith remained imprisoned. On a second visit to Liberty Jail, Brigham and Heber were able to spend more than an hour reporting to the prisoners and getting their counsel. Smith had mellowed by his jail experience. The Lord "has chosen his own crucible to try us," he declared, "a trial of our faith equal to that of Abraham or any of the ancients." Such trials, he asserted, "only give us the knowledge necessary to understand the minds of the ancients."[35]

Once Brigham had done all he could to effect a safe removal from Missouri, he and the Saints had to decide whether to gather again immediately, and if so, where? Smith said in March that "places for the location of the saints" must be found, and "the saints ought to lay hold of every opening, in order to obtain a foothold on the earth."[36]

In the meantime the Saints had scattered. Most of them headed east to Quincy, Illinois, where the community gave them assistance and welcome. Quincy was becoming a de facto headquarters of the church in exile, with Brigham, Wilford Woodruff, and John Taylor all there by mid-March, making plans to bring in their families.[37] Orson Hyde later returned, made a full confession of his errors, and was soon reinstated in the Quorum of Apostles.[38]

On April 17, just as the last Saints were leaving Far West, Brigham presided over a conference in Quincy at which George A. Smith, only twenty-one years old, was sustained as one of the Twelve. The Twelve then held a council with other church officials. They discussed the question of whether they should return briefly to Missouri. It was dangerous to go there, but they remembered the revelation saying they would depart for their mission to Europe from Far West.[39] Some present "considered the Lord would take the will for the deed and did not expect we would go to fulfill it." But Brigham "felt differently, and so did the Twelve who were with me." After each of the Twelve separately expressed his feelings, Brigham announced "that the Lord God had spoke and it was our business to obey, and the Lord would take care of us." All present agreed to go and fulfill the revelation.[40] The next day, unaware that Joseph and Hyrum Smith and the other Liberty Jail prisoners had been allowed to escape and were already on their way to Illinois, Young, Orson Pratt, Taylor, Woodruff, and George A. Smith, accompanied by Alpheus Cutler, the master builder for the Far West Temple, set out for Missouri.

On their way to Far West, Brigham characteristically "helped the Lord fulfill His prophecy." On the twenty-first they encountered the missing apostle, John E. Page, who was hurrying his family toward Quincy. The Page wagon had just tipped "bottom-side upwards" and John was "elbow deep" in soft soap, "scooping it up with his hands." Brigham requested that he return to Far West with the other apostles. With remarkable restraint, Page paused in his suds to reply that "he did not see that he could, as he had his family to take to Quincy." "Never mind, your family will get along," said Brigham. "I want you to go with us." John asked how much time he could have to get ready. "Five minutes," Brigham replied. They helped him reload his wagon, "he drove down the hill and camped, and returned with us."[41]

On April 25, Heber Kimball, who had gone on a special assignment to visit Joseph Smith, secreted himself in Far West. During the night, Elders Young, Orson Pratt, Page, Taylor, Woodruff, and Smith of the Twelve, along with about twenty Saints, all in peril of their lives, arrived by moonlight. In the predawn light the apostles rode into the public square of Far West.[42]

The small conference voted to excommunicate nearly three dozen of their former associates who had failed to remain loyal during the difficulties of the fall and winter. After Wilford Woodruff and George A. Smith received their ordinations as apostles, Alpheus Cutler directed the placement of a stone to commence the foundation of the temple. All seven of the apostles prayed in turn, according to their order in the quorum, and "the twelve took their leave of the Saints agreeable to revelation."[43] Before departing, some of the men wandered the deserted streets, observing grass where only months before foot and wagon traffic had packed soils hard.[44]

A week later, four miles outside Quincy, the Twelve had a happy reunion with Joseph and Hyrum Smith. Said Brigham of the occasion:

> It was one of the most joyful scenes of my life to once more strike hands with the Prophets, and behold them free from the hands of their enemies: Joseph conversed with us like a man who had just escaped from a thousand oppressions, and was now free in the midst of his children.[45]

Brigham was content to be one of those children. Defending Joseph Smith and leading in his absence had brought him prominence, but now his Prophet had returned. This early May reunion launched an unusual season of counsel and instruction, the Twelve meeting frequently and learning at the feet of their Prophet. For the first time the quorum would begin to have that relationship with Smith that, to the deep consternation of some, had earlier eluded them.

T H E bold return of the Twelve to Missouri under the leadership of Brigham was not the only symbol of a new era for the apostles. With the ordination of Woodruff and George A. Smith on April 26, Brigham for the first time had a quorum under his direction. Now united and confident, the impending departure for Europe gave the apostles added direction and purpose. Not all was positive, of course. There was controversy over apostles Hyde and William Smith, Parley Pratt continued to languish in Richmond Jail, Lyman Sherman had died before his ordination, and Willard Richards, still in England, had not yet been ordained. But the addition of Taylor, Woodruff, and George A. Smith, two of them veterans of Zion's Camp and the other a recent convert from Canada, strengthened the quorum immeasurably. While John E. Page had yet to associate closely with his brethren, his appointment also seemed promising. These were men who had weathered times of difficulty and trial, men of proven loyalty to Smith, to Brigham, and to the unfolding program of the church.

For the first time since the Missouri difficulties, the church met for an important conference under the direction of the First Presidency. By this time Sidney Rigdon resided in Commerce, upriver from Quincy, and his home was appointed the location for the next general conference in early October. That action, along with sanctioning Joseph Smith's purchase of Iowa lands directly across the river from Commerce, effectively established a new gathering place for the Saints. Smith had completed arrangements with Isaac Galland for the Iowa lands, and just before the conference had acquired property in Commerce. He also appointed William Marks to preside over the Saints at Commerce and instructed the bishops to reside there, making the beginning of what would soon be known as the Nauvoo Stake of Zion.[46]

Brigham, Wilford Woodruff, and their families arrived in Commerce on May 18 to find the surveyor hard at work. Although they regarded the location for the city beautiful and promising, there was only a handful of buildings scattered about, so the two apostles had to join others seeking shelter for their families across the river at abandoned Fort Des Moines (Montrose), Iowa.

On July 2, after dining at the Woodruffs', the Twelve and the Presidency assembled at Brigham's home for blessings and farewell instructions. According to Wilford Woodruff's marvelously detailed diary, the First Presidency blessed each apostle and his wife individually, promising that "if we were faithful we had the promise of again returning to the bosom of our families and being blessed on our missions and having many souls as seals of our ministry." The women, as well as the men, needed that assurance; they were being left destitute, some pregnant, most ill, thrown on the scanty resources of the impoverished church and their own resourcefulness.

Knowing that the apostles were seasoned missionaries, Smith did not advise them how to preach the gospel or give them instruction in administration and organization. Nor did he tell them how long they must be gone, where they should go, and how they should approach the people. But he was anxious to instill in them a good attitude—a spirit that would enable them to accomplish their goals. They must keep "the principles of mercy" alive; they must be quick to forgive an erring brother; they must remember that forgiving an enemy "before they ask it" would elicit God's equally prompt and merciful response. "We ought to be willing to repent of and confess all of our own sins and *keep nothing back* . . . and not seek to excell one above another but act for each others good . . . and not backbite and devour our brother." Wilford Woodruff's diary entry continues by noting the instruction that the apostles were to "act for each others good and honorably make mention of each others name in our prayers before the Lord and before our fellow men."[47]

On July 7, Brigham, Heber, and the others gave their farewell address to the Saints in an emotion-filled meeting. Brigham, according to the minutes, "bore testimony in the Spirit."[48]

The Twelve had a few last-minute councils with the Presidency, did what they could to make their families comfortable, and prepared a few personal belongings for travel. But their departure was delayed by malaria, or whatever debilitating sickness it was that swept through their riverside settlements in July. The apostles, their families, and neighbors were prostrated with chills and fever—hardly a settler escaped. Their mission looked impossible until, on July 22 ("a day never to be forgotten," wrote Brigham), the Prophet arose from his own bed of sickness and commenced to command the sick in the name of Jesus to be made whole. He crossed the river to Montrose and went from house to house. Said Brigham, "I arose and was healed, and followed him and the brethren of the Twelve" to other homes.[49] Woodruff reported that

> it was a day of Gods power. There was many sick among the Saints on both sides of the river and Joseph went through the midst of them taking them by the hand and in a loud voice commanding them in the name of Jesus Christ to arise from their beds and be made whole and they leaped from their beds . . . and followed Joseph from house to house and it was truly a time of rejoicing.

All of the Twelve were among the stricken, but they were determined, "sick or not," to fulfill their mission.[50] On Sunday, August 4, a day of fasting and prayer, the Prophet renewed his instruction to "go forth without purse or scrip, according to the revelations of Jesus Christ."[51] Woodruff and Taylor, therefore, left later that week. Able to walk at his departure, Taylor soon became so ill that George A. Smith caught up with him later and carried him along in his wagon. A letter from Taylor's wife, Leonora, dated September 9, 1839, reveals the conditions in Nauvoo: "This has been a distressed place since you left, with sickness. Allmost evry individual in evry family sick." She had carried "several pails" of water to Brigham Young and his family since every single member was so ill that not one could fetch "a drop."[52]

Yet ten days after Mary Ann was delivered of Emma Alice, Brigham was ready to go. His "History" entry for September 14, the day of his departure, states laconically:

> I started from Montrose on my mission to England. My health was so poor I was unable to go thirty rods to the river without assistance. . . . I left my wife sick, with a babe only ten days old, and all my children sick and unable to wait upon each other.[53]

He prevailed on a church member with a horse, Israel Barlow, to take him to Heber's house in Nauvoo. He had to be helped to the river in order to cross, and at Heber's he remained sick for four days. When they left together, still tottering, Brigham had to be helped to the wagon. His sister Fanny urged him not to go until he was well. Stubbornly, he replied:

> "Sister Fanny, I never felt better in my life." She was a very eccentric woman and looking at me with tears in her eyes, she said, "You lie." I said nothing but I was determined to go to England or to die trying. My firm resolve was that I would do what I was required to do in the Gospel of life and salvation, or I would die trying to do it.[54]

The two apostles made a sad picture. According to Wilford Woodruff, Brigham and Heber "were without a second suit to their backs, for the mob in Missouri had taken all they had." Brigham's wardrobe, as he commented wryly, "had not much of a ministerial appearance," for his cap had been made out of "a pair of old pantaloons" and he wrapped himself in a quilt for want of an overcoat—a need supplied him by the New York Saints.[55] Nor was Heber any better off. Vilate also was bedridden; only by supreme effort did she rise to cheer him off with a wave of her hand.

Long would Brigham and Heber, Mary Ann and Vilate, remember that parting. In a letter written after their arrival in England, Heber reminisced to Vilate:

> I will tell you, my Dear, that time will be remembered by me as long as time lasts. Fore no man has ever suffered as much as I did in my feelings. No more do I ever wish to while I live on earth. I think if ever one man did I have left all fore the Caus of Christ.[56]

Brigham's feelings were similar, but he seldom loitered in sentimentality. His first letter to Mary Ann, written only hours after parting, explained debts that he owed and monies he had left her to pay them with, ending with a balance of $2.72 for herself.

> This is allmost rob[b]ing You I [k]now. But I doe not now wht elce to doe. Brother Joseph [Smith] has pledged himself that the wives of the Twelve should have what they wanted. . . . I doe feele as thou the Lord would provide for you and me.[57]

Having neither passage fare nor clothing for their journey, Brigham went on to explain their intention to "goe through the Churches" or branches of the church along the way instead of the shortest route by water "so that we can recru[i]t up and get what Clothing we shall want."

Frail shadows of their healthy selves, Brigham and Heber made it only as far as Quincy before they had to stop for several days to gain enough strength to continue. There Brigham visited for the last time with his father—old, ill, worn down by the Missouri persecutions. John died shortly after Brigham and Heber left Quincy.[58]

Despite illness, Young kept up his diary. His short entries convey his gratefulness to the Saints along the way for their indispensable assistance: "The frends and Brothern convaid ous [conveyed us]," or "We ware kindley treated and nurst up and helped to pursue our jorney. . . . M[a]y the Lord bless them."[59]

Because of illness and their desire to visit the branches, where they preached and counseled as well as received assistance, the journey to Kirtland required seven weeks. For ten years Brigham and Heber had been companions and associates; never did they rely more on one another than now. At first Heber nursed Brigham, who was weaker. A month later Heber, very ill, was administered a mistaken dose of morphine by a drunken doctor and nearly died. He came to his senses to find Brigham attending him "with a fatherly care, and manifesting much anxiety in my behalf." "Don't be scared, for I shan't die," Heber told his friend. The experience was a traumatic one for both Young and Kimball. Later in the month Heber had strength enough to write about it in detail. He told his wife that "it tock the docter and his wife and Br Brigham all nite to keep a breth of life in my body."[60]

Brigham's record of that journey reveals the wry sense of humor that gave him some much-needed distancing from pressures. A catalyst may have been his association with George A. Smith, the twenty-two-year-old cousin of Joseph Smith who had just been appointed an apostle and who joined Brigham and Heber at Quincy. George A., also ill, was so weak and thin that he appeared an old man.[61] Nevertheless, his journal, like that of Brigham and Heber, is full of good humor and optimism.

Crossing Illinois, Brigham, Heber, and George A. spent the night with a fellow Mormon. Upon seeing George A.'s bottle of tonic bitters, the host exclaimed: "You are a pretty set of Apostles, to be carrying a bottle of whiskey with you." Brigham notes simply that an explanation of the contents "appeased his righteous soul, so that he consented to have us stay over night."[62] The wryness has an edge to it as Brigham tells of the next night, when a doctor called upon them. "Relating over the . . . brethren's ill health, he shed many tears, but he did not have quite sympathy enough to buy [us] a chicken or give [us] a shilling, though he was worth some four or five hundred thousand dollars."[63]

George A. was so sick that his eyesight was impaired, and Brigham "had to wait on him while traveling, and select his food and put it on the plate, as he could not tell one dish from another." At one inn where they had stopped, Brigham overheard two guests gossiping while he was settling the bill. " 'Do you know that old gentleman who came in on the stage?' " one queried. When the answer was no, he then asked, " 'Do you know that young man that waits on him?' " Brigham does not say whether he gratified their curiosity, but clearly he enjoyed retelling the story.[64]

Kimball's father-in-law, traveling from Commerce with other elders, came upon Heber in his severest illness and left him sadly, certain he would never see him alive again.[65] But a few days later Heber was well enough to stay up and nurse Brigham through another relapse.

Having received $13.50 in donations, the pair now set out to travel by stage as far as their money would take them. At each terminal Brigham would reach into his small trunk, pay the fare, and note that they had just enough to go one more leg. Wrote one who heard Brigham later tell the story:

> They did not expect to be able to travel far with the stage for lack of means, but at every stopping place, when Bro. Young went to his trunk to pay his fare, he found money to pay their fare to the next stopping place, and so on until they got through and had 50¢ left, and took their meals regular, and always when he needed money he found it in his trunk.[66]

When they reached Kirtland on Monday, November 4, Brigham totaled up what he had disbursed to discover that it amounted to more than $87. He suspected that Kimball had put the money there from a purse that he had not disclosed, but Heber insisted this was not so. The money had to "have been put in his trunk by some heavenly messenger," they decided, "who thus administered to our necessities daily as we knew we needed."[67] Brigham, who had always said "he was willing to believe a *big* story, if it was true," had no idea how the money got there "except by some unseen agent from the Heavenly world to forward the promulgation of the Gospel."[68]

They remained in Kirtland for two weeks. Brigham noted in his diary that, while most strove to serve the Lord, there was "some devision of sentiment among the Brothern."[69] On Sunday, November 17, Brigham preached in the morning and John Taylor in the afternoon. From Kirtland they took a lake steamer east toward New York. At night heavy weather transformed the tranquil waters that Young had so enjoyed during the day. He wrote:

> The wind arose about one o'clock in the morning. I went up on deck and I felt impres[sed] in spirit to pray to the Father in the name of Jesus for a forgiveness of all my sins and then I fe[l]t to command the winds to sees [cease] and let ous goe safe on our Jorney. The winds abated and Glory and [h]ouner and prase be to that God that rules all things.[70]

Young later recorded two instances during this leg of his journey that had significance to him. One had to do with counseling a branch of the church that was in confusion because the gift of tongues had been among them and they "supposed that everything which was spoken in tongues was immediate revelation from God." Speaking as a man of some experience with the gift, he

> taught them that when they spoke in tongues the language might be from the Lord, but with that tongue they spoke the things which were in their hearts, whether they were good or evil; the gift of tongues was given for a blessing to

the Saints, but not to govern them, nor to control the elders, or dictate the affairs of the church.

For that, said the apostle, "God had placed . . . apostles, prophets, helps and governments."[71]

Shortly after, Brigham met with the family of his cousin Phinehas Brigham, whose son was a young Baptist preacher. The visit was unproductive, but Brigham's history offers a commentary on how his own mind had reacted to Mormonism eight years before. He told the family that he had studied all the religions,

> for I desired to know the truth, and found I could put all their doctrines, when simmered down to truth, into a snuff box of the smallest class. . . . But when I found Mormonism, I found it was higher than I could reach with my researches, deeper than I was capable of comprehending, and calculated to expand the mind, and lead mankind from truth to truth, from light to light, from grace to grace, and exalt him . . . to become associated with Gods and the angels.[72]

That Brigham's illness did not leave him unmarked is indicated by the fact that, upon his arrival in New York, he slipped when jumping onto a ferryboat and fell against an iron ring on the dock, dislocating his shoulder. As his concerned companions gathered about him, Brigham had Reuben Hedlock roll him onto his back; then he instructed Reuben and Heber to hold him down while fellow apostle Parley P. Pratt, a foot against his ribs, pulled steadily on his hand. Brigham himself "guided the bone with my right hand back to its place. The brethren wound my handkerchief round my shoulder and helped me up." "When I came to a fire," he continues, "I fainted, and was not able to dress myself for several days."[73]

They arrived in New York City in late January 1840 and spent the next five weeks holding meetings, baptizing, and raising funds. According to Heber, who arrived somewhat later than Brigham after a side trip to the Victor-Mendon area, the apostles would have departed immediately for England if money for the passage had been available.

On March 7, 1840, Brigham and Heber and several others left New York harbor on board the *Patrick Henry* bound for Liverpool. Woodruff and Taylor had booked passage several weeks before. After a stormy voyage—"I was sick nearly all the way, and confined to my berth," said Brigham—they arrived in England on April 6, the tenth anniversary of the organization of the church. Remembering how Joseph Smith had told him before their departure that "when [you] land upon a foreign shore the same spirit [will] rest upon you that now rests upon me, to lead guide and direct," Brigham was full of emotion.[74] When he had both feet firmly on Liverpool's docks, he said, "I gave a loud shout of hosannah . . . I felt that the chains were broken, and the bands that were upon me were burst asunder."[75]

6 ✤

The British Mission

We find the people of this land [England] much more ready
to receive the gospel, than those of America, . . . for they have
not that speculative inteligence, or prejudice, or prepossession,
or false learning, call it what you please, which they have there
[in America].[1]

E N G L A N D in 1840 was at once the most advanced and the
most depressed nation of Europe. On the one hand, it had become the first industrial nation, half of its people living in urban manufacturing or mining communities. On the other hand, the enclosure movement had uprooted millions of
yeomen, small farmers, and cottagers who, crowded into the new industrial centers, eked out an existence at starvation wages. Poverty was widespread, sanitation
poor, and schooling available primarily to the upper class.

Three years earlier, Alexandrina Victoria, age eighteen, had been crowned
queen. Intelligent and self-assured, in 1840 she had married her first cousin,
the sober and sensible German Prince Albert of Saxe-Coburg-Gotha, inau-
gurating an era of unprecedented peace, progress, and enlightenment. The
invention of the spinning jenny, the power loom, and the steam engine—and
the ensuing introduction of the factory system, the railroad, and the steam-
ship—had revolutionized England's economy and placed it in the center of
world manufacturing and commerce. At the same time, the country's writers
and politicians had given it a social and intellectual leadership that placed it
in the forefront of Western culture. Keats, Shelley, Wordsworth, and Byron;
Sir Walter Scott, Dickens, and Thackeray; Tennyson, Carlyle, and the Brown-
ings; Lord Melbourne, Sir Robert Peel, and Benjamin Disraeli—these were
names to respect, admire, and conjure with. England had magnificent harbors,
magnificent buildings, and magnificent palaces. And yet, partly as a consequence of her challenging industrial innovations, she also had millions who
were abysmally poor.

To be sure, England had enacted the Reform Bill in 1832, marking the
first step in the adoption of modern democracy. The existing system of par-

liamentary representation was reformed to eliminate political inequalities and to extend the franchise; the balance of power was shifted to the industrial and commercial classes. Partly as a result of this reform, slavery was abolished in the colonies in 1833, and the 1834 Factory Act took the first steps toward protecting children from the worst abuses of the industrial system. The act forbade the employment of children under nine and restricted the labor of those between ages nine and thirteen to forty-eight hours per week or nine in a single day. Children under thirteen were to have two hours' schooling per day. These regulations, however, applied only to employment in textile factories. Also, in 1834, the new Poor Law limited the payment of charitable doles to sick and aged paupers, and established workhouses where able-bodied paupers were put to work.

Despite these tentative beginnings of social legislation, the bulk of England's fifteen million inhabitants in 1840 were destitute, not able to vote, and poorly educated. Masses of displaced country workers crowded London, Liverpool, Manchester, and other industrial and commercial centers, barely subsisting in areas that were polluted, unsightly, and unhealthful. Working with the indigent in 1840–41 had an ineradicable influence on Brigham Young. In the years to come, he would dedicate much of his energy to assisting these and their kindred poor to emigrate to the Latter-day Zion in the West.

Into the English milieu in 1837 had gone Mormon apostles Heber Kimball and Orson Hyde, along with Joseph Fielding and Willard Richards. Distributing tracts, preaching, and working with the unemployed and needy, they had baptized several hundred persons and established a small, unstable LDS community before all but Fielding returned to America in 1838.

John Taylor, Wilford Woodruff, and Theodore Turley landed at Liverpool on January 11, 1840. Taylor remained in Liverpool to visit the relatives of his wife Leonora; Woodruff and Turley traveled north to Staffordshire and thence into Herefordshire. All three had success in their preaching.

In April arrived Brigham Young, Heber Kimball, Orson and Parley Pratt, and the youthful George A. Smith. Standing on the bow of their ship as they sailed into Liverpool, the apostles observed with mounting excitement Europe's leading seaport. On the margins of the crowded docks with their swing bridges were gigantic fireproof warehouses used for storing tobacco, cotton, wool, grain, and other produce. In the harbor were scores of vessels of all kinds, sailing in with foodstuffs and raw materials, and sailing out with manufactured goods made in "the workshop of the world."

Intent on their religious mission, however, Brigham and his companions, after docking, immediately gathered privately to partake of the sacrament of the Lord's Supper, to thank God for His care and protection, and to pray "that our way might be opened before us to accomplish our missions successfully." Within a few days they met Taylor and Richards. "I was so emaciated from my long journey and sickness," Brigham wrote, "that he [Willard] did not know me."[2]

Three days after their arrival, they went by train to Preston, marveling that the way out of Liverpool was an underground passage lighted by lamps, through which they passed without benefit of engine. At Preston, long a linen center and now suddenly transformed into manufacturing cotton, they were met by Joseph Fielding, who had directed Mormon affairs in England after Kimball's departure in 1838. Fielding noted in his diary that the apostles "look thin and weather beaten . . . but they are in good Spirits."[3] News of their arrival spread so rapidly that by April 12, their first Sunday in England, some five or six hundred Saints gathered in the Preston Cock Pit, historic meeting place for dissident groups. There the seven of the Quorum of Twelve then present "bore testimony to the work, and spoke with power."[4]

Later that week, still in Preston, the apostles met for four days of council and conference in what one of them called "the first Council of the Twelve among the Nations." As the "Standing President of the Twelve," Brigham was in charge.[5] The first order of business was to ordain Willard Richards to the apostleship, as authorized by the July 8, 1838, revelation. There were now eight apostles in England. Three others (Orson Hyde, John E. Page, and William Smith) did not fill the mission to Britain, although Hyde was there for a brief period in 1841 on his way to Palestine. One vacancy remained in the quorum.

Brigham now directed a "general conference" of the Saints in England at which nearly sixteen hundred were present. The conference approved Brigham's proposal to publish the Book of Mormon, a hymn book, and a monthly periodical "for the benefit and information of the church." The new publication was to be called the *Latter-day Saints' Millennial Star*, with Parley Pratt as editor. The Twelve concluded by encouraging groups large or small to emigrate to America. Brigham insisted that no one "that has money" go to America "without assisting the poor according to our council."[6]

Within two weeks of landing, Brigham and his associates had launched a full program of proselyting, publishing, and preparing for the emigration. One task was left: sending a report to Joseph Smith on what they had decided and done. In the packet dispatched to him were copies of the minutes, several letters, and a brief report. The preface contains a millennial flavor:

The gospel is spreading, the devils are roaring; as nigh as I can learn the priests are howling, the tares they are binding up, the wheat is gathering, and nations are trembling, and kingdoms are tottering: "Men's hearts are failing them for fear, and for looking for those things that are coming on the earth."

Always deferential to the Prophet, Brigham attached a personal note to the minutes, his own writing obviously "cleaned up" by scribe Willard Richards:

If you see anything in, or about the whole affair, that is not right: I ask, in the name of the Lord Jesus Christ, that you would make known to us the mind of the Lord, and his will concerning us.[7]

To mark the end of the planning period, the apostles met at the home of a convert, Alice Moon, at Penwortham; two miles from Preston, for an evening of celebration. Forty years earlier, she said, she had received a bottle of rare vintage wine for her marriage. She had forgotten to open it then. She likewise had forgotten to open it when her first child was born. She still had the bottle and did not wish to disappoint Providence by leaving it untouched. The apostles accepted her gift, blessed it, and each drank a glass.[8]

W I L F O R D Woodruff had already hit a rich vein in Herefordshire. A pastoral county in southwest England, famous for Hereford cattle and for the production of fruits, hops, cider, and grain, Hereford was "ripe for Mormon plucking" because of the prevalence of several congregations of dissident Methodists called United Brethren. When he first arrived there in the spring of 1838, Woodruff had spent the night at the home of John Benbow, a well-to-do farmer at Frooms Hill who was a United Brethren. Interested in what Woodruff told him, Benbow invited him to preach in a large room of his house. With its sacred books, emphasis on prophecy and the millennium, and claim to apostolic authority exercised through a lay priesthood, the gospel preached by Woodruff appealed to the Brethren (the term included women as well as men), and Benbow and his wife were baptized, along with several other members of the congregation. Soon the Brethren superintendent, Thomas Kington, and his household were baptized. Woodruff reported:

> I also baptized about forty preachers of the same order, and several others belonging unto other churches, and about 120 members of the United Brethren, which opened around forty doors or preaching places.[9]

It was to this ripe field that Brigham and Willard Richards now went with Woodruff.[10]

Brigham had had experiences with religious controversy in New York, New England, and the American Midwest, but he had never seen anything that compared with England. A nation with a long history of free expression, the British were lavish with their criticisms as well as their praise, throwing vegetables as well as coins. The streets and parks were filled with the noise of reformers, preachers, do-gooders, and eccentrics spouting slogans, scriptural verses, and crying alarm.

As Brigham was to discover, not just Herefordshire but all England was in a state of religious excitement, and this may well have given the Mormons a better audience than a more apathetic society would have done. A century earlier, John Wesley had sought to make religion more vital in the lives of individual Christians, with the result that there was a lively debate within the established church, marked by an outpouring of pamphlets and tracts that were intended to overcome the supposed spiritual complacency. The result had been the formation of an Evangelical movement within the church more interested in personal salvation than in outward appearances. Eventually, and somewhat reluctantly, the Methodists found themselves outside the Anglican fold.

As they prospered, at least partly because of their enthusiasm and diligent work habits, the Methodists themselves became "middle class" and failed to supply all the religious wants of the poor. A "fundamentalist" schism produced the Primitive Methodists, and a break-off in turn from that group had spawned the United Brethren in Lancashire. To these and other splinter groups and individual "seekers," Mormonism had an undeniable appeal. Their belief in universal salvation, their habit of mutual aid and assistance, their self-discipline, their doctrine that individuals could advance from human stature to the divine, their theme of emigration to a Promised Valley in the West—all of these were attractive to the "honest but poor" who had suffered from the social and economic dislocations of contemporary "fair Albion."

To George A. Smith Brigham wrote, with his characteristic spelling, that there was a "grate caul for preaching in this regon of contry"; i.e., Herefordshire northeast to Worcester and southeast to Bristol. The working classes, he wrote, "are wanting to hear the word preached." But the pastors were not so eager:

> I have had an intervue with a Priest, one a Baptist the other a Methodst. But they are jest like the rest of the Priest[s]. They have jest relegon enuph to damb them—no inclenation to even inquire after the gospel of Jesus Christ. This is a wicked place but there is a fue that want to be saved.[11]

To Joseph Smith he wrote: "Almost without exception it is the poor that receive the gospel." For these humble, teachable people, Brigham wrote, "simple testimony is enough."[12]

For a month Brigham directed the transformation of the converted United Brethren into organized branches.[13] His simple, direct preaching was effective, and his experience in working with people helped speed the process. But the Mormon activity incited intense sectarian feelings. The week beginning Sunday, May 17, is illustrative. Woodruff preached in the morning; Young, in the afternoon. While Brigham preached, according to Woodruff,

> opposers made much disturbance and was determined to break up the meeting. Elder Young rose up in the power of the Priesthood and in the name of the Great God and according to the laws of the land commanded order. Two of the brethren went to the door to keep order. Elder [Willard] Richards was one of them and they were enabled to overcome the enemy and peace was again restored. We administered the Lords supper and confirmed five, and ordained four.[14]

The next day, May 18, had traditionally been a feast day among the United Brethren, and so they held a celebration for the Saints. The apostles' day started at 5:00 A.M. with Woodruff baptizing several—and more throughout the day. Young and Richards confirmed them as they came out of the water. At 4:00

P.M. Brigham addressed the approximately one hundred who were gathered. After dinner Brigham again delivered a short address followed by more confirmations and ordinations and still more baptisms. In his diary Brigham tersely noted, "spent the day with the Brothering. They had a tea party. We had Prayrs[,] confirmed several, ordained a nomber. There was 20 Baptized."[15]

It was also on this day that a "notable miracle was wrought by faith and the power of God." Mary Pitt, for six years confined to bed, had not been able to walk for eleven years before that without crutches. Woodruff wrote: "Elders Young, Richards, and Woodruff lade hands upon her and rebuked her infirmity and her ancle bones received strength and she now walks without the aid of crutch or staff."[16]

Later the next day Brigham was on his way to Manchester, and Woodruff and Willard Richards resumed the work of baptizing and confirming. Soon the Bran Green and Gadsfield Elm branches of the United Brethren were converted into a conference of the Latter-day Saints, with Thomas Kington as presiding elder. The Herefordshire conference now comprised 33 Mormon churches with 541 members.[17]

F E W of the early British converts to Mormonism had seen the Book of Mormon, none had read and studied church literature; the need for a hymn book was imperative. As Brigham said, "The brethren had laid by their old hymn books and they wanted new ones; for the Bible, religion, and all is new to them."[18]

Brigham was able to obtain a loan of £350 from John Benbow and Thomas Kington to produce 3,000 copies of the hymn book and 5,000 copies of the Book of Mormon. While many of the hymns were of Anglican and Protestant provenance, some had been written in the 1830s by William W. Phelps, Parley Pratt, Emma Smith, and other Mormons. The hymn book was ready for distribution by June, the Book of Mormon by February 1841. An ornately bound copy of the latter was presented to Queen Victoria before Brigham left the country.

The *Millennial Star* was first issued at Manchester in late May 1840, shortly after Brigham's arrival; the second issue was out by June 17. (Brigham had instructed editor Pratt to go ahead and publish 2,000 copies and he, Brigham, would see that the bill was paid.)[19] Twenty-four pages in length, the publication was the primary means of communication for the British mission. The *Star* published revelations and instructions from Joseph Smith, letters of apostles and mission leaders reporting progress in Britain and elsewhere, selections from the Book of Mormon until the British edition was out, editorials and doctrinal articles by Brigham Young and other apostles, and comments on "signs of the times" that were considered a harbinger of Christ's imminent return. Readers received advice on organization and procedures, temperance, honesty, and chastity. Regular features included "Questions and Answers" and "Questions and Answers for Children." The publication was noticed in the

London literary periodical, *The Athenaeum,* on April 3, 1841. Mormonism, said the writer,

> is making rapid progress in England, particularly in the manufacturing districts; and it is also spreading in Wales. Furthermore, its converts are not made from the lowest ranks; those sought and obtained by the Mormonite apostles are mechanics and tradesmen who have saved a little money, who are remarkable for their moral character, but who are exposed to delusion from having, as Archbishop [Samuel] Sharpe expressed it, "studied the Bible with an ill-balanced mind."[20]

While arranging and preparing for the publication of the hymn book and the Book of Mormon in Manchester, Brigham had a chance to visit the city.[21] About one hundred miles north of Hereford and about equidistant from Liverpool and Preston, Manchester was probably chosen as his headquarters city because of its location and its facility for printing. The living conditions of its two hundred thousand inhabitants were dismal. Its more than a hundred smoke-blackened factories were nearly all devoted to the spinning and weaving of cotton. Deplorable and unhealthful as were the working conditions, living conditions were a degradation. The city's inhabitants huddled in back-to-back houses intersected by narrow lanes, each neighborhood sprinkled with open cesspools into which garbage, night soil, and ashes were thrown. Many people lived in cellars. Since the city had no public park, and the impact of the Evangelical and Dissenting movements was to forbid the opening of libraries, art galleries, museums, and zoological gardens on Sundays, the desperate and hungry factory hands in many cases ended up stupefying their misery with gin and beer. Few were satisfied that the church could do anything for them: "We want more bread and less Bibles, more pigs and less parsons."[22]

Brigham tried to reassure himself by keeping busy—writing his fellow apostles, preaching "the new and everlasting covenant" to large congregations (including an audience in Carpenter's Hall), and organizing groups who wished to emigrate. "My labor has ben such that I am quite unwell," he wrote Willard Richards. "But I keepe going with all my might."[23] His "hard work," however, did not interfere with his sense of perspective. Cognizant of his responsibility as president of the apostles, he concluded a letter to Richards with the warning:

> Be carful not to lay this letter with the New Testament writings. If you doe som body will take it for a text after the Mallineum [Millennium] and contend about it. . . . Now my Dear Brother you must forgive all my noncense and overlook erours.[24]

His fellow apostles enjoyed these little expressions of Brigham's contagious enthusiasm and good humor. As Heber Kimball wrote his wife, "There never was better feelings among the Twelve than at this time; all things go well."[25]

On June 1, Brigham and Heber met with a company of forty-six Saints to organize them for their journey to Nauvoo. They appointed John Moon priesthood leader, gave each one of them a blessing, asked them to take along a bundle of letters to the apostles' families in Nauvoo, and, with John Taylor, joined the emigrants on the *Britannia* to help them get comfortably situated. After fond farewells, the ship set sail on June 6.[26]

Brigham sent along with Moon's company two letters and several small gifts for Mary Ann, locking them in a little box. In a separate envelope he enclosed a note and the key to the box. Unfortunately, the two letters have not survived, but the cover note, dated June 2, 1840, concludes:

> I must closen up my letter and say fare well. Sister Moon or Brother Moon will deliver the little present to you. Brother Kimball send[s] you a little smeling bottle just to let you know that he thinks of my famely.[27]

Brigham must have sent a small amount of cash as well, for he wrote of his gratitude to God for permitting him to help his wife and children buy "a morsel of bread, it is not me but the Lord that has done it through me."[28]

How much he knew of Mary Ann's condition is unclear. The situation of both the Young and Kimball families during the winter of 1839–40 was desperate. Her own means exhausted, Mary Ann Young one day left the older girls with the rest of the children while she crossed the Mississippi in an open boat, her baby bundled tight against the cold. She hoped to obtain food from the Nauvoo bishops. Years later one Nauvoo veteran described her arrival that stormy November day:

> with her baby Alice in her arms, almost fainting with cold and hunger, and dripping wet with the spray from crossing the river. . . . I tried to persuade her to stay, but she refused, saying, "the children at home are hungry, too." I shall never forget how she looked, shivering with cold and thinly clad. I kept the baby while she went to the tithing office. She came back with a few potatoes and a little flour, for which she seemed very grateful, and taking her baby with her parcels . . . weak as she was from ague and fever, wended her way to the river bank.[29]

After this terrible winter the worst had passed, and by spring letters from America began to report "I saw sisters Pratt, Kimball, Young, Woodruff, Turley, Smith. . . . They and their families are well."[30]

Brigham must have had his family very much on his mind when, a few days after the departure of the Moon company, he had a dream—or, as he called it, a "night vision."

> I first dremed of being at home in the Stat[e]s. I first saw Elizabeth. I asked her whare her mother was. She said she was about the house. She soon came in. I shook hands [with] her hart[i]ly as I had don with Elizabeth. I embraced her in my arms and kissed [her] 2 or 3 times and asked hir whare my four children was.

She and Elizabeth both ansard and said they ware at [s]chool and . . . loved there books. My wife says we feele well but you must provide for your own families for the Church are not able to doe for them.[31]

The next day he repeated to Mary Ann in a lengthy letter: "I thought that I had got to takare of my own famely fore the Church would not be able to doe much for our famelies." He told her of material for "a butiful Calico frock kaften" for her and Vilate Kimball, courtesy of Henry Moon, and said he would like to see her in the frock when he returned. After a report of the progress of the work, he promised, "the Lord being my helper I will doe as much and as fast as posable, for I feel that I with my Bretherin will be wonted with our families eare long. Fore if the Lord dont come out of his hiding place before long I am mestaken."[32]

As long as he had to be away from his family, wrote Brigham, he was as happy to be in England as anywhere.

They are as loving a set of people as ever I saw in my life. Y[e]a they are more so in their appearance than the Americans. But my soul says sweet home sweet home. My blesed famely, yes my kind and loving family, how sweet is home. . . . When the time has fully com and the Lord says goe home, my hart then will leap for joy.

Finally, Brigham assured Mary Ann that he fully realized the extent of her personal sacrifice:

I think much about you having the [care of] such a large famely upon your hands and no one to see to or doe enything for them but your self. Your task must be grate. I shall endevor to send to your assistence as often as I can. . . . To Elizabeth may the Lord bles you and keep you humbel and Violate, be good girles and pray for me that the Lord will enable me to doe his will. I sub[s]cribe myself, yours in the bonds of love, matromony, and the everlasting Covenent.[33]

Brigham Young's concern for his own family made him sensitive to the feelings of others—and anxious to help where he could. Jenetta Richards, the wife Willard had married soon after his arrival in England in 1837, had not been well, and Brigham thought Willard should be with her. Approaching the matter humorously, Brigham wrote Willard:

Now as to the other question about Jennet, thus saith the scripter he that provideth not fore his own household has—but perhaps he had not hou[s]e. Well has he got a famely? Yes he has got a wife. Then let him see that she is taken care of and her hart comforted. But stop; say som, why doe you not tak care of your famely? I doe when circumstances doe not render it otherwise. There is a difference betwene three months jorny and a fue [h]ours ride. Now I say to answer my own feelings, com as soon as you can leve things there. This is not by relevation nor by commandment, so put it not with the anapistles of the New Testament. But Brighcm sayes come and see your wife.³⁴

Richards went immediately to his wife.

On July 6 the Saints met together in a conference at Manchester to settle difficulties. We do not know of many of these problems, but Joseph Fielding, who saw it as a time of "great Instruction and Warning to the Church," told of a case in which a man had done some ugly things and placed the blame on an evil spirit. Very well, said Brigham, "the blame must be laid on that spirit, and if we could get at him we would cut him off from the Church. But we do not know how to get hold of him unless we take hold of the person possessed by it."³⁵

o n September 5, as a company of two hundred Saints gathered at the port to sail to America under Elder Theodore Turley, Brigham and Willard Richards were in the Manchester office of the *Star* preparing a lengthy letter to Joseph Smith and his counselors in Nauvoo. The heart of the report was a recital of the social and economic conditions in England. The apostles were appalled that the ministers and factory masters had such control that "many simple souls who believe our message dare not be baptized" because starvation could be the result. They commiserated with men out of work, families starving, women and children begging to survive.³⁶ These conditions led them to make every exertion to aid the emigration of as many Saints as possible. Knowing the poverty and distress, reported the apostles to the First Presidency, "we . . . have made use of our own credit among the brethren" to bring the poor along with the rest.

> Brethren, our hearts are pained with the poverty and misery of this people, and we have done all we could to help as many off as possible to a land where they may get a morsel of bread, and serve God according to his appointment; and we have done it cheerfully as unto the Lord, and we desire to ask you have we done right? Or is it a right principle, for us to act upon, to involve ourselves, to help the poor Saints to Zion?

They closed with many questions, some urgent.

> Our motto is go ahead. Go ahead, and ahead we are determined to go till we have conquered every foe. So come life or come death we'll go ahead, but tell us if we are going wrong and we will right it.

Letter in hand, Brigham and Willard went to Liverpool to meet the departing Saints. On September 8 a steamer towed the ship *North America* out of port, Brigham and Willard on board with the emigrants. After the fifteen-mile tow, Young and Richards returned to shore with the steamer, then traveled back to Manchester.[37]

O N October 6, 1840, the Twelve met in Manchester for the third general conference since their arrival. Brigham's thinking and preparation for the conference are indicated by a still-extant small folded paper with his handwritten notes on problems to be discussed:

> Whare shall the Book of Mormon [be published]?
> Who shall take charge of the Maleneal Star if P. Pratt does not come?
> Is it best for some of the 12 to goe home this fall and come back next Seson?
> What time shall the next company goe to America and how shall they be organised to goe?
> Who shall have athority to ordane officers in the Churches?
> Will the Church help Brother Richards?
> Who shall make or prepare the endex to the Book of Mormon?[38]

This agenda would largely be followed, and in a real sense the October conference, important for establishing policy and new precedents, would be Brigham's conference. Ordinations were performed, disciplinary cases were acted upon, a fund was established to support missionaries with insufficient means, and missionaries were assigned to their places of labor. Total membership was reported to be up 1,115 since July, and there were 70 churches and 1,007 members at Herefordshire.[39]

Several letters that Brigham wrote to Mary Ann during the fall and winter of 1840 have survived. They document plainly that the demands of publication continued to occupy a large portion of Brigham's energy and that invariably, as every new publisher learns, everything connected with it took longer than anticipated. In mid-October he and Heber, just returned to Manchester, prepared to visit Preston and Liverpool "on som buysness concerning the Book of Mormon." If they could finish the business, it was their intention to spend part of the winter in London (some of the other apostles had begun preaching there) and perhaps make a short visit to Hamburg, Germany, where one missionary was working. If the typesetting and printing had started about the time that they purchased paper in July, by this time it should have been far advanced. Young also carried the financial responsibility for the *Star*; he was much relieved when he learned in October that Parley Pratt had returned the day before from America. He was now free "to goe to other places to preach and attend to business." As late as mid-January he was still apologizing that "the printing of the Book of Mormon goes slow to what the hymn book did. It is a grate job though it is about don and desposed of." Since it "rest[s] upon my sholders," he knew it must be done before he could leave for America. Not until February were the first unbound copies of the book ready; binding and business details continued for several weeks after that.[40]

Brigham wrote to Mary Ann in October that, although the English "broth-erin and sisters would pluck out there eyes" for him and his brethren "if it ware nessary," the apostles needed "help in the vinyard." He hoped for elders that would follow counsel and keep within bounds:

> I have not herd who is acoming but I trust they will be good men that will be sent, for [s]churely it requires men of strong mind and determined persistence to due all things right, and then due nothing more.

Within this letter he wrote a note to his brother Joseph Young, senior president of the Seventy, urging him to send more elders, "but for Heven sake due not send men here that is to[o] big to be counseled." Even without more elders, however, "the work of the Lord is roling on in this contry. The Elders are going in every direction to preach. The people are receiving there testemony and they are building up churches in meny parts of the land." Unfortunately, this "causes much per[se]cution. We have Baptised some of the old Westl[y]ans, which makes them [their ministers] feele verry uneasy."[41]

Brigham had earlier organized Manchester elders into a preaching corps that occupied some forty stations throughout the city to conduct street meet-ings and announce the central meeting at the large Carpenter's Hall. The men would first meet together for a priesthood meeting and then disperse to their assigned stations. On November 8, Brigham sent the men home rather than to their stations. He had heard that the Methodists had complained, and Manchester's mayor had instructed the police that morning to arrest all street preachers. All twenty arrested were quickly released when they proved to be Methodists.[42]

Brigham was delighted with the Manchester ministers who tried to keep their members away from the Mormons by telling them "if you don't . . . you will want to goe again and you will be druv away by them. They are so intising you cannot keep away if [you] goe once." Indeed, the delusion was so powerful, said the preachers, that after joining the Mormons people would even pay their own passage to America "to the promist land." Brigham commented dryly that, unfortunately, not all were deluded enough to pay their passage, and a few had even said they would not go unless their way was paid.

Brigham learned through a letter from Vilate to Heber Kimball that his (Brigham's) family "were needy." Their house was hardly a shelter, and daugh-ters Vilate and Elizabeth were both sick with the chills.[43] This news prompted Young to write:

> I aske my Hevenly Father to preserve my family till I returne home. How I long to see my famely or [k]now they are well and provided for so that they doe not suffer for food and rament, and I know that the Church is poor and it is as much as they can doe to attend to without doing enything for my famely. I know they woul[d] . . . if they could. . . .

Sister Vilate says your house could hardly be cau[l]d a shelter. This makes me fee[l] bad but I will doe [all] I can for you to help you to make you and the children comfortable while I am in the vinyard. . . . I dremed last night of seeing the house whare you live and that it looked very open and cold. I feele for you. . . .

During the last of November and early December Brigham, Heber, and Woodruff spent twelve days in London, where they preached on Sunday and two evenings in each week and visited the "sights."[44] Although they did not expect to attract many converts, and regarded their presence in London as of primarily symbolic significance, Brigham and his associates would not have missed the opportunity of seeing the world's largest city. What they saw helped them to understand the complexity of the leading society of their day. For London, with its two million inhabitants, well illustrated the paradox of England—the magnificence and the squalor; the opulence and the destitution. Their diaries mention rope dancers, greengrocers' boys, and skaters at Kensington Gardens; a flea circus, pre-Christmas pantomimes, and a Punch-and-Judy show. They heard the cacophony of political and mystical diatribes in Hyde Park and firsthand accounts of the flogging of poor girls in the workhouse. They witnessed a procession of royal carriages, featuring twenty-four beautifully matched cream-colored horses whose sleeping stalls, they were informed, had beds that "are better than those which half the people in London sleep upon." They were doubtful of the attention shown to Queen Victoria and her husband; Heber expressed surprise, in a letter to his wife, at "the stur thare is made over a little queen at the same time thousands [are] starving to deth fore a little bread."[45]

Brigham, Heber, and Woodruff visited Buckingham Palace and some of the worst slums. They saw St. Paul's Cathedral, including the whispering gallery and the steeple, even going into the brass ball on top of the steeple, which could hold twelve people. They also observed beggars with stunted growth and halting speech who were dying for lack of food. They went to the tunnel under the Thames and the monument near London Bridge erected in commemoration of the dreadful fire of 1666, and attended the College of Surgeons and the National Gallery. They spent hours at the Tower of London, where the kings held their festive tournaments and pompous ceremonials and where were exhibited equestrian statues of the most celebrated kings, together with their lords and ladies; the crowns and jewels of many of the rulers; instruments of torture, and the ax once used for beheading. They did business with the Bank of England, of which Brigham was later accused of being the largest stockholder, and toured the British Museum where they examined papyri, mummies, sepulchers, marble statues, and other antiquities.

Of all their visits, they spoke and wrote most about Westminster Abbey. Clearly, it had impressed them in an indelible way. The most noted church in Great Britain, there the sovereigns of Britain were crowned. The stained glass windows, the fine old tapestry, the Venetian glass mosaics, the rich marble of the interior, the royal burial vaults, the many memorials on the walls, the statues of prominent men and women, the congregated bones of people who had filled history with their deeds and the earth with their renown—the Mormon visitors were fascinated. Brigham would have echoed Woodruff's comment that London was "as profitable a school to me as any I have ever met with in my travels"—a beautiful, inspiring, and yet a depressing, woeful city.[46]

Although Brigham and his companions had gone, "Jonah-like," to and fro, "endeavoring to get some door open where we could warn the people and search out the honest in heart . . . we found the whole city given to covetousness . . . and all manner of abominations." They concluded that London was "a perfect depot of the systems of the nineteenth century, containing 666 different gods, gospels, redeemers, plans of salvation, religions, churches, commandments, orders of preaching, [and] roads to heaven and to hell."[47] Only a handful had converted to Mormonism.

B R I G H A M left London by rail on December 11 to resume his schedule of visits and conferences. But with the new year the apostles realized their stay in England was drawing to a close. On January 15, 1841, Brigham announced to Mary Ann that

> on the 6 day of Apriel 1841 we hold a Councel of the Twelve with the officers of the Church for the purpos of arrangen the affares of the Church so that we can leve. I think we shall start for home then, and make ouer way as fast as we can. I believe this is the feelings of all the Twelve. This is all I can say upon the subject, the will of the Lord be don.[48]

The labors he had set for himself about completed, Young finally allowed himself to think about going home. Apparently the heavy demands of young children and her own poor health had prevented Mary Ann from writing often. Just before he wrote to her in January, he received a long letter from her further turning his heart toward home. He expressed sorrow at her illness and awareness of the difficulty of her tasks even with health. "I pray for you and the children continuly," he wrote, "it is all I can due. I cannot help you about your daly work." He reaffirmed that he felt they were in the hands "of the Lord God of Israel," although he also admitted feeling a great desire for them. He was certain that the time went faster for him than for them because of the variety and demands of his mission. His responsibilities weighed so heavily upon him that he had time for little else: "If I would give up my mind to think of my famely it would destract me and I should not be fit for the work the Lord has set me about." But this time he was distracted. Mary Ann had written that "little Mary Ann cried the other night and did not want to goe to bed till she had kneled down and praid for Father." Deeply touched, Young responded: "Bless the little creater [creature]. How I want to see hir."[49]

Immediately after writing to Mary Ann, Brigham penned letters to the other members of the Twelve notifying them to be ready to sail in early April. His letter to George A. Smith was no doubt typical:

> The Twelve are agoing to meet on the last day of March or the first day of Apriel for . . . such business as will be nessary . . . before they goe home. I believe it to be the minds of all the Bretherin to goe home emed[i]atily after the confrence. . . . What say you about the matter. I say I am for home if the Lord will that I goe. If this dos not meet your mind you must let me know.[50]

Earlier, on December 15, 1840, Joseph Smith had written a letter advising the Twelve to return to America in the spring, but it did not arrive until late February, well after Brigham had decided to do precisely what Joseph counseled.

Smith's letter did provide his answers to the numerous questions Brigham and his associates had earnestly raised in May and September. He approved of their publishing activities, but he did not wish to comment on the long list of questions. "You are more conversant with the peculiar circumstances than I am, and I feel great confidence in your united wisdom." The Prophet then offered a poetic comment. The successes they had achieved, he wrote, must have increased their confidence in God, in the Gospel, and in themselves,

> like the gallant Bark, that has braved the storm unhurt, spread her canvass to the breese, and nobly cuts her way through the yielding waves, more conscious than ever of the strength of her timbers and the experience and capabilities of her captain, pilots and crew.

Shortly after reading the Prophet's letter, the apostles received an epistle from the First Presidency entitled "A Proclamation to the Saints Scattered Abroad."[51] It contained information about developments in Nauvoo and renewed emphasis on the importance of the gathering:

> It is true the idea of a general gathering has heretofore been associated with most cruel and oppressing scenes, owing to our unrelenting persecutions at the hands of wicked and unjust men; but we hope that those days of darkness and gloom have gone by. . . .

The gathering was necessary, declared the proclamation, for only by a "concentration of action, and a unity of effort" could the Saints accomplish the great work of the last days. In addition to the temporal benefits of such action, in no other way could a temple be built and the Saints saved spiritually.

M O S T of the English Saints needed no urging to emigrate. Even before the apostles mentioned the gathering, they desired to see the Prophet, to live among the Saints, to go to America. Brigham wrote to his brother Joseph Young in October 1840:

> The Saints have got a start for to gether to America and goe they will, and nothing can stop them. . . . They have so much of the spirit of getherin that they would goe if they knew they would die as soon as they got there or if they knew that the mob would be upon them and drive them as so[o]n as they got there. They have the spirit of the times here as well as the Church there.[52]

The season's emigration opened in early February with final preparations for the sailing of the *Sheffield*.[53] Three apostles (Young, Taylor, and Richards) had contracted for the ship, purchased provisions, and arranged many of the stores. To accompany each shipload of English Saints, Brigham appointed an American elder—someone capable of being a leader as well as one who could transact the American end of the business without unnecessary costs.

On the morning of February 7, Young and several hundred others watched as the *Sheffield* carried the 235 New Orleans–bound Mormons down the river and out to sea. Four days later the three apostles appointed three men to serve as the presidency on the ship *Echo*, which sailed with 109 Saints on board.[54] In March, Young assisted with the departure of the *Alesto*.

When not directly involved with the ships and emigrating Saints, Brigham supported the movement with numerous letters to keep the other apostles informed and coordinate their efforts so that money, provisions, emigrants, and a ship came together for a successful company. His February 13 letter to George A. Smith illustrates the process of planning and preparation:

> We wish you to Call the Churches together in your part and ascertaine emeditly how meny of the Bretherin can be reddy to sale by the 10 of March next, as we shall fit out another Company then. . . . Let us know by the 25 of this month. Let us have the names of all, and the ages of all children under 14 years. Children from one to 14 will goe 2 for one. Under one year they goe free.[55]

Smith was instructed to appoint an agent to handle the money for passage and provisions. Brigham continued:

> As soon as we find out the name of the Ship and the day of Saling we shall wright and let you know what time to send your agent and also what day your famelies must be here. . . . Our advice is for all to goe that can in March, as they will goe by New Orlenes. . . . [much cheaper than] by New York—and such as cannot goe then had better stay till the last of August or September and then sale for New Orleans.

When Brigham received a letter stating "all willing but none able to gather at present" because they lacked the means, he replied:

We say goe, or at enny other time when they chose. Our surkler [circular] is no law but advice in consequence of the expence. The vessles are now fild to over-flowing that are leving for America. The passage will be much higher after this till fall agan—but we say to the Bretherin goe when you can.[56]

Between ship departures Young continued his travels, visiting the elders and preaching. He also prepared a communication for the *Star* on family prayer: "Heads of families," he admonished, "should always take the charge of family worship."[57]

On April 1, the Twelve assembled in Manchester to begin their final labors in England. Orson Hyde had arrived, which meant that nine of the Twelve were there assembled for council—the most to be together since soon after their call in 1835. Summarizing the meetings, Woodruff wrote in his diary that "perfect union and harmony prevailed in all the deliberations of our Councils for the last four days."[58] The membership tallies showed a total of 5,864, up nearly 2,200 since the last conference and more than 4,300 since their first conference one year before.[59] In addition, approximately 800 had emigrated and were not counted here, for a total membership present and emigrated of 6,674. Subtracting from the 1840 membership of 1,541 leaves an increase in one year of 5,133. If one counts a few backsliders, the total number of converts approached 6,000. Clearly the Twelve had provided the impetus for a Mormon community that eventually sent more than 38,000 Britons to Nauvoo and to the Salt Lake Valley by 1870.

In his parting remarks, Brigham was concerned to instruct English leaders in church administration and procedure. All the British branches were orga-nized into conferences and presiding elders appointed over them.[60] Parley Pratt, the apostle who would remain in England, would preside over the whole. Amos Fielding was appointed emigration agent in Liverpool.

A beautifully decorated cake from New York, a present from the wife of George J. Adams to the Twelve, graced the evening meeting. Appropriate hymns and "a powerful and general feeling of delight" animated the seven hundred in attendance as the cake was served. Joseph Fielding thought the cake a fitting symbol "of the good things of that land from whence it came, and from whence they had received the fulness of the gospel." Brigham and William Miller then sang the hymn, "Adieu, my dear brethren," after which Brigham dismissed the congregation by invoking the blessing of "the God of our fathers" that each member would have the "wisdom and grace to act each your part in the great work which lies before you."[61]

T H E Y all left Liverpool on April 21, 1841, a departure that was delayed because of Saints gathering to sail on the same ship, a round of farewells, and final purchases. Already, noted Brigham, the shipmasters were looking foward to the "large business" that Mormon emigration promised.[62] As they departed, one of Woodruff's converts, a man who had already aided many of the poor to emigrate, gave Woodruff a purse of gold to assist him in his journey home; he divided it with his fellow apostles so that none of the Twelve left England with empty pockets.[63]

Brigham later summarized his year in England:

> We landed . . . as strangers in a strange land, and penniless, but through the mercy of God we have gained many friends, established churches in almost every noted town and city in the kingdom of Great Britain, baptized between seven and eight thousand, printed 5000 Books of Mormon, 3000 Hymn Books, 2500 volumes of the Millennial Star, and 50,000 tracts, and emigrated to Zion 1000 souls, established a permanent shipping agency, which will be a great blessing to the Saints, and have left sown in the hearts of many thousands the seeds of eternal truth, which will bring forth fruit to the honor and glory of God, and yet we have lacked nothing to eat, drink or wear: in all these things I acknowledge the hand of God.[64]

The return journey, unlike the trip out, was fine until they were "becalmed on the banks of New found Land" and Brigham "was verry sick and destressed in my head and stomick." In one of his few moments that was less than determinedly cheerful, he admitted, "I felt as though I could not endure menny such voiges as I had indured for two years or sence I started on my mision and ware it not for the power of God and his tendere mercy I should despare. But the Lord is my strength."[65]

The other passengers were also discouraged, and their grumbling galvanized Brigham. He summoned the other apostles, they "agreed to humble themselves before the Lord and ask Him to calm the sease and give us a fair wind. We did so and the wind emeditly changed and from that time to this it has blone in our favor." As the *Rochester* came into New York harbor on May 19, Brigham's journal notes expansively, "Fine morning. My native land looks good to me."[66] He was never to leave it again.

The route between New York and Nauvoo was enlivened by two or three minor accidents: a car caught fire on the train, the boat out of Pittsburgh was picking its way through water so low that it "rubed on the botom several times" and they finally ran aground, and an accident with steam a few days later scalded a woman, her daughter, and her grandchild.

No account of their actual arrival in Nauvoo on July 1, 1841, has survived. Joseph Smith, pleased with what had been achieved, visited Brigham in his home and conveyed a special revelation to him:

> Dear and well beloved Brother Brigham Young, verily thus saith the Lord unto you, my servant Brigham, it is no more required at your hands to leave your family as in times past, for your offering is acceptable to me; I have seen your labor and toil in journeyings for my name. I therefore command you to send my word abroad, and take special care of your family from this time, henceforth and forever. Amen.[67]

Welcome words for both Brigham and Mary Ann. Although their trials were by no means over, never again would Brigham leave his family so destitute and for so long as he had during the 1840-41 British mission.

The final entry in his journal covering this period—and his first entry since his return home in July—was written on January 18, 1842. It is all poignant understatement: "This evening I am with my love alone by my fireside for the first time for years. We injoi it and feele to prase the Lord."

7 ✤

Nauvoo

We moved in to our new house on Wensday the 31 of May
in the year 1843. I prase my God for the privelege of a house.[1]

O N his return from England, Brigham found his family living
in a small, unfinished hewn-log cabin, "situated on a low, wet lot, so swampy
that when the first attempt was made to plow it the oxen mired." After the
city was drained, however, "it became a very valuable garden spot."[2] As he
had time available, and with the Prophet's permission to provide for his family's
needs, Brigham began chinking the cabin, preparing a garden, building a
temporary shed for his cow, setting out an orchard, and draining, fencing,
planting, and cultivating his lot. As the ground was too damp for an underground cellar, he built one aboveground with inner and outer brick walls with
about four or five inches between them for dead-air space, the outer arched
over with a vaulted brick roof. "Frost never penetrated it," he declared, "although in summer articles would mildew in it."[3] The cellar was essential for
storing fruits and vegetables for winter use and for cooling milk and meats.

O N August 10, 1841, a little over a month after Brigham and his fellow apostles
returned to Nauvoo, Joseph Smith called the available members of the Twelve
to a meeting at which he made a startling announcement. Henceforth, he said,
the Twelve must assume "the burthen of the business of the church in Nauvoo,
and especially as pertaining to the church lands, settling of the Saints after
their arrival, and selling church lands."[4] This new assignment meant that the
Twelve now had formal responsibilities within a fully organized and functioning stake of Zion.

Smith called a special conference of the Saints for August 16 to explain
his action and have it ratified by the church. Six of the apostles were present—
Brigham, Heber, Orson Pratt, John Taylor, George A. Smith, and Willard
Richards. Unfortunately, Joseph Smith's youngest child died on August 15,
and the Prophet was not present for the first session. Brigham therefore opened

the conference, was voted to the chair, and proceeded to direct the calling of missionaries and the settling of immigrants.

Joseph Smith presided over the second session and announced that the main purpose of the conference was

> that the Twelve should be authorized to assist in managing the affairs of the Kingdom in this place [Nauvoo, church headquarters] which he said was the duties of their office &c. Motioned seconded and carried that the quorum of the twelve be authorized to act in accordance with the instructions given by president Joseph Smith in regulating and superintending the affairs of the Church.[5]

Henceforth, the minutes make clear, the Twelve had authority to administer the affairs of the church wherever and whenever the Prophet directed. Willard Richards's brief diary entry adequately summed up their new position: "Conference—Business of the Church given to the 12."[6]

From this time Joseph Smith would rely on the Twelve to manage many of the day-to-day affairs of the church. As president of the Twelve, Brigham would become, along with the Prophet's brother Hyrum and two or three others, one of his intimate circle of confidants, advisers, and administrative assistants.

In some respects the new assignment seemed to be merely an extension of work that the Twelve had undertaken on an ad hoc basis before: They had earlier been instructed to call and appoint missionaries, they had preached the gathering in the East and England, and they were responsible for settling the gathered Saints around Nauvoo after they arrived. But as subsequent events demonstrated, the new general responsibility for "the business of the church in Nauvoo" marked a new plateau of authority. For example, in September 1841 Brigham was elected to the Nauvoo City Council and, with the exception of absences on short-term missions, served during all the years the Mormons were there. He was also inducted into the Masonic lodge that had been organized in Nauvoo in 1841. (For a short period he had been a Mason in western New York before he joined the Mormons.) But, although he received the first three degrees, there is no indication that Brigham was particularly interested in or active in Masonic affairs.[7]

In a more ecclesiastical capacity, Brigham and the Twelve henceforth directed the proselyting activities of the church, whether in the immediate region of Nauvoo, in the United States and Canada generally, in Great Britain and continental Europe, or in the South Pacific; supervised the ingathering of Saints from the East, from Great Britain, and from elsewhere; acted as land agents and as settlement directors for new converts coming into the region; and directed the collection of tithing and other contributions toward the construction of the Nauvoo House, a hotel, and the Nauvoo Temple. For the latter purpose they established, in the summer of 1841, a tithing recorder's office and tithing storehouse. The record books show regular contributions of grain, meat, vegetables, clothing, horses, wagons, cattle, hogs, sheep, butter, and eggs. One of Brigham's recurring responsibilities was pricing the items that came in on tithing.[8] Most of the receipts were distributed to the families of workmen on the temple. The Twelve also oversaw the publication program of the church, including the newspaper, *Nauvoo Neighbor*, the monthly, *Times and Seasons*; a Nauvoo edition of the Book of Mormon; and a supply of doctrinal and historical tracts and pamphlets.

Most importantly, the Twelve consulted regularly with the Prophet on church doctrine and practice, an opportunity that became increasingly important as they approached the time to dedicate the temple.

F O U R new doctrines or practices were introduced to the Twelve by the Prophet in the fall and winter of 1841–42. The first was the performance of baptisms for the dead. If everyone had to be baptized as a prerequisite for salvation, those who died without hearing the gospel could be baptized only by proxy. This, at least, was the rationale, first set forth in a revelation issued by Joseph Smith. One of the first portions of the Nauvoo Temple to be completed was a font where baptisms for the dead—living persons acting as proxy—could be performed. Completed in November 1841, the font was dedicated on November 8. Brigham offered the dedicatory prayer.[9] The first baptisms in the new font, a ceremony in which Brigham participated, were performed on November 21.

The second new doctrine or practice was plural marriage. In 1831, while studying the Old Testament with Oliver Cowdery, Joseph Smith became persuaded that plural marriage was a biblical principle and that in restoring all correct ancient practices God required it for the Latter-day Saints. Although there is some evidence that Smith (and possibly Cowdery as well) married plural wives in Kirtland, he unquestionably began to introduce the principle to some associates in the spring of 1841, while the Twelve were still in England. The latter found out about this on their return. Quietly, hesitatingly, in private conversations with each apostle, Joseph explained that he now believed plural marriage to be a divine requirement. Brigham later described his emotions on first learning about plural marriage:

> Some of these my brethren know what my feelings were at the time Joseph revealed the doctrine; I was not desirous of shrinking from any duty, nor of failing in the least to do as I was commanded, but it was the first time in my life that I had desired the grave, and I could hardly get over it for a long time. And when I saw a funeral, I felt to envy the corpse its situation, and to regret that I was not in the coffin, knowing the toil and labor that my body would have to undergo; and I have had to examine myself, from that day to this, and watch my faith, and carefully meditate, lest I should be found desiring the grave more than I ought to do.[10]

He must have held long and earnest conversations with Mary Ann and his close associates of the Twelve. Others had similar reactions.[11]

Some of Brigham's rationalizations about the adoption of this practice are revealed in his conversation shortly afterward with "a professor in a Southern University." The following is from Brigham's history:

> In order to explain the principle [plural wives], I asked the gentleman if he believed the Bible, and was a believer in the resurrection. He said he was a believer in the Old and New Testament and in the resurrection. I then asked him if he believed parents and children, husbands and wives would recognize each other in the resurrection. He said he did. Also, if parents and children would have the same filial feeling towards each other which they have here; and he said he believed they would, and that their affections would be more acute than they were in this life.

Brigham then said to him:

> We see in this life, that amongst Christians, ministers and all classes of men, a man will marry a wife, and have children by her; she dies, and he marries another, and then another, until men have had as many as six wives, and each of them bear children. This is considered all right by the Christian world, inasmuch as a man has but one at a time. Now, in the resurrection this man and all his wives and children are raised from the dead; what will be done with those women and children, and who will they belong to? and if the man is to have but one, which one in the lot shall he have?

The professor replied that he had never thought of the question in this light before, and said he did not believe those women and children would belong to any but those they belonged to in this life.

> "Very well," said I, "you consider that to be a pure, holy place in the presence of God, angels, and celestial beings; would the Lord permit a thing to exist in his presence in heaven which is evil? And if it is right for a man to have several wives and children in heaven at the same time, is it not a consistent doctrine that a man should have several wives, and children by those wives at the same time, here in this life, as was the case with Abraham and many of the old Prophets? Or is it any more sinful to have several wives at a time than at different times?"

The professor answered that he could not see that it would be any more inconsistent to have more wives in this life than in the next, or to have five wives at one time than at five different times. He was finally forced to admit that "it is a correct principle and a Bible doctrine, and I cannot see anything inconsistent in it."[12] (It is interesting that there was no consideration of a woman having plural husbands, yet Brigham's rationale would also seem to fit that situation.)

LINCOLN CHRISTIAN COLLEGE

75944

After a few weeks of study, conversation, and prayer, Brigham reluctantly accepted the doctrine. With Mary Ann's consent he married his first plural wife in June 1842, Lucy Ann Decker Seeley, the ceremony being performed by Joseph Smith. Born at Phelps, Ontario County, New York, in 1822 of Dutch and English parents, Lucy was eleven when she and her family moved to Portage County, Ohio, in 1833. They soon joined the Mormons. At the age of sixteen she married William Seeley, also a Latter-day Saint, and they moved to a Mormon settlement in Missouri where Lucy had her first child, Isaac. Along with other Mormons, Lucy and William were driven from Missouri. In Illinois two more children were born, Harriet and an unnamed stillbirth. Lucy's husband began to abuse her, then abandoned her, and she was informed that he had died. After she and Brigham were married, they became the parents of seven children, including one son (Feramorz) who attended the United States Naval Academy at Annapolis.[13]

These first plural marriages were performed secretly, the revelation commanding its practice was not set down in writing until July 1843, and the practice itself was confined to a limited group until after the Mormons moved to the Great Basin.

In the meantime, a third preparatory ordinance or ceremony introduced privately to the Twelve shortly after baptism for the dead and plural marriage was "the full endowment." There had been washings and anointings in the Kirtland Temple, but the full endowment, as introduced in the spring of 1842, was a sacred ceremony in which participants observed a series of dramatic renderings of episodes that illuminate the plan of Christian life and salvation. The endowment also included the making of "covenants" or promises to live chaste, obedient, and Christian lives. Brigham noted in his journal on May 4, 1842, that he, Heber Kimball, and Willard Richards met with Joseph and Hyrum Smith. Joseph "taught the ancient order of things for the first time in these last days, and [I] received my washings, anointings, and endowments."[14] A year later, on May 26, 1843, the same group met again. In Brigham's words, Joseph Smith "administered to us the first ordinances of endowment, and gave us instructions on the Priesthood and the new and everlasting covenant."[15]

A fourth set of instructions related to "sealings" of children to parents and of persons with unbelieving or worldly parents to faithful families. In special ceremonies Brigham was sealed to his parents, his children were sealed to him, and a number of young men were sealed to Brigham as his spiritual sons.

Brigham, Kimball, and Richards were expected to introduce these new beliefs and practices to other members of the Twelve and of the church. When Joseph and the Twelve had completed this work, by the summer of 1843, Joseph then organized, among those who had received these teachings and ordinances, an "Anointed Quorum" or "Holy Order" that met periodically in the Prophet's office or home to discuss the "higher things" of the gospel. Women—the wives of the Twelve and other church officers—were also members of this group, including Mary Ann and Fanny Young Murray, Brigham's widowed sister. This group met regularly for prayer, sermons, theological instruction, and other spiritual exercises beginning in the fall of 1843.[16]

Although these practices were introduced only to an inner circle, there were inevitable leaks. A few of the faithful murmured about "secret" and "abominable" practices, and those who had reasons to fear the buildup of Mormon power began to mount hostile campaigns.

I N connection with his duties, Brigham was often "on the road," and served two short-term proselyting missions himself. The first of these was a mission to various towns in Illinois to counteract anti-Mormon propaganda, from September 9 to November 4, 1842.

Welcomed into Illinois for humanitarian and political reasons in 1839, the Mormons were watched with growing mistrust by other residents in the region. The rise in population, the impact of bloc voting, and the growing strength of the "Nauvoo Legion"—the Mormon militia—were sources of alarm. The legislature had granted a charter with wide powers to Nauvoo, and Smith, in order to prevent a repetition of the experiences in Ohio and Missouri, took an expansive view of his powers. In nearby Warsaw, Thomas Sharp, editor of the *Warsaw Signal*, used every opportunity to demonstrate that Joseph Smith was "a dangerous man." Then, in the summer of 1842, John C. Bennett, an opportunistic convert who had become mayor of Nauvoo and a general in the legion, was charged by Smith with attempting to seduce several Nauvoo women under the guise of polygamy. Drummed out of the church, Bennett went on the lecture circuit against the Mormons, published articles in local and national newspapers, and collected these into a widely selling book called *The History of the Saints; or, An Expose of Joe Smith and Mormonism* (1842). Bennett's exposé became public on the eve of statewide elections, and both candidates for governor called for repeal of the Nauvoo charter. In May 1842, an attempt had been made to murder Lilburn W. Boggs, the Missouri governor who had led the drive to "exterminate" the Mormons in that state. State officials blamed Porter Rockwell, a bodyguard of Joseph Smith. Although Rockwell and Smith both denied it, there was some circumstantial evidence. The Mormons were accused of murder, of seeking political domination, and of immoral practices.

To counteract Bennett's charges and the generally bad publicity the Saints were receiving, Brigham, Heber Kimball, George A. Smith, and Amasa Lyman—all apostles, and many others under their direction—were sent on preaching missions to Illinois cities where Bennett had spoken. Brigham and his associates held conferences in Lima, Quincy, Payson, Atlas, Pittsfield, Apple Creek, Jacksonville, Springfield, and Morgan City. Brigham's journal suggests the kind of activities in which they engaged:

> *Lima:*   We preached to a large congregation . . . and showed the falsity of Bennett's statements.

Quincy: Elders Kimball, Smith, Lyman and myself held a conference. . . . We exposed the course of Bennett and the mobocrats, and disabused the public mind, to some extent, of the prejudices recently imbibed. Governor [Thomas] Carlin attended one meeting.

Payson: I endeavored to get the affidavits against Dr. J. C. Bennett inserted in the *Whig* and *Herald,* . . . but they refused to print them on any terms. I returned to Nauvoo, and had a number of them struck off as handbills for circulation. I proceeded to Atlas, and . . . preached in Col. Ross' brick-house.[17]

Shortly after his return from this mission, Brigham nearly lost his life. His own account gives the details:

November 26, 1842. I was suddenly attacked with a slight fit of apoplexy [loss of consciousness]. Next morning I felt quite comfortable; but in the evening, at the same hour that I had the fit the day before, I was attacked with the most violent fever I ever experienced. The Prophet Joseph and Elder Willard Richards visited and administered unto me; the Prophet prophesied that I should live and recover from my sickness. He sat by me for six hours, and directed my attendants what to do for me. In about thirty hours from the time of my being attacked by the fever, the skin began to peel from my body, and I was skinned all over. I desired to be baptized in the river, but it was not until the 14th day that brother Joseph would give his consent for me to be showered with cold water, when my fever began to break, and it left me on the 18th day. I laid upon my back, and was not turned upon my side for eighteen days.

Then came a frightening experience that led to what we now call mouth-to-mouth resuscitation:

When the fever left me on the 18th day, I was bolstered up in my chair, but was so near gone that I could not close my eyes, which were set in my head— my chin dropped down and my breath stopped. My wife [Mary Ann], seeing my situation, threw some cold water in my face, that having no effect, she dashed a handful of strong camphor into my face and eyes, which I did not feel in the least, neither did I move a muscle. She then held my nostrils between her thumb and finger, and placing her mouth directly over mine, blew into my lungs until she filled them with air. This set my lungs in motion, and I again began to breathe.[18]

A student of medical history, Lester Bush, has suggested that Brigham probably had scarlet fever, along with a secondary infection that prolonged the fever.[19] His recovery was slow. Partly because of the cold winter he was not able to leave his home until mid-January, nearly eight weeks after the first fit of apoplexy. Even then he was weak, and as late as the next August he was still not "wholly recovered from my last winter's illness."[20]

Nevertheless, Brigham was able to build a new home for Mary Ann, symbolic of his increasing importance in the community. Pride is reflected in the following entry in his journal:

> *May 31, 1843.* I moved out of my log cabin into my new brick house, which was 22 feet by 16, two stories high, and a good cellar under it, and felt thankful to God for the privilege of having a comfortable, though small habitation.[21]

The large downstairs room with its cooking hearth and "bustle oven" served as kitchen, dining room, and the "keeping" center of family activities. At the time five children were in the family. Elizabeth, now seventeen, had married and moved out, and Vilate, at twelve, was temporarily in Salem, Massachusetts, studying music. With Mary Ann at the time were Joseph, eight; Brigham, Jr., and Mary Ann, six; Alice, three; and Luna, nine months. In terms of contemporary values the house must have cost Brigham about $400 in labor, valued at $2 per day. During the summer of 1844 he constructed wings one story high on each side of the residence, one wing to serve as a bedroom and the other, with an outside entrance, to serve as an office. In restored form the home is still open to visitors.[22] Meantime, Lucy Ann remained in the home her first husband had provided for her some five blocks to the northeast of the house Brigham had built for Mary Ann.

Brigham's relationship with Mary Ann continued to be pleasant. She declared later that their life, while exacting, was palliated by their joint feeling that Brigham was doing the right thing in laboring for the good of "the Kingdom."[23]

BRIGHAM'S second short-term mission started on July 7, 1843, and lasted until October 22. Accompanied much of the time by Wilford Woodruff and George A. Smith, Brigham's assignment involved some supervisory work and proselyting in the East. But the principal purpose of the mission was to raise money for the temple and the Nauvoo House. In anticipation of their service as church financial agents on this journey, someone proposed that the Twelve ought to be bonded. Joseph Smith agreed. "The Twelve," he said, "are the most suitable persons to perform this business. . . . [They] were always honest and it will do them no hurt to bind [bond] them." "I go in for binding up the Twelve solid, putting them under bonds."[24]

As a young man Brigham had resisted making a pledge of abstinence from liquor because such a pledge would interfere with his free agency—he thought it a higher order of morality to do right without being bound or compelled; now, for similar reasons, he resisted the bonding proposal. It reflected, he felt, on the honesty of the agents, and was a move in the direction of "muzzling the ox that treadeth out the corn."[25] Joseph responded, somewhat lightheartedly, that "the idea of not muzzling the ox is a good old Quaker song; but we will make the ox tread out the corn first, and then feed him."[26]

The conference adopted the bonding plan and stopped all agents from collecting funds except the Twelve. John M. Bernhisel, Joseph Smith's family doctor, became bondsman for Brigham, for the sum of $2,000.[27]

Brigham's mission journal contains frequent and sometimes delightful entries for most of the days he was away:

Item: Joseph Smith had announced a revelation in 1833 counseling against the use of tobacco, liquor, tea, and coffee. How strict should local officers be in insisting on compliance? Brigham's answer: "I said I considered it wisdom to use all things put into our hands according to the best judgment God would give us: wisdom was justified of her children."[28]

Item: Joseph Smith was arrested without a proper warrant at Dixon, Illinois, by Missourians who sought to get him across the border into Missouri, where he could be tried without going through the obstacle of extradition. Joseph's brother Hyrum asked the local militia to intercept the kidnappers before they reached Missouri. The general of the militia said he would not go until the expense of the expedition was raised. Brigham told them to prepare to leave; he would personally guarantee the money. In two hours, he wrote, "I succeeded in borrowing $700 to defray the expenses of the expedition."[29]

Item: Brigham heard the preaching of one of the apostles, John E. Page: "He hammered the sectarian churches unmercifully." Brigham "exhorted him to be mild and gentle in his teachings and not fight the sects, but endeavor to win the affections of the people."[30]

Item: Brigham was asked whether any officer in any branch of the church could say that his word was law and must be obeyed. Answer: "He can say that his word is law, but does that make it so? Yes, if he has the law of God, and delivers it, otherwise it is not."[31]

Item: Can a branch of the church make bylaws on the principle of expediency, which are not specified in any revelation? Answer: "Yes, if they wish they may make laws to stick their fingers in their eyes; but it is like the man who habituated himself to sticking his finger into a knot-hole, in a board partition, every morning, until custom compelled him to do it. Having omitted it one morning, he felt so curiously at the breakfast table that he could not eat—he then bethought himself, went and put his finger into the knot-hole, and returned with a good appetite and ate a hearty breakfast."[32]

One day Brigham and his colleagues went on a picnic to Gloucester Point, on the Delaware River, near Camden, New Jersey. In the evening, for recreation, they had a debate on the topic "Is the prosperity of any religious denomination a positive evidence that they are right?" John E. Page contended for the affirmative; Jedediah M. Grant, for the negative. Each defended his position with much spirit. Asked to decide the question, Brigham first tried to reduce the tension:

I told them I was reminded of the anecdote of the negro's attempt at shooting a squirrel. His master having occasion to be absent from home, charged him to be sure and not meddle with his guns and ammunition; but no sooner had the master got fairly out of the way, when the negro's curiosity prompted him to try one of the master's guns. He accordingly took one down which had been loaded for some time, and went into the woods. He soon saw a squirrel, and crept up a hill behind a log and fired. But the gun, being heavily charged, knocked the negro over, and he rolled down the hill. Upon gaining his equilibrium and realizing his defeat, he looked up from the ground where he lay, and seeing the squirrel jumping from tree to tree as if conscious of victory, cried, "Well, well, cuffy, if you had been at the other end of the gun you would have known more about it."

After the laughter, Brigham gave his decision "that the prosperity of any people was not positive evidence of their being right."[33]

A few days later, Brigham and George A. Smith stayed overnight with a Brother Atkinson, near Bordentown, New Jersey, in a large frame house that Brigham understood had been built about 1690. The house "was so infested with bed-bugs that we could not sleep," wrote Brigham.

> Brother George A. Smith gave it as his legal opinion that there were bed-bugs there which had danced to the music at the battle of Trenton, as their heads were perfectly grey. We took our blankets and retreated to the further end of the room, and, as the bugs followed us, I lit a candle, and as they approached, caught them and burnt them in the candle, and thus spent the night.[34]

Still later, in Boston, "at the request and expense" of a local elder, Brigham visited the noted phrenologist O. S. Fowler. Fowler examined his head and gave him a chart, which Brigham appended in his journal, adding this comment:

> After giving me a very good chart for $1, I will give him [Fowler] a chart gratis. My opinion of him is, that he is just as nigh being an idiot as a man can be, and have any sense left to pass through the world decently. And it appeared to me that the cause of his success was the amount of impudence and self-importance he possessed, and the high opinion he entertained of his own abilities.[35]

Other typical Brigham observations in his 1843 diary:

On choosing local leaders: "They should control themselves and bring their passions into subjection to the law of God, then preside over their wives and children in righteousness, and this will qualify them to preside over branches of the church."[36]

On lawyers: "When any man who calls himself a lawyer takes a course to break peace instead of making it, he is out of the line of his duty . . . and let him receive pay like any laboring man. . . . To cure lawing, let us pay attention to our own business. . . . The grand object before us is . . . to mind our own business and let others alone; and suffer wrong rather than do wrong. . . . If any of you wish to know how to have your bread fall butter side up, butter it on both sides."[37]

I T was while he was on this mission that Brigham received a letter from Mary Ann that brought news of sickness at home. The letter was being written "while our little family is quietly resting in bed, which has been very seldom for four weeks past," Mary Ann said.

> I was taken with enfluensy and Colamorbus [cholera morbus] the first. Brigham [Jr.] was taken with the scarlot feever. Before he recovered the three little girls were taken. Mary had the Canker so she did not swallow for ten or eleven days anything but drink . . . a litle fish flesh once. Vilate was taken very sick one week since with scarlot feever. The Colamorbus took hold of her yesterday in a very severe manner so she appeared nigh unto Death, but through mercy of God and the utmost exertion she is quite comfortable. . . .

Thankful that the children were now recovering, Mary Ann concluded:

> I do not want to say things to you to trouble you. You must excuse me for saying so much about the distress we have passed through. . . . May the Lord bless you and make you an instrument of doing much good. You have all our Prairs. I am yours in bonds of the everlasting Gospel.[38]

Ten days after this letter was written, the Youngs' six-year-old daughter, Mary Ann, died of what was diagnosed as "dropsy and canker."[39] This little girl, the twin of Brigham, Jr., was the lovely "little creater" who refused to go to bed until she had prayed for her father.

Brigham himself was plagued with a relapse of his illness of the winter before. He wrote Mary Ann:

> I have ben verry sick with my old complaint. Feele some better today. . . . I was sick and distressed about four days and nights. Hardley got enny sleep. I suffered much. I took some pill[s], was anointed. Had hands laid on me Thursday night. My distres continued till about 12 o. c[lock]. I laid down, went to sleep. Had a good nights' rest. Have ben perty well ever sence.
> When I was so sick I thought if I could only be at home, I should be thankful. There is no place like home to me. . . . You and I must take some masurs [measures] to recover our helth or we shall not last a grate meny years; and I want that we should live meny years yet and due much good on the earth.[40]

I N Nauvoo, as in Kirtland, Joseph Smith insisted on carrying forward his vision of a theocratic kingdom. He played an active role in the political and economic life of Nauvoo and maintained tight ecclesiastical control. He was supported in this endeavor by Brigham, Heber, and the other apostles. Not all his other associates did, and of course there were people in the nearby communities of Carthage and Warsaw who were fearful of the growing strength and power of the Mormon community in Illinois. (One of the few Illinois politicians who advocated tolerance and fairness toward the Mormons was Abraham Lincoln. Although there is no evidence that he ever met either Joseph Smith or Brigham Young, as a member of the Illinois House of Representatives he voted for the act to grant a charter to Nauvoo, personally congratulated Mormon lobbyists on its passage, and was sympathetic with their problems, both then and later.)[41]

In September 1843, a group of anti-Mormons gathered at Carthage, the Hancock County seat, and promised military support to apprehend the Prophet, countering the theocratic control over Nauvoo with boasts that they were prepared to go beyond law to violence. Anti-Mormons were emboldened even to threaten the governor, should he attempt to protect the Mormons in their rights: "If he opens his head we will punch a hole through him! He dare not speak! We will serve him the same sauce we will the 'Mormons!' "[42] Joseph Smith was harassed with writs, suits, arrests, and threats of assassination.

In March 1844, Joseph assembled the Twelve and other Mormon leaders to establish a council that could serve as a legislative body for the theocratic society. Some fifty men were organized into a Grand Council or Council of Fifty. They met periodically until territorial government was established in Utah in 1851. Brigham's diary entry says simply: "Met in councel at Br J. Smith's store in company [of] about twenty to orginise ourselves into a compacked boddy for the futher advenment of the gospel of Christ."[43] In his history, however, he expands the entry to read:

> Joseph commenced the organization of a Council for the purpose of taking into consideration the necessary steps to obtain redress for the wrongs which had been inflicted upon us by our persecutors, and also the best manner to settle our people in some distant and unoccupied territory; where we could enjoy our civil and religious rights, without being subject to constant oppression and mobocracy, under the protection of our own laws, subject to the Constitution. The Council was composed of about fifty members, several of whom were not members of the church. [Recent research has shown that all were church members.]
>
> We prepared several memorials to Congress for redress of grievances, and used every available means to inform ourselves of the unoccupied territory open to settlers. We held a number of sessions, and investigated the principles upon which our national government is founded; and the true foundation and principles of all governments. Joseph Smith was appointed chairman, William Clayton, clerk, and Willard Richards, historian of the Council.[44]

As if he had a foreboding of his impending death, Smith also called the Twelve together, on or about March 26, 1844, and gave them a dramatic charge to "bear off the Kingdom." As they later recounted the moving experience, the Prophet seemed depressed and opened his heart about his "presentiments of the future." He explained that "some important scene is near to take place," that perhaps he would be killed, and that as a precaution he must give the Twelve all other keys and powers that he held. Then, if God wills, "I can go with all pleasure and satisfaction, knowing that my work is done, and the foundation laid on which the kingdom of God is to be reared. . . ." He counseled them about what lay ahead, then continued,

> saying, while he walked the floor and threw back the collar of his coat upon his shoulders, "I roll the burthen and responsibility of leading this Church off from my shoulders on to yours. Now, round up your shoulders and stand under it like men; for the Lord is going to let me rest a while." . . . After he had thus spoken, he continued to walk the floor, saying: "Since I have rolled the burthen off from my shoulders I feel as light as a cork. I feel that I am free. I thank my God for this deliverance."[45]

"To us," wrote one of the apostles later of the event, "were committed the Keys of the Kingdom, and every gift, key and power, that Joseph ever had."[46]

DISAPPOINTED with his failure to get national support to protect the Saints, Joseph Smith decided early in 1844 to run for president of the United States as a way of publicizing the Mormon plight. This action infuriated his opponents, but offered an opportunity for the apostles to carry his social and religious message throughout the nation. On May 21, 1844, Brigham, Heber, and Lyman Wight, who had been ordained an apostle in April 1841 while Brigham and Heber were in England, left on a preaching mission in support of Smith's candidacy. While waiting for a boat at Fairport, Ohio, on Lake Erie, Brigham started a letter to Mary Ann: "I feele lonsom. O that I had you with me this somer I think I should be happy. Well I am now [happy] because I am in my cauling and duing my duty, but [the] older I grow the more I desire to stay at my own home insted of traveling." Continuing the letter some time later from Albany, New York, Brigham wrote that he had not had much sleep and was "perty well tired out," adding:

> Last night I felt for somtime as though I had got to get a new const[it]ution or [I would] not last long. How I due want to see you and [the children]. Kiss them for me and kiss Luny [Luna] twice or mor. Tel hir it is for me. Give my love to all the famely. I nead not menshion names. . . . Dont you want for eney thing. You can borrow monney to get what you want. . . . After taking a grate share of my love to your self then deal it out to others as you plese.[47]

Among other places, Brigham and his companions preached in St. Louis, Cincinnati, Pittsburgh, and Kirtland (where Brigham visited with his brother John Young and his sister Nancy Kent). He then went to Salem, where he spent two or three days with his daughter Vilate, who was living there with church member friends while she attended school and learned to play "the pianna." This visit was followed by preaching appointments in Lowell and Boston.

Meanwhile, events in Nauvoo were disquieting. A small group was opposed to new developments there—the organization of the Council of Fifty, the revelation on plural marriage, and the completeness of ecclesiastical control. These people publicly declared their opposition to the Prophet and his policies, organized a competing church, and began publication of the Nauvoo *Expositor*, which contained inflammatory allegations about Mormon marriage practices and policies. Joseph Smith and the city council declared the paper libelous and a public nuisance endangering the peace, and the paper and its press were destroyed. This presented an issue on which all could unite—freedom of the press. Thomas Sharp of the Warsaw *Signal* editorialized: "War and Extermination is Inevitable, Citizens ARISE ONE AND ALL." Smith and his city council were charged with inciting a riot, Governor Ford ruled that the Mormons must submit to the processes of the Carthage court, Smith was arrested and placed in the Carthage jail.

On the evening of June 27, despite Governor Ford's personal guarantee of safety, a mob made up of Warsaw and Carthage militiamen, their faces blackened, broke into the jail, stormed up the stairs, killed Joseph and Hyrum Smith and wounded Apostle John Taylor who, with Willard Richards, had spent the day with the Smiths.[48]

Brigham later wrote in his journal that in Boston, on June 27, he was sitting with Wilford Woodruff in the railroad depot waiting for a train. "I felt a heavy depression of spirit, and so melancholy I could not converse with any degree of pleasure."

Still in the Boston area, Brigham began to hear rumors of the assassination for the first time on July 9. One week later, he and Orson Pratt were at the home of a Brother Bement in Peterboro, New Hampshire, when they heard a letter read from a Nauvoo resident giving particulars of the murder. "The first thing which I thought of," Brigham said in his journal, "was whether Joseph had taken the keys of the kingdom with him from the earth; brother Orson Pratt sat on my left; we were both leaning back on our chairs. Bringing my hand down on my knee, I said the keys of the kingdom are right here with the Church."[49]

While awaiting the arrival of other apostles, Brigham received a confirmation of the sorrowful news from Mary Ann:

My Dear Companion. I set down to communicate a few lines to you at this time. My heart is full. I know not what to write to comfort you at this time. We have had great afflictions in this place since you left home. . . . You have now been gone allmost six weeks. I have not had a line from you since you left home. I have not time to write much now. We are in great affliction. . . . Our Dear Br. Joseph Smith and Hiram has fell victims to a verocious mob. The great God of the creation only knows whithe[r] the rest shall be preserved in safety or not. We are in tolable good health at presant. I have been blessed to keep my feelings quite calm through all the storm. I hope you will be careful on your way hom and not expose yourself to those that will endanger your life. Yours in hast[e]. If we meet no more in this world may we meet where parting is no more. Farewell.[50]

Brigham and Pratt immediately sought to establish contact with other members of the Twelve. They found Heber Kimball and Woodruff in Boston, laid over a week until Lyman Wight arrived. They were joined at Albany by Orson Hyde (and Orson Pratt and Wilford Woodruff, who had gone on to New York while Brigham waited for Wight). Though we have no record of their conversations, they must have engaged in earnest discussions of the church's future. Traveling by stagecoach, lake boat, and buggy, the group arrived in Nauvoo on August 6, "where," as Brigham wrote, "we were received with joy by our families and friends."[51]

Brigham wrote to his daughter Vilate after his return home:

It has been a time of mourning. The day that Joseph and Hyrum were brought in from Carthage to Nauvoo it was judged by menny boath in and out of the church that there was more than five barels of tears shead. I cannot bare to think enny thing about it.[52]

But Brigham was not to have the luxury of just shedding tears. The church faced a crisis of survival.

8 ✦

City of Joseph

Here is Brigham—have his knees ever faltered? Have his lips ever quivered? Did he ever flinch before the bullets in Missouri?[1]

A F T E R Brigham and the Twelve arrived in Nauvoo on August 6, they learned the extent of the bewilderment of their fellow Saints, unsure of their future. To use Wilford Woodruff's phrase, "they [the Saints] felt like sheep without a shepherd."[2] There were connivings by would-be leaders, and it seemed imperative that the Twelve settle matters so as to avoid divisiveness.

The morning after their return, the apostles met at the home of John Taylor, who was convalescing from his wounds received in Carthage jail. They learned that on Sunday morning, August 4, a substantial congregation had assembled for the traditional Sabbath worship service, where they were addressed by the popular orator Sidney Rigdon. Rigdon, who had served as one of the First Presidency since 1833, had become disenchanted with Joseph Smith and had, indeed, gone to Pittsburgh, away from church headquarters, a few days before the Prophet's death. Smith had wanted to release him from his position in the Presidency, but the conference of Saints, after an impassioned plea by Rigdon, had voted in October 1843 to sustain him. On his return to Nauvoo on August 3, Rigdon had contended that he had received a revelation (referred to contemptuously by Wilford Woodruff as a "second class vision") directing him to serve as a "guardian" for the church. In the hope of having his leadership ratified, Rigdon had called a meeting for August 8. Parley P. Pratt and Willard Richards, who were in Nauvoo at the time, had tried to delay any definite decision until the remainder of the Twelve returned. Fortunately for those supporting the Twelve, they came back on August 6.

After the round of discussion on the morning of August 7 at the Taylor home, Brigham called a meeting for the same afternoon of the apostles, Nauvoo Stake High Council, and all high priests. Rigdon, of course, was present at that meeting; upon the invitation of Brigham, he said that he had been ordained as "a spokesman to Joseph Smith" and had come to Nauvoo "to see that the church is governed in a proper manner." Joseph Smith, he asserted, despite his murder "sustains the same relationship to this Church as he has always done." Since he, Rigdon, "was commanded to speak for him," the Saints had to acknowledge that revelations from Joseph Smith would have to come through him, Rigdon. "The Kingdom is to be built up to Jesus Christ," Rigdon declared, "through Joseph. . . . The martyred Prophet is still the head of this church."[3]

Brigham's response was: "I do not care who leads the church, even though it were Ann Lee [founder of the Shakers]; but one thing I must know, and that is what God says about it." As president of the Quorum of the Twelve, Brigham said, "I have the keys and the means of obtaining the mind of God on the subject. . . . Joseph conferred upon our heads all the keys and powers belonging to the Apostleship which he himself held before he was taken away, and no man or set of men can get between Joseph and the Twelve in this world or in the world to come."[4] The confrontation between Rigdon and Brigham was already clear, but it would become even sharper.

The next day, August 8, the Saints gathered at 10:00 A.M. at the outdoor prayer meeting called earlier by Sidney Rigdon. Church authorities occupied seats on the stand, but because the wind was blowing from a direction behind the congregation and toward the stand, Rigdon, in order to make himself heard, left the stand and climbed into the back of a wagon behind the congregation so the wind would carry his words toward the audience. The listeners, estimated by Brigham as five thousand, turned around on their benches and faced the wagon. They did not see Brigham as he made his way to the stand to occupy the seat vacated a few minutes earlier by Rigdon. Usually a fluent, impassioned speaker, Rigdon talked slowly and in a labored manner. His long "discourse" (one and a half hours) discussed the Mount of Olives, the Brook Kedron, Queen Victoria, and a variety of other topics. He awakened no emotions; they heard from him no words that marked him as the true leader.[5]

At the end of Rigdon's speech Brigham spoke. "My hart was swolen with compasion to[w]ards them," he wrote in his diary, "and by the power of the Holy Gost, even the spirit of the prophets, I was enabled to comfort the harts of the Saints."[6] He spoke only briefly. He told the audience that he would much rather have returned to Nauvoo to mourn for the dead Prophet for thirty days than to attend so hastily to the business of appointing a new shepherd. But he had "perseved a spirit to hurry business . . . menny wanted to draw off a party and be leders." He announced that an assembly of the leaders and members would be held at two o'clock that afternoon.

Whatever Brigham's words, whatever his appearance and manner, some of those present were startled by an occurrence that they regarded as miraculous.[7] Benjamin Johnson, a young man of twenty-six, said that he was seated between the stand and the wagon and that, as he turned from the wagon to face the stand, he saw Brigham stand up. "But as soon as he spoke I jumped upon my feet, for in every possible degree it was Joseph's voice, and his person, in look, attitude, dress and appearance; [it] was Joseph himself, personified;

and I knew in a moment the spirit and mantle of Joseph was upon him."[8] Mosiah Hancock, who was only fourteen, wrote, "Although only a boy, I saw the mantle of the Prophet Joseph rest on Brigham Young; and he arose lion-like to the occasion, and led the people forth."[9] George Q. Cannon, a boy of fifteen, declared that "it was the voice of Joseph himself; and not only was it the voice of Joseph which was heard, but it seemed in the eyes of the people as though it was the very person of Joseph which stood before them. They both saw and heard with their natural eyes and ears, and then the words which were uttered came, accompanied by the convincing power of God, to their hearts, and they were filled with the Spirit and with great joy."[10] Wilford Woodruff later stated, "If I had not seen him with my own eyes, there is no one that could have convinced me that it was not Joseph Smith."[11]

However one tries to explain it—the downcast spirits of the Saints, who had mourned Joseph's passing for forty days; their yearning to be comforted by their lost leader; their disappointment with Rigdon, whose ambition had diluted his sincerity; their surprise at the presence of "Brother Brigham," who was thought by many to be still on his way back from Boston, and Brigham's talent for mimicry—the diaries, letters, and later recollections of many of those present testify to an experience that persuaded them that Brigham was the new Joseph. Late in 1844 a correspondent to the *Times and Seasons* boldly inquired: "Who can't see that the mantle of the prophet (using a figure) has fallen on President Young and the Twelve? Who can't see that the same spirit which inspired our beloved brother Joseph Smith, now inspires President Young?"[12] Two months later, during the October conference of 1844, Albert Carrington remembered that when Brigham Young was giving his conference address he, Carrington, "could not see anyone but Joseph speaking" until Brigham got through addressing the congregation.[13] It was not uncommon for people to see Joseph speaking through Brigham many years after "the mantle had fallen on him."

Whatever took place, miraculous or not, Brigham's presence and manner must have quieted the anxieties of the Prophetless Saints. And they had found, as they thought, divine confirmation that he was to be their new leader.

At the afternoon meeting, again attended by several thousand, the major address was by Brigham. It was long—about two hours in length. Brigham spoke in an "open, frank and plain" manner about the proposed guardianship, Rigdon's alienation from Joseph for the previous two years, the necessity of building upon the foundation left by Joseph, and the proper role of the Twelve. "You cannot appoint a prophet," Brigham said, "but if you let the Twelve remain and act in their place, the keys of the kingdom are with them and they can manage the affairs of the church and direct all things aright."[14] Other talks were delivered by Amasa Lyman and Parley P. Pratt, apostles, and by W. W. Phelps, a church publisher. Phelps, who had been asked by Rigdon to defend his point of view, actually contended for the authority of the Twelve.

Brigham then arose and asked the basic question: "Do you want Brother

Rigdon to stand forward as your leader, your guide, your spokesman?" At this juncture Rigdon asked Young to put the other question first; that is, "Does the church want, and is it their only desire to sustain the Twelve as the First Presidency of this people? All those in favor, raise your right arm to the square." The minutes of the conference and the diary entries of several of those present show that there was a universal or nearly universal affirmative vote.[15] "If there are any of the contrary mind, every man and every woman who does not want the Twelve to preside, lift up your hands in like manner." Again, the minutes of the conference show "no hands up."

After a few additional remarks, Brigham then asked for a series of votes of support on specific measures:

Is it the will of this congregation that they be tithed until the Temple is finished?

Is it the mind of this congregation to loose the hands of the Twelve, and enable us to go and preach to all the world?

Will you leave it to the Twelve to dictate about the finances of the church?

Will it be the mind of the people that the Twelve teach what will be the duties of the bishops in handling the affairs of the church?

Will you leave it to the Twelve to appoint a patriarch to the church to replace our beloved brother, Hyrum Smith?

Will this congregation uphold Brother Rigdon in the place he occupies by the prayer of faith and let him be one with us and we with him?[16]

While the minutes of this conference and the diary entries of several of those present show a unanimous affirmative vote to each of these propositions, there were some who remembered a few dissenters. William C. Staines said there were "a few dissenting voices," and William Adams wrote that "out of that vast multitude about twenty voted for Rigdon to be Guardian."[17]

Brigham wrote in his diary that evening: "The church was of one hart and one mind; they wanted the Twelve to lead the church as Br. Joseph had dun in his day."[18]

From that point, Sidney Rigdon essentially disappears from Mormon history. Although sustained in full fellowship by the Nauvoo conference, he continued to assert claims superior to those of the Twelve, and was excommunicated on September 8. Brigham's diary comment is that Rigdon insisted that "all things had [been] shone to him . . . but he did not tell what the saints should do to save themselves."[19] Rigdon returned to Pittsburgh and the following spring organized a "Church of Christ," which attracted a few who opposed the Twelve, felt Joseph Smith was a fallen prophet, or rejected polygamy. He began publication of the *Latter-day Saints' Messenger and Ad-*

vocate. By 1847 this small organization had virtually disintegrated, although Rigdon continued for another thirty years to try to rally support.

I N the weeks and months that followed the vote of support for the Twelve, Brigham's diary shows him meeting almost daily to discuss policies and give instruction to local and general church officers. He was also consulted by widows needing food and housing, by mistreated wives, by immigrants wishing to start new businesses, and by political leaders seeking Mormon votes. Nauvoo moved ahead, the people seemed to be united on goals, and there was an atmosphere of exuberance.

In one matter, however, Brigham made a tactical error. When he returned to Nauvoo the evening of August 6, he became so involved with the machinations of Sidney Rigdon that he apparently failed to visit Emma, the widow of Joseph Smith. A woman of intelligence and culture, Emma had been a partner of Joseph Smith in several business operations, a spokeswoman for him in political matters, and his confidante in many enterprises. Not a submissive woman, Emma was determined to maintain her "rights" as widow of the Prophet and mother of his five living children. Preoccupied with setting the Nauvoo Saints on the right path and persuaded that she was opposed to his leadership, Brigham may not have seen Emma until several weeks after his return.[20]

During this time misunderstandings accumulated between them. Just prior to their imprisonment in Carthage jail, Joseph and Hyrum Smith had crossed the Mississippi River, ostensibly to seek refuge somewhere in the Rocky Mountains. But after they had camped their first night in Iowa they received a missive from friends and Emma in Nauvoo, urging them to submit to the authorities, which they did. Brigham thought this had been misguided advice. If the Twelve had been there, he reasoned, Joseph never would have been delivered to "the law."[21] In the struggle over succession, Emma declared that the rightful head of the church was either Rigdon or the president of the Nauvoo Stake, William Marks.[22] Brigham and Emma also disagreed over the doctrine of polygamy, Emma asserting that it could not possibly be a divine principle. She played the part of the kind sister-in-law to William Smith, despite his excommunication for disloyalty and instability.

Finally, there was the Nauvoo Legion episode. In September 1844, Governor Thomas Ford, acknowledging that the Mormons were in danger of being driven from Illinois as they had been exiled from Missouri during the winter of 1838–39, had gone with officers of the state militia to Nauvoo, commissioned Brigham lieutenant general of the Nauvoo Legion, the Mormon militia, and advised the Mormons to keep drilling and conducting exercises in order to prevent armed invasion by mobs from Carthage, the center of anti-Mormonism. Assuming that Joseph's military costume went with his office, Brigham sent a note to Emma asking her to lend him the Prophet's uniform and sword, and his favorite horse. Emma resented doing this. Brigham also accused Emma of taking a portrait and ring from Hyrum's widow, Mary Fielding, and never returning them. Emma, on the other hand, charged Brigham and the Twelve with taking Joseph's long wool cloak.[23]

All of these quarrels were merely preparatory to a major struggle between Brigham and Emma over the disposal of Joseph's properties. Both loved Joseph and had certain rights to his papers and properties. There was inevitable disagreement, and among two such strong and proud personalities, the dispute could be acrid.

The church had revolved around Joseph Smith so surely that little distinction had been made between property that was his and Emma's and property that was the church's. Under Brigham's direction, the Twelve in December 1841 had created the office of trustee-in-trust to handle properties belonging to the church, and Joseph Smith was named to that office. But legal niceties had not always been followed; in some difficult cases, they could not. An example was the so-called Hotchkiss Purchase of five hundred acres of land in Nauvoo. This land was bought by the First Presidency, Joseph Smith, Hyrum Smith, and Sidney Rigdon, for church members to live on, but the First Presidency had to pledge their personal credit before the purchase could be consummated. Did the land belong to the church or to the First Presidency in a private capacity? Some of the properties in Smith's name were acquired in part with money earned by Emma, who took in boarders. Was Joseph's general store his or the church's? Was the steamboat his or the Saints'? And did his financial papers rightly go to Brigham or did they belong to Emma and her lawyer? One can sympathize with Emma's desire to obtain for herself and her children what was rightfully theirs. One can also appreciate that Brigham, as head of a church with thousands of destitute members, and charged with completing the temple and managing affairs for the welfare of the organization, wanted to assure that the interests of the church were safeguarded.

This is not the place to detail the specifics of what properties went to Emma and what was obtained by Brigham for the church, but Emma always thought Brigham and the apostles tried to cheat her out of properties rightfully hers (she claimed all of the properties in Joseph's name), and Brigham believed that Emma had forced the apostles to give her properties paid for by the labor and tithing of church members. The truth is that both suffered when the Saints were driven from Nauvoo in 1846, because the value of the properties declined sharply. Emma's city lots were of little cash value; Brigham found it difficult to sell the church's property to any buyer, at any price.

Brigham's failure to express his sympathy to Emma soon after his arrival in Nauvoo and his ineptitude in dealing with her in the months that followed must have caused him many heartaches. Perhaps the most significant result of the schism was that Emma's son Joseph III decided to split with "Utah Mormonism" in 1860 because of his objection to polygamy and other doctrines and practices of "the Brighamites." He served as first president of a competing group, the Reorganized Church of Jesus Christ of Latter Day Saints, now

headquartered in Independence, Missouri, with some two hundred fifty thousand members. The confrontation between Brigham and Emma had a poetic
ending—both died calling Joseph's name.[24]

Brigham was truly sad about losing Emma and Joseph III, but he showed
little anxiety about the dissidence of James J. Strang. An imaginative and
capable leader, Strang had been baptized in February 1844 by Joseph Smith
himself and had gone to Burlington, Wisconsin, to investigate a new gathering
place for the Saints. When he learned of Smith's death, Strang sent a letter,
which he claimed had been written by Smith, naming him president of the
church and designating Voree, Wisconsin, as the new gathering place. By the
time a copy of this letter reached Nauvoo, the Twelve were firmly established
in control of the church. Brigham and his associates branded the letter a forgery
and confirmed Strang's excommunication by the conference of elders in Michigan. Strang, however, continued to proselyte, gathered a body of believers
to Voree, and eventually won over three former members of the Twelve who
had lost their standing—William E. McLellin, John E. Page, and William
Smith. For a time he also had the support of William E. Marks, former president of Nauvoo Stake, John C. Bennett, George Miller, and, reportedly, Lucy
Mack Smith, Joseph's mother, and other members of the Smith family. Most
of Strang's backing evaporated, however, and at no point did he represent a
numerically significant challenge to Brigham's leadership. In 1849 he relocated
his colony on Beaver Island in northern Lake Michigan, and the next year he
was crowned King of the Kingdom. He was assassinated by a disgruntled
follower in 1856.[25]

D U R I N G the months that followed Joseph and Hyrum Smith's deaths
Brigham and the apostles supervised the construction of the Seventies Hall, a
concert hall, and the Nauvoo House. Heber Kimball and Willard Richards
replaced their log homes with two-story brick houses in 1845, and the authorities
began the erection of a home for Lucy Mack Smith. There were other projects:
construction of a Mississippi River stone dike intended as a ship dock and
waterhead for shops and machinery, organization of the Nauvoo Agricultural
and Manufacturing Society, and the establishment of the University of the
City of Nauvoo.

But the most important project in terms of human and financial resources
was the temple. Considering the enormous investment it would require, with
the probability that many or all of the Saints would ultimately have to abandon
Nauvoo, Brigham originally had misgivings about the project—and there must
have been others who contended that the investment was not worth it. In his
holograph diary, under Friday, January 24, 1845, Brigham reported that Kimball
and Bishop Newel K. Whitney came to his house. They conducted some of
the sacred ceremonies they had been taught by Joseph—washings, anointings,
and prayers—then, Brigham wrote, "I inquaired of the Lord whether we should
stay here [in Nauvoo] and finish the templ[e]. The ansure was we should."

From that time on, Brigham and the Twelve met often with the temple committee, women organized to raise funds, and craftsmen mobilized to do the work. By the fall of 1844, limestone blocks for the second story were laid and the first of the large sunstones was raised into place. By the late spring of 1845 the trumpet stones and capstones had been positioned. Workers assembled the roof, finished the interior, carved a stone basin and oxen for a permanent baptismal font, and plans were made for a formal dedication of the whole building in April 1846.

At the end of 1845, Nauvoo had about eleven thousand residents, rivaling Chicago as the largest city in Illinois. Visitors from the East and England were writing complimentary things about it. In a letter of June 27 to Wilford Woodruff in England, Brigham expressed his own satisfaction:

> Nauvoo, or more properly, the "City of Joseph," looks like a paradise. All the lots and land, which have heretofore been vacant and unoccupied, were enclosed in the spring, and planted with grain and vegetables, which makes it look more like a garden of gardens than a city; and the season has been so favorable, the prospect is, there will be enough raised within the limits of the corporation to supply the inhabitants with corn, potatoes, and other vegetables. Hundreds of acres of prairie land have also been enclosed, and are now under good cultivation, blooming with corn, wheat, potatoes, and other necessaries of life. Many strangers are pouring in to view the Temple and the city. They express their astonishment and surprise to see the rapid progress of the Temple, and the beauty and grandeur of Mormon looks. Many brethren are coming from abroad, who seem highly delighted with the place and all its appendages.[26]

The emergence of Nauvoo out of a swamp on the edge of the Mississippi was, in a way, a symbol of America's heroic age. The sturdy homes, the magnificent temple, the presence of the five thousand immigrant-converts who were in the process of becoming Americans—these must have impressed the city's many visitors.

Just how Brigham Young's family fared during these years is not certain. His diary deals almost exclusively with church and community activities. We do know that he had married Harriett Cook and Augusta Adams Cobb as plural wives in 1843; and by the time of Smith's death he had also married Lucy Ann's sister, Clarissa Decker, by whom he subsequently had five children. By the time Brigham left Nauvoo in February 1846, he had been sealed to Clarissa Ross (by whom he had four children), Margaret Maria Alley (two children), Emmeline Free (ten children), and Margaret Pierce (one child). He also agreed to look after some of the plural wives of Joseph Smith. Three of these to whom he was sealed later gave birth to his children: Louisa Beaman (five children), Emily Dow Partridge (seven children), and Zina D. Huntington Jacobs (one child). Five others were simply "caretaker" marriages, older women or spinsters. The most important of this group was Eliza R. Snow, who, though certainly not a connubial wife, lived in Brigham's Lion House in Salt Lake City and was an acknowledged leader of the women of the church.

The reason for Brigham's marriages to Joseph's wives is not difficult to imagine. Old Testament practices dictated that one should marry his dead brother's wife or wives and "raise up seed" to him.[27] One of Brigham's older daughters, Susa Young Gates, states that after Joseph's death her father went to Joseph's widowed plural wives and "told them that he and his brethren stood ready to offer themselves as husbands" in accordance with Old Testament tradition, so that posterity for the dead brother might be born in his life. Subsequently eight of Joseph's plural wives were sealed to Brigham for the remainder of their mortal lives. There is no evidence that Brigham proposed to Emma and, considering their unfriendly relationship, it is doubtful that either would have given any thought to such an arrangement.[28]

Thus, by February 1846 Brigham's family consisted of twelve wives and nine children, besides several foster children. If we exclude the children of the plural wives' previous marriages, Brigham's family consisted of the following (February 1846 ages in parentheses):

Elizabeth (20) and Vilate (15), children of Miriam Angeline
Mary Ann Angell (42), with children: Joseph A. (11), Brigham, Jr. (9), Alice (6), Luna (3), John W. (1)
Lucy Ann Decker (23), with her own two children and Brigham Heber (1)
Harriett Cook (21)
Augusta Adams Cobb (43), with her daughter Charlotte by a previous marriage
Clarissa Decker (17)
Clarissa Ross (31)
Emily Partridge (21), with son Edward (1)
Margaret Alley (20)
Louisa Beaman (30)
Emmeline Free (19)
Margaret Pierce (22)
Zina D. Huntington Jacobs (24)

A F T E R the Prophet's death Brigham continued to convene the Council of Fifty that Smith had established, and to make preparations for eventual removal from Nauvoo. Smith had authorized Lyman Wight and Bishop George Miller to establish a Mormon colony in Texas, and Brigham encouraged this effort until it became clear that they would not be satisfied with anything short of a general exodus to Texas. Believing that his Council of Fifty assignment took precedence over the instructions of the Twelve, Wight refused to join in the exodus to the Great Basin and was finally excommunicated in 1848. Another expedition leader was James Emmett, appointed to explore Oregon and California, who, without the sanction of the Twelve, left Nauvoo in September 1844 with about one hundred people. Because of his efforts to enforce a communal way of life, however, the endeavor ended up in disorder, and Emmett was ultimately disfellowshipped. As the completion of the temple came nearer, additional "ambassadors" from the church were appointed to negotiate with the British and United States governments about sites for settlement.

Mormon group political action, group economic controls, group religious practices did not mesh well with the democratic sentiments of the frontier. Even Governor Thomas Ford, according to one Hancock County militia colonel, was reported to have declared to an anti-Mormon group, "It's all nonsense, you will have to drive these Mormons out yet!" The colonel asked, "If we undertake that, Governor, when the proper time comes, will you interfere?" To which Ford replied, "No, I will not, until you are through."[29]

Brigham and the apostles avoided politics and endorsed no candidates for election, but that was not enough. In September 1844 preparations got underway to raise an anti-Mormon force to drive out the Saints. Notices appeared in the papers of Hancock and surrounding counties of a prospective "wolf hunt" by anti-Mormon night riders. Fearful of a general uprising, Ford gathered a militia force of about five hundred men and went to Carthage. For the time being, an anti-Mormon massacre was avoided. The commander of the unit, General John J. Hardin, remained in Hancock County during the winter.

Non-Mormons were infuriated that the Nauvoo charter permitted the city to operate its own government, including law enforcement and judiciary, separate from the county. Any Mormon in the county accused of a crime could get a Mormon jury that would acquit him. Hatred of the Mormons increased as their community continued to grow and prosper.[30]

The Mormons' enemies demanded both the repeal of the charter and the disbandment of the Nauvoo Legion. When the Illinois legislature revoked the charter, on January 24, 1845, the Mormons were left without police protection or a civil government. Brigham's stopgap solution was to use the governmental machinery of the church. A countywide militia or police force was composed of "quorums" of twelve men acting as "deacons" under the supervision of "bishops" who patrolled the streets day and night and served as bodyguards to the apostles and other church authorities. Brigham called this provisional government "The City of Joseph." Four months after the revocation of the charter, in April 1845, the center of the town was incorporated as a new town and the old police were appointed en masse to serve it. The disincorporated Nauvoo Legion was reorganized as the New Police. The arrangement was apparently satisfactory; Brigham wrote in his journal on April 14:

The deacons have become very efficient looking after the welfare of the saints; every part of the city is watched with the strictest care, and whatever time of night the streets are traveled[,] at the corner of every block a deacon is found attending to his duty.[31]

The Nauvoo Legion continued on an extralegal basis as an instrument of internal control and as a means of defense. Guards were posted to prevent people going into or out of the city without permission of the authorities. Brigham even encouraged the formation of a Junior Legion, of some two hundred fifty boys, who trained every week during the summer of 1845.[32]

At the same time as these arrangements were being effected, Governor Ford wrote to Brigham on April 8:

> Your religion is new, and it surprises the people as any great novelty in religion generally does. They cannot rise above the prejudices excited by such novelty. . . . If you can get off by yourselves you may enjoy peace; but surrounded by such neighbors I confess I do not foresee the time when you will be permitted to enjoy quiet. . . .
>
> I would suggest a matter in confidence. California now offers a field for the prettiest enterprise that has been undertaken in modern time. It is but sparsely populated by none but the Indian or imbecile Mexican Spaniard. . . . Why would it not be a pretty operation for your people to go out there, take possession of and conquer a portion of the vacant country, and establish an independent government of your own subject only to the laws of nations. You would remain there a long time before you would be disturbed by the proximity of other settlements. If you conclude to do this your design ought not to be known or otherwise it would become the duty of the United States to prevent your emigration. But if you once cross the line of the United States territories you would be in no danger of being interferred with.[33]

BRIGHAM and his associates knew they would have to leave Illinois eventually, but they wanted to stay until the temple was finished and adequate preparations were made for their intended removal. Based on the deliberations of the Council of Fifty and Quorum of Twelve, begun while Joseph Smith was alive and continued after his death, the choice was narrowed down to the "Oregon and California country." Other possibilities—Texas and Vancouver Island, for example—were considered as places for colonies but were not appropriate for the massive migration of Latter-day Saints. Interested only in unsettled areas where they would not alienate "old settlers," they narrowed their alternatives still further. During the winter of 1844–45, the Quorum of Twelve read the journals of fur trappers, the reports of government exploring parties, and newspaper articles about Western travelers. They also talked with people who had spent time in the "Rocky Mountain region." They learned that there were at least two contiguous unsettled areas, both of which they might occupy: the valley of the Great Salt Lake, sometimes referred to in a broader setting as Bear River Valley, and Utah Valley, the valley north of

Utah Lake and southeast of Salt Lake Valley. Either or both of these intra-montane locations would provide the desired isolation, thousands of acres of arable land, and a suitable base for expansion into irrigable patches between the Rockies and the Sierra Nevada. By mid-1845 Brigham and the Twelve had definitely decided on the Salt Lake Valley as the most suitable site for a settlement.[34]

The church newspaper, the *Nauvoo Neighbor*, began to carry articles about California and Oregon and as early as March 1845 gave detailed coverage of the Western explorations of John Charles Frémont.[35] A few months later, Lansford W. Hastings was in Nauvoo promoting a removal to California, which then included the Great Basin region. The *Neighbor* published extensive extracts from Hastings's book,[36] and, beginning in September 1845, from the unpublished Frémont journals. The final issue from this source closed with this gratifying comment:

> The Rocky Mountains, . . . instead of being desolate and impassable . . . embosom beautiful valleys, rivers, and parks, with lakes and mineral springs, rivaling and surpassing the most enchanting parts of the Alpine regions of Switzerland. The Great Salt Lake, one of the wonders of the world . . . and the Bear River Valley, with its rich bottoms, fine grass, walled up mountains . . . is for the first time described.[37]

On September 9, Brigham convened the Council of Fifty and made pre-liminary plans to send 1,500 men to the Great Salt Lake Valley.[38] Nauvoo's neighbors, however, would not wait. Early in September, almost simultaneous with these definite indications of imminent removal, a mob of three hundred began the systematic burning of outlying Mormon homes and farms. Brigham reported on September 15 that forty-four buildings had been destroyed. These included houses, a blacksmith shop, a chair factory, a soap manufactory, hay-stacks, and later, maturing fields of wheat. The terrified Saints, upon Brigham's advice, fled to Nauvoo, and 134 teams and wagons were sent from the city to aid in the evacuation. Brigham declared:

> I said . . . I was willing they should do so [burn the houses], until the surrounding counties should be convinced that we were not the aggressors, peradventure they may conclude to maintain the supremacy of the law by putting down mob violence and bringing offenders to justice.

He advised the Saints to prepare for a siege:

> There is grain enough growing within ten miles of this city, raised by the saints, to feed the whole population for two years if they were to sit down and do nothing but gather it in and feast upon it, and worship God.[39]

Nevertheless, the burnings continued. More than two hundred houses, barns, shops, and granaries were destroyed in the fall of 1845 and some Mormon men were murdered and their wives and daughters raped.

Governor Ford felt there was little he could do in the face of overwhelming public sentiment against the Mormons. In a meeting of priesthood leaders to determine policy, Brigham and the Twelve were joined by a committee sent by the governor, consisting of Judge Stephen A. Douglas; Major General John J. Hardin, commander of the Illinois State Militia; and two others. By noon of October 1 the following agreement had been reached:

1. The Saints, who a few weeks previously had ceased planting winter wheat, would continue the same policy as proof of their intention to be gone before the next harvest.

2. They would leave in the spring as soon as the grass was high enough on the prairies of Iowa to support their livestock without grain feeding, and the ice was out of all the waterways. (This would normally be about the last week in April or the first week in May.)

3. The Mormons were to appoint trustees to remain at Nauvoo to sell the property of those who had not been able to dispose of it by springtime, and a detachment of troops would be stationed at Nauvoo to prevent a resurgence of mob violence against those who were making plans to leave the city.[40]

In preparation for their journey "as soon as the grass is green and the water runs," Brigham wrote to Sam Brannan, publisher of the Mormon newspaper in New York, instructing him to take a company to the Bay of San Francisco. The president also sent John Brown, a young Mississippi scout who had moved to Nauvoo, to Mississippi to organize a migration of southern Mormons to the Salt Lake Valley in the spring of 1846.[41] Calculations were made by Parley Pratt, Orson Spencer, and W. W. Phelps as to what each family should require for the journey "across the Plains."[42]

The October 1845 general conference was held, for the first time, in the nearly completed temple. Measures were taken to perfect the organization of the church and to adopt regulations that would speed up preparations for leaving. The key resolution of the conference was similar to what Brigham had earlier presented prior to the removal from Missouri. According to the minutes,

> President Brigham Young moved that we take all the saints with us, to the extent of our ability, that is, our influence and property; seconded by Elder [Heber] Kimball, and carried unanimously. Elder Brigham Young continued: "If you will be faithful to your covenant, I will now prophesy that the great God will shower down means upon this people, to accomplish it [the move] to the very letter.[43]

In an "Epistle to the Church" sent out at the end of the conference, Brigham declared that the Mormon community faced "a crisis of extraordinary and thrilling interests"—namely, "the exodus of the nation of the only true Israel from these United States to a far distant region of the west." This is "a new epoch, not only in the history of the church, but of this nation." The planned exodus was not necessarily a calamity, but a part of the "merciful design in our Heavenly Father towards all such as patiently endure these afflictions until He advises them that the day of their deliverance has come."[44] "Therefore," he went on, "dispose of your properties and inheritance [land], and interests for available means, such as money, wagons, oxen, cows, mules, and a few good horses adapted to journeying and scanty feed. Also for durable fabrics suitable for apparel and tents." Brigham concluded:

Wake up, wake up, dear brethren, . . . to the present glorious emergency in which the God of heaven has placed you to prove your faith by your works, preparatory to a rich endowment in the Temple of the Lord, and the obtaining of promises and deliverances, and glories for yourselves and your children and your dead.[45]

Late in November 1845, special rooms in the temple's attic story were plastered and painted and borrowed carpets laid. Brigham and Heber placed the curtains their wives had made for the windows. On November 30 there was a dedication, and ten days later the first group of Saints passed through the endowment ceremony in the top-floor compartments. Thereafter, "temple work," the performance of ordinances for the living and the dead, proceeded night and day, without interruption. Brigham noted in his holograph diary on January 12 that for many days he had been giving himself "entirely to the work of the Lord in the Temple. Almost night and day I have spent, not taking more than four hours upon an average out of twenty-four to sleep, and but seldom ever allowing myself the time and opportunity of going home once a week." Wives were sealed to husbands and, by the ceremony of "adoption," leaders adopted members and families as their own children. These ceremonies, in which the leading roles were taken by Brigham and Heber Kimball, continued until February when the Twelve left Nauvoo. By then the ordinances had been administered to more than five thousand people.

T H E evacuation of the Saints from western Illinois was originally planned for April 1846, but two new threats prompted an early, hasty exit. The first was an indictment against Brigham Young and eight other apostles accused of harboring a Nauvoo counterfeiting operation conducted by transient river traffickers. Government officials tried to serve the warrants, but failed when William Miller put on Brigham's overcoat and cap and left the temple where the apostles were gathered and stepped into the president's carriage. The

waiting marshals arrested Miller and took him to Carthage before they discovered that they had only a "bogus Brigham."[46]

The other threat, probably unfounded but accepted as genuine at the
time, was the warning by Governor Ford and others that federal troops in St.
Louis were planning to intercept the Mormons and destroy them. Colonel
Thomas L. Kane, a member of a highly placed, politically active Pennsylvania
family, became a friend of the Mormons in 1846. He claimed he had inside
knowledge that federal seizure was a real possibility. Brigham believed him,
and repeated the charge several times in later life. It now seems that the rumors
were circulated precisely in order to induce the Mormons to leave sooner than
they had planned.

On Sunday, January 18, 1846, Brigham wrote in his diary that he had
convened a meeting in the temple of all the "commandants" of the companies
appointed to "lead out" in the journey west. How many, he asked, would be
"ready and willing to start at a moment's warning, should necessity require
it?" He had been advised of the "evil intended toward us," he said, "and that
our safety will depend on our safe elopement from this place before our enemies
should intercept and prevent our escape." Brigham wrote that "every man
[present] felt willing to yield to the circumstances that surrounded us and do
whatever was considered best for the common interest of all." They also indicated, he wrote, that they were willing "to be used and to let their property
be used" for the purpose of accomplishing "this wise and preconcerted elopement." Brigham then appointed a committee of five to dispose of all property
and effects left behind, including the temple and the Nauvoo House.

The public decision to leave was made on February 2; the first group,
church authorities and their families, crossed the Mississippi on February 4.
In succeeding days several hundred left and assembled in temporary camps in
Iowa. Brigham, who had remained behind to help administer endowments to
Saints who begged him to do it, crossed with his wagons the evening of
February 15, and joined the group to which he had been assigned at Sugar
Creek, nine miles into Iowa. Brigham's contingent consisted of fifteen wagons,
and fifty members of his family. His brother Joseph was left in charge of
Nauvoo. On February 24 the temperature dropped to twelve degrees below
zero, freezing over the Mississippi and permitting great caravans to cross on
the ice. By mid-May more than ten thousand Saints had crossed the Mississippi.

Brigham and the Twelve developed the military-style organization Joseph
Smith had initiated on a minuscule basis in Zion's Camp. Fifty families formed
the basic unit of travel. Each fifty was subdivided into ten, led by a captain
who maintained discipline, supervised the march, and oversaw the work of
guards, herdsmen, commissaries, and so on. Brigham dubbed these moving
companies the Camp of Israel and unhesitatingly used ancient Israelite motifs
in his letters and speeches. By mid-June he and Heber had reached the Missouri
River and established temporary headquarters on the lands of the Potawatomi

Indians. The east bank camps were at the present location of Council Bluffs, Iowa, at what the Mormons came to call Kanesville; the west bank camps, at present-day Florence, near Omaha, Nebraska, at what was called Winter Quarters.

The original plans called for the movement of several hundred men to the Great Basin in 1846, and this continued to be Brigham Young's intention as late as June 1846. The Journal History of the Church for June 28, 1846, notes that "Pres. Young proposed sending a company from this [Missouri River Valley] to Bear River Valley [apparently Salt Lake Valley] in the Great Basin, without families, forthwith." In a general council later the same day, Brigham warned: "If the church is blown to the four winds and never gathered again, remember I have told you how, when and where to gather."[47] Young dictated a letter to President James K. Polk, giving details of his plans:

> The cause of our exile we need not repeat; it is already with you, suffice it to say that a combination of fortuitous, illegal and unconstitutional circumstances have placed us in our present situation, on a journey which we design shall end in a location west of the Rocky Mountains, and within the basin of the Great Salt Lake, or Bear River valley, as soon as circumstances shall permit, believing that to be a point where a good living will require hard labor, and consequently will be coveted by no other people, while it is surrounded by so unpopulous but fertile country.[48]

Two developments caused them to postpone the dispatch of an advance company until the spring of 1847. The first was the realization of the amount of planning necessary to move a large body of people. The second was the recruitment of the Mormon Battalion. In January, Brigham had instructed his nephew Jesse C. Little, the church's envoy in the East, to "take every honorable advantage of the times you can" to get assistance from the government for the Saints' migration west. The church hoped to obtain a contract from the Secretary of War to build a series of forts to protect the developing Oregon Trail. Little was able to discuss the proposal with President Polk, despite his preoccupation with the declaration of war on Mexico. Polk authorized the enlistment of 500 Mormon soldiers to go by land to California in support of the army of General Stephen Watts Kearny. To Brigham this arrangement would provide "hard cash" income to the Mormons, would guarantee government permission to camp on Indian lands and use grass and timber, and would assure the transportation, at government expense, of 500 men to the West Coast.[49]

Confident that the battalion would be a help, Brigham moved from camp to camp, speaking before campfires and from wagon tongues, and managed to induce 500 Mormon boys and men to leave their families and enlist. They moved out of the Mormon camps at Council Bluffs on July 20, marched to Fort Leavenworth, Kansas, and then on to San Diego, California, in what was quite possibly the longest march of infantry to that date in American history.

Because of the battalion recruitment and other factors, therefore, Brigham wrote to the Nauvoo trustees in September that the intention of the Saints was to winter at Council Bluffs and build a community where they could leave their families for a season and in the spring of 1847 "start for the Bear River Valley, find a location, plant our seeds, build our houses, etc.," and the next season take their families.⁵⁰ During this same period the Jesuit priest, Father De Smet, met the leaders at the Mormon encampment and gave a glowing report on the Salt Lake Valley, further confirming them in their decision a year earlier.⁵¹ A comment of Willard Richards suggests that the church leaders had even gone so far as to become acquainted with irrigation techniques necessary in the Great Basin. Speaking of the necessity of leaving the majority of the people at Winter Quarters for another winter, Richards gave the following argument against attempting to move the entire body of the Saints:

If we go 5 or 600 ms [miles] to put in a crop this spring we shall probably be too late as the drought comes on much sooner in that region of country than it does here, thus you see we will have to be careful and select a location where we can irrigate everything that we put into the ground, which will doubtless require considerable of labour to build a dam, cut races or make troughs [ditches] sufficient to water a farm of that size.⁵²

During the winter of 1846–47, then, Brigham further strengthened the organization of sixteen thousand Saints spread out over several hundred miles of prairie, established an internal mail service, built a grist mill, organized relief teams to bring the families who hadn't yet left Nauvoo to the main body, sent several apostles to England to oversee the missionary and emigration apparatus in that country, and continued to interview persons about the geography of the Far West. On January 14, 1847, he announced "The Word and Will of the Lord" to the Camps of Israel to move West. His acknowledged skill in organizing and directing that migration, and its epic nature, were to have a lasting impact on the Mormons—and on Brigham himself.

9 ✤

The Pioneer Trek
to the Great Basin

I could a deal easier saw up this house and eat it for Indian
meal and give satisfaction than go over the mountains. . . . I
just do the thing that I know to be right and the Lord blesses
me.[1]

D U R I N G the winter and early spring of 1847 the entire Camp
of Israel had "resounded with the sounds of intelligent, well directed labor."[2]
Wagons had to be built and outfitted, horses and oxen sturdy enough to
withstand the rigors of a thousand-mile journey had to be procured, foodstuffs
and other supplies for the trek had to be gathered, and sustenance and protection of those who would remain behind had to be arranged. As leader of
the migration, however, Brigham was sometimes frustrated. Disgusted at the
plodding progress on the wagons, he warned some at a meeting in early March
that "if you come here again and don't report them fitted out, I'll rub your
ears for you—worse than I have done tonight."[3] By early April more than
seventy wagons were fitted and ready to roll.

A relatively small party was to make the initial crossing of the plains,
laying a trail for the larger companies of Saints to follow. This first band, most
of them handpicked by Brigham and his fellow apostles, "consisted of 143 men,
3 women [Clara Decker, Brigham's plural wife; Harriet Decker, Lorenzo's
wife; Ellen Sanders, Heber's plural wife], and 2 children—148 souls. They had
a boat, a cannon, 70 wagons and carriages, 93 horses, 52 mules, 66 oxen, 19
cows, 17 dogs, and some chickens."[4] Six of the party were apostles and ten
had participated in Zion's Camp. Originally, Brigham had intended to take
only men, but his brother Lorenzo contended that Harriet, whose asthmatic
condition was exacerbated by the Missouri lowlands, should make the trek
with them. When Harriet pled that she needed company, Brigham agreed that
Clara, who was Harriet's daughter by her first husband, and Heber's Ellen

might also go. Lorenzo also took his six-year-old son Lorenzo, and a stepson, Perry Decker, about the same age.

APRIL 5–18:

"I am anxious to . . . be about my errand."

The first several days of the journey amounted to a series of fits and starts. Heber Kimball and six of his teams were first to leave Winter Quarters on April 5; over the next two days they traveled about ten miles, heading west.

Meanwhile, Brigham and the others had remained at Winter Quarters to participate in the church's general conference on April 6. Addressing the congregated Saints, Brigham admitted that "I am anxious to leave this place and be about my errand. . . . the principle of eternally preaching and never practicing is folly." He admonished his followers to "pray for yourselves, and your enemies. Pray that God may soften their hearts until we are out of their grasp." Ever the pragmatist, he concluded by advising residents of Winter Quarters to "give up all farming and fencing until this place is fenced in, and make a good Stockade."[5]

The next day Brigham joined the pioneer camp, which then continued on to the Elkhorn River. While at that location, the news reached camp that Apostle Parley Pratt was at Winter Quarters, having returned from England— whereupon Brigham and members of the Twelve made a return trip to greet him. They rejoined the camp on April 11, finding the company on the west side of the Elkhorn, having rafted across the river on the previous day.

Dawn of April 12 saw Brigham and several others returning once again to Winter Quarters; Elder John Taylor had arrived from England, and was due a welcome from the brethren. Taylor had brought with him a substantial sum of money contributed by the Saints in England, as well as several scientific instruments for use on the journey: "two sextants, two barometers, two artificial horizons, one circle of reflection, one telescope; all of which were exhibited to us in the evening and boxed up so that we could take them along."[6]

According to previous agreement with Brigham and the Twelve, the pioneers traveled only about twelve miles during this final absence of their leaders. Encamped on the banks of the Platte River, about forty-seven miles from Winter Quarters, they awaited the arrival of their camp's full complement—and the real beginning of the journey west.

During this hiatus Thomas Bullock, official camp clerk, had his first encounter with Indians. He recorded that

> while in the act of hitching my cattle to the wagon, four Omaha Indians came rushing down upon us, waiving their standards covered with Turkies Feathers, hallowing and yelling, like Savages, . . . one had the boldness to come to my Wagon and attempt to take the front of my Wagon Cover to make him a head dress, but I repelled him, and he went away in anger.[7]

Late in the afternoon of April 15 Brigham and his companions finally rejoined the camp. Early the next morning, a "gloomy, windy, and cold" day, the little band assembled to organize themselves and invoke divine blessings upon their undertaking. "After being numbered and formed in two lines in a circle around the wagon carrying the leather boat," recorded Norton Jacob, "all kneeled down, when Brother Brigham addressed the Lord by prayer and dedicated the mission and all we have to the Lord God of Israel. . . . President Young now proceeded to organize the camp."[8] The camp broke in midafternoon and traveled about three miles, stopping for the night near a stand of cottonwood. Brigham and Heber rode on horseback several miles ahead of the company in order to scout the next day's route.

On Saturday, April 17, following an eight-mile stint on the trail, afternoon found the party at the edge of another grove of cottonwoods, where they camped to make preparations for Sabbath observance. Here Brigham introduced a new organizational structure, this one conforming to military protocol with himself as lieutenant general and others designated as colonel, first major, second major, and captains of companies (tens). "Orders from General Young," according to Wilford Woodruff,

> were for the whole regiment to journey in a compact body as we were in an Indian country; for every man to carry his gun loaded; for the cap locks to be shut into a piece of buckskin with caps handy to slip on in an instant in case of an attack; flint locks with cotton or tow in the pan, and a powder flask attached to prime lock; the object of this caution is to prevent accidents. Every man is to walk beside his wagon and not to leave it unless he is sent away. Strict rules and discipline are necessary while traveling through a hostile Indian country.[9]

The Sabbath dawned cold and blustery—so unpleasant, in fact, that the camp agreed to dispense with worship services for the day, although members of the Twelve "retired to the woods to counsel together."[10] Toward sunset, Brigham called company captains together and proceeded with a final bit of organizational business. The camp, he announced, would be governed by the following regulations, as recorded by clerk Bullock:

> At 5 A.M. the horn should be blown and every man then arise and pray, attend to their cattle, and have every thing done, in order that all may start by seven o'clock, that each extra man should travel on the off side of his team, with his gun loaded over his shoulder, that each driver shall have his gun so placed that he can lay his hand on it in a moment, that every gun shall have a piece of leather over the nipple, or in the pan of his gun, having their caps, and Powder Flasks ready for a moment's warning.
> The brethren will halt for an hour to have dinner, which must be ready cooked. When the Camp comes to halt for the night, the front of every man's wagon shall be outwards where the fires shall be built, the horses to be all secured inside the circle. At ½ past [eight] the horn will be blown when every man must

retire to their wagons and pray, and be in bed by 9 o'clock except the night guard, all fires to be put out at bed time, all the Camp to travel in close order, these orders to continue in force until further orders. The Captains were also instructed to drill their men.[11]

While they were now fully organized, no one knew quite what to expect from the journey; but there was no turning back, and the Great Plains stretched before them in a pristine, menacing, tantalizing expanse. They would know hunger, exhaustion, illness, backbreaking labor, threats of Indian attack, and the ever-present danger of wild animals. At the end, "in the valleys of the mountains," perhaps a new Zion.

APRIL 19–30:
"The Camp is in good helth and first rate sperits"

When the travelers broke camp early on the morning of April 19, it was with nature's blessing—fair weather, calm and pleasant, easy traveling over dry, sandy river bottoms, the landscape dotted with small lakes. That evening, camped after logging some twenty miles, several of the men made a fishing expedition to one of the lakes, returning with "a snapping turtle, four small turtles, one duck, two small cat fish, and two creek suckers."[12]

At this point William Clayton, a conscientious journal keeper with an eye for detail, began to mull over the problem of maintaining an accurate record of mileage. "I walked some this afternoon in company with Orson Pratt," he wrote, "and suggested to him the idea of fixing a set of wooden cog wheels to the hub of a wagon wheel, in such order as to tell the exact number of miles we travel each day. He seemed to agree with me that it could be easily done at a trifling expense."[13] Nearly a month later (and only after Clayton's repeated urgings), such a device—called an odometer—was constructed and put into operation by Appleton Harmon. Its precise measurements proved to be of great value to pioneer companies making the trek in years to come.

The Mormons had determined to march west along the north side of the Platte River, and for several hundred miles that body of water was in constant sight. "It is the most singular river I ever beheld," wrote Wilford Woodruff:

It is from three quarters to a mile wide and its shores and bed one universal body of quicksand. It is a rapid stream, yet in many places a person can wade across. Frequently the whole bed of the river is covered with but a few inches of water and at other places it is deep and rapid. . . . Horses and cattle can walk down to the edge of the river and drink, like walking on the edge of a smooth sea beach, and sometimes while walking on the apparent hard beach or bed of the river a man or horse will suddenly sink into the quicksand. . . . Many men and horses have been lost in this way on the Platte.[14]

Heber Kimball discussed the river in context of their daily fare:

The country is beautiful and pleasing to the eye of the traveller, notwithstanding there is only the same kind of scenery from day to day, namely on the left the majestic Platte, with its muddy waters . . . the river frequently hid from view by the many handsome cottonwood groves, before and behind, on the right and left a vast, level prairie, and on the right at a distance the continued range of majestic bluffs.[15]

In the quiet of late evening on April 20, Brigham's thoughts turned back to his home at Winter Quarters, his wife Mary Ann, and his children. Ninety-five miles now separated them; but he could at least take a few moments to pen a note to "My dear companion partner in tribulation":

I should have writen to you by Br. Rockwood but had not time. The Camp was to be organized and a gratedeal [great deal] to be dun to prepare for mooving. On Sunday I should have writen but did not feele able to. I lade abed and thaught of a grate deal I should like to say to you. The Camp is in good helth and first rate sperits. They have never felt better in their lives. I think my helth has verry much improved yesterday and today. You menshend in your letter that you herd I lay on the ground the night I left home. I did but due not think it hurt me, but when I arived in camp I found myself complet[el]y tired out. I thank you a thousand times for your kind letters to me more especely for your kind acts and still more for your kind hart. I pray for you and the children continualy and for all of our famely. I due think the Lord has blest me with one of [the] best famelyes that eney man ever had on the Earth. I due hope the children will be good and mind there mother when I am gon.

Brigham then included some fatherly advice to his two sons, Joseph A. and Brigham, Jr., ages twelve and ten:

My son Joseph you *must not goe away from home* and Brigham also must stay at home. How due [you] sapose I would feele when I come home and find one of my children dest[r]oyed by the Indens? I pray this may not be the case.[16]

The camp's first encounter with a large body of Indians occurred as they passed a Pawnee village on April 21. The Indians appeared friendly enough (especially when offered gifts of powder, tobacco, flour, and other trinkets), but warned Brigham against killing their buffalo, insisted that the pioneers turn back, "and other talk of the same import—all of which showed to us the influence of the traders, the Missourians and others were using with the Indians against us, and which bade us be on our watch."[17] Not willing to take chances, Brigham ordered a heavy guard to watch through the night. They saw Indian fires all around them, "but a few guns and other demonstrations let them know that we were on hand."[18] Two days later, six hundred Pawnees, still feeling protective about their buffalo (and likely covetous of the camp's collection of horses), were very much in evidence.

Then there was the Loup Fork of the Platte to be navigated, a tributary "three to four feet deep and very rapid and about 300 yards straight across."[19] The crossing was later recalled as one of the most difficult fords of the entire journey. Wrote Heber:

> When I jumped into the river I was astonished at the strength of the current, for it was all I could do to stand on my feet. . . . We saw that it was wearing the men and teams down and they could not long endure it. President Young gave orders that no more wagons should cross tonight. . . . The wagons make a noise when crossing the quick sands, as though they were rolling over a very rough stone pavement and it seems as though they would shake to pieces.[20]

It was with weary thanksgiving that the last wagon reached the Fork's south shore in late afternoon of April 24. The group moved on about three miles, then set up camp near a small lake

Next day was the Sabbath, a welcome respite from the rigors of the trail. Thomas Bullock found it an idyllic scene:

> The Camp arose at the sound of horn, attended to their cattle, and observed it as a day of rest, for meditation, prayer and praise. All was harmony, peace, and love, and an holy stillness prevailed throughout the day. The principal sounds heard, were the tinkling of the Cow Bells, and the screams of Wild Geese as they flew past our Camp. The sky was beautiful with a South Wind.[21]

A worship service was held in late afternoon, during which Brigham addressed the camp.[22] "We do not anticipate any attack by the Indians to kill any of the men, but to steal horses," he explained; "the purpose of the guard is to look after our horses."[23] There was wry humor in Brigham's official motion "that any one who wants to murmur, go to Henry G. Sherwood, who will do the business for them."[24]

Brigham's comment regarding the Indians' intentions was substantiated that very night—a small contingent of horse-hungry warriors caused a general camp alarm before daylight. Their attempt was foiled; but before another day had passed, the persistent Pawnees had made off with two steeds. Irked, Brigham and several others made a fruitless search for the animals. The men were then reminded by Brigham to attend to their horses.[25]

By week's end, they had traveled more than two hundred miles from Winter Quarters. The days were generally dry, cold, and cloudy. The roads were "extremely dusty and the strong wind blows it into the wagons and everything is covered."[26] Grass for the stock was plentiful most days; fuel for campfires, however, was becoming scarce and cold suppers the usual fare. Frontier ingenuity, coupled with recent evidences of buffalo along the trail, soon provided a solution: "The camp have found a good substitute for wood in the dried buffalo dung which lies on the ground here in great plenty, and makes a good fire when properly managed."[27] Buffalo chips ("as modest folks calls it"[28]) thus became a major source of fuel on the desolate prairie lands.

MAY 1–31:
"If we do slay when we do not need,
we will need when we cannot slay."

The first day of May was cold (thermometer at thirty degrees) and windy, but fraught with a sense of high excitement.[29] During the day's travel, Brigham and his companions caught their first glimpses of buffalo. Now, for many days, there would be hundreds of thousands of the animals, crowding the trail, close-cropping the vegetation, coloring the wind with the stench of their numbers, yet never failing to pique the fascination of men whose paths crossed theirs.

William Clayton described the wild buffalo's appearance as "somewhat singular":

> The color of the back and about half way down the sides is a light brown, the rest is a very dark brown. The shoulder appears slightly rounding and humped. When running, the large shaggy head hangs low down, about half way in height between the ground and the top of the shoulder. They canter like any ox or cow, but appear far more cumbersome and heavy, especially about the fore parts, which look larger than they really are on account of the long, thick matty hair. They run tolerably fast, but a good horse will easily gain on them. They will run a long time without diminishing their speed. Their meat is very sweet and tender as veal.[30]

Most of the day was devoted to a spirited buffalo hunt by ten or twelve of the camp's official hunters, resulting, by late afternoon, in the killing of ten animals. The meat was distributed equally among the companies of ten. "We had plenty of good [buffalo] meat for supper; it is much better than beef," wrote George A. Smith.[31] Apparently the meat also had a singular effect on the digestive system, for a day later George A. recorded that "I ate heartily of buffalo meat, and was routed out very early by its effect."[32] Wilford Woodruff added, a few days afterward, that "I was quite sick with the diarrhea; the change from salt to fresh meat is affecting a number in camp."[33]

Indian war parties were never distant. One of their tactics was to set prairie fires in the Mormons' path, making feed for their teams and horses virtually nonexistent for miles in all directions. "The wind blew the ashes of the burnt grass in all directions," wrote Bullock, "which caused us to look like [chimney] sweeps. However by washing, after our halt, we were enabled to discern each other again."[34]

On Tuesday, May 4, Brigham found a few minutes to complete his letter to Mary Ann, begun two weeks earlier. Writing from "About 20 miles above the head of Grand Island," he assured her that

I want to wright a long letter but have not time. We are all perty well at present though my labour has b[ee]n verry hard for me on the jorney. I pray for you continualy. . . . I am glad you are not a going to come on this sumer for I want to be with my famely when they come this jorney. . . . I want the bretheren to help my famely whilst I am gon and not supress them. Joseph and Brigham be good boys and mind your mother and Ales [Alice], Caroline, little Johne and finely all my children and famely be you blest for ever and ever.[35]

Through the next several days, buffalo continued plentiful. Concerned by the avidity with which camp hunters pursued the shaggy-headed beasts, Brigham issued an ultimatum that "there should be no more game killed until such time as it should be needed, for it was a sin to waste life and flesh."[36] He was to repeat this injunction time and again, warning that "if we do slay when we do not need, we will need when we cannot slay."[37]

Brigham's patience sometimes wore thin. "Yesterday there was no one with the cows," Brigham pointed out, "and they started twice to go to the Buffalo and I had to run my horse twice to bring them back, in doing which I lost a good telescope. I did not know then that Erastus Snow was the driver for that time. If I had, I should have known that he would not go out of his road one rod, he is so lazy." A sharp exchange took place between the two men, Erastus soon promised to do better, and Brigham's expensive new British spy glass was recovered.[38]

The Indians' habit of burning the prairie, together with the collective appetite of the buffalo and antelope population, made it increasingly difficult for the Mormons' animals to find adequate nourishment. By mid-May, journal entries similar to Wilford Woodruff's were commonplace: "The feed is so short and teams so weak that we are unable to travel but a short portion of the day."[39]

Mindful of the companies that would follow, Brigham and other camp leaders deemed it advisable to leave periodic messages along the trail. On May 10 the first of these was prepared. Thomas Bullock made out a copy of the laws regulating the camp and read it to Brigham who declared, "That's Scripture," and proceeded to seal it up and enclose it in a box, which was then attached to a twelve-foot pole. On the outside was written in red chalk "Open this and you will find a letter." On the reverse, "Look in this, 316 miles from Winter Quarters. Bound Westward. Pioneers." Brigham suggested that Bullock write, on the upper right-hand corner, "Platte Post Office."[40] Similar messages would be left approximately every ten miles for the remainder of the journey.

By the end of May, Brigham had become increasingly disturbed by the behavior of many in the camp. He called a general meeting on Saturday, May 29, and summarily declared:

I am about to revolt from traveling with this camp any further with the spirit they now possess. I had rather risk myself among the savages with ten men that are men of faith, men of mighty prayer, men of God, than to be with this whole camp when they forget God, and turn their hearts to folly and wickedness. . . . I am now resolved not to go any farther with the camp unless you will covenant to humble yourselves before the Lord and serve him and quit your folly and wickedness. For four weeks past nearly the whole camp has been card-playing, and checkers and dominoes have occupied the attention of the brethren, and dancing, and niggering [presumably, "putting on acts"] and hoeing down, all has been in the act continually; now it is quite time to quit it.[41]

At the conclusion of his hour-long discourse in a similar vein, Brigham "very feelingly and tenderly blessed the brethren. . . ."[42]

The upbraiding had its desired effect; later in the day they again "pursued our journey in peace." According to Heber, "No loud laughter was heard, no swearing, no quarrelling, no profane language, no hard speeches to man or beast, and it truly seemed as though the cloud had burst, and we had emerged into a new element, a new atmosphere, a new society and a new world."[43]

JUNE 1–30:
"Bridger . . . said he would give one thousand dollars
for a bushel of corn raised in the Basin."

Late on the warm afternoon of June 1, they made camp on the north side of the Platte River opposite Fort Laramie (also called Fort John).[44] Owned by the American Fur Company and managed by James Bordeaux, the fort served as a permanent residence for about eighteen families and was a popular stopping-over place for traders and emigrant companies.[45] On June 2, Brigham and a few others crossed the river and were graciously received by Bordeaux, who strongly recommended that they continue their journey on the south side of the river, offering to ferry their wagons across at a reasonable rate of payment. Wilford Woodruff recorded that during the conversation, Bordeaux took occasion to mention that "Gov. Boggs [of Missouri] passed here a short time before us. He talked much about the 'Mormons,' warned the Fort to watch us. Mr. Birdoe remarked that he did not think the 'Mormons' could possibly be any worse than Boggs himself. We concurred."[46] Ferrying began at sunrise the next morning and was completed by the following morning.

On the south side of the river the pioneers were joined by the Robert Crow company, a party of seventeen Saints from Alabama and Mississippi who were part of a larger group that had headed west, according to Brigham's January 1846 instructions, failed to locate the main body of the church along the trail (due to the decision to wait until 1847), and wintered at Fort Pueblo, now Colorado. The Southerners brought with them news of a "sick" detachment of the Mormon Battalion, which had left the battalion at Santa Fe and gone to Pueblo. The Crow company, except for a small party that returned to Pueblo to lead the Mississippians and battalionists to Brigham's destination, joined Brigham's group for the remainder of the journey to the Salt Lake

Valley. By noon the expanded company had once again taken up their march, this time following the Oregon Trail.

As the altitude increased and the road became steeper, often broken by treacherous inclines and descents, the long, level stretches of sandy river bottoms fast became only memories. "We think that we fully work our road tax," commented Orson Pratt, "for we have ten or twelve men detached daily, whose business it is to go in advance of the company with spades, iron bars, and other necessary implements to work the road."[47]

Slowly they worked their way up, down, and across the "rough broken country." While the design was to push continually westward, the band found itself "changing our direction evarry few minutes to wind around some point or gutter to pass some crick or confused mass of rocks which ley in fragments, or to avoid some steep [hill] that is to[o] rugged for our teams. At one point we ware a going NE when the point we want to make is S of W."[48]

A few days' travel from the place where their trail crossed the Platte River, Brigham sent a small party ahead with the leather boat, the *Revenue Cutter.* Arriving at the banks of the storm-swollen river just ahead of some Oregon-bound emigrant trains, the men offered their services and were hired to ferry the wagons' contents across the river while the wagons themselves were floated over. The emigrants paid $1.50 for each wagon and load, "payment being made in flour at $2.50 per 100 lbs." The earnings were divided among the members of the camp equally, which amounted to five and a half pounds of flour each, two pounds of meal, and a small piece of bacon. "It looked as much of a miracle to me," wrote Wilford Woodruff, "to see our flour and meal bags replenished in the midst of the Black Hills as it did to have the Children of Israel fed with manna in the wilderness."[49]

The main body arrived at a point near the Platte crossing on Saturday, June 12, where they camped and made preparations to observe the Sabbath. Following worship services the next day, Brigham met with camp officers to discuss the best method of getting the company across the river—100 feet wide, 15 feet deep, with a treacherously swift current. He proposed that four empty wagons, lashed together abreast, could be drawn across the river safely.

Brigham's plan, as it turned out, left something to be desired, as did a few other schemes. Wilford Woodruff reported:

We swam our horses and cattle, crossed our loads in the skiff, and at first tried the plan of floating our wagons by extending ropes down the river and attaching them to the end of the tongue, but the current would roll them over as if they were nothing but a log, wheels and bows appearing alternately upon the surface of the water, and two lashed together by means of poles placed under them shared the same fate. . . . The plan was abandoned as being too dangerous. The next plan was to try small rafts, but the difficulty of polling a raft in so deep and swift water was such that the wind, aiding the current, would not infrequently sweep them down from one to two miles before it would be possible to make the other shore. . . . In attempting to drag rafts across the current with ropes, the current would draw them under.[50]

By this time convinced that there must be a better way, Brigham sent men and teams to gather additional wood for a more elaborate raft. When the timber arrived at midmorning on June 16, "Prest. Young stript himself and went to work with all his strength, assisted by the Dr. [Richards] and the brethren, and made a first rate White Pine and White Cotton Wood Raft. . . . The new raft was in operation all day and worked well."[51]

Departing the North Fork of the Platte on the morning of June 19, they left behind a small contingent of about ten men whose assignment was to make a business of ferrying Oregon emigrants across the river, an arrangement that was profitable for the Mormons and a considerable help to the emigrant trains. Those remaining at the river were instructed to come west with the second pioneer company, due there in about a month.

Travel for the next few days was hardly a scenic adventure. The camping place on the evening of June 19, in fact, was declared by Woodruff to be "the most wretched of any ground we have found on the way." Brigham thought it might properly be called Hell Gate, as "the water tasted as though it ran through a bed of salt, salts, saltpeter, and sulphur."[52] The place was called Soda Springs, although Heber had other names for it: "It is one of the most humid, swampy, filthy, stinking places imaginable . . . a gloomy, cheerless, filthy place, most dangerous for cattle and unhealthy for families."[53]

That same evening, two scouts left camp to search out the next day's stopping place. According to William Clayton, they were accosted along the road by six men, clothed in blankets, who "had every appearance of being Indians." The scouts ignored them, but the Indians persisted by blocking the trail and motioning for the two horsemen to "go back." That tactic proving unsuccessful, the marauders "put spurs to their horses and were soon out of sight behind a higher piece of land." The scouts mounted the ridge and dis-covered a camp of Missourians—"and the six Indians were just entering the camp." Satisfied that the "Indians" were Missourians who were trying to keep them from a good campground, Brigham considered it to be "an old Missouri trick" and ordered his men to "press on a little faster and crowd them up a little."[54]

The Saints now passed over a hilly, sandy country. On June 21, stopping to rest on the banks of the Sweetwater River, they found themselves opposite Independence Rock, a "lengthy, high mass of rock, somewhat oval in form . . . has quite an isolated appearance, standing, as it does, some distance from the hills by which it is surrounded."[55] Having forded the river and camped for the evening, several of the men explored the rock, which was variously decorated with names of passersby.

They first sighted the Rocky Mountains late on the afternoon of June 23.

"In advance of us," recorded Horace Whitney, "at a great distance can be seen the outlines of mountains, loftier than any we have yet seen, the settling sun throwing its glancing rays athwart their summits, reveal[ing] them to our eyes covered with snow."[56] The final leg of their journey was in sight.

The Mormons were now gaining altitude and donning extra layers of clothing against the chilly mountain air. "Only in high altitudes was such a scene possible: abundance of good grass mingled with various plants and flowers upon the bottoms of the stream, and a few yards distant, were large banks of snow several feet in depth."[57] Sudden changes in temperature—from warm days to freezing nights—were later (mistakenly) thought to have contributed to a sudden outbreak of mountain fever in the camp.

The camp received visits from three men whose travels and explorations had taken them throughout the West. First came Moses "Black" Harris, a hunter-trapper heading east from Oregon with a small company of men on horseback. Having lived for nearly a quarter of a century west of the Rockies, his knowledge of the area was extensive. He was less than optimistic about the possibilities of settling the Great Basin, pointing to its scarcity of timber as a major drawback.

Next to make an appearance was James Bridger, the celebrated "Mountain Man," on his way to Laramie with a small company. His assessment of the basin was more promising, although he "considered it important not to bring a large population into the Great Basin until it was ascertained that grain could be raised; he said he would give one thousand dollars for a bushel of corn raised in the Basin."[58] Bridger apparently dwelt at considerable length upon his own expertise and experience, a self-glorification that did not sit well with some camp members. "From his appearance and conversation," wrote Howard Egan, "I should not take him to be a man of truth."[59] Wilford Woodruff was cautiously awestruck: "We found him to have been a great traveler, and possessed a great knowledge of nearly all of Oregon and California . . . if what he told us was true."[60]

On the evening of June 30, Samuel Brannan and two other men trudged into camp. Brannan had been appointed by Brigham during the winter of 1845–46 to colonize a settlement of Saints in California; he had sailed with a party of two or three hundred to the West Coast, via Cape Horn, in the spring of 1846. Now, he and his two companions had made the overland trek from San Francisco to convince Brigham that the Saints belonged in California. Brigham would not be persuaded, though Brannan "gave a very favorable account of the climate and soil of California."[61] Brannan and his companions eventually left for Pueblo to guide members of the Mormon Battalion to California for discharge.

On the last day of June, the Green River, storm-swollen to nearly 15 feet deep, a fast-moving 180 yards wide, had to be crossed. Profiting from their earlier experience, the Saints constructed two rafts and rigged them with rudders and oars. Over a four-day period the wagons were ferried safely across, their contents intact. The animals, as usual, made the crossing under their own power.

A number of the travelers recorded an increasing occurrence of "mountain fever" throughout the camp. "Several of the brethren were reported sick," according to Howard Egan, "and not able to drive their teams. The brethren are all taken alike, with violent pains in the head and back and a very hot fever."[62] The sickness, Orson Pratt reasoned, was "probably occasioned by suffocating clouds of dust which rise from the sandy road and envelop the whole camp when in motion, and also by the sudden changes of temperature."[63] Whatever its cause, the affliction gradually spread through the camp.

JULY 4–24:
"I felt that there the Saints would find protection and safety."

The Fourth of July was just another hot, dusty, mosquito-ridden day of traveling. "This," wrote Norton Jacob, "is Uncle Sam's day of Independence. Well, we are independent of all the powers of the Gentiles, that is enough for us."[64]

That same day, the five volunteers (among them Brigham's brother Phinehas) left the camp to retrace their trail, meet the second group of pioneers, and pilot them on to the Salt Lake Valley. Brigham and a few others accompanied the men as far as the ferry at Green River, where they met thirteen discharged members of the Mormon Battalion, "who were in pursuit of stolen animals which they had mostly recovered."[65] Returning with Brigham to the main camp, the thirteen were given a warm welcome.

Three days later the party arrived at Fort Bridger—"two double log houses about forty feet long each and joined by a pen for horses about ten feet high constructed by placing poles upright in the ground close together, which is all the appearance of a fort in sight."[66] Setting up camp near the fort, the men busied themselves for two days with horseshoeing and general wagon repairs. Most took a turn or two at trading with fort residents.

From Fort Bridger the terrain was "the most mountainous course we have yet seen."[67] Several of the men were ill and unable to manage their wagons without assistance. Thomas Bullock recorded that one afternoon the party "descended by two steep pitches, almost perpendicular, which on looking back from the bottom looks like jumping off the roof of a house to a middle story, then from the middle story to the ground and thank God there was no accident happened. Prests. Young and Kimball cautioned all to be very careful and locked the wheels of some wagons themselves."[68]

The pioneers were visited by Miles Goodyear, a mountaineer who had settled just east of where the Bear River flows into Great Salt Lake. Goodyear painted a glowing word-picture of the Weber River route to Salt Lake Valley. It was later agreed by camp members that he probably overstated his case "on account of his anxiety that we should travel through there, thereby making a road, and ensuring the passage of other emigrants in that direction."[69]

On the morning of July 12, Brigham was "attacked with fever," now diagnosed as Colorado tick fever, "a nonfatal viral illness transmitted by ticks found in most areas of the mountain west."[70] At noon he was forced to remain behind, and by evening he was "very sick . . . raving and insensible." He experienced excruciating headaches, high fever, and severe aches and pains in the back and joints. He was, as he described himself, "almost mad with pain."

Heber and a few others remained with him to offer what comfort and assistance they could. He was "a little better" the next day, and by noon of July 15 he felt well enough that he and Heber and their small rear company joined the main camp, which, at Brigham's direction, had proceeded on. They pressed on for a few more miles in the midst of a summer downpour. Soon after they had halted for the evening, Horace Whitney visited Brigham and "was glad to find him in a state of convalescence, and in tolerably good spirits, though his pale and emaciated countenance plainly testified that he had recently been quite ill in body."[71]

An advance group of twenty-three wagons and forty-two men, captained by Orson Pratt, had gone ahead to scout a road leading over the mountains. Finding the desired route, Pratt sent farther ahead a "small company of about a dozen with spades, axes, etc., to make the road passable, which required considerable labor."[72]

On July 17 Brigham was again "very sick" and had to stop. When word got around that he was "nigh unto death," a number of the men retired to a secluded grove to join in a prayer circle. It was fortunately a good location for stopping over, with fresh water and plentiful feed nearby; several men tried their luck at fishing. The following day, a Sunday, Brigham was "sensibly better," but the group repeated their prayers. On Monday, July 19, it was agreed that a small group would remain behind with Brigham while the others went onward. The President's health was "slowly improving."[73] Having prepared a bed for him in the back of a carriage, they broke camp before dawn on July 20 and were able to travel some twelve miles. But the difficulty of traveling so fatigued Brigham and others that they remained camped through the next day.

Orson Pratt's advance company continued to make laborious progress. Encamped near East Canyon Creek on July 20, Pratt wrote a detailed description of the road and terrain, leaving it in a conspicuous location for the benefit of the main company. His group then proceeded with their arduous trail-making.[74] Next day, Pratt recorded his first view of the valley of the Great Salt Lake:

> Brother Erastus Snow . . . and myself proceeded in advance of the camp
> down Last Creek four and one-half miles, to where it passes through a canyon

and issues into the broad, open valley below. To avoid the canyon, the wagons last season had passed over an exceedingly steep, dangerous hill. Mr. Snow and myself ascended this hill, from the top of which a broad open valley, about 20 miles wide and 30 long, lay stretched out before us, at the north end of which the broad waters of the Great Salt Lake glistened in the sunbeams, containing high mountainous islands from 25 to 30 miles in extent. After issuing from the mountains among which we had been shut up for many days, and beholding in a moment such an extensive scenery open before us, we could not refrain from a shout of joy which almost involuntarily escaped from our lips the moment this grand and lovely scenery was within our view.[75]

Descending into the valley with one horse between them, Pratt and Snow explored a bit, traveling some twelve miles before returning to their camp.

That evening, a letter was delivered to Pratt, written by Willard Richards and George A. Smith in response to Pratt's letter left along the trail. "We left Brother Young day before yesterday," they reported. "His health was improving, but he was not able to travel as fast as the camp. . . . Brothers Kimball, Woodruff and [E. T.] Benson and eight or ten wagons tarried with Brother Young. We expect they are coming leisurely on." The authors then detailed Brigham's instructions for proceeding with settlement of the valley:

President Young . . . felt inclined for the present not to crowd upon the Utes [Indians] until we have a chance to get acquainted with them, and that it would be better to bear toward the region of the Salt Lake, rather than the Utah Lake and find some good place for our seeds and deposit them as speedily as possible, regardless of a future location. . . .

We think that the views of President Young and Council would be carried out the most perfectly, by your continuing to prosecute the route, as you have hitherto done, until you arrive at some point in the Basin, where you could "hear" the potatoes grow, if they had only happened to have been there; then let all your mechanics, even to the rough hewers, be employed in fitting up plows, while all your horses and mules should be employed in small companies in scouring the country in every direction, so that by night you will be able to get a tolerable good report from the various companies and begin to judge where will be the best spot to put in the plows, and we hope to be there to hear the report, as we anticipate we will not be more than one day behind you; and we expect the whole camp will be on hand in a day or two following.

The time for planting is fully come, and we feel anxious to make every move that would facilitate the potatoe crop; it matters not where it is. The president thinks the Utes may feel a little tenacious about their choice lands on the Utah Lake, and we had better keep further north towards the Salt Lake, which is more of a warlike or neutral ground, and by so doing we should be less likely to be disturbed, and also have a chance to form an acquaintance with the Utes, and having done our planting shall select a site for our location at our leisure.[76]

It was late afternoon on July 22 when the main camp of pioneers, after a day of strenuous road work, caught their first full view of the valley, "the Salt Lake in the distance with its bold hills on its Islands towering up in bold relief behind the Silvery Lake."[77] "I could not help shouting 'hurra, hurra, hurra, there's my home at last,' " wrote Thomas Bullock, continuing:

> The sky is very clear, the air delightful and all together looks glorious, the only drawback appearing to be the absence of timber. But there is an ocean of stone in the mountains to build stone houses and walls for fencing. If we can only find a bed of coal we can do well and be hidden up in the mountains unto the Lord.[78]

Descending to the valley proper, the party set up camp "on the banks of a beautiful little stream which was surrounded by very tall grass."[79]

Under way by seven the next morning, the pioneers had to travel only about two miles and just over two hours to reach the intended camping and farming site. Within a few minutes of their arrival, Orson Pratt had gathered the men around him. Following a few introductory remarks, Pratt led the camp in "prayer to Almighty God, returning thanks for the preservation of the Camp, their prosperity in the journey, safe arrival in this place, consecrated and dedicated the land to the Lord and entreated his blessings on the seeds about to be planted and on our labors in this valley."[80]

The camp then lost no time in organizing their farming effort. Committees were appointed to look after every operation from plowing to planting to irrigation; at noon the first furrow was turned. Work progressed through the afternoon, and would continue in four-hour shifts daily from 4:00 A.M. to 8:00 P.M. until the project was completed.

Meanwhile Brigham, still weak from the ravages of "mountain fever," was approaching his own intimate encounter with the valley. "I ascended and crossed over the Big Mountain," he recorded on July 23, "when on its summit I directed Elder Woodruff, who had kindly tendered me the use of his carriage, to turn the same half way round so that I could have a view of a portion of Salt Lake Valley [from my bed in the back]. The spirit of light rested upon me and hovered over the valley, and I felt that there the Saints would find protection and safety. We descended and encamped at the foot of the Little Mountain."[81]

While the "spirit of light" enveloped Brigham with comforting assurance, and while Wilford Woodruff gazed with wonder on the "grand scene," others in his party, though relieved to see the journey's end, were less enthusiastic. Lorenzo's wife Harriet, who had been distressed throughout the journey by the lack of trees and other scenery, saw more of the same barren wasteland in the Salt Lake Valley. Looking over the country, she remarked to her husband, "We have traveled fifteen hundred miles to get here, and I would willingly travel a thousand miles farther to get where it looked as though a white man could live."[82] Lorenzo himself, ill and exhausted, was a long way from rejoicing on that hot, dusty July afternoon: "This day we arrived in the valley of the great Salt Lake. My feelings were such as I cannot describe. Everything looked gloomy and I felt heartsick."[83]

On July 24, "after crossing Emigration Kanyon Creek eighteen times," Brigham and his rear company joined the already bustling little settlement in early afternoon.[84] The entire Camp of Israel had arrived.

JULY 25–AUGUST 25:
"The city can be laid out perfectly square,
north and south, east and west."

July 25 was a Sabbath day of worship and thanksgiving; members of the Twelve spoke at morning and afternoon meetings, exhorting camp members to industry and upright behavior. Brigham, though still feeble, addressed the group briefly, outlining the specifics of Sabbath observance. "President Young . . . informed the brethren they must not work on Sunday, that if they did they would lose five times as much as they would gain by it, and they must not hunt or fish on that day. . . . He remarked there would be meeting every Sabbath in this place or wherever we stop."[85]

It took Brigham about three days to settle down to the business of planning his city. On July 28, he walked with the Twelve "from the north camp to about the centre between the two creeks," waved his hand and said, "Here is the forty acres for the Temple. The city can be laid out perfectly square, north and south, east and west." Woodruff recalled:

> It was then moved and carried that the Temple lot contain forty acres [later reduced to a more manageable ten acres] on the ground where we stood. . . . that the city be laid out into lots of ten rods by twenty each, exclusive of the streets, and into blocks of eight lots, being ten acres in each block, and one and a quarter in each lot. . . . that each street be laid out eight rods wide, and that there be a sidewalk on each side, twenty feet wide, and that each house be built in the centre of the lot twenty feet from the front, that there might be uniformity throughout the city. . . . that there be four public squares of ten acres each, to be laid out in various parts of the city for public grounds. . . . At 8 o'clock the whole camp came together on the Temple ground and passed the votes unanimously.[86]

Within a week, surveying had begun, and men not engaged in farming activities were put to work making adobes with which to build a temporary "fort"—a square of adjoining log cabins, all opening into an inner court or corral for the cattle, with an adobe wall around three sides of the outer perimeter as a protection against marauders. Within three weeks a wall had been constructed around the fort and twenty-nine log houses had been built in the fort, each eight or nine feet high, sixteen feet long, and fourteen feet wide. Four of these were built by Brigham. The chimneys were of adobe, the hearths of clay, and the roofs of willow boughs covered with earth. In one of these

Clara Decker lived, to be joined later by Eliza R. Snow. A chest Clara had brought was her only table; the bedstead was built into a corner, the walls forming two sides and cords wound tightly around pegs forming the "mattress."[87]

Approximately one hundred men of the advance company were expected to return to Winter Quarters with Brigham to prepare their families to move west the next year. Brigham announced on August 3 his intention "to have the ox teams start back on Monday next, and the horse teams in two weeks from that time."[88] He felt a heavy responsibility to provide adequately for those who would stay behind and the close to two thousand who would join them in the fall.

The general work of raising a city was accompanied by frequent explorations of the valley. One memorable expedition took place soon after the pioneers' arrival, when Brigham led a party of sixteen to the shores of the Salt Lake—and beyond. "All bathed in the Lake," reported Thomas Bullock, "which they found so very salt[y] that no man could sink in it and so warm that no one had a desire to retreat from it. A man could sit in it as in a Rocking Chair. . . ."[89] Days later, during a sermon, Brigham remarked that "we want all the brethren who are going back [to Winter Quarters] to go to the Salt Lake and swim. It is almost equal to vinegar to make you smart in the eyes and nose."[90]

The excursion back to Winter Quarters was three-faceted. A vanguard of eleven men, departing on August 11, would lead the way for the ox teams, which would follow in a few days; the two companies would meet near the Platte River, then travel leisurely to Grand Island (239 miles from Winter Quarters), where they would await Brigham's company. It was anticipated that all three parties would arrive at Winter Quarters together.

The first two companies having departed on schedule, Brigham called a special conference on the afternoon of Sunday, August 22.[91] The meeting centered around the welfare of the Saints who would remain in Salt Lake City. Among other things, Brigham warned camp members of the "folly of trading with the Indians here, for if we continued to do so, . . . we would always be molested with them, therefore, we should give them to understand that we were not permitted to trade at this place, but appoint a distant place for that purpose."[92] Four days later, the long trek back to Winter Quarters was under way.

AUGUST 26–SEPTEMBER 30:
". . . going to gad round the Fort . . . ,
or shall we go like respectable men?"

The return was neither as long nor as tedious as had been the trip west. More familiar with the terrain this time, with fewer wagons and less loaded, men and teams found the traveling considerably faster. "We were 42 days from this spot to Great Salt Lake City," wrote Thomas Bullock on September 17. "We are 23 days coming from Great Salt Lake City to this place, . . . or *19 days* quicker on return journey."[93]

There were joyful reunions when Brigham's party met and greeted camps of emigrant Saints on their way to Salt Lake Valley. The first of these companies, headed by Daniel Spencer, was encountered on September 4; the two groups spent an amiable evening together. Parting the next morning, several of Brigham's company, having found members of their families in Spencer's group, elected to return with them to the valley.

Not long afterward, stopping at noon along the banks of Little Sandy, the pioneers met Parley P. Pratt's company and stayed together for the afternoon and evening. Another day and twenty-six miles later they encountered three additional companies of Saints, clustered together on the banks of a small stream.

On the morning of September 7, having been apprised that John Taylor's company was encamped on the Sweetwater a few miles to the east, Brigham sent a messenger to request that they remain where they were until he and his group arrived. When the pioneers appeared in midafternoon, having traveled some fourteen miles through a heavy snowstorm, they found a banquet in the making. Thomas Bullock described the evening, which began with

> a supper in a Willow Grove for the Pioneers which was furnished with Roast and boiled Beef, Veal (they had killed the fatted Calf to make merry), Pies, Cakes, Biscuits, Butter, Peaches with Coffee, Tea, Sugar, Cream and a variety of the good things of life. About 60 sat down to the Table first time, the remainder at the second spread, also the 3 Frenchmen who have travelled with us from Fort Bridger and who are going to the States in our Company. Afterwards the brethren and sisters tript "the light fantastic toe" in the dance, making a large fire in the Willow Patches which they kept up until about 10 or 11 o'clock.[94]

During the next day or two, Brigham's party met with the final two companies of westbound Mormons on the trail at that time. One of them was Jedediah M. Grant's company, which included two of Brigham's wives, Eliza R. Snow and Margaret Pierce. Brigham, however, had not forgotten Clara Decker, the wife he had left behind in Salt Lake City, and took a few minutes to pen a note to "My dear Clary":

> While stoping here with the last company, where my famely is and expecting to start the male [mail] tomorrow for the valley I thought I would wright you a fue lines. My helth is good and has been sence I left the valley with the exception of one night. . . . I due feel to bless and pray for you. You have been a grate comfort to me this sumer. I miss your society. I wish you to live at [the] home of sister Eliza Snow.
>
> You must pray for me and my safe return. Give my love to your mother

[Harriet Decker Young, Lorenzo's wife], . . . I shall start as early in the spring [of 1848] as I can. . . .

I almost feele it my duty to return with the companies and see them safe through to the valle, O that I had my famely here.[95]

Brigham also took occasion, before the departure of the westbound company, to send along a special letter of advice about planting:

> As you are located in a new country and untried climate, and as we know the drouth to be great in the latter part of summer, we recommend that you begin to plant and sow such seeds [corn, grain, vegetables, etc.] as soon as the snow is gone in the spring, so that we might know by experiments whether it is possible to ripen grain in the valley before the summer drouth shall demand the labor of irrigation.[96]

It was with considerable chagrin that the eastbound Saints awoke on the cold morning of September 9 to find themselves between forty and fifty horses short, the Indians having stolen them during the night. Only about five of the animals were recovered, a circumstance that placed heavy burdens upon the remaining horses in camp. Brigham, Heber, and others who had been accustomed to riding on horseback could no longer do so. A similar incident later cost the camp eleven additional horses, but these were recovered following an "interview" between Brigham and the Indian chief in question.

Meanwhile, Clayton's ox teams had rendezvoused with the advance party of horsemen at the Upper Platte ferry on September 8; they were to continue on together. A week later, inexplicably, Clayton decided to speed up their progress, apparently disregarding Brigham's instructions to wait for the main camp at Grand Island. "In consequence of some things which have passed and some which at present exist," wrote Clayton, "I have concluded to go on as fast as circumstances will permit to Winter Quarters and I intend to start tomorrow. Some have opposed it, but not with a good grace. However, I have no fears that the council will censure me when they know the cause. If they do, I will bear the censure in preference to what I now bear."[97] Subsequent entries seem to indicate that the camp was doubly plagued, by shortages of provisions and by internal contention.

By September 24, less than a month from their leave-taking of Salt Lake City, Brigham's party had traveled more than five hundred miles and were approaching Fort John (Laramie). Gathering members of the camp around him early in the morning, Brigham enquired "if every man was going to gad round the Fort on our arrival there, without any regularity, or shall we go like respectable men?"[98] The unanimous vote was that "we all behave ourselves like Gentlemen, and mind our own business."[99]

Two wagons mired in a slough on September 29; while the brethren tugged them out with ropes, one of the camp's more adventurous canines killed a skunk—"a small black animal which stunk in a dreadful manner," wrote Thomas Bullock. "The dog then leaped into 2 other Wagons which it did not belong to, and kicked up a bad stink by rubbing itself against the clothes. On being put out, it went into the river to wash itself." Next day, the dog tried again: "Saw another skunk which 'Trip' seized behind, but immediately released his hold again on account of its offensive odor, which stunk all the neighborhood."[100]

OCTOBER 1–31:

"We have accomplished more than we expected. . . .

the blessings of the Lord have been with us."

Mild, pleasant weather accompanied the party into October, as did increasing numbers of buffalo, antelope, and Indians. Two of the three being fair game, camp hunters determined to provide a good store of meat, as many in the camp were virtually destitute of flour and other provisions. Unable to do much about the Indians, who were, as usual, horse-hungry, the travelers were at least conscientious about keeping up the guard. One afternoon, in fact, the lookout overreacted: "No sooner had some of the animals been loosed from the traces, than the cry of 'brethren, gather up your horses, a band of Indians is coming on us!' On close examination it proved to be a large herd of elk coming down the hill behind us."[101]

While plentiful game was a boon, herds of buffalo and antelope had virtually stripped the plains of greenery, creating a serious shortage of feed for the horses, some of which were "failing quite rapidly." Thomas Bullock recorded that "the brethren have to assist 'Jacob,' 'Moses,' and 2 or three other horses who are nearly worn out, to get on their feet every morning. We have several horses that are obliged to be driven loose every day and several are very weak, that we are afraid will 'give out' almost every day."[102] Horace Whitney's poignant journal entry may have reflected a general camp sentiment: "My pony continuing to fail rapidly to night, I turned him loose; considering that it was as well for him to live and be stolen by the Indians, as to die by starvation among us."[103]

On October 4, the travelers had come upon a guideboard posted by Clayton: "Camp of Pioneers, stopt here & killed & dried 30 buffalo cows, Sept. 28, 1847." From this news, camp leaders placed the ox teams' progress at about six days ahead of them. Because several of their horses were failing and they were in need of support and assistance, "it was deemed advisable to raise volunteers to go ahead on foot, and arrest the progress of the ox teams."[104] Twelve men volunteered for the mission, and Brigham prepared a letter to be carried to the ox team captains, instructing them to "stop, and kill buffaloes and dry the meat till we should come up, that they may relieve us of some of our wagons, or, at least, some of the loads in them."[105] But the ox teams were already hurrying on their way; the volunteers were simply unable to overtake them and finally gave up the chase, camping until the main group caught up with them on Saturday, October 16. Amasa Lyman, leader of the discouraged dozen, reported "that they had been down to Grand Island and there discovered evidences of the Ox Teams being several days ahead last Tuesday, that they were perfectly satisfied that the Ox Teams were running ahead at twenty-five miles a day, perfectly reckless of their promises and determined to leave us at the mercy of the weather . . . that it would be necessary for us to halt here and kill so much meat as would carry us to Winter Quarters. . . . Accordingly it was decided to go to the banks of the Platte and halt until we could get the buffalo meat, and then pursue our journey as best we could."[106]

Weary, disappointed, and concerned for their weakening horses, Brigham and his companions decided to camp and retrench for a day or two. They had hardly resumed their journey on the morning of October 18 when they met a company of sixteen horsemen, fresh from Winter Quarters and laden with provisions and grain, messages from the folks at home, and even a reinforcement of horses.[107] These, together with fresh meat killed by their hunters, made it possible to proceed with renewed energy toward Winter Quarters.

October 23 found the company encamped on the banks of the Platte River's Loup Fork. The plan was to ford the river early the next morning; however, high winds and shifting quicksands made the crossing too hazardous, and the attempt was delayed overnight. Finally successful, the Mormons camped at a deserted Pawnee village on the twenty-fifth. That evening a small detail was sent ahead to Winter Quarters, "to apprise the brethren there that we were close by, and to allay the anxiety that they might feel at our prolonged absence from home."[108]

Snow flurries and strong, chilly winds made the going uncomfortable, but visions of home, friends, and families so near at hand likely spurred the returnees to a more lively march than they had attempted for many days. "We halted only *once* during the day to water our horses," noted Horace Whitney on October 29—and by the afternoon of the thirtieth they were within easy traveling distance of Winter Quarters.[109] Gathering the men around him, Brigham called for a vote as to whether or not they should march ahead to their final destination that very night. Consensus was that "we should all remain in a body, horsemen and all, and go into town together" the following day.[110] But that last evening on the trail was far from lonely, for sunset brought a welcoming party from Winter Quarters—some twenty wagons, "many friends, bringing food and grain."[111]

The final hours and moments of the epic trek were recorded in Brigham's own words:

> Sunday, 31 [October]. When we were about one mile from Winter Quarters the wagons of the Twelve came to the front, when I remarked:
> Brethren, I will say to the Pioneers, I wish you to receive my thanks for your kindness and willingness to obey orders; I am satisfied with you: you have done well. We have accomplished more than we expected. Out of one hundred forty-

three men who started, some of them sick, all of them are well; not a man has died; we have not lost a horse, mule, or ox, but through carelessness; the blessings of the Lord have been with us. If the brethren are satisfied with me and the Twelve, please signify it (which was unanimously done). I feel to bless you all in the name of the Lord God of Israel. You are dismissed to go to your own homes. . . .

We drove into the town in order, about an hour before sunset. The streets were crowded with people to shake hands as we passed through the lines; we were truly rejoiced to once more behold our wives, children and friends after an absence of over six months, having traveled over 2000 miles, sought out a location for the saints to dwell in [in] peace, and accomplished the most interesting mission in this last dispensation.[112]

10 ✤

To Zion, 1848

Let all Saints who love God more than their own dear selves—
and none else are Saints—gather without delay to the place
appointed . . . to the mountains of the Lord's house . . .[1]

D U R I N G the 1847 trek, the time and energies of Brigham Young and his associates in the Twelve and Council of Fifty were absorbed by the immediate demands of pioneering. Formal meetings of the Twelve "and council" did not resume until they had returned to Winter Quarters in August and set about preparing the church for the migration west in 1848. The first such council listened to reports of what had transpired during the summer and discussed matters that needed immediate attention: How could they arrange to move the poor? Should they sell the temple? But with Brigham's nudging, the meetings quickly moved to another level of concern: what should be the organization of the church now that a new Zion had been established and the Twelve would soon be scattered on individual assignments? It was time, concluded Brigham, to consider the option of organizing a First Presidency and shifting the burden of administration to such Presidency, freeing up the Twelve for their designated responsibilities of traveling throughout the world.

In mid-November 1847, the Twelve began a series of lengthy discussions and prayer sessions that reached their climax on December 5 when they unanimously decided to organize a First Presidency under Brigham Young.[2] They also agreed that the President had the right to nominate his counselors—men who might come from outside the presiding quorums—and that the Twelve would then approve or "sustain" that selection. Heber Kimball and Willard Richards were accordingly nominated by Brigham and sustained by the Twelve. Three weeks later, on December 27, 1847, when a hall large enough to accommodate a public conference had been constructed, the new First Presidency was formally sustained by the Iowa members of the church.

The debate prior to that action is important because it set the stage for the structure of church government and for the subsequent assignments of the Twelve under the new Presidency.

There was no disagreement that the Twelve had the right to organize a First Presidency, nor was anyone hesitant to acknowledge that Brigham would, by right, head it. At issue was, as Orson Pratt put it, the "propriety or expediency now" of so doing when the church had prospered for three and a half years under a group leadership. Concerns voiced by Pratt and others about changing the arrangement attested to the full participation the Twelve had thus far enjoyed under Brigham's leadership. We have already noted that on August 12, 1844, within a few days of the Twelve's return to Nauvoo following Joseph's death, the Twelve sustained Brigham, Heber, and Willard as an executive committee of the quorum to manage the general affairs of the church. They had thereafter constituted a de facto Presidency. Nevertheless, the apostles did not welcome any arrangement that would diminish their involvement in direction of the church. "I am perfectly ready to act in any place as one of the Twelve in anything that may be necessary," declared the amiable George A. Smith, but was it necessary?

Brigham maintained that he had believed since Joseph's death that a Presidency would one day be required, and that the only question was when. Until now they had gone forth with an imperfect organization—whipping the apostates with one hand behind their backs, as it were.[3] He had remained unwilling "to broach the subject until I felt it duty," Brigham explained, and until he knew "the Spirit would let me do it." But during the return from the Great Salt Lake Valley "the Spirit [told] me [that] the Church ought to be now organized." The Twelve, Brigham explained, "must be cut loose [for] their mission [is] to all the nations of the Earth where the First Presidency [can] not go."[4] In the three and a half years since Joseph Smith's death, the Twelve had completed the temple, helped the Saints receive their endowments, managed the exodus from Nauvoo, and established a new Zion. Much of their headquarters responsibilities had thus been discharged, and it was again time to attend to concerns in other parts of the world.

As to their fear of losing influence, Brigham reminded the apostles of the precedent of Joseph Smith's Presidency, during which there were frequent consultations with the Twelve, along with their travel assignments.[5] But members of the Twelve recalled how Brigham had publicly chastised some of them for errors of judgment during the trek west. They were mortified that this had been done before it was fully aired in the quorum. Brigham responded with some vigor that public acts may require public chastisement and that, as their leader, he had an inescapable responsibility to condemn wrongdoing.[6] When the Twelve made errors, he was duty-bound to act in his office and speak his mind:

> If I have to mouthpiece, I have to be so in councilling, in dictating. . . . I know my standing before God. . . . As the lot is mine, dont quarrel with it. I am going to go it, the Lord being my helper . . . and if I see you going to the Devil I will

head you [off] and prevent you. . . . Gentlemen, I will chastise you when I please
and how I please and now help yourselves.[7]

The issue was broader than the matter of chastisement, of course. The
question was a basic one about the President's rights and responsibilities as
"the principal spokesman for God on earth." Like Joseph, Brigham insisted
he would not be trammeled. If he had to "run to my brethren before I can
speak before the public," it would be better to join Joseph in the grave. God's
spokesman cannot be "trammeled"; a basic matter of church government was
at issue.[8] When every apostle had expressed his feelings on this issue, Heber
Kimball summarized the position of the quorum by declaring that they could
not have a mouthpiece of the Lord if they insisted on telling him what he
could say and when and where. Rather, the Twelve should pray that Brigham
act in wisdom by the Spirit. Should that ever fail, and he speak in chastisement
unwisely, they should pray that they have the Spirit to bear it in patience. "I
will be free," Brigham insisted, and "if you tie me up you will see the whipple
trees and chains fly."[9]

As for the proper relationship between himself and the rest of the Twelve,
Brigham was forthright: "If this body [the Twelve] is the head of the Church
and I am the head of the Quorum [then] I am the mouthpiece and you are
the belly."[10]

Brigham's confidence in his own leadership—he consistently maintained
that he had the keys, the calling, and the Spirit as a guide—was such that he
assured his brethren he would counsel with them, but would not seek a sustaining vote before every move. The church was not a democracy where each
man or even each apostle cast a vote to see what God willed. Joseph Smith
did not test his revelations by open debate in the Twelve; nor would Brigham.
Having established this basic principle, however, he admitted that he had not
always acted in perfect wisdom. "I mean to improve by my tongue and guard
it more . . . I mean to improve," he said. "When I feel anything by the Spirit
of the Almighty there is no flinch here," he said, but

> I do mean that my tongue shall not offend my brethren. I shall and do want to
> grow with you. I feel towards the Twelve [the] same as I do my pet young ones,
> that I could put them in my pockets same as my Wives and Children. I mean to
> act according to the Holy Ghost. I want to put you in my pockets so that when
> I want to talk with you, I put my hand in my pocket, take you out and talk with
> you.[11]

Feeling that they had reached a unified position, the Twelve then met in
the newly constructed Log Tabernacle on December 27, 1847, and made public
their decision. Orson Pratt, who had contended most strongly against the
organization of the Presidency, conducted the business, explaining to the con-

gregation that "the time has come when the Twelve must have their hands liberated to go abroad among the nations of the earth." The Twelve had been faithful to Joseph's charge, declared Brigham in his remarks. "[We] have proven to God, Saints and all manner of sinners and devils that we can carry the Kingdom off triumphant."[12]

Sustained by the Saints assembled, buoyed up by a solemn "Hosanna Shout," Brigham proclaimed it one of the happiest days of his life.[13] Freed from administrative responsibilities, the Twelve accepted a variety of assignments. Some remained on the Missouri to preside over the Saints remaining behind when the Presidency moved to the Salt Lake Valley that spring; others took up duties in the East, or in Europe, to resume the work of conversion and gathering.

W I T H the completion of the trek, the next step was to gather the Saints to the Great Basin in ever-increasing numbers. With such a goal in mind, Brigham issued a lengthy epistle to the general membership of the church, dated December 23, 1847, calling upon Latter-day Saints throughout the world to "gather yourselves together speedily, near to this place [Winter Quarters], on the east side of the Missouri River, and, if possible, be ready to start from hence by the first of May next, or as soon as grass is sufficiently grown, and go to the Great Salt Lake City, . . . To the Saints in England, Scotland, Ireland, Wales, and adjacent islands and countries, we say, emigrate as speedily as possible to this vicinity."[14]

Brigham gave detailed instructions for the emigration—which routes to travel, appropriate clothing for the journey, the keeping of accurate historical records, advice on trading of goods and services, and a liberal dose of aesthetic and spiritual motivation:

> Let all Saints who love God more than their own dear selves—and none else are Saints—gather without delay to the place appointed, bringing their gold, their silver, their copper, their zinc, their tin, and brass, and iron, and choice steel, and ivory, and precious stones; their curiosities of science, of art, of nature, and every thing in their possession or within their reach, to build in strength and stability, to beautify, to adorn, to embellish, to delight, and to cast a fragrance over the House of the Lord; with sweet instruments of music and melody and songs and fragrance and sweet odours, and beautiful colours, whether it be in precious jewels, or minerals, or choice ores, or in wisdom and knowledge, or understanding, manifested in carved work; or curious workmanship of the box, the fir and pine tree, or any thing that ever was, or is, or is to be, for the exaltation, glory, honour, and salvation of the living and the dead, for time and for all eternity. Come, then, walking in righteousness before God, and your labour shall be accepted; . . . for the time has come for the Saints to go up to the mountains of the Lord's house, and help to establish it upon the tops of the mountains.[15]

By May of 1848, nearly two thousand Saints were ready to make the journey under Brigham's direction. "Every exertion," wrote a member of the company, "is making to go West."[16]

Thomas Bullock, who had kept a detailed journal of the 1847 trek, again accepted responsibility for chronicling the day-to-day events of the 1848 "camp." He did so with a comparative eye, frequently evaluating the journey's progress in light of "what it was last year when pioneering."[17] Bullock's painstaking census of Brigham's division included 397 wagons, 1,229 souls, 74 horses, 1,275 oxen, 699 cows, 184 loose cattle, 411 sheep, 141 pigs, 605 chickens, 37 cats, 82 dogs, 3 goats, 10 geese, 2 beehives, 8 doves, and a solitary crow.[18]

After spending several days on horseback between Winter Quarters and Elkhorn assuring that everything was in order, Brigham and his immediate family departed May 26. Brigham's own notation reads, "On the 26th I started on my journey to the mountains, leaving my houses, mills and the temporary furniture I had acquired during our sojourn there [Winter Quarters]. This was the fifth time I had left my home and property since I embraced the gospel of Jesus Christ."[19] Others in the division having arrived during the last days of May, Brigham organized his division into groups of hundreds, fifties, and tens, with corresponding leaders. General camp instructions were: "Not to abuse cattle but take care of them; not to yell and bawl or make any noise nor to be up at nights; but attend prayers and go to bed by nine and put out the fires."[20]

By June 3, when the first wagons pulled out of the Elkhorn encampment, the emigrants had ferried nearly three hundred wagons across the river, established workable camp regulations, and had begun to function as a responsible unit. They had also welcomed three new babies and buried three small children and a young mother.

One disturbing incident occurred almost at the very start. A rule had been established that no wagon in the procession should stop, because this would cause a break in the train and encourage an Indian attack. Lucy Groves attempted to climb out of her wagon while it was in motion. Weak from having given birth just ten days before, she slipped and fell in front of the front wheel. It ran over her body and broke three ribs. Her husband was standing close by and grabbed her as quickly as he could to prevent the hind wheel from running over her too. But her leg was broken as well. Brigham went to her immediately, set her leg, and gave her a blessing assuring her that she would reach Salt Lake in good condition.

Lucy's children had to walk from then on, as the bed upon which she lay took up all the room in the wagon. Her thirteen-year-old daughter assumed her mother's tasks—cooking, washing, caring for the little children. But on the ninth day out, when it seemed that the leg was knitting satisfactorily and Lucy soon would be up, the daughter accidentally stumbled over her mother's leg, breaking it a second time. This time the pain was so severe that Lucy cried out in agony at every step the oxen took. She finally told her husband that he would have to pull out of the train and stop. When Brigham saw the wagon pull to one side, he stopped the entire train and rode back to where Lucy was. Tears were falling down her cheeks as she explained the situation and urged him to go on without them. Brigham replied that he would do no such thing; he would not leave any of his people alone. Instead, he made camp for the night, sawed off the tops and bottoms of the legs of the poster bed so there was nothing left but the frame around the mattress and the springs, which were laced across pioneer style. He fastened this to the wagon bows so it would swing easily, like a hammock. He then renewed his blessing to Lucy, promising her she would live many years. He rode by her side for several days to make sure that she had no further trouble. "With his gentle kind manner," wrote Lucy's grandson, "he won the love of Lucy and her posterity forever."[21]

One of Brigham's teamsters, Oliver Huntington, who had just returned from a mission to England, wrote that on the way up the Platte River, through the Black Hills and other desolate portions of the trail, they occasionally made camp early in order to take advantage of good camping grounds.

> On such occasions [Brigham] would walk around the great corral formed by the 270 wagons formed in a circle, and when he came to a teamster or others that offered him an inviting occasion to sit down and "chat," down he went on the wagon tongue, ox yoke, or anything else convenient, not refusing even the earth, where there were a few bunches of grass.
>
> On some of these occasions I enjoyed personally his visit, and there on that old flat wagon tongue with the end resting on an ox-yoke, we sat and talked of the many places we were both acquainted with in Preston, Clithero, and other shires and towns in England.
>
> Then turning conversation to the West, he related incidents in pioneering his way to the great valley of Salt Lake, the year previous, 1847.
>
> Those conversations to me were fairly enchanting. I listened with that attention that never allows the mind to forget.[22]

Following the north bank of the Platte River, the unwieldy troupe moved so slowly that Brigham became concerned. Calling his captains together on the evening of June 6, he suggested that they "perfect their organizing." They would form smaller companies that would travel double file. Slower teams would start an hour earlier than the others; if they had not arrived at the night's camping place in time to join in the corral, they would simply form a line inside.[23]

B Y mid-June the company had arrived at the west side of the Loup Fork encampment, on a northern tributary of the Platte, and the men were busy getting their wagons across the river's swift current and shifting quicksands; "Pres. B.Y. in person crossed & recrossed back & fourth, untill he saw all over safe."[24]

On the afternoon of June 15 a messenger, accompanied by rain, hail, thunder, and lightning, rode into camp with the news that several days earlier Heber Kimball's camp at Cedar Creek had been attacked by Indians. The fracas had left two of Kimball's men wounded, an ox killed, and four Indians dead. Alarmed, some of Brigham's company formed an impromptu scouting expedition, "but no discovery was made of Indians."[25] Within a few days Kimball's group had caught up with Brigham's, and no further incidents were reported.

The tasks of herding and guarding, wrote Oliver Huntington, "together with my daily tasks, kept me beat down and wore out all the time. The women were as well drove beat down as the men."[26] Yet some among them could not resist viewing the trek as high adventure. Louisa Barnes Pratt, who had apparently begun the journey with considerable misgivings, recorded a growing appreciation for the simple pleasures of pioneer life. She and her companions began to enjoy climbing mountains to pick fruit, were inspired by "the grandeur of nature" and delighted by "the wild flowers on the banks of the rivers."[27]

Brigham was less inspired by nature than by the exemplary behavior of the Saints. "Never has there been a people of the same number since the days of Enoch [the ancient prophet who "walked with God"] that has journeyed under the same circumstances with less murmuring and complaining than this people has," he declared. "From the spirit I have seen manifested, I am inclined to think that the peace, love, and union that is in the Camps of Israel will continue to increase." Realist that he was, however, he told the camp in their fourth Sunday meeting since leaving Winter Quarters that he wanted all to understand before they went any farther "that if it was for the riches, honors, glory, comfort, and enjoyment that they expect to receive in this world, they had better have stayed in the states or in their own country." "You can get apples and peaches as easily in Pittsburgh as in the Salt Lake Valley," he declared. "Should any want to return now, I will have you guarded safe back to Winter Quarters. But if it is for the reward of immortality and eternal life beyond the veil, then persevere and live so as to obtain it."[28]

The Platte River country, scenic as it was by Louisa Pratt's standards, made difficult going for teams and wagons. Punishingly hot, dusty days (during one of them, reported Hosea Stout, "One ox of John Alger melted and died"), soft ground, and sandy ridges combined to slow their progress to sometimes fewer than ten miles per day. Wood and water were fast becoming scarce; "Had to use the bois de vache or buffalo chips for fuel which were damp which made rather an unfavorable impression on our women relative to being entirely confined to them before we get to our journey's end."[29] Each day's journey usually meant the digging of a new well, as Platte River water was unsuitable for drinking.

Some days later, Brigham faced again—this time on a much larger scale—the same problem he had encountered on the 1847 march: the wanton, reckless killing of buffalo by his men. As in the previous year, he had appointed camp hunters to kill only enough meat for consumption by the pioneers. But by the first day of July, when swarms of buffalo had appeared like "black clouds in the prairie," allegiance to Brigham's instructions had dissolved in the wake of hunting fever, which "seized on the brethren and they, regardless of the previous arraingements to let hunters kill our meat, often ran and left their teams pursuing & shooting at the buffalo all day. Many were killed and left out, & but few brought into camp." Brigham was incensed and "reproved the people for the course they had taken." Thomas Bullock disgustedly recorded the names of five men who had killed and wounded five buffalo and left them on the prairie to waste. Only one brought a tongue into camp: "A wicked destruction of life and scores in the camp wanting meat to eat this day."[30]

Louisa Pratt, who had likely never seen a buffalo before, was quite taken with the beasts:

> Nothing could be more exciting than to see them in large droves or herds, marching as orderly as a company of soldiers; nothing seemed to daunt them. If they were headed towards our traveling companies, we would make a wide passage for them to cross our path; and they would march along so majestically with their great bushy heads, turning neither to the right or left, not seeming to notice us at all; while we would stare at them with breathless anxiety, thinking how easily they might crush our wagons and do us great injury were they to become furious. The men would not fire upon them when they were near us, but follow them to their haunts, capture one, kill, and haul it to camp with two yoke of oxen. The meat would keep sweet without salt till perfectly dried.[31]

July 4 again had its ironic overtones. "Today," recorded Hosea Stout, "is our Nation's annaversary or birth day of her liberty while we are fleeing exiles from her tyranny & oppression."[32] Bullock chose this day to bring the mileage record up to date: "The Pioneer Camp [of 1847] was 30 days travelling from the Horn to this place. This Camp (B.Y.'s) also 30 days travelling from the Horn to this place. Pioneers travelled 27 days, lay by 3. This Camp travelled 21 days, lay by 9. Average 14⅔ Miles per day."[33]

A few days later Brigham and his company had an encounter with a group of disenchanted Mormon settlers heading east from Salt Lake City. The two camps were on opposite sides of the river at Ash Hollow, about 380 miles from Winter Quarters, on July 8. Bullock reported the exchange:

> On the opposite side the river James Field, Sears, Stodham and Waters from the [Salt Lake] Valley, with Mr. Rashiaw [phonetic rendering of French pronunciation of Richards], an Indian trader, were camped. The four brethren were going back with their families to get a fit-out for the Pacific. One of them reports that they cannot die there unless they take poison, and the other that they die too sudden. They give contradictory reports. They seem to stagger because a good man (Bishop Foutz) should die (Foutz was poisoned by eating wild roots) and are afraid nothing can be made there. Wm. Weeks [architect of the Nauvoo Temple who had apparently been involved in some questionable business dealings] had

run away from Ash Hollow two days ago. He was afraid to see Brigham. Field
conversed with Prest. Young some time. He [Brigham] told Field when he saw
Weeks to tell him he shall not have any peace in his mind until he comes to the
valley and makes restitution for the wickedness he has committed and cursed him
in the name of the Lord, and also tell him we can build a Temple without his
assistance, altho' he (Weeks) says we cannot. The People said "Amen."[34]

Oliver Huntington took time on July 9 to comment on the general condition of the camp—and to record an incident that caused Brigham to chuckle:

As yet the camp and in fine, all the camps had got along well, and with few
accidents. Three had been run over in our camp and one wagon turned over
which was brother Gates'. He blamed his women severely for it, and what mortified
him worse than all, it disclosed a bottle of wine; before unknown. The wagon
turned square bottom side up, no one in it. That night he quarreled with his wife
and whipped her. The guard about 11 o'clock saw it and when the hour came to
cry, he loudly cried 11 o'clock, all is well and Gates is quarreling with his wife like
hell.[35]

Not many miles outside of Ash Hollow, the flat monotony to which the
pioneers had become accustomed gave way to dramatic bluffs lined with cedar
shrubs. The crossing at Castle Bluff Creek was complicated by tenacious quicksand, but the task was accomplished "by doubling teams and patience." Farther
on were the Ancient Bluff Ruins, which, according to Oliver Huntington,
"very closely resembled the ruins of castles and towns in the old countries.
There is a large portion of bluffs along here very high and in shapes and
appearance like ruins of art." By July 12 they had come in sight of Chimney
Rock; later they set up camp "about a mile beyond our Old Pioneer Camp
Ground of 22 May last." Here they were approached by a company of Sioux
Indians, described by Hosea Stout as "very friendly and altogether the best
looking and neatest Indians I ever saw. Proud spirited & seemed to disdain
to beg & the men would seldom condescend to trade in small articles like
moccasins but would have their Squaws do it."[36]

O N E Sabbath in mid-July, as Bullock was "busy preparing the Mail for the
Valley," Brigham went to his wagon and instructed him "to write an Epistle
to the Saints in the Valley. He told me I had been a copyist long enough and
from henceforth I must write all the Epistles and Letters and told me to dive
right strait into the Spirit of it." Later that evening, three mail carriers were
appointed to ride to the Salt Lake Valley with "205 letters from Winter Quarters
and about 54 since starting. Also sent 6 General Epistles, 5 Newspapers, the
Statistics of the Camps, and tied same up in my yellow handkerchief."[37]

While encamped near the Ancient Bluff Ruins, a mare belonging to Captain E. Miller was bitten by a rattlesnake. By next morning the horse was
"verry bad, not able to travel." Because of diverse opinions among company

leaders, it was determined that the entire company would "lay by" until the following morning. "Soon after," recorded John D. Lee,

> Squire Wells, Pres. B.Y.'s Aidecamp rode up to enquire the cause of our delay. . . . In the mien time Capt. John Wakeley & Wilson G. Perkins returned, said that they Saw Pres. B.Y., told him the cause of the delay of the co. He replied that it would not do to stop a whole co. because a Horse was bitt by a snake, to go & tell Capt. E. Miller to mix the spirits of Turpentine with Tabacco, wash the wound, Pray for the recovry of the Beast & start her on, for should the co. stay till morning they will likely have more horses bit. Just before this information reached camp Capt. J.D. Lee discovered that one of his Horses was bit by a snake on the under Jaw. He however fortunately used the Pres.'s remedy which soon counteracted the poison. At this instruction the whole co. gathered up their teams and roled out.[38]

Despite the often tortuous physical aspects of the journey, not to mention the weight of his leadership responsibilities, Brigham refused to let himself be burdened unduly. In order that his body could keep pace with his mind, as he expressed it, Brigham joined with his fellow migrants in occasional dancing, songfests, and comical readings. "About Dark" on July 20, "Capt. J.D. Lee & Wilson G. Perkins rode to Pres. B.Y.'s Camp, found them enjoying themselves firstrate upon the melodious charm of the drum & violin."[39] One young woman, traveling with the same body but in a different company from Brigham's, recalled an exasperating visit to Independence Rock: "We heard so much of Independence Rock long before we got there. They said we should have a dance on top of it, as we had many a dance while on the plains. We thought it would be so nice, but when we got there, the company was so small it was given up. . . . We had not a note of music or a musician. I was told afterwards by some of the girls that we had travelled with that they had a party there, but President Young had all the music with him."[40]

After several difficult days bucking "the heaviest sandy road we had since we started and no grass of any importance," Brigham's company doubled their teams and crossed the Platte to its south side, where they joined the Oregon Trail. On July 22 they passed Fort Laramie, crossed the Laramie River without incident, and set up camp in the early evening, surrounded by "Plenty of Timber and Choke Cherries. The mountain scenery interspersed with Cedar and Pine Trees looks pretty to me," wrote Bullock. He also noted that the 1847 camp took forty-eight days from Elkhorn to Laramie, and the 1848 company took the same amount of time.[41] The general attitude was expressed by one of the travelers when he wrote: "We are as comfortable and happy as most of the stationary communities. For if we have not all that our wants may call for, we have the art of lessening our wants, which does as well." Nevertheless, wrote Huntington, "cattle are dieing off as though we did not need them any more. Every day takes some. Seven since we stopped here."[42]

About 2:00 P.M. on July 23, Louisa Beaman Young was delivered of male twins, "which verry much delighted Pres. B.Y., the Father of the children."[43] Both mother and twins were apparently in good health and arrived safely in the valley less than two months later.

From Laramie the party approached the Black Hills, and conditions worsened. Higher altitudes brought cold weather, frequent drenching rain and hail storms, sharp mountain ridges and steep stream banks to navigate. Men, women, and animals took sick, causing delays and frustration. Brigham himself had been very ill, perhaps with a viral infection; Bullock reports visiting Brigham's camp on July 30: "Saw him; he was very sick yesterday, confined to his bed and wagon, but is able to be up this morning. Praise the Lord."[44]

Brigham's condition was not helped by the elements. During an early-afternoon shower on August 2, some of the men stopped to gather large hailstones to heat for water. As the camp resumed their journey over the hill to Box Elder Creek, they observed "a tremendous shower" coming toward them. "We got in a gulley," reported Bullock, "huddled up to prepare for it, when it came rushing down upon us as if it were going to sweep our wagon tops away. The thunder kept up one unceasing roll and was awful. I was very thankful when all was over. We again hitched up and started, but the ground being so very slippery, we could not go in the road, but went over the sage bushes for better convenience. Rough work for wagons."[45]

When the rains abated, clouds of choking dust engulfed the travelers. On August 4, 619 miles from Winter Quarters, Bullock recorded that they "rolled away thro' the Sage and Grease Wood plains, having a very dusty road, or as Prest. Young calls it, a dull yellow day." Feed for the animals, he added, "is more scant on this journey than it was on the Pioneer trip, or return journey, scarce any being seen." The next day, a "dull autumnal morning," he worried that "the Wolves strike up a most doleful melancholy howling and are in greater numbers than they have been. Every time I hear them I all but tremble for the safety of some of our Cattle, they being very weak." Indeed, by mid-August, following a disheartening series of livestock deaths (including Brigham's "Charlie Colt"), Bullock observed, "It appears that the way to the Valley of Life for the Saints is thro' the Valley of Death to our Cattle, and it appears as if we are to get to our Journey's end by a miracle, or very narrowly indeed."[46] Many of the animals had died after drinking water from alkali springs.

By August 10 the company had crossed Muddy Creek ("about the worst creek to cross on the route"), forded the Platte for the last time, attended to ailing oxen and battered wagons, ascended and descended challenging Prospect Hill, and were encamped near Independence Rock in the Sweetwater valley, where sage trees grew "10 feet high and as thick as my body." After crossing Grease Wood Creek and traveling several miles over "a very heavy sand road," a number of men in the company fell to gathering supplies of saleratus, "large lakes of which lay like fields of snow crusted sometimes six inches deep over the ground." Soon after the project had begun, "the Prest. rode up in his

Carriage at the time and with Axe in hand commenced operations."⁴⁷ Later in the afternoon Brigham and others climbed Independence Rock for a brief exploration.

Between August 12 and 21, Bullock recorded four separate crossings of the winding Sweetwater River. Grazing for the animals along the river's banks had improved somewhat, although many still went hungry and several died each day of starvation or water poisoning. Long sand hills, steep ascents, and heavy gravel roads took their toll of men, teams, and wagons alike. And the weather was growing colder; most mornings brought "ice on the water pail sufficiently strong to hold the water if turned bottom up."⁴⁸

In the face of such hardship, Hosea Stout recorded with enthusiasm on August 17: "The express met us today from the [Salt Lake] Valley giving us the joyful information that a large number of teams and waggons were on the way to meet us." True to the report, Brigham's brother Lorenzo Young and several others arrived on the twenty-eighth, with promises that 50 wagons and 150 yoke of oxen were on their way. When the larger group pulled into camp two days later, they found an ailing President Young, who earlier in the day "had a severe attack of chills, lay down and slept." Apparently revived by the excitement of the occasion, Brigham greeted the company warmly, "conversed much, over-exerted himself and went to bed very sick."⁴⁹ Meantime, the party from "the valley" reported that their harvest was over and they had reaped 10,000 bushels more than were necessary to feed those already in the valley, so there would be plenty for those coming. "Corn done [as] well as that in the states," they reported, but "wheat suffered much from the crickets and a lack of proper knowledge of irrigation. . . ."⁵⁰

The cold, rainy, and generally miserable days of early September did little to dampen either the "hideous howling" of the wolves or the dogged determination of the Saints. Brigham, still weak but "on the mend," announced his intention of traveling to Pacific Springs, nearly thirteen miles distant, and encouraged "those who are ready, to clear out." It was a steep climb to the dividing ridge of the South Pass, and their descent was accompanied by a heavy thunder and hailstorm. "Came to a halt when it was dark," recorded Bullock, "and kindled a large fire to be a guide to the teams behind, but the wind and rain put out the fire and I went out to pilot them in. The rain and dark rendering it miserable." The next morning was equally miserable, but for Bullock, at least, there was some compensation: "A beautiful rainbow seen, very near the Earth and spans only over ten waggons and apparently three times the height of the wagons. The lowest I ever saw and very beautiful."⁵¹

By September 3, the company was traveling in view of the snow-covered Wind River mountain chain. During the day, an incident occurred that served to demonstrate Brigham's blend of compassion and discipline. The camp met two families who had left the valley and were returning to Missouri to live. President Young, according to Bullock, "gave them a very severe lecture on their going to serve the Devil among our enemies. On finishing, he told them to go in peace, but never to return to the Valley, until they knew they were Saints indeed, and their names would be blotted out of remembrance." Then, added Bullock, "he gave them 25 lb. Meal to feed them."[52] Later in the day came three additional men from the valley; but they had wagons and oxen to assist the westbound travelers on the remainder of their journey to the Salt Lake Valley.

After a brief stop at Fort Bridger on September 12, the company continued on a southwesterly course toward Evanston and the Bear River. At this point the roads became rougher, the streams swifter, the ascents steeper, and the descents more treacherous in the wake of heavy rains. Bullock wrote that "on reaching the 'Muddy Fork' (which was dry) I found Prest. Young driving his team, who then requested me to ride with him in his carriage. He had a few newspapers which I read to him thro' the day. This day," Bullock added, "has been the coldest we have had, a perfect cutting wind, which benumbs many." The next morning it was "snowing rapidly & so we hurried on to decend out of the clouds & make our decent down a very steep hill for near two miles; our teams litterally slid down."[53]

Between September 17 and 19, a "gathering" apparently took place among the Saints preparatory to their entry into the Salt Lake Valley. Throughout the journey various companies had been in the lead position, with others strung out behind them over many miles. In fact, Brigham's company was rarely in the forefront, for the president and his companions were often to be found assisting companies who had suffered illness, injury, or mechanical break-downs. But now, nearing the end of their long march, those ahead of Brigham's group stopped and waited. "This halt," wrote John Pulsipher, "was in honor of President Young, the leader of Israel. The companies that have traveled ahead of him, except a few stragglers, stopped and waited until he passed into the valley in his place, at the head of the joyful multitude." When Brigham passed, all fell into line behind him.[54]

Now the long train began its final assault on the Rocky Mountains—only a few short days from the valley, but over some of the roughest terrain the travelers had encountered, "winding thro the deep canyons and over the passes from one creek to another, traveling in every direction but east." Crossing Kanyon Creek meant doing so as many as thirteen times, in addition to "many Springs which are very miry and bad to cross" and the Weber River, "which was deep and flowed rapid." Steep, muddy, uneven roads, together with weakened teams and exhausted drivers, made for an inordinate number of break-downs and other mishaps as wagons lurched up and down mountainsides, rammed into tree stumps in the road, and bogged in the mire of soggy stream beds. Nevertheless, by late afternoon on September 20, Brigham's group and others had finally clawed their way to the summit of Big Mountain, "the highest one we had to ascend on this journey. Here we had a view of the south part of the [Salt Lake] Valley & like old Moses could 'view the landscape o'er' while many hills and bad roads yet intervened." Bullock's joy was unabashed:

"Then we pulled thro' to the top of the Mountain; on reaching the summit and again seeing the Valley my soul could not refrain crying out Hosanna to God and the Lamb for ever, Amen."[55]

Brigham and his immediate company, having taken the lead, entered the Salt Lake Valley on September 20. John Taylor, senior apostle in the Salt Lake Valley, started out on horseback to meet the president, astride "a Spanish pony." As they were riding across the fort where most of the people were living, his horse reared, Taylor was injured, and he could not proceed. Upon his arrival Brigham called to see him. According to Mary Isabella Horne, who was present, Brigham remarked that Taylor's horse was like many people, "only the people had the stiffness in their necks and the horses had it in their legs."[56]

The last wagons rolled into the main fort four days later. That afternoon Brigham addressed a large congregation of Saints at the Bowery (an open-air meeting place covered with limbs and leaves), erected for public meetings on Temple Square. He commended the people for their "industry" and expressed his "joy in being able to come here in safety. That this is the place he had seen before he came here & it was the place for the Saints to geather."[57]

At the end of a 1,031-mile journey, Thomas Bullock recorded "86 travelling days at an average of 12 miles per day; 36 days lay still. Total 122 days from Winter Quarters to Great Salt Lake City."[58]

And Hosea Stout wrote, in turn, of a sweet but hard-won victory over time and circumstance that would have expressed Brigham's feeling:

> Thus ends this long and tedious journey from the land of our enemies, & I feel free and happy that I have escaped from their midst. But there is many a desolate & sandy plain to cross. Many a ruged sage bed to break through. Many a hill and hollow to tug over & many a mountain & canon to pass. And many frosty nights to endure in mid-summer.[59]

Brigham had made his long trek to Zion for the last time. He was in his new home, where he would spend the next twenty-nine years.

11 ✣

The Colonizer President

My soul feels hallelujah, it exults in God, that He has planted
this people in a place that is not desired by the wicked. . . .
I want hard times, so that every person that does not wish to
stay, for the sake of his religion, will leave. This is a good
place to make Saints, and it is a good place for Saints to live.
It is the place the Lord has appointed, and we shall stay here
until He tells us to go somewhere else.[1]

T H E Great Basin, an area approximately the size of Texas, was
the region situated between the Rocky Mountains on the east, the Colorado
River on the south, the Sierra Nevada Mountains on the west, and the watershed of the Columbia River on the north. Its boundaries included nearly
all of the present state of Nevada, most of Utah, the southeastern corner of
Idaho, the southwestern corner of Wyoming, a large area in southeastern
Oregon, much of southern California, and a strip along the eastern border of
California. The most characteristic features were the Great Salt Lake in the
north and the Grand Canyon of Colorado in the south.

In the center, as if to split the basin in two parts, was the Wasatch Range
of the Rockies, running north and south, which dwindled in its southern end
into a series of high, wide, undulating mountain plateaus. One of the dominant
ranges of America, the Wasatch had snow-clad peaks varying from 10,000 to
12,000 feet above sea level. West of the Wasatch was the salty, dry, unyielding
Great Basin desert land, broken by isolated ranges and rich in minerals. To
the east were the towering Uinta Mountains and Uinta Basin, drained by the
Colorado, which were wild and canyonated—not easily traversed or cultivated.
The outstanding characteristics of the Great Basin were its isolation, aridity,
and the scarcity of timber and game. Missouri Valley trading posts were twelve
hundred miles away, transportation to and within the region was difficult, and
rainfall varied from five to sixteen inches per year.[2]

The Mormon communities first founded by Brigham Young were located
along the creeks at the base of the western slopes of the Wasatch. The Great

Salt Lake Valley, the Saints' first semiarid Shangri-la, was a level strip of land from fifteen to twenty miles wide and from twenty to forty miles long, between Great Salt Lake and the Oquirrh Mountains on the west, and the Wasatch Mountains on the east. It occupied the center of what geographers have called the Wasatch or Salt Lake Oasis—an irrigable strip of land from two to twenty miles wide and some two hundred miles long, lying at the western base of the Wasatch. The immense amphitheater, originally with few trees, but abundant grass along the creek banks, was supplied with culinary and irrigating water by many mountain streams. It furnished excellent mill sites, had ample facilities for grazing, and was only occasionally traversed by Indians. Said Brigham:

> We have been kicked out of the frying-pan into the fire, out of the fire into the middle of the floor, and here we are and here we will stay. God . . . will temper the elements for the good of His Saints; he will rebuke the frost, and the sterility of the soil, and the land shall become fruitful.[3]

Within little more than one hundred years, the Salt Lake Oasis would provide a home for almost a million Latter-day Saints.[4]

I N 1847 Brigham had selected a central ten-acre location as the site for a temple. He had chosen the block east of the Temple Block for his own acreage and had allowed the other apostles to select lots around this central location. Salt Lake City was then surveyed and divided up into 114 blocks of ten acres. Each block contained eight lots of one and one-quarter acres. Only one house could be constructed on a lot, and this dwelling had to be set back twenty feet from the front of the property.[5] The streets between the blocks were eight rods wide, enough to enable an ox team with wagon to turn around. The general distribution of these lots began after Brigham's return, in September 1848, when he and Heber supervised a lottery, slips of paper with numbers being drawn by family heads.

A second plat of sixty-three additional blocks to the east of the original plat was next surveyed and distributed. The 177 blocks in these two plats were divided into nineteen ecclesiastical wards, with a bishop in charge of each. Spreading toward the south and west of the city were five-acre plots to provide small farming lands for mechanics and artisans. Farther out, ten- and twenty-acre lots were distributed to those who wished to farm. The number of the land parcel drawn by each person was recorded by Thomas Bullock. One did not pay for the land but was required to provide $1.50 for surveying and filing fee. Bullock's receipt was each man's title to his land. Unmarried men were not given a land allotment, but polygamists were entitled to receive one for each family. Widows and divorced women who were heads of families also participated in the drawings.

The basic land policy for the new commonwealth had been established by Brigham in a talk given July 25, 1847, his first full day in the valley:

No man will be suffered to cut up his lot and sell a part to speculate out of his brethren. Each man must keep his lot whole, for the Lord has given it to us without price. . . . Every man should have his land measured off to him for city and farming purposes, what he can till. He may till as he pleases, but he should be industrious and take care of it.[6]

With regard to general policy, Brigham declared:

We do not intend to have any trade or commerce with the gentile [non-Mormon] world, for so long as we buy of them we are in a degree dependent upon them. The Kingdom of God cannot rise independent of the gentile nations until we produce, manufacture, and make every article of use, convenience, or necessity among our own people. We shall have Elders abroad among all nations, and until we can obtain and collect the raw material for our manufactures it will be their business to gather in such things as are, or may be, needed. So we shall need no commerce with the nations. I am determined to cut every thread of this kind and live free and independent, untrammeled by any of their detestable customs and practices.[7]

On the lot adjoining City Creek that Brigham had chosen for himself he built, in the fall of 1848, a row of log houses on what is now First Avenue, just east of State Street, in downtown Salt Lake City. In these log houses, collectively called Harmony House, were placed his wives and their children. To the south of this "old log row" he built, in 1854, a sun-dried adobe structure to which white plaster was added. This was known as the White House (or sometimes the Mansion House), and in this home were placed Mary Ann and her five children—Joseph A., twenty; Brigham, Jr., eighteen; Alice, fifteen; Luna, twelve; John W., ten. (By this time, Mary Ann, as the "senior wife," was referred to as Mother Young.) Situated on the brow of a hill, with a long line of steps leading up to it and with trees and flower gardens, the White House commanded a view of nearly the entire valley. It is said to have been the first house in Utah with a shingled roof. Of old colonial design, it served for a period as the official headquarters for both church and state in the territory. Nearby were a carriage house, barn, and other outbuildings.

Brigham also supervised the erection of a large adobe house fronting on what was called during his lifetime Brigham Street (now South Temple Street). Still standing, this two-story structure, faced with cement, was constructed with a tower surmounted with a gilded beehive, and thus came to be known as the Beehive House. Beginning in 1855, it served as Brigham's official residence as governor and president of the church. In charge of the house was Brigham's first plural wife, Lucy Ann Decker. At the time she had four children—Brigham Heber, nine; Fanny Caroline, five; Ernest Irving, three; and Shemira, one. Three additional children were born to Lucy during the next six years—Arta De Christa, in 1855; Feramorz Little, 1858; and Clarissa Hamilton, 1860. Some other wives lived for brief periods with Lucy, helping with the housekeeping, cooking, washing, and entertainment.

In 1856 Brigham put up an impressive three-story, thick-walled adobe structure, called the Lion House because of the crouching lion on the portico over the front entrance. Designed by Brigham's brother-in-law, Truman Angell, the Lion House, in which as many as twelve families lived during their growing-up years, was designed to harbor a plural household. This gabled building consisted of twenty-five apartments or rooms. The basement or ground floor included a school and recreation room, washroom or laundry, kitchen, dish room, and dining room on the west side, and pantry, buttery, coachman's room, weaving room, ash house for making soap, and general cellar on the east side. The main floor included a parlor or prayer room and then several rooms for wives with small children on each side. The second floor had twenty single rooms, ten on each side, some of them with fireplaces, others with stoves. These were for the caretaker wives and for older children. The general Young family get-together was at "supper" at five o'clock, followed by a family meeting or "home evening," "family fun," and prayers at 6:30 P.M. An average of about fifty family members sat down to meals.

The activities at the Lion House included school from nine to ten, recess till eleven, dinner at twelve, school again at one-thirty, recess from two-thirty to three, and out by four. The women took turns ironing at night so that there was always someone up to watch out for fire. (Brigham made regular fire inspections of all his properties.) Typical breakfasts were toast, eggs, milk, and stewed fruit. Dinner in the middle of the day, at least when food was plentiful, might consist of beef or lamb, bear or elk or goose, with chicken on Sunday. Supper was not a heavy meal, and usually featured cornmeal mush with cheese, fresh fruit, and bread.[8]

Between the Beehive House and Lion House was the one-story President's Office—really a western extension of the Beehive House—where Brigham and his counselors and clerks met for informal discussions, for conversations with fellow church officers and members, and for "interviews" with visitors.

Designed to be self-sufficient, Brigham's compound included a gristmill, barns and corrals, granaries and outbuildings, a store or commissary, a schoolhouse, and a small private cemetery. By the time he had completed the Lion House, Brigham had eleven connubial wives (those he stayed with on occasion) and thirty-five living children, not counting several caretaker wives and several foster children. His compound was a sizable operation, comparable to a southern plantation, with blacksmith shops, carpentry shops, and assorted other enterprises serving primarily his family and those he looked after. Entrance to the estate, which was surrounded by an eight-foot cobblestone wall, was on the south through the Eagle Gate—a large wooden, hand-carved eagle over a timbered archway mounted on four stone pillars. The Eagle Gate was also the entrance into City Creek Canyon, and for many years city residents paid a toll when entering the canyon on excursions for wood.

Some idea of the size of Brigham's property in the 1850s can be calculated from a "Deed of Consecration," which conveyed all of the property held in his own name to the church. The listed property in 1855, valued at approximately $200,000, included his city compound, valued at $85,000; other city lots valued at $29,000; and farms valued at $24,000. On his properties were 350 range cattle, nine horses, nine mules, fifteen cows, and five pigs. He owned eight wagons, seven carriages and buggies, one sleigh, one threshing machine, several plows and harrows, and such personal property as a gold watch and chain, three silver watches, six clocks, and assorted beds and bedding, crockery and tableware, stoves, and household furniture.[9]

What was life like for one of Brigham's wives? The experience of Zina D. Huntington Jacobs, whom Brigham married at Winter Quarters in 1846, may have been typical. In Nauvoo, Zina had been married to Henry Jacobs, by whom she had two sons. She was later separated. She and her sons were in Brigham's company that journeyed to the Salt Lake Valley in 1848. After living several weeks in her wagon, she moved into one of the log houses on "log row." These homes were "comfortable and shut out the cold," but "the dirt roofs were scarcely protection from rain." Like the other wives, she was fully occupied with household duties—making candles, soap, starch, molasses; carding, spinning, dyeing, knitting, and weaving; and looking after sick children and friends. She gave birth to her first child by Brigham in 1850, a daughter, also named Zina.

When the Lion House was completed in 1856, Zina and her children moved into that building, where she reared not only her own children, but the four of Clarissa Chase, a sister wife who died in 1858. A cheerful person, Zina was the midwife and nurse for most of Brigham's family. She later became an officer of the Relief Society, the woman's auxiliary of the church, and was placed in charge of several programs that were important to Brigham's program of self-sufficiency.[10] Of Brigham, Zina declared, "No man could be more careful of women while bearing their children, thoughtful & kind as far as means could be obtained than was Brigham Young. . . . My two sons, step-sons of his, I do not remember of his ever even speaking sharp to them. In clothes, etc., they shared with his own."[11]

In a January 1856 letter to a sister wife who lived in central Utah, Zina mentions that most of the Young children were down with the measles. "We were just counting them up that had had them [the measles]. Seventeen children and Sally [an Indian foster child of Brigham]. All doing well. . . . The union among the girls [sister wives] is an example in Isreal and truly do I believe the Lord was well pleased with us as a family. . . . Our kind love to all and our dear Husband [Brigham] in particular."[12]

Brigham himself moved from the Old Fort (in 1848), to Log Row (1849–54), to the Mansion House (1854–56), and to the Beehive House (1856–77). Like other Salt Lake Valley dwellers in the early years, he and his family were often short on food and clothing. The days were passed in hard work and preparing for a better future. In general, his wives reared their children without his presence, except for morning and evening prayers and the family meeting after supper, where he read from the Scriptures, presented a short homily, listened to some of the older children sing or play the piano, and gave instruction and advice. Brigham usually "led" in the family prayer as the family knelt behind their chairs in the "parlor" or prayer room each evening. One child later recalled his father's earnestness in prayer when he was continually interrupted by a child of three who was running about and squealing. Exasperated, Brigham arose, took the child to its mother, and returned to his knees and closed his eyes to complete the prayer.[13]

M U C H as he enjoyed being with his family, Brigham devoted nearly all his waking hours to the task of supervising the affairs of the church. Approximately sixteen thousand people were in the Missouri River Valley in 1846, ready for migration to the Great Basin. About sixteen hundred journeyed to the Great Basin in 1847, another three thousand in 1848, and an average of three to four thousand per year until, by the end of 1852, essentially all the Mormon refugees from Illinois were in the Salt Lake Valley. Then began the migrations from Great Britain and Scandinavia, at the rate of approximately three thousand per year. Counting natural increase, and allowing for some desertions to California and elsewhere, by 1857 there were about thirty-five thousand Saints in the Basin, and by 1869 approximately seventy-five thousand. At Brigham's death in 1877 there were about one hundred twenty-five thousand.

To supervise this migration Brigham established in 1849 the Perpetual Emigrating Fund Company, an independently administered arm of the church that supervised the gathering and shipping in Liverpool and the reception and reshipping in New Orleans (before 1854), New York City (after 1854), St. Louis, Winter Quarters (or one of the other frontier outfitting points), and the Salt Lake Valley. The fund (called the PEF in nearly all Mormon literature) collected annual donations in the Great Basin and elsewhere, for financing the ocean voyage, the trip up the Mississippi or by train from the East Coast to the frontier, and the journey by wagon across the plains to the Salt Lake Valley.

Immigrants usually arrived in September or October and spent the winter in one of the nineteen Salt Lake City wards. Men who could work were normally employed during the winter on church public works, helping to erect the tabernacle, the temple, the social hall, the theater, or building roads, canals, fences, walls, or herding church livestock. In the spring the immigrants were organized into colonizing companies and sent to settle a community south or north of Salt Lake City. Some five hundred Mormon communities were founded during Brigham's lifetime, most of them at his suggestion or with his approval.

In settling his people, Brigham at first suffered from a piece of bad advice, whose inaccuracy he did not discover until 1858. Lansford Hastings had told Mormon leaders in Nauvoo that the region north of the Salt Lake and Weber river valleys was too cold to grow crops. This was reaffirmed by Jim Bridger

Earliest known photograph of Brigham
Young, probably taken in Nauvoo,
Illinois, in the early 1840s.

Joseph Smith, Jr., founding prophet
of the Church of Jesus Christ of
Latter-day Saints.

Cabinet made by Young.

Home built by Young in New York State
for his first wife, Miriam Works.

Mormon temple in Kirtland, Ohio.
Young worked on this building, which
was completed in 1836.

Mormon city of Nauvoo, Illinois,
ca. 1845.

Brigham Young's residence in Nauvoo, built by him in 1843.

Young and his second wife, Mary Ann Angell, and their children. After a painting done in Nauvoo in 1843.

RIGHT: Brigham Young in 1847, about the time of the departure of the first pioneer company for the Salt Lake Valley. BELOW: Mormon pioneer company crossing the Plains to Utah.

Heber C. Kimball, early New York friend
who accompanied Young to Utah as
companion and counselor.

lard Richards, cousin, missionary
npanion, and counselor to
gham Young.

LEFT, ABOVE: Daniel H. Wells, mayor of Salt Lake City, superintendent of public works, general of the Nauvoo Legion, and counselor to Young.

LEFT, BELOW: Orson Pratt, Mormon missionary and theologian, and fellow apostle of Young.

ABOVE: Wilford Woodruff, missionary and apostle whose diary recounts many important events in Young's life.

when the advance party reached his fort. The exploring party sent out by Brigham during the early weeks in the region in 1847 concurred. The opinions seemed to be confirmed in the winter of 1855–56, during a drought, when he sent 2,000 head of cattle belonging to the church to Cache Valley in northern Utah, to winter. Only 420 survived.[14] In 1856 he went north to Fort Hall in present-day Idaho and reported the country along the Snake River to be "a sterile, barren, desert country."[15] "The further we go north," he said, "the less good characteristics are connected with the valleys, except in the articles of fish, water, and in some instances, timber."[16] During this period Brigham thought in terms of a line of settlements running south from Salt Lake City to southern California.

In 1849 Brigham commissioned a large exploring party, under the direction of Parley Pratt, to explore the country south to the Virgin River (Rio Virgen) in southern Utah. This group reported many suitable sites for settlement in the southern country, and these formed the basis for the expansion of the Salt Lake base. After settlements had been organized in north and south Salt Lake Valley and along the Weber and Ogden rivers in 1847–48, new communities were opened up in Utah Valley (Provo), Salt River Valley (Nephi), Sanpete Valley (Manti), Sevier Valley (Richfield), Little Salt Lake Valley (Parowan, Cedar City), and on into Las Vegas, Nevada, and San Bernardino, California. Even after the completion of the railroad in 1869, Brigham continued to push settlers into eastern Utah, Arizona, New Mexico, and southern Colorado.[17]

Concentration on the settlement of locations to the south meant that colonists were sent into an environment less favorable (i.e., drier and with less dependable streams for irrigation) than that of the Salt Lake Valley. Saints comfortably established in the headquarters valley and immigrating Saints, primarily European, who wanted to remain in the Salt Lake Valley were not always anxious to move on to these isolated southern colonies. Moreover, the necessity of autarchy forced Brigham to recommend the growing of cotton and other crops that they would not have raised if he had not directed them to do so.

Remembering the unfortunate experiences of the Mormons in Ohio, Missouri, and Illinois, the Mormon leadership was determined to discourage the encroachment of "Gentiles" into the territory. They were equally determined to avoid dependence on non-Mormons for provisions and supplies. Mormons must occupy all habitable spots in the region and must use every exertion to be self-sufficient. In giving encouragement to those called to settle some "hardcase" areas, Brigham came to emphasize not how the prospective site compared with the Salt Lake Valley but how it would be in a few years as the result of their united effort. He would claim that the Salt Lake Valley was a similar desert at the time of its settlement, and that just as the Lord had led them to the valley with good results, so the Lord was now directing them to settle other areas. Brigham also prophesied that God would ameliorate the climate to help them overcome the harsh environment to which they were sent.

This rhetoric was successful in inducing the settlement of such inhospitable areas as southern and eastern Utah, southern Nevada, and central Arizona.[18] One of his talks in the Old Salt Lake Tabernacle is typical:

> The miracles wrought in the days of Moses for the deliverance of the children of Israel from Egyptian bondage as they are recorded in the Old Testament, appear to be wonderful displays of the power of God. . . . The children of Israel, it is written, were brought out of Egypt . . . to inherit a land flowing with milk and honey; we have assembled in these distant valleys for the trial of our faith. They were delivered out of a dreadful bondage, leaving none behind; we have willingly . . . left . . . friends, parents, companions, &c., behind. The distance to their land of promise was but a few miles from the country of their bondage, while a great many of this people have traversed over one-half the globe to reach the valleys of Utah.[19]

Four kinds of colonies were established under Brigham's direction in the 1850s. First, there were settlements intended to serve as temporary places of gathering and recruitment before convert-immigrants moved on to permanent settlements in the Great Basin. An example is Genoa, in Carson Valley, Nevada. Originally known as Mormon Station, later Reese's Station, it grew into a town that was used as a subsidiary gathering place for Saints from the West Coast. Because Brigham saw Genoa as mainly a funnel, he declined to recruit people from the Utah valleys to settle there. He explained to Parley Pratt that neither California nor Carson Valley was meant to be a permanent settlement:

> I am not particularly disappointed that there is no place in California for the gathering of the Saints. If the whisperings of the Spirit are to come to the valley of the mountains it is a happy whispering to you, and them and very satisfactory to me. Neither am I desirous that any should remain at Carson Valley who wish to come here. These places are only fixed that those who are disposed may be gathered and not left to wander like sheep without a shepherd.[20]

In the 1850s a string of Mormon way places was set up along immigration routes to raise grain and hay, maintain ferries, and store supplies. Several such settlements were maintained for periods in present-day Nebraska, Wyoming, Nevada, and California.

A second group of colonies was established to serve as centers for the production of necessary commodities: iron and coal; cotton, flax, molasses, and sugarcane; cattle and sheep. In one of his earliest formal addresses, Brigham advised: "Produce what you consume; draw from the native element, the necessaries of life; . . . let home industry [i.e., Mormon industry] produce every article of *home* consumption."[21]

Third, at least four colonies were founded as the hub of various missions to the Indians. These included Harmony, in southern Utah; Las Vegas in southern Nevada; Lemhi, in northern Idaho; and the ill-fated Elk Mountain

Mission in eastern Utah. Brigham's instructions to Rufus Allen, one of the missionaries in Harmony, were typical:

> . . . you know that we look upon that place [Harmony] as a rendezvous for all the missions in that region for the present—a place where they can come to and find a home—a place to send out from and direct, as circumstances shall require. It is desirable that it should rather increase than diminish—that grain should be raised—schools should be established, and a nucleus established where Indians can come with a degree of assurance of receiving not only knowledge and wisdom, but the common necessaries of life, also instruction in the art of husbandry, and the arts of civilized life.[22]

Fourth, permanent colonies were established to provide homes and farms for the hundreds of new immigrants who arrived in the Salt Lake Valley the preceding fall. As Brigham found it increasingly difficult to visit each settlement during the summer, he was amazed at their growth and the necessity of finding new sites for colonization. He commented in a letter to his son Brigham, Jr., in England:

> It is almost a matter of surprise even to us, who have traveled more or less every Summer throughout the Territory from the first of our settlement here until the present, how the people have increased and are still increasing and spreading abroad. We have been traveling steadily all this summer which is just past, remaining but a very short time in the City between our trips, yet there are a great number of settlements that we have been unable to visit for the want of time. The time is not far distant when the cry will be heard, "the place is too strait for me: give place to me that I may dwell." And Zion will lengthen her cords and strengthen her stakes and break forth on the right hand and on the left.[23]

In 1857 he covered eight hundred miles in a trip north and east of Salt Lake City and found many areas that could be settled. As he reported to Orson Pratt:

> We saw enough to satisfy us, had we hitherto been ignorant of the fact, that the world is not yet overpeopled. And, there are thousands of acres of good arable and pasture land where thousands of the honest and industrious poor now immured in factories and other civilized prisons, could sustain themselves and thrive as industrious bees of Deseret's hive [the Saints named their territory after the Book of Mormon term for hives of bees], breathing a pure and wholesome air, free to do all the good they can to the human family and to themselves.[24]

With respect to northern Utah and southern Idaho, however, Brigham learned almost disbelievingly of the rich possibilities for colonization. In 1856, a year of heavy drought and grasshopper infestation, nine families obtained Brigham's permission to move from Tooele Valley, west of the Salt Lake Valley, to the southern end of Cache Valley, in northern Utah. Although Brigham was fearful of short seasons and summer frosts, they found the climate delightful and were able to raise a "good crop" of grain the next summer. Reluctantly persuaded of the region's potential, and faced with the necessity of finding places to settle several hundred families uprooted by the Utah War, Brigham suggested they try Cache Valley. Five settlements were established there in 1859, and an additional dozen settlements in the years immediately following. By 1866, the region was being referred to as "Utah's granary."[25]

T H E Mormon colonization effort in Utah was not accomplished through the initiative and direction of Brigham alone. A great deal of the drive for new settlements came from individuals and groups who wanted to move to certain areas. Those wishing to resettle usually asked Brigham's permission. His answer was not always affirmative. In some cases, he was apprehensive of the threat posed by hostile Indians; in others, he was concerned that the proposed area for settlement was too distant from other communities. In 1851 he counseled John D. Lee and those who were to go with him from Parowan to the Rio Virgen that they should "tarry another season before you go; by that time you and they can provide means for the sustenance of your families, while you go and explore the country, find a location, build a fort, and prepare for your families." There was also another reason for waiting, since "by that time also, another emigration will have arrived, and your places be readily filled up, as will also your own company be strengthened."[26] To still another group who asked about forming a new settlement, he replied, "I am perfectly willing you should go there and make a settlement but we must consider whether it will be safe or not," and then followed this permission with detailed instructions to assure safety and success.[27]

It was not unusual for Brigham to couple permission to settle with detailed directions. When a company was formed to create a cotton farm on the Rio Virgen, Brigham told the leader to construct a brush dam across the river, flood the land, and then build houses. They were to raise only cotton "and about ¼ of an acre of Tobacco, the leaves of the latter to be dried in the shade—for which you had better prepare a small shed." Brigham told them to build another shed where water could be kept constantly running through in which to keep the wagons, "as otherwise a few months, in that dry climate, will ruin the best we have."[28]

One of Brigham Young's most common directives or requirements was that the settlers provide a fort as quickly as possible and refrain from taking women or children to the new location until their safety could be assured. Sometimes he even specified the dimensions. To one group of would-be colonizers he gave these instructions: "Your fort walls must be 12 feet high 4 feet thick either good stone or good dobies and laid in lime mortar."[29] Another group was told to make their fort 16 feet high and 4 feet thick, with the additional advice that "the doors should be narrow and double and made out of 2-inch plank, and the port holes should not be less than 12 feet high from the ground."[30]

When a bishop asked Brigham about settling on the city lots at Scipio, Utah, Brigham replied that before giving a definite reply, "I should want to know the size of the city lots, and whether one man will own a number of lots and cause the houses to be widely scattered. If the city lots are not too large, and one man owns one lot only, and the people build close together, then the movement would not be so objectionable." He suggested in a postscript that "they could take up a block and settle it and then another block and so on, then they would be close together and could assist one another in case of emergency."[31]

The task of recruiting people to colonize new settlements was handled in a variety of ways. In many cases men or families were selected individually by Brigham and called as colonizing missionaries. Some were expected to stay in their new location for life and to help build up that portion of the Kingdom. Others were told to stay there temporarily before moving on to another new settlement. In picking colonists for a settlement, Brigham tried to make sure that it would have a fairly balanced group of members. He chose some with particular crafts or manufacturing skills so that the necessary services would be readily available. He would often select men from several of the older communities and then add some newly arrived immigrants to provide a mixture of seasoned pioneers and newcomers. In settling southern Utah he called twenty-eight families, most of whom were converts from the southern states, to move to that area to grow cotton. To found settlements in Iron County, Brigham sent a company of English, Scottish, and Welsh miners and iron manufacturers to establish an iron foundry.

Brigham sometimes called specific individuals, even reading off their names at general conference meetings, to a particular colonizing mission. But just as often he simply appointed a leader of a new settlement and gave him authority to recruit those who would go with him. To settle Sanpete County, for example, Brigham appointed Isaac Morley and two counselors to establish Manti. They were told to choose others to go with them, with the recommendation that they pick mostly young men with families. Within a week there were fifty to one hundred families planning to leave for Sanpete Valley in the next few days.

Orson Hyde, in charge of establishing a settlement near Fort Bridger, chose some of the settlers himself and read off a list of thirty-eight names from the stand at general conference. However, he augmented this group by calling for volunteers, gathering another fifty-three men within two weeks of sending the first company on its way. In giving permission to Phinehas W. Cook to go to the mouth of Salt Creek (Nephi) and to take some men with him, Brigham stressed that it should be a purely voluntary matter for those who went. "I do not wish one man to go unless he wants to," Brigham wrote, "and those that wish to go have my permission."[32]

When the decision was made to establish a settlement in Uinta Valley in northeastern Utah, Brigham wrote the leaders in Utah County asking for 150 volunteers. He specified, "We would like to have good substantial men who are and wish to be saints and who prefer to live with saints, than those who for the sake of gain continually entice into our midst the wicked and ungodly."[33] He also invited those in Sanpete to consider settling Uinta Valley as well. After announcing that an early party was already forming and planning to leave as soon as possible, he said, "It is probable that some of the brethren in Sanpete would be pleased to avail themselves of the opening now presented in Uinta, if so I wish you to inform such as are *suitable* and *would prefer* to go there that their so doing promises to be beneficial to them and will be gratifying to us."[34]

Men should be "suitable" and should really want to go. To a group petitioning to return to Rockport from Wanship, Utah, he wrote:

> I do not wish to give you any counsel upon this subject, nor to assume any responsibility connected with it. You can do as you please. I have given so much counsel to the brethren respecting their locations and the proper methods for them to adopt to secure themselves, their families and stock, and have had it disobeyed, that I do not feel encouraged to counsel and take the responsibility of their scattering.[35]

Clearly, it is not accurate to say that Brigham ruled his people with an iron hand, making all decisions and paying no attention to individual preferences.

Nevertheless, it is easy to understand how some observers have felt that Brigham moved his people about like pawns on a chess board—like a general planning an attack. Surely Brigham would have known of some of the sacrifices his people made to establish new colonies, to preach the gospel in locations far removed from the Great Basin, to surrender their summer's work to drive to the Missouri River to pick up immigrants from abroad. The hardship inflicted on the wives and children by some of these "calls" must have been particularly severe. Did it cause any second thoughts in Brigham? Apparently not. There are many examples of his compassion. He was not "cruel," as some contended, although he was capable of giving strong advice or chastisement that might have seemed beyond the call of his pastoral duty. Nor was he oblivious to the needs and desires of his people, though he thought his people should place their time, their property, and their skills at the disposal of the Kingdom. In short, he was a determined and forceful leader, but not always.

F O U R challenges to Brigham's ingenuity during the early years in the Great Basin were: (1) the institution of a suitable system of exchange; (2) the management of the "crisis" that came with the discovery of gold in California in 1848; (3) the development of the resources of the region and the starting-up of industries; and (4) the establishment of state or territorial government. Isolated as it was from the paths of trade, the Mormon community had to be largely self-sufficient during these early years. There was no national currency before the Civil War, and in any case the Mormons could not expect any significant amount of capital from "outside" investors or developers. Brigham's solution was to develop an internal system of exchange based on locally produced coin and currency and tithing produce. Each settlement had a bishop (or, in some smaller settlements, a presiding elder or "president") who was instructed to establish a tithinghouse or bishop's storehouse to receive (and disburse) tithing contributions, almost invariably "in kind." Under the supervision of the bishops these receipts were paid out to widows and orphans, the sick and disabled, and to those laboring on public works. Transportable items, such as grain and cattle, were taken to Salt Lake City to a general tithing storehouse and yard on the temple lot, immediately west of Brigham's compound. There the receipts were used to support public hands (those doing public works) and buy needed supplies and equipment in the Missouri Valley.

Here, for example, are the general tithing office receipts for 1854–55, together with the disbursement of the same and the amount of property in the hands of the trustee-in-trust (Brigham):

Tithing receipts in cash (U.S. coins, drafts on Eastern banks, and locally produced gold coins, and gold-backed paper)		$56,383
Tithing receipts in produce		57,646
15,807 bushels of grain at $1.50 to $2.00	$30,062	
79 tons of hay at $12	940	
12,212 pounds of flour at 6 cents	733	
12,467 bushels of potatoes, beets, and onions at 80 cents	10,689	
13,847 heads of cabbages, pumpkins, squashes, and melons at 6 cents	831	
5,520 pounds of beef at 7 cents	386	
29,567 pounds of pork at 16 cents	4,731	
9,127 pounds of butter at 25 cents	2,282	
4,267 pounds of cheese at 15 cents	640	
2,077 dozen eggs at 18 cents	374	
7,780 pounds of salt at 4 cents	311	
2,238 chickens at 20 cents	448	
375 pounds of soap at 15 cents	56	
1,021 pounds of wool at 40 cents	408	
131 loads of wood at $6.00	786	
Miscellaneous produce	3,969	
Tithing livestock		58,932
691 head of oxen at $37.00	25,892	
192 cows at $35.00	6,720	

909 young stock at $25.00	22,270
90 horses at $45.00	3,800
2 mules at $80.00	160
9 hogs at $10.00	90
Tithing labor	
Service rendered on labor tithing (valued at an average of $2.00 per man-day)	43,674
Total Tithing	$216,635

Of these receipts, there were disbursed to public hands and used for other public purposes: cash to the amount of $56,167; produce valued at $43,067; and virtually all of the livestock receipts. The church had retained 7,000 bushels of wheat, valued at $14,000; small amounts of grain and vegetables amounting to $907, and had on hand in its possession merchandise and supplies and equipment, as follows:

In the Tithing Storehouse	$12,667
In Church Historian's Office	989
In *Deseret News* Office	26,268
In Building Trades Shops and Yards	23,993
On Church Farms	34,269
Desk and supplies in President's Office	1,000
Total	$99,186

The accounting showed buildings owned by the central church valued at $259,762, as follows:

Deseret (Church) Store	49,000	
Temple wall	28,000	
Temple foundation and stone	23,400	
Council House	25,000	
Church Barn	3,800	
Tabernacle	16,000	
Social Hall	13,600	
Endowment House	5,900	
Sugar House and property	41,000	
Livingston Kinkead & Co. Store	6,100	
Perry's Store	3,600	
President's New House (Beehive)	29,200	
Miscellaneous Shops and Facilities	15,162	
Other Valuable Properties		$35,378
Value of other city property	6,735	
Woolen machinery stored in St. Louis	15,000	
Stock on hand in Liverpool Office	29,597	
Stock on hand in Welsh Office	4,825	
Less liabilities	20,779	

The clerk lists the value of all assets of the central church, clear of all indebtedness, at $614,130.[36]

It is evident that, depending as he did on receipts in kind, Brigham's managerial task was far more complicated than the same function in communities with monetary economies. How, for instance, did one transform contributions of calves, lambs, and pigs into fare for ocean voyages, the purchase of oxen for the hauling of emigrants across the Plains, the acquisition of machinery for the manufacture of wool? Some idea of Brigham's financial problems can be had by imagining what it would be like if the receipts of New York City consisted of barley, Mesabi iron ore, fresh goat's milk, volunteer labor, freshly sheared sheep's wool, summer squash, and worn-out clothing.

Brigham had some caustic comments about the kind of tithing that came in. For example, the following in 1852:

> Walk into the storehouse, and examine for yourselves. To be sure there was an old silk dress put in for $40, that had been lying for years rotting in the chest: this is a specimen of the rest. What are such things worth to our workmen? Why, nothing at all. We wish you to put in strong and substantial clothing. Good, strong, homemade stuffs make the most suitable clothing for those who are building up the public works.[37]

Or this in 1855:

> Some were disposed to do right with their surplus property, and once in a while you would find a man who had a cow which he considered surplus, but generally she was of the class that would kick a person's hat off, or eyes out, or the wolves had eaten off her teats. You would once in a while find a man who had a horse that he considered surplus, but at the same time he had the ring-bone, was broken-winded, spavined in both legs, and had the pole evil at one end of the neck and a fistula at the other, and both knees sprung.[38]

Occasionally, there were bishops and tithing clerks who were not entirely honest in handling the tithing. The goose and cheese that came in as tithing would end up on their dinner tables instead of in the storehouse for payment to the poor or those on the public works. Brigham said he had discovered a number of such cases:

> When a good, handsome cow has been turned in on tithing, she has been smuggled, and an old three-titted cow—one that would kick the tobacco out of the mouth of a man who went to milk her—would be turned into the General Tithing Office, instead of the good cow. If one hundred dollars in cash are paid into the hands of a Bishop, in many instances he will smuggle it, and turn into the Tithing Office old, ring-boned, spavined horses, instead of the money. I am inquiring after such conduct, and will continue until I cleanse the inside of the platter.[39]

Such malpractice was not the rule, but it was common enough to evoke an occasional sermon on the subject.

Despite repeated attempts to separate his own family accounts from those of the church and maintain separate ledger books, the accounts are usually interwoven, as the enterprises were. There is no clear-cut way to distinguish Brigham the Family Provider from Brigham the President of the Church. Brigham tried to explain this:

> Some may think that my personal business is so mixed up and combined with public [church] business that I cannot keep them separate. This is not the case . . . Hiram B. Clawson, John T. Caine, and Thomas Ellerbeck are the clerks who keep the books of my private business; and the Trustee-in-Trust has his clerks, of whom David O. Calder is the chief. Horace Whitney, Joseph Simmons, and Amos M. Musser are his associate clerks, and they keep the books pertaining to the public business. . . . If brother Calder wishes one hundred or a thousand dollars, if I have it, he borrows it of Hiram B. Clawson and pays it back; and so also brother Clawson borrows of him and returns it. . . . Brigham Young and the Trustee-in-Trust are two persons in business. When you speak of Brigham Young as Trustee-in-Trust, he is one man; and when as Brigham Young, he is another. . . . If you want to know anything about the money, item by item, how it has been obtained and how expended, our books are open.[40]

To Brigham, who "owned" properties or who furnished funds was a secondary consideration:

> In reality, we should have only one mess chest, one place of deposit, one store house, one "pile," and that is the kingdom of God upon the earth; it is the only store-house there is for Saints, it is the only "pile," the only safe place of deposit, the only place to invest our capital. This is rational to me; and all who contend for an individual interest, a personal "pile," independent of the kingdom of God, will be destroyed. . . . The gold, the silver, the wheat, the fine flour, buffalo, the deer, and the cattle on a thousand hills, are all His, and He turns them whithersoever He will.[41]

Although willing to open the books for legitimate inquiries, Brigham did not welcome criticism of his use of church funds. On one occasion, he heard complaints about his project in the 1850s to build a wall around the city, as well as around Temple Block and his own estate. His reply was more testy than usual:

> Some have wished me to explain why we built an adobe wall around this city. Are there any Saints who stumble at such things? Oh, slow of heart to understand and believe, I build walls, dig ditches, make bridges, and do a great amount and variety of labor that is of but little consequence only to provide ways and means for sustaining and preserving the destitute. I annually expend hundreds and thousands of dollars almost solely to furnish employment to those in want

of labor. Why? I have potatoes, flour, beef, and other articles of food, which I wish my brethren to have; and it is better for them to labor for those articles, so far as they are able and have opportunity, than to have them given to them. They work, and I deal out provisions, often when the work does not profit me.

I say to all grunters, grumblers, whiners, hypocrites and sycophants, who snivel, crouch and crawl around the most contemptible of all creatures for a slight favor, should it enter my mind to dig down the Twin Peaks, and I set men to work to do so, it is none of your business, neither is it the business of all earth and hell, provided I pay the laborers their wages. I am not to be called in question as to what I do with my funds, whether I build high walls or low walls, garden walls or city walls, and if I please, it is my right to pull down my walls tomorrow. If any one wishes to apostatize upon such grounds, the quicker he does so the better; and if he wishes to leave the territory, but is too poor to do so, I will assist him to go. We are much better off without such characters.[42]

T H E second problem with which Brigham wrestled was the Gold Rush. Six discharged members of the Mormon Battalion were working with James Marshall when the gold discovery was made at Coloma, California, and they and their companions found other rich deposits, including the fabulous Mormon Island. More than sixty of their comrades were working for John A. Sutter in the immediate vicinity, while another hundred Battalionists from the San Francisco Bay region were among the first to reach the gold fields. Sam Brannan, who had led the Mormon company from New York to San Francisco in 1846 and established the Mormon agricultural settlement of New Hope, not far from the gold fields, was the first to announce the discovery. More than three hundred Mormons were at work on Mormon Island in July 1848, according to William Tecumseh Sherman, who accompanied the governor of California on a tour of the gold fields at that time. The Mormons could have made the most of their fortunate ground-floor opportunity if encouraged to do so.

But Brigham was adamant against any wholesale Mormon "desertion" of their Promised Valley. "We are gathered here," he wrote, "not to scatter around and go off to the mines, or any other place, but to build up the Kingdom of God."[43] The Salt Lake Valley, Brigham said, ". . . is a good place to make Saints, and it is a good place for Saints to live. It is the place the Lord has appointed, and we shall stay here until He tells us to go somewhere else."[44] The Sacramento Valley, he said, was unhealthy—morally and physically. "If you Elders of Israel want to go to the gold mines, go and be damned."[45] He wanted to hold the church together. "When I see some of the brethren going away," he said, "I feel like a mother seeing her child in the midst of the ocean, or in the roaring flames. We are gathered here, not to scatter around and go off to the mines, or any other place, but to build up the Kingdom of God."[46]

He even thought that the average person would be better off economically by remaining in the Great Basin. He told those who wanted to go to the mines that he would remain here, mind his own business, help to build up the

Kingdom of God, and when they returned from the mines he would agree to count dollars with them.[47]

Despite his insistence about remaining in the Great Basin, Brigham did seek to make the most of the opportunity the Gold Rush presented. He permitted members of the Mormon Battalion to stay in California to earn money, by prospecting or otherwise, before returning to the Salt Lake Valley. In fact, he called some fifty-two young men, primarily former members of the battalion, to go to California to mine gold for the church.[48] To protect the interests of the church in California, he sent two of his apostles, Charles C. Rich and Amasa Lyman, to California to minister to the Saints who were there and to establish a colony in southern California at San Bernardino. "The harvest of '49," as the impact of the Gold Rush has been called, was helpful to Brigham and his associates in that earnings from the Overlanders (people who traveled overland from the eastern United States to the West Coast) and gold from California financed much of the immigration of the 1850s and assisted in the purchase of needed machinery and equipment.[49]

D E D I C A T E D to the development of local resources, Brigham mobilized his commonwealth to make the most of what God had blessed them with— but four signal efforts were unsuccessful. These were attempts to produce beet sugar, iron products, wool, and lead.[50]

Sugar. When Apostle John Taylor, as a missionary in France, observed a beet sugar factory in operation at Arras, he reported the experience by letter. Excited with the prospect of rendering the Great Basin Kingdom self-sufficient in this expensive item (sugar sold for upward of forty cents per pound in Salt Lake City), Brigham instructed Taylor and other French missionaries to secure funds, designs, personnel, equipment, and seed preparatory to establishing a beet sugar industry in Utah.[51] With the assistance of converts in France and the British Isles, Taylor organized the Deseret Manufacturing Company with capital of $32,000, purchased 1,200 pounds of "the best French Beet seed," and ordered $12,100 worth of machinery from Faucett, Preston & Co. of Liverpool, designed to produce from five to ten tons of sugar per day.

The story of the transport of this heavy machinery across the ocean to New Orleans, up the Mississippi to St. Louis and up the Missouri to Fort Leavenworth, and by multiple ox teams across the mountains and plains to Utah is one of persistence and hardship. Upon its arrival in Utah, the company's resources exhausted, Brigham found it necessary, as trustee-in-trust, to take over the enterprise. He assigned it to the Church Public Works Department, which alone in the territory had the equipment and men needed to construct the factory and put it into operation. A factory of "Sugar Works" was erected on the Church Farm, four miles south of Salt Lake City, in what is now Sugar House.

While the construction was being undertaken, two seasons went by in which farmers were urged to plant beets in the expectation of exchanging them for sugar. The anticipated completion of the factory was used as a talking point to get farmers to continue, possibly against their better judgment, to devote their energies to beet production, the thinning, weeding, and harvesting requiring particularly arduous labor. Brigham attempted to reassure them:

> There is not the least doubt we can make the Sugar from the Beet; we shall never give it up, nor cease our operations, until we manufacture everything we can eat, drink, or wear, from the native element, and make the earth itself, like the garden of Eden.[52]

But the factory was a failure. Over a seven-week period in 1855, more than 22,000 bushels of beets were ground into molasses, but the operatives never succeeded in converting it into sugar.[53] To add to the difficulties, the sugar beet crop failed in 1855 and 1856 because of drought and grasshopper destruction of the seed. While the First Presidency sought "the blessing of the Lord, that no failure of the kind will again thwart our wishes, and that we shall soon be able to furnish, from the beet, sugar sufficient for home consumption," Brigham eventually became convinced that Utah's beets were too alkaline to refine into sugar, or that the enterprise was not worth the effort required to establish it.[54] The only salvage—the equipment—was used for such varied purposes as the manufacture of linseed oil, paper, iron, and wool. The factory building housed, in turn, wool carding machines, a machine shop, and a paper factory.

M. Mollenhauer, the expert sugar-maker imported to superintend the operations, blamed the lack of success on the failure of the company to order "retorts"—the cast-iron ovens in which bones were burned to make the animal charcoal needed to clarify and purify the beet juice before it could be made into sugar. Retorts were not ordered later, because "the company received such opposition from quarters not expected, it was broken up and disheartened." Architect Truman O. Angell said the greatest need was "a set of strangers to run said factory."[55]

Whatever the reasons for failure—chemical, mechanical, financial, or administrative—Brigham shifted to advocacy of the culture of sorghum cane. Several dozen horse- and water-powered molasses roller mills were established by private individuals and communities to crush the cane and squeeze out the juice. The juice was then boiled down until it became a thick golden syrup. Molasses remained the principal source of sweet in the territory until well after Brigham's death.

Wool. In the fall of 1849 Brigham wrote to the church president in England requesting that he send, "if possible," woolen and cotton machinery, together with a company each of woolen and cotton manufacturers, the following spring.[56] In February 1851, at Brigham's request the legislative assembly appropriated $2,000 "to encourage the manufacture of wool in Great Salt Lake County."[57] The resolution also included a pledge by the legislators "to use for ourselves and in our families, only domestic manufactured clothing as soon as a sufficient quantity of it can be furnished to supply the market." The company was organized in Paris by John Taylor in March 1851, and plans were made for the export later that year of men, sheep, and machinery.

While some of the personnel went to Utah in 1852, some operatives and the machinery remained in St. Louis. In succeeding years, one difficulty or another prevented the transportation of the machinery to the Salt Lake Valley, and it was not until 1862 that a long train of mule teams—part of the church teams dispatched under the auspices of the Perpetual Emigrating Fund in that year—finally took the last of the equipment into the valley. The factory was established on Big Kanyon Creek, near Salt Lake City, and referred to as "Brigham Young's Woolen and Cotton Factory"; it was assembled and put in motion in 1863, with 240 spindles, thus providing the first commercial market for wool in the territory. It was also the first woolen factory of its size to be operated in the West.

The lack of success in establishing a large-scale territorial wool manufacturing industry was apparently due to the insufficiency of sheep and the heavy losses because of the severity of winters, wolves, and disease; and also the inability of the population to make wool manufacturing worthwhile, considering the fact that the work could be done in the home. One of the "shepherd boys with Scotch collies" brought to Utah by the PEF woolen company in 1852 later reported that the church sheep had been "devoured by wolves and coyotes," and so he was employed on one of Brigham's farms during the remainder of the 1850s.[58]

Iron. When Parley P. Pratt's expedition discovered iron and coal in southern Utah in 1850, Brigham decided to start a colony at nearby Parowan to raise crops to support an iron enterprise. In November 1851, after the first harvest had been completed, a group of thirty-five men skilled in mining and manufacturing was called to found the Pioneer Iron Mission at Cedar City, some twenty miles south of Parowan. Committees of these "iron missionaries" were appointed to lay out a village, erect a fort, dig a canal, plant a cooperative farm, construct a road to the coal deposits, build a road to the timber, and locate materials with which to build a small blast furnace. On September 28, 1852, less than a year after the mission had been established, the blast was put to the furnace, and "a small quantity of iron run out, which caused the hearts of all to rejoice."[59] The iron was used in making horseshoe nails and a pair of andirons (called dog-irons).

Meanwhile, Brigham and other church officials took steps to enlarge the iron mission and give it a strong financial and technical base. In September 1851, while the agricultural missionaries were harvesting their first crop, Brigham wrote to church leaders in Europe, asking them to search out "brethren who could make different kinds of iron from magnetic iron ore" and send them to the Salt Lake Valley.[60] Franklin D. Richards and Erastus Snow, presidents of the British and Scandinavian missions, held a special European conference of the church in London at which they presented before the assembled thousands the necessity of helping to create an iron manufacturing industry in Utah. Obtaining the names and addresses of "wealthier brethren," Richards and Snow spent most of the next month visiting them. Finding "a general readiness on their part to receive our counsel, and employ their funds as we thought best for the making of iron in these valleys," they visited various ironworks and obtained general information "on the subject of making iron."[61]

The Deseret Iron Company was organized in 1852, and with the assistance of experienced ironmasters, Snow and Richards arranged for the purchase and transportation of various kinds of iron-making machinery and then hurriedly embarked for the New World.[62] They arrived in the Salt Lake Valley in August 1852, in time to be present when the Iron County delegation took the first supply of precious molten iron to Brigham. Warmly complimented by Brigham for their success in organizing a company and securing Old World capital, Snow and Richards were advised to establish works in Iron County as rapidly as possible. The territorial legislature caught the contagion of this enthusiasm and appropriated $5,000 "to advance the Iron interests in Iron County."[63]

The bulk of the territorial appropriation was expended in the spring of 1853 on explorations for a superior vein of coal and the construction of a suitable wagon road to it. For a time the mine produced coal at the rate of 100 tons per week. The company also employed John James of the Victoria Iron Works, Wales, to construct a small air furnace in which to try the experiment of fluxing the richer ores without the blast. This furnace, completed in the summer of 1853, was built of adobe and rock and had a funnel 300 feet long through which smoke was conveyed to a chimney stack forty feet high. A casting house was also constructed.

Despite the enthusiastic and hopeful labor of the missionaries, however, a number of circumstances delayed the work. It was planned to put the blast to the furnace near the end of July, but news reached the southern settlements that an Indian war had started. The iron work was suspended and the colonists were instructed to devote their "persevering industry" to erecting extensive fortifications and securing grain, hay, and wood for the winter. On September 3, the community was visited again by "a terrible flood" that "swept down Coal Creek, carrying before it all bridges and dams, completely inundating the site of the works, and sweeping off much of the Company's property."[64] Twenty- and thirty-ton boulders were deposited with the debris. The remainder of the year was required to rebuild the dam and repair the breaches.

Brigham, however, continued to support the colony and took measures to nurse it along. He called Isaac C. Haight, recently returned from a mission to England, to go to Cedar City and "take charge of the iron works."[65] He also denied the petition of a number of the colonists asking for "release" from the Iron County mission:

> If you were now on a [proselyting] mission to France or England or any
> other part of the earth, you would not sit down and counsel together about going

to get your families, or about going home till your mission was ended. This [iron mission] is of quite as much importance as preaching the Gospel. The time is now come when it is required of us to make the wilderness blossom as the rose. Our mission is now to build up stakes of Zion and fill these mountains with cities, and when your mission is ended you are at liberty to go.[66]

During the spring of 1854, after the completion of the fort, coal was hauled on sleds and the furnace was again put into operation. Some iron was made, but repeated experimentation had impaired the workability of the furnace, and it was necessary to construct a new one. This task occupied the attention of the iron company during most of the year. The red sandstone furnace, built under the direction of Elias Morris, foremost carpenter and building contractor in the territory, was twenty-one feet square and thirty feet high, required 650 tons of rock, and had a capacity of ten tons per day. The blast was made by a new large blowing apparatus powered by a waterwheel. Six coke ovens were also built in order to supply the furnace with good coke.

Recognizing the many unexpected obstacles the company had to contend with, Brigham and his associates were not yet discouraged. After all, they reasoned, the experience gained in the first two years augured well for future success. Responding to Brigham's suggestion, the legislature advanced the company another $4,840 in 1855. As trustee-in-trust of the church Brigham provided an equal amount.[67]

In anticipation of Brigham's visit to Cedar City in the spring of 1855, every effort was made to institute a successful run. In order to keep the furnace burning, a large quantity of sagebrush was pulled and piled before the flue. On the first twenty-four-hour run, 1,700 pounds of "good iron" was produced. By constant effort, another ten tons was manufactured in April. It was from some of this iron that the company made the only casting that survives—a bell cast by the public works department in 1855, whose ringing called the colonists to church.

Having solved, as they thought, the technical problem of producing iron, the next step was to acquire more workers. A call was made in May 1855 for 150 wagoners, miners, colliers, lime burners, timbermen, quarrymen, brick and stone masons, carpenters, machinists, charcoal burners, and furnace men, besides fifty teams to haul fuel and ore. By the fall of 1855, the ironworks was reported to be "progressing first-rate," with a "hot blast, which operates complete," and "several tons of castings of various descriptions," and with other "good iron" manufactured in November. The uncertainty of the waterpower, however, hampered operations during the winter of 1855–56 when the stream was frozen for three months. Coal was also inaccessible during the same period.[68] An attempt was made to overcome this dependence on waterpower by the installation of two thirty-horsepower steam engines, at least one of which was supplied by Brigham.

Other accidental factors hampered operations in 1856. When the furnace was started up in June, for example, the hot blast pipes accidentally burned out, chilled the furnace, and they had to "blow out" without producing any iron. Everything was in order by the first week of August, and the furnace started up once more, but an untimely drought caused a failure in the water supply and they had to blow out again. Finally, the grasshopper plague of 1856, which devastated virtually the entire territory, forced the iron colonists to devote most of their efforts to securing enough food to keep their families from starving.

More difficulties occurred in 1857. The danger of floods forced them to move the scene of their operations to higher ground. A new site was laid out, complete with lots for homes, public buildings, and ironworks. This relocation occupied the colonists for several weeks. When they were ready to resume manufacturing operations, they received word from Brigham "to suspend all business and take care of the grain as the United States were sending troops into the Territory to oppress the Saints, and force officers upon us contrary to our wishes and the constitution."[69] Convinced that the Utah Expedition was seeking to repeat the kind of persecution to which the Mormons had long been subject, the iron missionaries, along with other Mormons, began a series of military drills and exercises.

Almost a year was devoted to various kinds of service connected with the Utah War. When that question was settled, in 1858, the company built a new furnace, but "for the want of fuel and the lining giving way," they had to blow out.[70] There were two more successful trial runs in September and October 1858. But by that time the company was ready to give up and the works was officially closed. Almost ten years of labor had resulted in nothing more than a few andirons, kitchen utensils, flatirons, wagon wheels, molasses rolls, and machine castings. Small volunteer, cooperative industry was simply unable to cope with the problems associated with developing a major resource. (Since World War II, when the Defense Plant Corporation built the Geneva Steel Mill, Iron Mountain has furnished iron for the only major steel factory in the Great Basin.)

Lead. In June 1855, Brigham called thirty men to go to Las Vegas Springs, in what is now southern Nevada, to serve as missionaries to the Indians. During one of their exploring expeditions they discovered outcroppings of lead at Cottonwood Springs, thirty miles southwest of Las Vegas. Some specimens of this ore were taken to Brigham during the winter of 1855–56. He was sufficiently interested to call Nathaniel V. Jones to go to Las Vegas in February 1856 with a group of thirty others to search for ore and "go into the lead business."[71]

After two months of intensive exploration, Jones's party returned to Salt Lake City and reported the prospect to be "exceedingly flattering," although the nearest running water was twelve miles away, and there was an almost complete lack of grass to feed the animals. Immediately, preparations were made to send a company to work the mine.[72] In July 1856, Jones left with three companions, two four-mule teams, and necessary tools and supplies. The company carried a letter instructing bishops of the southern settlements to respond to Jones's calls for men and other assistance in prosecuting the work.

Supplied with food, feed, and equipment by the Indian missionaries, and also by tithing houses in Utah, the lead missionaries first constructed a road to the top of the high mountain where the lead was situated. While some of them were locating materials for a furnace as far as seven miles away and painstakingly carrying the materials to the mine, others were hauling several tons of lead ore to Cedar City, Provo, and Salt Lake City. When the furnace was finally put to the blast in September, they found to their disappointment that the local materials would not withstand the fire. Rather than waste time experimenting with local materials with possible risk of failure, Jones left most of his co-workers in Las Vegas and returned to Salt Lake City—more than five hundred miles distant—to secure the construction of a bellows, blast furnace, and hearth by the Church Public Works employees. Returned from Salt Lake in December 1856 with the necessary supplies and equipment, Jones and others began smelting on Christmas Day, and within two weeks about nine thousand pounds of lead was produced. Most of this was taken to Salt Lake City with teams previously dispatched by Brigham and made into bullets by the public works.

Despite this seeming success, Jones and company decided late in January 1857 to abandon the mine as unprofitable. The ore was yielding "only" 20 to 30 percent lead, there were many impurities that caused much of the lead to burn up during the smelting, and washing was impractical since the nearest stream was 12 difficult miles away. Provisions and forage for the animals had to be hauled 230 miles over a difficult road, and the Indians were causing trouble. The property was abandoned, with only sixty tons of ore having been mined.

As with the iron mission, which failed on a mountain of 200 million tons of 52 percent iron ore, the Las Vegas Lead Mission expired on a rich silver-bearing galena. Very near the mine from which Jones and company obtained lead the fabulous Potosi silver mines were "discovered" by non-Mormons in 1861.

T H E boldness of Brigham's design in attempting to provide the economic foundations for a commonwealth is clearly evident. That in each case the responsibility and control eventually passed into his hands was due partly to the lack of private capital and partly to the belief that all institutions in Mormondom ought to be under the influence of the priesthood. While this assured a concentration of efforts in developing the region, it also involved the danger of tying the hands of the "experts" who were engaged in the active management of these enterprises. Brigham and his appointed lay leaders were outstanding colonizers and were dedicated to the Kingdom, but the more the specialists depended on them for leadership, the more the specialized industries were apt to suffer from inexpert direction. Brigham himself admitted, in 1855, that he had just learned why the iron company had to build a new furnace every time a "blow out" occurred. Up to that time, he had thought that the iron workers were merely "dilatory."[73] Even after the works was abandoned, he attributed the failure not to the lack of suitable coal, not to the lack of capital, not to the lack of technical prowess, but to the spirit of self-seeking among the iron missionaries:

> Again, all that has been said, and all the praying that has been done, and all the faith that has been exercised, and all the combination and union of effort among the Saints have not brought to pass one say of the President's in regard to iron; he said, let there be iron, but there is no iron yet. Br. Wells has told you the reason, this morning. A man says, "I am going to make iron, and I will have the credit of making the first iron in the Territory. I will have the credit of knowing how to flux the ore that is found in these regions, and bring out the metal in abundance, or no other man shall."[74]

It is quite possible that the sugar, wool, iron, and lead enterprises, and perhaps others, would have been more successful if knowledgeable private interests had been allowed a freer hand in the day-to-day direction, a stronger voice in the making of basic decisions, and an opportunity to share in any profits. Brigham was not entirely free from errors of judgment, and some of his attempts to industrialize were premature.

12 ✚

President of the Church

I want present salvation. I preach, comparatively, but little
about the eternities and Gods, and their wonderful works in
eternity; and do not tell who first made them, nor how they
were made; for I know nothing about that. Life is for us, and
it is for us to receive it today, and not wait for the millennium.
Let us take a course to be saved today, and, when evening
comes, review the acts of the day, repent of our sins, if we
have any to repent of, and say our prayers; then we can lie
down and sleep in peace until the morning, arise with gratitude to God, commence the labours of another day, and strive
to live the whole day to God and nobody else.[1]

As president of the Latter-day Saints Brigham Young had several
roles to fill. He was an organizer, a preacher, a pastor, and a theologian. Like
Augustine, Loyola, Luther, and Wesley before him, Brigham added to his
charismatic qualities the ability to provide for continuity, to delegate, and to
magnify his impact by his organizational skills. His achievements as a religious
organizer are impressive. Confronted with persecution, internal tension and
schism, the lack of regularized machinery for missionary proselyting and immigration, and the relief of the destitute, he had to choose a permanent
location, move thousands of people across the Great Plains, institute a shep-
herded migration from Europe, and establish new settlements in the West.
And all this under intermittent harassment from the federal government.

The specific religious organizational tasks he had to perform during the
early years in the Great Basin were (1) the organization of wards or congregations in the Salt Lake Valley and in each subsequent settlement of Latter-
day Saints; (2) the appointment of a bishop in charge of each; and (3) the
selection of new apostles to take the place of those who had dropped away
from the faith before the church went west. Above all, he had to choose an
inner circle of advisers and administrators who would carry out his program

and "look after the Saints." With respect to this, he of course began with his counselors in the First Presidency, Heber Kimball and Willard Richards, who met with him regularly, advised him on appointments and programs, and assisted with his many administrative tasks. Heber's specific assignment was to superintend marriages, baptisms, sealings, and other religious ordinances in the Salt Lake Endowment House, which was built to take care of these ceremonies until the completion of the Salt Lake Temple many years after Brigham's death.[2] A fine writer, Richards was the first editor of the *Deseret News* and assisted Brigham in drafting the "epistles" of the First Presidency and the Twelve, Brigham's letters to church and government officials, and his official messages as governor.[3] When he died in 1854, Richards was replaced by Jedediah M. Grant, a thundering but clever and entertaining speaker, who was also mayor of Salt Lake City.[4] He lived only two years after his appointment to the First Presidency, however, and was replaced in 1856 by Daniel H. Wells. Tall, redheaded, dignified, and perceptive, Wells succeeded Grant as mayor of Salt Lake City, served as Church Superintendent of Public Works, and was lieutenant general of the Nauvoo Legion.[5] Kimball was Brigham's counselor until his death in 1868, when he was replaced by George A. Smith, who had been a leading colonizer and popular preacher, and served also as Church Historian and Recorder. Rotund (close to 250 pounds), with a wig, false teeth, and hideous spectacles, he had a lively sense of humor and was a favorite with Utah's Indians, who referred to him as "non-choko-wicher," meaning "man who takes himself apart."[6]

Besides Kimball and Richards, Grant and Wells, and George A. Smith, Brigham's "inner circle" of advisers and administrators in the 1850s and 1860s included Edward Hunter, who supervised the bishops throughout the church, directed the welfare program, was a key officer of the Perpetual Emigrating Fund Company, and oversaw the general tithing storehouse in Salt Lake City;[7] Brigham's brother, Joseph Young, who was Senior President of the Seventies of the church and therefore a respected leader of many missionaries, colonizers, and local leaders;[8] and Albert Carrington, an alumnus of Dartmouth and former teacher and lawyer, who was Richards's successor as editor of the *Deseret News* and Brigham's secretary for twenty years. There was also one female adviser and coworker and non-connubial plural wife: Eliza R. Snow, once a plural wife of Joseph Smith and "Zion's poetess," who was placed in charge of "the sister's work" in the Endowment House, in the wards and stakes, and indeed throughout the church. Remarkably astute, "Aunt Eliza," as she was often called, was independent-minded and helped to assure recognition and appreciation for the work of both women and intellectuals in building the Kingdom.[9]

One other personality, who at all times was a leading counselor of Brigham via special courier, was Thomas L. Kane. Scion of a prominent Pennsylvania family, Kane had read in Philadelphia newspapers of the Mormon exodus from Nauvoo in 1846, attended a Mormon meeting, and felt impelled to visit their camps at Winter Quarters. He helped in the negotiations that led to the call of the Mormon Battalion, was impressed with Brigham and his followers, and vowed, as a non-member, to be their "second in an affair of honor." Brigham had an almost reverential regard for Kane, whom he addressed as "Our Friend" or "Our Special Friend."[10]

In addition to the inner circle, there were other Saints called upon for important ad hoc tasks. Among these were John M. Bernhisel, a tall, dignified physician who was Utah's non-voting delegate to Congress in the 1850s; and his replacement, William H. Hooper, merchant and banker, whose pleasing personality enabled him to make many friends for the church in the 1860s.[11]

With the assistance of the Quorum of the Twelve and his inner circle, Brigham, in February 1849, organized the Salt Lake Saints into nineteen wards, each a kind of separate community within the greater city; created wards at each of the settlements in the Salt Lake Valley and north and south of the valley; called groups of people to colonize new locations; and sent missionaries to such distant places as Copenhagen, Hamburg, Paris, northern Italy, Constantinople, India, the Cape of Good Hope, Malta, Hong Kong, Chile, and the South Sea Islands. A key role in the direction of the missionary work and colonization, of course, was played by the Twelve Apostles: Parley Pratt went to California and Chile, but was assassinated near Van Buren, Arkansas, in 1857; Orson Hyde helped colonize Wyoming and Nevada and later became "senior elder" in the Sanpete and Sevier valleys in Utah; Orson Pratt oversaw missionary work in Great Britain; John Taylor went to France; Wilford Woodruff served as George A. Smith's Assistant Church Historian; and Amasa Lyman supervised the Latter-day Saints in California. Ezra T. Benson, who was ordained an apostle by Brigham in 1846, was in charge of some settlements west and north of Salt Lake City. The four new apostles ordained by Brigham and Heber in 1849 played similar roles. Charles C. Rich, in addition to being a general in the militia, for several years ran the Mormon settlement at San Bernardino, California. Lorenzo Snow proselyted among the Waldensians in northern Italy. Erastus Snow, Lorenzo's distant cousin, also initiated Mormon missionary work in Scandinavia, while Franklin D. Richards was a British missionary and leader of the Mormon community in the Ogden and Weber valley area.[12]

Other church-oriented programs that were organized by Brigham and his counselors and advisers in the 1850s were related to education and recreation. Each bishop was asked to establish a grade school in his ward. Most of these were ungraded; that is, unseparated by age groups. And most operated only three or four months a year during the winter. Supported by local tithing and other donations and by "tuition payments" in kind by families to the teacher, they assured *some* education during the early years of the territory.[13]

Mormons attracted attention among Overlanders because they sometimes held dances in the evening at their camps on the plains. To provide a facility for periodic dances in the Salt Lake Valley, Brigham appropriated out of tithing receipts enough commodities to support workmen to build a social hall in downtown Salt Lake City. Periodic dances, opened and closed with prayer and conducted under strict supervision, were held there, as were plays by local and visiting theatrical groups, and other cultural events—musical recitals, lectures, magic performances. Brigham believed in providing "wholesome" entertainment for Latter-day Saints, and the Salt Lake example was followed in other Mormon communities.[14]

Not all these programs worked satisfactorily. Ward dances were sometimes interrupted by "troublemakers"; ward schools were often suspended because of epidemics, natural disaster, or lack of a teacher; and missionary work was not always blessed with success. Brigham was generally considered to be a practical genius but, like Don Quixote, he was also capable of tilting at windmills. While some programs, considering the circumstance and resources, were brilliantly conceived and executed, there were also failures. Here are two in the field of missionary work, suggesting that Brigham's limited knowledge of the world made failure inevitable.

In 1852 he called Levi Savage, Jr., on a mission to Siam (Thailand). Savage had been a member of the Mormon Battalion as it marched to San Diego and had married shortly after his arrival in Utah in 1847. His wife had died after bearing a son. He left the infant with a sister, traveled overland to San Francisco, and embarked for Calcutta. From there he found passage to Rangoon, but never reached Siam. He spent depressed months living as a dependent upon kind English colonials. He converted no one and finally came back to America. He reached the Missouri River in August 1856 and headed west with the handcart emigrants of that year, arriving in the Salt Lake Valley four years after his departure.[15]

Hosea Stout, chief of police and militiaman in Nauvoo, and sometime lawyer-legislator in Utah with no language capability, was sent with two companions on a proselyting mission to China. Stout left Salt Lake City on October 20, 1852, "and took my departure to a nation whose language, manners, and customs I knew not." He first traveled overland to the Mormon colony at San Bernardino, California, arriving there a month later. He secured passage on a ship and, with two others, arrived in Hong Kong on April 27, 1853. Finding that "the Chinese were not inclined to receive the Gospel," Stout and his companions returned to America in the fall of the same year. "We feel that we have done all that God or man can require of us in this place," he wrote at the time of his departure from Hong Kong. "We have preached publickly and privately as long as any one would hear and often tried when no one would hear. . . . And thus it is this day we do not know of one person in this place to whome we can bear our testimony of the things of God or warn to flee the wrath to come." When he reached home in December 1853, poor and weary, he found his wife Louisa and infant son dead, his house occupied by strangers, and his family dispersed. "I remain as a blank on earth," Stout wrote a week after returning, "a monument of disappointed hopes."[16] His diary entry on the day he returned to Salt Lake City is also poignant: "I left them [his family] by the command of the Lord to preach the gospel in foreign lands, and returned but not to them. . . . I gazed upon the sad wreck of all my hopes in silence while my heart sank within me. . . ."

T H E leading mechanism for education, entertainment, spiritual rejuvenation, and intellectual stimulation in pioneer Utah, however, was the weekly Sunday afternoon service in the Old Tabernacle and the periodic meetings in other settlements when visited by Brigham and/or one or more of the apostles or other church leaders. The Old Tabernacle, constructed of adobes on the south-west side of Temple Square in 1852, seated about twenty-five hundred people and resembled a large lecture hall with choir seats behind the speaker's stand. Brigham presided at these worship services. They began with a rousing con-gregational hymn, followed by a prayer by a church authority, and another hymn, perhaps more subdued. The Sacrament of the Lord's Supper, consisting normally of bread and water, was blessed and distributed to the congregation while one or two returned missionaries spoke. Then Heber or one of the apostles spoke, followed by Brigham, who generally took the remainder of the time—often as much as an hour. After Brigham's talk a closing hymn was usually sung by the congregation and a final prayer by a church authority dismissed them.

Fortunately, nearly all of the sermons delivered by Brigham in the Old Tabernacle in the 1850s were taken down by stenographers. Many were pub-lished in the *Deseret News*. Others were printed in the annual compilation of *Journal of Discourses*.

Since he was untrained, in a formal sense, having never had a course in homiletics, Brigham's sermons rambled, were weak in organization, and would not be published among the great "literary" sermons, as would, for example, those of Henry Ward Beecher, DeWitt Talmage, or Lorenzo Dow. Brigham's sermons were not works of art, they often contained New York–New England provincialisms, they were not committed to paper in advance, they were never rehearsed with careful attention to pace, gestures, crescendo, and diminuendo.

Nevertheless, Brigham's messages were well thought out, suggest re-markable mental power, and were well adapted to his audiences. They were "fireside chats," an informal "talking things over" with his people, and a reading of the sermons indicates that he knew where he was going and was effective in getting there. Moved by the "Spirit," mixing up subjects as diverse as women's fashions, the atonement of Christ, the forthcoming events associated with the Second Coming, and recollections about Joseph Smith, Brigham was able to keep his audiences enthralled, amused, in tears, and at the very least awake for as long as two or three hours on some occasions. In the course of his remarks he would respond to critics, hold forth inspiring visions of what to expect, call up recollections from his own past experiences, nag and cajole, amuse with lighthearted whimsy, comment on the news of the day in its relation to the Saints, teach doctrine from the scriptures and from his own prophetic understanding, encourage and buoy up—all by use of pungent, colloquial language and frequent anecdote, and invariably within a general atmosphere of optimism and faith that communicated confidence to the wavering and downhearted. Many are the entries in the diaries of the listening Saints like this one of Wilford Woodruff: "Attended meeting. Heard Brigham Young speak. Could have listened to him all day."[17]

Although Brigham would have insisted that he preached from the Bible, he had no hesitancy in interjecting his own speculations. He had "a holy reverence and belief in the Bible"; he believed it to contain "the words of life and salvation"; he thought that those who followed the doctrines of the Bible would make "splendid husbands," "excellent wives," and "obedient children"; a nation that would follow biblical principles would become "wealthy and happy." Nevertheless, unlike many Protestant sermonizers of his day, he did not regard the Bible as the infallible "Word of God." Biblical texts sometimes contradicted each other, and there were ambiguities in the theologies and world views of the various writers. "Many precious things may have been rejected in the compilation and translation of the Bible," he declared.

> I have heard some [ministers] make the broad assertion that every word within the lids of the Bible was the word of God. I have said to them, "You have never read the Bible, have you?" "O, yes, and I believe every word in it is the word of God." Well, I believe that the Bible contains the word of God, and the words of good men, and the words of bad men; the words of good angels and words of the devil; and also the words uttered by the ass when he rebuked the prophet [Balaam] in his madness. I believe the words of the Bible are just what they are.[18]

Brigham was capable of humorous references even on serious topics, as is suggested by the following excerpt from a sermon of October 8, 1854, that has remained unpublished. The talk dealt with the creation of the world.

> When the Lord had organized the world, and filled the earth with animal and vegetable life, then he created man. . . . Moses made the Bible to say his wife was taken out of his side—was made of one of his ribs. As far as I know my ribs are equal on each side. The Lord knows if I had lost a rib for each wife I have, I should have had none left long ago. . . . As for the Lord taking a rib out of Adam's side to make a woman of, it would be just as true to say he took one out of my side.
>
> "But, Brother Brigham, would you make it appear that Moses did not tell the truth?"
>
> "No, not a particle more than I would that your mother did not tell the truth when she told you that little Billy came from a hollow toadstool. I would not accuse your mother of lying any more than I would Moses. The people in the days of Moses wanted to know things that was not for them, the same as your children do when they want to know where their little brother came from, and

he answered them according to the level of their understandings, the same as mothers do their children."[19]

His humor was not always lighthearted, however, whether in sermons or personal conversation. There were instances in which it seems to have been more calculated to wound than to amuse. He did not like pretentious people who put on airs and aped the fashions of the world, and he sometimes tried to "cut them down to size." He was in his office on one occasion discussing some business with a family; the door had been left ajar. A group of people walked by, and Brigham noticed the tall, handsome, immaculately dressed figure of John Taylor, president of the Quorum of Twelve Apostles. In a voice hardly muffled, Brigham exclaimed, "Well, if there isn't Prince John!" The elegant Taylor overheard the remark and came back to say, "As a person, Brigham Young, you can be awfully small; but I still respect you as a great leader."[20]

P A R T L Y as a follow-up to his preaching and partly inherent in his role as leader of his people, Brigham was expected to be a pastor, a family counselor, a financial adviser. People asked him where to build a home, how to find a spouse, whether to open a shop, how to collect a debt, when to plant potatoes, how to handle a confrontation with the Indians. Of the thirty thousand surviving copies of letters signed by Brigham, at least ten thousand are responses to letters directed to him for advice on personal and family problems.

While he tried to be patient and Solomonlike in his capacity as counselor, he privately wished that people would exercise greater patience and skill in solving their own problems. "When men have wives and cannot, or do not, live happily, and throw their family troubles, disputes, and cares upon me, or take a course by which their wives do so," he grumbled, "I think it wise for them to exercise a little patience and strive to learn wisdom in the conduct of those matters, that I may not be so frequently troubled with family difficulties. . . ."[21] To someone wanting advice about buying a neighbor's farm, he wrote:

> This is a subject about which I have no counsel to give, as I do not know the circumstances fully, and really have nothing to say about it. There are wise brethren in your vicinity with whom you can converse on the subject and from whom you can obtain counsel, which, with the aid of the light of the holy Spirit within yourself, ought to be a sufficient guide in this matter. A little reflection will enable you to perceive that it would not do for me to meddle with affairs of this kind.[22]

When an earlier decision of his was brought to his mind by one of the parties, Brigham replied, "Situated as I am, I cannot charge my mind with all the particulars of such cases; they are too unpleasant to me to have any wish to retain the recollection of them, and I dismiss them from my mind as soon as possible."[23]

Brigham kept his mental balance by freely expressing his reactions to impossible situations, often in light and humorous ways, and by sympathizing with people facing difficult problems. When a man from Farmington called upon him to ask what to do about his second wife—who had told him she would steal from him if he didn't provide her enough and yet refused to get a divorce—Brigham replied that she was admittedly a "hard case," but there was little he could do to alter the situation.[24]

In all of this Brigham did not take himself too seriously. When a certain Elizabeth Green wrote to him in 1851 to have her name removed from the records of the church because she had decided to become a spiritualist, Brigham's answer was:

> Madam: I have this day examined the records of baptisms for the remission of sins in the Church of Jesus Christ of Latter Day Saints, and not being able to find the name of "Elizabeth Green" recorded therein I was saved the necessity of erasing your name therefrom. You may therefor consider that your sins have not been remitted you and you may consequently enjoy the benefits therefrom.[25]

Brigham learned that one of the Salt Lake bishops was selling liquor in his store. This was not proper for any Latter-day Saint, let alone a bishop. Brigham wrote him the following letter:

> Dear Brother: I write to request you *not* to sell any more whiskey or alcohol, or any description of spiritous liquor, no matter who may call upon you to purchase. And in case the plea is made that some will die unless the liquor can be had, be pleased to tell them to first call upon me and get an order for the coffin. . . . We have seen as much drunkenness about our streets as we care about seeing, and they all acknowledge that they got their liquor at [your] still.[26]

A third example of Brigham's light approach is a letter to a church member in central Utah who was disturbed about recurring fears that he was about to be murdered. Brigham's reply:

> Now, I do not think that anybody wants to slay you, unless it be your wives. The servants of the Lord do not want to do it; but if the women want to slay you, I do not know that we can help it, as we did not have to slay you to have you take wives.[27]

Brigham found it difficult to deal with people who were perplexed by what he regarded as minor decisions, such as what to eat and drink, what cut of clothes to wear, what color their house should be painted, and how to keep the Sabbath day holy. Being a Latter-day Saint was more important than making such petty choices. When he was in England, he ran into a number of Sabbatarians who objected to his shaving on the Sabbath; he should shave on Saturday and skip Sunday. Brigham responded, "I will shave on Sunday morning, if I have not time to do so on Saturday." We in America have our own customs and traditions on matters like this, he said. "And if I wish to go to meeting and worship God, it is just as acceptable to do so on Saturday as on Sunday." Brigham called to mind Adam Clark, of whom it was said, "If the clock struck twelve on Saturday night, and he happened to have but one shoe blacked, he would drop the blacking and brushes, and go to meeting next day with one shoe blacked and the other unblacked." That might be esteemed a pious example by some, said Brigham, but to him it was "a waymark to the kingdom of folly."[28]

As a public figure, Brigham was a mixture of idealism and pragmatism. The idealistic path of service to his people intertwined with the pragmatic goal of preserving his status, power, and influence. At any given time, for instance, it would have been hard to tell whether he considered his acknowledged opponents (federal appointees, apostates) or some of his more contrary followers the greater enemy. An example of the latter was his sometime business agent Edwin D. Woolley. A loyal but plainspoken former Pennsylvania Quaker, Woolley's rejoinders sometimes matched Brigham's own, and irritated the president. Bishop Woolley (he was longtime bishop of the Salt Lake Thirteenth Ward) was not satisfied with the social hall as a place for ward entertainments and in 1861 constructed an elegant addition to his ward meetinghouse for use as a place of recreation. Called "the Assembly Rooms," the structure was lavishly furnished and decorated. At the dedication Brigham, who hated the trappings of luxury, said he would not counsel parents to send their children there because it was "only fit for folks of the caliber of Presidents of the United States or Congressmen."[29] Bishop Woolley not only used the Assembly Rooms for ward dances and parties, lectures and classes, but also dared to rent it to non-Mormons for similar purposes. Brigham complained publicly that the bishop was allowing "a sacred house" to be used for profane purposes. After one such discussion, which was pointed if not heated, Brigham remarked caustically to the bishop: "Well, I suppose now you are going to go off and apostatize." "No, I won't," retorted Edwin. "If this were your church I might, but it's just as much mine as it is yours."[30]

Brigham could hardly fail to respect that response. He is said to have commented once that if Bishop Woolley should fall off his horse while crossing the Jordan River on the way to his pasture, those searching for him should not expect him to be floating downstream; they would more likely find him swimming upstream, obstinately contending against the current.[31] Brigham had a number of run-ins with such recalcitrants, but not all of them remained as loyal as Woolley.

I F Brigham was a religious leader, was he also, to any degree, a contemplative; that is, a person with a frequent experience of encounter with God? Certainly no one would suppose the hyperactive, down-to-earth Brigham engaged at any time in transcendental meditation, although one can imagine pensive thoughts coming to him as he traveled long distances uninterrupted in his buggy. But there would have been no emptying of the mind or focusing on the One. He believed God's revelations were based on natural principles—and not likely to be conveyed by ineffable experiences. Did he have an interior life of rich spirituality? The answer is probably yes, based upon two clues. He did pray— in private, in his family circle, and in council meetings and congregations. And he was a devoted participant in temple ceremonies. There Brigham, removed from the ordinary routine of life, could experience an approach to God.

That the temple meant a great deal to him is demonstrated both by his insistence that the Nauvoo Temple be completed before the Saints left that city and by the major investment he made in the erection of the Salt Lake and St. George temples. Brigham's first public act upon locating the site for Salt Lake City was to place down his cane and say, "Here we shall build a temple to our God."[32] Construction began after an elaborate ceremony in 1853 at which there was a dedication at each of the four cornerstones of the structure. Dozens of men and teams worked more or less steadily on the project during all of Brigham Young's presidency. When he found that the temple could not be finished during his probable lifetime, Brigham dedicated ground in St. George for a less imposing temple. It was completed in 1876, less than a year before he was to die. It gave him great satisfaction to be able to revive and revise the temple ritual taught him by Joseph Smith. A bold and bluff leader who could wheel and deal when he had to, Brigham was also responsive to the chords of celestial music as mediated through a liturgical experience of profound significance to him and his followers. His entire religious existence was not absorbed in his activities as organizer and as preacher.

W H A T were Brigham's theological contributions? In his sermons, which he called "discourses" because he did not follow the model of conventional talks, did he present articulated statements of Mormon religious positions? A reading of his hundreds of available sermons suggests that, although he was a vigorous thinker, he was not a systematic theologian. One could hardly summarize his "discourses" and produce a *Summa Theologiae* of Mormonism. But he was concerned about "sound doctrine" and did function as a theologian by using the Bible, Book of Mormon, Doctrine and Covenants, and remembered statements of Joseph Smith as a body of material that required explaining, reconciling, and clarifying.[33] He tried to make sure that everything printed or taught under church auspices passed the test of orthodoxy. After some materials that contained errors had appeared from the British mission office, he expressed his concern about "unsound" doctrines and reminded the brethren there to exercise vigilance so that "no ideas or doctrine be published at the Office in Liverpool, or at any other point in the Missions under your presidency, which will not bear the strictest investigation."[34]

It would be impossible in this space to discuss how Brigham dealt with the many topics in Mormon theology, but unquestionably his cosmological and doctrinal ideas, influenced as they were by the scripture and the teachings of Joseph Smith, set the pattern and context of Mormon work and worship for his own and future generations. If later Mormonism has tended to shift away, to some extent, from Brigham's theology, it has occurred not by any formal repudiation of his doctrines but by giving a different emphasis.[35]

Brigham had, first of all, a philosophy of eternity, eternity for him being synonymous with endlessness.* "There never was a time when there were not Gods and worlds, and when men were not passing through," he said. (7:333; also 1:352, 13:270) "There never has been a time," he said, "when there have not been worlds like this, and there never will be a time when there will not be worlds organized and prepared for intelligent beings to dwell upon." (8:81)

Brigham's cosmos consisted of uncreated time and space, material elements, laws and principles that condition the structure of the universe, and the intelligence that constitutes the basis of human personality.[36] There was no immaterial substance; spirit was "refined matter." Recalling a sermon delivered by a "Christian" minister on the soul, Brigham expostulated:

> After laboring long on the subject, he [the minister] straightened himself up—he was a fine looking man—and said he, "My brethren and sisters, I must come to the conclusion that the soul of man is an immaterial substance." Said I, "Bah!" There was no more sense in his discourse than in the bleating of a sheep or the grunting of a pig. (14:198)

This refusal to divide reality into two distinct realms—material and immaterial, temporal and spiritual—elevated the role and worth of the material world in Mormondom.

God, for Brigham, was a craftsman, a scientist, who molded the material elements into various shapes and forms according to His designs. But God did not make the world out of nothing:

> Worlds are made of crude element which floats, without bounds in the eternities—in the immensity of space; an eternity of matter—no limits to it, in its natural state, and the power of the Almighty has this influence and wisdom—when He speaks He is obeyed, and matter comes together and is organized. We take the rock, and the lime from the mountains and burn it and make mortar with lime and sand and lay the foundation of houses, and rear the superstructure with bricks, stones, adobies or lumber. We bring these elements together and

---

* Because of the numerous quotations from Brigham Young's sermons in the *Journal of Discourses* which appear in the remainder of this chapter, I have given, after each such quotation, the volume and page of the *Journal of Discourses* in which it appears. From this point on in the chapter, reference notes will be given only when other sources have been used.

organize them according to our pleasure. We should teach our children that God has so organized the earth from the rude, rough native element. (13:248)

Creation, in other words, was organization—the shaping of inert elements into superior forms. "To assert that the Lord made this earth out of nothing," said Brigham, "is preposterous and impossible. God never made something out of nothing." (14:116)

The most conspicuous characteristic of Brigham's universe was its never-ending activity. "All creation is in progress," he said. All visible nature was going through a process of growing and increasing, although there were cycles of growth and decay. An example of the latter was human death, which separated the body and spirit. (1:350, 3:276–77)

God's structuring of the organized universe fell within the parameters of natural law. God and man, science and religion, were all dependent upon and conditioned by the order of nature. Said Brigham:

My religion is natural philosophy. You never heard me preach a doctrine but what has a natural system to it, and, when understood, it is as easy to comprehend as that two and two equals four. All the revelations of the Lord to the children of men, and all revealed doctrines of salvation are upon natural principles, upon natural philosophy. (4:202–3)

God's creation of any world, therefore, occurred according to eternally "fixed laws and regulations, by which the elements are fashioned to fulfill their destiny in all the varied kingdoms and orders of creation, and this process of creation is from everlasting to everlasting." (11:122)

God's intervention in the world was analogous to a chemist's operation in the laboratory. All of God's "productions come according to natural principles." (8:115, 9:255) An individual who does not understand the laws and principles of chemistry may be mystified by what goes on in the lab.

The world was filled with strange events, but no event, however inexplicable, was really supernatural. "They have all transpired upon natural principles." (4:203) The real problem is insufficient understanding:

What is a mystery? We do not know, it is beyond our comprehension. When we talk about mystery, we talk about eternal obscurity, for that which is known, ceases to be a mystery; and all that is known, we may know as we progress in the scale of intelligence. . . . Things transpire almost every day in our lives which we class under the term mystery, for want of a better term. What does it mean, in reality? Why, nothing at all. (1:274)

We may call certain events miracles, but that is because of our lack of understanding:

> There is no such thing, in reality, as a miracle, except to those who do not understand the "Alpha and Omega" of every phenomenon that is made manifest. To a person who thoroughly understands the reason of all things, and can trace from their effects to their true causes, mystery does not exist. (2:91)

Not that Brigham rejected Jesus' miracles—only the interpretation people gave them.

> When the only begotten Son of God [Jesus] was upon the earth, he understood the nature of these elements, how they were brought together to make this world and all things that are thereon, for he helped to make them. He had the power of organizing, what we should call, in a miraculous manner. That which to Him was no miracle, is called miraculous by the inhabitants of the earth. (1:270)

The miracle of changing water into wine, for example, was a "chemical process" and "can be done by the persons who understand the process." (1:270)

All of this suggested that, as man acquired knowledge and understanding, he could approach godhood. Life was a great school, providing the opportunity of acquiring knowledge and experience so that human beings might become "more perfect even as our Father in Heaven is perfect."

> Our religion embraces chemistry; it embraces all the knowledge of the geologist, and then it goes a little further than their systems of argument, for the Lord Almighty, its author, is the greatest chemist there is. (15:127)

"Mormonism," said Brigham, "embraces all truth that is revealed and that is unrevealed, whether religious, political, scientific, or philosophical." (9:14)

"Truth" included both descriptive natural law and prescriptive moral law. Both were necessary to the perfection of man. The morally neutral laws of science describing the behavior of matter were fused with the moral law pre-scribing perfection for individuals and societies. Men and women could achieve "perfection" by the exercise of godly virtues: compassion, sympathy, love, and unity. Especially unity.

> If we should build up and organize a community, we would have to do it on the principle of oneness. . . . A city of one hundred thousand or a million of people could be united into a perfect family, and they would work together as beautifully as the different parts of the carding machine work together. (16:170)

Power seeking, greed, envy, and selfishness were destructive, bringing about poverty, unhappiness, disorder, strife, and disintegration.

God, for Brigham as for Joseph Smith before him, was once a "man" on another planet who had "passed the ordeals we are now passing through; He has received an experience, has suffered and enjoyed, and knows all that we know regarding the toils, suffering, life and death of this mortality, for He has passed through the whole of it, and has received . . . exaltation." (11:249) God, said Brigham, "is a being of the same species as ourselves; He lives as we do, except the difference that we are earthly, and He is heavenly . . . in either case we are of one species—of one family." (4:217)

God is the father of Jesus the Christ, and also of all the spirits of men. God the Father, Jesus His Son, and the Holy Ghost constitute the Godhead, and Brigham and his fellow Saints, as with other Christians, addressed their prayers to God the Father in the name of Jesus Christ. While Brigham regarded the atoning role of Jesus in much the same way as other Christians of his day, he did regard Adam, the first earth man according to Genesis, as a more exalted personage than many contemporary Christians did.[37] Indeed, Adam was a kind of hero; an oft-quoted phrase from the Book of Mormon was "Adam fell that man might be; and men are that they might have joy." Brigham thus adopted a doctrine known in the history of theology as "the happy or fortunate fall." Adam would stand at the head of the human race on the Day of Judgment. Following the same concept, Brigham once said that there were several Adams, for it was a title used to designate several generations of fathers of the human race. Indeed, in one of his off-the-cuff sermons Brigham once went so far as to say that "He [Adam] is our Father and our God, and the only God with whom we have to do." (1:50, 4:216–17)[38]

Brigham's understanding of this "Adam-God" doctrine, which was never adopted by the church, is unclear. Certainly, one finds many statements by Brigham in both published and unpublished sermons declaring that it is a believer's responsibility to worship God in the name of Christ, with no mention of Adam. Perhaps that was Brigham's way of emphasizing the ongoing, expansive potential of Adam's descendants. In the eternities ahead, human beings would have the potential of peopling earths and in that sense being gods and goddesses—Adams and Eves.[39]

Brigham's sermons suggest that he saw God, angel, man, spirit, intelligence as merely different names designating related beings in various stages of development. Man is in the middle stage. Intelligence and spirit, when prepared, entered mortal existence and became "man." God derives His greatest satisfaction from the efforts of His children to "walk in His footsteps." (8:116) Man is a God in embryo, with a capacity for endless growth, development, and joy. (2:125, 7:149, 286)

Man's mission and responsibility, his destiny and privilege, Brigham insisted, was to build society—to plant trees, gardens, and vineyards; to build houses, shops, and meetinghouses; to dig ditches and dugways; to organize colleges, concerts, and study groups. (13:305) In his first "General Epistle to the Saints," written after his elevation to the Presidency of the church in Winter Quarters in December 1847, Brigham set forth some of the requirements for building a Zionic community "in the tops of the mountains":

... the Saints should improve every opportunity of securing at least a copy of every valuable treatise on education—every book, map, chart, or diagram that may contain interesting, useful, and attractive matter, to gain the attention of children, and cause them to love to learn to read; and, also every historical, mathematical, philosophical, geographical, geological, astronomical, scientific, practical, and all other variety of useful and interesting writings, maps, etc. . . . from which important and interesting matter may be gleaned. . . .[40]

In a subsequent sermon Brigham reflected:

How gladly would we understand every principle pertaining to science and art, and become thoroughly acquainted with every intricate operation of nature, and with all the chemical changes that are constantly going on around us! How delightful this would be, and what a boundless field of truth and power is open for us to explore! We are only just approaching the shores of the vast ocean of information that pertains to this physical world, to say nothing of that which pertains to the heavens, to angels and celestial beings, to the place of their habitation, to the manner of their life, and their progress to still higher degrees of perfection. (9:167)

"The whole object of the creation of this world," said Brigham, "is to exalt the intelligences that are placed upon it, that they may live, endure, and increase forever and ever. We are not here to quarrel and contend about the things of this world, but we are here to subdue and beautify . . . the whole face of the earth, until it shall become like the garden of Eden." (7:290, 1:254)

If mobs expelled the Saints, Brigham promised, the latter would continue to build wherever the Lord led them. He had himself built and lost six homes (Mendon, New York; Kirtland, Ohio; Far West, Missouri; Montrose, Iowa; Nauvoo, Illinois; and Winter Quarters, Nebraska) and he kept on building. "All the heaven we shall ever have," he told the Saints, "is the one we make for ourselves." (9:170)

For Brigham, every activity of man's daily life was part of religion. Theology must be pulled earthward. "We cannot talk about spiritual things," said Brigham, "without connecting with them temporal things, neither can we talk about temporal things without connecting spiritual things with them. . . . We, as Latter-day Saints, really expect, look for and we will not be satisfied with anything short of being governed and controlled by the word of the Lord in all our acts, both spiritual and temporal. If we do not live for this, we do not live to be one with Christ." (10:329)

N O N E of his contemporaries supposed that everything Brigham spoke was to be regarded as official Mormon doctrine, or that all of his counselors and advisers agreed with everything he said. Since his sermons were not written in advance and since, in almost every instance, he did not use notes, relying entirely on the inspiration of the moment, he occasionally got carried away and expressed himself more strongly or less thoughtfully than he might have done if he had given carefully planned sermons. His closest advisers rarely took issue with his opinions, but one who did was Orson Pratt, a senior apostle, leading authority on Mormon theology, and a speculative scientist and philosopher. The ongoing controversies between Pratt and Brigham indicate how far the President was willing to go in tolerating differing points of view on key doctrinal questions.[41]

Pratt was influential in formulating the Mormons' idea of God, the religious basis of polygamy, the pre-earthly existence of spirits, the resurrection, and the doctrine of the gathering of Israel. But there were significant differences between his approach and that of Brigham. When Pratt dwelt on the divine attributes of God, Brigham found it necessary to remind the Saints that they worshipped God, a corporeal being, not His attributes. When Pratt emphasized the omniscience, omnipresence, and omnipotence of God, Brigham pointed out that God was a developing being still in the process of growth—still progressing in knowledge and wisdom. Pratt thought doctrinal positions should be rational and consistent, systematically presented and defended, and reconcilable with extant written scriptures. Brigham believed in continuous revelation and that the voice of God coming through the Prophet in an inspired sermon had more relevance than what had been written several generations earlier in an accepted inspired book. In any case, Brigham contended for the simple gospel. "When I read some of the writings of such philosophers," he said, in 1857 after listening to one of Pratt's long, involved, abstractly reasoned arguments, "they make me think, 'O dear, granny, what a long tail our puss has got.'" (4:267)

Once when Brigham advised Pratt that certain of his writings were not "sound doctrine," Pratt replied that he realized it was not his prerogative "to teach publicly that which the President considers to be unsound." But he hoped "that you will grant me as an individual the privilege of believing my present views, and that you will not require me to teach others . . . that which I cannot without more light believe in."[42] Brigham contended that, as the Lord's mouthpiece, he had an obligation to assure that the Saints were taught correct doctrine. Convinced that his own views were based on the written canon, Pratt was reluctant to admit error. Convinced *he* was right, Brigham nevertheless was loath to publicly criticize and demean Pratt, whose mind and energy were among the church's most valuable assets. Brigham feared the dangerous effects of Pratt's logic; Pratt feared the dangerous extremes to which Brigham might go in his impromptu sermons. Thus there was a continuous tension between Pratt the philosopher and Brigham the Prophet.

There were many public run-ins between the two over twenty years, until Brigham's death in 1877. But in every instance, there were resolutions that left Pratt with a measure of freedom in speaking and writing and Brigham with a measure of control over the doctrinal pronouncements coming from Pratt's indefatigable and persuasive pen.

Sometimes the reprimands could be acrimonious. For example, in 1857 Brigham declared:

> With all the knowledge and wisdom that are combined in the person of brother Orson Pratt, still he does not yet know enough to keep his foot out of it, but drowns himself in his own philosophy, every time he undertakes to treat upon principles that he does not understand. . . . His vain philosophy is no criterion or guide for the Saints in doctrine. (4:267)

Pratt's reply to these sniping criticisms was:

> So far as I have ever preached abroad in the world, and published, one thing is certain, I have not published anything but what I verily believed to be true, however much I may have been mistaken, and I have generally endeavored to show the people, from the written word of God, as well as reason, wherein it was true. . . . Previous to declaring a doctrine, I have always inquired in my own mind, "Can this doctrine be proved by revelation given, or by reason, or can it not?" If I found it could be proved, I set forth the doctrine but if I found there was no evidence to substantiate it, I laid it aside. (2:58–59)

Brigham had no doubt of Pratt's competence in theology. "The trouble between Orson Pratt and me," he once said, "is I do not know enough and he knows too much. I do not know everything."[43] (He was not implying that Pratt did!) Pratt, on the other hand, said:

> I am willing to take President Young as a guide in most things but not in all. President Young does not propose to have revelations in all things. I am not too loose in my agency. I have said many things which President Young says is false. . . . I do not believe them to be false. . . . When Joseph [Smith] teaches anything and Brigham seems to teach another contrary to Joseph . . . I believe them as Joseph has spoken them. . . . President Young said I ought to make a confession of what I do not believe. I am not going to crawl to Brigham and act the hypocrite and confess what I do not believe. I will be a free man. . . . It may cost me my fellowship but I will stick to it if I die tonight. . . . O Lord God Almighty, I believe what I say.[44]

Although some of his associates recommended it, Brigham refused to entertain the thought of trying Pratt for his fellowship. "I do not have it in my heart to disfellowship people who believe differently," he said. "I seek merely to correct men in their [improper] views."[45] With respect to Pratt he stated, "I am determined to whip Brother Pratt into it and make him work in the harness. . . . If Elder Pratt was chopped up in inch pieces," he added, "each piece would cry out Mormonism is true!"[46]

Shortly before Brigham's death, Pratt acknowledged to Young that "it has been only through your great forbearance and long suffering, and the patience of my Quorum, that I have been continued in the high and responsible calling of the Apostleship to this day. . . . I am determined to be one with you, and . . . humbly submit, in all matters of doctrine and principle, my judgment to those whose right it is, by divine appointment, to receive revelation, and guide the Church."[47]

I F Brigham Young was not a systematic theologian like Pratt, he did have certain characteristic emphases, a power of mind, a trenchant vigor, and a recognition of the earthly role of religion that deserve more respect than he has usually been given. If he was not on the level of St. Augustine—a great preacher, an incandescent candle of individual spirituality, a creative synthesizer and major theologian, not to mention philosopher of history, combatant of heresy, and administrator-organizer—he nevertheless possessed the ingredients of what the Latter-day Saints have come to place within a single word: prophet. For Saints, despite his humanity—or perhaps because of it—he was a man for all seasons, exactly what they needed during the crucial generation following the death of their founding prophet.

13 ✦

Indians: Friendship
and Caution

Why should men have a disposition to kill a destitute, naked
Indian, who may steal a shirt, or a horse and think it no harm,
when they never think of meting out a like retribution to a
white man who steals, although he has been taught better
from infancy?[1]

THERE were approximately twelve thousand Native Americans
in the region claimed by Brigham Young and his followers in 1847 and succeeding years. These included Gosiutes in the northwest, Paiutes in the southwest, Navahos in the southeast, Shoshonis in the northeast, and Utes (or
Utahs) in the center. These Indian nations were not well organized, and usually
took the form of scattered bands that operated quite independently of each
other. In comparison with most Indian nations in the Midwest and East, they
lived a marginal life, barely subsisting on what the region afforded.

The first important contact the Mormons had with any of these groups
was in the fall of 1847, after Brigham, Heber, and others had gone back to
pick up their families in the Missouri Valley. A group under the leadership of
Wanship, a small Ute band, had fought the rival Little Wolf's band and,
although losing two men, took two teenagers, a boy and a girl, as prisoners.
One Ute, Batiste, offered both prisoners to the Mormons for sale. When the
Mormons recoiled at the suggestion, Batiste said if they did not buy them he
would kill them. When the Mormons continued to hesitate, Batiste killed the
boy and returned with the girl. Accepting Batiste at his word, Charles Decker,
Brigham's brother-in-law, agreed to give Batiste a gun for the girl. Decker
then gave the girl to his sister Lucy, Brigham's first plural wife, to raise. Lucy
named her Sally and reared her as her own. She later became chief cook in
the Beehive House and married the Ute chief Kanosh as a plural wife, but
Kanosh's first wife, in a fit of jealousy, murdered her.[2]

Brigham had dealt with Indians in the Midwest before his trek to the Salt Lake Valley. Before leaving Nauvoo, he sent delegations to meet and negotiate with Indians for permission to camp on their lands. He met with Potawatomi chiefs in Iowa and asked for permission to pass through their territories, offering gifts and building improvements in return. As the wagons moved into Omaha country, Brigham continued to arrange negotiations, smoke the peace pipe, and work out mutually agreeable arrangements with the tribes. He proposed paying the Omahas and providing help for permission to camp for two years at what became Winter Quarters. When Indians began stealing stock from the river bottoms and some Mormons strongly urged killing them, Brigham suggested instead the use of guards and defensive measures or whipping as a last resort. His approach was to be friendly, promote peace, trade fairly, avoid extreme reactions or retaliation, and maintain distance.

Joseph Smith had taught that Indians were a remnant of scattered Israel, a fallen race whose ancestors' history was outlined in the Book of Mormon. Mormons were under a special obligation, he said, to redeem the "Lamanites," as the Indians were called in the Book of Mormon, and to teach them the ways of civilization and the spiritual truths of the Restored Gospel.

Accepting these views, Brigham saw Indians as being under a curse (according to the Book of Mormon account), which explained their internecine warfare and degradation. With the help of the Saints they would become a "pure and delightsome" people.[3] Though they were culturally inferior to whites— "naturally savage, revengeful, and prone to wander about and lead vicious, idle, and criminal lives"—they were a "people of destiny."[4]

"In some respects," he wrote to the head of the Las Vegas Indian mission, "they are already superior to the whites," alluding to their "simple heartedness and honesty."[5] He minimized Indian thefts, noting that the Saints had suffered much more from whites of bad character than from Indians, and that he would much rather take a chance for fair treatment from Indians.[6] In responding to Mormon settlers who were upset at Indian depredations, he "alluded to the ignorance of the untutored savage, and that to be rigid in our exactions and requirements of them would be to invoke a judgment upon ourselves, which if our Heavenly Father exacted would preclude the exercise of that charity which we sought after at His hands."[7]

He urged his followers not to kill Indians for stealing. Stealing was a far worse crime for a white man, who had been taught otherwise all his life, than for an Indian, to whom it seemed natural and sensible:

> . . . the truth is, their sense of matters and things differs so much from ours that we often find it difficult to bear with their indignities and ignorance. . . .
>
> What to us is a deep insult and outrage, to them is a small matter, of little consequence; on the other hand, a thing of minor importance to us becomes to them a thing of great moment.[8]

He cautioned against becoming too familiar with Indians. "Treat them kindly, and treat them as Indians," he said, "and not as your equals." Obviously, whatever acculturation Brigham hoped to accomplish with the Indians was to be done from a position of white superiority.

Out of these attitudes grew Brigham's policies in dealing with the Indians: his attempts to civilize and "raise them up," his notions of fairness and forbearance, his willingness to chastise and punish severely when necessary. He did not see them as having a superior or prior claim on the region; whatever the resistance from the Indians, the Mormons would not be driven from their home in the Great Basin and would continue to found new settlements and expand irrigated acreage.

BRIGHAM'S decision to settle near the Great Salt Lake was based in part on information he had learned about the Indians in the area. He hoped to avoid crowding either the Shoshonis in the north or the Utes in Utah Valley. The initial contacts between Mormons and Indians in the Salt Lake Valley helped confirm the wisdom of this decision, for as bands from both tribes came in to trade, disagreements erupted between them. The Shoshonis claimed that the Utes were overstepping their boundaries and offered to sell land to the Mormons, hoping perhaps that they would serve as a buffer between the two native groups. Brigham responded by directing his people not to trade any more guns and ammunition and by enunciating a position regarding the land that was suited to Mormon interests. Discouraging the idea of paying the Shoshonis for the land or even for the use of it, he noted that doing so would only encourage other tribes to ask for payment too. "The land," he said, "belongs to our Father in Heaven and we calculate to plow and plant it and no man will have power to sell his inheritance for he cannot remove it; it belongs to the Lord."[9] The Indians claimed all the land as their own and the right to a share of the grain raised in return for the use of this land. Neither Brigham nor any of his associates paid serious attention to such claims.

Brigham insisted that the Mormons had never pushed the Indians off the land but had always "consulted" them, "and they not only evinced a willingness but a strong desire to have us settle upon them . . . ," even to the point of being unhappy when their valleys were not chosen for settlement.[10] They stood to benefit, he thought, from having closer facilities to trade and get provisions. In 1850 Brigham asked the Ute chief Walkara (Walker) if he desired to sell his land. Walker responded by saying he did not want the Mormons to buy it but it was all right to settle on it. Brigham assured him that "our Father the Great Spirit has plenty of land for you and for the Mormons."[11]

Brigham's report of a peace meeting with both Utes and Shoshonis also implies acquiescence on the part of the Indians. When asked to sell their land, they replied that it did not belong to them "but that if we would make a settlement on Green river they would be glad to come and trade with us."[12] Brigham may have given too much weight to this limited statement, for there is evidence of Indian opposition to Mormon settlement at Green River and elsewhere.[13]

For about a year and a half the Saints generally enjoyed peaceful relations with the Indians. When Brigham returned to the Missouri Valley in 1847, the Salt Lake High Council implemented his instructions to trade honestly with the Indians but to maintain strict separation from them. In hopes of preventing individual disputes with the Indians, a few Mormons were designated traders.

But the Indians continued to steal horses and kill cattle. In 1849 Brigham sent Colonel John C. Scott of the Nauvoo Legion with a company of militia into Utah Valley. Scott and his men found the Indian camp and, when the Indians refused to surrender, killed the men and took the women and children back to Salt Lake City. Five days later the Mormon leadership decided to establish a settlement among the Utes in Utah Valley. The settlers assured the natives that they would not deprive them of their land or their rights, that there was room enough for all. But clearly the Utes were edgy, and Brigham, fearing an uprising, took steps to try to prevent it. His plan involved restructuring and expanding the Nauvoo Legion, directing the Provo Saints to finish their fort quickly and stay inside away from the Indians, and limiting trading with the Indians to two men. He also sent conciliatory messages to Walker, the Utah chief.

In June of 1849, Walker met with Brigham and other leaders and invited the Mormons to settle on his lands in San Pitch (Sanpete) Valley. In return Brigham offered to help the Indians grow crops, teach them to read, and enlighten them concerning their history. At first the new settlement of Manti was basically a mission to the Indians to help them become accustomed to white men's ways of life. Mormons and Indians in Sanpete Valley generally were able to cooperate and help each other, each side effectively policing its own renegades.

At Provo, however, early in 1850 the injudicious murder of a native named Old Bishop by three Mormons resulted in a rash of thefts and threats. When the increased "sauciness" was reported to Brigham (without any mention of the Old Bishop provocation), he repeated his earlier directions to use wisdom and forbearance, saying that if the Mormons killed Indians for stealing they must answer for it. Then, however, Isaac Higbee came to plead his case personally, saying that every citizen of Provo favored killing the Indians off, and the suggestion received unanimous recommendations from his associates as well as the encouragement of Captain Howard Stansbury of the U.S. Army Corps of Engineers, who was surveying the region. Still not knowing about Old Bishop, Brigham ordered out the militia to exterminate all the "hostile" Indians while saving women and children and those who asked for peace. The expedition accomplished much in the way of eliminating Indians but nothing in the way of producing a lasting peace, despite Brigham's attempts to heal the breach by returning property and prisoners to the natives as soon as possible. Rather, the Provo campaign was taken as a model for later responses, as reports of depredations were increasingly responded to with military force and the killing of Indians, as at Ogden and Tooele.

By the time of the expedition to Tooele in June of 1851, the policy of extermination was being reversed. In rescinding earlier orders to trap Indians and kill them, General Daniel H. Wells of the Nauvoo Legion noted that pursuing them was costing more time and money than the value of what they had taken. Brigham was recognizing that "it is cheaper by far, yes hundreds and thousands of dollars cheaper to pay such losses, than raise an expedition . . . to fight Indians."[14]

Another solution to the "Indian problem" that Brigham considered in these first years was complete removal. Frustrated in his attempts to civilize the Indian, finding him troublesome, hostile, and increasingly an obstacle to expanding settlements, Brigham at the end of 1850 asked Utah's delegate to Congress, John M. Bernhisel, to try to get the government to arrange for removal of the Indians from Utah Territory to more suitable areas elsewhere. "We would have taught them to plow and sow, and reap and thresh," he wrote, "but they prefer idleness and theft." Removal, he said, would be better for the Indians themselves as well as promoting the "safety of the mails" and the "progress of civilization." Once settled, the Indians should be taught agriculture, science, and religion by farmers and missionaries sent by the government.[15]

Nevertheless, Brigham later admitted the Indians' rights to the land upon which the Mormons were living, saying that those who wished to come back and live near the settlements had a right to do so.

> This is the land that they and their fathers have walked over and called their own; and they have just as good a right to call it theirs to-day as any people have to call any land their own. They have buried their fathers and mothers and children here; this is their home, and we have taken possession of it, and occupy the land where they used to hunt. . . .

He noted the lack of game and fish and restated again the responsibility of the Mormon farmers toward the natives: "It is our duty to feed these poor ignorant Indians; we are living on their possessions and at their homes." He backed off from taking too much blame, however, insisting that "we are not intruders, but we are here by the providence of God." The Mormon responsibility was not to depart and leave the land to the Indians but to stay, raise grain enough to feed them, and treat them kindly.[16]

T H E summer of 1853 brought a rash of Indian attacks on Mormon settlements that came to be known collectively as the Walker War, since the Ute warriors of Chief Walker were responsible for most of the attacks. Much of the difficulty resulted from Brigham's attempts to halt the Indians' ongoing trade with

Mexicans, who came to get children to take to Mexico as slaves. In April of 1853, Brigham Young met Pedro Leon, one such trader, and told him that such traffic was illegal in Utah, in spite of his license from the governor of New Mexico. Brigham then issued a proclamation forbidding arms traffic with the Indians and sent a thirty-man detachment south to warn settlers to be on their guard. It was feared that the Indians might be incited by the Mexicans.

Tension was in the air. Brigham reminded his people that they had avoided Indian massacres so far because they had always been ready. "When we first entered Utah," he said, "we were prepared to meet all the Indians in these mountains, and kill every soul of them if we had been obliged so to do. This preparation secured to us peace."[17] If Walker should become hostile, "he shall be wiped out of existence, and every man that will follow him."[18] Federal Indian agent Jacob Holeman feared that, given Brigham's strong language, the militia might get carried away and "may go farther than the conduct and acts of the Indians should justify." But his fears did not come to pass. A month later he reported that the disturbances had quieted down and complimented Brigham on having "promptly laid hold of the matter, and checked it at once."[19]

The lull did not last long. During the summer of 1853, Brigham was faced with many Indian depredations. The main thrust of his policy consisted of defensive preparation, a preference for making life and property secure and avoiding hostilities. He emphasized the importance of forts, directing in his General Order No. 1 that "the policy of constructing forts and occupying them be adopted and rigidly enforced." Settlers were not to retaliate or threaten the Indians but were to act strictly on the defensive.[20] Brigham's military directives emphasized the need for efficiency, energy, and dispatch in intelligence gathering and communication. He advised securing the stocks that were left—even to the point of sending them to Salt Lake City for safekeeping—rather than fruitlessly trying to recover those the Indians had taken. He was "entirely unwilling that men should be sent out after the Indians" for fear of losing more men and animals and increasing the Indians' fears.[21]

Brigham was concerned about the instability and rashness of his people, whose reactions were not unlike those of most Americans on the frontier. Either they were so complacent that they did not bother to take ordinary precautions such as closing doors, traveling in groups, and keeping arms close at hand, or they were all up in arms afraid that "all the Indians in the mountains are coming to kill off the Latter-day Saints," an eventuality that he himself had "no more fear of . . . than I have of the sun ceasing to give light upon the earth."[22]

Superintendent of Indian affairs by August 1853, Brigham forbade any trafficking of arms and ammunition with the Indians and revoked all licenses for trade. Five days later he softened this by sending explanatory letters to several military commanders authorizing them to continue to furnish small amounts of ammunition for hunting to Indians known to be friendly.[23]

When he had done all he could to rally and restrain his people, Brigham could look at the Walker War as a necessary means of chastening. Walker, he said, "is helping me to do the will of the Lord to this people, he is doing with a chastening rod what I have failed to accomplish with soft words. . . ."[24] The disturbances would "tend to teach us union, and learn us to be more diligent in listening to counsel, and in walking in obedience to the commandments of the Lord."[25] From the Mormon point of view, the war had the good results of expediting the harvest and stirring people to fortify their settlements and prepare themselves as they had been counseled to do all along. On the negative side, there were twelve Mormon deaths and stock losses perhaps as high as four hundred.[26] The war also halted the progress of many projects in the territory, such as the construction of the capitol at Fillmore and the attempts at iron manufacture in Cedar City.

Brigham continued to have difficulties with Walker. The following summer the chief became irritated at the citizens of Nephi for building their fort, feeling it was designed to keep him and his people from going into the city as they pleased. Brigham replied that the fort would be a protection for Walker from his enemies. Walker "threw away the letter and called Brigham Young a fool, saying he had been in the mountains longer than Brigham Young, and he was not afraid. He did not know what the Mormons meant by building forts." He grumbled that Brigham did not know how to treat a chief like him, demanding letters clearing him from blame in recent murders, and setting arbitrary terms for trade.[27]

A shrewd leader who foresaw the eventual destruction of his traditional way of life as a result of the Mormon presence, Walker had, on occasion, professed warm friendship toward Brigham; at other times he had demonstrated both anger and fear. In one conference with Brigham, he acknowledged that the Mormon's advice to him had been good and that he had been a fool for rejecting it. Yes, the Mormons had been friends to the Utes and had "used them well." Yes, they were glad the Mormons had settled on their lands. Yes, they wanted to trade with the whites. Yes, they loved Brigham: "ooa, we all love you." As if to prove all this, Walker arose, said a prayer, lifted his pipe to "Too wats" the Great Spirit, asked him to bless the pipe, then smoked it, and passed it to Brigham and his "chieftains" to do the same.[28]

Periodically, Brigham sent letters and presents (cattle, clothing, guns, grain, tobacco) to the chief, and Walker's responses became more and more respectful. By the time of his death, early in 1855, Walker was willing to say that Brigham really had been his best friend. Brigham's language in these diplomatic exchanges is illustrated in his letter of January 22, 1855, written less than a month before the chief's death.[29]

To Captain Walker, our brother: . . .
    I am much pleased . . . to hear from you, that your heart is inclined to peace, and that you are preaching to the Utahs continually that they must not war either with the white or red man. This is good, very good, and I want you to weary

not in thus well doing. Tell them we are their very best friends they have on the earth. We shall vary not, nor turn, either to the right hand or the left. We are their friends. While the sun shall shine and the moon shall give her light we are still their friends. And the reason is, Friend Walker, that I have before told you. [It is] because the Red Men have descended from the same fathers and are of the same family as the Mormons, and we love them, and shall continue to love them, and teach them things that may do them good.

And now, Brother Walker, you have never known me to be ought but your steadfast, undeviating friend. No two faces, nor double meaning, . . . have I ever shown you, and I never shall. But I will, as I always have, preach peace to all men, and I will tell the Snakes not to hurt the Utahs, and that the Utes are the friends of the Snakes and want peace like the Mormons. . . .

No, I have not thrown you away, nor do I mean to, altho some of my people might think you more to blame than they ought to think, for they do not all understand properly, neither do I approve of what some of my people think and do, with respect to the Indians. But you know some of your people are not wise in their actions, neither are some of mine, and we must mutually forgive. . . .

I now send you six large plugs of tobacco, that you may smoke in peace with your friends, remembering that I am one [friend] whilst ever you sojourn upon the earth, earnestly seeking your true welfare, and praying for blessings to descend upon you whilst your actions are guided by the Spirit of Truth.

Brigham Young

T H E most prominent theme in Brigham's Indian policy in the 1850s was patience and forbearance. Early in 1853 he advised the settlers at Fillmore "to give an inch or even a foot, to lose a dime or even a dollar rather than endanger their property or lives."[30] He continued to emphasize always being ready, using all possible means to conciliate the Indians, and acting only on the defensive. In sending an expedition to Fort Hall, he instructed, "You must be careful not to give any occasion, but bear and forbear, and give them no pretence or cause of provocation."[31] Brigham found it difficult to restrain many whites. One sheriff wanted an armed force so he could go against the Indians and "kill every damn Rascal."[32] Brigham replied that it was not necessary to call forces into service at the time. "The loss of a few cattle does not justify a retaliation sufficient for White men to kill the offenders," he wrote. "This is Indian politics in their savage state, and the white men's should be of a higher grade."[33]

Since more was needed in dealing with the Indians than simply trying to pacify them with presents and using military force when necessary, Brigham formally instituted, in the fall of 1851, a program of teaching Indians to farm by appointing three men as "farmers to the Indians." Paid $600 per year, these men were to work with individual tribes at Fillmore, Sanpete, and Harmony. Originally, their assignment was to grow produce to be used in pacifying the Indians; later their work expanded to include teaching the Indians themselves how to farm.

In one of his earliest meetings with Walker, Brigham told him, "We want you to learn to raise grain and cattle and not have to go and hunt and be exposed to other Indians, but build houses, raise grain, and be happy as we are."[34] Neither Walker nor other native leaders responded with enthusiasm to Brigham's suggestions. "They seem disposed to hang around and loiter about the settlements begging their provisions from day to day," Brigham reported.[35]

He repeatedly asked Washakie, the Shoshoni chief, to consider finding some good land to farm so he and his people could settle down and have schools. He offered to send men to help them, but Washakie was never really interested, despite making some halfhearted requests for assistance from time to time.

The Indian farms did experience some success. Brigham wrote to Thomas L. Kane about the harvest feast held in Parowan. All the Indians who had helped to raise the grain were invited, and 154 Piedes attended. Some Utes in the area were also invited but declined. Brigham commented, "Less hypocrisy there, than in the higher circles of Society, where they plan your destruction, while they eat your broth."[36]

When the Mormons opened relations with the Navahos in 1854, Brigham reminded the leader of the Mormon company that the Navahos were settled Indians who cultivated the land. He gave instructions to encourage Navaho efforts to care for themselves by taking along plows, spades, shovels, hoes, picks, and other farming implements.[37]

The effort to establish Indian farms really got off the ground with the arrival of Garland Hurt as the new federal Indian agent in February of 1855. He and Brigham agreed on many basic principles and were able to cooperate in developing some thriving farms during the following two years. Hurt asked Brigham's opinion, which largely coincided with his own, as to the desirability of such farms and requested suggestions from him of suitable sites. Brigham suggested locations in Utah, Juab, Sanpete, Millard, and Iron counties, noting that the Indians were already there "and would feel it a grievance to entirely leave the scenes of early childhood and cherished memories"—a definite change from his earlier desire to have them removed from the territory. He further recommended that the sites be near to hunting grounds and that the farmers appointed to run the farms should not "farm for the Indians at the expense of the government as is to[o] often the case but . . . learn them to farm raise grain cattle &c and to keep and preserve property."[38]

The Indian farms established by Hurt with Brigham's blessing and encouragement were thriving in three locations by the summer of 1856: Corn Creek, in Millard County; Twelve Mile Creek in Sanpete County; and near the mouth of Spanish Fork Canyon in Utah County. In 1857 there were more than seven hundred acres under cultivation and the farms were expected to yield crops valued at $24,752. The farms did not completely achieve the hoped-for objectives, however, since the Indian participation was generally limited to herding cattle and helping with harvesting.

But Hurt became alarmed when he discovered that the Mormons taught not only agriculture but also Mormonism. At Santa Clara in southern Utah among the domestic and agreeable Piedes, the missionaries were told to go live with the Indians, learn their language, and become close to them. "We intend at the April 1855 Conference," Brigham wrote, "to increase the missions among the Indians in their various locations—we feel it our duty to turn our attention more and more to the scattered remnants of Israel."[39] New missions were established at Elk Mountain in southeastern Utah; Las Vegas in south-western Utah, now Nevada; on the Salmon River in northern Idaho; and among the Cherokee nation in present-day Oklahoma. Hurt was fearful that the missionaries would tell the Indians that the Mormons were their friends and other Americans their enemies. He thought little of the caliber of men being called as missionaries—"rude and lawless young men, such as might be regarded as a curse to any civilized community."[40] There may have been some justification in his assessment, since Brigham was known to have asked local leaders to round up all the men who were asking to go off to the mines and call them on missions to the Indians instead, for "men that can go and dig gold certainly can go and assist in the redemption of the children of Israel, a far greater more important and profitable employment."[41]

Brigham advised baptizing Indians who desired it, ordaining the chiefs and head men to the priesthood, and having them attend church meetings and take the Holy Sacrament. The missionaries were to teach the Indians to be clean and virtuous and to start schools for them. Brigham's objective was to "form such connections and ties among them as can never be broken off, that we may be able to control and influence them as we shall see best for their good, and the good of Israel."[42] Again, forbearance and maintaining peaceful relations were of utmost importance in pursuing this aim. "For my part," he told the missionaries in Las Vegas, "I would rather that you or any of the rest of the missionaries would leave and come home than to pursue such a course as will lead on to angry and hostile feelings between you and the Lamanites."[43]

None of these missions accomplished the hoped-for results. Some were abandoned or destroyed due to Indian troubles; others were terminated by the U.S. Army occupation of Utah in 1858. Even when giving up an unsuccessful mission such as the one in Las Vegas, however, Brigham hoped to maintain good feeling with the Indians. He instructed the leaders to leave their rooms and gardens in the hands of some of the best Indians and try to manage their departure so the natives would regret their going and possibly then be ripe at a later time for another contingent to bring them "truth and salvation."[44]

A L T H O U G H Brigham hoped to convert the Indians, he also wanted to help them become more "civilized." He advised Indian agent Stephen Rose to maintain an influence with the Indians that would "inspire them with the superiority of civilization, and lead them from their savage acts, and wandering mode of life."[45] In emphasizing the necessity of unity to the inhabitants of Fillmore, he wrote that only then could they "exert a salutary and benign influence upon the Natives who surround you, and overcome the savage propensity of their at present degraded natures. You will then be able to control them for good. . . ."[46] This condescending attitude was standard in white approaches to Indians in the nineteenth century. But in Brigham's mind the good of the whites did not have to be chosen over the good of the Indians; ultimately the two races would benefit mutually from the relationship he advocated.

The main elements in these attempts to make the Indians more civilized included—besides farming and religion—living in houses, literacy, paying for what they received, and adopting Christian morals. Brigham's direction to Isaac Morley in Manti to build a comfortable house for Arapeen, successor to Walker, was one of many attempts to get the natives to live in houses rather than wickiups and to have a stable existence in fixed locations rather than a nomadic one.[47] For the most part, the Indians were not comfortable in such strange dwellings.[48] Brigham also offered on many occasions to teach the Indians to read and write—especially the children, as he eventually despaired of being able to effect changes in the generation already grown.

Soon after the Walker War disturbances, Brigham wrote a letter to several chiefs. He assured them of his willingness to help them and also told them what he wanted to do:

> I shall want the Indians to work for what they get from the Whites, as we have to do, or pay in skins, and quit begging, for we all have to work for what we have, and I wish the Indians to learn to work and live comfortably, and also learn to read and write, and I will help them to do so all I can.[49]

When he sent a batch of clothing donated in Salt Lake City for the destitute Indian women and children in Iron County, he set down the rules for its distribution:

> I deem it the best policy to require the Indians to pay in labor for every article, as it has a much better tendency than to bestow upon them in idleness, besides it learns them to work and to depend upon their own exertions for a subsistence.[50]

That Brigham meant business is indicated by his submission of a suggested price list and by his informing the leaders that these items were being charged to their account, which they could pay for in grain, labor, animal skins, or whatever came to hand.[51]

Brigham encouraged the members of the expedition to the Navaho nation to teach morality by example, which should be strictly fair and honest with no fraud or looseness.[52] He advocated stronger measures as well. When Dimick

Huntington reported that the Indians of the Gosiute tribe engaged in a "whore dance, which was lewd and wrong," Brigham said he should whip them to cause them to desist.[53] When Brigham heard that some of the employees on Garland Hurt's Indian farm were "gambling, drinking liquor, swearing and setting bad examples before the Indians," he wrote about his strong concern and explained:

> It has ever been my aim, in all my intercourse with the Natives, to teach them by example as well as precept, and to endeavor to exercise a good wholesome and salutary influence over them, in order if possible to bring them to appreciate the benefits arising from a civilized existence when contrasted with their own.

He asked Hurt to dismiss any person guilty of "whoring, drunkenness, gambling, using profane language, or any other vile, or idle practice, or example which might prove pernicious to them [the Indians]. . . ."[54]

Brigham took special pleasure in reporting that, "not infrequently," he had seen Indians driving teams and performing other common labor in the southern Utah settlements and "Indian children playing with those of the inhabitants; clothed, fed and schooled the same as their own."[55] He told Arapeen, "We hope to see the time when you and all the Lamanites, will become the same as we, that we may be one in all things, that your people may learn to work, and raise grain, vegetables and stock, and live in houses as we do."[56]

In order to facilitate acculturation of the Indians, Brigham approved of the missionaries' marrying Indian women—particularly the daughters of chiefs or leading warriors. (He remained silent when Walker and Arapeen requested Mormon women.) Brigham also sanctioned the adoption of Indian children into Mormon homes. Upset at the Indian practice of selling children into slavery in Mexico, Brigham found that the Indians resented his interference with their trade and then looked to the Mormons to pay for the children. So Brigham advised his people to "buy up the Lamanite children as fast as they could, and educate them, and teach them the Gospel, . . . and said that the Lord could not have devised a better plan than to have put us where we were in order to accomplish that thing."[57] When he asked the legislature to pass a law forbidding slavery, Brigham emphasized that the Mormon purchase of Indian children was a different matter—a means of purchasing them into freedom rather than slavery—and made sure the law included provisions limiting the time of indenture and the conditions. Some of the known fifty to sixty Indian children raised in Mormon homes became acculturated to white Mormon ways and intermarried into the society, while others either died or never were comfortable in either white or Indian society.

If necessary, Brigham resorted to what might be called forced acculturation. One example is the case of Little Soldier and his band, who were making trouble in the Ogden area by pilfering, burning, and other depredations. Brigham's solution was an inventive one:

> I have considered the matter, and concluded that the best thing that can be done with that band is to distribute them out among the inhabitants of the district to labor and earn a living. . . .
> If the Indians will stay where you place them with the brethren, it will very much improve their condition, and there will be no fear of them going hungry or naked. Just take them and distribute them in families to the brethren; and tell them they must work, and tell the brethren they must exercise patience and forbearance, but require them to work, pay them reasonable wages in food and clothing day by day, and in such articles as they need, for themselves and families. In this way they will be disposed of very much to their own advantage and benefit and to the relief of the community, who will also find it much cheaper to support them in this manner, and they will do something towards their own support; as it is, the people have them to sustain.

Dimick Huntington was to explain the plan to the Indians as a means of gaining quicker compliance. "But be this as it may," Young directed, "you must have it done."[58]

Predictably, the Indians were angry at first, but eventually became reconciled to the idea. Four months later Brigham reported to the Indian commissioner that "upon their promising good behaviour, Little Soldier's band have had their arms delivered up to them, and have been permitted to go out and come in at their pleasure; and happily have thus far complied with their compact, and are behaving commendably."[59]

Although Brigham cautioned against expecting too much too soon from the natives, he eventually decided that they could not be civilized. He blamed this on the curse placed upon their ancestors by God. After a quarter-century of interaction with them and attempts to influence and help them, he perceived them as "so wild that you cannot tame them," a "dark and benighted" people who "want to sit on the ground in the dirt, and to live by hunting, and they cannot be civilized."[60] For Brigham, as for countless other white men, the attempt to fit the Indians into the mold he desired had not succeeded. Brigham's Indian policy did not encompass respect or recognition for the values and outlook of their culture; he cannot fairly be portrayed as enlightened in a sense that would satisfy the militant Native Americans of today. Nonetheless, viewed in the nineteenth-century context, when ruthless exploitation and genocide were all too common, Brigham displayed moderation and a willingness to share.

14 ✛

Governor of Utah

I am and will be Governor, and no power can hinder it, until
the Lord Almighty says, "Brigham, you need not be Governor
any longer," and then I am willing to yield to another Governor.[1]

W H E N Brigham Young and Heber Kimball were preparing to
leave the Salt Lake Valley in August 1847 in order to rejoin their families in
Winter Quarters, they appointed "Uncle" John Smith, uncle of Joseph Smith
the Prophet, to be stake president, with Charles C. Rich and John Young,
Brigham's brother, as counselors. Twelve men were chosen as a high council.
This stake presidency and high council remained as the governing body of the
Salt Lake community until the return of Brigham and Heber in the fall of
1848.

The Mexican cession of the Great Basin region to the United States had
occurred in February 1848, when Brigham was still in Winter Quarters. When
he reached the Salt Lake Valley, hopeful that Congress would create a Mormon
state, he summoned a convention on March 4, 1849, at which a committee
was appointed to draft a constitution for a provisional state government. The
"State of Deseret" was named after a Book of Mormon term for honeybee,
signifying industry and cooperation. Eager to make their state as large and
self-sufficient as possible and still not claim territory important to other claimants (California and New Mexico), the Mormons envisioned Deseret to include
all of the Great Basin and the Colorado River Valley—all of present-day Utah
and Nevada, southeastern Idaho and southwestern Wyoming, western Colorado and New Mexico, northern Arizona, southeastern California, and southeastern Oregon. Within the proposed region were about 265,000 square miles
of desert, mountain, and lake land—in essence, all the area from the Rockies
to the Sierra, the northern watershed of the Great Basin to the Gila. It also
included the Pacific Ocean port of San Diego in order to provide an entry
place for emigrants to the Great Basin by way of the Isthmus of Panama.

Although the constitution of Deseret, which was quickly approved by local voters, called for the election of officials on the first Monday of May, Brigham and his advisers decided to hurry things along. So the election was held two days following the convention at a public meeting on March 12. In a vote of 674 persons Brigham Young was elected governor, with his counselors, Heber Kimball and Willard Richards, elected, respectively, as chief justice and secretary of state. Other high church leaders were elected to other positions.[2]

The hastiness of the vote was not the only deviation from the newly created constitution. Some prescribed offices were not filled while other offices not mentioned in the constitution were created and filled. The supreme court members were chosen by popular vote instead of by joint session of the legislature. The explanation for these deviations is found in the fact that Brigham and the Council of Fifty, meeting the day before the convention began, had already drawn up a slate of officers (slightly different, as it turned out, from what came out of the convention) and had instructed the marshal to advertise the election for March 12. This slate and date prevailed over that enacted by the convention, which suggests the informal manner in which Brigham and his coterie of associates ran things.[3]

The election marked the first official designation of their political supremacy and began a nine-year period when the reins of political and ecclesiastical authority were united under Brigham's leadership—a situation that was natural and efficient from the viewpoint of the Mormons but drew criticism from those less tolerant of the mingling of church and state power. Brigham was nevertheless confident that Congress would admit Deseret to the Union: "Brethren," he said in a speech on July 8, 1849, "we are going to have a state government."[4] This push for statehood seems paradoxical in the light of his expressed belief that internal conflicts would bring the United States government to the brink of collapse. In one colorful but hyperbolic statement made in 1849 he went so far as to declare: "God Almighty will give the United States a pill that will puke them to death, and that is worse than lobelia. I am prophet enough to prophesy the downfall of the government that has driven us out. . . . Wo to the United States! . . . I see them greedy after death and destruction."[5]

Until the legislature took hold of the law-making process in 1850, Brigham continued to oversee the work of the legislative council, which handled such matters as appointing officials, hearing reports from various committees, and approving public works projects. On one day, for example, his secretary mentions that he went with a surveying party and spent two days checking the river and banks in order to decide upon a site for a dam.[6]

During the two eventful years of its existence, the State of Deseret, under Brigham's active leadership, created a state university (now the University of Utah); organized and fixed the boundaries of seven counties; regulated the control of streams, timber, and grazing; prohibited the sale of liquor and ammunition to the Indians; incorporated and granted municipal charters to five cities; and incorporated the Church of Jesus Christ of Latter-day Saints.[7]

Brigham's own involvement is suggested by the following entry in his office journal for one typical day in January 1850:

> As Governor of the Provisional State of Deseret I [today] approved of Ordinances providing for the organization of the Judiciary; Concerning Revenue; Offering a Bounty for killing Wolves; For taking out the river Jordan; Also Big Cottonwood and other creeks for irrigating and other purposes; Providing for State and County Commissioners on roads; And Providing for the location of Counties and Precincts.[8]

Meanwhile, John M. Bernhisel, Wilford Woodruff, and Almon W. Babbitt were in Washington, D.C., carrying petitions to Congress for approval of the proposed state.[9] In its petition the constitutional convention had called attention to the failure of Congress to provide a form of government for any part of the territory ceded to the United States by the Republic of Mexico and declared that in the absence of civil authority anarchy had prevailed, that the revolver and bowie knife had been the highest law of the land, that there was a large enough population to support a state government, and that recognizing Deseret would assure the preservation of the constitutional rights of the people. The memorialists asked for admission into the Union as a state, or "such other form of civil government as your wisdom and magnanimity may award to the people."[10]

Although Bernhisel and Woodruff had been sent to Washington with a request for territorial status, upon consulting in Pennsylvania with Thomas L. Kane, that "special friend" of the Mormons, they modified the document to request statehood. "You are better off without any government from the hands of Congress than with a territorial government," Kane advised, reasoning:

> The political intrigues of government officers will be against you. You can govern yourselves better than they can govern you. . . . You do not want corrupt political men from Washington strutting around you, with military epaulettes and dress, who will speculate out of you all they can.[11]

When Brigham became aware of the reluctance of Congress to take action on a matter that involved intense sectional controversy, he decided to explore President Zachary Taylor's suggestion that Utah join with California to petition for statehood together, with an agreement to split into two states in 1851. Brigham commissioned Amasa Lyman to meet with a convention in California and to work out whatever terms he could. His reasoning is revealed in part in his letter to Lyman:

> . . . we shall continue to press our suit at Washington for independence, hoping to obtain the same before the joint petition from your western convention arrives there. Should such an event occur, it can do neither party any harm, for the west will then come in alone.

No man in all our councils will consent for a moment to wear a broken yoke. Should our petition, which has gone forward, fail, the one here proposed will catch us, and before the yoke of the consolidated state can reach over the Sierra Nevada and fasten on us, 1851 will arrive, and the yoke will be broken. Thus, while government is using us to save the nation, we are using them to save ourselves.[12]

This theme of using whatever the federal government provided to the benefit of Deseret surfaced many times during Brigham's rule as territorial governor and even later. California rejected the idea of shared statehood, however, and decided to press its own case for statehood.

The whole question of the establishment of governments in the West, as it turned out, was inseparably interwoven with the problem of slavery. The Treaty of Guadalupe Hidalgo, by which New Mexico, California, and Utah were ceded to the United States, carried the potential of upsetting the balance between "free states" and "slave states." Northern states argued that as long as the region remained unorganized, the Mexican law prohibiting slavery was operative. Southerners, on the other hand, insisted that the United States Constitution guaranteeing the protection of slaves as property was in force. Both the Northerners and Southerners preferred the organization of territorial governments, thus assuring national sovereignty. Thinking that most of the settlers would be Southerners, Southerners expected the territories to be pro-slavery. Expecting to maintain a majority in Congress, Northerners thought that by organizing territories they could insure the prohibition of slavery.

Only a compromise could assure a satisfactory resolution of the conflict. Hardly aware of the geography of the region ("The ignorance of the collected wisdom of the nation in regard to our region of country is most profound," wrote Bernhisel),[13] and having nothing against either Hispanics in New Mexico or Mormons in Deseret (plural marriage was not publicly declared until 1852), Congress, under the leadership of Henry Clay, approved the Compromise of 1850 under which California was admitted to the Union as a free state; territorial governments, with no specification with respect to slavery, were established for Deseret and New Mexico, to comprise all the land acquired under the Treaty of Guadalupe Hidalgo not included in the boundaries of California; and certain other provisions were adopted with respect to Texas, fugitive slaves, and Washington, D.C. Sectionalists tried by every available means to amend the bill to favor the wishes of their respective constituents, and when all of these failed, the Omnibus Bill, as it was called, was passed on September 9, 1850, and on the same day signed by President Millard Fillmore.

Congress did not like the name "Deseret"—too much like "Desert," they reasoned—so the territory was named after the Yutas or Utah Indians, "dwellers in the tops of the mountains." Brigham's contemporary comment about the failure of the statehood petition was remarkably restrained: "When the constitution of Deseret was adopted, and its boundaries were established therein, the actual settlers of Deseret outnumbered western California five to three.

Notwithstanding which, a strong exertion has been made by Congress to receive California into the Union, to the exclusion of Deseret, though our petition for admission was equally before them."[14]

F I L L M O R E appointed Brigham Young as first governor of the new territory and superintendent of Indian affairs. The appointment had by no means been a foregone conclusion. Almost a year earlier, Thomas Kane had told Wilford Woodruff and John Bernhisel of his unsatisfactory discussions with President James K. Polk about a government for the Mormons. Polk "did not feel disposed to favor your people," and had men of his own picked out to be appointed as governor and other officials. Kane had argued on behalf of Brigham as governor. "His head is not filled with law books and lawyers' tactics, but he has power to see through men and things."[15]

President Fillmore had been more willing to consider appointing Mormons as territorial officers. Bernhisel, reporting to Brigham on the day that the bill establishing the territory passed the House of Representatives, said that the president had "signified his willingness to make the appointments from our number," but Bernhisel was not sanguine about a slate of all-Mormon officers being approved by the Senate.[16] Five days later, reporting that Fillmore was "quite favorably disposed," Bernhisel assured Brigham that he had little doubt about his appointment. Fillmore was, however, concerned about Brigham's loyalty. "He inquired whether you would support the administration if you should be appointed," Bernhisel wrote. "I replied that I thought you would."[17] Bernhisel's next letter, written on October 2, congratulated Brigham on his appointment, which had been confirmed two days before. Although the final set of officers contained both Utah Mormons and non-Utah Gentiles, Brigham retained his position as political leader in the territory. (Bernhisel was subsequently elected the territory's first delegate to Congress.)

Bernhisel's letter did not reach Salt Lake City until December, and official word did not arrive until nearly the end of January. Brigham's sister, Fanny Young Murray, mentioned the fanfare that greeted her brother as he returned from a visit to another settlement soon after the news was known:

> . . . the people rallied, and a large company went out to meet him:—last night about sunset, he was ushered into the city, with the roaring of cannon, the band of music and a company of horsemen that look'd like immortals, several carriages, and many footmen.

Fanny said she hoped "his robes of honor will not deprive him of his robe of righteousness." She described Brigham as looking "very thoughtful and contemplative" when he came to visit her later that evening.[18]

A few days later, on February 3, Brigham took the oath of office and became Utah's first territorial governor and superintendent of Indian affairs. The oath was administered by his close friend, Daniel H. Wells, who was serving as chief justice of the State of Deseret. Young's territory, which had been trimmed in the compromise bill, was still an impressive 187,923 square miles. This was one-eleventh of all the land under the American flag and five times larger than New York or Pennsylvania.[19]

BRIGHAM had scarcely begun his term before he faced problems in dealing with the non-Mormon territorial officers appointed by the federal government. The new officers trickled into Utah during the summer of 1851, with the last, Judge Perry E. Brocchus, arriving in August. By the end of September they had all left the territory, later reporting to President Fillmore that Brigham Young's irregular procedures, despotism, and hostility toward the United States made it impossible for them to function.

The areas of conflict between Brigham and these officers foreshadowed continuing problems he had to deal with in various forms throughout his governorship: money and appropriations, the relationship of the Mormon church to the United States government, and the issue of church and civil power being concentrated in Brigham's hands.

Personality conflicts exacerbated the misunderstandings. Broughton D. Harris, secretary for the territory, drew up a list of grievances concerning Brigham's official performance of his duties. He pointed out irregularities in the census and election that had been held previous to his arrival: the governor's proclamation was faulty, aliens were allowed to vote and act as officers at the polls, officers not authorized to be voted for were elected, and the results were never properly declared to the public by the governor. He accused Brigham of squandering the $20,000 appropriated for government buildings and using it to pay Mormon debts. He also complained of Brigham's repeated attempts to get from him the $24,000 he had brought for territorial expenses.

Chief Justice Lemuel G. Brandebury had minor personal complaints. Brigham had refused to see him on the two occasions when Brandebury attempted a visit. But Judge Brocchus experienced a personal confrontation with Brigham in a church conference meeting that, along with Harris's concern about keeping the $24,000 out of Brigham's hands, was the impetus for the speedy departure of the judge. Brocchus asked the territory for a block of marble to be used in erecting the Washington Monument. He also tried to explain that the United States government was neither an enemy of the Mormons nor responsible for their persecutions, and he chastised his listeners for their expressions of hostility. He also apparently made comments that were interpreted as aspersions on the virtue of the women in the audience.

Brigham criticized Brocchus as "either profoundly ignorant, or wilfully wicked." There would be "either a pulling of hair or a cutting of throats" if he permitted such political discussion to continue. He subsequently invited Brocchus to apologize at a later meeting, but the judge declined. Their exchange of letters during the rest of September did not succeed in convincing Brocchus that he was incorrect or in persuading him to stay.

W H A T kind of governor was Brigham in these first months of his territorial governorship? To the federal officers, he was a law unto himself in consequence of his power as church president and the almost complete allegiance of his followers. "In a word," they said, "he ruled as he pleased, without a rival or opposition, for no man dared question his authority."[20] They saw themselves in the frustrating position of having to rely on Governor Young but finding him uncooperative, both because of his hostility toward the government and because of his arrogant belief that he could rule without them. They reported that in refusing to see Chief Justice Brandebury, Brigham had said that "he did not wish an introduction, for none but Mormons should have been appointed to the offices of the Territory, and none others but d——d rascals would have come amongst them."[21] Brigham Young, they said, claimed "that he had ruled that people for years and could rule them again; that the United States judges might remain in the Territory and draw their salaries, but they should never try a case if he could prevent it."[22] The federal officers were made to feel superfluous and "seemed to be looked upon as the mere toys of the Governor's power—he treating them as he pleased, according to his capricious humor—sometimes encouraging a hope for a better state of affairs, to make the next outbreak of hostility and insult the more marked and humiliating."[23] They claimed that Brigham said he would "kick any man out of the Territory who attempted to dictate to, or advise him in his duty."[24]

Brigham, for his part, felt he had acted honestly and efficiently, if not exactly according to form, in taking the census and making the legislative apportionment, and he criticized the outside officers for their tardiness in arriving at their posts. He claimed that the money appropriated should have been used to defray the costs of the 1850–51 legislature during the long wait for the officers to arrive, and he complained that once in place the officers had taken no initiative to attend to their duties.[25]

Brigham made no secret of his dislike for Brocchus. Nearly two years later Brigham said he did not drive the officers away but did

> . . . chastise the mean ruffian, the poor miserable creature, who came here by the name of Brocchus, when he arose before this people to preach to them. . . . It is true, as it is said in the Report of these officers, if I had crooked my little finger, he would have been used up, but I did not bend it. If I had, the sisters alone felt indignant enough to have chopped him in pieces.[26]

Brigham was probably not exaggerating his influence. His potential power of life and death, although not exercised by him, would have contributed to the sense of personal danger experienced by Brocchus and the other officers.

Brigham's assessment of Brandebury was kinder. Noting a few years later that Brandebury was writing for lawyers now and then but had not achieved much success or power, Brigham called him "a tolerably good man" and said that "if he had done as I counselled him, he would have stayed here, and let that other judge go. Mr. Brandebury was a good sort of a man, he never had any difficulty with me, and would have done well, if he had only had sense enough to know that he could not obliterate 'Mormonism.' "[27]

It is doubtful that Brigham felt any uneasiness or guilt about his actions. His explanations have the ring of a self-satisfied but misunderstood man—slightly on the defensive, ready to see opposition and persecution in little things, but sure of his rightness and confident of his power. He certainly did not miss the outside officers, for despite his occasional complaints about the difficulty of carrying on territorial business with several offices unfilled, he simply made adjustments where necessary—appointing the one remaining judge, Zerubbabel Snow, as temporarily in charge of all three judicial districts, for example—or selecting people of his own choosing, like Willard Richards as *pro tem* territorial secretary.

When John Bernhisel wrote Brigham about the report of the outside officers, his response was generally calm. He was not at all alarmed concerning the final outcome. He felt sure that if the government should decide to send troops and outside officers to rule over them, the citizens of the United States would protest and prevent it. But he also considered the possibility that all would not work out well and pronounced himself ready to make yet another migration to be free from "bondage and oppression" even if it meant death and hardship for the Saints. He expressed willingness to move to a faraway "bleak, barren and inhospitable" place and "leave this so recently and so ardently sought asylum to its wonted desolation, without an inhabitant to sing the requiem of departed liberty."[28] Here was the seed of the idea to vacate the territory if the government pushed too hard.

A M O N G all the charges and complaints made by the outside officers, the uniting of civil and religious authority in the hands of Brigham Young inspired their severest criticism. It was this same concentrated power that President James Buchanan later rebuked when he decided to remove Brigham as governor. Without non-Mormon territorial officials, Buchanan believed that "there no longer remain[ed] any Government in Utah but the despotism of Brigham Young."[29] Brigham's power was particularly threatening because of the strong popular support he enjoyed and the tightly organized structure at his disposal—a difficult arrangement for an outsider to penetrate or to oppose.

Federal appointees also complained of the lack of separation of powers—legislative, executive, and judicial—under Brigham's governorship:

> The Governor had been accustomed, as many of the leading men there informed us, to enter the legislative hall, under the provisional State government, and dictate

what laws should or should not be passed, and the court and jury rooms to indicate what verdicts should be rendered, and he had given us ample evidence that he was equally omnipotent and influential with the Mormon people under the territorial government.[30]

Brigham's lack of concern about following strict formality in arranging for elections and his obvious influence over the legislature provided evidence of such unhealthy mingling. So did the casual way in which the legislature was convened in Fillmore in 1856. (At Brigham's suggestion, the state capital had been moved out of Salt Lake City to a point about 150 miles south, which was named after the president, either as a gesture of gratitude or in an attempt to curry favor with him, or both.) Both houses met as one, along with county judges, apostles, and various officials, all of whom joined in the discussion and voted on the bills.

It was well known that the church leaders selected the candidates for the territorial legislature, and with only a single slate of names the election process was little more than a ratification. When Brigham passed through Parowan on his tour of southern settlements in May 1851, for example, he oversaw the nomination and election of the representatives to the legislature, the delegate to Congress, and the local officials, after recommending that the citizens be "united" in their selection of officers.[31]

Brigham showed an easy flexibility in handling political matters. A good example is his impulsive decision in the middle of a church meeting in 1853 to deal with the political business of reelecting John Bernhisel as delegate to Congress.

It came into my mind when brother Bernhisel was speaking, and the same thing strikes me now, that is, inasmuch as he has done first-rate, as our delegate in Washington, to move that we send him again next season, though it is the Sabbath Day. I understand these things, and say as other people say, "*We are Mormons.*" We do things that are necessary to be done, when the time comes for us to do them. If we wish to make political speeches, and it is necessary, for the best interest of the cause and kingdom of God, to make them on the Sabbath, we do it. Now, suffer not your prejudices to hurt you, do not suffer this to try you, nor be tempted in consequence of it, nor think we are wandering out of the way, for it is all embraced in our religion, from first to last.

Brother Kimball has seconded the motion, that Doctor Bernhisel be sent back to Washington, as our delegate. All who are in favour of it, raise your right hands. (More than two thousand hands were at once seen above the heads of the congregation.)

This has turned into a caucus meeting. It is all right. I would call for an opposite vote if I thought any person would vote. I will try it, however. (Not a single hand was raised in opposition.)[32]

Two years later, however, Brigham stated in meeting that he did not intend to elect Bernhisel in the same fashion as before but wanted to learn if he was willing to return first.[33] There was presumably no problem concerning Bernhisel's election once his assent was obtained. As Brigham wrote in July, "We shall vote for Doctor John M. Bernhisel for our Delegate to Congress at the next general election, on the 1st Monday of August next, which I presume will be generally satisfactory to the people of Utah. . . ."[34] Brigham's control is further shown by the fact that the previous fall he had offered this position to Thomas L. Kane, who declined. He told Kane that the Mormon council and "other prominent citizens" all concurred unanimously in approving of his nomination and assured him that "you know this people well enough to be certain that they will vote as they may be counselled, hence you will have no dubiety as to the result of the election. . . ."[35]

Again in 1857 Bernhisel was essentially chosen at a meeting in the Bowery on Sunday, the day before the slated election. Brigham explained:

But I don't see why to-day isn't just as holy, and why we shouldn't take a vote today. Brother Bernhisel, brethren, has done well enough in Congress, though nobody's of much use there; and if it's worthwhile to send anybody to Washington, I guess we might as well send him back; if he can't do us any good, he won't do us any harm. So all of you that are in favor of sending Brother Bernhisel back, will please rise.[36]

"Accordingly," added the Sacramento *Daily Union*, "the whole audience arose."[37]

In some cases Brigham attempted to distinguish between his two "hats" and to specify in which capacity he was acting, but the line was never completely clear. Once in general conference, for instance, he preached a sermon about the use of the canyon resources and then made a motion for dealing with the problem. After a unanimous vote in favor of his motion, he urged the judges of not only Salt Lake County but the other counties as well to "take due notice, and govern themselves accordingly." The order, he explained, "does not come from the Governor, but from the President of the Church."[38] In this instance the disposition of natural resources was being dealt with by religious authority rather than by the political apparatus that normally would handle such matters. On the other side of the coin Brigham recorded: "As Governor, I signed letters of commendation to the missionaries for Continental Europe."[39]

Far from having qualms about this mixing of power, Brigham saw it as a positive force for maximizing good results. "In all my official transactions I have acted in accordance with the Priesthood," he said. "The Priesthood assists me to honor, to preserve, to see, and understand the welfare of the Government I am acting for, and enables me so to do a thousand times more effectually than I could if I had not this Priesthood; and if anyone can produce documents to prove that any governor has magnified his office better than I have, let him bring them forth."[40]

A S territorial governor, Brigham did not always enjoy a friction-free relationship with Washington. One continuing difficulty was getting and keeping federal officers with whom he could work effectively. There were also many problems concerning appropriations (money was a constant concern), censuses, and land that had to be worked out with various federal departments.

Brigham did not have a negative opinion of all federal appointees. He thought well of some non-Mormons, such as Judges H. Reid and Leonidas Shaver, who succeeded Brocchus and Brandebury. He wrote to Bernhisel that Reid and Shaver "conduct themselves very gentlemanly thus far, appear frank, and friendly in their deportment and are universally liked, and respected in their Offices by the people, and I would prefer to have them remain if possible."[41] These judges apparently responded in kind, were not overly troubled about the religious and social peculiarities of the Mormons (polygamy was being preached publicly for the first time), and saw Brigham in a kindlier light rather than as the despot depicted by the earlier set of officers. Chief Justice Reid commented:

> I have made up my mind that no man has been more grossly misrepresented than Governor Young, and that he is a man who will reciprocate kindness and good intentions as heartily and freely as any one, but if abused, or crowded hard, I think he may be found exceedingly hard to handle.[42]

Judge Shaver was succeeded in office by W. W. Drummond, one of the most disliked federal officers to be appointed to a post in Utah. Notice of his arrival indicates one reason: "Associate Justice Drummond (and Lady!!!) arrived in Salt Lake City."[43] Drummond's open immorality and his refusal to function in agreement with the court system in Utah elicited critical comments from several church authorities. At Fillmore during the legislative session Brigham commented, "The Judge is not here as a king or as a Monarch—he is nothing but a boy."[44]

After Drummond's hasty departure, ostensibly to Carson (in present-day western Nevada) to hold court but actually to return to the States via California and Panama, Brigham commented on his lack of intelligence and common sense in attempting to hold court in Carson under a new law before it was even in force.[45] Drummond should be removed from office, Brigham argued, "as he has often and in various ways transcended his authority, and demeaned himself very much like a dog or wolf, viscious [sic] and brutal, whining and snappish, vain as a peacock and ignorant as a jack-ass."[46] Drummond was all too typical of those Brigham denounced as the "infernal, dirty, sneaking, rotten-hearted, pot-house politicians" being sent to Utah. "We will rid ourselves of as many such white livered, blackhearted, sycophantic demagogues, as the Administration shall send," he said, "though they be like the locusts and frogs of Egypt."[47]

Securing a territorial secretary with whom Brigham would work effectively was not easy. With the first appointee, Broughton D. Harris, there was too much mutual suspicion. When Harris left, Brigham made his trusted associate Willard Richards secretary *pro tem* on October 15, 1851. In the summer of 1852 the new appointee, Benjamin G. Ferris, arrived for a stay of approximately six months. Upon his departure, Richards again took over the work but once again was not officially appointed (although he was paid $1,800 by the federal government for work he had done).[48] Brigham was greatly disappointed that the appointment went instead to Almon Babbitt.

Babbitt, a Mormon, had not compiled a reassuring record. Although he had been sent to Washington as a special delegate to petition for statehood, his image as a sharp political horse trader who was also trying to advance his own interests did little for his reputation back home. In 1850 Thomas Kane recommended that Babbitt not be retained as delegate.[49] As bearer of a $20,000 appropriation for public buildings in the territory, Babbitt wanted to give over only part of it to Brigham. He cautioned the governor that the apportionments and elections would be illegal unless a census was taken—which Brigham thought unnecessary as there had just been one recently.[50]

A year later, despite brushes with Brigham and other church leaders, Babbitt was still considered within the fold. Brigham had him speak in a church meeting once as a testing device:

> I was glad to hear brother Babbit speak this morning. He wondered why he had been called to the stand to speak, and could not conceive of any other reason, except it was that the people might know whether he was in the faith or not. He guessed pretty nigh right. He has been gone some time, and travels to and fro in the earth, playing into law up to the eyes, mingling with the bustle of the wicked world. Has he got any faith? We think he has. I wanted to hear him speak, and to know what his feelings were, and if the root of the matter was in him. . . .[51]

Babbitt became secretary in June of 1853 and had the longest tenure of any secretary during Brigham's term of office. He seems to have performed many of his duties satisfactorily and to have ably represented the interests of the territory in his communications with the Treasury and other government departments. Yet he had several disagreements with the governor. By the end of 1853, Brigham suspected that Babbitt was attempting to secure the position of chief justice of the territory and even thought that might be an improvement. "If we could have the right one appointed Secretary," he wrote to Bernhisel, "it might be as well to make the exchange."[52]

To Brigham, Babbitt always seemed to be making excuses for not getting or turning over money for various territorial projects. Babbitt, for his part, had to account to the Treasury Department and wheedle needed funds out of the officials there. Brigham once asked Bernhisel to find out whether Babbitt really could not pay out any funds for the penitentiary, as he had claimed. Babbitt's penny-pinching bothered the governor. He claimed that Babbitt carefully counted out the candles for use by the legislature, watched them closely, and snuffed them out immediately when regular business was ended, saving them all—long or short—for later use. Even worse, "the Governor has been required to cut a good share of the wood burned by the Assembly, and still more economical, that burned in the Secretaries office."[53]

In October 1856, after Babbitt disappeared and was later presumed killed by Cheyenne Indians on the plains, Brigham appointed William H. Hooper as secretary *pro tem.* Babbitt's death was more of a relief to Brigham than anything else. "If Almon Babbitt were here—thank God he is not—he would have found fault with everything," he said in a speech to the legislature two months later. "If there is anything I have been thankful for, it is that we have a Secretary that is heart and hand with us. My heart is glad every moment of time that we have the privilege of coming together and not have a quarrel on hand."[54] Like most officials sent west, Babbitt, although a Mormon, saw his job as representing the United States government rather than cooperating with Brigham's plans. To someone as accustomed as Brigham to ruling his own way, such officers were obstructionists at best, enemies at worst.

Brigham once asked Bernhisel to see if he could get an adjustment made in the Organic Act of the Territory that would "give the Governor the same authority and powers to act in the Secretary duties, during the Secretary's absence, as it now does the Secretary during the Governor's absence." Yet Brigham saw some redeeming features in Babbitt and before his disappearance had hopes for him: "Still, for our part, he has done well, at times, and could again if he would give his common sense fair play."[55]

M U C H of Brigham's frustration as governor centered on the question of money. Payments for territorial expenses were often insufficient, slow in arriving, or disallowed by government officials. When the problems became especially irritating, Brigham sometimes said Utah would be better off without any money from the government at all.

Brigham was allotted an annual salary as governor of $1,500 plus $1,000 as superintendent of Indian affairs. The governor's office was also entitled to $1,000 in "contingent funds" each year. As soon as Brocchus, Harris, and Brandebury left the territory, questions arose regarding the payment of these contingent funds; in November 1851, the government withheld the $1,000 until such time as allegations made by officers against Brigham were proved untrue. This attitude of "guilty until proven innocent" rankled Brigham. He continued to request the $1,000 over the next several months, even explaining that he had "personally expended more than twice that amount during the past year for the Government."[56] But Washington continued to refuse to honor his drafts. Even two years later, difficulties regarding this issue continued, as Brigham was told that he owed $1,000 to the contingent funds account, that an earlier payment had been an advance, and that he had exceeded the allotted amount anyway.[57]

The governor's office probably did exceed the appropriations for contingent fund expenses. Brigham once complained to Bernhisel, "The usual annual appropriation of one thousand dollars, to defray the contingent expenses of this office, has never been sufficient, in consequence of the high price of fuel, rent, clerk hire, &c." Brigham asked for an additional appropriation of $500. On the other hand, Brigham's salary as governor may well have supported some of his activities as church president, since drawing lines between the two roles was almost impossible. The instructions to Bernhisel to devote all of his salary toward the liquidation of Perpetual Emigrating Fund debts was not untypical.[58]

Throughout his governorship Brigham perceived the federal government as being reluctant to pay the money justly allotted for territorial expenses. His letters to Bernhisel are filled with detailed questions, instructions, and information pertaining to financial matters and a fair amount of grumbling as well. "The appropriation you mention has not arrived," he noted in one letter, "and the slow motion of the Departments in all that relates to Utah is very vexatious, and troublesome, aside from being unjust; and even after the most tedious delays, they seem disposed to still farther tramel our affairs by very trivial exceptions, but all will work out for good."[59] By 1856 Brigham was feeling more impatient:

> All we want of the Government is for them to pay their just debts, and administer the Government in righteousness. We do not want their appropriations of money nor arms. Let them and their gold perish together. God forbid that we should be in any great degree dependant upon them. . . . They have never paid the least regard to our estimates. And when an appropriation is made they will keep it in the department until they can get an opportunity to throw it into somebody's hands for disbursement who is as corrupt as themselves, and whom they know will squander it away.[60]

The federal government had appropriated $20,000 for the erection of public buildings in the territory. Originally, the plan was to erect a statehouse in Union Square in Salt Lake City. But toward the end of 1851 it was thought best to purchase some accommodations temporarily in Salt Lake and meanwhile begin work on state buildings at the newly located seat of government in Fillmore. Accordingly, the money was used to purchase from the church part of the newly completed Council House, the value of which Brigham Young set at more than $45,000. The government took a dim view of this course, and a long string of letters, accusations, justifications, and explanations followed. Eventually, in 1854, the shift was made to renting the rooms in the

Council House. The bills for the expenses of locating the new seat of government were questioned and disallowed by Washington.

Trivial matters could take much time. There was, for example, the problem of the government mules Brocchus had brought into the territory. Brigham wrote that one mule furnished to the territory had died of disease and asked for confirmation as to whether the animals were in fact government property. He was told that he was charged $330 for the value of the three mules. If he wished to be released from this charge he must 1) get an affidavit from a "disinterested person" regarding the death of the one mule; 2) turn over the other two to the appropriate army officer "together with harnesses, if any were received by you"; and 3) send the receipt for the mules to the Treasury Department.[61] Accustomed to direct action and results, Brigham had little patience with the workings of government bureaucracies.

Another matter was public arms, which the government sent to the territory even though they had not been requested. "To tell you the truth about those public arms," Brigham wrote to Bernhisel, "we do not want them, we would rather not have them. It will only prove a source of discomfort to us, annoying, and I fear, serious detriment." He said he would keep them safe if they were sent but did not like being responsible for them. Since the government sent only old out-of-date muskets anyway, Brigham said, they were of little or no value. An additional fear was that, inadequate as the arms were, the Mormons might at a later time be asked to give them up for use against themselves after they had grown to depend upon them. "No," Brigham wrote, "we do not want them but prefer to depend upon our own resources—then we know where we stand."[62]

D U R I N G Brigham's governorship, in an attempt to gain greater autonomy, Utah Territory made at least four additional attempts to gain admission to the Union as a state after the first application had resulted in territorial status instead. The territorial legislature sent memorials to Congress year after year (1852, 1853, 1854), all of which were ignored. Finally in 1856 a full-scale convention was held, a constitution was adopted, and another memorial was prepared. Prospects seemed so poor by then that it was never formally presented.

Brigham's correspondence reveals his great concern with achieving statehood as well as his motivations. He discussed tactics and possible allies in his letters to John Taylor and John Bernhisel.[63] When the memorial was drafted in March 1856, Brigham expressed confidence and optimism. In asking Thomas Kane for his aid, Brigham said:

> We strongly desire to become a state. We consider, that we possess all the elements, ability, power, and claims requisite for State Government. If we have been sufficiently scolded, thumped, thrashed, and beaten for youth and infancy; let us emerge from the leading strings, and assume our place among this family of nations.[64]

Frustrated by the constraints of territorial status, Brigham wrote to Franklin D. Richards that they were "trying to extricate ourselves from the forms and trammels of a Territorial Government and emerging into a free and Independent State."[65] Brigham encouraged Bernhisel not to despair, "for you know that our path sometimes leads through gloomy scenes. . . . I trust that when our application is fairly before them it will be favorably considered and acted upon. The Lord will control all for our good." Brigham saw state government for Utah as inevitable and went on to say, "They might just as well give us a state government now as at any other time for they cannot help doing it much longer, and the question might just as well be met now as ever."[66]

He seemed to be more interested in independence than in union.[67]

> All we care about is for them to let us alone, to keep away their trash and officers so far as possible, to give us our admission into the Union just as we are, just as we have applied for it or as near as may be to let us take care of ourselves, and they may keep their money, their lands and in fact everything which they can.[68]

One might conclude that Brigham and his followers sought to join the United States in order to be free from it.

Brigham's disenchantment with the United States grew worse in 1857 when an incursion of federal troops became a strong possibility. In a speech shortly after news of the approaching troops reached them, Brigham suggested that perhaps it was time for cutting all ties with the United States:

> I shall take it as a witness that God designs to cut the thread between us and the world, when an army undertakes to make their appearance in this Territory to chastise me or to destroy my life from the earth. . . . As for the rest, we will wait a little while to see; but I shall take a hostile movement by our enemies as an evidence that it is time for the thread to be cut.[69]

Frustrated as territorial governor, thwarted in his repeated applications for statehood, Brigham had little alternative but to accept the continuing territorial arrangement and unloose occasional hyperbolic bombast.

I N his role as governor Brigham dealt with such diverse responsibilities as seeing to the establishment of a county in Carson Valley and arranging for the formation of a boundary line with California, corresponding with the governor of another state regarding a question of child custody, and meeting with university regents to help develop the Deseret Alphabet. The latter represented an attempt on his part to invent an alphabet that had a separate symbol for each of the thirty-eight sounds in the English language. This, he thought, would assist immigrants from Scandinavia and other non-English-speaking groups in grappling with the problems of spelling and pronunciation. The Book of Mormon and other texts were published with the new symbols, and classes of instruction were held throughout the territory, but, like George Bernard Shaw's campaign for simplified spelling, it proved to be a losing battle.[70]

Many petitions arrived at the governor's office, mostly asking pardon for crimes or forgiveness of fines. Most of the pardons granted by Brigham were to men convicted of larceny, which might have brought a sentence of up to several years of hard labor, sometimes with a ball and chain, plus a fine of $50, $100, or $150. Many of these larceny convictions involved non-Mormon emigrants passing through Utah. Brigham felt his clemency ill repaid when some of these men then told false stories about the Mormons. He complained about the resulting unequal press notices:

> The testimonials of hundreds and thousands of emigrants who came, received our hospitality and passed on their way with good feeling, not having been molested, but on the contrary, very essentially assisted on their toilsome journey, although published at the time in many of the papers, seem now to be laid aside and forgotten, and the half dozen thieves who not succeeding in stealing their way through, and happening to be caught, tried, and sentenced to expiate the just penalty of their crimes, by hard labor with ball and chain (in lieu of a penitentiary which is not yet provided) but finally through the clemency of the Executive were pardoned, can publish their falsehoods and have them trumpeted by the press and continually kept before the public.[71]

On occasion Brigham issued pardons for murder convictions, usually on the grounds of extreme youth and/or a conviction based on circumstantial evidence. He sometimes had questions concerning his jurisdiction and authority for granting pardons. He wrote both Kane and President Franklin Pierce, for example, to ask if he had the right to grant a pardon to a man convicted in a U.S. District Court; meanwhile, he issued a reprieve from the death sentence.[72]

Brigham had a close relationship with the territorial legislature. He attended sessions regularly and was actively engaged in their deliberations and decisions. This involvement had its bothersome side for him, however, and he finally "requested the privilege of going in and out of the House without being molested by their rising."[73] He described his relations with the legislature as being characterized by "agreeable concord" and "pleasant harmonious feelings"—but the body was, of course, essentially hand-picked by him. However, there were occasional difficulties. Brigham once lectured the members about making light of another person's religion and using the name of the Deity in vain. "I remarked that it grieved and hurt my feelings when present on any occasion where such things were allowed."[74] He also smoothed some ruffled feathers, refusing to accept the resignations of members who had quit when they felt Brigham had bad feelings toward them, and reassuring them of his support and concern.[75]

Although he approved almost every act of the legislature as a routine matter, he would occasionally suggest an amendment. On one of the rare occasions when he vetoed a bill—an act designed to encourage the manufacture of window glass—it was both because of the state of territorial finances and because of private plans he knew to be already underway for beginning such an operation.[76]

Brigham's official proclamations and messages to the legislature illustrate his practice of injecting religious elements into what would elsewhere have been purely political documents. His proclamation setting aside January 1, 1852, as a day of praise and thanksgiving mentions not only God, but also Jesus, celestial glory, the Holy Ghost, Kolob (according to Mormon belief, the star nearest the throne of God), and the Holy Priesthood. He gave detailed instructions on how to observe the day: rising early, washing, caring for animals, fixing food, abstaining from evil and strife, donating food to the poor, and retiring early.[77]

Brigham was proud that Utah's public officials served without compensation (except for those whose services were paid for by the federal government) and that tax monies were used almost exclusively on direct public improvements. Still, he encountered difficulties in keeping the receipt of even these modest taxes current and asked often in his messages for more prompt collections.

Utah Territory's accomplishments in education were less than impressive, despite a number of legislative acts designed to promote learning. In his last annual message Brigham tried to put a bold face on this situation, noting that Utah had done more "proportionately" than any other state or territory in like conditions and that one could obtain an education elsewhere than in schools.[78]

He used these annual messages as a vehicle for the expression of his opinions on such issues as laws (the simpler the better), the national scene (full of commotion and corruption), and slavery. He commented on the national debate over Negro slavery, finding fault with both Northern and Southern positions. He felt blacks should not be treated as property but that they were destined to be servants and were not suited to be equal to white men or to hold civil or ecclesiastical office.[79] He was pleased with the way the legislature had handled the slavery issue in Utah:

> Happily for Utah, this question [slavery] has been wisely left open for the decision of her citizens, and the law of the last session, so far proves a very salutary measure, as it has nearly freed the Territory of the colored population; also enabling the people to control all who see proper to remain, and cast their lot among us.[80]

N O T all territorial governors, of course, served also as superintendent of Indian affairs, and thus there were some unique elements in Brigham's governorship. Like other superintendents, he distributed gifts of beef, cattle, blankets, shirts, and tobacco; licensed and supervised Indian traders; prohibited trading on Sunday; and placed a ban on liquor. Despite his vigorous efforts to eliminate liquor consumption, however, he found himself unable to control it completely. Of the violators he complained to the federal Indian commissioner with heat and anger, even if with some uncharacteristic language:

> Every power and influence will be exerted to keep this article [whiskey] from the Indians from the baneful influence of which, so much is to be dreaded, and if it cannot be done, it will be owing in a great measure to the emigration or the recklessness of such traders and assistants as are permitted to go amongst them, who for the sake of a pair of mocassins, would destroy every vestige of goodness yet lingering, and every prospect of advancement and reformation in store for these already heaven *knows* sufficiently degraded and ignorant savages. A man having one spark of the enobling aspirations of his nature within him, that would recklessly put the liquid fire to the lips of the untutored savage, knowing as all do the fatal consequences which inevitably result therefrom, it would seem could never again look his fellows in the face or enjoy even an *unquiet* repose, without hearing the wail of the unfortunate victim of despair, and being haunted with the murderous fury of a savage demon.[81]

Brigham's relationship with the Office of Indian Affairs (OIA) in Washington, in the absence of specific instructions, consisted mainly of his submitting vouchers and quarterly reports. He regularly complained about the financial arrangements (or nonarrangements) under which he was required to operate. The federal government, he assumed, was responsible for seeing to the needs of the Indians but did little to help him act effectively as its agent. Only a few months into his superintendency he wrote:

> The Indians are now more than ever carried away with the idea of receiving presents, these demands have to be met on every occasion, and you are probably aware how much money, means &c has been furnished this Superintendency for this purpose. Please sir, inform me what I shall do, shall I say to the Indians their great Father has no means to gratify their expectations?[82]

Instead he found that the Mormons still had to pay out much that was required to feed, clothe, and pacify the Indians. He asked repeatedly for money to purchase goods to keep on hand as presents but had to be content with buying them himself and then asking for government reimbursement, a constant source of irritation to him.

Finally, completely frustrated, he unleashed the following blast at the OIA:

> . . . nor do I care a groat, whether the Department, or the Government ever contribute a penny towards the support of the Indian relations; for the suppression of Indian hostilities, or any other public purpose, or object, in or for the Territory, of Utah. If they will only come out boldly, and say, that they do not wish, or intend to, instead of eternally thrashing in the dark, taking shelter behind such

trivial vain subterfuges, as such men as you can hatch up. I have not the confidence to believe, that we could make out a paper that would be satisfactory to your *sceptical brain*. Judging from the manner in which these matters have been treated by the Department, I should conclude, that you did not believe there was any Indians in this Territory, or if there was, that it was necessary to expend anything to maintain friendly intercourse with them.[83]

Brigham was also frustrated at the distinction made by the government between prevention of hostilities and suppression, with costs of the latter having to be submitted to the War Department. He complained in 1854 about his claims for depredations and oppressions of Indian hostilities then sitting unpaid in that department:

The United States Government do not appear to know that they have never yet paid a *solitary* dollar for the *suppression of Indian hostilities in the Territory*, although they and all the world do know that we have had more or less Indian difficulties since the winters of 1848 & '49.[84]

In fact, it rankled him that the government was willing to make greater appropriations for carrying out war than for preventing it in the first place.

One fourth part of the money annually expended in fighting the Indians, maintenance, and transportation of troops and attending incidental expences, rightly expended in peaceful operations, would not only leave thousands of Indians to cultivate the soil, cause them to raise their own subsistence, but maintain almost if not entire peaceful relations with them.

Parsimonious expenditures for such purposes is a mistaken policy, and proves far the most expensive in the end.

He suggested that the government appropriate $70,000 to $100,000 annually through the OIA (instead of the $10,000 he was receiving at the time for his superintendency) in order to avoid expenses of expeditions to deal with unruly Indians.[85] He pointed out that after the fighting was over there was always an extensive distribution of presents anyway, "which if properly distributed in the first instance might have averted the fight."[86]

Giving presents to the Indians took many forms. New settlers often needed to provide food for Indians who came begging. This was done both individually and on a community basis when provisions from the local tithing storehouse were handed out to Indians. More officially, Brigham Young used the judicious disbursement of presents to friendly Indians to prevent hostilities. He claimed that this policy "saved much calamity and bloodshed, and at comparatively trifling expense."[87] In recommending presents for Ute Indians meeting in a council to elect a new chief, he explained:

> The Indians always expect presents upon great occasions such as these, and indeed, they are never wanting in an excuse to beg, but I feel that when they are disposed to do right, as appears in the present instance to be the case, it is good policy to make some.[88]

He tried to make sure that the Indians would not come to expect presents as a matter of course. He used them as a "carrot" to obtain peace. "Now if we can be let alone," he told Chief Walker, "we shall be able to do more and more for you and your Nation every year."[89]

Brigham continually attempted to convince the Indians that the Mormon people could not provide for all their needs. He complained that "as yet it has been impossible for us to make them comprehend that it is not our personal duty to supply their wants, any further than charity connected with ability would prompt, but that their great Father at Washington claims it as his prerogative to see that all his red children are justly and reasonably provided for, and has super-abundant means to enable him to do so."[90] He had difficulty in obtaining funds from the government for this purpose.

As Brigham's policies broadened to include Indian farm efforts, he attempted to make the character of the presents reflect this change. When he sent agent George Armstrong south to the Indians, he instructed him to take in addition to the customary blankets, shirts, and tobacco, "some good strong hoes, grubbing hoes, axes, shovels and spades, and one or two plows if you can readily procure them."[91]

Guns and ammunition, on the other hand, were to be handed out sparingly. Brigham urged that ammunition not be given unless the Indians strongly demanded it, and then but little, "as plows, spades, &c, are much better for them." Nevertheless, he recognized that the Indians needed powder and lead and was willing to give them these when he felt they would use it for hunting game and not in hostile actions. He knew, too, that they could not be weaned from hunting all at once. "I realize," he said, "that occasionally they need to hunt, or feel wishful to do so. We do not expect them to abandon their natural pursuits all at once, but by degrees."[92]

One example of Indian hostilities against non-Mormon whites that involved action from Brigham was the massacre of Captain John W. Gunnison and several of his men while they were on a surveying trip in Millard County. The killings were apparently in revenge for the death of an Indian at the hands of an emigrant party that had passed earlier through the area. Brigham dispatched Dimick Huntington to assist the surviving officers. With the help of other Indians and local citizens, the remains were found and buried and many of the government instruments, notebooks, animals, and weapons were recovered and returned. Brigham was offended when the officer in charge, Brevet Captain R. M. Morris, refused to pay the bill for the expenses of the trip, saying he had not ordered out any party to assist him and insisting that the OIA would have to bear the cost.[93] Brigham wrote a sympathetic letter of

BRIGHAM YOUNG: AMERICAN MOSES

condolence to Gunnison's widow, enclosing a lock of her late husband's hair.[94]

In February 1856, a renegade band of Indians under the leadership of Tintic began stealing horses and cattle and killed several Mormon men and boys. Brigham had difficulty restraining the more hotheaded of his people. Armed with writs from Judge William W. Drummond, Thomas Johnson rode off after the Indians despite advice from George A. Smith "not to break peace with the Indians, nor kick up a war without the counsel of the Superintendent of Indian Affairs."[95] The next day Brigham issued a notice to the inhabitants of the territory urging them to remain cool, to disband their large posses, and to arrest no Indian unless he was absolutely known to be guilty. "The Agency in the Territory has the authority and right to dictate regarding the Indians," he wrote, "and will call upon the civil authority when necessary." His own suggestion was to send a man or two to Cedar Fort quietly to attempt to take the Indians when the situation had cooled down.[96] The posse was on its way, however, and in the resulting confrontation both Indian and white lives were lost.

Within a week Brigham had no alternative but forceful retaliation. He wrote to Bernhisel, "We very much regret to have to proceed against them, but are compelled to use the strong arm of power to preserve the lives, and protect the property of our citizens."[97] But he instructed his military officers to try to hire friendly Indians to recover the stock, saying "you need not be particular about the price."[98] By June, Tintic appeared to be repentant and sent word that he wanted to come in to the settlements and make peace.[99]

Occasionally Brigham would recommend the use of courts of law in dealing with Indian depredations. When Squash, a "turbulent fellow," continued stealing cattle and giving trouble to the citizens of Springville, Brigham suggested to the mayor that he take Squash and try him in court, first imprisoning him with a ball and chain. He cautioned the mayor to make sure he had an airtight case (eyewitnesses, for example) and to wait until all was ready, then take Squash unawares. This, he said, would be a lesson to him and a deterrent to other Indians.[100]

A L T H O U G H Brigham held impressive titles—president of the church, governor of Utah Territory, superintendent of Indian affairs—and unquestionably sought to remain in full control, he often remarked that he cared little for grand titles and liked to keep the common touch. His daughter relates that when he was governor a traveler addressed him with all of his federal, military, and religious titles, to which Brigham replied, "Sir, you have omitted my most cherished titles: Carpenter, Painter and Glazier."[101] More offensive to him was the fawning and sycophancy he often encountered because of his position as governor. He expressed disdain for worldly position and especially for those who demeaned themselves catering to it:

As for the pride that is in the world, I walk over it, it is beneath me. To see men who are called gentlemen of character, sense, taste, and ability, who pass through this city, and come bending with the recommendation, saying, "Governor Young this," and "Governor Young that"—it makes me feel to loathe such hypocritical show, in my heart. . . . If they would come to me and say, "Brigham, how are you?" or, "I want to speak to you, &c.," with a good honest heart in them, instead of "Governor Young," "Governor Young," in a canting tone, with hearts as black and deceitful as hell, they would command that esteem from me which is due to an honest man.[102]

Almost from the beginning of his governorship Brigham had to deal with the possibility of his removal from office. There were complaints from disgruntled federal officers, publicity about polygamy, and concern about concentration of power. Before the end of 1851, the federal officers had made their report in Washington, and Bernhisel feared Brigham would lose office. General Alexander Doniphan of Missouri—the man who in 1838 had courageously refused to turn Joseph Smith over to a mob—was rumored to be his successor, and the assumption was that he would be accompanied by a military force.[103]

Brigham's response seems acquiescent compared with later occasions when he asserted his intention to remain governor. Although expecting matters to work out all right, he indicated that if he should be supplanted "it would be nothing but what could be easily survived," and told Bernhisel that should any non-Mormon or nonresident be named governor, "I should as soon General Doniphan would be that man, as any I know of."[104]

In 1853 Brigham made some comments that would later find wide circulation as examples of arrogance. On more than one occasion he reassured his listeners that he had no fear that Franklin Pierce would remove him from office.[105] He told of Almon Babbitt's advice to him not to sign his name as governor on the constitution for state government that Deseret had originally sent to Washington because it would "thwart all your plans." Brigham had replied that he would sign anyway. In a public "discourse" he stated, "I am and will be Governor, and no power can hinder it, until the Lord Almighty says, 'Brigham, you need not be Governor any longer,' and then I am willing to yield to another Governor."[106] A year and a half later, he was still explaining and defending that statement, insisting that he had not claimed that the U.S. president could never remove him but was only acknowledging the Lord's hand in the affairs of men:

The newspapers are teeming with statements that I said "President Pierce and all hell could not remove me from office." I will tell you what I did say, and what I now say; the Lord reigns and rules in the armies of the heavens, and does His pleasure. He walks in the midst of the people, and they know it not. He makes Kings, Presidents, and Governors at His pleasure; hence I conclude that I shall be Governor of Utah Territory, *just as long as He wants me to be*; and *for* that time, neither the President of the United States, nor any other power, can prevent it.[107]

Brigham's four-year appointment as governor was due to expire in 1854. At the end of 1853, Bernhisel told Pierce that the people of Utah strongly desired Brigham to be retained, and the president assured him that he had no intention of removing the governor and would not do so without further consideration and consultation with Bernhisel. Pierce added, however, that there were some difficulties about Brigham's reappointment.[108] Brigham appears to have been puzzled by this. He asked Bernhisel for an explanation of those "difficulties."

> Do you know to what he [Pierce] aludes? If you do I shall be obliged to you if you will intrust them to me, and if you like myself are ignorant about what they are, will you please to ascertain what they may be, and inform me in your next. I tell you however to give yourself no uneasiness in the matter. Office I have never courted nor do I expect to of this administration, but I expect to be Governor "the difficulties in the way" thereof to the contrary notwithstanding.[109]

Brigham had some support outside of Utah. Parley P. Pratt held a discussion in San Francisco on the subject, "Is it expedient for the government to appoint Brigham Young or any other Mormon governor of Utah?" and with an audience composed of lawyers, editors, merchants, priests, etc., succeeded in getting a vote of one-third in favor of the reappointment.[110] In Utah, meanwhile, a memorial from the mostly Mormon territorial legislature to the president and Senate expressed the desire of the members and their constituents for the reappointment. A general petition saying much the same thing was signed by all the territorial officials, the leading merchants of Salt Lake City including the non-Mormons, and the military officers in Lieutenant Colonel Edward J. Steptoe's command, including Steptoe himself. (Steptoe was head of an army engineering unit charting the possible location of a transcontinental railroad in 1855.) Steptoe was probably reassured by the peaceful conditions and general accord in Utah at the time and could see no point in attempting to take office himself.

In December 1854, Bernhisel reported that President Pierce was probably planning to appoint a non-Mormon of high character on the ground that such a man would treat the Saints justly and speak well of them, thus helping to remove some of the prejudice against them. Although Bernhisel continued to press for Brigham's reappointment, he reported that it was not at all certain. A close friend of the president told Bernhisel that he had no idea how great the opposition was to Brigham Young's reappointment.[111]

In January 1855, Bernhisel sent news of the choice of Steptoe as Utah's governor. Brigham had already heard "vague reports" of Steptoe's appointment but passed them off, noting that most of the officer's friends didn't believe he would accept the position anyway.[112] (The prediction was accurate; Steptoe decided not to become Utah's governor.) Bernhisel explained the reasons Brigham had not been reappointed:

> I think the President would have reappointed you but for the tremendous opposition on account of the "peculiar institution" [polygamy] which is so repugnant to the feelings of the people of these States, and the gross perversion of the language represented to have been used by you on two different occasions at the Tabernacle . . . that you threatened that you would not yield obedience to your successor, nor lay down the robes of office with which you had been invested by the people; that you asserted in March last that no power but the Almighty could remove you, and that you intimated if the President should appoint another Governor he would be lynched whenever he made his appearance in Utah; that you defied the Federal Government, and that you would declare war against it, in the event that it should choose to assert its authority in the Territory of Utah. . . .

Yet Bernhisel held out an interesting prospect: "If matters move on peacefully and harmoniously for a year or two under the new Governor, which I have no doubt they will, much of the prejudice excited against us . . . will be removed, and I think that you can be reappointed, indeed I understood the President to intimate as much."[113]

Brigham treated Steptoe courteously and expressed his willingness to relinquish the governorship to a good and honorable man. If Steptoe had received the commission as governor and had accepted it, "I would have taken off my hat and honored the appointment; and this people would have been just as passive and submissive as ever they could be to me." He paid Steptoe the compliment of saying that "if there was going to be a gentleman called upon to be our Governor, there is not a man, out of the Kingdom of God, that I would listen to sooner, and feel more confidence and cordiality towards, than to him."[114]

Brigham's feelings do not seem to have been just for public consumption. In a letter to Bernhisel when the appointment was only rumor, Brigham said, "It is all right, let it be as it will. Col. Steptoe has evinced a friendly feeling since his sojourn with us, and I hope it may continue whether he becomes Governor or not."[115] And to Apostle Erastus Snow, Brigham indicated that he was "well pleased" with Steptoe. He also expressed his acceptance of whatever the result as the will of the Lord. "In regard to the appointment of another Governor, or my own reappointment, they can do as they please, or rather as the Lord pleases to have them, and it is all right with me. If no one else acknowledges the hand of the Lord in such things, we do."[116]

Still, it was no doubt a relief to Brigham when Steptoe left for California with his troops.[117] He saw the outcome of this episode as further evidence of the will of the Lord. He noted that President Pierce had been in office long enough and had had enough pressure to remove him from the governor's office. Yet it had not been done, "though we nearly thought it was when Colonel Steptoe received the appointment; but the Lord operated upon the Colonel to continue his march to California." He concluded that the Lord still wanted him to be governor: "When He wishes another Governor here, the proper person will be on hand; until then, there is no power beneath the heavens that can simply remove the present Governor of Utah, much less the loyal people who inhabit these mountains."[118] Statements like these, which some considered arrogant, continued to flow from him. "I am still acting Governor," he wrote to John Taylor, "no doubt very much to the annoyance of the administration."[119] "I am still governor of this Territory to the constant chagrin of my enemies."[120]

It apparently was a source of pleasure to Brigham to be able to retain his office in the face of national opposition. To those who wondered why he remained in office, and to Congress, which was asking the president that same question, he retorted, "I can answer that question; I hold the office by appointment, and am to hold it until my successor is appointed and qualified, which has not yet been done."[121] Indeed, when Bernhisel reported to Brigham that Steptoe had arrived back in Washington from California, he noted that there had not yet been a governor appointed for Utah.[122]

Brigham's situation was not always clearly understood, even by his church associates. He corrected Charles C. Rich, telling him, "You are misinformed in regard to my being re-appointed Governor; I still hold over, but not by re-appointment."[123] A year later, in 1857, he expressed his appreciation to Thomas Kane for his influence, ascribing his continuation in office to Kane's efforts and the "Providence of God."[124] At this time there were once again rumors that President Pierce would appoint a new governor for Utah before leaving office, but Brigham seemed not to give these reports much credence. "How long they have talked and tried," he sighed. "Wonder if they will not again try to appoint a New Gov'. They have tried so often perhaps they will get tired of trying."[125]

When James Buchanan became president in 1857, Bernhisel met with him to ask that Brigham Young be retained as governor, assuring him as he had Franklin Pierce that no other man would be as acceptable and that Young enjoyed the entire confidence of the people of Utah. Buchanan feared that sending Brigham's name to the Senate would raise a storm. Bernhisel told Buchanan he understood that, which was why he did not ask that Brigham be reappointed but just held over.[126]

Just before news of Buchanan's Utah Expedition reached Brigham, Thomas Kane wrote describing his "policy of staveing off appointment for Governor until fall, as after that time he thinks the administration will drop the matter."[127] At the same time, Brigham's son, John W. Young, was writing a defense of his father, which appeared as a letter to the editor of *The Mormon*. "Brigham Young will resign the Governorship of Utah without a word when his successor is appointed," he wrote, "and there is no possible chance of any collision between the Mormons and the General Government unless President James Buchanan should appoint some hot-headed, blood-thirsty fool as Governor of Utah, who will go beyond all law, all reason, and all good sense, and attempt to rule the people with a high hand."[128]

John W.'s words were prophetic, for Buchanan did not appoint such a man as governor, and despite the threatened presence of an army, Brigham did yield his governorship with remarkably little fuss.

15 ✦

The "Invasion" of Utah

Citizens of Utah—We are invaded by a hostile force who are
evidently assailing us to accomplish our overthrow and destruction.[1]

As a part of the law enforcement system of the State of Deseret,
Brigham Young had created a small force of Minute Men who were prepared
to leave at a moment's notice to pursue Indian or white raiders in order to
recoup stolen cattle or horses. So efficient and dedicated were these young
men that they began to take on a sinister aspect to those who observed the
workings of the Mormon system from afar. Taking some poetic license from
the short-lived, nonofficial Mormon vigilante group in Missouri, they were
sometimes referred to as Danites or Destroying Angels. They played and
continue to play a major role in western fiction, and many readers have imag-
ined Brigham as a military dictator with a personal army of avengers who
carried out his orders to capture, torture, and kill people who crossed him.
But that the Minute Men were anything more than a group willing to undertake
arduous labors for their governor and church president has never been demonstrated.

In 1856 Brigham called the Minute Men to help him establish a series of
way stations between the Salt Lake and Missouri valleys to assist the three
thousand or more immigrants who "gathered" to the Salt Lake Valley each
summer and fall. The enterprise, called the Brigham Young Express and Carrying Company, secured the government contract to carry the mail to Utah,
established a pony express system, and built way stations at nine locations. It
was a considerable enterprise, involving a heavy investment of men, livestock,
and provisions. But it did not take into account the vagaries of federal policy.
On July 1, 1857, operatives of the Y. X. Company, as it was sometimes called,
stopped at the federal post office in Independence, Missouri, to pick up the
mail. The postmaster refused to give it to them, and although he was instructed
to offer no reason for his refusal, the Y. X. representatives soon learned that
on June 10 the government had canceled their mail contract. This decision,

they learned further, was coincident with a plan to send a large consignment of federal troops to Utah.

It was to be a secret operation, if something involving five thousand federal troops, teamsters, suppliers, and hangers-on can be called secret, and the Mormons could only conclude that it was a repetition of Missouri and Illinois—they were to be put down or driven out.

Abraham O. Smoot, mayor of Salt Lake City, was in charge of the mail going east from the city in June, and it was he who first learned of the operation. He made immediate plans to hurry back to Utah to tell Brigham. Knowing that he enjoyed Brigham's full confidence, Smoot ordered the Y. X. agents to close up their stations and return with stock and provisions to Utah. At Fort Laramie he teamed up with Porter Rockwell and Judson Stoddard, trusted Minute Men and Y. X. employees. On July 18, the three "hitched up two spans of our best animals to a small spring wagon" and reached Salt Lake City on July 23, averaging more than 100 miles per day.[2]

Prior to their arrival, Brigham and his family and several thousand associates and followers had gone to Big Cottonwood Canyon, south and east of Salt Lake City, to celebrate the tenth anniversary of the entrance of the pioneers into the Salt Lake Valley. It was there that public announcement of Washington's designs was made.[3]

W H A T led President James Buchanan to send some twenty-five hundred army regulars and about as many teamsters, blacksmiths, suppliers, and other civilian auxiliaries to Utah? Why did he decide to appoint a non-Mormon governor of the territory?

The Mormons, who had sought to settle in a land no one else wanted so they could follow their religious practices without hindrance, found themselves caught up in the national controversy over slavery. When the Kansas-Nebraska Act, granting popular sovereignty on the question of slavery to those two territories, was passed in 1854, abolitionists were horrified. Dissatisfied "anti-Nebraska" men reacted by forming a new party, the Republican party, to resist the extension of slavery into the territories. In opposing the principle of popular sovereignty, Republican orators began to use the example of Utah, whose citizens would certainly vote to support plural marriage. By 1856 Republicans were insisting on the right and duty of Congress to "prohibit in the Territories those twin relics of barbarism—Polygamy and Slavery."[4]

The Democrats, not wishing to imply support of polygamy by their support of slavery, became just as outspoken in denouncing Mormon marriage practices.[5] An action calculated to "put them down" would at once attest to Democratic abhorrence of the Mormons' "peculiar institution" and demonstrate to Southern extremists that Washington would not tolerate rebellion. Buchanan, the Democratic victor in 1856, was particularly influenced by some federal officials who had visited Utah and whose letters and reports suggested that the Mormons did not have the proper respect for the United States or its laws and institutions, and that federal appointees in Utah were powerless to discharge their official duties. Buchanan therefore decided to appoint as governor of the territory Alfred Cumming of Georgia, who had been Indian commissioner in Missouri. Believing that the Mormons would not accept a new governor unless forced to do so, Buchanan also ordered General William S. Harney of Fort Leavenworth, Kansas, to take command of a substantial military force that would accompany Cumming and ensure his installation. All of this was decided without investigation and, more important, without notifying Brigham Young or anyone else in Utah.[6] The president's order to General Harney, dated June 29, 1857, and as amended by his message to Congress in December, read as follows:

> The community and, in part, the civil government of Utah Territory are in a state of substantial rebellion against the laws and authority of the United States. . . . As Chief Executive Magistrate, I [am] bound to restore the supremacy of the Constitution and laws within its limits. A new civil governor is about to be designated, and to be charged with the establishment and maintenance of law and order. Your able and energetic aid, with that of the troops to be placed under your command, is relied upon to insure the success of his mission, . . . [they are sent] to aid as a *posse comitatus*, in case of need, in the execution of the laws.[7]

The Utah Expedition, as it is referred to in military annals, began in July and August 1857. Harney was later replaced by Albert Sidney Johnston, later a leading Confederate general in the Civil War, who accompanied the force to Utah.

The news of the troops' approach, as conveyed by Smoot, Rockwell, and Stoddard, was met by the immediate resolution of the Saints to resist, if the "mob" tried to force its way into the territory. The rhetorical response was fiery. Heber Kimball said:

> Send 2,500 troops here, our brethren, to make a desolation of this people! God Almighty helping me, I will fight until there is not a drop of blood in my veins. Good God! I have wives enough to whip out the United States; for they will whip themselves.[8]

Some eastern publications ran cartoons showing Brigham urging his wives, holding infants high, to charge the U.S. soldiers. Such cartoons were titled, "Brigham's Breast-works."[9]

Brigham's immediate reaction seems, in retrospect, to have been remarkably restrained. He had received some advance indication that his people could expect hostile action from Washington. In a sermon delivered on June 7, he revealed that "some poor, miserable people" had been telling him that the Mormon people would soon be forced to leave their Great Basin retreat.[10] In a sermon delivered two days after the announcement of the "invasion," he said:

I am a Yankee guesser, and I guess that James Buchanan has ordered this Expedition to appease the wrath of the angry hounds who are howling around him. . . . Russell and Co. will probably make from eight to ten hundred thousand dollars by freighting the baggage of the Expedition. What would induce the Government to expend that amount of money for this Territory? Three years ago they appropriated $45,000 for the purpose of making treaties with the Utah Indians. Has even that diminutively small sum ever been sent here? It is in the coffers of the Government to this day, unless they have stolen it out, or improperly paid it out for some other purpose. . . .

I swore in Nauvoo, when my enemies were looking me in the face, that I would send them to hell across lots, if they meddled with me; and I ask no more odds of all hell today. If they kill me, it is all right; but they will not until the time comes, and I think that I shall die a natural death. At least I expect to. . . . Catching is always before hanging. . . .

What are they angry at me for? Because I will reprove men for their iniquity, and because I have such influence here—the very thing they are all after. . . . There is no influence, truth, or righteousness in the world, only what flows from God our Father in the heavens. . . .

What is now the news circulated throughout the United States? That Captain Gunnison was killed by Brigham Young, and that Babbitt was killed on the Plains by Brigham Young and his Danite band. What more? That Brigham Young has killed all the men who have died between the Missouri river and California. . . . Such reports are in the bellows, and editors and politicians are blowing them out. . . .

I will make this proposition to Uncle Sam. I will furnish carriages, horses, the best of drivers, and the best food I have, to transport to the States every man, woman, and child that wishes to leave this place, if he will send on at his own expense all those who want to come to Utah; and we will gain a thousand to their one. . . . It would have been much better to have loaded the waggons reported to be on the way here, with men, women, and children, than with provisions to sustain soldiers; for they will never get here without we help them. . . .[11]

The more Brigham pondered the deliberate failure of the president to notify him of his replacement and of the dispatch of the army, the more suspicious he became of Buchanan's motives. Was the approaching army yet another mob ready to annihilate the Mormons or drive them from their homes?

By early August he had decided on his course of action. "Citizens of Utah," he stated in a broadside proclamation dated August 5,

> We are invaded by a hostile force who are evidently assailing us to accomplish our overthrow and destruction. . . . Our opponents have availed themselves of prejudice existing against us because of our religious faith, to send out a formidable host to accomplish our destruction. We have had no privilege, no opportunity of defending ourselves from the false, foul, and unjust aspersions against us before the nation. The Government has not condescended to cause an investigating committee or other person to be sent to inquire into and ascertain the truth, as is customary in such cases. . . .
>
> The issue which has been thus forced upon us compels us to resort to the great first law of self preservation and stand in our own defense, a right guaranteed unto us by the genius of the institutions of our country, and upon which the Government is based. Our duty to ourselves, to our families, requires us not to tamely submit to be driven and slain, without an attempt to preserve ourselves. Our duty to our country, our holy religion, our God, to freedom and liberty, requires that we should not quietly stand still and see those fetters forging around, which are calculated to enslave and bring us in subjection to an unlawful military despotism. . . . This is, therefore,
>
> 1st:—To forbid, in the name of the People of the United States in the Territory of Utah, all armed forces, of every description, from coming into this Territory under any pretence whatever.
>
> 2nd:—That all the forces in said Territory hold themselves in readiness to march, at a moment's notice, to repel any and all such threatened invasion.
>
> 3d:—Martial law is hereby declared to exist in this Territory, . . . and no person shall be allowed to pass or repass into, or through, or from this Territory, without a permit from the proper officer.[12]

A few days later, he wrote in his personal diary: "Fixed my determination not to let any troops enter this territory, . . . and make every preparation to give the U.S. a Sound Drubbing. I do not feel to be imposed upon any more."[13]

Brigham mustered the Nauvoo Legion, ordered that no grain or other staple was to be sold to passing emigrants or speculators, arranged for fortifications to be built, and instructed his Minute Men to harass the army and supply trains. He also sent out exploring groups to locate oases where the Saints could survive if forced to abandon their homes.[14]

On September 7, 1857, Captain Stewart Van Vliet of the quartermaster corps arrived in Salt Lake City to arrange for supplies for the incoming troops and to assure Mormon leaders of their peaceful intentions. He interviewed Brigham and his associates, inspected their resistance measures, and attended a public meeting in the Old Tabernacle where Mormon speakers recounted their persecutions in Missouri and Illinois and pledged unanimous support of Brigham's resistance policy. Van Vliet was persuaded that the Mormons were

not in rebellion and that they had some justification for their defensive preparations. Unsuccessful in making his quartermaster arrangements, he returned
to the expeditionary force and then to Washington and became a strong advocate of peaceful reconciliation.[15] He was accompanied by Utah delegate
John Bernhisel, who carried letters to Brigham's friend, Thomas L. Kane.

The day after Van Vliet's departure, to prepare his people for any eventuality and to persuade Washington that if it encroached on Mormon territory
the army would be resisted, Brigham reissued his August 5 proclamation as
territorial governor declaring martial law. All that we ask for, he stated, is that
"the Constitutional rights which pertain unto us as American citizens" be
extended to Utah, "according to the spirit and meaning thereof, and fairly and
impartially administered."[16] Under this authority, he sent out about one hundred
"Mormon Raiders," as the Minute Men now referred to themselves, to harass
the army and ordered the Nauvoo Legion, under command of Daniel H.
Wells, to the eastern front (Echo Canyon) to face the oncoming troops. The
instructions to the Raiders were:

> On ascertaining the locality or route of the troops, proceed at once to annoy
> them in every possible way. Use every exertion to stampede their animals, and
> set fire to their trains. Burn the whole country before them and on their flanks.
> Keep them from sleeping by night surprises. Blockade the road by falling trees,
> or destroying the fords when you can. Watch for opportunities to set fire to the
> grass on their windward, so as, if possible, to envelop their trains. Leave no grass
> before them that can be burned. . . . Take no life, but destroy their trains, and
> stampede or drive away their animals, at every opportunity.[17]

One early action of these Raiders was to burn two prize and expensive Mormon
outposts in what was then eastern Utah (now western Wyoming), Bridger
and Fort Supply, which government forces had expected to occupy. They also
burned three freight trains, out of a total of forty-one, comprising seventy-
four large wagons. The supplies destroyed made Brigham wince: about seventy
thousand rations of desiccated vegetables, four tons of bread, four tons of
coffee, eighty-four tons of flour, forty-six tons of bacon, three thousand gallons
of vinegar, and seven tons of soap—enough to last the entire army three
months. They also captured fourteen hundred of the two thousand head of
cattle accompanying the expedition.[18]

When the federal commander, Colonel Edmund B. Alexander, reached
the borders of Utah Territory, Brigham sent him a message that, in his position
as governor, he was "impelled by every sense of justice, honor, integrity and
patriotism to resist what I consider to be a direct infringement of the rights
of the Citizens of Utah and an act of usurpation and tyranny unprecedented
in the history of the United States."[19] Despite Alexander's assurances that the
citizens would not be harmed by the army, Brigham had too often seen "armies
in our country, under color of law, drive this people, commonly styled 'Mor-

mons', from their homes, while mobs have followed and plundered at their pleasure, which is now most obviously the design of the General Government, as all candid thinking men know full well." If the army was really sent to "protect" the people, "why did not the Government send an Army here to protect us against the savages, when we first settled here, and were poor and a few in number?"[20] Since he had as yet had no official notice that the army had been sent by the government, he felt it his right to treat them as a mob.[21] As governor, Brigham ordered Alexander to take his troops and leave, but warned that the Mormons had counted the cost of possible conflict and would not surrender their rights.[22]

A tragic incident occurred during the Mormon mobilization that has left a scar on the image of Brigham Young and Mormonism to this day.

In his message justifying the Utah Expedition, Buchanan charged that Brigham had "tampered with the Indian tribes, and excited their hostile feelings against the United States."[23] Why this merited the speeding of an army to Utah is not explained, but there is little doubt that the Mormons, in the words of one Indian agent, "accidentally or purposely created a distinction in the minds of Indian tribes of this [Utah] territory between the Mormons and the people of the United States."[24] This issue, though apparent earlier in Brigham's superintendency, came to a head during the tense period of the government-Mormon face-off in the fall of 1857. The three points of the triangle—Mormon–Indian–United States—were played off against each other in a variety of ways. Indeed, Brigham's handling of Indian relations during his last few months as superintendent focused largely upon this problem.

Although he reported to the commissioner that he always tried to "create in them [the Indians] some respect for their great father the President,"[25] the Indians could not fail to recognize some distinction between Mormons and other Americans. When the Mormons told Walker they were building a fort at Nephi to keep out the Americans in case they came to drive the Mormons away, the chief offered to help the Mormons fight the Americans—but also threatened to become friends with the Americans instead, should the Mormons "shut him out" by building the fort.[26]

To Brigham, Buchanan's concern about the distinctions made by the Indians was misplaced. The Indians themselves, he said, had made the distinction at the time when the emigrants to California first began passing through the territory in 1849. Finding that they were shot at by the emigrants but fed and clothed by the Mormons, and that the Mormons had left the United States because of conflict with Americans, they could not help making the distinction. Nevertheless, Indian agents' reports did have an effect in influencing government officials to take action against the Saints. When the army reached the edges of the territory, Brigham suspected them of trying to enlist the Indians to fight against the Mormons. Even the report of troops being on the way, he wrote, had influenced the Indians to make attacks on Mormon herds, that "they seemed to think if it was to be war they might as well commence and begin to lay in a supply of food when they had a chance."[27] Reports began to filter in that the troops were offering Indians presents and trying to hire them to steal Mormon livestock, that the commander had offered Indians $150 for each Mormon they would bring him, and that the army filled the Indians' heads with tales of atrocities committed by Brigham and his people. Indian attacks in Tooele County and on the Mormon fort at Lemhi, Idaho, were seen as results of incitement or bribery by the federal troops.[28]

However nefarious or innocent the distinctions created before the coming of the troops, there was some indication that Brigham did attempt to acquire Indians as military allies against the U.S. Army. There were several instances when Brigham asked Indians to remain neutral.[29] But there were also reports of an expedition into the Bear Lake area involving several conferences with Indians and instructions to them, and letters to church leaders in southern Utah indicating that there were probably attempts to secure their alliance. In August, right after the news of the troops' approach reached Utah, Brigham wrote to missionaries in Nebraska territory and among the Cheyenne and Sioux, urging them to impress upon the Indians the importance of their being friends of the Mormons so as to save themselves, "for they must learn, if they do not know it now, that if they do not help us to whip our enemies they [federal troops] will whip us both if they can."[30] On the same date he wrote to Jacob Hamblin in southern Utah, reminding him to conciliate the Indians "and seek by works of righteousness to obtain their love and confidence, for they must learn that they have either got to help us or the United States will kill us both."[31]

Finally, on September 12, Brigham sent a letter to Jeter Clinton that, allowing for some rhetoric, hints that he had some control over the actions of Indians in the territory:

> For years I have been holding the Indians, the check rein has broken, and cousin Lemuel is at length at large; in fact he has been already collecting some of his annuities. Day after day I am visited by their Chiefs to know if they may strike while "the iron is hot." My answer depends on Mr. Buchanan's policy—if he does not mete out justice to us, the war cry will resound from the Rio Colorado to the head waters of the Missouri—from the Black hills to the Sierra Nevada—travel will be stopped across the continent—the deserts of Utah [will] become a battle ground for freedom. It—peace and our rights—or the knife and tomahawk—let Uncle Sam choose.[32]

Unbeknownst to Brigham, the most tragic event in Mormon history had occurred just the day before that letter was written. A company of Arkansas immigrants, headed for California, had been joined before they reached Utah by a group of horsemen called "Missouri Wildcats." Perhaps because of the lateness of the season, they had decided to take the southern route, via the Spanish Trail, and headed for southern Utah. Traveling at a time when the territory was under martial law, they had tried, without success, to buy grain and supplies. Some of them had boasted about participating in the Haun's Mill Massacre and other mob actions against the Mormons. Some had expropriated supplies from Mormon farmers. And some suspicious Mormons thought they were a reconnoitering party in advance of the main federal army. But the gravest circumstance was the belief of Indians in central Utah that members of the train had poisoned their wells and that some of their stock, and some of their tribesmen, had died. The Indians determined to attack them.

By the time the company reached Mountain Meadows, in southern Utah, the Indians laid siege. Meanwhile, they asked their Mormon "friends" to help them wreak their revenge. Warily, the Mormons, outnumbered now by the Indians in the region, declined. Pressed by the natives, local leaders on September 7 sent a courier to Brigham asking him what to do. The courier, Captain James Haslam of the Iron County Militia, reached Salt Lake City in three days—a remarkable time for horse travel over that 250-mile distance. Brigham's reply, written immediately, was as follows:

> President's Office
> Great Salt Lake City
> Sept. 10, 1857

Elder Isaac C. Haight:

Dear Brother:—Your note of the 7th inst. is to hand. Capt. Van Vliet, Acting Commissary, is here, having come in advance of the army to procure necessaries for them. We do not expect that any part of the army will be able to reach here this fall. There is only about 850 men coming. They are now at or near Laramie. A few of their freight trains are this side of that place, the advance of which are now on Green River. They will not be able to come much if any further on account of their poor stock. They cannot get here this season without we help them. So you see that the Lord has answered our prayers and again averted the blow designed for our heads.

In regard to the emigration trains passing through our settlements, we must not interfere with them until they are first notified to keep away. You must not meddle with them. The Indians we expect will do as they please but you should try and preserve good feelings with them. There are no other trains going south that I know of. If those that are there will leave, let them go in peace. While we should be on the alert, on hand, and always ready, we should also possess ourselves in patience, preserving ourselves and property, ever remembering that God rules. He has overruled for our deliverance thus once again, and He will always do so if we live our religion and be united in our faith and good works.

All is well with us. May the Lord bless you all the Saints forever.

Your Brother in the gospel of Christ.

Brigham Young[33]

According to Haslam's later testimony, he started back for Cedar City just four hours after he arrived in Salt Lake City. As he left Salt Lake, Brigham said to him, "Go with all speed, spare no horse flesh. The emigrants must not be meddled with, if it takes all Iron County to prevent it. They must go free and unmolested."[34] Haslam reached Cedar City about 11:00 A.M. Sunday morning, September 13, and delivered the message—two days too late.

Owing to provocations from the immigrants, the local settlers' fear of infuriating the Indians, and their own hysteria when they found that some of their impetuous young men had killed an immigrant going for help—thus leading the company to conclude that the Mormons were partners with the Indians in the siege—members of the local militia joined the Indians in killing some 120 immigrants, including all the women. Only eighteen small children were saved.

When the local Mormon Indian farmer John D. Lee brought word of the massacre to Brigham, he stated only that the Indians had done it. The details were so gruesome that Brigham Young wept. Valuable as a precise indication of what Brigham was told about the incident is Wilford Woodruff's diary entry for September 29, 1857:

> Elder John D. Lee also arrived from Harmony with an express and an awful tale of blood. A company of Calafornian emigrants of about 150 men women and children. Many of them belonged to the mob in Missouri and Illinois. They had many cattle and horses with them. As they travelled along south they went damning Brigham Young, Heber C. Kimball, and the Heads of the Church saying that Joseph Smith ought to have been shot a long time before he was. They wanted to do all the evil they could, so they poisoned beets and gave it to the Indians and some of them died. They poisoned the springs of water. Severel of the saints died. The Indians became inraged at them, caught [up with them] and they surrounded them on a prarie, and the emigrants formed a bulwark of their waggons and dug an entrenchment up to the hubs of there [their] waggons. But the Indians fought them 5 days untill they killed all their men, about 60 in number. They then rushed into their correll and cut the throats of their women and children except for some 10 children which they brought and sold to the whites. They strip[p]ed the men and women naked and left them stinking in the boiling sun. When Brother Lee found it out he took some men and went and buried their bodies. It was a horrid awful job—the whole air was filled with an awful stench. Many of the men and women were rotted with the pox before they were hurt by the Indians. The Indians obtain[ed] all there cattle horses and property. Guns to[o]. Their was another large company of emigrants who had 1000 head of cattle who was also damning both Indians and Mormons. They were afraid of sharing the same fate. Brother Lee had to send interpreters with them to the Indians to try to save their lives while at the same time they are trying to kill us.

> Brother Brigham, while [Brother Lee was] speaking of the cutting of the throats of women and children by the Indians down south, said that it was heart rending—that emigration must stop as he had before said.

On the basis of Lee's report, which he had no reason to discredit, Brigham reported to James W. Denver, the Indian commissioner in Washington, that this "lamentable" occurrence was "only the natural consequence of that fatal policy which treats the Indians like the wolves or other ferocious beasts."[35] Only many months later, from seemingly casual conversations with trusted associates, did Brigham learn the horrible truth that the members of the Iron County Militia, Mormons all, were full participants in the massacre.

B R I G H A M ' S role as commander in chief of the Nauvoo Legion required his participation, with Lieutenant General Daniel H. Wells, in directing military operations. Some of his work was tedious and routine, such as the preparing and signing of letters to the colonels and majors of various military districts asking them to raise a set number of men and report for duty. When Colonel Albert Sidney Johnston took command of the Utah Army, Wells was concerned that this would invigorate the force and give it the impetus to push into the valleys. In response to his anxious communications, Brigham ordered more letters written for mustering men and stayed up until 2 A.M. signing them.[36]

Brigham's letters were specific in directing the activities of his forces. He told the leader of a brigade to bring "crow bars, picks, and spades for the purpose of loosening up rocks from the tops of cliffs that may be hurled down to good effect when the signal is given for the same."[37] He gave instructions for stampeding animals, for rousing up the camps to prevent the soldiers from sleeping, and for stealing guns from the trains. To take advantage of the possible disaffection among federal troops, he detailed a careful plan that encompassed specific matters of time, placement, and sound. He suggested having someone with a clear and loud voice who was also a good rider go to the camp

> and upon the first opportunity, at about dusk of a still evening, approach within hailing distance on the windward side, and on a point or rise of ground if any, and shout something as follows: "Attention the camp" (to be repeated, perhaps, once or twice, till attention is attracted) "all who wish to fight the Mormons had better stay where they are; and all who do not wish to fight are advised to make for Salt Lake City at every opportunity, where they will be well treated, furnished with employment and permitted to proceed to California when they please."[38]

Brigham changed tactics in accordance with changed conditions. In mid-October he ordered his Minute Men to stop destroying the army's wagon trains, "for if the troops undertake to come in we shall fall heir to the property in their possession." This did not mean to leave the trains alone, for he counseled them to send any goods they could conveniently get hold of to Salt Lake City.[39]

While the expeditionary force was being prepared, the Church Public Works Department labored overtime in the interests of defense. Volunteer and employed workers labored "from sunrise to sunset," making guns, bullets, cannonballs, and canister shots. On the site of the old sugar works, a chemical laboratory was erected for the manufacture of gunpowder. On Temple Square, a shop produced revolvers. According to one observer, they turned out guns resembling Colts at the rate of twenty per week.[40]

Finally, Brigham ordered all the "outposts of Zion" and the missionaries located throughout the world to abandon their missions and "come home to Zion." This drastic action, made in the heat of defense preparations, involved the abandonment of the Salmon River mission in northern Idaho, the Elk Mountain mission in eastern Utah, the Mormon Station in Carson Valley, Nevada, and the settlement at San Bernardino, California. Also called home were several hundred missionaries stationed throughout the world.[41]

DESPITE the information that a new governor had been appointed for Utah, Brigham unsurprisingly continued to enjoy strong local support for his continuance in office. A memorial signed by many people in Utah, both Mormons and non-Mormons, was dispatched to Washington in October recommending that he remain as governor since he enjoyed the "unlimited confidence" of the people and had filled the office honorably.[42] In December the legislature stated their unanimous support for him, their willingness to sustain him in all his constitutional acts, and their refusal to accept other officers as long as the territory was being menaced by an army.[43] When the newly appointed Governor Cumming sent a letter to some of the Mormon troops ordering them to disband, they "Formd a Hollow Sq & after hereing the New Gov orders, we gave 3 Cheers For Gov Brigham Young which made the Kanyon ring."[44]

During the winter Brigham decided he would have to relinquish his governorship and recognize Cumming as the new governor. A "rumor" was current in December that Brigham would receive the soldiers kindly and install Cumming as governor if the soldiers would leave behind their weapons and enter peaceably.[45]

At the same time, Thomas Kane secured an appointment with President Buchanan and sought to mediate the dispute. He was willing to travel secretly to Utah at his own expense, without official position, in order to assure that Brigham was released as governor, Cumming installed, and the army permitted to establish a camp in Utah without opposition. The president, eager to achieve a peaceful settlement of an action that he now regarded as probably precipitate and that others believed was a blunder, agreed to write a letter stating that Kane had his confidence and was "recommended to the favorable regard of all the officers of the United States whom he would meet as he traveled."[46]

Leaving on a steamer from New York in January, Kane was accompanied by a black servant named Osborne, and he conveniently appropriated that name, traveling as Dr. A. Osborne, a botanist connected with the Academy of Natural Sciences of Philadelphia. The two debarked at Panama, crossed the isthmus, and sailed up the California coast, from which they hurried to the

Mormon settlement at San Bernardino. There they were assisted by two Mormon families, who arranged transportation for them to Utah and provided provisions and equipment.[47]

Colonel Kane, alias Dr. Osborne, arrived in Salt Lake City on February 25 and immediately held a series of conferences with Mormon leaders. Brigham's journal describes the result as follows:

> Colonel Kane . . . tried to point out a policy for me to pursue. But I told him I should not turn to the right or to the left, or pursue any course except as God dictated. . . . When he found that I would be informed only as the Spirit of the Lord led me, he was at first discouraged. Then he said, I could dictate he would execute. I told him that as he had been inspired to come here, he should go to the Army and do as the Spirit of the Lord led him, and all should be right.[48]

Brigham would not agree to a settlement, however, without assurances that the army would not come in with the governor.

Kane was in poor health, and when the wisdom of his proceeding on to the army encampment at Camp Scott was raised, Brigham declared:

> The Lord has sent you here, friend Thomas, and He will not let you die. No, you cannot die until your work is done. Your name will live with the Saints in all eternity. You have done a great work, and you will do a greater work still.[49]

About ten days after his arrival in Salt Lake City, accompanied by an escort of Mormons, Kane traveled to the army camps in Wyoming. As he neared the camps, he dismissed the escort and rode in alone. He was so exhausted that the soldiers had to take him from his horse. He insisted on transacting his business not with the military officers but with the newly appointed governor. He was able to persuade Cumming that he would be recognized by the Mormons as governor, that the Mormons were not in a state of rebellion against the government, and that the army should not be allowed to remain in Salt Lake Valley. The negotiations with army leaders were not as pleasant. One of Colonel Johnston's officers shot at Kane, narrowly missing him. Johnston dispatched an orderly to invite Kane to dinner, but the orderly placed Kane under arrest. With Cumming's approval, the diminutive Kane then sent a challenge for a duel to Johnston. The affair blew over quickly when Kane was informed that Johnston had not ordered the arrest.

Kane and Governor Cumming left Camp Scott, without military escort, in April. Although Brigham was reconciled to relinquishing his governorship, some of his close associates still resisted. As the office clerk recorded a conversation: "Bro's Wells and Smith said they disliked to have A. Cumming become, by any means, Governor of the Territory. . . . Prest. Young said he did not care anything about it: the Lord would overrule it for good, whichever way it happened."[50]

Brigham was still a little recalcitrant. He said he did not wish to see Cumming unless the new governor particularly desired an interview. If Cumming should want to speak to the people in the tabernacle to see if they wanted him, Brigham thought it might be good to have the building filled with women for the occasion, and he hoped that when Cumming arrived the feelings of the people would be "cold enough to freeze peaches."[51]

Cumming's meetings with Brigham, however, were generally amicable. Only a few things may have rubbed Brigham wrong—particularly when Cumming asked for Young's office. (Kane explained that Brigham's office was a part of his private residence.) He apparently felt accepted and well treated. He reported to Colonel Johnston after his first few days that he had been recognized as governor everywhere and had suffered no indignities or insults. Brigham had delivered records and seals to him and had "evinced a willingness to afford me every facility which I may require for the efficient performance of my administrative duties."[52]

Kane had what he called his "final and decisive" interview with Cumming on April 24. He wrote in his diary, "I am and know myself to be happy."[53] Kane then left the Salt Lake Valley, accompanied Cumming as far as Camp Scott, and then continued east. He reported to President Buchanan, who then arranged to have the Mormons "pardoned" and to locate the army no closer than forty miles from Salt Lake City. In his next annual message to Congress, Buchanan paid special tribute to Kane:

> I cannot refrain from mentioning . . . the valuable services of Colonel Thomas L. Kane, who from motives of pure benevolence, and without any official character or pecuniary compensation, visited Utah during the last inclement winter for the purpose of contributing to the pacification of the territory.[54]

The tribute of the Mormons was even more glowing. Reflecting Brigham's feeling, Wilford Woodruff wrote to Kane:

> You were an instrument in the hands of God, and you were inspired by Him to turn away . . . the edge of the sword, saving the effusion of much blood, and performing what the combined wisdom of the nation could not accomplish, changing the whole face of affairs, with effects which will remain forever.[55]

C U M M I N G ' S acceptance proceeded slowly. He addressed the Saints on April 25, after which Brigham said that the governor could not be received unless he used his influence to have the army withdrawn and reported favorably on the Mormons. He reminded Cumming that were it not for his [Brigham's] influence in restraining his people, "it is not for me to say where the United States army now within our borders would have been this day."[56] Gilbert Clements's comments at the same meeting illustrate the feelings of the people and their reluctance to accept Cumming. Clements said he had nothing against

Cumming personally and that he in fact seemed to be a good man; his only complaint was that Cumming was a stranger, unknown to the Mormons and not of their own choosing.

> . . . Shall we give up *him* who has governed us for years with such happy results— who has proved himself to be no summer friend, (one simultaneous "No!") who in our dark days of adversity and sorrow stood faithfully by us in every storm, who has been a co-partner with us in poverty, nakedness, and want, who has sympathised in all our afflictions, and led and guided us, as a tender parent would his child? I say shall we give up such a man, and allow a mere stranger to supplant him in our affections? (No Never, No never, from all parts of the house). The universal feeling of this people is that Gov. Young is, and ever will be our Governor.

Clements went on to say that it was not because of Brigham's prestige as church president that they wanted him as governor but because of the sound policy of his official acts, the impetus he had given to industry, his efforts in promoting public works, and his evenhanded administration of justice.[57]

Brigham's insistence that the army not come into the Salt Lake Valley stemmed from his feeling that there were trigger-happy men on both sides who would precipitate "incidents" that would lead to bloodshed. His solution, proposed to a special "Council of War" on March 18, 1858, while Kane was at Camp Scott negotiating with Cumming and Johnston, was "to go into the desert and not war with the people [of the United States], but let them destroy themselves." "Rather than see my wives and daughters ravished and polluted, and the seeds of corruption sown in the hearts of my sons by a brutal soldiery," he said, "I would leave my home in ashes, my gardens and orchards a waste, and subsist upon roots and herbs, a wanderer through these mountains for the remainder of my natural life."[58]

Three days later, in the regular Sunday tabernacle service in Salt Lake City, the meeting was resolved into a special conference of the church to consider what was called the "Sebastopol Plan," referring to the Russian evacuation of Sebastopol during the Crimean War two years before. The statement of the Russian general who evacuated Sebastopol had excited Mormon admiration:

> . . . it is not Sebastopol which we have left to them, but the burning ruins of the town, which we ourselves set fire to, having maintained the honour of defence in such a manner that our grandchildren may recall with pride the remembrance of it and send it on to all posterity.[59]

Brigham "presented the policy which he intended to pursue, which was to remove the grain and the women and children from the city and then, if needs be, burn it and lay the country waste."[60]

We are in duty bound to preserve life—to preserve ourselves in earth—consequently we must use policy and follow in the counsel given us. . . . Shall we take a course to whip our enemies? or one to let them whip themselves? or shall we go out and slay them now? We have been preparing to use up our enemies by fighting them, and if we take that course and shed the blood of our enemies, we will see the time, . . . when we will have to flee from our homes and leave the spoil to them.[61]

The next day he sent a special courier to Kane informing him of this decision:

We are now preparing to remove our men, women and children to the deserts and mountains, that our enemies may come in and complete their instructions to establish a military post at or near Salt Lake City, if that is their only alternative. . . . Will our enemies keep off and let us alone while we are removing, or are they so bloodthirsty that they will not be satisfied short of doing their utmost to destroy our lives? . . . If they come here and find neither people nor city, what will be their next move?[62]

The prospect of evacuating Salt Lake City and nearby settlements, said Brigham at the weekly tabernacle service the next week, "gives a spring to our feelings, especially since we for the first time have the privilege of laying waste our improvements, and are not obliged to leave our inheritances to strangers to enjoy and revel in the fruits of our labors."[63]

As directed by Brigham, the "Move South," as it was called, had two phases: the organization of parties to search out a new gathering place, should necessity require it, and the organization of the Move itself.

Exploring parties found a few "valleys" in the area of modern-day Nevada that might receive small groups of Latter-day Saints and would be impregnable against an army. As Brigham expressed it:

While small parties might be able to cross such a thirsty waste with comparative safety, an army would find it impassable, and the larger the force the more impracticable it would be. While few men might find enough water in a small seap or water-hole to allay their thirst, a thousand men and animals would find it totally inadequate. Such a desert would be a more formidable barrier than an army of forty thousand men.[64]

Recognizing that the Mormons would move again if they had to, "General" William Walker and a Colonel Kinney offered to sell to the church thirty million acres of land on the Mosquito Coast in Central America. Another proposition came to settle Sonora, in northern Mexico. Some officials in Washington seemed to regard the proposals as offering means of disposing once and for all of America's "Mormon question" and were prepared to recommend that financial inducement be offered the Mormons to accept. But Brigham, determined if at all possible to remain in Utah Territory, did not carry these negotiations to an advanced stage.[65]

While parties were "searching out the desert fastnesses" and church officials were considering moves outside the country, the wards and settlements in northern Utah were organizing for the Move South. At Brigham's suggestion, the Move was to be led by 500 families from Salt Lake City who had never been driven from their homes. These people were to be selected by bishops from "the poorest and most helpless" and their migration was to be "an ensample" to other wards and settlements throughout the territory. They were to be assisted in moving by men, teams, and wagons donated by other members of their own and nearby wards. Within a week after the Move had been announced, they had been organized and had begun their hegira, at the rate of about forty families per day.

The First Presidency, the Apostles, and the Presiding Bishopric supervised the organization of the remainder of the Saints.[66] In general, the church was divided into three groups: (1) those living in southern Utah who would not move, but who were instructed to send wagons, teams, and teamsters to northern Utah to assist in the Move; (2) those living in northern Utah who were young and vigorous and who would remain behind to irrigate crops and gardens, guard property, and set fire to the homes in case the Sebastopol treatment was ordered; (3) some thirty-five thousand Mormons living north of Utah Valley who would make the Move. Each ward was allotted a strip of land in Utah, Juab, Millard, or Iron county, as the immediate objective or resting-place. Those wards being carried by southern Utah teams were to go farthest south. The grain was to be moved first and then the families.

The Move was to be carried out in strict Mormon military order, each ward being organized into tens, fifties, and hundreds, with a captain over each. Each family was expected to transport furniture, in addition to food and clothing, so that personal and family possessions would not be burned, if that tactic were decided upon. Shavings, kindling, and dried grass were to be left in the entrances of homes to make the scorched-earth policy more effective. Initially, the housing at their destination would consist of the bodies of their heavy covered wagons, or canvas tents. Inevitably, some would live in dugouts and temporary board shanties and cabins. Whatever the shelter, the regular work of making a living—making butter and cheese, raising stock and poultry, spinning and weaving—would be continued as if in their former homes. Several hundred southern Utah wagons, complete with oxen, horses, and mules, came north to assist with the Move.

While bishops were organizing their wards, the public works department was preparing for the transportation of church properties southward. One group cached all the stone that had been cut for the Salt Lake Temple and leveled and covered over the foundations of this sacred edifice so that it would resemble a plowed field and remain unmolested by "desecrating maurauders." Another group boxed all of the tithing grain in bins holding seventy-three bushels each and transported it south to granaries specially erected for its reception in Provo. More than 20,000 bushels of wheat were hauled in this manner—almost 300 wagon loads. Additional wagon trains carried machinery and equipment to be housed in specially built warehouses and sheds. Still another group hauled the public machine shop, the *Deseret News* print shop, and other machinery and equipment to Fillmore and Parowan. All the church records, papers, and books were packed in boxes and shipped to Provo. Temporary public works mills and shops were set up in the principal settlements in central and southern Utah to grind wheat, repair equipment, manufacture armaments and munitions, and perform other public services.

The Move occupied a period of about two months, being virtually completed by the middle of May. This meant that several hundred wagons were constantly on the go during this period. One report states that an average of about six hundred wagons had passed through Salt Lake City daily during the first two weeks of May. Governor Cumming, of course, was in Utah during part of the Move South period and made several journeys along the line of caravans pleading with the people to return to their homes. On one trip he met 800 wagons. "Is there not some way to stop the moving?" he asked Brigham, to which the president replied that "if the troops were withdrawn from the Territory, the people would stop moving, but that 99 out of every hundred of the people would rather live out their lives in the mountains than endure the oppression the Federal Government was now heaping upon them." Brigham is also reported to have declared, "Our necks shall not be given to the halter. . . . I'm tired of this city."[67] As late as May 24, when the Move had been completed, Brigham Young and other church officials were giving serious consideration to burning Salt Lake City and all settlements north of it.

I T was clear to Cumming that, as he said to Brigham, "I can do nothing here without your influence."[68] Brigham was of course aware of the difficulty of Cumming's position. "The Gov. seems disposed to do all he can to make things right," he wrote to Bernhisel, "if he can only be recognized as Governor—an item which the people have not yet acceded to."[69] Meanwhile, Brigham continued to act as a governor might—directing fifty men to repair the road at the Point of the Mountain, for example, and threatening to call in the newly established currency if the people did not sustain it.[70] The people still saw him in that capacity as well. One man wrote to his sons:

> . . . to-day the ex-Governor is, in my sight, guiding this people in a severe trial, restraining, by his influence, the party opposed to peace, controlling their ruffled

tempers, maintaining order among them, and inspiring them with confidence in the Lord, ten thousand times more worthy of honor than any Governor, King, or Emperor upon the earth.[71]

Even the federal government was unsure about the details of the transfer of power from Young to Cumming. The comptroller of the Treasury months later was inquiring of the State Department as to just when Brigham had ceased to be recognized as governor and when Cumming had actually taken the oath of office.[72]

Three years before he yielded the role of governor, Brigham had said, "Though I may not be Governor here, my power will not be diminished. No man they can send here will have much influence with this community, unless he be the man of their choice. Let them send whom they will, and it does not diminish my influence one particle."[73] His words proved true. Looking back on this period, Brigham summed it up by saying, "I believe that Governor Cumming came to the conclusion that he was Governor of the Territory as domain; but that Brigham Young was Governor of the people."[74]

There was one sense in which Brigham retained the title as well as the power of governor. With the establishment of the "ghost" legislature of Deseret in 1862 following yet another unsuccessful attempt to obtain statehood, Brigham was appointed as governor by this shadow entity that convened each year right after the territorial legislature ended and was made up of the same members. It reenacted the same laws passed in the territorial legislature and listened to messages from their "Governor." The Gentile (non-Mormon) governors of Utah during the 1860s chafed under the limitations of their situation, but despite their efforts none succeeded in becoming more than a nominal ruler.

W I T H   respect to Indian affairs, Congress had passed an act on March 3, 1857, providing for a superintendent separate from the governor in the territories of Utah, New Mexico, Washington, and Oregon, and in August Jacob Forney of Philadelphia was appointed for Utah. He spent the winter at Camp Scott with the other federal appointees, during which time Utah had in effect two superintendents of Indian affairs. Throughout those tense months both Forney and Brigham Young expressed their desire to keep the Indians neutral, yet each suspected that the other was secretly tampering with them and using them.

Soon after Cumming took over as governor in the spring of 1858, Forney arrived and began his duties as superintendent. Brigham wrote his final report on June 30, closing his accounts and formally turning the office over to Forney, explaining that he had not felt able to lay down his duties while Forney was in Camp Scott and had waited until his arrival in Salt Lake City.[75] But when Forney received vouchers for Young's expenditures up to that date, he coolly replied that he had been appointed superintendent the previous August.

By a refference to the enclosed papers, I perceive, that you assume to exercise the authority vested in me. It is therefore quite obvious, that I can not be the medium of communication between the Indian Department and yourself, in transmitting these papers.

Whenever it suits your convenience, I will be pleased to receive the papers and property, belonging to the Un. States, in your possession.[76]

It took several years for Brigham's accounts with the government to be finally settled. An investigation was begun in 1862 into his claims to see if there was any fraud. Brigham's comment at the time, in a letter to delegate John M. Bernhisel, was caustic:

It occurs to me, if the clerks in the Indian Department are as punctilious and caviling with all accounts as they have been with mine, that they are entirely too immaculate for the corrupt position they occupy, and should be preserved for closing dead men's eyes.[77]

Payment of the accounts, totaling $34,145, was finally made in 1866, almost a decade after his superintendency ended.

Brigham Young's work as Indian superintendent received positive evaluations, despite its conflicts, difficulties, and alleged administrative lapses. Bernhisel reported that Senator Salmon P. Chase of Ohio had said "that no Governor had ever done so well by the Indians since William Penn as Gov. Young had done."[78] Brigham himself felt good about his work and took several opportunities to describe what he had accomplished. He made much of his own personal travels among the Indians. In 1854 he wrote to Thomas Kane:

I have traveled over several hundred miles this season among the Native Tribes, to conciliate their hostile feelings, and cause them to become friends. I have the proud satisfaction of having been eminently successful, and peace again smiles upon all our settlements, and that too without a resort to arms.[79]

The following year he estimated that he had traveled 800 to 1,000 miles per year among the Indians "and have never failed in exercising a very favorable influence upon them."[80] While he eagerly reported any success in his efforts to civilize and domesticate the Indians, clearly his most important priority was keeping them peaceful. He explained his philosophy and its success to Indian agent Garland Hurt and expressed pleasure that Hurt seemed to be in agreement with his course.

In contradistinction to the views, and policy acted upon by many others, I have always considered it far more economical to the Government, better for the Indian, more safe for the people of the Territory, and passing emigrant, to treat the Indians humanely, and if possible impress their minds to rectitude of character, and industry by moral suasion, and philanthropic acts rather than fight them, and hitherto, the effect produced has been salutary, and attended with success. . . .[81]

In fact, Brigham presented himself as so committed to his policy that "I would rather never receive a dime, than suffer their [the OIA's] interference in the policy which I have adopted towards the Indians, because it is humane policy, and one which must necessarily redound to their advantage as well as to the advantage of the settlements in the continuance of that so desirable blessing—peace."[82] Considering that the government had not given him any money or means in advance and had been slow in repaying, Brigham saw himself as more effective than the penurious government and claimed that "I have individually done more for the welfare of a downtrodden race, than has a proud and powerful confederacy."[83]

It has cost the Government hundreds of thousands of dollars more for the Indians in other territories than it has in this; and I have saved the Government hundreds of thousands of dollars, by keeping the Indians peaceable in Utah.[84]

Although Brigham no longer functioned as superintendent after the summer of 1858, he continued to be involved with Indians and to exert some influence over them. In the fall of 1858, for example, when there was trouble between the federal soldiers and the Indians, Chief Walker's successor, Arapeen, offered Brigham his people's help to drive the soldiers out, if Brigham should wish it. Brigham replied that there must be no war on the troops. Although he had little confidence in Forney, Arapeen was willing to follow Brigham's direction but said he would have taken on the Americans had Brigham not advised him otherwise.[85]

Brigham of course continued to deal with various Indians by means of church programs, especially missionary efforts. He attempted to get a tribe of Hopi Indians (Moquis) to move from their homeland in northern Arizona to a point closer to the Mormon settlements.[86] He also saw the fruition of his efforts to interest the Shoshoni chief Washakie in farming when two decades later a village consisting of about three hundred Shoshoni Indians was established in southern Idaho and northern Utah. In 1874 Egippetche, a leading Shoshoni, talked with Little Soldier about the possibility of taking up land and farming like whites. When Little Soldier agreed with the idea, Egippetche asked Frank Gunnell, an interpreter in Wellsville, Utah, to write about it to Brigham, who responded by calling George W. Hill to lead a mission to these Indians in April 1874. Hill was directed to locate the Indians in a gathering place where they could be taught agricultural techniques and eventually become self-supporting. The settlement, appropriately called Washakie, survived through several moves, many disasters, and crop losses and continued into the twentieth century.[87]

When the federal government finally set aside the Uinta Basin as an Indian reservation and paved the way for treaties to be made with the natives to extinguish the Indian title, Brigham, because of his known friendship for them, was asked by O. H. Irish, the current superintendent, to participate in the negotiations. He agreed, and although several chiefs were opposed to the treaty arrangements in the beginning, they also expressed confidence in him and appealed to him for advice. Brigham advised them to sign the treaty and accept the benefits offered therein, whereupon the chiefs agreed. Superintendent Irish, recognizing Brigham's influence with the Indians, wrote to Washington:

> The fact remains, however, as much as some might prefer it should be other wise, that he has pursued so kind and conciliatory a policy with the Indians that it has given him great influence over them. It was my duty and policy under your instructions to make use of his influence for the accomplishment of the purposes of the government.[88]

16 ✛

Babylon Wars: Zion Grows

> While strife and bloodshed are wasting the States, we continue
> to enjoy the rich blessings of peace, in whose various occu-
> pations, according to localities and season, the people are most
> industriously occupied.[1]

A T four o'clock in the morning of June 10, 1858, Brigham Young
and his wife Mary Ann, his counselors Heber Kimball and Daniel H. Wells,
nine members of the Council of Twelve Apostles, the church patriarch John
Smith, Brigham's secretary Albert Carrington, and three other men left Provo,
where they had established their families during the Move South, and drove
to Salt Lake City. They took the fourteen miles north to American Fork, where
they had breakfast, and then the remaining thirty-six miles to Salt Lake City,
arriving there at three o'clock in the afternoon. They went directly to Brigham's
mansion east of Temple Square and ate supper. All was deserted, except for
a few "valiant men" left behind to "look out after things" and set fire to the
city in case the army sought to occupy it. Since every home in Salt Lake City
was boarded up, Brigham asked the entire party to quarter at his mansion.

The purpose of the trip back was to hold a conference with Governor
Cumming and the peace commissioners sent to Utah by President James
Buchanan. Early in April, the administration had decided to dispatch a commission to bring the war, which was later estimated to have cost $15 million,
to an end. The commission consisted of two men: Lazarus W. Powell, forty-
six, former governor of Kentucky and now United States senator from that
state; and Ben McCulloch, forty-seven, Texas legislator, major general of the
state militia, Indian and Mexican fighter, and the first person proposed by
Buchanan to become the governor of Utah to replace Brigham Young. The
commissioners, now in Salt Lake City, had sent a letter inviting Young to
confer with them about the "unfortunate difficulties" between the Mormons
and the U.S. government.

Upon his arrival at his Salt Lake mansion, Brigham had written a diplomatic note to Powell and McCulloch stating, "I shall be happy to meet you

in the large room of the Council House tomorrow morning at 9 o'clock." He added, "I can assure you that it is with much pleasure I see for the first time a fair opportunity, through you, of correcting the misrepresentations in which the 'unfortunate difficulties' to which you have referred originated."

In the evening, Brigham and President Wells went to see Governor and Mrs. Cumming. Well pleased with Cumming's conciliatory attitude, Brigham had arranged for them to occupy William C. Staines's comfortable house, which had the finest garden in the territory. Heber Kimball furnished it with his piano, made in London, and Brigham gave Cumming some elegant chairs, china, and other items from his own houses. Told in advance that the peace commissioners were intent on taking a hard line, Brigham had left them to fend for themselves as best they could in their wagon until two weeks later, when the church provided them with one unfurnished room.

The next morning, the Mormon leaders met the commissioners in the Council House. The boarding had been taken off and the windows replaced for the occasion. At this first meeting, Governor Cumming and the new Indian superintendent, Jacob Forney, were interested observers, as were the entire company of Mormon officials. Tall and somewhat portly, Lazarus Powell was a commanding figure. His message was not hard to understand. He and McCulloch had been sent to Utah to see that law and order were established and to insist that the Mormons obey the constitution and laws and officers of the United States. The army would enter the territory on the president's order but would not injure the inhabitants. They had brought a presidential pardon for "the seditions and treasons heretofore . . . committed." He urged the Mormons to accept it.

Brigham was acutely disturbed that his people's fate rested with the commissioners rather than with Cumming, and said as much. Daniel Wells, Erastus Snow, and businessman Gilbert Clements reminded the commissioners of Mormon experiences in Missouri and Illinois, where the government had done nothing to help them. Cumming was a witness that the charges the administration had made about Mormon sedition were false. The president's proclamation did not apply to the Saints, they said, because they had committed no offense requiring a pardon. They were determined that their rights not be infringed upon.

In the evening there was a "private" meeting of Young, Kimball, Wells, and Elias Smith with the two commissioners. Acceding to the entrance of Johnston's army into the territory, Brigham wanted to be sure that it would not remain in Salt Lake City and that it would follow Cumming's orders. Insisting that they could whip the army if they had a mind to, Brigham and his associates said they would permit the soldiers to enter as proof of the Mormons' peaceful intentions and their willingness to comply with federal law. While the forty-two charges against them were false, they said, they would accept the pardon to save the lives of innocent men and women.

The next day, at a small public meeting, Powell announced that all difficulties between Utah and the United States had been happily settled. In a letter to the Secretary of War, John B. Floyd, the commissioners confirmed that peace had been established. To General Johnston they communicated the same news and asked him to issue a statement assuring the Mormons that he would not violate their property rights. Two days later, Governor Cumming issued his own proclamation of the end of the war and asked the people to return to their homes. Upon hearing from Powell and McCulloch, Johnston wrote the Mormons a letter that, while taking special pains to remind them of their previous misdeeds, nevertheless assured them that they would not be molested. The army, he said, "is as ready now to assist and protect as it was to oppose them while it was believed they [the Mormons] were resisting the laws of their government."

Upon his return to Provo on June 13, Brigham spoke to the Saints in American Fork. "The hand of God is visible in all things with us," he said. "He [God] has brought us to our present position of peace and has hedged up the way of our enemies."[2] He told the people that they should not return to their homes in Salt Lake and northern counties until it was ascertained that the army had lived up to its pledge of peaceful occupation.

Brigham learned almost immediately that there had been a departure from his understanding with the commissioners. Despite strong assurances from Cumming and the commissioners that the army would not move into Utah until the governor ordered it to, Johnston had set out for the Salt Lake Valley on the very day of Brigham's first conversations with Powell and McCulloch. Protesting bitterly over this breach of faith, Brigham could not very well reverse his decision. He did not want to fight the army, nor did he want to continue the exodus beyond Provo. But his suspicions were heightened, and he continued to caution his people against involvement in any incidents that would give the army an excuse to attack them. As his clerk recorded, "President Young feels rather dubious; [he is fearful] that the United States Government will not carry out their pledges towards us."[3] He approved a somewhat sarcastic *Deseret News* editorial stating, "We tender our thanks to President Buchanan for pardoning acts committed in holding the wrist to a hand grasping a weapon to destroy our lives, and that too for no breach of law on our part, for we emphatically affirm that all allegations of our disobedience to the Constitution and laws of the United States are untrue."[4]

Incensed that Johnston should have violated the agreement, Cumming wrote a caustic letter demanding an explanation. It became clear that the governor wanted to have done with the animosities and grievances of the past, while Johnston, having suffered the winter at Camp Scott because of Mormon guerrilla activity, desired his pound of flesh. To strengthen Cumming's resolve in dealing with Johnston, Brigham asked the governor to "use every precaution in your power, both as a citizen and our Chief Magistrate, to prevent any collision between the citizens and the army, and to carefully guard against everything that may give rise to such collision, lest the happy results just budding from an 'amicable and honorable' agreement be nipped by conduct that will cause every lover of our Republic to mourn for rights and liberty trampled in the mire."[5]

On June 26, Johnston's army marched through Salt Lake City. The first of the troops arrived at ten o'clock in the morning; the rear guard departed the city at five-thirty in the evening. The "valiant men" left in the city by Brigham to observe any possible troop movement reported that the army maintained the "strictest order and discipline." Colonel Philip St. George Cooke, in command of the cavalry unit, is said to have "passed through the city with his head uncovered, as a token of his respect for the Mormon Battalion," which he had commanded twelve years earlier. A different touch was provided by Fitz-John Porter, Johnston's adjutant. As his group approached Brigham's house, he rode up to the bandmaster and directed them to play "One Eye Riley," an obscene marching song with a thousand verses, most of them unprintable.[6] The army marched on to a bivouac eighteen miles west of the city, to a point "beyond the Jordan" River. Several days later Johnston established Camp Floyd in Cedar Valley, some forty miles south and west of Salt Lake City. Troops remained there until the outbreak of the Civil War in 1861.

o n July 1, 1858, five days after the army had passed through Salt Lake City peacefully, Brigham Young announced he was returning. Any who wished to do the same were now free to go back. The next day, the streets of Provo were crowded with families with their wagons, herds of cattle, and flocks of sheep, on their way back to their homes. Twenty-five of Brigham's family arrived in their Salt Lake homes that day. Others returned in the next day or two.

In order to show his good faith toward the government, Brigham notified Cumming that he was prepared to return all the livestock the Mormon Raiders had taken from government troops and supply trains the previous fall. This offer, amounting to some 1,200 head of horses and cattle, wrote Brigham, "is freely and voluntarily made through you to General Johnston, who will please to designate the time and place for its reception."[7]

Perhaps the main frustration for Brigham (and for Governor Cumming) during the year or two after the establishment of Camp Floyd was the difference in instructions received by the governor and by General Johnston. Secretary of State Lewis Cass assigned Cumming the task of upholding "the supremacy of the law."[8] The governor was authorized to employ a civil posse to enforce obedience, and if that should fall, he might call upon the army as a *posse comitatus*. Cass ordered that there be no interference "with any peculiar opinions of the inhabitants, however deplorable in themselves or revolting to the public sentiment of the country."[9]

Johnston's instructions, coming from Secretary of War Floyd, were different: "The community and, in part, civil government of Utah Territory are in a state of substantial rebellion against the laws and authority of the United States. . . . The prudence expected of you requires that you should anticipate resistance, general, organized, and formidable, at the threshold, and shape your movements as if it were certain."[10] Floyd's instructions stated that the three newly appointed judges—John Cradlebaugh, Delana R. Eckels, and Charles E. Sinclair—also might summon the troops as a *posse comitatus*, if they should feel that the performance of their duties required it.[11]

Cumming tried to understand the Mormons' grievances; Johnston saw the saints as insubordinate, a people who needed to be put down and kept down. It was obviously advantageous for Brigham to cultivate Cumming. It was also necessary to cool off his associates who were angered by the insults emanating from Johnston, the federal judges, and the occupying troops.

There was a succession of petty disputes between the judges and Mormon leaders—about the alleged failure of Mormon jurors to return judgments against fellow churchmen, about the attempts of the judges to pack their juries with transients, and about the jurisdiction of Utah's probate courts. The one action most deplored by Brigham was the request of Judge Cradlebaugh that a detachment from Camp Floyd be stationed in Provo to protect the court he held there. Johnston, who had a deep distaste for "despotic ecclesiastical law" in Utah, sent the troops with pleasure.

Although the soldiers were instructed only to guard prisoners and help maintain peace during a judicial investigation, their presence excited townsfolk to the point of hysteria. To the Saints who remembered Missouri and Illinois, these soldiers were a herald of "military despotism." Cradlebaugh, they feared, would use the army to round up and execute church officials without due process of law. Some local officials, including the mayor, were arrested. The city marshal promptly added two hundred policemen to his force. Johnston then sent ten additional companies of soldiers, bringing the total force camped in and around Provo to almost one thousand. It was a tinderbox that would have required very little to set off a terrible conflagration.

Cumming requested Johnston to remove the troops, but the general replied, "I am under no obligation whatever to conform to your suggestions with regard to the military disposition of the troops in this department, except only when it may be expedient to employ them in their civil capacity as a posse."[12]

Meanwhile, rumors reached Salt Lake City that Johnston had ordered the Fifth Infantry there. Lieutenant General Daniel Wells alerted his Nauvoo Legion units to prepare to repulse an assault. Guards placed outside Brigham's gate were instructed to "admit no person to enter his office only such as he had a mind to see." Five men slept there at night "in case of surprise," and an alarm bell was attached to the gate.[13] Brigham received several anonymous threats in the mail. In Manti young men claiming to be deputy U.S. marshals rode up and down the streets of the village, denouncing Mormon "murderers and thieves" and announcing the intention of the federals to "hang every God-damned Mormon President and Bishop." They concluded by "shouting at the top of their voices three cheers for Judge Cradlebaugh and three groans for Cumming, the God-damned old Jack Mormon."[14] In another incident, one Captain Turnley allegedly abused a Mormon and asserted that "Brigham Young should be hung on the highest tree" and the soldiers "intended to do it."[15]

Wells went to Cumming and asked "what should be done if that army moved into this city. . . . From threats made by Military Officers and others it is evident that their intention is to try and harrass and arrest Brigham Young, and it is also evident that were he [Brigham] in their hands, he would be massacred." The people, he said, will "not submit to have President Young dragged into a Military Court and murdered." Cumming responded by issuing a proclamation, which was little more than a public announcement of his frustration and helplessness. Many Mormons seriously believed that Cumming himself might be arrested by the military.[16]

So alarmed was Brigham that he went to the office of the governor at midnight and told him that "if he was not prepared to vindicate the duties of his office . . . the people were prepared for the emergency and would not tamely submit to a repetition of the Carthage Massacre."[17] But there was little Cumming could do except write Lewis Cass about Johnston's behavior. Cradlebaugh, having dismissed his grand jury as incompetent, was acting, in Brigham's view, as "accusor, prosecutor, witness, and juror at the same time."[18] Brigham talked seriously to his associates of another flight "into the mountains and desert."

Anxious to avoid a collision, Brigham counseled his people to restrain themselves. He sent his nephew, Feramorz Little, a colonel in the militia, to Utah Valley "to assist in smoothing the rough edges, and in keeping things quiet, he being favorably acquainted with many of the officers. . . ." He expressed his agreement with Cumming that

> it is the best policy to endure their insults and abuses, rather than condescend to resent them. They have evidently gone to Provo designing to raise a muss. We trust they will be disappointed. Their plans will again be frustrated, if the brethren will be wise, . . .[19]

He wrote George A. Smith, leader of the Utah Valley Saints:

> It is perfectly apparent to all who reflect carefully, that the foul-mouthed scurrility, ribaldry and profanity so commonly indulged in by some of the persons illegally and carelessly thrust upon Provo, are practised on purpose to evoke tumult and riot, purely to gratify the evil [anti-Mormons] and [to] harm those who would do right.
>
> I know of no way so effectual in foiling their designs as to let them severely alone, except so far as to use such means as you already have, and other like means for the removal of a nuisance so high handedly imposed upon you, but words are

wind, and it is easy to pass on the other streets, and then if the officers do not restrain their men and confine them strictly to the locality and duties which Judge Cradlebaugh has set forth in his charge, and other remarks and letters, at once enter complaint properly authenticated to the proper officers, and exercise the utmost forbearance till the nuisance can be removed upon the plan above named.[20]

With restraint, Brigham said, "this whole affair will fizzle out."

Ultimately, Brigham's approach was vindicated. Judge Cradlebaugh received a letter from the United States Attorney General, Jeremiah Black, instructing that "the judges appointed for that [Utah] Territory should confine themselves strictly within their own official sphere." The government, he said, "has a district attorney, who is charged with the duties of a public accuser, and a marshal, who is responsible for the arrest and safe-keeping of criminals." For the judges, he added, "there is nothing left except to hear patiently the cases brought before them, and to determine them impartially, according to the evidence adduced on both sides." Black stated that the governor was "the supreme executive of the Territory" and responsible for the public peace. He alone had power to issue a requisition for the movement of the troops from one part of the territory to another. "He alone could put the military forces of the Union and the people of the Territory into relations of general hostility with one another. The instructions given to the commanding general by the War Department are to the same effect."[21]

Cradlebaugh did not agree with the ruling, but he adjourned his court, the troops were returned to Camp Floyd, and the Mormons once more "settled down" to their normal pursuits. Secretary of State Cass later informed Cumming that his actions had Buchanan's approval. Territorial and military officials were instructed to support Cumming unconditionally. Secretary of War Floyd wrote to Johnston: "You will therefore only order the troops under your command to assist as a *posse comitatus* in the execution of the laws, upon the written application of the governor of the Territory, and not otherwise."[22]

A F T E R failing to achieve his purposes in Provo, Judge Cradlebaugh—still believing the Mormons to be guilty of criminal activity and deserving of being brought to justice—induced Johnston to assign a posse of some two hundred soldiers and an equal number of civilians to accompany him to southern Utah in the spring of 1859 to expose Mormon guilt in connection with the Mountain Meadows Massacre.[23] Cradlebaugh issued several dozen warrants for the arrest of local men supposedly involved in the atrocity, but did not succeed in arresting any of them. He remained convinced, however, that Mormons were at least partly responsible for the bloody deed. His reports to Washington elicited suspicions that plagued Brigham throughout the remainder of his life. Had the Mormons in fact participated in the massacre, as Cradlebaugh alleged? Was Brigham engaged in a desperate "cover-up" to save his people from massive federal retaliation?

A perusal of the evidence in the Mormon Church Archives and in government reports suggests that Brigham had accepted John D. Lee's account of September 1857 at face value, and that he did not know the full extent of Mormon involvement until the early 1860s—possibly as late as 1865.[24] According to the later court testimony of Jacob Hamblin, Mormon Indian missionary in southern Utah, Hamblin was in Salt Lake City on June 18, 1858, and told Brigham and George A. Smith that he was certain that Mormons had participated in the massacre.[25] Brigham's response, according to Hamblin's memory, was, "As soon as we can get a court of justice we will ferret this thing out, but till then, don't say anything about it."[26] This was just one week after the peace commissioners had offered a pardon, martial law was in effect, the northern settlements were abandoned, and the federal army was still on Utah's borders. To have revealed the possibility of Mormon involvement could have jeopardized the government's amnesty and brought on hostilities again.

Brigham resolved to put the burden on Governor Cumming. George A. Smith and Hamblin were Brigham's emissaries, presumably because they "knew" southern Utah. Hamblin's autobiography, written many years later, reported that Brigham asked him and Smith "to assure him [the governor] that all possible assistance would be rendered the United States courts to have it [the massacre] thoroughly investigated." During that meeting Smith, on his own behalf, "also urged upon Governor Cumming the propriety of an investigation of this horrid affair, that, if there were any white men engaged in it, they might be justly punished for their crimes." Cumming replied, according to Hamblin, "that President Buchanan had issued a proclamation of amnesty and pardon to the 'Mormon' people, and he did not wish to go behind it to search out crime." When Smith urged that it was a personal crime, "had nothing to do with the general officers of the territory," and therefore was "a fit subject for an investigation before the United States courts," Cumming "still objected to interfering, on account of the president's proclamation." Smith later commented: "If the business had not been taken out of our hands by a change of officers in the territory, the Mountain Meadows affair is one of the first things we should have attended to when a United States court sat in southern Utah. We would see whether or not white men were concerned in the affair with the Indians."[27]

Still wanting to know the "true story," Brigham sent Smith and Amasa Lyman to the area for a "thorough investigation." They conducted a two-day examination at Cedar City and a three-and-a-half-day "trial" at Parowan. Those questioned seem to have stuck by their vows to accuse the Indians of the tragedy and place no blame on themselves or their brethren. Nevertheless, on a later trip to southern Utah, in 1859, Smith was sufficiently disquieted to relieve some local church officers of their posts. As late as October 1859, he was still insisting that the deed had been done primarily by Indians, although he acknowledged that there was some evidence of Mormons being present in the last stages.[28]

Dissatisfied with this conclusion, Brigham declared to his close associates "in a private meeting" that "so soon as the present excitement subsides, and the Army can be kept from interfering with the Judiciary, he intends to have all the charges investigated that Judge Cradlebaugh has made such a stink about. And he will try to get the Governor and District Attorney to go to Washington County and manage the investigation of the . . . Massacre themselves."[29] Brigham later stated that he then went privately to Governor Cumming to raise the question once more:

> I told Governor Cumming that if he would take an unprejudiced judge [not Cradlebaugh] into the district where that horrid affair occurred, I would pledge myself that every man in the regions round about should be forthcoming when called for, to be condemned or acquitted as an impartial, unprejudiced judge and jury should decide; and I pledged him that the court should be protected from any violence or hindrance in the prosecution of the laws; and if any were guilty of the blood of those who suffered in the Mountain Meadow massacre, let them suffer the penalty of the law. But to this day [1863] they have not touched the matter, for fear the Mormons would be acquitted from the charge of having any hand in it, and our enemies would thus be deprived of a favorite topic to talk about, when urging hostility against us. "The Mountain Meadow massacre! Only think of the Mountain Meadow massacre!!" is their cry from one end of the land to the other.[30]

Still engaged in his acrimonious dispute with Johnston and the federal judges about his (and their) authority, Cumming apparently agreed with Brigham that the general and the judges had prejudged the blame and were anxious to seize on every excuse to pin responsibility on the Mormons. Relationships with both Mormons and Indians would remain more pleasant and stable if everyone would accept the idea that President Buchanan had issued a "pardon" for all Mormon offenses, and if there was any Mormon involvement it could be considered as having come under the pardon. "Moderation" should be the keynote.[31] Brigham said he had heard Cumming tell Charles Sinclair, one of the hostile judges, that he, Sinclair, "did not care about bringing the guilty [to trial] . . . , but that he wanted all the time to injure the leading men of the Mormon Church."[32] Frustrated by not acquiring evidence that Brigham himself had ordered the massacre, the judges preferred to leave the matter open in order to "inflame public opinion against our community."[33]

Sometime in the 1860s, however, Brigham was told that a few Mormons had been full participants in the killing and indeed had lured the Arkansas and Missouri travelers to their death. John D. Lee, Brigham's adopted son and valued friend, was released as bishop and was told privately to "gather your wives and children around you, select some fertile valley," in an out-of-the-way place, and keep away from the public eye. In 1870 he was excommunicated, along with two others. When Lee asked Brigham why he, Lee, had been allowed to retain his membership for thirteen years after the massacre and now was suddenly cut off, the president replied, according to Lee, "that they had never learned the particulars until lately." Lee was not bitter at Brigham's action, however: "I believe," he wrote, "that Prest. Young has suffered this to take place for a wise purpose & not for any malicious intent. My prayer is, may God bless him with light & with the intelligence of Heaven to comprehend the things of God & discriminate between truth & error."[34]

What were Brigham's feelings toward those Saints who had been involved in the massacre? From some of them he began to receive letters of confession, and his responses suggest he was not exactly in a mood to forgive and forget. To one who wrote that the deed "rests with a heavy weight upon my mind," and that "the bloody scene passes before me day and night," Brigham responded: "If you want a remedy, a rope around the neck taken with a jerk would be very salutary." He continued:

> There are courts of law and officers in the Territory. Appeal to them. They would be happy to attend to your case. If you are innocent you give yourself a great deal of foolish trouble. . . . Why do not all the Latter-day Saints feel as you do? Simply because it does not concern them. As to your faith being shaken, if the Gospel was true before the Mountain Meadow Massacre, neither that nor any other event that may transpire can make it false.
>
> When Gov. Cumming was here, I pledged myself to lend him every assistance in my power, in men and means to thoroughly investigate that matter, but he declined to take any action. This offer I have made time and again, but it has never been accepted. Yet I have neither doubt nor fear on my mind but the perpetrators of that tragedy will meet their reward. God will judge this matter and on that assurance I rest perfectly satisfied.
>
> If you are innocent, you may safely do the same; if you are guilty, better try the remedy.[35]

In 1861, during a trip to southern Utah, Brigham visited the scene of the massacre. A monument had been erected—a pile of stone with a wooden cross on top with the words, "Vengeance is mine and I will repay, saith the Lord." While meditating in front of the monument, Brigham declared that the legend should read, "Vengeance is mine and I have taken a little."[36]

DESPITE the irritations of the judges and Johnston's occupying army, of the search for the "truth" of the Mountain Meadows Massacre and the continuation of hostile public opinion, Brigham's major preoccupation in the 1860s was the emigration and suitable settlement of newly won converts from Great Britain and Scandinavia. Believing that the newly baptized must flee from "Babylon" and "come home" to Zion, he gave countless talks urging donations to the Perpetual Emigrating Fund and wrote hundreds of letters establishing and explaining emigration arrangements.

His messages reveal much about Brigham himself and his personal reactions to people and their problems. He had seen the miserable lives of the

English poor in 1840–41; in Utah, he believed, they could come to own property and live a life of dignity and self-improvement. The PEF could "gather Israel from all nations, and the poor can sit under their own vine and inhabit their own house, and worship God in Zion."[37] Moreover, the Second Coming of the Savior was near, and the millennial timetable called for swift action. "The nation in which we dwell," he wrote, "is surely ripening for destruction. Not many years will roll away before the sceptre will pass into the hands of the righteous, and the people who possess this land be governed by the oracles of the Almighty."[38]

The preferred emigration arrangement was always what would maximize the number that could be brought each season. Since the effort and expense involved in carrying extra luggage and more than minimal provisions would decrease the number of Saints that could be brought, those who migrated should not expect to come in comfort:

> The poor who can live in the States with little clothing, and little or no groceries, &c., can live equally as cheap on the road; and when once here, can produce the comforts of life by their industry. Souls are the articles for the Perpetual Fund to gather home, and that, too, as many as possible; and other things will be attended to in their time and place.[39]

Not only should unnecessary luggage be eliminated, but immigrants should plan on walking as much of the way as possible:

> Many of the English brethren and sisters think it a trifle to walk fifteen or twenty miles to hear preaching on the sabbath, and return home at evening, and then stand at their labor the remainder of the week; and can they not walk twenty miles per day for fifty days, for the sake of getting to their Father's house; to the home of the Saints in the Valley of the mountains?[40]

What about the aged and infirm? Did they not have a right to be carried to Zion? They did, but the energetic Brigham did not want any mollycoddling. Providing wagons for infirm persons to accompany those who walked might "encourage infirmity or rather laziness. . . . There would soon be but few able to walk if such arrangements were made."[41] The very aged and infirm, he explained, "should be brought in wagons in a separate train."[42] With most of their possessions left behind and with most of the immigrants walking, there would be a feeling of equality that was wholesome and boded well for the equalitarian society for which he longed.[43]

From the Great Basin side the requirements were heavy donations of teams, teamsters, and provisions to supply the PEF system. Brigham kept up a steady campaign of requests for contributions. "Come on, you tobacco chewers," he said. "Put your $1,000 into the Poor Fund and I will give you liberty to chew another year."[44] He himself donated extensively of his own wealth.

On different occasions, he put up some of his land and buildings to be sold and the proceeds given to "the Poor Fund." The White House, a flour mill, and house and farm in Sanpete County were examples of properties sold for this purpose.[45] All of his earnings for granting divorces ($10 per divorce bill) went into the PEF. All unclaimed livestock brought into the Estray Pound went into the fund, as did all sums paid by residents to redeem stock they had lost.[46]

Brigham urged merchants and other well-to-do Latter-day Saints to make contributions. "We consider [it] the duty of every Saint to help the poor Saints to gather home to Zion and use the means with which the Lord has blessed them to promote the cause of truth and righteousness upon the earth."[47] The following appeal to William H. Hooper is typical:

> If you are willing for me to draw on you for a thousand dollars to assist the poor to emigrate next season please signify as much in your next communication. I shall appropriate two thousand dollars for this purpose, and trust that you will find it convenient to donate the sum above mentioned.[48]

The most successful immigration device during the 1860s was the Church Train system. Recognizing the large number of converts in Great Britain and Scandinavia who were still anxious to migrate, Brigham worked out a new immigration procedure. In 1860 his nephew, Joseph W. Young, helped to prove that oxen could leave the Salt Lake Valley in the spring, carry flour to be deposited for the use of immigrants along the way, load freight and immigrants at the Missouri River, and return to the valley the same season in good time and full health.[49] Instead of commissioning agents to purchase the hundreds of oxen and horses needed each summer to haul the immigrants and their baggage to Salt Lake Valley—and that became increasingly difficult to do during the Civil War—Brigham decided to assign each ward and settlement to send an apportioned number of drivers, teams, and wagons to the Missouri Valley each spring for a "down and back" trip. They would pick up immigrants, at the rate of ten to twenty persons per wagon, and transport them back to Utah. (The war did not hinder this travel back and forth.) During the 1860s, when millennialistic expectations and anxiety to emigrate were at a high point, the Church Trains transported an average of three thousand immigrants to the valley each summer. Some twenty-five hundred men and seventeen thousand oxen were required for this enterprise.

Early each spring Brigham met with nearby bishops and wrote to those some distance away, instructing the Church Train volunteers to assemble on the edge of Salt Lake City during the last week in April, ready to leave for the Missouri Valley. A total of two hundred to three hundred wagons went back each spring, taking along such items as they had to sell or trade in the Midwest. They picked up immigrants who had left Liverpool in January and traveled to the Eastern Seaboard, then went by train to the Missouri outfitting post. With other needed freight and supplies, they were transported back to the valley, usually arriving in October. "The gathering of Israel," Brigham said, "is so important a part of the great work in which we are engaged that it occupies much of our thoughts, and we are ever anxious to afford it all just facilities and influence, even to the risk of infringing upon other requirements."[50]

After the immigrants arrived, Brigham gave them a steady stream of practical advice, both by sermon and by letters of instruction. This had to do not only with the care of livestock and crops but how to keep house, cook meat, bake bread, train girls to be good wives, and how to wash and dress children. He even ventured to tell them how to knit stockings, for, said Brigham, "when [your] stockings are finished they are like some of these knitted by machinery—a leg six inches long, while the foot is a foot and a half long; or the leg is only big enough for a boy ten years old, while the foot is big enough for any miner in the country."[51]

Some immigrants had more difficulty adjusting to life in frontier Utah than others, and Brigham was ready to give advice. In 1865 he received a letter from a British-born divorcée, converted in India, who had just immigrated. About fifty years old, she was "not used to any outdoor or indoor work, . . . we are brought up in India, . . . where there are many servants to work for us." She hoped to be able to teach reading, writing, arithmetic, knitting, and sewing to the children of Brigham or another "well-regulated family" and could produce good recommendations. Bothered by rheumatism, unable to tolerate the cold Utah winters, she wrote: "I cannot stir from the fireside, much less do outdoor work. I do not wish to live upon the Church for my entire support, but I shall do what I can to work a living for myself—shall make myself generally useful in a family if I have time from my other duties but will be excused cooking and washing."[52]

Brigham was frankly perplexed: "I really do not know what to do with you. It would not be convenient for me to take you into any of my families. My own folks have to work, carry water, wash, build their own fires, cook, &c., and mostly wait upon themselves." Then he added some homely advice about frontier Mormon hospitality:

> The Saints who gather here we are glad to see, and we feel to do all that we can to aid, comfort and counsel them; but it is as absolutely necessary for every man, woman and child who embraces this work and gathers to Zion to do all that he or she can to forward the work of God to build up Zion, and to aid in the redemption thereof. We, all of us, have as much as we can do to discharge the duties which devolve upon us. Our zeal in this labor, and the earnestness with which we pursue it, causes us sometimes to appear, in the eyes of the inexperienced, indifferent to the situation of new-comers. Still, this has a tendency to develop energy and self-reliance in the Saints that they could not otherwise have, were they not to be thrown on their resources.

I should advise you to get acquainted with the people around, and see if you can get situated to suit yourself; and then if you are not able to provide yourself as you need we will render you assistance.[53]

Mutual acquaintances tried to help, and Brigham himself offered his aid, but the woman could not accommodate herself to the climate and the rigors of frontier life. She asked if she might have assistance to return to England, where she had friends who might help her back to India. Although the president advised her to stay in Utah and try to fit in, she apparently left the territory after more than three years of maladjustment.[54]

Some immigrants left the faith. Of these Brigham wrote:

It is often the case that so soon as a man who never owned a cow or a pig nor any living animal gets here and begins to rise in regard to property that he forgets his God and all that has been done for him, and from thenceforth is not satisfied until he gets back into hell from whence he came. It is manifestly better for all such persons to remain and even die in the world without gathering at all so they die in the faith than come here only to apostatize and finally go to hell at last.[55]

A major frustration for the president was the failure of many immigrants to repay promptly any aid they had received on the journey. More conscientious repayment—which was done by crediting immigrants for labor on public works or for donations of cattle, produce, or other property acquired after they obtained employment in Utah—could have enabled the Perpetual Emigrating Fund Company to extend help to many hundreds more than it did; its effectiveness was constantly hampered by lack of the resources to which it was entitled. In September 1855, Brigham sent PEF debtors an exhortation through their bishops and presidents: "Will the Lord, Angels, and holy beings fellowship you if you longer neglect these matters, if you longer exhibit a careless indifference to this important subject? Will the church and the brethren sustain you in their faith and prayers, while the lamentations and cries of the worthy poor are filling the ears of the Almighty for release and deliverance? No, they will not; and if you do not act, feel, and do different, the withering curse of the Almighty will be upon you to darken your minds, to lessen your faith, and cause a famine spiritual and temporal to consume you."[56]

Brigham Young's day-to-day involvement with immigration matters tapered off after the coming of the transcontinental railroad. His resignation as president of the PEF Company in 1870 was part of this process. Cash, not manpower or oxen, became the key to passenger arrangements, and there were fewer worries about immigrant companies encountering problems en route. Nevertheless, he continued to betray an emotional involvement. In 1869 he wrote the editor of an eastern periodical to describe the way in which the Mormons had fulfilled their mission. He passed lightly over his people's accomplishments in conquering the desert and their material achievements. But this, he wrote, was not "by any means our greatest labor or chief success":

> A people possessing great enterprise, industry and frugality might have brought about these same results, the most conspicuous of our toil, but when we turn to the other phases of our mission and prove that Mormonism has sent forth its teachers to the ends of the earth, has gathered people of almost every tongue and creed under heaven, of the most varied educations and the most opposite traditions and welded them into one harmonious whole, one in faith and in practice, with the same hopes, desires and aims, it is then we see the results that prove its divine inspiration, and its affinity to the Gospel taught by Jesus and his Apostles. A creed that can take the heterogeneous masses of mankind and make of them a happy, contented and united people has a power within it, that the nations know little of.[57]

P A R T L Y because of the immigration, Brigham and his followers went through a period of geographical expansion after the Utah War. Some thirty new settlements were founded in 1859, and another sixteen in 1860, another thirty in 1861–63, thirty-one in 1864, and thirty in 1865–68. These included fourteen communities in Cache Valley, in northern Utah and southern Idaho; eleven in Bear Lake Valley, also in Utah and Idaho; additional ones were founded in Wasatch Valley, Sevier River Valley, and Sanpete Valley; and some twenty in southern Utah and Nevada.[58]

The decision to establish settlements in Bear Lake Valley suggests some of Brigham's methods and motives. At a meeting held Sunday evening, August 23, 1863, in Logan, "to take into consideration the immediate possession of Bear Lake Valley," Brigham asked for fifty men from Cache Valley to go over to Bear Lake Valley, about a day's horseback ride to the east, to build up a fort before winter. Several hundred Saints would be sent the next year under the direction of Apostle Charles C. Rich, to establish settlements north, south, and west of the lake. The president did not want "a single soul" to say anything about the enterprise—"otherwise it will be telegraphed to old Abe Lincoln by some of these officers, and then it will be made a reservation of immediately to prevent us from getting it." "Is the Bear Lake Valley in Utah Territory?" asked one person. "I don't know," responded the president, "neither do I care." He then asked the Cache Valley leaders to make a road to Bear Lake so he could visit the new settlements the next year. "Lay low, watch for 'black ducks,' " he concluded, meaning presumably federal military personnel. "We calculate to be the kings of these mountains. Now let us go ahead and occupy them."[59]

I N addition to immigration and colonization programs, Brigham was preoccupied in the 1860s with the construction of needed public works. These included the resumption of work on the Salt Lake Temple, the building of a new and larger tabernacle, work on the transcontinental telegraph line, and the construction of the Salt Lake Theater. Each of these projects involved the mobilization of several hundred men, taxed the resources of the community, and received Brigham's close attention. "Brigham's way" included the use of tithing labor and produce to pay the skilled people who were more or less regularly employed, and the sale of tithing cattle to get the cash or credit to buy needed supplies and equipment in the East and Midwest. Unquestionably the territory benefited from the many skilled laborers who had come from Great Britain, Scandinavia, and continental Europe, and the quality of the architecture reflects this. "Gathering the poor and providing facilities for their being the most profitably occupied after their arrival here," said Brigham, "are among the important duties devolved upon the Saints."[60]

Men were credited for this voluntary labor according to their skill. Average agreed-upon values for a day's work in the 1860s were:

Men with teams	$4.50
Carpenters	2.75
Masons	3.25
Machinists	3.25
Blacksmiths	2.75
Painters	3.25
Quarrymen	2.50
Common laborers	1.50

The hired hands were paid with tithing store credit, credit on their PEF loans, cash, and theater tickets.[61]

Work on the transcontinental telegraph was of a somewhat different order because Brigham operated under a cash contract. In 1860, on the eve of hostilities between the North and the South, Congress had passed the Pacific Telegraph Act, authorizing a subsidy for the completion of a telegraph line from the western boundary of the Missouri to San Francisco. Hiram Sibley, president of the Western Union Telegraph Company, organized two companies to accomplish the purpose—the Pacific Telegraph Company to run the line west from Omaha, Nebraska, and the Overland Telegraph Company to build the line east from Carson City, Nevada. Mormon cooperation was essential to both projects, in providing the necessary timber, transportation, and feed for livestock and subsistence for workmen. Brigham contracted with Edward Creighton and James Gamble, the Western Union contractors, to provide poles for almost a thousand miles of the line, as well as most of the labor, food, feed, and transportation. The line from Omaha to Salt Lake City was completed on October 17, 1861; Salt Lake City to Carson City was finished a week later. On behalf of the church, Brigham received $11,000 in gold for his assistance in the projects.[62] He also was given $10,000 in stock in the Overland company. "This was done to secure President Young's interest in the protection of said line," said H. W. Carpenter, president of the company.[63]

Brigham had a warmly approving attitude toward the performing arts. He had assisted in organizing a Deseret Dramatic Association in 1850 and set standards for the performers to follow. Actresses must be conveyed in his private carriage to and from the theater in order to prevent them from being exposed to improper society. All rehearsals and performances must be opened with prayer. Smoking and drinking were prohibited.

In 1860 he decided to commence construction of a theater, which was completed in 1862. Modeled after the famous Drury Lane in London, the imposing structure had a seating capacity of 7,500 people.[64] The auditorium had a parquet, dress circle, and three balconies. Fitz Hugh Ludlow described the theater shortly after it was built:

> I was greatly astonished to find in the desert heart of the continent a place of public amusement, which regarding comfort, capacity, and beauty has but two or three superiors in the United States. . . . My greatest surprise was excited by the remarkable artistic beauty of the gilt and painted decorations on the great arch over the stage, the cornices, and the moulding about the proscenium boxes. President Young, with a proper pride, assured me that every particle of the ornamental work was done by indigenous and Saintly hands.
>
> "But you don't know yet," he added, "how independent we are of you at the East. Where do you think we got that central chandelier, and how much d'ye suppose we paid for it?"
>
> It was a piece of work which would have been creditable to any New York firm, apparently a richly carven circle, twined with gilt vines, leaves and tendrils, blossoming all over with flaming wax-lights, and suspended by a massive chain of golden lustre. So I replied that he probably paid a thousand dollars for it in New York. "Capital!" exclaimed Brigham; "I made it myself! That circle is a cart-wheel, the wheel of one of our common Utah oxcarts. I had it waxed, and gilded it with my own hands. It hangs by a pair of ox-chains which I also gilded; and the gilt ornaments of the candlesticks were all cut after my patterns out of sheet tin."[65]

The grandly massive building, which dominated the Salt Lake skyline at a time when the temple was hardly up to ground level and the tabernacle not yet commenced, was made possible by the skilled labor of American and European immigrants, by Brigham's purchase of government surplus property when the army was ordered east at the start of the Civil War, and by the use of funds that had been previously collected to construct a Seventies Hall of Science. Total cost was estimated at $100,000.[66]

This was not to be a theater to dramatize themes important to the Mormon story or a "restored" Christianity; it was to be a professional organization, producing secular plays. It featured not only homegrown actors and actresses but the best of those from the East and Europe. "If I were placed on a cannibal island and given a task of civilizing its people," said Brigham, "I should straightway build a theater for the purpose."[67] Most church members were of the laboring class and had not "had an opportunity to cultivate their minds, to search into history of the nations of the earth, to learn the prejudices that are upon the people, their education, feelings, and customs."[68]

In particular, the theater could educate people about morals. As he said in a talk entitled "The Capacity of the Human Body and Mind for Improvement and Development," given at the theater's dedication ceremony,

> Upon the stage of a theatre can be represented in character evil and its conse-quences, good and its happy results and rewards; the weakness and the follies of man, the magnanimity of virtue and the greatness of truth. . . . The stage can be made to aid the pulpit in impressing upon the minds of a community an enlight-ened sense of a virtuous life, also a proper horror of the enormity of sin and a just dread of its consequences. The path of sin with its thorns and pitfalls, its gins and snares can be revealed, and how to shun it. . . . The Lord understands the evil and the good; why should we not likewise understand them? We should. Why? To know how to choose the good and refuse the evil; which we cannot do unless we understand the evil as well as the good.[69]

Traditional Christians were wrong to shun the theater; the relaxation the theater induces is healthy and desirable. "My mind labors like a man logging, all the time," he said, "and this is the reason why I am fond of these pasttimes—they give me a privilege to throw everything off, and shake myself. . . ."[70] Men and women should have opportunity for recreation and relaxation:

> Everything that is joyful, beautiful, glorious, comfortable, consoling, lovely, pleas-ing to the eye, good to the taste, pleasant to the smell, and happifying in every respect is for the Saints. Tight-laced religious professors of the present generation have a horror at the sound of a fiddle. There is no music in hell, for all good music belongs to heaven. Sweet harmonious sounds give exquisite joy to human beings capable of appreciating music. . . . Every sweet musical sound that can be made belongs to the Saints and is for the Saints. Every flower, shrub, and tree to beautify and to gratify the taste and smell, and every sensation that gives to man joy and felicity are for the Saints who receive them from the Most High.[71]

Actors and actresses were not evil people and could be (should be) models of proper conduct and behavior:

> I want you to pray for them [the actors and actresses] that the Lord Almighty may preserve them from ever having one wicked thought in their bosoms, that our actors may be just as virtuous, truthful, and humble before God and each other as though they were on a Mission to preach the Gospel.[72]

In order to protect the audience's happy disposition, Brigham forbade any morally or emotionally disturbing action:

Tragedy is favoured by the outside world; I am not in favor of it. I do not wish murder and all its horrors and the villainy leading to it portrayed before our women and children. I want no child to carry home with it the fear of the faggot, the sword, the pistol, or the dagger, and suffer in the night from frightful dreams. I want such plays performed as will make the spectators feel well; and I wish those who perform to select a class of play that will improve the public mind, and exalt the literary taste of the community.[73]

In order to produce "pleasurable emotions in the midst of the audience," Brigham thought it necessary to eliminate any language or action that would offend the audience. For example, he banned all profanity. Such expressions as "I swear" or "By Heavens" and the name of the Deity and other sacred words should be omitted in plays, he declared.[74]

Brigham also made regular inspections for fire safety. Alfred Lambourne wrote:

> Brigham Young was famed for completeness; he possessed a genius for details. Carefully, the President examined each water-tank, each barrel of salt. . . . He broke, with the end of his gold-headed cane, the thick crusts that had formed over the tops of the barrels of salt. I watched him shake his head and compress his lips; there came a frown upon his face. His orders for safety, one could see, had been neglected.[75]

Brigham's personal interest even extended to the costuming. His daughter tells of an incident in which one of "the brethren" was persuaded to give the very hair off his head when a leading lady so demanded:

> During the performance of play, Sara Alexander was made up as a blonde when the role called for a brunette. Father always took a keen interest in even these slight details and pointed the discrepancy out to her. Sara replied that she would dearly love to comply with his wishes in the matter and could very easily do so if she could only have the glossy black curls of John McDonald to adorn her own head. Brother McDonald was inordinately proud of his wonderful locks that reached down to his shoulders but when Father explained the situation to him, he hesitated only one brief moment and then said gallantly, "If the success of the play depends upon my hair, Brother Brigham, you shall have my hair."[76]

On occasion, he also lent furniture and other bric-a-brac for a production, and even some of his own clothing. George Pyper tells one such story:

> On one occasion David McKenzie [who doubled as one of Brigham's clerks], who played "Uncle Tom" in the first production of "Uncle Tom's Cabin," did not please President Young because he played the part without a dialect and because his coat was inappropriate. George Pauncefort, the company's preceptor, who played George Harris, had assured Mr. McKenzie that it was not right to play *Uncle Tom* with an accent. But the president thought otherwise and next

morning hastened to David's desk to tell him so. David said he might be able to prepare the negro dialect by the next evening but didn't know where to get the coat.

"Here it is," said Brigham, and he took off the old "Prince Albert" coat he was wearing and slipped it on "Uncle Tom's" back. The two men were of the same height, and so for the rest of the engagement "Uncle Tom" used a dialect and wore Brigham's coat—both with great success.[77]

The original actors and actresses, with the exception of the invited professionals, were expected to serve without pay, as if they were serving on missions for the church. Many of Brigham's daughters participated, as an example to reluctant parents of talented young players, and he did not hesitate to use his authority to "requisition" needed personnel. For example, the following note: "Dear Brother and Sister Colebrook: Would you allow your daughter Nellie to act upon the stage. It would very much please me. Your Brother, Brigham Young."[78] Tickets were sold by the tithing office and admission was commonly paid by receipt for the delivery of a quantity of produce, poultry, or livestock to the General Tithing Office. One of the actresses, Annie Adams Kiskadden, the mother of Maude Adams, wrote:

President Young . . . told us we were only doing our share towards the uplift of the community, in the same way as were the elders and missionaries who were sent into foreign fields to make converts; only our work, he said, was being done at home.[79]

Actually, of course, there was some compensation—they received complimentary season tickets for their families and special gifts, and the many staff parties were hosted by the management. But the "no pay" arrangement was bound to change. The actors, who included blacksmiths, carpenters, farmers, printers, housewives, and seamstresses, were often at rehearsals until midnight or beyond, and of course became professionals in attitude and training, if not in income. Annie Adams Kiskadden was there when the actors and musicians decided to insist that Brigham pay them. All of them met on the open stage.

He [Brigham] asked us to state our demands individually. There was deep silence. No one cared to make demands upon Brigham Young. First, it was something he was not used to and his temper was sometimes stern; second, he was in a position to refuse. Chief agitators were silent, seeming to be trying to hide within themselves, or behind their cravats, or inside of their collars. . . .

Finally David Evans, second violin in the orchestra and a shoemaker by trade, pulled his crippled frame up on his crutches and hit out straight from the shoulder. He told President Young quite caustically that we were being treated unfairly; that most of us were forced to earn our daily bread outside of the theatre, yet at the same time giving half of our daily lives to the playhouse. He told the President point-blank that the theatre was making oodles of money and that he could see no reason why the entertainers should not share in the profits. He made a speech that surprised and half-frightened every one of us present. . . .

Then, Phil Margetts . . . stated his case, and others followed. It was nothing short of a strike. No one quite said so, but the intimation was quite plain. It was no pay, no work. . . .

Brigham Young answered. He referred especially to Evans, half in pity, half in scorn. He said that he realized that Evans was a cripple and that if he (Evans) would leave his sack outside the First President's door, Brigham Young would see that it was kept well filled. This fired Evans to the breaking point. He struggled to his feet and spoke with the heat of a truly angry man. "President Young," he said, "I have had my flour sack at your store for more than a month, and I have been repeatedly told there was no flour."

The problem was, Evans went on to explain, that flour often sold on the open market for more than the tithing office price, which was $6.00 per hundred pounds. So when the outside market was high, people sold their flour and turned in other produce for tithing, leaving none available for "public hands."

Brigham tried every means to settle the matter without putting the local talent on salary. He would "make up" to Phil Margetts any income from his blacksmithing that he lost through work with the theater. He would guarantee to John Lindsay enough work as a carpenter with the theater to earn him a full income; and so on. But none of these offers suited the actors and "grumbling grew louder." Finally, Brigham agreed to draw up a salary list, not "magnificently large," but at least enough to let them know that they were "worth something."[80]

Both before and after the decision to grant compensation to local talent, Brigham required strict accountability from all performers. The rules and regulations stipulated that performers would be charged fifty cents for talking too loud in the "greenroom"; fifty cents for being late to a rehearsal; $5.00 for missing a rehearsal; $1.00 for failing to learn a part on time; and $1.00 for unnecessary delay in costume change. Coming to the stage under the influence of alcohol would cost a week's salary, and ad libs and improvisations were forbidden. And if an actor refused to play a role assigned him by the stage manager, he could forfeit his pay for the entire season. Similarly, musicians could be fined for tardiness, absence, loss of music, missing cues, missing the overture, and so on.[81]

Although Brigham often said he was opposed to tragic theater, he had in mind horrifying scenes of violence that would disturb the viewers. He did not ban plays, but was known to have censored scenes that were "left to the imagination of the horrible." When one visiting actor gave too realistic a hanging scene in Neck and Neck, the president's foot came down.

President Young was in his box that evening. As soon as the act was over, he went behind the curtain and stated that the scene should not be repeated in that manner on the Salt Lake stage. Mr. Stetson said the scene must be done just the same for the week, or he would cancel his engagement. President Young said he could please himself, but the scene should not be enacted that way again. And it was not; neither was the engagement cancelled.[82]

There was a similar censoring of a scene of *Oliver Twist*. The beating of Nancy was so bloodcurdling that Brigham ordered the scene withdrawn.[83]

During the years Brigham was the producer, really the manager-producer, the theater ran both new and old plays. Brigham's favorite plays were said to have been *The Lady of Lyons*, a romantic comedy by Edward Bulwer-Lytton; *The School for Scandal*, by Richard Sheridan; and Shakespeare and Boucicault. During Brigham's life the theater produced *Hamlet* nineteen times; *Macbeth*, eighteen; *Richard III*, fourteen; *Romeo and Juliet*, fourteen; *Othello*, ten; *Merchant of Venice*, nine; and many others. Brigham also produced two plays by local playwright Edward Tullidge and three by local writer Edward L. Sloan. And he instructed missionaries and agents in English-speaking nations to be on the alert to purchase playbooks for acceptable productions.[84]

Brigham was delighted that the example of the Salt Lake Theater spread throughout the territory. Nearly every settlement had its dramatic club, its thespian society, its group of players. Performances were sometimes in the chapel, doubling as a social hall, or in a separately constructed entertainment facility. With Brigham's blessing, there was a Scandinavian troupe that gave Danish performances in Salt Lake City, Cache Valley, Sanpete Valley, and in other areas where many Scandinavians had located. As Roberta Asahina has suggested, "Young realized a theater was the key to the community's psychological survival in the midst of the Great Basin wasteland. Certainly, the theater's imposing architectural structure softened the harshness of that barren environment. It also served as a symbol of civilization. The theater as a cultural center incorporated all the arts of literature, dance, music, and human talent. The outside world would learn that faith and works could overcome prejudice and distrust. Indeed, the Mormons could build an advanced nation in the middle of a desert. . . . Brigham Young's philosophies on recreation and theater laid the groundwork for Mormon art and amusement. To this day, music, dance, and drama are fostered in the community as important elements of the Mormon lifestyle."[85]

L O Y A L to the U.S. Constitution yet remembering past persecutions, desirous of being admitted to the Union as a state but still insecure in the aftermath of the Utah War, the Mormons had tried to remain largely independent of national politics. But they were well aware that national political events could affect their relationship with "the States." On December 20, 1860, the day South Carolina seceded from the Union, Brigham commented to William Hooper, Utah's delegate to Congress:

While the waves of commotion are whelming nearly the whole country, Utah in her rocky fortresses is biding her time to step in and rescue the constitution and aid all lovers of freedom in sustaining such laws as will secure justice and rights to all irrespective of creed or party.[86]

During the same month, Hooper wrote to George Q. Cannon that, as instructed by Brigham, he had again presented Utah's petition for admission as a state. He added:

I tell them that we show our loyalty by trying to get in, while others are trying to get out, notwithstanding our grievances, which are far greater than those of any of the seceding states; but that I consider we can redress our grievances better in the Union than out of it; at least we'll give our worthy "Uncle" an opportunity in engrafting us into his family; and if he doesn't want us, we must then carve out our own future.[87]

When the transcontinental telegraph was completed in October 1861, six months after the beginning of the Civil War, Brigham, in the first message sent over the wire from Salt Lake City, offered congratulations and then concluded: "Utah has not seceded but is firm for the constitution and laws of our once happy country."[88] After Georgia joined the seceding states, Governor Cumming left Utah to return there, much to the regret of Brigham. About the same time General Johnston, an ardent supporter of the Confederacy, also departed, but no tears were shed by Mormons.

The Mormons did not volunteer to fight for either side in the Civil War, nor were they invited to do so. Brigham tended to view the war as a divine retribution upon a nation that had allowed the Saints to be persecuted and driven out without extending a hand to protect them. He saw the bloodiness of the conflict as the possible beginning of the national dissolution that would precede the establishment of God's Kingdom on earth. He declared to one group:

I am neither an abolitionist nor a pro-slavery man. If I could have been influenced by private injury to choose one side in preference to the other, I should certainly be against the pro-slavery side of the question, for it was pro-slavery men that pointed the bayonet at me and my brethren in Missouri, and said, "Damn you we will kill you." I have not much love for them, only in the Gospel. I would cause them to repent, if I could, and make them good men and a good community. I have no fellowship for their avarice, blindness, and ungodly actions.[89]

Self-sufficiency, already a goal for the territory, received additional encouragement from the Civil War. Supplies from the East and especially the South obviously would not flow easily. In October 1861, Brigham called 309 families to go south to settle in what would now be called "Utah's Dixie." They represented a variety of occupations and were instructed to go in an organized group and "cheerfully contribute their efforts to supply the Territory with cotton, sugar, grapes, tobacco, figs, almonds, olive oil, and such other useful articles as the Lord has given us, the places for garden spots in the south to produce."⁹⁰ Brigham asked them to produce tobacco in order to eliminate "paying to outsiders from sixty to eighty thousand dollars annually for that one article." It was also hoped that the region would produce wine for the Holy Sacrament, medicine, and sale to "outsiders."⁹¹ The central colony was named St. George, after the popular apostle, George A. Smith.

Additional families were sent to St. George in 1862, 1864, and 1867. About three thousand people were called to Utah's Dixie in the early 1860s, and around three hundred more families went in the late 1860s and early 1870s. Some of the cotton grown was exported to the Missouri Valley where it was exchanged for machinery; some was freighted to California and traded for other products. Showing great personal interest in this colonizing project, Brigham erected a home in St. George and, beginning in 1864, spent each winter there.

Another opportunity Brigham took advantage of was calling a company of men to protect the overland mail route. Allegedly interfered with by Indians, and possibly Confederate sympathizers, those handling the mail had been subjected to threats. There had been losses of merchandise in transit. Brigham wired delegate Hooper that "the Militia of Utah [the Nauvoo Legion] are ready and able and willing to protect the mail line if called upon to do so."⁹² Finding that other troops could not be spared, President Lincoln wired Brigham Young—Young, rather than Utah's acting governor, Frank Fuller—"authorizing him to raise, arm and equip a company of cavalry for ninety days' service . . . to continue in service until the United States troops shall reach the point where their services are needed."⁹³ Within two days, Major Lot Smith, who had headed the Mormon Raiders during the Utah War, was on his way with a company of 120 men.⁹⁴

T H E Civil War proved to have far greater influence on Utah and the Mormons than Brigham ever anticipated. In 1862 Lincoln told T. B. H. Stenhouse, a Mormon journalist, that he intended to leave the Mormons alone:

> Stenhouse, when I was a boy on the farm in Illinois there was a great deal of timber on the farms which we had to clear away. Occasionally we would come to a log which had fallen down. It was too hard to split, too wet to burn and too heavy to move, so we plowed around it. That's what I intend to do with the Mormons. You go back and tell Brigham Young that if he will let me alone I will let him alone.⁹⁵

But this did not last long, thanks to the prejudices and ambitions of Colonel Patrick E. Connor. Connor, a suspicious Irishman, was to become a worthy antagonist to the equally suspicious and ambitious Brigham.

Born in County Kerry, Ireland, near the lakes of Killarney, Connor was taken by his parents to New York City as a child. He enlisted in the United States Army in 1839, at the age of nineteen. He fought in the Seminole War, was stationed for a period at Fort Leavenworth, Kansas, and was discharged as a private in 1844. He served with the Texas Volunteers in the Mexican War and was discharged as a captain in 1847. The Gold Rush lured him to California, where he engaged in mining, surveying, and ranching. With the outbreak of the Civil War, Connor, a strong Unionist, volunteered and was named colonel of the California Third Volunteer Infantry. In May 1862, the Volunteers were ordered to replace the Mormons who were protecting the overland mail route. Arriving at Fort Churchill, Nevada, early in August, Connor assumed command of the Military District of Utah, which comprised both Nevada and Utah. Leaving his command at Ruby Valley in eastern Nevada, he scouted the route to Salt Lake City in September. He quickly acquired strong views on the Mormons. As he said in his report to army headquarters at San Francisco:

> It will be impossible for me to describe what I saw and heard in Salt Lake, so as to make you realize the enormity of Mormonism; suffice it, that I found them a community of traitors, murderers, fanatics, and whores. . . . The people publicly rejoice at reverses to our arms, and thank God that the American Government is gone, as they term it, while their prophet and bishops preach treason from the pulpit. The Federal officers are entirely powerless, and talk in whispers for fear of being overheard by Brigham's spies. Brigham Young rules with despotic sway, and death by assassination is the penalty of disobedience to his commands.[96]

Connor, who was supported in his charges of disloyalty by the newly appointed governor, Stephen S. Harding, recommended that his troops be located on a "bench" of the Wasatch Mountains three miles east of Salt Lake City, where they could "command" the city. "If the general [Brigadier General George Wright, then commanding the Department of the Pacific from San Francisco] decides that I shall locate there, I intend to quietly intrench my position, and then say to the Saints of Utah, enough of your treason." General Wright approving, Connor moved about 750 soldiers to a sentinel shelf overlooking Salt Lake City and named it Camp Douglas, after Stephen A. Douglas, who had died a few months before.

Brigham's reaction to the establishment of a federal force above the city was expressed in three separate ways. First, he directed the bishops in Salt Lake City to ask the block teachers to constitute themselves as policemen to watch over the people and see that no "strangers" came into the ward boundaries without just cause and that no women of the ward, "no matter under what pretence," went to the army camp.[97] Second, he appointed a central committee to establish standard prices for articles that might be sold to the army, so that Mormon sellers would not be cheated. For several years prices

were set in annual "price conventions."[98] Third, he expressed his strong re-
vulsion at Connor's requirement that anyone offering to sell produce to the
army take an oath of loyalty to the Union:

> Now, right in the time of war there could not be a greater insult offered,
> nor one of a higher character than the Government have already offered to this
> corporation by locating that army within the limits of the corporation without
> asking leave. And then after doing this, tell this community that they must take
> an oath of allegiance before they can be allowed to sell anything to the army; for
> say they, "We rather mistrust that you are not loyal and we shall not allow you
> to bid at all." In regard to their location I wish to say, that after all the insult that
> has been offered, they are in the best place they can be in for doing the least
> injury. If they were at Camp Floyd or Camp Bridger they would go unrestrained,
> but here they cannot do much hurt. I feel that they will dwindle away. Col.
> Connor started, I am told, with 1,600 men and got here with a little over 600.
> . . . I cannot say what we shall do next time we hear of an army coming here,
> but hope we shall do right. . . .
>
> I hope the brethren will keep their families from that Camp; and let them
> alone and politely ask for what they want. To take the oath to furnish a dozen
> of eggs! I wonder who would do it for the privilege of selling a dozen of eggs!
> They make manifest their folly in all they do. . . . Let them come and say "Will
> you sell me a bushel of potatoes?" Then comes the answer "Do you want me to
> take the oath of allegiance? If you do, go to hell for your potatoes."[99]

Brigham and the colonel continued to flail at each other for the next several
months. Brigham accused Connor of aiming artillery pieces—nine-, twelve-,
and twenty-four-pounders—at an innocent populace with the intention of
setting up a military despotism; Connor charged Young with disloyalty and
treason. The suspicion on both sides eventually led to a situation that, from
this distant perspective, seems almost laughable. The ever-wary Mormons kept
Brigham informed of remarks made about him by Connor. On March 8, 1863,
one of these eager listeners overheard Connor talking to a federal judge, Thomas
J. Drake. The colonel was reported to have said: "These three men must be
surprised." The judge allegedly replied, "Colonel, you know your duty." Thinking this meant that Connor was planning to arrest Brigham, presumably on
the charge of polygamy, the well-meaning eavesdroppers reported this. And
it seemed plausible: Had not representatives of the colonel been "spying on"
the president's mansion? Had not one of these brought an instrument to
measure height and location? Had not seemingly drunken noncommissioned
officers "hung around" the president's home? Where there is suspicion, many
actions are misinterpreted.

Mormon guards raised a flag on top of the Beehive House as a signal
that there was imminent danger. Within an hour a thousand armed Mormons
gathered around Brigham's residence; another thousand arrived soon after.[100]
Stenhouse describes the situation:

The city was in commotion, and rifles, lead, and powder, were brought out of their hiding-places. On the inside of the high walls surrounding Brigham's premises, scaffolding was hastily erected in order to enable the militia to fire down upon the passing Volunteers. The houses on the route which occupied a commanding position where an attack could be made upon the troops were taken possession of, the small cannon were brought out, and the brethren prepared to protect the Prophet.[101]

There was apparently no truth to the story that the army intended to arrest Brigham and his counselors, but Mormons were taking no chances. For several weeks armed men were maintained around Brigham's mansion, and citizens were admonished to watch for signals if anything unusual took place.

The denouement was a fitting end to the comic opera. Three weeks later Connor, whose troops had earlier massacred an Indian village on the Bear River in southern Idaho, received word from San Francisco that, as the result of his "heroic conduct and brilliant victory" he had been appointed a brigadier general. That night the elated Volunteers sounded their cannon in salute. Mistaking this as the first salvo of an attack on their city, the Mormons sounded their signal cannon, hastily donned their clothes, and rushed to the Beehive House, only to hear the soldiers serenade their newly promoted general with band music.[102]

O N E other chapter in the Brigham Young–Patrick Connor confrontation had more lasting consequences. The Volunteers, largely veterans of the California and Nevada gold fields, made no secret of their desire to do some prospecting in the mountains around Salt Lake City. When argentiferous ore was discovered twenty-five miles southwest of Salt Lake City in September 1863, Connor delightedly planned to solve "the Mormon problem" by starting a mining boom. "I have no reason to doubt," Connor wrote his superiors, "that the Mormon question will at an early date be finally settled by peaceable means, without the increased expenditure of a dollar by Government, or still more important, without the loss of a single soldier in conflict."[103]

Connor organized a mining company, framed laws for the government of mining districts, promised military "protection" for miners in dispute with the Mormons, encouraged his officers and enlisted men to prospect by granting indefinite furloughs and furnishing provisions and equipment, and, above all, distributed exaggerated releases to the Eastern press advertising "rich veins of gold, silver, copper and other minerals" in Utah.[104] The colonel himself discovered the first silver-bearing rock in Little Cottonwood Canyon and erected a smelting furnace. He also founded an anti-Mormon newspaper, the *Daily Union Vedette*, the purpose of which was "to educate the Mormon people up to American views." His policy, clearly stated in public and in private, was best expressed in his own words:

My policy in this Territory has been to invite hither a large Gentile and loyal population, sufficient by peaceful means and through the ballot-box to overwhelm the Mormons by mere force of numbers, and thus wrest from the church—disloyal and traitorous to the core—the absolute and tyrannical control of temporal and civic affairs. . . . Mines of undoubted richness have been discovered, their fame is spreading east and west . . . and the number of miners of the Territory steadily and rapidly increasing. With them, and to supply their wants, merchants and traders are flocking into Great Salt Lake City, which, by its activity, increased number of Gentile stores and workshops, and the appearance of its thronged and busy streets, presents a most remarkable contrast to the Salt Lake of one year ago.[105]

Brigham's response was conditioned by the assumed unprofitability of mining development as well as by the desire to prevent a miners' stampede. Agreeing with Adam Smith's dictum that mining was "perhaps the most disadvantageous lottery in the world, or the one in which the gain of those who draw the prizes bears the least proportion to the loss of those who draw the blanks," Brigham said that "the people have spent twenty dollars for every one they have obtained from the mines."[106] Sermon after sermon and editorial after editorial were directed at Mormon farmers and mechanics, urging them not to "take to the hills," but to let the Gentiles "roam over the hills and make holes in the ground."[107] The following expression of Brigham is typical:

Instead of hunting gold we ought to pray the Lord to hide it up. Gold is not wealth, wealth consists in the multiplication of the necessaries and comforts of life. Instead of hunting gold, go and raise wheat, barley, oats, get your bread and make gardens and orchards and raise vegetables and fruits that you may have something to sustain yourselves and something to give to the poor and the needy.[108]

Only a handful of Mormons joined the Volunteers in the hunt for gold. The great majority were content to till their fields, anticipating improved prices for their produce. When there was a sudden upsurge of interest in mining prospects in some valley, Brigham dispatched telegrams urging all to "stay home and attend to your farms and do not think of gold mining."[109] He also took a paternalistic attitude toward the "gold-crazy" Volunteers. When the short harvest and unprecedented demand of 1863–64 forced the Mormons to ration their grain, Brigham directed the tithing offices to supply limited quantities of grain to the Volunteers—at the rate of $3.00 per bushel. The Volunteers also were allowed to purchase approximately five tons of flour per week, as well as beef and vegetables, though at what Connor regarded as "enormous and unreasonable prices."[110]

B R I G H A M had been supremely confident of the Great Basin Kingdom and his status in it throughout the 1850s. Mormon institutions gained strength, the ideals of Zion seemed increasingly realizable, there was no thought in his mind of compromise with "Babylon" or with his "Christian neighbors," whom he had happily left behind. The stone cut out of the mountain mentioned in the Book of Daniel was rolling inexorably forward and would eventually destroy all that opposed it. The time for the millennial return of Christ was being speeded up.

The 1850s were years of Mormon nationalism. Brigham and his "Mormon thunders"—Heber Kimball and Jedediah Grant—were strident and uncompromising in their rhetoric, were little worried about their worsening national image, and pulled no punches. "Zach Taylor is dead and in hell and I'm glad of it." "We have been on wheels for thirty years and we'll stay on wheels. Heaven help you if you get under the wheels." The urbane voices of men who urged caution and conciliation (Kane, Bernhisel, Hooper) did not prevail. Instead, there was harsh hyperbole, offensive rhetoric, and militant posturing. Missionaries were sent out to warn the nations and to defend the church. Brigham seemed to be administering affairs pretty much as he wanted to, despite warnings from his friends that he was pushing the level of tolerance unreasonably.

And then a succession of events shook his confidence: the failure of his costly iron and sugar ventures of the early 1850s, the grasshopper plagues and drought of 1855 and 1856, the harsh winter of 1855–56 that killed a large proportion of the cattle. During the Reformation of 1856 the Saints got carried away by the hellfire and damnation sermons of Grant, George A. Smith, and others, and a few felt justified in participating in the Mountain Meadows Massacre. Then in 1857 the United States Army marched on the territory, Brigham was removed as governor, and the territory was occupied by federal troops.

The year 1857 had marked the high point of Mormon nationalism. Brigham's realization that his rhetoric, and that of his associates, could have disastrous consequences; the impoverishment of the territory by the necessity of raising and supporting an army of defense; the disruption of families, wards, and communities by the Move South; Brigham's own situation in which he remained virtually under self-imposed house arrest, not making public appearances even to preach to the Saints—these events seemed to undermine his self-confidence. The uncompromising language, the militant stance, the violent imagery of his public "discourses" were abandoned. The master of bluff and fiery speech in the 1850s became a practitioner of the relaxed fireside talk of the 1860s. In the 1860s, as his letters show, he was willing to consider solutions, even if on middle ground.

Thus, the Civil War marked the end of the militant Kingdom. As the war raged, millennialism among the Saints soared. The nation was doomed; the old order would be destroyed and the Saints of God would usher in a new one. But when that conflagration ended with the nation intact, reunited, and eventually stronger than ever, everything had to be reassessed. Brigham sought to neutralize some of his followers' least acceptable practices.

He continued as the effective controller of Mormon destinies, to be sure. Strangely, some of this was a direct result of government policies. In order to punish the Mormons, the administration had failed to set up land offices in Mormon country. This left effective land control in the hands of the church. To deprive the Mormons of federal aid, Indian appropriations were meager. So Indian affairs remained in Mormon hands. On the other hand, antibigamy laws were on the books; Mormon foes continued to gain strength.

Whatever the outcome of events, both national and local, Brigham had complete confidence that God could be trusted to do whatever was in the best interest of His people. "The Lord sits in the heavens," he wrote one of his young missionaries, "and laughs at man's puny efforts to thwart His purpose and to render His word into promises of non-effect, and He will visit them with fierce indignation in His own due time."[111]

17 ✤

Governor and Counselor

Young man, fit you up a little log cabin, if it is not more than
ten feet square, and then get you a bird to put in your little
cage. You can then work all day with satisfaction to yourself,
considering that you have a home to go to, and a loving heart
to welcome you. You will then have something to encourage
you to labor and gather around you the comforts of life, and
a place to gather them to. Strive to make your little home
attractive. Use [white] lime freely, and let your houses nestle
beneath the cool shades of trees, and be made fragrant with
perfumes of flowers.[1]

B R I G H A M was not only civil governor and entrepreneur but
of course a religious leader as well. He established, maintained, and supervised
religious ordinances, rites, and special observances that symbolized sacred relationships between God and his people and bound together the Latter-day
Saints as a group distinct from the unconverted. These ordinances and rituals
included washings, anointings, "endowments," and "sealings" in the Endowment House in Salt Lake City. These were placed under the direct charge of
Brigham's counselor Heber Kimball; after his death in 1868, they were directed
by Daniel H. Wells.

One institution that Brigham considered particularly effective in the cultivation of spirituality was the weekly prayer circle. In this ceremony a group
of people, dressed in ceremonial clothing, met together in the Endowment
House, the Lion House, or a "dedicated" room of a local house of worship,
formed a circle, and offered up prayers to God. After prayer they often exchanged opinions and information, particularly on theological or doctrinal
subjects, or took turns in bearing testimony on gospel experiences and principles. They often listened to "discourses" on some subject—the meaning of
certain scriptures, church history, and occasionally even organizational and

"temporal" problems. Participants often covenanted to live more fully certain commandments.

Under Brigham's direction each member of the First Presidency and Twelve Apostles organized a separate prayer circle, so that there were as many as fifteen such groups in Salt Lake City. There were others in St. George, Manti, Provo, Ogden, Logan, and Paris, Idaho.[2] Less regularly, women held prayer circle meetings independent of the men. These began in Winter Quarters in 1846 and continued in the 1850s and 1860s in Utah. These intimate, spiritually oriented meetings complemented the public conference, the sacrament meetings, Relief Society meetings, priesthood meetings, and other public services of the church.

In leading the church, Brigham Young functioned through what might be called the President-in-council. Most commonly he consulted with the other members of the First Presidency. There were also ad hoc council meetings of members of the First Presidency, available members of the Quorum of the Twelve, the senior president of the First Council of Seventy (Joseph Young), the Presiding Bishop (Edward Hunter), and the Salt Lake Stake President (Daniel Spencer). Occasionally, depending on the matters to be discussed and the availability of members, men and women with special assignments were invited to participate in these council meetings.

The surviving minutes reveal that those present at these meetings gave advice openly and candidly, feeling free to differ with the president and their colleagues, both on matters of doctrine and on organizational and social policy. Discussions centered on such items as Indian problems, freighting goods from the Missouri Valley, the work of the bishops, operations of the Perpetual Emigrating Fund Company, the establishment of outlying settlements, work on the temple, forthcoming preaching tours, problems connected with publications, doctrinal matters, and assignments of the Twelve.

Two examples illustrate the decision-making process. On October 23, 1859, a council meeting was held to choose a new apostle. Parley P. Pratt had been assassinated in Arkansas in 1857 while returning home from one of his many preaching missions. The minutes show that there was a long discussion on how to proceed with the choice. Brigham suggested that each person write out a nomination or two, have the clerk or the nominator read the names, discuss them, and finally come to a meeting of minds. George A. Smith recommended that the First Presidency nominate the person, but Brigham said he preferred to hear the suggestions of the apostles. Finally, a few names were advanced. There was a discussion on proper qualifications for the apostleship. Particularly revealing is an exchange between Orson Pratt and Brigham. Pratt, possibly unwittingly using himself as a model, asked "whether we are to suggest men of experience, who have been tried and proven in many responsible positions, or those who are young and have not been called to important trusts in the Church." He clearly favored the former. Brigham, on the other hand, seems to have had in mind someone like himself. "If a man was suggested to me of good natural judgment," he said, "possessing no higher qualifications than faithfulness and humility enough to seek to the Lord for all his knowledge, and who would trust in Him for his strength, I would prefer him to the learned and talented." Orson Pratt responded, "If the Lord should designate a boy twelve years old, he is the person we would all be willing to sustain. But if left to my own judgment . . . I would select a man of experience who was tried in many places, faithful and diligent, and a man of talent who could defend the Church in any position in which he might be placed."

After some discussion the Twelve finally passed a motion that Brigham Young propose the new apostle. He nominated George Q. Cannon, a thirty-two-year-old missionary. The Twelve sustained Cannon as the new apostle without dissent. In advancing him, Brigham remarked: "He is modest, but I don't think he will let modesty smother his obligations to do his duty." Since Cannon was then in Great Britain on a missionary assignment, it was almost a year later, on August 25, 1860, that the available members of the Twelve assembled together to participate in ordaining him to the apostleship.[3] Cannon later served as Brigham's secretary and assistant president, as editor of the *Deseret News*, as Utah's delegate to Congress, and after Brigham's death as a member of the First Presidency. He was one of the most able, astute leaders the church produced in the nineteenth century.

A second example of Mormon decision-making is a council meeting that took place prior to general conference in April 1860, when the First Presidency and the Twelve spent two days discussing the extent to which they were free to present in their public "discourses" alternative views of certain doctrines. Each apostle, of course, had his own peculiar emphases and "hobby horses." Brigham, however, took seriously his own responsibility "to see that correct doctrine is taught and to guard the church from error." Orson Hyde, serving as president of the Twelve, expressed the prevailing ambivalence when he declared: "When the Prophet pronounces upon [revealed] doctrines, it is for us to repudiate ours, and sustain his. . . . As to whether we should sustain the Prophet in every scientifical subject, contrary to our own judgment, it might not be policy to say that, as [it] involves a principle of absolutism which would not look well."[4] An example of an expressed opinion of the Prophet that could not be regarded as revealed doctrine was a statement Brigham had made in 1849: "The President [Brigham] gave it as his opinion that the earth did not now dwell in the sphere in which it did when it was created, but that it was banished from its more glorious state or orbit or revolution for man's sake. Also that he did not think the tides were by the influence of the moon, but as the beating of a man's heart, the earth being a living body."[5] Brigham defended his own role by assuring his "Brethren" that his doctrinal pronouncements and policy judgments were influenced by the Holy Spirit. "I have revelations; if I don't, I don't magnify my calling." If he wrote everything that came to him via the Spirit, he said, he could "write revelations as fast as [a] dog trots."[6]

The net result of the two-day deliberation, aimed at salvaging the pride of the more independent and strong-minded while at the same time preserving the prerogatives of the president, was an agreement that all would "keep as far away from the precipice" as possible by avoiding the public discussion of debatable subjects—questions "that could put one in a rough place."[7] At the same time, they signed the following statement: "No member of the Church has the right to publish any doctrines as the doctrines of the Church . . . , without first submitting them for examination and approval to the First Presidency and the Twelve." Brigham was jubilant that all could unite behind this principle:

> This day I have seen the best spirit manifested. I have heard fifteen . . . men [the First Presidency and the Twelve], all running in the same stream. . . . I could cry out hallelujah! hallelujah! Praise to God who has been merciful to us and conferred on us His Holy Spirit.[8]

Despite "their sins, folly, and weaknesses," he said of the Twelve, "I will hold on to [them] . . . until I meet with them in my Father's Kingdom, to part no more, because they love God and are full of integrity." And this was especially true of Orson Pratt: "Brother Orson, I want you to do just as you have done in your apostleship."[9]

I N 1867 Brigham decided to expand his "council" or forum to include most of the leaders in the Utah community, both male and female. Recalling an earlier organization founded by Joseph Smith in Kirtland, Ohio, in 1833, he called it the School of the Prophets. The school held confidential sessions and was intended to establish consensus and maintain unity during the critical period just before and just after the coming of the railroad.

A similar organization, the women's Relief Society, was also reestablished at the same time to provide Mormon women with opportunities for leadership, self-expression, and service. While neither of these organizations established policy in the same sense as the First Presidency and Quorum of Twelve, they were devices by which the Presidency and Twelve extended their influence and accomplished goals that required a larger forum.[10]

The Salt Lake School of the Prophets had nearly one thousand members and met monthly and sometimes weekly under Brigham's direction during a seven-year period from 1867 to 1874. Branch schools were established in some twenty-five or thirty leading Mormon centers in the West. In general, the school attempted to preserve the self-sufficient, homogeneous, equalitarian, autonomous society that had prevailed during the 1850s and, to a lesser extent, the 1860s.[11]

BRIGHAM regarded it as part of his responsibility to visit each Mormon settlement in Utah at least once a year.[12] Originally, most of these visits could be made on successive weekends, when he conducted two-day meetings or conferences. As the number of settlements multiplied, he began the practice of an annual spring tour of the northern settlements and an annual fall tour of the southern communities. Some of these tours lasted several weeks and involved several dozen visits. The tours allowed him to observe conditions in each colony, giving practical advice and spiritual encouragement to the people, strengthening their resolve to accomplish given tasks, and perhaps offering some relief to their hard life. Brigham usually took along with him one of his counselors in the Presidency, three or four of the apostles, one or two of the presidents of the Seventies, a reporter for the *Deseret News*, the wives of some of the dignitaries, and teamsters for each of the wagons. Occasionally, local leaders joined the party, as it entered "their valley" or string of settlements. At each location two or three persons gave addresses, after which Brigham spoke, delivering, as one observer wrote, "sledge-hammer blows that warmed up the audiences" to go home and try harder. When settlements were close together, Brigham might speak three or four times a day; on other occasions the party traversed long stretches between settlements.

A person who accompanied one of his southern tours said that Brigham carried in his buggy something for every possible emergency—rawhide to mend the wagons, tobacco for the Indians, improved varieties of seeds for the farmers and gardeners. On the way he inspected territorial cotton factories, woolen mills, granaries, orchards, and church pastures. He chose sites for colonies, named villages, and made suggestions for the improvement of irrigation systems. He listened to stories of woe, heard complaints about bishops and husbands, and renewed friendships with old-timers who had been with him in Zion's Camp. He chastised, cajoled, and encouraged. A woman in southern Utah told him she had followed his advice and made all the clothes for her family during the preceding four years. He rewarded her by giving her ten sheep.[13] To the men in Fillmore, he said in 1865, "Ye Elders and young men, court up the girls and marry them and not let them go to the Gentiles. I cannot take them all."[14]

Mrs. Thomas L. Kane, who, with her husband and two sons, accompanied Brigham on one of the southern tours, reported:

> When we reached the end of a day's journey, after taking off our outer garments and washing off the dust, it was the custom of our party to assemble before the fire in the sitting-room, and the leading "brothers and sisters" of the settlement would come in to pay their respects. The front door generally opened directly from the piazza into the parlor, and was always on the latch, and the

circle round the fire varied constantly as the neighbors dropped in or went away. At these informal audiences, reports, complaints and petitions were made. . . .

They talked away to Brigham Young about every conceivable matter, from the fluxing of an ore to the advantages of a Navajo bit, and expected him to remember every child in every cotter's family. He really seemed to do so, and to be at home, and be rightfully deemed infallible on every subject. I think he must make fewer mistakes than most popes, from his being in such constant intercourse with his people. I noticed that he never seemed uninterested, but gave an unforced attention to the person addressing him, which suggested a mind free from care. I used to fancy that he wasted a great deal of power in this way; but I soon saw that he was accumulating it. Power, I mean, at least as the driving-wheel of his people's industry.[15]

A L L was not business and solemnity on these presidential tours. Heber Kimball's son Solomon, seventeen at the time, left a vivid account of Brigham's first trip to Bear Lake Valley, in May 1864.[16]

Nine officials started out in six light vehicles and a baggage wagon. By the time they reached Franklin, Idaho, 110 miles north of Salt Lake City, their number had increased to 153 men, 86 riding in vehicles, the remainder mounted on horses.

One of the travelers was George A. Smith, the young apostle Brigham had ordained in Missouri and who had since become a leading colonizer, Church Historian, and head of the Utah Valley Saints. Playful and full of fun, despite his 250-pound bulk, Smith was a popular companion as well as a persuasive speaker. On the fourth day, while traveling through the canyon east of Franklin, Smith's carriage broke down. With an extra the travelers had taken along for just such an emergency, they were soon on their way again. When they reached the large mountain dividing Cache Valley from Bear Lake Valley, they found the mountain so steep that all were compelled to walk except Smith, who was so heavy it would have been dangerous for him to undertake it. Horses were harnessed and hitched to singletrees, and the "portly" gentlemen, of which Brigham was one, held on to these with both hands and thus were pulled up the mountain. Several yoke of oxen were hitched to Elder Smith's wagon to haul him up, but by the time he reached the summit, the wagon was so badly broken that he was compelled to abandon it. He was placed on the largest saddle horse in the company and made another start.

When the travelers reached the head of Pioneer Canyon, on the Bear Lake side, they struck "mud, mud, mud." It had been raining all day. Four horses were hitched to Brigham's carriage, and several yoke of oxen to the baggage wagon. Most of those who had been riding in vehicles now had to walk once more. "To see that presidential procession waddling through the deep mud was enough to make any living thing smile," wrote Solomon Kimball. "Several times President Young's horses mired down to their sides, but with careful driving they got through all right."

The party arrived at the mouth of the four-mile muddy canyon at nine o'clock at night. They rested for an hour or so, fed their animals, and then drove down in the valley and finally reached Paris, the central settlement in Bear Lake Valley, at three o'clock the next morning. At that time, Paris consisted of thirty-four log huts with dirt roofs. The Bear Lakers gave the president and company an early breakfast of lake-grown trout, fried in butter, after which they took a nap.

The next day the party visited the various settlements in the valley. On Sunday, they held a meeting in front of Apostle Charles C. Rich's residence in Paris. Brigham gave a short sermon on the importance of "cultivating our own minds" as well as cultivating the soil. He named the settlement seven miles south of Paris St. Charles, after Apostle Rich. Elder Rich asked Brigham to name the creek as well. Brigham replied, "You may call it big water, tall water, large water, big creek, pleasant water, or rich water." With no attempt at poetry or euphony, it was called Paris Creek.

Brigham cautioned the settlers about the possibility of losing their stock to rustlers, urged each family to pray night and morning, and suggested they establish sawmills and gristmills. When they finished converting their houses from logs into adobe, he thought they should construct a road to Ogden Valley. He emphasized that they must live close together, ten families per block. They should fill up one block before anyone settled on another. "Then if you should be attacked by Indians, one scream will arouse the whole block." "Make your fences strong and high at once," he said, "for to commence a fence with three poles will teach your cows and other stock to be breachy [fence jumpers]. They learn to jump a three-pole fence, you add another pole and they learn to jump that, and thus they are trained to leap fences which would otherwise be sufficient to turn them."

Little children should not be sent out from the settlement to herd cattle or sheep, he admonished, but kept at home or entered in school. "Let every father and mother make their homes so interesting that their children will never want to leave it. Make your homes pleasant with foliage and beautiful gardens, with the fragrance of flowers and fruit blossoms. Teach your children to remember God, and that from Him proceeds every good thing."

One incident from this or a similar tour emphasizes Brigham's attraction to children. He had stopped at the home of Anson Call, a pioneer colonizer. Sitting in a circle around the fireplace after the afternoon service, Brigham invited Anson's little daughter to sit on his knee. During a lull in the conversation, he reached out and turned her head so he could look her full in the face. He started to tell her how pretty she was when she blurted out, "Your eyes look just like our sow's!" Anson was embarrassed, but Brigham took the child by the hand and headed for the door. "Take me to the pig pen. I want to see this pig that has eyes just like mine."[17]

O N September 1, a larger party left Salt Lake City for the southern tour.[18] It consisted of forty-eight persons, including Brigham, six apostles, some actors and actresses and musicians, and several family members. Brigham took Amelia Folsom Young, a plural wife he had married the previous year, and six of his children: Oscar, eighteen; Ella, seventeen; Fanny, fifteen; Jeannette, fifteen; Emily, fifteen; and Hyrum, thirteen. The party picked up a string band at Payson. When they reached Nephi, "every man, woman and child in the place was out in holiday attire. They lined both sides of the streets for blocks, and shouted praises to their leaders as they passed by. A brass band at the head of a company of cavalry, with colors flying, came out to meet the party, and discoursed sweet music. . . . Two meetings were held during the day, and a dance at night."

When they were ready to proceed the party "kidnapped" the Nephi band, "body and breeches," and took it along with them. For the remainder of the trip the band was an important adjunct. The reception in Fillmore was similar to the one in Nephi. "Just before the procession reached the Capitol Building, anvils boomed, cows bellowed, horses bucked, donkeys brayed, women shouted, youngsters yelled, and dogs yelped," while the local Indians looked on in puzzlement mixed with anxiety. They were favored with a banquet that included "armful after armful of the choicest fruits, meats, and vegetables of every variety"—custard pies, frosted cakes, preserved fruits, and other delicacies. The dance was held in the elaborately decorated Capitol Building and featured "Highland Flings," "Pigeon Wings," and other fancy steps. The actors furnished comical intermission entertainment. The dance ended at daybreak, as the band played "Oh, Dear, What Can the Matter Be." On Sunday a worship service was held at which the speakers referred to "conditions, circumstances, and situations that were both amusing and pathetic, often causing the congregation to alternate between laughter and tears."

Succeeding days saw the party in Kanosh, Beaver, Parowan, Cedar City, Pinto, Pine Valley, and finally at St. George, where they remained three days and four nights. They visited Santa Clara, where they felt "a great outpouring of the Holy Spirit." On their return to St. George, they came across "an old gentleman with a heavier load than his team could pull over a bad place on the road." "President Young," wrote the company historian, "stepped out of his carriage, and with a wave of his hand cried out, 'Come on, boys, let's help this good old farmer out of his troubles!' " One day Brigham spied some little boys playing marbles with pebbles. He stopped his carriage, reached into his travel bag, and gave them a full set of genuine marbles."

When they passed Hurricane Hills on one of their side trips to a settlement, the children were amused that Brigham joined his associates in rolling stones down the thousand-foot sheer mountainside in order to watch them as they went bounding into the big boulders below. In the process, Apostle Wilford Woodruff, as he lifted a large stone from its place, was stung by a scorpion. A crowd gathered around shouting suggested remedies. Some advised a drink of liquor, but not a drop could be found. Others suggested the application of chewing tobacco. They located a man who had a chew, tied it onto the apostle's finger, "and in a short time the poison was killed."

On a trip to Toquerville, as they sat down to dinner, Brigham "noticed that the teamsters are not present, to which he took exception. He always insisted upon the drivers eating at the first table, and often said, 'They do the work while we play.' "

The cavalcade visited a dozen or more additional communities on the return trip, and after a month's tour finally arrived in the Salt Lake Valley on September 29. When they reached Gardner's Mill, on Big Cottonwood Creek, in the southeast part of the valley, they were met by Presidents Kimball and Wells and a large party of Salt Lakers. "It seemed as if all the people in Salt Lake county were in line," wrote Wilford Woodruff. "There were the city fathers, brass and martial bands, private citizens, and everybody who could muster an outfit. And how they made the dust fly from then on until they reached President Young's residence on Brigham street, at just 5:15 o'clock p.m. Here the company disbanded, going to their several places of abode, congratulating themselves that they had enjoyed the time of their lives." John D. Lee witnessed a similar homecoming celebration in 1867 and asserted that twenty-five thousand people, divided into companies, formed an escort five miles long to greet Brigham.[19]

WHILE the tours helped Brigham in governing the territory, they were more important in maintaining his acquaintance with his followers. Men and women visited him regularly in his Salt Lake City office to discuss their personal and family affairs, but the tours enabled him to visit his people in their own homes and local settings. Many individual conversations on visits or in his office were followed with letters making his oral counsel more explicit. Of special interest, because of what his counsel reveals of Brigham himself, are his admonitions on medical treatment and his advice to husbands and wives.

Brigham vigorously opposed the "heroic" school of medicine of his day that emphasized bleeding, harsh "poison" medicines (calomel, arsenic, and opium), and brutal surgery. The orthodox doctors did not understand "the system of man," in Brigham's judgment: "A worse set of ignoramuses do not walk the earth. . . . I could put all the real knowledge they possess in a nut shell and put it in my vest pocket, and then I would have to hunt for it to find it."[20] His experience was that if you took one group of people who patronized doctors and the same number who doctored themselves "according to nature and their own judgments," there would be less sickness and fewer deaths among those who did not rely on physicians. Although he conceded that doctors were necessary to set broken bones and perform "skillful surgical aid," he himself "had never been under the necessity of calling a doctor to my family for forty years," i.e., since his first marriage.[21]

As an individual, I am free to confess that I would much prefer to die a natural death to being helped out of the world by the most intelligent graduate, new or old school, that ever scientifically flourished the wand of Esculapius or any of his followers.[22]

"I see no use for them [doctors] unless it is to raise grain or go to mechanical work."[23]

As the state of the art in medicine improved in the late 1860s and 1870s, Brigham became more reconciled to doctors and their cures and began to patronize them and use their medicines. Ever believing in territorial self-sufficiency, he called a number of young men and women on missions to go east to obtain medical degrees. Women in each settlement were appointed and trained to serve as midwives.[24] Among the men he called to become a doctor was his nephew, Seymour B. Young, who cared for him during the last three years of his life and, along with others, attended him during his final illness.

It is clear that Brigham was influenced by Joseph Smith and his cousin, Willard Richards, both of whom believed in the Thomsonian (after Dr. Samuel Thomson, early-nineteenth-century practitioner in New York and New England), or botanic "system," which emphasized treatment by herbs, along with judicious use of vomiting, purging, and the application of heat. Above all, Brigham believed in faith healing; that is, prayer and "administration by the laying on of hands" by men and women set apart as healers. In 1846 he wrote the soldiers of the Mormon Battalion: "If you are sick, live by faith, and let surgeon's medicine alone if you want to live, using only such herbs and mild food as are at your disposal."[25] Similarly, in a general epistle in 1852 Brigham offered the following advice:

> When you are sick, call for the Elders, who will pray for you, anointing with oil and the laying on of hands; and nurse each other with herbs, and mild food, and if you do these things, in faith, and quit taking poisons, and poisonous medicines, which God never ordained for the use of men, you shall be blessed.[26]

But faith and administration, he said, are not sufficient. People should use their knowledge and wisdom to do all they could to cure themselves and those who depend on them. For one who is sick to ask the Lord to heal him without using his own healing remedies is equivalent to a farmer asking God to cause his wheat and corn to grow without his first plowing the ground and casting the seed. "It appears consistent to me," he said, "to apply every remedy that comes within the range of my knowledge, and to ask my Father in heaven, in the name of Jesus Christ, to sanctify that application to the healing of my body."[27]

In addition to mild foods, herbs, fasting, resting, cleansing, and patience in body-healing processes, Brigham recommended the "Word of Wisdom," a revelation announced by Joseph Smith in 1833 that advised the Saints, among other things, to avoid liquor, tobacco, tea, and coffee. Brigham often referred to this principle in his "discourses" and urged the Saints to obey it. He had quit the use of tobacco himself and knew that others could do so, so he was particularly explicit about the evils of tobacco chewing:

> Many of the brethren chew tobacco, and I have advised them to be modest about it. Do not take out a whole plug of tobacco in meeting before the eyes of the congregation, and cut off a long slice and put it in your mouth, to the annoyance of everybody around. Do not glory in this disgraceful practice. If you must use tobacco, put a small portion in your mouth when no person sees you. . . . I do not charge you with sin. You have the "Word of Wisdom." Read it. . . .
>
> Some men will go into a clean and beautifully furnished parlour with tobacco in their mouths, and feel, "I ask no odds." I would advise such men to be more modest, and not spit upon the carpets and furniture, but step to the door, and be careful not to let any person see you spit; or, what is better, omit chewing until you have an opportunity to do so without offending.[28]

Brigham chastised chewers for giving public meeting places the odor and appearance of a cattle yard, forcing women to draw their clothes through besmeared areas, and not paying sufficient attention to where they "drop their nuisances."[29] Good health, good taste, and good economics suggested that they overcome the habit and be good Saints. By this abstinence, and by teaching their families to do likewise, means could be saved and devoted to emigration, the construction of temples, and the support of missionaries.

One trial for Brigham was the toothache, which reached unbearable levels in 1857. As a young man, Brigham had taken up the chewing of tobacco, especially when his teeth hurt; apparently the tobacco tended to relieve the pain. But with his arrival in the Salt Lake Valley in 1848, considering the Word of Wisdom and the importance of good example, he decided to quit the habit. He was proud of being able to do so. For some time he kept a plug of tobacco in his hip pocket, and whenever the desire to chew threatened to overcome him he would take it out and say, "Who is going to be master, you or me?" With his usual "grit and determination," he would put it back in his pocket. This determination continued for nine years; that is, until 1857, when the pain in his teeth and gums became so unendurable that he resorted to tobacco once more. One problem, he acknowledged, was that he feared a tooth extraction "for fear I should faint away." He eventually overcame these feelings and in 1860 began to have his worst teeth pulled. Unfortunately, his first experience was almost devastating. In October 1860, a Provo dentist pulled two of his teeth, one of them rotten and the other "the best tooth in my head while the other rotten one still remained." During these periods of pain and removal he chewed "a little in wisdom." By this time, however, he had become disgusted with the number of young men in the territory who had picked up the habit from their parents and neighbors. In July 1860, aching teeth or not, he stopped the use of tobacco and began to get his delinquent followers to do the same. When additional teeth were removed in 1861–62, he assuaged the pain by rubbing on gunpowder and burnt alum. Finally, in 1862, the last five of his teeth were extracted and he was fitted with a set of dentures that suited him "exceedingly well" and gave him "great satisfaction." The set cost him $100.[30]

Basically, however, Brigham's health was good throughout the early 1860s. On July 7, 1861, his clerk reported: "The health of the President is very good. Yesterday in his two sermons he occupied two hours and a half, and today is not fatigued by the labor. Thus his health enables him to deliver long sermons in the bowery where his voice reaches to the remotest part, and to join in the dance with freedom, strength, and buoyancy of spirits."[31]

T H E thousands of letters that Brigham sent out in response to requests for advice on marital and family matters testify to his functioning as a kind of pastor-not-in-residence. Perhaps it was easier to confide in him than in a local bishop—perhaps his weekly tabernacle sermons, filled with counsel on personal and community problems, gave settlers confidence that his instruction would be both fair and practical.

When Brigham heard that one man did not treat his wife well, he wrote:

> From what I learn, and observe myself, you do not conduct yourself nor keep your house as becomes a saint, and I wish you to reform in these particulars, and treat your wife kindly, and as a wife should be treated, and keep an orderly, quiet house, unless you prefer to incur severer treatment than a brotherly hint.[32]

It was the husband's duty, Brigham wrote, to make his wife happy. If his wife was discontented, it was the husband's responsibility to make things right. To a man who complained that his wife did not have good feelings toward him, Brigham wrote:

> Woman's nature craves affection, she must have man's love and society, or she cannot be thoroughly happy, and nothing will disappoint her more than to be denied this. Treat her lovingly, take her to your bosom, give her every privilege a wife ought to have, and when you have done this, and maternity begins you will find that her feelings will not be then as you say they are now. You say your wife complains you are too fast with her, my opinion is, she means you are too slow.[33]

Brigham did not respect men who were so weak or ineffective as to let their wives boss them or lead them. He wrote to one bishop concerning a ward member having difficulty with his wife:

> I am rather of the opinion, that she has been in the habit of dictating her husband, or what we would call wearing the Broadcloth. I do not know this from

personal observation, but judge from the appearance of Bro. Bridges, that, he is a great lover of women, and lets them do with him just about as they please.[34]

One man had permitted his wife to "take in gentile boarders" and thus had "exposed her to temptation." There were resulting jealousies, disagreements, and fault-finding. Brigham told the husband that he was to blame— he was more interested in making money than in his wife's virtue. He concluded:

> . . . but if you wish me to answer the question whether wives have a right to go to parties without the consent of their husbands, I would answer no; but they have as much right to do so as husbands have to expose their wives to the society of the ungodly . . . by inviting such characters into their houses and nourishing and cherishing them therein.[35]

He concluded his letter by saying that they should "wean their affections away from gold and silver" and have regular family prayers.

Brigham believed that families had an obligation to care for parents and grandparents. He told one man to take his mother to live with him. "Her health is feeble and she needs care in her old age, and you should have her live with you and look after her kindly and considerately," he wrote. "If you were to have her live alone she would be likely to get lonesome and give way to melancholy."[36]

On the other hand, obligation to one's parents did not include putting up with everything. For example, Brigham advised one family to move their mother so as to promote greater family harmony. "I think it would be greatly to the advantage of all and be productive of more peace and happiness if you would move your mother away from here and take her down to Lehi," he wrote one member. "My sole motive in making this suggestion is to promote the good and happiness of all concerned."[37]

Church members also had a duty to care for and support their grown children when they required it. Brigham explained to one inquirer that Mormonism required its members to provide for relatives, especially their children:

> Your son Charles has been married for some time, his wife had some property, and they have struggled, probably to the best of their ability, for a subsistence, but appear to be unable to provide for themselves. *How much* have you and your two sons assisted them? Upon what righteous principle do you excuse yourselves for thus neglecting them, and casting them upon the charity of the public, or turning them over to burden the hands of the Bishops?
>
> You are probably ready to ask what my counsel in this matter is to you and your two sons. It is for you to at once provide comfortable shelter, food, and raiment for Charles and his wife, and continue so to do, as in duty bound, letting them assist therein according to their ability, and not so neglecting them as to cause them to appeal to others for the comforts of life.[38]

On one occasion a woman wrote to Brigham from San Francisco, explaining that she had lost her husband, was poor and friendless, and wished to return to her childhood home in Utah. Brigham wrote to her father and brother, telling them to get together and arrange to have her brought to Utah and taken care of.[39] To the father of a woman recently divorced, Brigham asked, "Will not your circumstances warrant you, and do you not think it would be your duty to take care of her and her family?"[40]

Many letters were addressed to Brigham asking his approval for a marriage, whether plural or single. One young woman asked whether she should marry an older man as a plural wife or a younger man closer to her own age as his first wife. Brigham recommended that she should marry the younger man, cautioning her to maintain her womanly reserve in any case—that should the young man "not reciprocate your feelings and wishes in this matter, of course your good judgement and natural womanly feelings will at once suggest to you the impropriety of urging the subject."[41]

In sending a new clerk to the bishop at Manti, Brigham wrote:

> Br. Jacob is now without wife, family, and home, and goes to your place to begin the world anew in regard to family and finances, and I shall be pleased to have you show him such facilities as may be consistent for making him comfortable and conducing to his success. Should he see a sister whom he may think would make him a good wife, I can recommend him as a good, kind faithful man and brother.[42]

In giving his permission to someone to marry a plural wife (every plural marriage required his written approval), he attached certain conditions:

> I am willing you should get yourself another wife, with this proviso, that you will treat her as a wife should be treated. . . . When men take unto themselves a wife . . . they must receive the gift with all thankfulness and conduct themselves in such a manner that their families can have confidence in them as men of God.[43]

Normally, he would not give permission for a man to take a plural wife unless his first wife consented. When one woman went to Brigham and complained that her husband was seeking to marry a plural wife without her permission, Brigham wrote the bishop a word of caution:

> I do not wish you to give him [the prospective husband] a recommend [to marry] without you feel perfectly satisfied that he ought to have an addition to his family in this way, (if he can keep what he has and be the means of their salvation he will do excellently) and you are assured he is reconciled with his family in the matter and has made it right with his present wives. He must do this before he has my consent to take this step.[44]

When a local leader asked about the desirability of giving permission to a man to marry an Indian girl, the president's counsel was equally cautious:

If you ascertain that the Parents of the Indian girl given to Ira Hatch are still of the same mind, and the main body of the Indians would not object to the union; and the result would be beneficial to the mission: and the girl is old enough, and matured sufficiently to bear children without injury.

This will be his authority to go ahead, and do as he has done, proving himself the Indian's friend.[45]

The usual concerns of maturity and parental and societal approval had added to them the additional question of how this would affect Mormon-Indian relations.

Occasionally personal traits made a man unsuited for married life, and Brigham would advise him not to marry at all. He told one colonizer that he would gladly agree to his request to marry if he would do what he must to retain such blessings after having received them.

But you are naturally inclined to be a little wild, and to draw away from settlements to places unpleasant and unsafe. I understand that you have lately been expressing a wish to settle in Uinta Valley, and until you can tame your thoughts and actions so far as to be willing to live where a family can be safe and have a reasonable opportunity for social enjoyment and improvement, I am of the opinion that it will be altogether best for you to continue to lead the life of a hermit, for I know of no woman worth a groat who would be willing to agree with your wild unsocial ways for any length of time.[46]

Brigham Young was not only called upon to advise members about their marital decisions but often consulted by parents about the appropriateness of their children's marriage choices. By and large, he took the position that parents should let children make such decisions themselves. Rarely did he recommend that a parent step in and take action against the child's desires. "When my daughters wish to marry," he said, "I permit them to exercise their own choice, for they are certainly the parties most concerned, simply giving them such counsel upon the point as my judgement may at the time dictate."[47] When asked for direct counsel about whether a young woman should marry a certain man, he inquired into the situation and, finding that her affections were directed toward the man, "counselled her, as I would my own daughter under like circumstances, that is, to marry him."[48] Brigham would go to some lengths to persuade a parent that disapproval of a child's marriage plans was unwarranted. To one father he wrote:

I learn from very good authority, that your daughter Martha and Wm. Batchelor are desirous of marrying each other, and would do so, only for your disapprobation.

My counsel to you is, to give your daughter her choice, and let her do as she pleases in this matter, believing it will prove the most judicious course for you to pursue, and result in the happiness of all parties concerned.

I have heard that Bro Batchelor sustains a general Good character, is going on a mission and do not see why you should feel so much prejudiced against him.[49]

Mormon society in nineteenth-century Utah had built into it a certain amount of pressure to marry. This was true for young people who were encouraged to marry at an early age, for already married men who experienced some pressure to add to their families by taking plural wives, and for women who felt the force of the imperative to join themselves to some worthy man, both for reasons of order and security and to get on with the business of bearing and rearing children. In answering a letter from a man in the East concerning polygamy and sexual matters among his people, Brigham described the general Mormon approach, which included the advocacy of early marriage.

In answer to your question regarding secret vices, such things are very rare, in fact are almost entirely unknown amongst this people. We strive to teach the young correct principles with regard to the beauty of holiness and virtue, and the value of their existence in this life; while we encourage early marriages, we frown down every approach to sin or immorality; thus the percentage of the married is very large, and as a general thing the people marry young.[50]

Pleased as he was with the marriage record of the Mormons, Brigham also felt compelled to assure concerned individuals that they were not under any compulsion to marry. Marriage was not necessary for entrance into the Celestial Kingdom:

You ask can a man be saved with but one wife? if he can, in what Kingdom? I answer, a man can be saved in the Celestial Kingdom with no wife at all, and a woman with no husband, and of course, then, a man can be saved in the Celestial Kingdom with but one wife.[51]

The Brigham Young Letterbooks contain literally thousands of letters in which, in reply to the complaints of wives, he counseled men to give adequate support to their spouses and children and threatened to disfellowship those who, after being warned, persisted in their neglect. But there were cases in which it was clear to Brigham that the husband was doing all he could to provide. He replied to one woman by outlining in detail the extent of her husband's support, advising her to be more frugal, and telling her that if this did not suit her she might find herself divorced with no support at all:

Your husband has written to me . . . that he has furnished you with 7117 pounds of flour since Feb. 7, 1857, and 110 pounds of meal and shorts; he also states that he has furnished you with wood until within a week or so past, during which time he was without wood himself; I also understand from his letter that he has paid all school bills, except a balance of $18.00 on a school bill for two of your children who will do nothing for [him]. . . .

I certainly think, so far as I can understand the matter, that it would be well for you to listen to your husband, and to teach your children to do so; and for both yourself and children to study and practice industry and economy. Should such a course not please you, I may, in case further complaints come to me, advise you to get a bill from your husband when he will *entirely* withdraw his support from you.[52]

The next most frequent complaint of the letter writers was that of mistreatment or abuse. In almost every case where there were serious problems of physical and emotional mistreatment or abuse, Brigham counseled divorce. In less serious situations he advised forgiveness, kindness, and attentiveness. The husband "should try and bind his folks to him, and by his love, manifested in word and action, operate upon this woman so she will cling to him instead of being alienated from him."[53]

When Brigham was called upon to deal with marital problems, his first approach was to try to get the offending party to mend his or her ways—to provide support, to stop mistreating the spouse, or to quit complaining. Once the offensive behavior had been stopped, he often had to assist in healing the emotional gaps that had opened up in the relationship. In most of these cases he tried to get the marriage partners to meet with him together for "joint counseling" and discussion of their difficulties, to stay in problem-plagued marriages as long as possible, and to make every attempt at reconciliation and forgiveness. He wrote one wife in words a modern marriage counselor would understand: "It will be best for you and Thomas to agree upon some time, and call on me together, for it is tedious, and unsatisfactory to listen to discrepant statements from different individuals at different times."[54]

Brigham advised resignation and acceptance of something less than perfection in marriage. One woman who wanted a divorce heard the advice that she not leave her husband but "make for herself all the happiness she could here, but not expect heaven here, but prepare so as to get it in due time."[55]

When marital problems could not be solved by counseling or through reconciliation, divorce became the alternative. Although not an advocate of divorce, Brigham was nevertheless fairly liberal in granting it, especially in cases of plural marriages. As Brigham explained in answer to a query from Sacramento, people of any religion could get a divorce; they must be residents "or declare their intention to become such." Grounds for divorce included "habitual drunkenness, wilful absence for more than one year, impotency after marriage, conviction for felony, brutal conduct, incompatibility, &c." Court costs did not exceed twenty dollars, and there were no fees for counsel unless by agreement.[56]

Brigham explained to another official that divorces were given to women, not to men. One man who wanted to divorce his present wife and marry another got this comeuppance from Brigham: "If Bro. Jas. [omitted] really wants to marry, he had better take his old wife and keep her instead of giving a divorce. It is the woman's place to apply for a divorce and not the man's."[57]

Yet the rights of men were not entirely unprotected. To one woman who was asking for a divorce when her husband was away, Brigham replied that she should wait until his return and see if difficulties could not be worked out. When she persisted, he responded, "Should you still wish a bill [of divorce], it will be well for you to attend to it when Thomas is at home, as it will not be given when he is absent."[58]

As to child custody and visitation, Brigham presumed in favor of the mother as the parent most suited to care for the children. Sometimes he had to speak strongly to the fathers to get them to give the children to their mothers. But he might step in to insure that the father had reasonable access to his children. He told a mother and her parents that "I deem it proper, right and just to now require you all to at least be generous and let James see the child and have its likeness taken, and permit the child to be occasionally taken either by its mother or father on a visit to the house of James' mother."[59]

Brigham could become impatient with those who always seemed to be splitting up, reuniting, splitting again—never sure of just what they wanted. He said about one couple, "I do not think that they had better go together again, unless they intend makeing the reunion permanent."[60] He wrote to a bishop concerning an old couple who had a history of separations and reconciliations:

> If you can get the old couple that you write of, who came together after they had been divorced, and again wish to be separated permanently, to come together, stand back to back and then both walk straight forward without turning round, and thus travel onward, it would be a long time before they would meet, this perhaps might be a suitable separation![61]

There were many instances when the situation became quite complex. One woman, married to her second husband, apparently was not happy with him but had not been sealed to her first husband and was in a quandary as to what steps to take. Brigham explained that there were two courses open to her:

> The first, and in my judgement the best, is for you to be sealed to your first husband, br. Wallace acting as proxy for him in the ceremony, which would have been the better plan when you were first married to br. Wallace; and then, if you prefer it, secure a shelter that will be reasonably comfortable for the accommodation of yourself and children, doing what you can for your own and their support, in which br. Wallace promises to assist you as much as he may be able, and not to interrupt you and your children in living by and laboring for yourselves. If this course should not suit you, you are also at liberty to get a bill of divorce from br. Wallace. These two are the best methods for changing your present

condition that I am now aware of, and you are at full liberty to take your choice between them, or to remain as you are now situated, just as you may prefer.[62]

This advice is noteworthy as an example of Brigham's ability to lay out in some detail the various options available, to offer advice to a degree, and yet to allow the individual a free choice—a good example of effective counseling technique.

Brigham did not try to solve domestic problems all alone. As the church population increased and the ecclesiastical and judicial system functioned more smoothly, he made use of lower-level church leaders, particularly bishops, and turned many of the matters concerning divorce and family problems over to the probate courts—which were usually presided over by the bishops anyway.

He used the bishops and other local leaders in a variety of ways. He often asked them to investigate situations and find out what was going on with particular families. Brigham asked Lorin Farr, for example, to "make enquiry of the Bishop at Mound Fort, and any other reliable source, from which you can obtain authentic information relative to the case, and write in the particulars" to help him in dealing with a couple wanting to divorce.[63] He asked another bishop, "What kind of person is she? What are the circumstances under which she has left [her husband]? Are they such as she describes?"[64] Brigham also asked bishops and other local leaders for direct advice about what to do with certain cases. "You probably know about all the circumstances of this case," he wrote one bishop, asking him to pass on whatever he knew, together with his recommendation.[65]

Beginning in the 1870s, Brigham referred people to the probate courts. He instructed a bishop: "With regard to Bro. Wm. [omitted]'s case, let it be referred to the Probate Court, so that Sister [omitted] can have a Bill of Divorce, and the proper steps taken to secure her a good maintenance. When this is done, if Bro. [omitted] refuses to abide the decision, cut him off the Church."[66] Probate court action was particularly advisable in cases that involved property. Brigham explained to Elias Smith why he had referred a certain case to him.

> Sister Katy [omitted], the bearer of this note, has called upon me with regard to difficulties with her husband. I have directed her to lay her case before you, considering you to be the proper person to take action in the matter. She particularly desires to talk to you regarding a certain property deeded to her by her husband which is now likely to be taken from her, as he has now mortgaged it to Bishop Raleigh. Feeling confident that you will do what should be done in the matter. . . .[67]

The probate court was also an important resource in cases regarding child custody. "Your better course, under your circumstances," he told one woman, "is to apply to Judge Z. Snow, who will award you your rights and doubtless the children. After you obtain the Judge's decision, Wesley [omitted] cannot touch anything or interfere with you without rendering himself liable to the law."[68] He also urged a woman who wished to be divorced from her husband, who was "hopelessly insane," to "apply to the probate court where you are and state all the facts in the case and let the court decide what is your right in the matter."[69]

A S a leader of his people, Brigham had charisma. He kept effective and judicious associates to assist him. He was pragmatic and flexible in his counsel. He was neither dictatorial nor rigid and uncompromising in his approach to the many domestic problems brought to his office. He was also realistic enough to realize that not everybody would take his advice. "It goes in at one ear and out at the other—it is like the weaver's shuttle passing through the web." Or, to change the image, he and his people were like boys with sleds: "We go up hill very slowly, but quickly rush down again. We are too apt to be slow to learn righteousness, and quick to run in the ways of sin."[70] Nevertheless, both he and his followers had come a long way since his early impatience with people's failings and sins.

18 ✦

Public Image and
Private Reality

Letter for the Perusal of My Family

I do not wish to complain of you without a cause, but
at prayer time lately I have noticed that one has been visiting,
another has gone to see Mary, and another to see Emily, etc.,
etc. My family . . . will acknowledge that my time is precious
to me as theirs is to them. When the time appointed for our
family devotion and prayer comes, I am expected to be there;
and no public business, no matter how important, has been
able to influence me to forego the fulfillment of this sacred
duty which I owe to you, to myself, and to God.

My counsel, which I expect you to receive kindly, is
to be home by six-thirty each evening so as to be ready to
bow down before the Lord to make . . . acknowledgements
to Him for His kindness and mercy and long-suffering towards
us. . . .

Your strict attendance to my wishes in this respect will
give joy to the heart of your Husband and Father.[1]

A T the end of the Utah War and Move South, Brigham Young
was fifty-seven. His health was reasonably good, despite his persistent rheumatism. His family was one of America's largest. Sixteen wives had borne him
forty-six children, of whom thirty-eight were still alive. He had married some
twenty women, of whom four had died. His children ranged in age from less
than one to thirty-three. His oldest son, Joseph Angell Young, had already
accomplished a proselyting mission to England, and several sons and daughters
had married. His personal property, as distinct from church property, consisted
of at least a dozen homes, three farms, and tens of assorted vehicles—buggies,

carriages, wagons, and sleighs. His outward mien was calm, and his people—there were approximately forty thousand Mormons in Utah Territory in 1858—gave every appearance of honoring him.

Brigham's public image elsewhere was to a significant degree influenced by the Saints' practice of polygamy (properly, polygyny). Plural marriage, taught and practiced by Joseph Smith and other Mormon leaders at least as far back as 1841, was not publicly announced until August 29, 1852, at a conference in Salt Lake City. The reasons for that delay are not difficult to imagine. It was practiced by a small minority "for righteous reasons" and was therefore not a matter of wide concern. It was also a revolutionary practice, abhorrent to many Christians, largely regarded as uncivilized, and calculated to bring opprobrium on the Saints. Not until they had been in their Promised Valley for five years and attained territorial status within the nation did they feel secure enough to "go public" with their "peculiar" institution. Chosen to make the announcement was Orson Pratt, who marshaled evidence to support the claim that the practice was scriptural, had divine approval, would prevent the licentious practices of "the world," and was protected by the United States Constitution because it was a religious practice, and the Constitution guaranteed freedom of religion. Until that announcement the practice was not publicly acknowledged and was, by some people (not Brigham), denied.[2]

While the revelation on plural marriage inspired a political crusade against the Mormons, resulting in the dispatch of the Utah Expedition in 1857 and the passage of antipolygamy legislation in 1862 and succeeding years,[3] another consequence was that Mormonism was catapulted into the national and international arena as an object of friendly and unfriendly humor, the subject of innumerable editorials and feature articles. Salt Lake City became a must stop on any western itinerary: the reading public was eager for firsthand reports and commentaries. Some of this interest, of course, was prurient in nature: what kind of a man would marry twenty wives? What kind of woman would permit herself to be married to a man who already had several wives? Among those who spent weeks in Salt Lake City to report on Brigham Young, the Mormons, and their social system were a French and an English scientist, Jules Remy and Julius Brenchley; the editor of the New York *Tribune* and later presidential candidate, Horace Greeley; a celebrated English explorer, Richard Burton; the youthful Samuel Clemens, later to achieve fame as Mark Twain; the American art critic and writer, Fitz Hugh Ludlow; humorist Artemus Ward; and two influential British writers and opinion makers, William Hepworth Dixon and Sir Charles Wentworth Dilke. Each wrote a best-selling travel account in which Brigham Young and the Mormons were central features. Not surprisingly, the reports, if basically favorable, were not always consistent.[4]

Remy and Brenchley, who spent a month in Utah in 1855, had at least four contacts with Brigham.[5] They found in him a "Mormon pope" of "superior intellect," "unusual strength of mind," "remarkable talent and profound ability in combining the heterogeneous elements of which his people are made up."[6] He was acutely observant of men, events, and surroundings; he could "philosophize with authority, if not polish, on Voltaire," they wrote, then make suggestions as to road conditions, provisions to carry on a journey, and how to deal with Indians. He was reserved yet affable, cautious of strangers but courteous, quick thinking yet deliberate in response and judgment. This, Rémy and Brenchley concluded, was not an ordinary man but one who fully belonged to "the rank of great men who appear at distant intervals, now to confer upon nations a benefit, now to serve as a scourge."[7] On a more personal basis they found him to be distrustful of strangers, polite and respectful—"a fine and delicate tact"—and "not without a certain kind of natural eloquence." In appearance he was something like "an honest farmer":

> He is a man of fifty-four years of age, fair, of moderate height, stout almost to obesity. He has regular features, a wide forehead, eyes which convey an idea of finesse, and a smiling expression of mouth. . . . Nothing in his manners indicates a man of the higher classes.[8]

Four years later, the white-hatted, baby-skinned, reform-minded *Tribune* editor, Horace Greeley, spent ten days in Salt Lake City. On July 13, 1859, he conducted his widely reported two-hour interview with Brigham (mentioned in the Prologue), an interview that the Librarian of Congress has said was the first published in-depth news interview with a public figure in the history of American journalism.[9] Greeley described Brigham as a modest, pleasant man. In his responses to Greeley's many questions, Brigham showed canniness, humor, a homey eloquence, and an ability to get to the point without bogging down in disputation or equivocation.[10] In response to the inevitable question, "What is the largest number of wives belonging to any one man?" Brigham responded, "I have fifteen; I know no one who has more; but some of those sealed to me are old ladies whom I regard rather as mothers than wives, but whom I have taken home to cherish and support."[11]

In August 1860, a year after Greeley's visit, Brigham was attended by Captain Richard Burton, "of the British Army," as the church clerks dutifully noted, but recognized around the world as "the famous Orientalist and explorer."[12] Dark and romantic-looking, he had passed himself off in Mecca as a pilgrim and in an Arabian harem as a merchant. It was his interest in Mormon polygamy that brought him to Utah. Originally intending to stay twelve days, he remained three weeks, and interviewed Brigham at least twice. Actually, Brigham, who had read much about him, kept him busy answering questions about Africa, Arabia, and India. Altogether, Burton reported, Brigham had the appearance of "a gentleman farmer in New England."

> His manner is at once affable and impressive, simple and courteous; his want of pretension contrasts favorably with certain pseudo-prophets that I have seen, each

and every of whom holds himself to be a "Logos" without other claim save a semi-maniacal self-esteem. . . . He assumes no airs of extra sanctimoniousness, and has the plain, simple manners of honesty. . . . There is a total absence of pretension in his manner, and he has been so long used to power that he cares nothing for its display. The arts by which he rules the heterogeneous mass of conflicting elements are indomitable will, profound secrecy, and uncommon astuteness.[13]

In physical description of the prophet, Burton wrote that he had "a calm, composed, and somewhat reserved expression: a slight droop in the left lid made me think that he had suffered from paralysis, I afterwards heard that the ptosis is the result of a neuralgia which has long tormented him. For this reason he usually covers his head—except in his own house or in the tabernacle."[14]

Mark Twain visited Salt Lake City with his brother Orion in the summer of 1861, though he did not write about it until 1870.[15] His report of the interview with Brigham is so brief and so facetious that one might question whether it took place. But Brigham's secretaries verified the visit by a notation for Wednesday, August 7, 1861: "Mr. Clements, Secy of the Territory of Nevada, who was on his way to Carson, accompanied by his Brother and one other gentleman" were introduced to the president.[16] It was on their second day in the Mormon city, wrote Twain, that they put on their white shirts and paid a visit to "the only absolute monarch in America."

> [Brigham Young] seemed a quiet, kindly, easy-mannered, dignified, self-possessed old gentleman of fifty-five or six [he was actually sixty], and had a gentle craft in his eye that probably belonged there. He was very simply dressed and was just taking off a straw hat as we entered.[17]

They spoke, according to Twain, of Utah, the Indians, Nevada, and "general American questions." Twain tried to "draw him out" on the Mormons' high-handed attitude toward Congress, "but he never paid any attention to me. . . . He merely looked around at me, at distant intervals, somewhat as I have seen a benignant old cat look around to see which kitten was meddling with her tail." At the end of the interview Brigham reportedly patted Twain on the head and asked Orion, "Ah—your child, I presume? Boy, or girl?"[18] The next morning Clemens left Great Salt Lake City "a good deal confused as to what state of things existed there—and sometimes even questioning in my own mind whether a state of things existed there at all or not."[19]

Few Utahans would have recognized the name of Fitz Hugh Ludlow, the twenty-seven-year-old New York art critic who crossed the Great Plains for his health in 1863.[20] Yet Ludlow was well known in American literary circles for his 1857 confessions of a college drug addict. His contact with Brigham occurred at the Mormons' Fourth of July ball in 1863, where they engaged in a brief repartee.[21] Ludlow's appraisal: Brigham was more youthful than his years, frank and straightforward in look, and mannerly to a degree astonishing to anyone who knew that "his early life was passed among the uncouth and illiterate." He had a "perfect deference to the feelings of others with absolute certainty of himself and his own opinions."[22]

Like Remy, Greeley, and Burton, Ludlow was convinced of Young's "absolute sincerity of belief and motive. [He] is the farthest remove on earth from a hypocrite."[23] In the end, Ludlow seemed to admire Young's Yankee "uncornerableness"—that is, his wit and resourcefulness.[24] Nevertheless, his power "is the most despotic known to mankind . . . such power resting in one man's irresponsible hands is a crime against the Constitution."[25]

In 1864 Artemus Ward came to Salt Lake City to give one lecture, but stayed a month because of an attack of fever.[26] He later capitalized on his Utah visit through comic essays including "A Visit to Brigham," "Brigham Young's Wives," "A Mormon Bill of Fare," "A Mormon Romance," "A. Ward among the Mormons, Reported by Himself, or Somebody Else," and *Artemus Ward: His Travels among the Mormons.*[27] In spite of their jocular tone, from Ward's and his manager E. P. Hingston's writings one can obtain a lifelike report of Brigham Young in the 1860s.[28] Ward noted the sandy hair, the clear, sharp eyes, and the hard, firmly set lips; the robust health, pleasant face, and jolly manner.[29] During the convalescence from his illness, he saw Brigham at a ball in the social hall. "The Prophet is more industrious than graceful as a dancer," he wrote. "He exhibits, however, a spryness of legs quite remarkable in a man at his time of life."[30] Another evening he saw the president at the theater:

> Brigham Young usually sits in the middle of the parquette, in a rocking-chair, and with his hat on. . . . When the play drags he either falls into a tranquil sleep or walks out. He wears in winter time a green wrapper, and his hat is the style introduced into this country by Kossuth.[31]

After he left Utah, Ward made the most of his experience. From the podium and by pen he made wisecracks about real Mormons and about the imaginary patriarch who walked out of a romantic play because he couldn't tolerate the silliness of the hero making so much fuss over one woman. But for the most part the humor was harmless and gentle. "They say that when an immigrant train arrives Brigham Young has all the women march up and down before his block and gobbles up the prettiest ones," Ward said. But he added that "they" meant "anti-Mormons" and followed the rumor with two pieces of Mormon defense.[32]

Hepworth Dixon was the forty-six-year-old editor of the failing but still distinguished London literary magazine, *The Athenaeum.*[33] His intellectual contributions included biographies of Admiral Robert Blake, Francis Bacon, and William Penn, and social commentaries on prison life and poverty among the working classes. From an 1866 summer in America he wrote the two-volume *New America* and two supplementary volumes entitled *Spiritual Wives*. Sir Charles Wentworth Dilke was the twenty-three-year-old son of the proprietor of *The Athenaeum* and grandson of a notable English critic/journalist. Later he would earn distinction as an editor, defense scholar, and radical politician. Dilke cut his teeth on the Mormons, whose colony he sought early in a world tour and described in *Greater Britain: A Record of Travel in English-speaking Countries During 1866 and 1867*.[34] Both Dixon and Dilke enjoyed the sense of unwrapping the mystery of Mormonism. As Dixon wrote, "We went out in search of an old world, and found a new one. . . . In the heart of solid societies and conservative churches, we find the most singular doctrines, the most audacious experiments. . . ."[35]

Dixon's narrative suggests that Brigham paid the Britons particular attention, granting them four interviews, inviting them to accompany him on church business, and admitting them to private councils. From Dixon's pen we have an image of Brigham welcoming a train of six hundred arriving immigrants. "You have been chosen from the world by God," Young told the immigrants. "Rest for a day or two. . . . Don't bother much about your religious duties. . . . Be of good cheer. Your first duty is to learn to grow a cabbage, an onion, a tomato, a sweet potato, to feed a pig, build a house, plant a garden, rear cattle, bake bread—to live. Your next duty is to learn English, the language of these latter days. The rest will be added to you in the proper seasons."[36] We see Brigham presiding at a meeting of the chief bishop of the church with the bishops of city wards, pointing out the object of business—to place the new immigrants in self-supporting situations—and adding with a sly little smile, "This is one of the labors of our bishops." Observing that two hundred bricklayers, carpenters, tinmen, farm servants, etc., were "placed" within a few minutes, Dixon commented to himself, "I confess, I could not see much harm in it."[37]

Dixon described Brigham as "a man of lowly birth, of keen humour, of unerring good sense." His mind too pragmatic to comprehend or sympathize with scholars like Orson Pratt, said Dixon, Brigham was cautious, even disdainful about Pratt's cosmogonies, but officially tolerated intellectuals. Asked about women, Brigham told Dixon, "They will be more easily saved than men," and then chuckled as he added, "They haven't sense enough to go far wrong." Brigham, Dixon wrote, was a minister of mirth, providing an earthly kingdom of plenty and enjoyment for his citizens through the theater, socials, picnics, and economic development. He recognized the political uses of polygamy, that is, dispensed the favor with an eye to maintaining his hierarchy. He also thought that Brigham "in the sphere of his knowledge, and his customs, [was] an honest man."[38] In Dixon's perception Brigham's "mastery of all the springs of action" made him a Moses, mythological in vision and wisdom.

Young Dilke was far more succinct. Brigham Young claimed to be a prophet, he wrote, which meant political philosopher.[39] "After all, Brigham said to me the day before I left, 'the highest inspiration is good sense—the knowing what to do, and how to do it.' " For Dilke, Brigham was really one of Bentham's utilitarian deists, whose revelation is written in utility:

[Brigham] sees that a canal from Utah Lake to Salt Lake Valley would be of vast utility to the Church and people—that a new settlement is urgently required. He thinks about these things till they dominate in his mind, and take in his brain the shape of physical creations. He dreams of the canal, the city; sees them before him in his waking moments. That which is so clearly for the good of God's people, becomes God's will. Next Sunday at the Tabernacle, he steps to the front, and says "God has spoken; He has said unto His prophet, 'Get thee up, Brigham, and build Me a city in the fertile valley to the South, where there is water, where there are fish, where the sun is strong enough to ripen the cotton plants, and give raiment as well as food to my saints on earth.' Brethren willing to aid God's work should come to me before the Bishops' meeting."[40]

Well, then, is Brigham Young "a white man" (a frontier term for a decent fellow)? "Given his foundation, yes."

Brigham and his associates had received a good deal of negative treatment by the press. As subjects of ridicule the Mormons, especially their leader, were hard to resist. Like every performer who hastens to read reviews after a concert or stage play, the Mormons thought positive statements fair and objective, while criticism was usually considered unfair. Thus, when Dixon returned to Utah in 1874, he was cheerfully received. A Salt Lake City newspaper described him as author of "one of the fairest and most impartial works on the various religions of the United States, including Mormonism, which has appeared."[41]

M O S T of the visitors to Mormon country in the 1850s and 1860s were impressed, both with Brigham and with the accomplishments of "his people." Later visitors (e.g., those who reported on them in the 1870s) found any instinctive liking they had for Brigham so in conflict with their abhorrence of polygamy and authoritarianism that they tended to read malevolence into his manner and appearance. Thus, Justin McCarthy, Irish politician, editor of the London *Morning Star*, and social novelist, concluded, "I do not say that Brigham Young was a Tartuffe [hypocrite], but I know now how Tartuffe ought to be played . . . to render the part more effect . . . [more] natural and lifelike than I have ever seen it. . . ."[42] John Hanson Beadle, whose bitter pen was emboldened by his belief that Mormonism was "a hideous moral gangrene" and a system of "petty tyranny," thought Brigham to be "a strange compound of imposter and fanatic," a leader "at once sagacious and unscrupulous."[43]

Whatever the period, it is clear that "Brigham copy" had a ready market. Readers wanted inside information on what he looked like, how he talked, who his associates were, where he lived, what he ate, and, especially, whom he slept with. This curiosity was left forever unsatisfied, for no observer was admitted to the inner sanctuaries to discover and reveal the intimacies of his family life.

When Brigham's family returned to Salt Lake City after the Move South to Provo in 1858, Mary Ann moved back into the Beehive House, where she had lived since 1854. She remained there until 1860, when she moved to the "White House on the Hill" that Brigham had built for her. After she left the Beehive House, Lucy Ann Decker, with her seven children, took residency there for the remainder of Brigham's life. At the time Lucy moved into the Beehive House, Brigham deeded it to her on the condition that "no matter what his reverses or financial conditions may become, she was never to mortgage or give him the Beehive House." Lucy Ann lived there until 1888, when she sold the house to John W. Young, a son of Brigham and Mary Ann.

There were, in addition, twelve families in the Lion House; one childless wife, Susan Snively, in the farm home in south Salt Lake Valley (Forest Farm); Eliza Burgess, with one son, in the home he had built in Provo; and, after 1865, Lucy Bigelow and three daughters in a home he built in St. George.

Lucy Ann's and Brigham's daughter Clarissa, who remained in the Beehive House until its sale, has left a recollection of life there in this, Brigham's official mansion, office, and sanctuary.[44] It was built for entertaining: the rooms were spacious, the parlors splendid, the furnishings rich. Square, green-shuttered, thickly walled with adobe, it was planned by Brigham in the colonial style of New England. In this home were entertained Ulysses S. Grant, William T. Sherman, Ralph Waldo Emerson, Mark Twain, Horace Greeley, and the celebrated midget Tom Thumb.

Brigham usually slept and ate breakfast in the Beehive House. His private bedroom, on the main floor just opposite the sitting room, was light and airy. Sixteen feet square, it contained a washstand, Franklin stove, desk, a few comfortable chairs, and a cupboard that might contain hard candy, raisins, or fruit to give to children and guests. At the head of the bed was a small table, water pitcher, and a high brass candlestick with a box of matches. The door on the west opened into his private office, which also opened to "Brigham Street" on the south. On the left side, as one walked in from the street entrance, were the three desks of his church clerks; on the right were the desks of his three private clerks. A door to the east opened into his private office—a plain room about twenty-five feet square. A large writing desk and money safe, tables, sofas, chairs, and a carpet made up the furniture of the room. On the wall at his back, as he sat at his desk, was his Nauvoo Legion sword, rifle, and lance, none of which he had used since 1844.[45]

According to Clarissa, Brigham had his breakfast between nine and ten in the morning, often with Clarissa, whom he referred to as "Clarie." Clarie tied a bib over his beard in order to protect it from crumbs and milk. His "ordinary" breakfast consisted of cornmeal mush and milk, or hot doughnuts and syrup. Occasionally he enjoyed squabs from the pigeon house and some delicacy from the garden such as strawberries or blackcaps (small black raspberries). His only hot drink was a "composition tea," made from herbs and spices.[46]

After breakfast he might have a session of "barbering" and then go to his office, where he remained until supper unless outside errands were necessary. In Salt Lake City, Brigham did not eat lunch.

When he went out, Brigham wore a rather high hat, a Prince Albert coat, and either a green cape or gray shawl over his shoulders. In the summer he wore light prunella cloth suits with white shirt and neck cloth and a Panama hat.

As an official residence of the church president, the Beehive House functioned also as a "home" for some incoming immigrants until they were placed. Clarissa said that her mother once complained that everyone who didn't have any other place to go was sent to her. Many who arrived in Utah without family, especially Danish, Swedish, German, and Welsh girls who needed to learn English before they were "placed," stayed to work for the Youngs.[47] "By the time mother was through training them," wrote Clarissa, "they were all good housekeepers." About that time they would get married.

Besides the young women who assisted in the home, all of the men who worked on the estate, usually about eighteen in number, ate at the Beehive House. "Father never allowed us to call anyone who worked upon the place 'servants,' " wrote Clarissa. They were always "the men or girls who helped with the work."[48]

Saturday afternoons Brigham often took some of his family to the Warm Springs Bath. "Father liked to bathe there because of the medicinal value of the water."[49] It must have given him relief from the rheumatism from which he suffered. They were driven there in a light carriage by "Black Isaac," a coachman who had earlier been a servant of Joseph Smith.

If Brigham had his breakfast in the Beehive House, he had dinner, usually called supper, in the west side of the basement of the Lion House. An average of something like fifty members of the family ate there. Lucy, who was an excellent cook, presided over the Lion House kitchen from the time it was built in 1856 until 1860, when she moved into the Beehive House to entertain the official guests. The childless "Aunt" Twiss then took over the Lion House kitchen and directed it until after Brigham's death.

The children were taught by Harriet Cook in the basement of the Lion House until Brigham built his own schoolhouse in 1865. Brigham also maintained a "recreation room" and erected a platform that could serve as a stage for family theatrical productions and variety shows. Later in the 1860s, he constructed a long porch the length of the west side to serve as a gymnasium. There were horizontal ladders and straight ladders, horizontal bars, backboards to straighten shoulders, jumping ropes, hoops, roller skates, wooden swords, dumbbells, swings, and big balls to kick and roll about. He kept teachers to instruct the children in gymnastics, fencing, and solo dancing. The roof of the porch was used for sleeping quarters by the older boys and girls in the summer.

Further recreation took place in a family swimming pool or "fount," located east of the Beehive House, back (north) of the schoolhouse. Supplied with water from City Creek, the pool was about twenty feet square and four or five feet deep. "Father," as the children called Brigham, insisted that bathing costumes be modest; they consisted of linsey dresses and pantalets for the girls and shirts and overalls for the boys. For dressing purposes, Brigham converted an old bandwagon into a bathhouse located near the pool. The fount was also used for baptisms.

At family dinners, usually at five-thirty, Brigham sat at the head of the table, Eliza Snow at his right, Twiss at his left, and each family, as a unit, with assigned places around the long table. After the dinner, Brigham would go to his room, light a candle in the tall brass candlestick, move into the sitting room across the hall, and call everyone to prayers, to be held in the parlor of the Lion House. The family was often joined by Brigham's brothers Joseph and Lorenzo. Brigham would step to the glass cupboard, take down the prayer bell, go to the door, give three rings, and take his "chair" in the center of the parlor. When all the family was gathered, he would discuss "topics of the day." The family would sing some familiar songs—old-time ballads or religious songs or both. This would be followed by a "program"; that is, children reciting poems and singing songs they had learned, older children playing musical instruments and singing, groups of them putting on skits, and, occasionally, a one-act play written by one of them. In the group singing Brigham would join in with his strong bass voice. At the end of the program they would all kneel while Brigham offered the evening prayer. Clarissa remembered a common theme in these prayers: "Bless the church and Thy people, the sick and the afflicted, and comfort the hearts that mourn."[50]

After prayers, members of the family dispersed to their apartments. The younger children would be put to bed. The wives and older children would talk and read and play until bedtime. On winter evenings the children would make popcorn or molasses candy. Brigham often enjoyed a bowl of fresh popped corn with sugar and cream.

Those who went out for the evening would take their lamps and place them on a table near the door. Upon returning, each would carry the lamp back to his room. The person who returned latest—evident by his lamp being the last one on the table—bolted the outside door for the night.

On Sunday evenings the older girls were permitted to entertain their boyfriends in the parlor. There might be as many as ten such couples in the parlor on a given Sunday evening in the middle 1860s. Clarissa recalled the occasion when the group decided to dim the lights by placing a barricade of books around the lamp. All went well until the door slowly opened and there stood Brigham, with a candle in his hand. He took one look around the room and then walked to the table where he removed the books one by one until the proper light shone forth. Then, turning to the subdued group, he said,

"The girls will go upstairs to their rooms, and I will say good night to the young men."[51]

Brigham was particular about his girls' male companions. Young men were closely questioned and scrutinized. Susa, the first child born in the Lion House, told of an incident that took place during the late 1860s, when she was in her teens:

> On one occasion, just as he [Brigham] was stepping into his carriage, he saw a strange young man about to enter the house gate. Instantly the flood of usual questions was poured out upon the embarrassed youth. Apparently not quite satisfied with the answers given, father asked, abruptly:
> "Are you a Mormon?"
> "Well," floundered the lad, "slightly."
> Father burst into his quiet, mellow laugh, and often afterwards, in speaking of the young man, whose name was Scipio Africanus Kenner, would jocosely call him Skippio Sinner.[52]

There was an affectionate relationship between Brigham and his children. But the kindness that characterized it included a firmness "that neither humiliated the child nor lowered his own self-respect."[53] Discipline was mainly an educational process of example and precept: "It is not by the whip or the rod that we can make obedient children," Brigham believed, "but it is by faith and by prayer, and by setting a good example before them."[54] If children knew the feelings of their parents when they did good or evil, "it would have a salutary influence upon their lives; but no child can possibly know this, until it becomes a parent. I am compassionate therefore towards children."[55] If parents wish children who are not contentious or quarrelsome, they should always be good-natured themselves.

> Never allow yourselves to become out of temper and get fretful. Why, mother says, "this is a very mischievous little boy or little girl." What do you see? That amount of vitality in those little children that they cannot be still. . . . They are so full of life . . . that their bones fairly ache with strength . . . and activity. . . . Do not be out of temper yourselves. Always sympathize with them and soothe them. Be mild and pleasant.[56]

Governing the home by violence and dictatorship was antipathetic to Brigham:

> I do not believe in making my authority as a husband or a father known by brute force; but by a superior intelligence—by showing them that I am capable of teaching them. . . . If the Lord has placed me to be head of a family, let me be so in all humility and patience, not as a tyrannical ruler, but as a faithful companion, an indulgent and affectionate father, a thoughtful and unassuming superior. . . .[57]

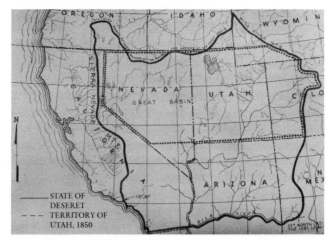

STATE OF
DESERET
- - TERRITORY OF
UTAH, 1850

State of Deseret 1849–51

ain Street in Salt Lake City, about
62. Note water flowing through
igation ditches on either side of
 street.

George Q. Cannon, Mormon apostle and Young's secretary and counselor.

Young's friend and counselor George A. Smith.

The "Mansion House" or "White House," built
by Young in Salt Lake City in the early 1850s.

Official residences and offices of Young in Salt
Lake City, built in the 1850s. *Left to right:*
The Lion House, the President's Office,
and the Beehive House. The stone wall was
erected around the property in 1856.

BELOW: Mary Ann Angell, second wife of Young and the "Mother Young" of Utah. LEFT: Young's first plural wife, Lucy Decker.

RIGHT: Eliza Roxcy Snow, a
plural wife of Brigham Young
and a leader of Mormon women.
BELOW: The Young brothers,
about 1856. *From left:* Lorenzo,
Brigham, Phinehas, Joseph,
and John.

The interior of Young's office, as drawn
for *Harper's Weekly* in 1871.

Mormon farmer and family returning
from a visit to Salt Lake City, 1870.

Young and other notables on one of their summer
visits to a Mormon settlement. Young usually rode
at the head of such a train, driving his own team.

The Mormon Tabernacle and Salt Lake City,
about 1867.

Brigham Young, about 1873.

One daughter recalled the many occasions when he amused babies by taking them on one knee and commencing a musical "too-roo-loo-rool-lool-or-loo," which would always "dry up any incipient torrent on a baby's cheek." And the office journals of his clerks likewise mention the solicitude and personal attention he would give to child visitors bringing messages from their mothers.[58]

The schoolhouse, across the street to the east of the Beehive House, contained a high-ceilinged, long-windowed room with a brass bell in its spire. There was a small wing attached as a private room for the teacher. School began at nine o'clock, summer and winter. All grades met at the same time until the opening of the University of Deseret in 1868, when those who had completed grammar school attended classes there. Brigham also employed a "phonographer" to teach the children shorthand, and musicians so the children could learn voice and how to play the piano, organ, harp, and other instruments. One of Brigham's daughters organized the first music department in the territory at Brigham Young Academy (later Brigham Young University) in Provo.

At the north end of the Beehive House on the first floor was the family "store" kept by John Haslam. There each wife had a charge account. In this store were staples, notions, drugs, dried peas and apples, calicoes, and candy.

Behind the Beehive House and the Lion House were a carpenter shop, laundry house, pigeon house, shoe shop, blacksmith shop, flour mill, barns, corrals, and gardens. There was an orchard of fruit trees, raspberry bushes, blackberry, currant and gooseberry bushes, strawberry plants, and beehives.

During the 1860s, in order to assure self-sufficiency and at the same time provide fine clothing for his wives and daughters, Brigham attempted to start a silk industry. For that purpose he imported mulberry trees and silkworms from France. There were a number of such trees in his orchard and a small cocoonery. Trees were also planted on his Forest Farm, and a large cocoonery with a capacity of two million silkworms was maintained. A convert from northern Italy, Susanna Gaudin Cardon, gave instruction in spinning and making silk, and a number of silk dresses, blouses, scarves, hats, and other items of wearing apparel were made by the family.

The home at the Forest Farm was designed by Brigham, and he directed its construction, which featured a gabled roof and porch all the way around. Brigham's blooded livestock were kept there, and all of the butter, eggs, milk, and cheese used by his family were produced there.[59]

The entire downtown compound was surrounded by a cobblestone wall nine feet high, with gates at convenient intervals. In front of the office was a guardhouse, where someone was on duty to keep out intruders.

I N the 1860s Brigham added three wives to his household. Mary Van Cott Cobb, Ann Eliza Webb Dee, and Harriet Amelia Folsom. He married Mary Van Cott in 1865, when he was sixty-four and she twenty-one. She was the daughter of John Van Cott, a New York Dutchman, who was a member of the First Council of Seventy of the church from 1862 until his death in 1883. Brigham had great respect for Van Cott and gave him several important church appointments. As a teenager, Mary had married James T. Cobb, a teacher in Salt Lake City, whose mother, Augusta Adams Cobb, had looked after and taught Brigham's daughter Vilate in Massachusetts in 1844. James and Mary had one daughter. When the marriage was later dissolved, Brigham agreed to be sealed to Mary. In 1870 she gave birth to Fannie, the last of Brigham's fifty-seven children, who lived to be eighty and was Brigham's final child to die. Mary died in 1884, at the age of forty.

Twenty-three-year-old Ann Eliza Webb Dee was the daughter of Chauncy G. Webb, a teacher in Kirtland. Tall and slender,with dark blue eyes and dark brown hair, Ann Eliza married James Dee, a plasterer, in 1863. She bore him two children before divorcing him for neglect and cruelty. As with many hundreds who wrote to Brigham asking him for a divorce, Ann Eliza's mother told of her concern for the ill treatment her daughter was receiving from Dee—he choked her, kicked her, and in other ways vented his violent temper upon her. Brigham responded with assurances that he would take steps to help the daughter. He then wrote to the probate judge, saying, "I am somewhat familiar with the case, and think her entitled to a Bill [of Divorce]."60 Ann Eliza met Brigham in the summer of 1867, when he, his brother Joseph, and George Q. Cannon were attending services near Chauncy Webb's farm in Little Cottonwood. Her parents urged her to cultivate him. He responded to the plea of the family and her own entreaties. No children were born of the marriage. Ann Eliza later divorced Brigham, left the territory, lectured widely against the Mormons, and was married at least two more times.

Amelia, as she was usually called, became a favorite of many Utah residents. A native of New York and second cousin of Frances Folsom, wife of President Grover Cleveland, she was the daughter of William H. Folsom, the church architect. Tall, fair, and musically talented, Amelia was twenty-four when she married Brigham in January 1863. No children resulted from the marriage, although it is not credible to think that the relationship was purely platonic.

Asked about the courtship some years later, Amelia said, "President Young was naturally dignified, but was always at ease with company." After the marriage, she took up residence in the Lion House. "At that time," she remembered, "there were seventy-five of us in the family, including the hired help." When Amelia was asked whether her married life was happy, she replied, "I should certainly dislike to think otherwise. . . . We were all members of the same family, and treated each other as such. I would sacrifice anything for the surviving wives of President Young, and their feeling toward me I think is the same." When a reporter told Amelia that she had the reputation of being Brigham Young's favorite wife, she replied: "I can't say that he had any favorites. He was equally kind and attentive to all in his lifetime, and left each surviving wife an equal legacy." When asked if she believed in plural marriage, she replied, "I certainly do. . . . There is no reason why a polygamous marriage

may not be as happy as the ordinary marriage, if it is entered into understand-
ingly." Commenting on her lack of children, she said, "I am constantly sensible
to the fact that children would have been an inestimable source of comfort
and company to me at the present time." However, she added, "visits back
and forth with the surviving wives of President Young add great pleasure to
my home life."[61]

Brigham often took Amelia to social and cultural events, and she went
with him on his tours of the southern settlements. An expert piano player and
teacher, she was always exquisitely dressed and impeccable in her manners and
cordiality.

He believed that he indulged all his wives. Contemporary testimony seems
to support his feeling that they were women of spirit. Of the schoolteacher-
wife Harriet Cook, Brigham said she would make a good sheriff: if she once
determined to get her man, she would get him. When told about a husband
who had blackened his wife's eye, Brigham declared, "I have women in my
family that would have killed that brother in a moment if he had treated them
in the way he has [her]." He went on, "I [endeavor to] govern my family by
kindness. I tell them what is right and I get them to obey me without whipping
them. If I cannot get my family to do as I wish them without quarreling with
them, I will not say a word about it."[62]

B R I G H A M appears to have been a reasonably fair and generous husband.
Four large family account books record all of the withdrawals of Brigham, his
agents, and his wives. One finds regular "purchases" of food, cloth, household
necessities, and other commodities by his various families: needles, calico,
matches, tea, and cutlery. Among Brigham's letterbooks are many missives
that contain his instructions to Mormon purchasing agents directing the buying
of some item for himself, one of his family, or one of his households. He
could be very specific. For example, when ordering 1,200 yards of carpeting
he insisted that no red material be included. "I want *red* entirely *rejected*," he
wrote, "and let the colors be selected of the yellow, brown, cinnamon, orange,
white, black, blue, green, &c., &c., altogether excluding red, if convenient so
to do."[63] His New England Puritan heritage was showing.

The following order is typical of the variety and detail—everything from
wire to olive oil, from codfish to water closets, along with the usual household
furnishings and clothing materials:

> I have concluded to have my garden wire fencing wove here, and wish you
> to purchase for me and forward to the terminus One Ton of No 9 galvanized
> wire, the $1,000 to cover cost and freight to terminus; I also wish you to purchase
> for me two dozen large bottles of pure olive oil for my own use; four or five
> quintals of best freshly cured codfish; needles and silk and thread, assorted colors,
> for sewing machines; two latest pattern water closets; sixteen window shades and
> fixtures, the shades to be 57 inches high and 36 inches wide, the body to be green,

with such ornamentation as your taste may select; 1 doz good, stout chairs suitable for a parlor or sitting room; 1 doz good chairs for bed rooms and upper parlor; six single mattresses of the best quality; 200 yds of the best three ply carpeting; one looking glass plain gilt frame, 2 feet 7 inches in width from outside to outside, length to suit yourself; calicoes, delaines, best bed ticking, 200 lbs feathers, bleached and plain domestic, as I spoke to you about, for family use.[64]

Brigham maintained his sense of humor in the business of buying and selling. In 1871, when David P. Kimball, president of the Paris, Idaho, stake, asked to purchase some rope, Brigham replied, "The rope was sent to catch the Bear Lake Monster [akin to Loch Ness] and if it cannot catch a Serpent, it is at least some gratification to know it is used on a ferry boat. You are welcome to the rope, all I ask for it, is the [privilege?] to use the ferry when we come to visit you."

That Brigham could be fussy is revealed in several letters:

I have several times sent in various ways for *black kid* gloves for my own use, but have seldom succeeded in procuring any to suit me; for this reason I wish you to procure for me 1 doz pr's of best French kid gents gloves (*goatskin*, not sheepskin), assorted sizes, numbers 10, 11, and 12, and forward them by the first trusty responsible person coming all the way through, for changing hands on the route shifts the responsibility, and articles often fail in coming to hand.[65]

If you have not already purchased the opera glasses, I wish you to purchase only *three* in Europe and *three* in New York City, instead of twelve in each place as previously advised. If you should have already purchased the twelve in Europe, all right; that will do, and you then need not buy any in New York. I wish them nicely cased in *roan* calf instead of patent leather, and strapped for carrying on the shoulder.[66]

He was very proud of the fact that the local and general authorities of the church were not supported out of tithing, but, instead, earned their own livelihood "by the labor of their own hands, like the first apostles."[67] Brigham's enterprises, involving both those necessary to support his families and those he maintained to assist the church, were extensive. Among his financial records is a list of his 183 employees as of December 24, 1864. Curiously, the list also gives the number in the family of each employee. The total of those supported from Brigham's private payroll came to 1,079. The list contains an even 100 people in Brigham's own family, including wives, children, adopted children, and others he regarded as under his personal care. The personal and family enterprises, with the number of employees, was as follows:

Gristmills and flour mills	21
Cotton factory	15
Salt Lake Theater and Social Hall	20

Building construction (carpenters, masons, plasterers, shingle makers)	18
Barn, yard, and garden	18
Forest Farm	7
Sawmills and lumberyard	6
Teamsters	6
House and commissary	5
Barber shop and harness shop	3
Bakery	4
Cabinetmakers and chairmakers	5
Nail factory	1
Canyon work (getting out wood)	22
Office clerks and business agents	10
Blacksmiths	7
Carriage driver, clothes cleaner, weaver	3
Henry B. Wilde's hands (mining coal at Coalville)	10
Sons doing various jobs for him for pay	2
Total	183

The year after this count, Brigham opened up his family schoolhouse, adding one full-time teacher to the list. (When the school was in the Lion House, Harriet Cook and other family members taught the children as a part of their assignments.) When the University of Deseret opened in 1868 for regular course work at all levels—primary, secondary, and advanced—Brigham's family made up the largest single group attending. In October 1869, Brigham paid tuition for thirty-three persons, including seven not in his own immediate family. The eldest was twenty-four, and one was only nine. Brigham believed that girls ought to attend school along with the boys, and more than half of the thirty-three for whom he paid tuition were young women. His daughter Susa edited the college paper, the *College Lantern*, believed to have been the first student magazine in the Mountain West.

Two examples will suggest Brigham's interest in serving as a "father" to young people. "B.F." (for Brigham Frederick) Grant, son of Brigham's counselor Jedediah M. Grant, was only a few weeks old when his father died in 1856. His mother made moccasins out of deerskins for sale and did housework for several families, and then, when B.F. was two, married and went to Denver, Colorado, to live. Little B.F. was left with his grandmother. He later was given to a family living in Richmond in the Cache Valley. In 1868, at the age of twelve, he "ran away" with a freight train headed for the Montana mines, and remained there for two years. Learning that he was Jedediah Grant's son, a Mormon freighter invited him to return with him to Salt Lake City, where he went to work in a coal yard. Somebody informed Brigham of his presence in the city, and Brigham sent word that he wanted to see him.

The president greeted B.F. with "a father's handshake," and learned what he had been doing. When Brigham offered him easier work—a job in one of his stores—B.F. replied, "I haven't got sense enough to work in a store—I can't read or write." "Tears rolled down the president's cheeks," wrote B.F. as he remembered the interview. "He took out his handkerchief, wiped them off, and said: 'My boy, come and live with me. I will give you a home, clothe you, and send you to school. You can work during the vacation for me.'"

B.F. accepted the offer and remained with the president's family for two years. He reported that there were six other orphaned boys and girls living in the family at that time, and he, for one, was "a real member of the family." Ultimately, however, B.F. decided he wanted to go to California where some friends of his were making "big money." Brigham tried to dissuade him, told him it was a mistake to leave school and the home he had provided. When he saw that B.F. was determined, Brigham fitted him out with a trunk full of clothing and other necessaries. There was a tearful session in the family evening prayer service, and a subsequent meeting alone with Brigham the next morning when the president gave B.F. a $100 greenback and some fatherly advice. In writing of the episode, B.F. said that Brigham had two outstanding characteristics. On the one hand he was "very stern and had a positive way of saying and doing things." On the other hand "he had a kind and loving way that was like a loving mother for her child. With his spirit of discernment, he was able to decide which of these attitudes was appropriate so that justice and right should prevail."⁶⁸

Ellis Reynolds was the oldest of four children born in a farming family in Pleasant Grove, Utah. She was fourteen when her mother died and she had to become the homemaker.⁶⁹ Within a year, however, her father remarried, and Ellis went to live with her grandparents who lived in an adjoining settlement. She was discontented there and made occasional visits to Salt Lake City to attend musical and dramatic performances, general conference, and to visit family friends and relatives. On one of these "nights out" she met Zebulon Jacobs, a son of Zina D. H. Jacobs Young, one of Brigham's plural wives. Ellis was warmly received by the Young family. Shortly thereafter Brigham visited Pleasant Grove to hold a meeting. At a party held for him in the evening Brigham saw and chatted with Ellis, was impressed with her vivacity and intelligence, and invited her to join him in one of the dances. The next day he sent her an invitation to come live in the Beehive House and attend school with his own children. This was in 1864, when Ellis was seventeen; she accepted.

She knelt with the Young family in prayers, sat in one of their boxes at the theater, was privately tutored in the Beehive House, and occasionally joined others on some of Brigham's tours. After two years she married Milford Shipp and moved into her own home. Determined to keep up her learning, however, she arose at four each morning and studied for three hours before her household began to stir. When she was twenty-eight, with three children, she obtained the support of Brigham, her husband, and others, and went to Philadelphia to earn a degree at the Woman's Medical College. Upon her return to Utah she specialized in obstetrics, diseases of women, and minor surgery. She was active in women's organizations of the church, a delegate to the National Council of Women, had additional children, and lived to be ninety-two. To a whole generation of young women, she was living proof that Brigham really meant it when he declared, in her hearing:

> We believe that women are useful, not only to sweep houses, wash dishes, make beds, and raise babies, but that they should stand behind the counter, study law or physics [medicine], or become good bookkeepers and be able to do the business in any counting house, and all this to enlarge their sphere of usefulness for the benefit of society at large. In following these things they but answer the design of their creation.[70]

A L T H O U G H Brigham could be kind to orphans, aspiring students, and helpless widows, he expected a full day's work from his employees. In the case of men he hired to labor in the canyon, this meant from dawn to dark. When he learned that they were "in the habit of observing ten hours labor, and making short time at that, and do not perform faithful labor from morning till night," he set them straight about what he expected:

> Now what I want is good faithful labor and no 10 hour system about it for which I expect to pay, and if there is anyone among you, who does not feel to give it, I do not want to board him in the Kanyon, but want him to leave forthwith. If a man cannot be as faithful, and work as well for me when there is no one to watch over him, as when there is, I do not want him to work for me, and I have directed that all or any such men, be discharged unless they can do better.[71]

In his business dealings he was equally firm, whether as trustee-in-trust for the church or as a private entrepreneur. In 1855 Brigham purchased from a Brother Cooley "all the interest" Cooley possessed in Big Cottonwood Canyon, including "mill saws, tools, and all property belonging thereto or used there about, logs, lumber and every description of property; also including all of his rights and privileges in the Kanyon" and then was surprised to learn that Cooley was "taking quite active measures in sawing, getting out lumber &c from his Mill." Brigham sent his agent, Feramorz Little, to inform Cooley that he had come to take possession. Although Brigham thought it was a clearly understandable situation, he still indicated a willingness to discuss and to make sure there was mutual agreement and understanding about what was going on.

> If I bought anything at all of Bro. Cooley I bought the whole. If Bro. Cooley does not want to stand to the bargain which he made with me then let him say so, but if he does then let him deliver to you all the property. . . . If it is not his understanding that we are to have the logs which are cut, and all the lumber on

hand as well as the balance of the property, let him come down and see me and we will try and get an understanding before we go any further in the business relating to the purchase.[72]

When his lower mill did not do much business, Brigham dismissed some of the workers and also the manager, asking him to "please deliver up the key and everything connected therewith to my son, John W. Young, in whose charge I have placed the Mill and appurtenances thereunto belonging."[73] In the case of one rather tenacious employee, Brigham tried to be kind but had to be rather blunt:

> I have informed you several times that I could dispense with your further services in my employ; the last time I mentioned this was prior to the First of last April at which time I told you I wanted you to quit.
> I wish you now to consider yourself dismissed from my Service. My children are now large enough to do a good deal of labor, and I am in a position to get along without your help.
> I have tried to be as kind to you as possible thus far, and I still wish to be kind to you; but I do not need your services any more, and I will feel obliged to you, if you will quit.[74]

On the other hand, a man who had borrowed a yoke of cattle from Brigham eight years previously received from him this sarcasm:

> When you have kept the yoke of cattle you had from me 8 years longer, then call on me and remind me at the end of 16 years, again that you owe me a yoke of cattle, & of course say nothing about the use of them for twice 8 yrs. You know what is right, do it & don't trouble me. I am the friend of the virtuous & good.[75]

When some of the men he hired in 1864 to work on a national railroad survey threatened to quit, Brigham impatiently wrote them, pointing out their "ingratitude" in the light of his having treated them more than fairly, and asked them to shape up and get to work as they had agreed.

> Now I wish to say to all such that I consider their action in this matter the heighth of ingratitude, to say the very least of it. They mostly came to me and offered their services, and I plainly told them what was required, and what wages I should pay, and they consented to go. I kept them here under wages some five or six weeks doing nothing, waiting Mr. Reed's [the federal engineer] arrival. I am furnishing their families with flour at $6.00 per hundred when I could get at the rate of $10. or $12 in gold for it, and other provisions proportionately cheap, and now all I demand of them is that they shall fulfil their agreement and go on and finish the job like honorable men, and not try to take an advantage of me now because they think I cannot get another set of hands in season to carry on the work.

They will probably all want work again. I would not like their course in this matter to be such as to debar them from the confidence and employ of good men. I wish you to read this communication to all who are dissatisfied, and tell them to stop their grumbling and growling as I did not hire them to do that, but to attend to their work and do whatever is required of them in Camp.[76]

Although Brigham tried hard to be fair, he did not like to be taken advantage of. Not surprisingly, there were those, even among his own people, who grumbled and felt they had not been treated properly. It must have been easy to envy someone who was well fixed and who so obviously enjoyed the esteem of most of the community. By and large, however, especially among those who knew him best, there was agreement that Brigham was both fair and generous. He had been honest and hardworking his whole life and did not think it too much to expect the same from others.

BRIGHAM had some sons who were pretty "wild" as they grew up; he had daughters who married non-Mormons, and he once remarked that "the Lord owed him a grudge for something and paid him off in sons-in-law."[77] Two of his plural wives divorced him, and members of his family sued the church for some of his property after his death. Nor did he succeed in persuading all of his visitors that Mormonism represented no threat to the nation or to good Christian morals. Nevertheless his family relationships, considering their complexity, were remarkably good. And most of the visitors to Mormon country who observed Brigham as husband, father, and employer as well as church and civic leader were favorably impressed.

19 ✦

Protecting the Kingdom

Speaking of the completion of this [transcontinental] railroad, I am anxious to see it, and I say to the Congress of the United States, through our Delegate, to the Company, and to others, hurry up, hasten the work! We want to hear the iron horse puffing through this valley. What for? To bring our brethren and sisters here.[1]

W H E N the word of General Robert E. Lee's surrender at Appomattox reached Utah in April 1865, Brigham's reaction was not entirely one of relief. He feared that the forces of Reconstruction, now that slavery had been slain, would turn their attention to Mormon polygamy, that other "twin evil" in the Republican platform of 1856. Brigham wrote to his son Brigham, Jr., and Daniel H. Wells, both in England.

The workers of wickedness . . . would really like, now that the war east [Civil War] appears to be off the hands of the Government, to have attention drawn to us here, and troops to be sent to break us up. They openly avow their intention to break the power of the priesthood and to destroy our organization.[2]

Brigham's apprehension was increased with the visit, in June 1865, of Speaker of the House Schuyler Colfax, editor Samuel Bowles of the Springfield (Massachusetts) *Republican,* and reporter Albert Richardson of the New York *Tribune.* So famous for his public piety that he was nicknamed "the Christian Statesman," Colfax came with certain prejudices and, not surprisingly, found his prejudices strengthened as the result of his visit.

Brigham tried hard to impress Colfax during each of three encounters in his eight-day stay in the Mormon capital. In the course of the first visit, at Colfax's apartment in the Salt Lake House, the party expressed their desire to attend a Sunday service. Brigham inquired what they would prefer as a subject for his talk. He was willing, Brigham said, to speak on anything they wished, even polygamy. But the visitors asked him to talk on something different—

anything he pleased.[3] On Sunday, then, Brigham preached in the Temple Block Bowery to about six thousand on the "Personality of God—His Attributes— Eternal Life, Etc." Emphasizing the centrality of Christ in Mormon theology, it was a typical Sunday afternoon sermon. But it was somewhat rambling and unlike the polished sermons of the professional ministry. It contained, wrote Bowles, "bare and bold statement" and "coarse denunciation," and was punctuated with such Vermont provincialisms as "leetle," "beyend," "disremember," and "they was."[4]

For their second interview, Colfax and his party walked to the Young compound with its nine-foot stone and mortar wall, on past the sentry who kept a revolver at his side, and into the president's office. There, in an airy, high-walled room surrounded by maps, daguerreotypes, account books, and armchairs, Young and his visitors enjoyed a long, rambling conversation on Indian policy, gold seeking, freight costs, Mormon history, and especially "plurality." What struck Richardson was Young's insistence that the Mormons had prospered with God's help. "We cannot be annihilated," Brigham said. Bowles wrote:

> The Mormons are eager to prove their loyalty to the government, their sympathy with its bereavement, their joy in its final triumph—which their silence or their slants and sneers heretofore had certainly put in some doubt—and they leave nothing unsaid or undone now . . . to give assurance of their rightmindedness. Also they wish us to know that they are not monsters and murderers, but men of intelligence, virtue, good manners and fine taste.[5]

After many flattering assurances and a hearty goodbye, Speaker Colfax and the journalists departed for Carson City, Nevada. Brigham wrote a close associate that they had seemed gratified by the reception and the beauty and industry of the city. "They could only see one thing that was lacking to make us a state and put us upon a very respectable footing."[6] Unfortunately that one thing (the refusal to abolish plural marriage) colored Colfax's, Richardson's, and Bowles' perception of Mormonism as a whole, and Brigham was not flattered by the dispatches that soon appeared. It was clear that, in cooperation with Colonel Patrick Connor and the local non-Mormon community, the visitors were determined to press hard against the Mormons in order to remove this "foul and filthy ulcer upon the body politic."[7] Bowles summarized his recommendation in *Across the Continent*:

> We all saw that the time had come for a new departure, for a new policy by the Government. The conflict of sects and civilization, growing up there in Utah, will soon solve the polygamous problem . . . if the Government will make itself felt in it with a wise guardianship, a tender nursing, a firm principle.[8]

It was such "wise guardianship," guided by "firm principle," that Brigham feared.

Federal interference occurred the very next year, over the control of liquor and gambling in Salt Lake City. Ever since Colonel Connor's Volunteers had arrived, there had been complaints about "a great many drunken people on the streets to be taken up by the police and by the provost guard." With Brigham's prodding, Salt Lake City had tried prohibition, but the "traveling community" insisted on liquor, and the city found it necessary to "control it so that all who are weak may not abuse themselves with it."[9]

In 1865, with the end of the war, federal troops and the traveling public were less willing to submit to control and discipline. So the city moved from licensing saloons to creating a monopoly. A new ordinance barred everyone but city agents from manufacturing, buying, or selling "spiritous, venous and fermented liquor." Profits from the liquor monopoly were to go to the city treasury, and existing licenses were allowed to run out. The ordinance also barred private billiard and gaming places, giving the city sole right to operate such. Illegal liquor or gaming operations were termed "nuisances" to be removed or abated.[10] This procedure suppressed the drinking of liquor to a considerable extent and, as far as Brigham was concerned, did "a great deal of good."[11]

In April 1866, in order to tighten its control over "nuisances," the city added a new enforcement clause. Anyone suspecting a public nuisance place to be in operation could swear an oath to that effect to the mayor or an alderman. If investigation proved the claim, the marshal could "take possession of such house or place, with the gaming tables, and all other instruments or devices used for the purpose of gaming and may demolish such instruments or devices or hold the same, including liquors and bar fixtures."

Fearing the "seize and destroy" possibilities, non-Mormons, who had apparently organized private clubs that sold liquor, sent a petition to the commanding officer at Camp Douglas, Colonel Carroll E. Potter, and a telegram to his superior in Washington, D.C., General Grenville M. Dodge. The petition stated that the ordinance might have the result of demolishing property "without due course of law." The telegram to Dodge produced a response to Potter from General William T. Sherman, endorsed by Dodge. It read:

In the month of April a telegram was received from American Citizens that their lives and property are in danger, received by General Dodge. Let the troops at Ft. Bridger and Camp Douglas be employed to protect the Gentiles [interesting that Sherman should have called them Gentiles], and let the Mormons know that if they injure the Gentiles they shall have to pay the penalty. Give them to understand that the people of the United States are only waiting for some pretext to destroy them root and branch.[12]

Colonel Potter requested a face-to-face meeting with Brigham, Salt Lake City Mayor Daniel H. Wells, former Mayor Abraham O. Smoot, and others. (No explanation is given for the failure to invite Governor Charles Durkee.) According to a verbatim transcript, the long meeting started with a warning. "I do not want the policemen to go and seize on property under this ordinance and destroy it," Potter declared, "until it is tried in the proper courts of law."[13]

After lengthy discussion, cross-criticism, and expression of pent-up feelings by both sides, Brigham promised, "If private property is infringed upon illegally or unjustly, you will have my assistance, as an individual, to the utmost." "That is enough," Potter replied.[14]

Eventually, as non-Mormon influence grew with the continuing development of mines, the city abandoned its monopoly and reestablished the old system of issuing licenses for places for saloons and places of amusement.

During the same period that the city was dealing severely with saloons, places of amusement, and other "nuisances," Brigham and his associates sponsored a boycott against unfriendly merchants. He had become "fed-up" with merchants who continued to charge "exorbitant prices," particularly by those who used their money and influence against the Mormons. Brigham had no objection to the "friendly" Gentiles who contributed generously to local enterprises, willingly paid taxes, and said good things about the Mormons on their eastern buying trips. But why, he wondered, should the Mormon community support men who were draining the financial strength of the territory?[15]

To one group Brigham explained the Mormon use of the word Gentile:

> "Gentile," or "gentilism," applies only to those who reject the gospel, and will not submit to and receive the plan of salvation. . . . It does not apply to any, only those who are opposed to God and His kingdom. . . . Whoever has been in our councils would never make the application of a "gentile" to a man or woman, simply because he or she was not baptized, for that has nothing to do with it either one way or another.[16]

The Gentile merchants of Salt Lake City (several of whom were Jews) found it difficult to recognize which of them were regarded as friendly and which unfriendly, and interpreted Brigham's expostulations to be directed against the entire group. A group of them, representing some twenty-three firms, sent an open letter to Brigham and "Leaders of the Mormon Church," offering to sell out at 25 percent less than the "cash valuation." Brigham's reply, the next day (December 21, 1866), declared that the offer to sell was exorbitant— "we, as merchants, would like to find purchasers upon the same basis." Gentiles were free to "stay" or "go" as they pleased.

> We have not sought to ostracise any man or body of men because of their not being of our faith. The wealth that has been accumulated in this Territory from

the earliest years of our settlement by men who were not connected with us religiously, and the success which has attended their business operations prove this. In business we have not been exclusive in our dealings, or confined our patronage to those of our own faith. . . .

There is a class, however, who are doing business in the Territory, who for years have been the avowed enemies of this community. The disrupture and overthrow of the community have been the objective which they have pertinaciously sought to accomplish. They have used every energy and all the means at their command to put into circulation the foulest slanders about old citizens. . . . While soliciting the patronage of the people and deriving their support from them, they have in the most shameless and abandoned manner used the means thus obtained to destroy the very people whose favor they found it to their interest to court. . . . What claims can such persons have upon the patronage of this community, and what community would be so besotted as to uphold and foster men whose aim is to destroy them? Have we not the right to trade at whatever we please, or does the Constitution of the United States bind us to enter the stores of our deadliest enemies and purchase of them?[17]

"My counsel to the Latter-day Saints," said Brigham the following Sunday in the tabernacle, "is to let all merchants alone who seek to do evil to this people. Those who will do well, deal righteously and justly, will be one with us in our financial affairs. . . . Sustain those who sustain this kingdom, and those that fight against it, cease to sustain them."[18]

Apparently Brigham's strategy was effective. A few of the firms left the territory, others remained, and, indeed, some are still in operation in Salt Lake City to this day.

Consistent with his remarks against building up "enemy" merchants, Brigham directed admonitions to the women who did most of the buying of imported goods. If the territory was to be independent and self-sustaining, he believed, they must develop home industries. And, indeed, many persons did make clothes for themselves and for their families. The order lists of the tithing stores show a greater demand for fabrics than any other imported commodities. Wives and daughters of public works employees and other tithepayers asked for bolt after bolt of calico, factory, shirting, and flannel as well as the more luxurious delaine, lawn, cambric, and gingham.[19] To help satisfy this demand without imports, Brigham encouraged the milling of wool and cotton. Women were urged to take up spinning and weaving and thus do the entire cloth manufacturing task from the raw material to the finished garment.

Although the campaign enjoyed some success, the purchase of imported goods continued to drain the Great Basin economy.[20] Despite injunctions to dress in homespun, Mormon women (and men too) wore Eastern fabrics whenever their purse permitted.

It was not that Brigham wanted to sever all contact with the outside world. When the transcontinental telegraph line was planned in 1861, as we have seen, the church contracted to construct the line from Wyoming to the border of California. By this means, the Latter-day Saints not only obtained the service that the telegraph permitted but also gained valuable experience. When the end of the Civil War in 1865 made it possible to purchase materials, the church organized the Deseret Telegraph Company and organized its people to build a 500-mile regional line that would connect the various Mormon settlements with each other and with the transcontinental station in Salt Lake City.[21]

A campaign was launched to collect the necessary funds to purchase the wire and other materials needed to equip such a large system. Each local community was assigned the responsibility of constructing, equipping, and staffing that part of the line running through the settlement and halfway to the next community. The $56,000 in cash with which to buy wire and other equipment was collected during the winter of 1865–66 and sent to Salt Lake City. At the same time, each community furnished wagons, teams, drivers, and provisions for a "Church Wagon Train" of sixty-five large wagons, which in the spring of 1866 traveled to the Missouri River to pick up wire and material and freight it back to Utah.

Each settlement large enough to maintain a station was asked to send one or two young men or women to a school of telegraphy held in Salt Lake City during the winter of 1865–66. These young people regarded their call as a church mission and were supported by their parents or local communities with food and clothing.

Under the direction of local priesthood groups—deacons, elders, Seventies, and high priests—the line was surveyed, poles were cut, and means were collected. The line was well along toward completion when work was suspended to concentrate on crops in the spring of 1866. By the time the Church Train arrived in October with eighty-four tons of wire, insulators, batteries, and other equipment, volunteer teams were ready to put up the wire and connect the line. The local women's Relief Societies participated by feeding the workmen and washing their clothes. By the first of December, the line from Salt Lake City to Ogden was connected. By the middle of February 1867, a line more than 500 miles long was in operation.[22]

As was customary with all such enterprises, it was dedicated by Brigham, who sent the following as the first message over the line:

> In my heart I dedicate the line which is now completed and being completed to the Lord God of Israel, whom we serve, for the building up of His Kingdom, praying that this and all other improvements may contribute to our benefit, and the glory of our God; until we can waft ourselves by the power of the Almighty from world to world to our fullest satisfaction.[23]

In subsequent years the line was extended, also with contributed labor, to join virtually all Mormon settlements from southern Idaho to northern Arizona, and most of the mining districts in Utah and southeastern Nevada.

By Brigham's death in 1877 there were approximately twelve hundred miles of wire, with sixty-eight offices or stations. The operators continued to be supported by voluntary donations until the end of the century, when the line was absorbed by Western Union. During Brigham's life, it was strictly a "people's line"; charges for correspondence via telegraph were nominal, and news passed over the wire to all settlements almost as quickly and as cheaply as it was received in Salt Lake City.

It was perhaps the only major telegraph line in the United States constructed and operated by a church, and it facilitated the administration of Brigham's kingdom, increased the security of the outlying settlements from attacks of Indians, and helped pioneers in scattered villages to overcome feelings of isolation and loneliness. The line was also of some value to the United States Army. The first news of General Custer's defeat by the Sioux reached the world through the agency of the Deseret Telegraph. Brigham was determined to have a line "in the hands of, and under the direction of the Priesthood of God."²⁴ He wanted to appropriate the techniques of the outside world without becoming financially beholden to it.

B R I G H A M Young had long anticipated the end of physical isolation in the Great Basin. As early as 1852 and 1854 he signed legislative memorials to Congress petitioning for a transcontinental railroad to pass through Utah. He felt that the rapid and far-flung system of colonization would benefit from railroad connections with Salt Lake City. In addition, the process of emigration to Utah would be speeded by having a railroad connection between the Missouri River and Salt Lake City. As a token of his support, when the Pacific Railroad Act was passed on July 1, 1862, Brigham subscribed for $5,000 worth of stock in the newly organized Union Pacific Railroad Company, and became a director in 1865.

Just as the railroad would make it easier for Mormon emigrants to reach Utah, however, it would likewise facilitate non-Mormon arrivals. The inevitable transformation of a self-sufficient economy into a specialized one would threaten the economic and political independence of the territory. The Mormons would find it more difficult to discourage the importation of eastern manufactured goods; the establishment of a powerful non-Mormon business community was inescapable.

Brigham's first and most persistent response to the economic challenge presented by the railroad was jawboning, a stepped-up campaign to discourage the purchase of imported luxuries. Included in the ban were tea, coffee, alcohol, and tobacco—items proscribed by Joseph Smith's "Word of Wisdom"—and also fashionable clothing and elegant furniture. (This was after Brigham had resolved to stop using tobacco.)

Despite Brigham's long opposition to the "outside" development of mining in Utah, his support of the railroad meant that he was fostering the very agency that would make Utah mining profitable. Brigham's nemesis, Colonel Patrick Connor, who had been refused a colonelcy in the U.S. regulars, was mustered out of the Volunteers as brevet major general in 1866 and resumed his campaign for mining development. More interested in mineral exploration than anti-Mormonism, he founded smelting companies, invested in mines, and organized mining districts.[25] Despite his continuing efforts to undermine Mormonism, Connor was an honest man, and a mutual respect developed between him and Brigham. Brigham reportedly said of the colonel, "Men have been here before him; to our faces they were our friends; but when they went away they traduced, vilified and abused us. Not so with Connor. We always knew where to find him. That's why I like him."[26] Thanks to Connor's promotional activities and to the railroad, the production of nonferrous metals in Utah increased during the first year after the completion of the railroad from $190,000 per year to $1.5 million per year.[27]

One part of Brigham Young's response to the coming of the railroad was his mobilizing the Schools of the Prophets to carry out a six-point program: landowners were instructed in methods of securing property titles; labor and funds were solicited to finance branch railroads within the territory; locally owned cooperative merchandising and manufacturing enterprises were established; wages in key industries were reduced in order to improve the competitive position of Utah exports; boycotts of hostile Gentile establishments were stepped up; and all members of the schools pledged to observe the Word of Wisdom, thus cutting imports. Moreover, the central or Salt Lake school, in Brigham's name, contracted with the Union Pacific and Central Pacific railroads to grade all of the transcontinental line in Utah, thus bringing cash revenue to Mormons and inhibiting the influx of non-Mormon laborers.

As the railroads approached Utah from the east and west, Brigham was disappointed in the choice of a northern route that would bypass Salt Lake City. The rails were joined at Promontory, Utah, on May 10, 1869. Both Union Pacific and Central Pacific defaulted on their construction contracts. The losses to the Mormon economy were staggering: $500,000 in cash and even greater aggregate losses to the subcontractors, merchants, and laborers. In an effort to compensate for these losses, Brigham decided to build a "cooperative" Mormon railroad to connect Salt Lake City with the line at Ogden. The railroad, called the Utah Central, was put together with the $500,000 worth of iron, construction equipment, and rolling stock that the bankrupt Union Pacific had used as a substitute payment on its obligations. Upon the completion of the thirty-seven-mile road, on January 10, 1870, a "grand dedicatory celebration" was attended by an estimated fifteen thousand Saints. With a steel mallet made in the church public works Brigham drove the last spike, also made at the public works of native Utah iron and bearing the emblem of a beehive, the initials U.C.R.R., and the engraved inscription "Holiness to the Lord." After a formal prayer by Wilford Woodruff, Brigham did a little boasting:

Since the first day that we first trod the soil of these valleys, have we received any assistance from our neighbors? No, we have not. We have built our homes, our cities, have made our farms, have dug our canals and water ditches, have subdued this barren country, have fed the stranger, have clothed the naked, have immigrated the poor from foreign lands, have placed them in a condition to make all comfortable and have made some rich. We have fed the Indians . . . , have clothed them in part, and have sustained several Indian wars, and now we have built thirty-seven miles of railroad. . . . I thank the brethren who have aided to build this, our first railroad. . . . They have worked on the road, they have graded the track, they have laid the rails, they have finished the line, and have done it cheerfully "without purse or scrip."[28]

The evening the Utah Central was finished, Brigham completed the organization of the Utah Southern Railroad, to run south from Salt Lake City—at first, to Sandy, where a line then went east to the mines at Alta and west to the mines at Stockton; then to Provo, the center of Utah Valley; then on to Juab; and eventually to Frisco, near Beaver, where silver and lead mines were exploited. A "Mormon road," called the Utah Northern, was also constructed from Ogden north to Logan, then to Franklin, Idaho, and eventually to Dillon, Montana, where it connected with the Northern Pacific Railroad. All of these were "Mormon" roads, managed by Brigham and his associates until they were sold, in the late 1870s, to the Union Pacific.[29] The Mormon railroads were not particularly profitable, but they were needed, they served the economy, and they helped to assuage the bitterness of the Mormons at the failure of the two transcontinental railroads to satisfy their construction contracts with cash.

In October 1868, in an attempt to route more importation of goods through Mormon hands, Brigham organized Zion's Cooperative Mercantile Institution (ZCMI). The purpose of this company, he said, was "to bring goods here and sell them as low as they can possibly be sold and let the profits be divided with the people at large."[30] To be successful, ZCMI needed not only the patronage of most Mormons but also the participation of the merchants. Brigham developed several policies to obtain that end. Every establishment conducting business with ZCMI had a sign placed over the main entrance inscribed, "Holiness to the Lord: Zion's Cooperative Mercantile Institution." This not only publicly blacklisted any establishment lacking such a sign but it also discouraged the faithful from being seen in nonparticipating firms. To assure maximum participation of the firms owned by Mormons, Brigham asked all merchants to turn over their inventories to ZCMI in return for stock. When some merchants balked, Brigham prepared to establish a church-supported wholesale establishment in Provo. Since this would have ruined most nonparticipating firms, Gentile and Mormon alike, the threat was sufficient to persuade recalcitrant merchants to cooperate. The institution opened for business on March 1, 1869.[31]

ZCMI was intended to be not only a retail emporium but also the "Parent Wholesale Institution." Under the direction of Brigham and the Twelve, local general store cooperatives were organized during the months that followed in some 150 different settlements.[32] In most cases, each of these was managed by the bishop (and his wife or wives), and the policies were established by an elected board of management. The local "coop" was expected to purchase all imported goods from ZCMI. As it earned "profits," each store was expected to use the earnings to establish local tanneries, gristmills, dairies, butcher shops, molasses mills, blacksmiths, sawmills, carding machines, and woolen mills. The establishment and support of local stores and industries was one of Brigham's answers to the challenge presented by the approach of the railroad.[33]

The cooperative movement fulfilled its purposes, both financially and in broader economic terms. ZCMI made immediate profits, with dividends by 1873 amounting to more than $500,000, on an original investment of $280,000. Many smaller non-Mormon merchants were squeezed out of the competition, and the larger non-Mormon firms such as Walker Brothers and Auerbach Brothers experienced temporary declines and less expansion than otherwise expected upon the completion of the railroad.[34] ZCMI branches were later established in several locations in the region. A church-sponsored cooperative bank, the Bank of Deseret, was set up in Salt Lake City; large textile factories in Provo (Provo Woolen Mills) and Washington (Rio Virgen Manufacturing Company); ironworks (Great Western Iron Company) in Cedar City and Salt Lake City; and a large boot and shoe shop at the Salt Lake City ZCMI.

A T the time the School of the Prophets was organized, Brigham appointed Eliza Snow, his caretaker wife who had been the plural wife of Joseph Smith, to mobilize the women. Although primarily assigned "to visit the sick and the helpless and the needy, and learn their wants, and, under their Bishops, collect the means necessary to relieve them,"[35] the women of the Relief Society became full partners with the School of the Prophets.[36] Their objectives were to prevent or diminish female extravagance; inform themselves on political matters so they could lobby effectively against anti-Mormon legislation; establish a woman's commission store as an outlet for their handicraft and home manufacturing; and direct the education of their daughters.

Brigham was particularly concerned about the influence of "Babylon" on women's fashions. Contemporary fashion he considered "most useless, unbecoming, and ridiculous." The Grecian Bend, he said, gave women a hump on their backs that made them look like camels; mutton-legged sleeves "took seven yards for the sleeves, and three for the dress"; and long trains would drag up the dirt, raise a dust, and represented a waste of many yards of cloth.[37] Rather than spend their money on "useless articles that do no good to the body of the persons who use them," Latter-day Saint women should make contributions to such worthy causes as the transportation of the "pure in heart" from abroad.

The third pillar of support for Brigham's attempt to preserve his independent commonwealth was the Young Ladies' Retrenchment Society. Recognizing that a generation of girls brought up "under the gospel covenant" were still too young to be active in the Relief Society, Brigham spoke to Eliza Snow about the desirability of forming a church-sponsored organization for young women. They decided that he should begin with his own daughters. He delegated Eliza to notify all his daughters over the age of twelve to attend a special meeting in the parlor of the Lion House. It was the evening of November 28, 1869, six months after the "Joining of the Rails" at Promontory. Bathsheba Smith (wife of Brigham's counselor, George A.) accompanied Eliza as she made the notifications and was present at the meeting. When he saw Bathsheba there, Brigham notified George to come as well. George and Bathsheba were the only "visitors."

Eight deliberate rings of the prayer bell, located in a niche in the hall, brought his daughters and spouses into the long, low-ceilinged parlor. The chill of the evening had been removed by the Lady Franklin stove; the glass lamps were lit. After the opening prayer, the president addressed his daughters and wives as follows:

> All Israel are looking to my family and watching the example set by my wives and children. For this reason I desire to organize my own family first into a society for the promotion of habits of order, thrift, industry, and charity; and, above all things, I desire them to retrench from their extravagance in dress, in eating, and even in speech. The time has come when the sisters must agree to give up their follies of dress and cultivate a modest apparel, a meek deportment, and to set an example before the people of the world worthy of imitation.

Brigham said he was "weary" of the manner in which "our women seek to outdo each other in all the foolish fashions of the world": in the dishes they want to set before invited guests for dinner, in the manner in which they wasted their time in aimless conversation and gossip, and in their insistence on having ruffles, panniers (hoops), and other "foolish and useless trimmings and styles." He went on:

> I have long had it in my mind to organize the young ladies of Zion into an association so that they might assist the older members of the Church, their fathers and mothers, in propagating, teaching, and practicing the principles I have been so long teaching. There is need for the young daughters of Israel to get a living testimony of the truth. Young men obtain this while on missions, but this way is not opened to the girls. More testimonies are obtained on the feet than on the knees. I wish our girls to obtain a knowledge of the Gospel for themselves. For this purpose I desire to establish this organization and want my family to lead out in the great work. . . . We are about to organize a Retrenchment Association, which I want you all to join, and I want you to vote to retrench in your dress, in your tables, in your speech, wherein you have been guilty of silly, extravagant

speeches and lightmindedness of thought. Retrench in everything that is bad and worthless, and improve in everything that is good and beautiful.[38]

After expressing their feelings, the family members voted to support the president in this new venture. An election was then held and Ella Young Empey, twenty-two years of age, was chosen "presidentess" of the association. She selected as her counselors Emily Young Clawson, twenty; Zina Young Williams, nineteen; Maria Young Dougall, nineteen; Caroline Young, eighteen; Dora Young, seventeen; and Phebe Young, fifteen.

Under the direction of Eliza Snow, the girls then met separately, drew up articles of association and resolutions, and named their organization the Young Ladies Department of the Cooperative Retrenchment Association. Meetings began in December and continued through 1870 and succeeding years.

News of this association spread through Salt Lake City and Utah Territory. Within a year there were similar organizations in the Salt Lake Valley, Ogden, Logan, Provo, Bountiful, and Brigham City. Most were established under the direct supervision of Eliza Snow. In the summer of 1870, a senior department of older women was organized. All of the organizations drew up resolutions related to the objectives Brigham had proposed in the original meeting of his family. Typical resolutions of the young women were the following:

> Resolved, inasmuch as cleanliness is a characteristic of a Saint, and an imperative duty, we shall discard the dragging skirts, and for decency's sake those disgustingly short ones extending no lower than the boot tops. We also regard "panniers," and whatever approximates in appearance toward the "Grecian bend," a burlesque on the natural beauty and dignity of the human female form, and will not disgrace our persons by wearing them. And also, as fast as it shall be expedient, we shall adopt the wearing of home-made articles, and exercise our united influence in rendering them fashionable.[39]
>
> Resolved, that as Saints being accountable to God for the use we make of the abilities and intelligence he has given us, we are determined to devote our time and talents in governing ourselves, storing our minds with useful knowledge, and improving every opportunity afforded us of qualifying ourselves to fill useful and honorable positions in the kingdom of God.[40]

As the organization "caught on," the name was shortened to Young Ladies' Retrenchment Association. In 1878, with the focus changing from retrenchment to self-improvement it became the Young Ladies' Mutual Improvement Association, or YLMIA. In this century the name was changed to Young Women's Mutual Improvement Association (YWMIA), which it still has to this day. The organization now has several hundred thousand members, with subgroups in each of the ten thousand or more Mormon wards throughout the world.

The fourth pillar of support for the protection policy was the University of Deseret, which, having been in abeyance since the early 1850s, Brigham opened in 1868 in order to give training to young men and women in the liberal and pedagogical arts and to provide an opportunity for a cultural and artistic center in Zion.[41]

For the first year, with more than seventy students in attendance, the university featured instruction in geography, grammar, music, business, banking, bookkeeping, mathematics, and business practice. The second year, Brigham recommended the appointment of one of his employees, John R. Park, as president, and the university was fully reborn. A native of Ohio, Park was one of forty physicians who appeared in Utah during the Civil War. Most of them went on to the West Coast or returned to the East and Midwest at the end of the war. Park, however, cast his lot with the Mormons. Only thirty-six in 1869, he had had teaching experience while taking medical training, and proved to be a remarkable university president. The first class consisted of 223 students, 120 males and 103 females. Classes were taught in modern languages; classical languages and literature; mathematics; physical and biological sciences; ancient, medieval, and modern history; rhetoric; astronomy; and physical education.

Brigham participated in a number of the extracurricular activities, including attendance at the University Ball, with dancing continuing until three in the morning. Taking a supervisory interest, he frequently attended meetings of the Board of Regents. His counselor, Daniel H. Wells, served as chancellor. A minute of the Board of Regents meeting of March 29, 1871, says that Brigham supported a proposal to give less emphasis to "the dead languages"—Latin and Greek. He "thought the classics had been used by the learned to keep the unlearned in subjection and ignorance."[42] Among other things, Brigham sent Dr. Park on a mission to the eastern states and Europe with the stated purpose of investigating various educational institutions and systems.[43] Park and an associate visited Ireland, Scotland, England, Italy, France, Switzerland, and Germany.

One result of the tour was increased agitation for free schools. Brigham opposed the idea. While he sought to have his own children educated, instructed each of the bishops to see that a school was maintained in his ward, and often sermonized about the importance of education, he did not establish a system to see that it was adequately supported.

Some say they are not able to send their children to school. . . . I think I would rise in the morning, wash myself, take a little composition [tea], and try, if possible, to muster strength enough to send my children to school, and pay their tuition like a man. When you have done this, if you are still unable, apply to some of your neighbors to assist you. . . . I know such persons are weak and feeble; but the disease is in the brain and heart—not in the bones, flesh, and blood. Send your children to school.[44]

The responsibility of paying for the schooling, he was insisting, rested primarily on the parents. He objected to free schools—that is, tax-supported schools—because they could not be conducted on a religious basis.[45] When John Chislett, an English convert who had apostatized, began agitating for free, nondenominational schools in 1873, Brigham publicly rebuked him. Chislett replied with an open letter that must have cut to the quick: "I did not expect a man like you," he wrote Brigham, "who cannot write a correct sentence in his mother tongue, and hardly spell half-a-dozen consecutive words correctly, to approve the proposition."[46] By the time of Brigham's death in 1877, free school sentiment was widespread, and the legislature was making appropriations to local school districts.

I T was inevitable that Brigham would be challenged on his protective policies. It was probably also inevitable that one of his challengers would be one of his "pets"—William S. Godbe. A native of England, the thirty-six-year-old Godbe went to Utah in 1851, became an assistant to a leading merchant, Thomas Williams, and soon was a leading businessman in his own right. Having enjoyed a meaningful religious experience when he was converted to Mormonism, Godbe served as a counselor to the bishop of the Salt Lake Thirteenth Ward from 1865 to 1869 and as a city councilman; he had entered into a polygamous marriage. Associated with Brigham in several important ventures, Godbe was clearly a man of talent and influence.

Godbe had become acquainted with a number of British intellectuals in the 1860s, including the mercurial Edward W. Tullidge and the brilliant and imaginative E. L. T. Harrison.[47] In January 1868, they began publication of an independent literary periodical, *The Utah Magazine*, the first issue of which asserted, "For some years we have felt that a great encroachment of power was being made by the ruling priesthood of our Church, beyond that allowed by the spirit and genius of the Gospel. We have also perceived that a steady and constant decline was taking place in the manifestation of the spiritual gifts, as well as in the spirituality of our system as a whole, and that as a Church we were fast running into a state of most complete materialism." Then on a trip to the East in the summer, Godbe and Harrison confessed to each other additional doubts about Mormonism—the seeming expediency of some of the revelations, the doubtful authenticity of the Book of Mormon story, the absence of magnanimity in Brigham's character, and the lack of commercial sense in some of his policies. Despite their misgivings, each enjoyed respect and friendships in Utah, and was successful in his enterprise. In New York, in an anguish of faith, they resorted to prayer and were visited, they asserted, by "a band of spirits" that gave them answers to their many questions. For their edification and understanding they received "a constant stream of communication by means of audible voices from a number of most distinguished historical personages."[48] One of these, they declared, was the recently deceased apostle, Heber C. Kimball, whom both men had admired. They were told that much of Mormonism was true and should be preserved. What was false should be eliminated.

Upon conveying their "extraordinary experience" to their friends in Utah, Godbe and Harrison were joined by Tullidge, Eli B. Kelsey, William H. Shearman, T. B. H. Stenhouse, and Henry W. Lawrence. All but Kelsey were British converts, all were loyal, faithful, well-educated local officers of the church, and all were or had been merchants. To them the Great Basin Kingdom was (in Ronald Walker's phrase) "an anachronistic vehicle for Brigham Young's personal power."[49] *The Utah Magazine* began to reflect this "New Movement." Among other things, it agitated for greater freedom of thought. "There is," wrote Harrison, "one fatal error, which possesses the minds of some, it is this: that God Almighty intended the priesthood to do our thinking."[50] In October 1869, the magazine published an article on "The True Development of the Territory," which discussed the difficulties of the people of Utah and suggested that they ought to give more attention to mining.

Brigham was furious. At a meeting of the School of the Prophets, the names of seven sponsors of the magazine and sympathizers were called. When they did not respond, Brigham demanded that they be disfellowshipped. The next day Godbe, Harrison, and Stenhouse were visited by a committee composed of former British missionaries, Orson Pratt, Wilford Woodruff, and George Q. Cannon, who attempted reconciliation. But the effort failed. The committee found the three to be in "the dark" and Harrison especially with "a bitter spirit."[51]

On the following Saturday, the "rebels" appeared at the School of the Prophets. Prepared for thundering anathemas, they were called to repentance by Brigham with surprising restraint. He dismissed the charges against everyone but Harrison and Godbe and called on them to speak. After Godbe had frankly stated his position, Brigham followed him "with aggravating mimicry, turning everything into ridicule."[52] Harrison, however, was defiant and directly challenged Brigham. The result of the meeting was that Godbe and Harrison were notified that they would be tried for their membership before the High Council the following Monday.

The October 25 trial, which took place before the Salt Lake Stake Presidency and High Council, with the First Presidency and Quorum of the Twelve and a number of local bishops and others in attendance, brought out with remarkable clarity the basic tension in the church between those who contended for freedom of individual belief about policy and those who insisted upon unity and conformity. Considering the continuing attempts of federal officials to undermine the Mormon kingdom and the efforts of non-Mormon politicos in Utah to subvert Mormon control, Brigham wanted the Saints to show solidarity and union. As he saw it, Godbe and Harrison were trying through their magazine to cast doubt on the leadership, to sow discord, to foster disunity.[53]

The charge against the two men "for harboring the spirit of apostacy" was made by George Q. Cannon, the Liverpool-born, forty-two-year-old apostle who had served as Brigham's secretary, editor, and delegate to Congress. (He was known as "smooth-bore Cannon" in Washington circles.) After reading selections from "Steadying the Ark," "The Real Representative of the Most High," "The True Development of the Territory," and "Justifiable Obedience," editorial articles that had appeared in recent issues of *The Utah Magazine,* Cannon declared: "They [Godbe and Harrison] clearly manifest an intention to destroy as far as possible . . . the teachings and the influence of the First Presidency among the people."

George Goddard and John B. Maiben, teachers of the Salt Lake Thirteenth Ward who had visited Godbe and Harrison to determine their current worthiness, reported that they had asked how the defendants would respond if called upon "to go to some remote part of the territory to build it up." Godbe had replied, "That depends on the circumstances and the position of life I happen to be in at the time." Apostles Orson Pratt and Wilford Woodruff, close friends of Godbe and Harrison, had accompanied Goddard and Maiben. Pratt testified that Godbe and Harrison tended to "ignore in some measure the authority of or the right of the Presidency of this Church . . . to counsel and dictate in all matters, whether they be temporal or spiritual." When Godbe had pointed out to his visitors that he had followed Brigham's counsel in investing in the unsuccessful Utah Produce Company, which had planned to transport goods from the West Coast up the Colorado River and thence overland to Salt Lake City, Pratt had replied, "It is far better for us to lose our property and our wealth and have it all swept from us by obeying counsel than it is to disobey that counsel and retain our property. . . . This very loss of our property might be in the mind of God one means of our salvation." Being "opposed in their hearts to this Church guiding and dictating in all matters," Pratt said the dissidents "were bordering apostacy if not already entirely apostatized."

Godbe then responded eloquently about the right of an individual church member to disagree with the First Presidency on matters of policy. "I do claim in all solemnity and in sincerity that I have not apostatized. The truth is just as dear to me today as it ever was." They had started the magazine with the consent and approval of Brigham, he said; they had not opposed measures with a disrespectful spirit, "but in a spirit of temperance, moderation, and respect to men whom we love, and whose antecedents have been of such a character to inspire us with the purity of their intentions and their honesty as men."

Harrison said he believed in the priesthood control of policy but not in the infallibility of the priesthood. "I do not believe in according to them [the First Presidency] the right to dictate me into a course which I consider wrong, morally wrong." He also denied the right of Brigham and other general church authorities to expel a person from the Church if he does not see eye to eye with them upon matters of doctrine provided he state that difference. . . . This principle of compulsion is wrong. . . . It is my right to honestly canvas the teachings of those that are placed over me. . . . I believe in the right to discuss freely, provided I do it respectfully and moderately, any measure or principle that may be presented. I do not believe I have the right to be rabid in regard to my use of vindictive language, but provided I am temperate—provided I accord to others the same privilege I do myself, I believe that men should be guided entirely by their own light and intelligence. . . . I observe man's fallibility. I presume I see as little fallibility in Pres. Young as in any man, but I see some; I cannot see but there are points where he appears to miss it. . . . I do not believe in the principle of implicit obedience, unconditional obedience without the judgment being convinced. . . . If it is apostasy to differ with the President on some points, I am an apostate because I honestly differ with him. I do protest that I differ in a spirit of love and due regard for him. . . . I cannot see the wisdom of some of his measures. . . . I have differed with him on the mineral development of the Territory.

Harrison then bore his testimony that Mormonism was a true doctrine, that Joseph Smith was a true Prophet of God, that polygamy was a true principle, that the Great Basin was the gathering place appointed by God, and that Brigham Young was the legal successor of Joseph Smith. He disagreed, Harrison said, only on one point, "and that is in accepting the infallibility of the guidance of the Church without any exceptions."

Before Brigham made his own response to Godbe and Harrison, he asked George A. Smith to reply. Smith's statement, also eloquent, reflected the siege mentality of the Saints. They were fighting federal officials who were trying to force them to conform to national standards of political, economic, and social behavior. They also had to combat the hostile Gentiles in their midst. Now some hitherto loyal Saints were defiantly waging a campaign to force the "kingdom" to accommodate.

Now brethren, . . . we know that all the world are against us. We know that every court, sect, and denomination, and all political organizations are for our destruction, but we trust in God. He has led us through our President Joseph Smith and Brigham Young—through a thousand dangers seen and unseen. . . . And here rises up some men to unite with the world in getting up a division. The rule on which we ought to work is this: get together and discuss what we have to say, and not draw out or sneak out without hearing what is to be said about it. But the first thing we know we find them [Godbe and Harrison] publishing and insinuating to the world that the people here are oppressed and that their liberties are taken away. They will unite with all the enemies of Zion to bring down vengeance upon the heads of the Saints. . . . I protest against any man or any motive or spirit . . . that will tend to destroy it [Zion].

Smith reminded the group of the conflict in Kirtland when, except for the stubborn loyalty of Brigham and Heber Kimball, some elders who believed that Joseph Smith did not know how to manage temporal affairs would have brought about his ouster:

> Numbers of Elders, embracing the highest order of Priesthood, took the ground that they had a right to question his right to dictate the church in temporal things. They acknowledged that Joseph was a prophet, but they said he had gone into darkness and fallen. They would profess to be full in the faith, they would preach the Gospel and all that, but they would set aside some revelations that were not exactly right in their opinion. . . .
> The same tune is heard over again. "Oh, I have such confidence in Bro. Brigham! Such confidence in these brethren. Such confidence, kindness, and good feeling. I only want to cut their throats! . . . Their protest [magazine articles] is to say to the world and the church, "We are misled, we have no liberty, we are tied up, we have no freedom of speech. Send an army to protect us. Come here and sustain us."
> Latter-day Saints do not fellowship a man who draws the sword to destroy them; do not fellowship a man who invites all hell to come and cut our throats; do not fellowship a man who publishes lies concerning us and misrepresents us. . . . I think there is a studied scheme to divide this Church and break it up; and if there ever was a strong evidence of apostasy it is in that protest. . . .
> "We know more than everybody else; all the rest of you are fools. The Priesthood that has built up and guided this Church and gathered us and brought us here is blind, and we have the right to fight against the Priesthood. We have the right to publish as Elders of Israel against Zion. We have all these rights." This is what they will say. I say our rights are few. We have the right to do right, and we have no right as Elders in Israel to do wrong.

Finally, Brigham rose to speak. His remarks were calm, temperate, more sorrowful than vengeful, confident but not with the sarcastic tone he sometimes used when attacked.

He began with a story illustrating his belief that the disagreement had been magnified out of its true significance. The story dealt with a British king who took his son to the House of Lords to let him see how things went— how they legislated for the nation, how they dealt with great national affairs. When the son had sat and listened until he was tired, he asked the king: "Father, why did you bring me here?" "That you might learn how little wisdom it takes to govern a nation," was the king's reply. "I mention this," said Brigham, "to show you how little wisdom it takes to raise an excitement in the midst of wise men."

As to the existence of freedom to think and act in the church, Brigham's response was:

> Where is our liberty? In truth. Where is our freedom? In truth. In the truth of God. In truth no matter where it is found. Where is our strength? In truth. Where is our power and our wisdom? In truth. It is truth that we want, it is truth that

exalts us. It is truth that makes us free. It is truth that will bring us into the celestial kingdom.

And as for the question of trying the case of the dissenters:

> I should be perfectly willing to take this case and try it before the daughters of Israel, and not have one present over fifteen years old, and let them decide the matter.

Even the dissenters had argued that Mormonism was true.

Now, said Brigham, what would happen if every person goes his or her own way? "What confusion, what discord, what discontent, what hatred would soon creep into the bosom of individuals, one against the other?" What happens in a family if a child has the privilege of dictating? "I have as much power in this family as my father or mother." If the mother says to one, "You go and make the beds," and to another, "Wash up the dishes," the girls would disobey her orders and think they had as much right to dictate as she had. Brigham continued: "Are we the Church and Kingdom of God? The family of Heaven? Yes. . . . We have made no bargain to gather up to Zion to raise confusion."

He had a duty to lead, Brigham said, and he was trying to do so according to his best light. "It is my right and duty to do it—were it not, I should not say it. I have never sought but one thing in this kingdom, and that has been to get men and women to obey the Lord Jesus Christ in everything. I do not care what they say of me, if they will live so as to help build up his [the Lord's] kingdom."

As for his management of temporal affairs, Brigham was defensive:

> Brother William [Godbe] has mentioned time and time again, as have others, wherein I made failures in losing money. I would ask, "Who gave you your money? Where did you get it? How much did brother William own when he came here? How much did others who invested in those things own when they came here? Did they have anything? . . . They came to these valleys like most of us, naked and barefooted. As for myself, I owed for the teams that brought my family. Did we run to the gold mines to get capital to raise our grain? to get the timber from the mountains? to make our farms and build our houses? No. But this [Utah] Magazine says go to the gold mines or you cannot do these things. . . . Let those who want to go to the mines do so, and when they have been one or ten years, I . . . can buy every ten of those who go to the mines with one who stays at home. . . . What is the result when every man is for himself? Why the devil is for the whole of them.

As to the matter of thought control:

> Now the Priesthood will not do your thinking, but it will help you to think correctly. . . . There is no person that knows anything about the Priesthood that

calculates the Priesthood is going to do the thinking for him or any one. We work in harmony with our Savior. He works in harmony with his Father, and we cooperate with the Son for the salvation of ourselves and the human family. The Son has, according to the wisdom and the design of the Father, become the Savior or the heir of this earth . . . and He calls upon His brethren to be co-workers with Him.

As to the design of his economic policies:

> I wish to elevate the whole people, and I am looking forward to the time when we will put our hand into the one purse. I am teaching that doctrine. I urge it upon the people. If we ever build up Zion we will be one. . . . I expect to see the time when everything will be laid at the hands of the bishops and [each] will dispense it to [his] whole ward.

> We must have the Lord to rule over us. . . . God has devised [the Plan of Salvation] for the children of men to bring them into submission and strict obedience to what he has revealed. This prepares a person to become a God and a son of God. For a man to become a God and a son of God and to reign eternally in the heavens requires strict obedience. Will they have dominion? Yes. Crowns? Yes. . . . My liberty is to do right and serve my God and build up his Kingdom.

> I want to say to you that the spirit of the Lord was with me in bringing the people to these vallies. . . . I do not pretend to be infallible, but the priesthood that I have on me is infallible. . . . Any man that wants to dissent from us has a right to do so. If he is not disposed to go with us, he has a right to go some other way. But we have the same liberty to go the road the Lord wishes us. . . . I will leave it to the people to do as they have a mind to. I have the right to counsel them and they have the right to take my counsel or let it alone, just as they please.

The stake president expressed his belief that Godbe and Harrison should be "cut off" from the church "and be handed over to the buffetings of Satan until they repent." The decision was moved, seconded, and carried unanimously by the High Council. Brigham then took the extraordinary step of placing the decision before the whole assembly. All sustained the decision but six people. These six were, or became, "Godbeites" and continued to advocate their "liberal" policies in the months that followed.

T H E excommunications of Godbe and Harrison were not followed by a wholesale purge; indeed, some of the dissidents, having failed to become martyrs, found it necessary to force their own excommunications by letters of resignation.

Shortly after the trial, the group began regular preaching and organized the Church of Zion. Amasa M. Lyman, one of the apostles, himself called into question several times earlier for his unorthodox interpretation of the Atonement and for his confidence in spiritualism, was chosen president, and the group enjoyed some temporary success.

Believing the new faith to be "the thinnest of whitewash of anything I've ever been acquainted with," Brigham's policy was to "let the fire blaze away."[54] Within a few months, Brigham was writing his son, Brigham Heber, a missionary in Zurich, the following appraisal:

> The Godbe Planchette Church, of which you have doubtless heard, is not making the progress its founders and advocates anticipated, but it is picking up a class who have already apostatized and who, like a drowning man, are ready to catch even at a straw. Their doctrines are as antagonistic to God and his righteousness as hell is opposed to heaven. They ignore the efficacy of the atonement, and they practically repudiate celestial marriage on the plea that the principle may do in the heavens, but they are not pure enough for it on the earth.[55]

At no time did any more than a few score adults—certainly not more than two hundred—join the new church. By the time of Brigham's death the movement was essentially dead.[56]

Gentiles and free-thinking Mormons, however, organized the Liberal party to contest the Mormons politically, and *The Utah Magazine* was converted into the *Mormon Tribune*, which published anti-Brigham, anti-Mormon articles and editorials. Only the movement's children, the *Tribune* and the Liberal party, survived Brigham.

20 ✠

Responding to the Challenges of the 1870s

> I want you to be united. If we should build up and organize
> a community, we would have to do it on the principle of
> oneness, and it is one of the simplest things I know of. A city
> of one hundred thousand or a million people could be united
> into a perfect family, and they could work together as beau-
> tifully as the different parts of the carding machine work to-
> gether. Why, we could organize millions into a family under
> the order of Enoch.[1]

W H E N Brigham Young and his associates agreed to the passage
of a legislative act giving the women of Utah the right to vote, making them
the first females in the nation to vote in municipal and territorial elections, it
was more an afterthought than the result of careful deliberation.[2] The initial
stimulus was the threatened congressional passage of an anti-Mormon bill.

In the course of proposing legislation to promote civil and political rights
for the blacks just freed from slavery in the South, the Radical Republicans
in control of Congress took steps to reform the social structure of Utah as
well. In December 1867, Senator Aaron Cragin of New Hampshire offered a
bill that would have placed control of the Nauvoo Legion and the selection
of its officers under the federally appointed governor, forbidden officers of the
church to solemnize marriages, given authority to the federal marshal to select
all jurors, taxed church property in excess of $20,000, and eliminated trial by
jury in cases involving polygamy. Brigham was outraged. After reading the
bill in the newspaper he wrote to delegate William H. Hooper in Washington:

> He might have added to it that no Mormon shall be allowed to vote on any
> occasion whatever, nor hold office in Utah or in any Territory, or State of the
> Union.
> I have a proposition to make to Cragan, [Benjamin] Wade and all such men.

When my old [servant] has been dead one year, if they will wash their faces clean they may kiss his ———.
I hold all such men in the greatest contempt and fear not their wicked deeds.[3]

As Brigham anticipated, the bill did not pass.[4] But two years later, a bill was introduced by Congressman Shelby M. Cullom of Illinois that had a better chance of passage because it was less extreme. This measure proposed to place in the hands of the U.S. marshal and U.S. attorney responsibility for selecting jurors. Polygamy cases would be confined to the jurisdiction of federal courts, and plural wives would be deprived of immunity as witnesses in cases involving their husbands. The act also proposed abolishing Utah's "marked ballot" by which it was possible to determine how each person voted.[5]

The Cullom Bill, which passed the House and was accepted by the Senate Committee on Territories, had the women of Utah in "high dudgeon," as Brigham expressed it.[6] Five thousand of them held a massive "indignation meeting" in the Salt Lake Tabernacle. In setting the theme of the meeting, Eliza Snow stated:

> Our enemies pretend that in Utah woman is held in a state of vassalage—that she does not act from choice but by coercion—that we would even prefer life elsewhere, were it possible for us to make our escape. What nonsense! . . . Were we the stupid, degraded, heart-broken beings that we have been represented to be, silence might better become us; but, as women of God—women filling high and responsible positions—performing sacred duties—women who stand not as dictators, but as counselors to their husbands, and who, in purest, noblest sense of refined womanhood, being truly their helpmates—we not only speak because we have the right, but justice and humanity demand that we should.

Aside from manifesting their protest against the Cullom and Cragin bills, the women adopted the following resolution:

> That we acknowledge the institutions of the Church . . . as the only reliable safeguard of female virtue and innocence. . . . We are and shall be united with our brethren in sustaining them against each and every encroachment.[7]

It was in the aftermath of the meeting that Brigham and other Mormon leaders—both men and women—decided it would be helpful if the Utah legislature should pass an act granting women suffrage. The Wyoming legislature had approved a suffrage bill in December 1869, just a month earlier, so there was precedent. The *Deseret News*, with Brigham's consent, had supported the enfranchisement of women since the idea had been advanced in the East in 1868.

One scholar has suggested that the person who first planted the idea of granting female suffrage in Brigham's mind was Augusta Adams Cobb Young, his fifth wife.[8] One of the famous Adams family of Massachusetts, wife of

Henry Cobb and a friend of suffragist Lucy Stone, Augusta had heard Brigham preach when he was in Boston in 1843, converted to Mormonism, and with her two smallest children went to Nauvoo where she was sealed to Brigham on November 2, 1843.[9]

Whoever was the initiator, Brigham pushed the idea. He saw female suffrage as a means of demonstrating that the image of the ignorant and helpless Mormon woman was inaccurate. He also seems to have recognized that the enfranchisement of Mormon women would rally the eastern-based female suffrage organizations and congressmen favorable to women voting and that these lobbyists would counter the attempts to pass the Cullom Bill. After the matter was discussed in some detail with his inner council on February 9, the legislature passed the bill unanimously the next day. Under the influence of the effective lobbying of Mormon women leaders, the acting governor, S. A. Mann, signed it on February 12.[10]

Two days after the signing, municipal elections were held in Salt Lake City. Twenty-five women, the vanguard of thousands who voted in succeeding elections, exercised their new right. Seraph Young, Brigham's niece, was said to have been the first woman to cast her ballot, and Brigham's daughter Susa was the second.[11]

Almost immediately, as Brigham had hoped, the woman's suffrage movement, in the words of Beverly Beeton, "gave the Mormons a national stage upon which they could demonstrate that polygamous wives were intelligent beings capable of thinking for themselves and therefore willing participants in plural marriage, not the downtrodden slaves painted by lecture-bureau circuit riders."[12] Although the Utah act did not provide that women could hold political office, it was nevertheless a revolutionary step. They began serving on party central committees, attending party caucuses and precinct nominating meetings, participating on juries, and one became a practicing lawyer. Women were increasingly appointed to territorial boards, and when Utah achieved statehood and could elect to allow women nominees for office, there was a woman mayor, a woman state senator, and a woman delegate to a national political convention. But the immediate reaction to the new involvement was perhaps best illustrated in the following entry in the diary of Mary Jane Mount Tanner:

> I attended a meeting today for electing delegates to the County Convention. Political meetings are something new to me. There were several ladies present, and we said "aye" sometimes by way of exercising our rights, and went home feeling the importance of our positions.[13]

S U F F R A G E established Mormon credibility with women's rights leaders. It also propelled Mormon women into the national suffrage movement. One of Brigham's daughters, Susa, became an officer of the National Women Suffrage Association and an officer of the International Congress of Women. Eliza

Snow had helped to foster the new image of Mormon women. "No woman in Zion," she said, "needs to mourn because her sphere is too narrow." As far as Brigham was concerned, women were free to pursue activities "suited to their sex." And his view of what was suited to their sex included fields as diverse as banking, medicine, journalism, education, and business.[14]

In 1872 Brigham's grandniece, Louisa Lula Greene (granddaughter of Brigham's sister Rhoda and John P. Greene), who had attended the University of Deseret during the year 1868–69, was approached by a Salt Lake City publisher about putting out a magazine by and for women.[15] Only twenty, Lula (as she was usually called) wrote to her aunt Eliza Snow asking her advice. Lula wondered whether she should instead be praying for the right man to come along so she could marry and have children. Eliza checked with Brigham to be sure there was no objection from him. Brigham not only relayed his sanction, but in Lula's words, "said he would gladly appoint me the mission and bless me in it." Eliza advised that it was more important to teach mothers how to bring up children properly than simply to have children which may or may not be brought up properly. True, you should prepare yourself to become a mother, she wrote. But "is it not as important that those already born should be cultivated and prepared for use in the Kingdom of God as that others should be born?" So Lula became founding editor of *The Woman's Exponent*, a biweekly published "for the benefit, education, and development of thought of all the sisters in the Church." Each of the issues contained poetry, fiction, editorials, sermons by church officials and Relief Society leaders, and news briefs from home and abroad. (Except for a short-lived magazine published by Abigail Scott Duniway in Oregon, it was the first magazine by and for women west of the Mississippi.) The magazine, edited by Emmeline B. Wells after the first seven years with Lula as editor, continued until 1914, when it became the official organ of the women's Relief Society and the name was changed to *Relief Society Magazine*.

Although it was an advocate of Mormonism, *The Woman's Exponent* was an independent journal and was read with respect by the women of Europe and America who wished to know the opinions and attitudes of Latter-day Saint women. The motto carried on the masthead for many years was: "The Rights of the Women of Zion, and the Rights of the Women of all Nations." While independent, however, it was supported primarily by the Retrenchment Associations and by the members of the Relief Societies.

A S mentioned earlier, Brigham lacked confidence in Gentile male physicians. In the first place, they were "a set of ignoramuses" who were "too lazy to delve and hoe like others [and] made people ill in order to get a living by doctoring them." In the second place, the Saints should rely on home care and faith healing. "When you are sick," he said, "call for the Elders, who will pray for you, anointing with oil and the laying on of hands; and nurse each other with herbs, and mild food, and if you do these things, in faith, and quit taking . . . poisonous medicines, which God never ordained for the use of men, you shall be blessed."[16] Childbirth, he thought, should be taken care of by midwives.

Often, however, women did not have the skills to perform the medical tasks brought to them. Martha Coray wrote Brigham that her daughter had died, apparently in childbirth, and she wrote pleading that "a class of students, women suited in mind and temper to the calling, be established in every settlement" to learn better medical practice. Shortly after the receipt of this letter—and perhaps after several other such suggestions—Brigham called his nephew Seymour Young and several women to go to the medical schools in the East to qualify as physicians.

So in December 1873, Romania B. Pratt, wife of Parley Pratt, Jr., departed for New York to study medicine. Leaving her five children, one a small baby, in the care of her mother, she studied for one year, after which she returned to Utah. Without money to complete her training, she turned to Brigham who, in turn, asked Eliza Snow and the Relief Society to assist. In minutes of Relief Societies throughout the territory are notations of contributions "for the sister that is studying medicine." Three years later, Dr. Romania Pratt returned home to establish a practice and to set up schools of medicine, midwifery, and nursing.

In addition to encouraging his nephew to pursue medicine, Brigham began sending some of his sons east to study engineering, architecture, and other fields. Willard, Brigham's eighth living son, attended the United States Military Academy at West Point, New York, 1871–75, and graduated fourth in his class with a commission in the Corps of Engineers. Alfales (pronounced Affluss) studied at the University of Michigan, 1875–77, finishing with a degree in law. Joseph Don Carlos went to Rensselaer Polytechnic Institute at Troy, New York, 1875–79, graduating in engineering and architecture. And Feramorz Little Young studied at the United States Naval Academy at Annapolis, 1874–76, and at Rensselaer, 1877–79, where he graduated with honors in engineering but died shortly thereafter.[17]

Notwithstanding these and other "scholar missionaries," Brigham preferred to have adequate schools of higher learning in Utah. The coming of the railroad had brought Episcopalians, Presbyterians, Methodists, Baptists, and Congregationalists, and many of them, supported by eastern missionary societies of their own faith, had established denominational schools. Although these mission schools did not succeed in converting LDS children, as they had been intended to do, they did lead to the upgrading of Mormon schools. Indeed, they were such an improvement over existing Mormon schools that some Mormon bishops were tempted to employ urbane Gentile teachers full-time in the ward schools. This unnerved Brigham:

What better is the man that can dress himself nicely and labor in a schoolhouse six hours a day, than the man who works ten or twelve hours a day hewing rock?

Is he any better? No, he is not. Are you going to pay him for his good looks? That is what some of our bishops want to do. If they can get a man, no matter what his moral qualities may be, whose shirt front is well starched and ironed, they will say—"Bless me, you are a delightful little man! What a smooth shirt you have got, and you have a ring on your finger. You are going to teach our school for us." And along comes a stalwart man, axe in hand, going to chop wood, and, if he asks, "Do you want a teacher?" though he may know five times more than the dandy, he is told, "No, no we have one engaged." I want to cuff you bishops back and forth until you get your brains turned right side up.[18]

But an adequate response to the spread of Gentile schools obviously involved more than jawboning. In 1875 Brigham donated land for the establishment of the Brigham Young Academy in Provo; and in 1877 he provided land near Logan for Brigham Young College, later transferred to Utah State University. He also made plans for the founding of a Brigham Young Academy in Salt Lake City but was unable to complete the legal transactions before his death. The Brigham Young estate and the church later joined in establishing the LDS College there; it operated until 1894 when it became part of the University of Utah.

Brigham took considerable interest in these schools. He said he intended Brigham Young College at Logan to be a "free educational institution to accommodate from 500 to 1000 young people," who can acquire "a liberal and scientific education as complete as can be found in any part of the world." Under his arrangements, each student, in addition to acquiring a liberal education, must learn "a trade, such as blacksmithing, carpentry, wheelwright, masonry, etc., and also scientific farming and stock raising." Each young woman, and he hoped there would be as many women students as men, would learn "to spin, weave, cut, sew, dairying, poultry raising, flower gardening, etc." Ideally, he wanted every student to spend one-third of the time on the farm, garden, or in shops. Theology and church doctrine would also be taught. Upon graduation students would be equipped free with a set of tools for a particular trade, a team and wagon, farming implements or household devices, so that they would begin to produce immediately. His ideas may have been influenced by Oberlin College, Ohio, not far from Kirtland, a coeducational institution where the students cleared land, built buildings, raised crops, sold products, and were to a large extent self-supporting under a policy of mutual cooperation, high standards, and interest in self-improvement.

The first principal of Brigham Young College was Ida Ione Cook, who had taught in Brigham's school in Salt Lake City and at the University of Deseret. Eventually, the college became a liberal arts institution until it closed in 1925, its resources transferred to Utah State Agricultural College and Logan High School. There were classes in Mormon scripture, church history, Old and New Testament as well as in the liberal arts, sciences, and trades.[19]

In order to assure that the academies would cater to women as well as men, Brigham provided that each school have on its board of trustees at least one woman. Women were also assigned other tasks. Earlier mention was made of the cocooneries managed by the women to produce silk. In 1875 the women formed the Utah Silk Association with Zina Diantha Huntington Young as president. A counselor to Eliza Snow in the presidency of the Relief Society, Zina traveled throughout the various settlements providing leadership to the Relief Societies, always including a special message encouraging and instructing the women in the tending of worms—how and how much and when to feed them, and the methods of retrieving the silk from the cocoons. It was an exciting day for the women of Ogden when they presented to Eliza Snow the first dress made entirely of Utah silk.

Late in the fall of 1875, Eliza began suggesting to the women that they should prepare home manufactures for display in the Women's Pavilion of the Centennial celebrations in Philadelphia. As items accumulated, the legislature, finding territorial finances "more embarrassed than for many years past," refused to provide the $3,000 necessary to ship the women's display and arrange for its care. So, at Brigham's suggestion, the women exhibited goods at the Utah territorial fair and then turned the exhibition into a commercial venture and sold on commission the items they were displaying. The women continued to manufacture their quilts, silk lace, fichus, wax flowers, crochet work, mottoes, and bedspreads, this time for sale on commission.

Brigham gave women an assignment in agriculture; they were to store and save wheat. He turned to Emmeline Wells, who related the incidents surrounding this assignment as follows:

> Just after October conference, in 1876, President Young sent for me to come to his office and instructed me to write an editorial urging the sisters to begin laying up grain against a day of need. . . . President Young said: "I have called upon and urged the brethren to lay up grain against a day of want, and they do not follow my advice; they excuse themselves by saying their wives and daughters want the proceeds of the grain to buy hats and bonnets," etc. In fact, he gave me quite a dissertation on the excuses made by the brethren, and then explained that if the sisters were told to save grain they would not sell it.[20]

The women began the purchase of wheat, organized gleaning parties to reap some of the "wasted harvest"; cajoled husbands and bishops into building granaries for the storage of their wheat; and by the time of Brigham's death, less than a year later, they reported that more than ten thousand bushels had been stored and about a dozen granaries built.

Brigham knew the power of women leaders to get things done and depended heavily on them to help in all his reforms. He said:

> I may preach to the female portion of this community until I am as old as Methusaleh [without avail]; but when they, the sisters themselves, take hold to

reform they will wield an influence that will be successful, and will save many thousands of dollars yearly to the community. It is utterly vain for me to try to exert such an influence.[21]

T H E success of the Young Ladies' Retrenchment Association was so gratifying to Brigham that he decided the young men needed something similar, something in addition to their priesthood responsibilities. Thus, in the summer of 1875, he called Junius F. Wells, the son of his counselor Daniel H. Wells and Hannah Free, to organize societies for mutual improvement. According to the twenty-one-year-old Wells, the president instructed him as follows:

> We want to have our young men enrolled and organized throughout the Church, so that we shall know who and where they are, so that we can put our hands upon them at any time for any service that may be required. We want them to hold meetings where they will stand up and speak—get into the habit of speaking—and of bearing testimony. These meetings are to be for our young men . . . for their mutual improvement. There is your name: The Young Men's Mutual Improvement Soci—Association."[22]

Young Wells called a public meeting in the Thirteenth Ward meetinghouse. Henry A. Woolley, son of the Thirteenth Ward bishop, was chosen president. One of his counselors was B. Morris Young, son of Brigham; the other was Heber J. Grant, son of Jedediah and future president of the church. Junius then organized other associations in the wards in Salt Lake City, then moving on to wards north and south of the central city. Perhaps as many as one hundred different organizations were formed within the next few months. Ultimately, general officers were appointed, with an advisory board, to supervise all the ward and stake Mutual Improvement Associations. The name, easily shortened to MIA, seemed so popular that the Young Ladies adopted it, calling themselves, after 1878, the Young Ladies' Mutual Improvement Association, later the Young Women's MIA.

These groups usually met weekly and conducted programs that included prayer, group singing, lectures, debates, parliamentary procedure, the production of plays, the reading of poetry, and musical performances. Brigham's teenage children were among the strong supporters of these Young Men and Young Women associations.

One night the Thirteenth Ward MIA was having a dance in the ward assembly hall. According to Heber Grant, who was the twenty-year-old chairman of the affair, the hall was packed; shortly, Brigham himself entered and slapped ten dollars down on the table. (Admission was $1.50.) "Is that enough to pay for my ticket?" he asked. Heber said, "Plenty!" "I do not know whether or not he expected any change, but he did not get any," said Heber. The bishop had given them permission to have only three round dances, since church leaders, including Brigham, thought round dances (waltzes) were more evil than square dances. While the president was there, the three round dances were used up, so Heber instructed the band leader to play a fourth and went to sit by Brigham to see his reaction.

> President Young said: "They are waltzing." I said, "No, they are not waltzing; when they waltz they waltz all around the room; this is a quadrille: He [President Young] turned to me and laughed and said, "Oh, you boys, you boys."[23]

T H E S E moments, light and happy ones for Brigham, were marred by three deaths in successive months during the summer of 1875. Emmeline Free Young, the mother of ten of Brigham's children and said to have been his "favorite" until he met Amelia Folsom, died in July at age forty-nine; Joseph Angell Young, the oldest child of Mary Ann, partner with Brigham in building the transcontinental railroad, and president of Sevier Stake, died in August at age forty-one; and on September 1, Brigham's first counselor and close friend for forty-two years, George A. Smith, died at his Salt Lake City home at age fifty-eight. Brigham's long and happy association with George A., and his sense of loss in the death of this loyal, articulate, and jolly counselor, caused him to weep openly during the funeral. For many Saints, it was the first time they had seen Brigham cry.

A L T H O U G H the protective movement did much to soften the impact of the "railroad invasion," it did not prevent the clash of values. Those opposed to the Mormons and their institutions continued their hostile activities. Ulysses S. Grant's vice-president was Schuyler Colfax, whose negative opinion of the Mormons had been strengthened by his visit to Utah while Speaker of the House. Grant and Colfax stepped up the drive against the Mormons, and in 1870 appointed as chief justice of the territorial supreme court James B. McKean, earlier identified with the Republican party in New York when it began its campaign against the "twin relics of barbarism," slavery and polygamy. The first relic having been eliminated, Grant sent McKean to Utah to root out the second.

McKean accepted his assignment with a sense of mission fully equal to that of the Mormons. Said the chief justice:

> . . . the mission which God has called me to perform in Utah, is as much above the duties of other courts and judges as the heavens are above the earth, and whenever or wherever I may find the Local or Federal laws obstructing or interfering therewith, by God's blessings I shall trample them under my feet.[24]

McKean violated judicial procedures established by the territorial legislature, denied criminal jurisdiction to the Mormon probate courts, and refused to grant citizenship to aliens who were involved in plural marriages or who believed them to be acceptable.

McKean's principal target was Brigham Young. On October 2, 1871, Brigham, now seventy, was arrested on a charge of "lascivious cohabitation." Apostle George Q. Cannon, counselor Daniel H. Wells, and one of the Godbeites, Henry W. Lawrence, were also arrested, although the chief object of the prosecution was Brigham. He was "dragged into court" on October 9. Judge McKean was exultant. His prepared statement was widely published:

> It is therefore proper to say that while the case at bar is called *The People versus Brigham Young*, its other and real title is *Federal Authority versus Polygamic Theocracy*. The government of the United States, founded upon a written Constitution, finds within its jurisdiction another government—claiming to come from God—*imperium in imperio*—whose policy and practice, in grave particulars, are at variance with its own. The one government arrests the other in the person of its chief, and arraigns it at his bar. A system is on trial in the person of Brigham Young. Let all concerned keep this fact steadily in view; and let that government rule without a rival which shall prove to be in the right.[25]

Brigham could be vitriolic and caustic when he felt the occasion demanded it, but this time he placed his opponents at a disadvantage by sitting respectfully and quietly in front of the judge for almost an hour. As Nels Anderson commented, "This time the lion did not roar."[26]

The not unpredictable result was that many Salt Lake Gentiles, including at least two prominent lawyers, came to Brigham's defense. As he left the courtroom, "feeble and tottering from his recent sickness," many felt respect and sympathy for the "old man."[27] One who volunteered to serve as his attorney was Major Charles H. Hemstead, former editor of the anti-Mormon *Union Vedette*. Though he had always opposed Mormon domination, he was, in this instance, even more opposed to the arbitrary power politics of the emerging "Gentile Ring"—a group of perhaps a dozen federal appointees and associates who opposed Mormonism so fanatically that they were willing to use questionable means to counter the influence of Mormon leaders.

Because of his poor health, Brigham asked the court's permission to make his usual winter visit to St. George. McKean set the trial for the following March. Brigham had started for St. George on October 24, but took his usual time, visiting the various settlements en route. He had no sooner reached his Dixie retreat than word came by telegraph that McKean had changed his mind and decided to schedule the trial for December 4. It would have been impossible for Brigham to get back in time, a fact the judge and the prosecuting attorney, Robert N. Baskin, must have known; if the trial did begin on that date, the court could then brand Brigham a fugitive from justice.

The judge then set another date, January 2, 1872; when the court convened, Brigham was there: he had made the trip from St. George through deep snow and severe weather. The prosecutor asked that bail be set at the impossible figure of $500,000. Brigham's old enemy, Colonel Patrick Connor, offered to share the bail. McKean finally decided to hold Brigham in custody, although he was permitted to remain in his home under guard by the U.S. marshal. He was required to pay the guard $10 per day; the guard was there for 120 days.

Brigham was never brought to trial, for on April 15 some of McKean's judicial errors caught up with him. In a case taken to the U.S. Supreme Court, it was ruled that McKean had permitted the marshal to draw juries illegally. The court quashed all other pending indictments, including the charges against Brigham.[28]

But Brigham's set-to with McKean was not over. Ann Eliza Webb Young, urged on by Baskin and other members of the Gentile Ring, decided to sue for divorce and separate maintenance. Asking for $1,000 per month pending a hearing, $6,000 lawyer's fee, a payment of $14,000 when the divorce was granted, and a final award of $200,000, she estimated Brigham's income at $40,000 per month.

When the case came before him in February 1875, Judge McKean ordered Brigham to pay Ann Eliza $500 per month and $3,000 to defray the cost of the trial. But Brigham's lawyers, knowing they could never persuade the court on the matter of his income, adopted a technical defense. They alleged that when the so-called "marriage" had taken place, Ann Eliza, unbeknownst to Brigham, was the undivorced wife of another man and that she knew Brigham had a legal wife living.

Brigham refused to pay the bill as the judge ordered, for which McKean held him in contempt of court. He was fined $25 and sentenced to a day in prison. March 11, 1875, the day of the sentence, was cold and stormy, but the seventy-three-year-old Brigham was taken to the penitentiary for twenty-four hours.[29]

A few days later McKean was removed by the Grant administration and replaced by Judge David Lowe of Kansas. When Lowe heard Brigham's case on April 24, he ruled that there could be no legal alimony claim because there was no evidence of legal marriage. But a fellow judge, Jacob Boreman, reversed Lowe and ordered that Young be imprisoned until the debt was paid. Once more, he was permitted to occupy his home in the custody of the marshal. Brigham did not yield, so the guard stayed at his expense until November 12, when Alexander White, the new chief justice, reviewed the case and released him from custody. White's appointment was not confirmed by the Senate, so he was replaced by Michael Shaeffer, who suggested a compromise; Brigham paid $3,600, a fifth of the alimony then due. The case was finally dismissed in April 1877, just a few months before Brigham's death.[30]

During the same year the Ann Eliza case first came up for trial, in October 1875, President Grant visited Salt Lake City and Brigham arranged a meeting with him. As Brigham was introduced, he removed his hat, as did the president, and said, "President Grant, this is the first time I have ever seen a president of my country." Grant nodded and introduced Brigham to Mrs. Grant, and they spent a half-hour in pleasant conversation.

Grant's arrival was on Sunday, and as he was carried up South Temple Street from the depot to Temple Square, several thousand Sunday School children were on each side of the street to give the presidential party a hearty greeting. The president inquired of his escort, Governor George W. Emery, whose children they were. Emery replied, "Mormon children." "For several moments the president was silent," wrote Edward Tullidge, "then he murmured, in a tone of self-reproach, 'I have been deceived.' " Tullidge also wrote that Mrs. Grant attended an organ recital in the tabernacle and was much moved by what she saw and heard. She is reported to have told ex-delegate Hooper, "Oh, I wish I could do something for these good Mormon people."[31]

O N E person who had rendered important service for Brigham in the early 1870s was apostle John Taylor. Not one of Brigham's close friends and advisers, Taylor, an Englishman who was perhaps a little envious of Brigham's power, had been a close associate of Joseph Smith and was, indeed, with the Prophet when he was murdered. He had been editor of the Nauvoo *Times and Seasons* and co-leader of the large company of Saints that went to the Salt Lake Valley in the fall of 1847. He was assigned to open up the French and German missions in 1849 and while there published *The Government of God* (Liverpool, 1852), an important study that has continued to be a basic doctrinal reference work of Mormonism.

Upon his return to the Salt Lake Valley in 1852, Taylor was elected a member of the legislative council, but resigned in 1855 to preside over the Eastern States mission and publish a church periodical, *The Mormon*. He returned to Utah in 1857 and was active and fearless in defending the church and denouncing the preachers and politicians who were mounting anti-Mormon crusades. He was once more elected to the legislature, became speaker of the House, probate judge in Utah County, and sometime territorial superintendent of education. Tall, kingly, a magnetic figure with prematurely gray hair, Taylor was an eloquent speaker and skillful writer.[32]

Brigham made particular use of Taylor's talents. When the Cullom Bill was being debated in 1869, Vice-President Schuyler Colfax went to Utah on a second visit with the intended purpose of giving support to the Godbeites and trying to persuade traditional Mormon leaders to make concessions to public opinion. There is some evidence that he sought Godbeite support for a move to send federal troops to Utah. "General Grant, who has crushed the Confederacy, can now settle the Mormon question once and for all with the sword." Apparently, the Godbeites talked him out of this. "If the government interferes and sends troops," they insisted, "you will drive the thousands back into the arms of Brigham Young who are ready to rebel against the one-man power."[33]

On October 5, 1869, Colfax delivered a major address on the portico of the Townsend House in Salt Lake City, in which he declared:

I have no strictures to utter as to your [the Mormons'] creed on any really religious question. Our land is a land of civil and religious liberty, and the faith of every man is a matter between himself and God alone. You have as much right to worship the Creator through a President and twelve apostles of your church organization, as I have through the ministers and elders and creed of mine. . . . But our country is governed by law, and no assumed revelation justifies any one in trampling on the law.[34]

On a church proselyting mission in Boston at the time the talk was published, Taylor immediately wrote a detailed reply that was published in the New York *Tribune* as well as in the Salt Lake *Deseret News*. His religious faith, agreed Taylor, "is a matter between God and myself alone." But plural marriage "emanated from God and cannot be legislated away. It is part of the 'Everlasting Covenant' which God has given to man. . . . Take this [celestial marriage] from us and you rob us of our hopes and associations in the resurrection of the just." Taylor continued:

Loyola did not invent and put into use the faggot, the flame, the sword, the thumbscrews, the rack and gibbet to persecute anybody; it was to purify the Church of heretics, as others would purify Utah. "Ours," says Mr. Colfax, "is a land of civil and religious liberty, and the faith of every man is a matter between himself and God alone,"—providing God don't shock our moral ideas by introducing something we don't believe in. If He does, let Him look out.[35]

In short, wrote Taylor, eastern society should clean up its own house before coming to purify the Mormons. Prostitution, infanticide, divorce, crime, drunkenness were all worthy objects of the vice-president's attention.

When he returned to Utah, Taylor was the lion of the valley. Never had the Mormon case been so masterfully presented. The national publicity given Taylor's reply stung Colfax to make a rejoinder, which he did in a letter so effective that everyone supposed, and historians generally agree, that the reply was written by one of the Godbeites, possibly Edward Tullidge. Taylor then responded with a series of five letters to the New York *Herald* that were then reproduced by the *Deseret News* and distributed worldwide. They formed an eloquent statement of the Mormon side of the conflict with the federal government. They detailed the weaknesses and abuses of Utah's federal appointees—"petty lords of misrule"—and they reasserted Mormon rights in a way that many readers in the nation could understand, if not approve. "Taking it all in all, this is doubtless the most important discussion in the history of the Church," wrote Mormon historian B. H. Roberts.

The great reputation of Mr. Colfax as a speaker and writer; the fact that he had for many years been a member of Congress and accustomed to debate, together with the high station he occupied at the time of the discussion, gave it a national importance. It occurred, too, at a critical time in the history of the Church. The Republican party had pledged itself to the accomplishment of two objects: the suppression of slavery and polygamy. Slavery it had abolished; and it was now expected that polygamy would receive its attention. There was also, just then, an effort being made by prominent and wealthy members of the Church, to destroy the influence of President Brigham Young, or, if that failed, to weaken it by dividing the Church into parties.[36]

In the years that followed, during Brigham's struggles with Judge McKean and other federal officeholders, Taylor's pen continued to be active in challenging Utah's "carpetbag" judges, governor, and the so-called Gentile Ring. His articles were cogent, elegant, and forceful, yet marked throughout by a tone of fairness and candor.

With this as background, Brigham—in a meeting of the Twelve held in Sanpete County in June 1875—clarified for the church Taylor's position as his rightful successor. Of the original apostles, only Brigham, Orson Hyde, and Orson Pratt survived. But, as we have seen, in 1839 Orson Hyde had left his position on the Twelve because of differences with Joseph Smith. Hyde later returned to the Twelve and, with no objection, took his former position. When Brigham was elected president of the church and chose Heber Kimball and Willard Richards as his counselors, Hyde therefore became president of the Twelve and was sustained in that position by the general conferences of Saints from 1848 to 1875. Orson Pratt also had apostatized for a brief period in 1842–43 and had later resumed his former place with the Twelve behind Hyde.

When Hyde and Pratt left the church, Brigham now contended, they lost their seniority and Taylor and Wilford Woodruff automatically moved into their places. So, under correct procedure, Taylor was the senior apostle, Woodruff next, with Hyde and Pratt next in line. This clarification was ratified by members of the Twelve and subsequently by the general conference in Salt Lake City in October. In announcing the decision to the Saints, Brigham turned toward Taylor and declared: "Here is the man whose right it is to preside over the council in my absence, he being the senior Apostle." It was now official that Taylor would be in charge in the event of Brigham's death. It would be a different kind of leadership than Brigham's, but it would be one that Brigham had arranged.[37]

T O T A L economic unity had been the goal of Brigham's policy since he had assumed control of the church in 1844; indeed, he had viewed God's people as an organized, unified community from the time of his baptism in 1832. He reminded his followers of this vision in the 1870s. After he accepted the Gospel, he said, he felt that "we shall be one."

> I felt that I should no longer have need to keep a day book and ledger in which to keep my accounts, for we were about to consolidate and become one, that

every man and every woman would assist by actually laboring with their hands in planting, building up and beautifying this earth to make it like the Garden of Eden.[38]

This vision of "becoming one" never left him, and he felt he could not face Joseph Smith in the next life unless he had made every effort to establish a system in which the Saints had "become one." The general success of the cooperative movement in the territory had persuaded him that the Saints were now ready to live an even higher law of economic oneness, the United Order of Enoch, named after an Old Testament personality named Enoch who established such a perfect society that the whole city he led was "translated"— i.e., taken up into heaven.[39] "The time will come," said Brigham in commenting on the cooperative movement, "when this cooperative system which we have now partially adopted in merchandizing, will be carried out by the whole people, and it will be said: 'Here are the Saints.' The time will come when we can give all into the storehouse of the Lord and have our inheritances [farms, shops, etc.] given out by those who will be appointed; and when we have had sufficient for the support of our families, the [surplus] supplies will be given into the storehouse of the Lord. Will there be any rich and poor then? No."[40]

The cooperative movement was a step toward the ultimate goal of developing a completely self-contained Latter-day Saint community, with emphasis on local production of every needful thing, without financial or other aid from outside the realm of the church. If cooperation was practical in each separate field of economic activity, how much better a cooperative of cooperatives that would organize all fields of economic activity under one directing head. This is what Brigham decided to implement in the winter of 1873–74 among the people of St. George and other southern Utah communities.

The president had been particularly impressed with the cooperative system of the northern Utah community named after him, Brigham City.[41] As early as 1864 Lorenzo Snow, an apostle, had established there a mercantile cooperative in which a number of people took shares. As profits were made, the people received dividends in goods rather than in money. Cash resources were husbanded, others were encouraged to buy capital stock (the price of which was only five dollars a share), and within four years the cooperative decided to establish a tannery. They produced their own boots and shoes and harness, using hides from their own livestock. The next year they began erecting a woolen mill to produce textiles. They continued to follow the policy of paying workers with locally produced goods and declaring dividends only in their own merchandise. By 1873, more than fifteen branches or departments had been established covering most sectors of industry and agriculture. Almost every conceivable good and service from brooms to hats was produced in one of these fifteen departments. They established a colony at Mantua to raise flax and one in southern Utah to raise cotton. Production jumped impressively.

Brigham City was regarded as one of the most prosperous and progressive settlements in Utah. For the few things its citizens had to order from Salt Lake City, they traded some of their "valley tan" leather and some of their famous home-produced cheese.

When the depression of 1873 hit Utah, many communities experienced unemployment, low prices, and poverty—but not Brigham City, which experienced its greatest year of expansion in 1873. And through the efforts of Lorenzo Snow and others, the Brigham City Cooperative Commonwealth was widely publicized. Newspaper reporters wrote how Brigham City people built homes for the poor and widows, set up a department to provide labor for tramps and benefit from feeding them, and planned to locate their shops and factories on a twelve-acre square around the center of town and run streetcars from the square to various parts of the town and the railroad station. Brigham City came to the attention of English social reformers, one of whom, Brontier O'Brien, said the Mormons had "created a soul under the rib of death."[42] Edward Bellamy spent a week in Brigham City observing the operation of the cooperative while doing research for *Looking Backward*.[43]

Meanwhile, other communities were undertaking similar arrangements. Once the federal government approved land titles in Utah, Brigham again began to consult lawyers on how the Law of Consecration and Stewardship could be introduced without having the property deeded over to the church as under the original plan. The Order of Enoch should be established, he decided, according to the Brigham City plan, that is, it should be done on a city-wide basis. Cooperatives must be instituted. People should get their pay in what they produce. Everything should be organized. A fund must be accumulated to purchase machinery and supplies from the East. All residents should be economical and live as one big family.

In one of his talks Brigham expressed his ideal of how a big family conducted after the Order of Enoch might live:

> I will tell you how I would arrange for a little family, say about a thousand persons. I would build houses expressly for their convenience in cooking, washing and every department of their domestic arrangements. Instead of having every woman getting up in the morning fussing around a cookstove or over the fire, cooking a little food for two or three or half a dozen persons, . . . she would have nothing to do but to go to her work.
>
> Let me have . . . a hall in which I can seat five hundred persons to eat; and . . . cooking room attached to this hall; and there is a person at the further end of the table and he should telegraph that he wanted a warm beefsteak; and this is conveyed to him by a little railway, perhaps under the table. . . . "What do you want to take with it?" "A cup of tea, a cup of coffee, a cup of milk, piece of toast," or something or other . . . it is conveyed to them and they take it. . . . And when they have all eaten, the dishes are piled together, slipped under the table, and run back to the ones who wash them. We could have a few Chinamen to do that if we did not want to do it ourselves.

This system would greatly economize on the labor of women. After prayers and breakfast,

> each one go to his work. Here are the herdsmen—here are those who look after the sheep—here are those who make the butter and the cheese, all at their work by themselves. Some for the kanyon, perhaps, or for the plow or harvest, no difference what, each and every class is organized, and all labor and perform their part.

Brigham said he would not have cows, pigpens, or outhouses in the city. There would be little railways to convey feed to the pigs, cows, and horses. He would build an ideal city:

> Gravel our streets, pave our walks, water them, keep them clean and nicely swept, and everything neat, nice and sweet. . . . There would be a variety of houses. . . . Our houses built high, sleep upstairs, have large lodging rooms, keep everybody in fresh air, pure and healthy. Work through the day, and when it comes evening . . . repair to our room, and have our historians, and our different teachers to teach classes of old and young, to read the Scriptures to them; to teach them history, arithmetic, reading, writing and painting; and have the best teachers that can be got to teach our day schools. . . . The youth would have a good education, they would receive all the learning that could be given to mortal beings. . . .

Brigham went on to say that a well-organized society would not have nearly as much waste as present societies. All members would be tending to their own specialty; they would have "the most improved machinery" for all their work; and they would take advantage of every device for providing comfort and convenience:

> A society like this would never have to buy anything; they would make and raise all they would eat, drink and wear, and always have something to sell and bring money, to help to increase their comfort and independence. . . . Do you think we shall want any lawyers in our society? No, I think not. . . . Would you want doctors? Yes, to set bones.[44]

W H E N Brigham went to southern Utah during the winter of 1873–74, he decided to introduce his new communitarian system in St. George.[45] After a series of talks and conferences, in which local members indicated their enthusiasm for the project, he organized the first cooperative community at St. George in February 1874. It was called "The United Order of the City of St. George," and after its pattern Mormons got the name "United Order." It followed the Brigham City pattern, with two differences: 1) To install the system, every person was asked to contribute his economic property to the United Order—not all his property, but his productive property—in return for which he would receive capital stock. The order would thus be provided with the enterprises and the capital with which to institute the system immediately.[46] 2) There was to be spiritual as well as temporal union, so a long list of rules was drawn up according to which each person should live. There was to be no lying, backbiting, or quarreling. All were to live like good Christians. They were to pray daily, not use liquor or tobacco, and obey their leaders. To emphasize the spiritual aspect, each person was rebaptized and made new covenants. The words spoken at this baptism were as follows:

> Having been commissioned of Jesus Christ, I baptize you for the remission of your sins, for the renewal of your covenants with God and your brethren, and for the observance of the rules of the holy United Order which have been said in your hearing, in the name of the Father and of the Son and of the Holy Ghost.[47]

After the St. George United Order was formed, Brigham and his associates organized similar orders throughout southern Utah. They then went north to Salt Lake City in April and May 1874. In every settlement along the way, they founded a United Order patterned after those established in southern Utah.

But in Salt Lake City they realized that a community-wide United Order would be impossible because of the large number of non-Mormons and because of the size of the city. So they organized separate United Orders in each of the city's twenty wards.[48] These United Orders were to be merely corporations to which people subscribed for shares, set up for the purpose of promoting some particular enterprise. For example, one ward built a hat factory; another, a soap factory; another, a tannery; another ward maintained a tailoring establishment.

The Mormons next established United Orders throughout northern Utah. In Hyrum and Bear Lake, the Brigham City plan was followed. In some of the smaller communities, the St. George plan was adopted.

Beginning in 1875, still another type of United Order was created. These were communities with a communal way of life in which people contributed all of their property to the United Order, had no private property, shared more or less equally in their common product, and lived as one large family. The first of these was founded at Orderville, in Kane County. It lasted for eleven years and was successful until it began to introduce a system of differential wages.[49] Similar communal organizations functioned in Kingston, Utah; Bunkerville, Nevada; and in several Arizona communities. These were almost completely self-sufficient in every respect. There was no private property, and the people ate at a common table. Labor was directed by a board of management and life was regulated by a United Order bugler who signaled for them to rise, to eat, to attend to prayers, to go to work, etc. They wore clothes from the same bolt of cloth. Some suggested that it all resembled army life, except for its voluntary nature and, of course, the brotherly love.

Some of the United Order organizations lasted into the 1890s, but most of them were relatively short-lived. There were different reasons for their discontinuance. In some cases it was a grasshopper plague; in others, the leading men were placed in jail for the practice of polygamy; in still others, it was bickering and lack of cooperation. Some of the "human" problems are illustrated in the experience of Orderville. Orderville had been founded in an atmosphere of dire poverty, and the common action that took place in the order made it possible for the members to eat and dress better than they had for years—better than many residents in surrounding settlements where United Orders were not functioning. But then rich mines were opened at nearby Silver Reef, and Orderville's neighbors, profiting from this boom, suddenly found themselves able to buy imported clothing and other store commodities. The Saints in Orderville became "old-fashioned"; their floppy straw hats, gray jeans, valley tan shoes, and one-room shanties became objects of ridicule and derision. Orderville adolescents began to envy the young people in other communities. The strength of the community ebbed away.

I T is clear that Brigham's dream of establishing a homogeneous cooperative community did not come to fruition. Many Saints felt that, while the United Order may have been a step in the right direction, it was unduly confining and restrictive of economic freedom. They were prepared to cooperate willingly in the digging of canals, the construction of roads and public works, and in the establishment of new enterprises; and they felt obligated to live the higher kind of life enjoined by the rules of the United Order. But they still preferred private stewardships to tightly organized cooperation.

Most of the orders had been discontinued by the time of Brigham's death.[50] Within ten years, all of them were abandoned as a formal system. Only the objectives, the injunctions to live "like Enoch and his people," and the unselfishness the movement had promoted, outlived the Young era. After Brigham's death the Saints continued to give much of their disposable income to the Kingdom, tended to hold their property in the interests of the communities where they lived, and maintained a system that was unquestionably more idealistic than the typical western community. But while continuing to respect the principles of oneness and equality, they refused to accept Brigham's United Order as the unique means of carrying out those principles. While this must have been saddening to Brigham, he could feel that, at the least, he had discharged his obligation to institute oneness. He could now face his Prophet Joseph by saying that he had tried.

21 ✤

The Last Year

I feel as young as ever. I am 75, and shall not be here many
years more. All I want now is to die and see all my people
peaceful, prosperous, and happy.[1]

H I S three-quarters of a century notwithstanding, Brigham
Young's last twelve to eighteen months were among the most productive of
his life. Although he had periods of ill health, he continued to be active in
running the affairs of the church and concerned about a number of problems
and developments in the territory.

He began the centennial year 1876 by sending a large colonization mission
to the Little Colorado River in northeastern Arizona. Early in January he gave
the Quorum of the Twelve the duty of seeing that the projected two hundred
missionaries were called and that the right kind of men were chosen. The
Twelve met with the bishops, and before the month was half over Arizona
mission discussions were held throughout the wards of Salt Lake County.
Brigham was pleased with the promptness of the response and described the
vision he had of how this small beginning would expand and the church spread
throughout the southern lands:

> Nor do I expect we shall stop at Arizona, but I look forward to the time when
> the settlements of the Church of Jesus Christ of Latter-day Saints will extend right
> through to the City of Old Mexico, and from thence on through Central America
> to the land where the Nephites flourished in the Golden era of their history, and
> this great backbone of the American Continent be filled, north and south,
> with the cities and temples of the people of God. In this great work I anticipate
> the children of Nephi, of Laman and Lemuel [native Indians] will take no small
> part.[2]

By January 22 the two hundred colonists were receiving Brigham's counsel.
He told them he wanted no "babyism" in this mission; they would not find
"ready cooked pigs and turkeys" but would have to begin from scratch.

When you leave our settlements you will find a hard rugged road to travel, and if you expect to have clothing you must make it. We want men that can fit themselves out. We would not give much for those that need others to fit them out. When you get there, fence your land, and secure your rights to it. Learn how to take care of yourselves. There will be mining going on within 80 miles of where you are going; pay no heed to them, but attend to your work.[3]

At another meeting of the missionaries at which they were divided into four companies, Brigham gave them further advice and direction. The teamsters always were to unhitch the teams. They were to be kind to the Indians, to "feed them, set them to work, and dont quarrel with them, or the agent." They should study the laws of Arizona Territory so they would not be vulnerable to lawyers' traps. The young men were to "take a wife with them, be economical, and learn how to live." They were being sent early so they would be able to raise a crop right away, and they were to hold onto their crops and not look for a market to sell them. He even gave the men advice about how to deliver babies.[4]

In March Brigham wrote Lot Smith and the other company captains advising that they settle about fifty men in each place, that settlements should be about five miles apart but no more than twenty-five, that they should build on solid ground, erect corrals as soon as possible, and distribute the mechanics (skilled artisans) equally among the companies.[5] Whether or not the settlers needed this specific advice, they tried to follow it. Within a month Brigham noted that the four settlements (Sunset, Brigham City, Obid, St. Joseph) had been formed. Farming had begun the day after the missionaries' arrival, and they were busy putting in crops, making gardens, and building houses.[6]

Meanwhile, other missionary thrusts were going forward in the Southwest. Brigham sent the following advice to Daniel W. Jones in El Paso regarding his mission into Mexican territory:

I feel that it would be wise for you to visit the old original blood [Indians] as much as possible. Let the Catholic church alone. If its members wish to hear the truth, expound it to them as to any other people, but do not debate with them, and as to the curses of the priests, you need not regard them as much as you would a mosquito in the season of the year when these insects trouble. Be cautious in your labors and movement, do not court opposition, but move steadily on, presenting the truths of the Gospel to those who will hear you and inviting all to become partakers of the blessings of the Gospel of the Son of God.[7]

Brigham was also reconsidering immigration plans and routes. In particular, he was thinking of bypassing the use of Union Pacific Railroad facilities because of the

high handed, oppressive and exacting course pursued by the officials of the Union Pacific Railroad, which he [Brigham Young] feels we have endured uncomplainingly long enough and he is willing to shew those gentlemen that the Latter-day Saints can get along without them. Since the commencement of 1868, our elders going out on missions have paid the company more than $31,000. And now they threaten to cut off the half fare tickets to our Missionaries because *one* of those tickets has fallen into the hands of a scalper.[8]

Brigham pointed out that the church paid the Union Pacific an average of $100,000 per year for missionaries and immigrants alone, "yet they threaten and snarl every time they have the slightest pretext until I am tired."[9] Instead, he was considering using wagons and teams from Omaha, or bringing the immigrants to Denver or Cheyenne and thence by road to Utah. He also thought of transporting them as far into the Southwest as possible and then moving them directly into the new settlements being built in Arizona.

As Brigham approached his seventy-fifth birthday, he noted that "after the busy season attendant on the meeting of the Legislature, the fitting out of the Arizona missionaries, etc., a short period of repose will be grateful to my feelings."[10] When general conference was held in April, he presided over its first two days but was absent the last two days because of a severe cold.

D U R I N G the previous winter Brigham had not made his usual trip to the milder climate of St. George. The death of his counselor, George A. Smith, in September 1875 may have been a factor in delaying him from heading south as soon as usual.[11] The work of getting the Arizona mission effort under way may have been another consideration. In any case, Brigham did not leave for St. George until May 1, 1876. Arriving there eight days later, he visited the temple, now under construction, going to the top of the main building and the tower. He spoke at the local conference, expressed satisfaction with the progress being made on the temple, and let it be known that he wanted the structure to be completed by the following April so that general conference could be held there.[12]

On Brigham's seventy-fifth birthday, June 1, the citizens of St. George put on a gala celebration. He was serenaded by a band early in the morning and then by the St. George choir. At a fast and prayer meeting in the tabernacle, addresses by James G. Bleak and by Brigham's daughter Susa Young Dunford (later Susa Young Gates) were followed by a "searching and powerful exhortation" by Brigham himself. After the program a dinner was held at the home of a prominent churchman to which forty veteran pioneers, all men over seventy years of age, had been invited. No women pioneers had been invited, and none of Brigham's own family. According to his daughter Susa, who was in St. George, Brigham "looked quizzically over the table full of old men, and remarked: 'You will excuse me. I am going home to my family. You have invited all the living tombstones in the country to remind me that I have one foot in the grave; so let them enjoy themselves. I am going home.' "[13]

Actually, according to the diary of Charles L. Walker, who was there,

Brigham remained some time with the "old folks" and "cake and wine were passed around." When he returned to his St. George home he was met at the gate by "a number of young misses," mostly his own daughters, dressed in white. They held baskets of roses and strewed petals along his path while singing an original song that Walker had composed for the occasion. "He [Brigham] was much pleased at this demonstration of innocence, and tears rolled down his cheeks as he gazed on the little folks." All the family and hired help then settled down to a surprise chicken dinner—a second dinner for Brigham.[14]

A few days later, at a Sunday afternoon meeting in the St. George Tabernacle, Brigham saw "Charley" and asked him for an original copy of the song he had composed for the dedication of the temple. Walker wrote:

> After meeting I went home and got the song and took it to him. He treated me very kindly and asked me to sit beside him and take dinner with him. I spent the time very pleasantly and found him to be very polite, genial, and sociable, and I felt quite at home in chatting over the work on the Temple, old times, and other general topics. In bidding him goodbye, he took my hand in both of his and said, "God bless you Br. Charley, and God has blessed you hasn't He?" It seemed that in an instant all the blessings I had ever recei[v]ed were before me. My emotion was too much to answer him, and I chokeingly said, "I have learned to trust in the Lord."[15]

Eleven days later, on June 13, Brigham left St. George to return to Salt Lake City.

O N E event that marred Brigham's satisfaction was the trial in Beaver, that same year, of his long-trusted friend, John D. Lee, for his part in the Mountain Meadows Massacre. Just one hundred miles northeast of St. George, Beaver was close enough for Brigham to be informed regularly of every development. Prodded by anti-Mormon Gentiles, the solicitor general had finally given his approval to a campaign to net at least one massacre participant, and John D. Lee was tracked down, arrested, and placed in the territorial penitentiary to await trial. During this period, several prominent federal officials offered Lee freedom and money in return for involving Brigham in the massacre. A man of staunch integrity, whatever his other faults, Lee refused: "I chose to die like a man [rather] than to live as a villain."[16]

The trial, as Brigham might have anticipated, was a thinly disguised attempt to incriminate the church president. A perusal of its minutes suggests that the real object of the prosecution was to use John D. Lee as a symbol, rather than to try him individually. For example, Robert N. Baskin, in his statement to the jury, said that in reality "the Mormon theocracy" was "responsible" for the "heinous crime" perpetrated at Mountain Meadows. "It seems to me," he said, "that a part of the Mormon Religion is to kill—and a part and parcel of it—and a great part of it is to shed human blood for another. . . . There is no use to disguise it when counsel said that the Mormon Church was on trial—I am willing to accept the gentleman's statement." Baskin went on to compare the Lee case to the Dred Scott case in which, he said, Dred Scott was a symbol, but "the whole system of negro slavery was involved." So it was with the Mountain Meadows affair: "Inasmuch as this crime was concocted by the leaders of the Mormon Church . . . , and the further fact shows it was the result of a secret and misterious [sic] organization which strikes misteriously and secretly and seals the lips of those who participated in it, . . . I am willing to accept the gentleman's proposition, that it is the Mormon Church that is now on trial." Baskin then went on to involve Brigham Young: "I do hold Brigham Young responsible; I do hold the system which has carried out, which distinctly teaches and carries out in its preaching and practices, the shedding of human blood to atone for real and imaginary offenses. I hold, I arraign this iniquitous system, and the leaders of the church."[17]

The prosecution's attempt to fasten the crime upon the Mormon church and its leaders, not surprisingly, influenced the Mormon jurors to acquit Lee. To convict him would have been tantamount to convicting themselves and their church. The four non-Mormon jurors voted for conviction, so there had to be a second trial.

The failure of the first trial led the federal solicitor to instruct the territorial prosecutor to make no attempt to implicate the church and its leaders: try Lee, and Lee alone. The intentions of the government were unmistakable, and the Mormons, whether as jurors, witnesses, or deponents, cooperated. Lee was convicted of having committed a murder, taken to the location of the massacre, and executed as expiation for the crime. No further prosecutions were undertaken.[18]

When the U.S. marshal asked Lee if he had any last words, he replied that he did not have much to say; he was not afraid to die. His chief regret was that he had to leave his wives and children "on the mercies of this cold world." Then he said that he had been intimately acquainted with Brigham, George A. Smith, and Daniel H. Wells, of the First Presidency. He wished that they had come to comfort him. (Smith was, of course, dead by this time.) "I have traveled with them; stood guard over them; I have kept them at my house; I have been with them in their homes; and we have been the most intimate of friends. Now in my time of trouble they do not come to comfort me."[19]

B R I G H A M returned to St. George for the last time in November of 1876, but during the three months between these visits he was busy with work in Salt Lake City, staying there almost all of the time except for a brief trip to attend a conference in Logan on August 27.

The Arizona mission continued to engage his attention and concern. Problems were beginning to surface, and Brigham tried to encourage and prod the missionaries to stay with their calling. He wrote to the presidents of the settlements telling them that difficulties were to be expected and "you will have to make many experiments, some of which may prove failures, until you become acquainted with the peculiarities of the soil, the climate and other surroundings." Brigham was concerned about reports of "murmuring" and members inclining toward apostasy and said, "We want none such to remain with you, lest they poison the camp with the leaven of their ill-feeling. . . . The selfishness and individuality that have characterized the labors of some of our brethren should not find a place with those called to this mission."[20] He gave the colonizers permission to extend and expand into new areas should some of the brethren feel discouraged with their present location.[21]

By September Brigham had learned that the settlements on the Little Colorado were running short of provisions. He set up a plan for gathering provisions from the Saints in the Cache Valley and urged the missionaries to practice rigid economy and to double up in the settlements if necessary.[22]

To spur the colonization effort, James Brown was sent to visit the various Mormon villages, lecture on missionary work among the Indians, and recruit volunteers. In his letter of authorization to the bishops, Brigham emphasized that hundreds could be accommodated, for "the rich valleys south and east of the Little Colorado offer homes for hundreds of those who desire to extend the curtains of Zion in that direction." Although some apparently believed that "it is better to be called by the authorities to such a mission than to volunteer," Brigham pointed out that those who waited for such a call were "slothful servants" and encouraged them to sign up on their own.[23]

In his instructions to the pioneers in the Southwest, Brigham repeatedly stressed that the policy was "to extend cautiously and gradually as the dictates of the Spirit of God shall direct." He left the details up to the settlers themselves. "We will leave it with you, as you are on the ground, to decide how many settlements, one or more, you will relinquish for the present and which camps you will concentrate in."[24]

Another topic strongly on Brigham's mind was temples. No sooner had he returned from St. George than he announced further plans for that temple. "Our present intention," he wrote to Albert Carrington, "is to go to St. George immediately after next October Conference, dedicate that portion of the Temple that is finished, organize the Priesthood, and commence to give endowments, baptize for the dead, etc."[25] A big push for temple building was under way by the fall of 1876. Brigham sent a message to a bishops' meeting in September that "he hoped the Brethren would continue their Temple donations, for another [temple] would shortly be commenced, and there would be no slackening off in the calls for this purpose, and if some thought otherwise, they would certainly be mistaken."[26]

During the summer months Brigham visited the bishops' meetings to correct some of their ideas about church organization and described in detail the responsibilities and functions of each quorum at both the general and local levels. He had the Council House rededicated when the bishops resumed meeting there after a gap of ten years. He assigned the Relief Society to organize a commission house that would dispose of homemade articles manufactured by the members.[27]

Brigham also continued to promote the United Order. He noted in September that "the United Order is being sought after by many of the Saints; they cherish the desire to understand its principles more perfectly, feeling assured that it is a requirement of the Almighty, which they and their children must eventually obey." He went on to point out how living the United Order, and the other commandments, could be a route to independence and self-government for the church. "If we as a people would only obey the voice of God and submit to His requirements in all things the reins of power would soon be placed in our hands, and instead of being governed, we would have the privilege of governing."[28] One question that arose was whether it was a good idea to join various family branches together in the United Order. Brigham expressed his fear that such an organization "will have a tendency to induce and foster a spirit of clannishness and exclusiveness, a thing that we are especially anxious to avoid. Neither do we think that selfishness will be as effectually rooted out by this plan as it will under the more comprehensive system advocated by myself and the brethren associated with me." He suggested consulting with the bishop and deciding together what course would be best. Perhaps betraying the ambivalence of one aware that others did not share his enthusiasm, Brigham effectively placed the decision on the local level. "So far as we are concerned," he said, "we have no objection."[29]

Despite his positive assertion that people were eager to enter the United Order, Brigham found much resistance. He told the bishops that "he had been inspired by the gift and power of God to call upon the saints to enter into the United Order, or Order of Enoch, and that now was the time, but he could not get the people to enter into it. He had cleared his skirts if he never said another word about it."[30] The assumption that Brigham was a dictator whose will was law does not hold up against evidence of his frustration in establishing the United Order.

B R I G H A M ' S health during the summer and fall was beginning to decline somewhat; there were urinary problems caused by an enlarged prostate, and a flaring up of rheumatism. "Since my return from the South," Brigham noted in August, "I have suffered some little from rheumatism, which has kept me considerably in my room. Now I am thankful to say that I am very much better, and my lameness has almost entirely left me."[31]

He was not allowed a life of retirement free of care. Legal problems became more numerous and complex. He wished his son Alfales had finished his studies and been admitted to the bar, "for you could materially help me in the numerous vexacious suits that are being brought against me to rob me of my property." He went on to describe the hypocrisy of the federal judges:

The present bench appears to be not only willing but anxious to give my possessions away to anyone who has the effrontery to ask for them. If I met three
highway robbers, who demanded my money or my life, I should know what to
do, but these worse than highwaymen, despoil me under the pretense of the law,
which they and all the world knows who know anything about the matter, does
not give them the shadow of an excuse for acting as they do.[32]

The Ann Eliza divorce case still plagued him. Charged with contempt of
court for not paying the alimony ordered by the judge, Brigham delayed his
winter trip to St. George. "If the Judge is corrupt and bitter enough to decide
against me," he wrote in a letter to his son, "I shall go to prison, [unless] my
mind very much changes, if I have to remain there all the rest of my days, for
I certainly shall not pay the plaintiff or her lawyers one cent."[33] When the
judge ordered his property sequestered, Brigham decided to repossess it as
soon as it was sold. "I do not think they will find anyone foolish enough to
purchase it under the circumstances," he said. "This order is altogether without
sense, reason, justice or law. But then some of our judges always act as though
the Mormons have no rights which they are bound to respect."[34]

Still observant, and anxious to give the good counsel expected of a prophetic
leader, Brigham focused on social issues in the city. He was concerned about
order in church meetings and asked the bishops and counselors to "use all due
diligence in preserving the utmost quiet and good order in the New Tabernacle
during Conference."[35] He recommended that meetinghouses not be used for
dancing and parties, yet in the absence of other suitable facilities, some leeway
was allowed.

> The question was raised by Bp Thomas Taylor as to whether dancing parties
> are to be tolerated in our Ward Houses this winter as Prest. Young had expressed
> his disapproval of them being held in a room used for Worship and yet, they
> were being held in some of the wards. He thought there ought to be a proper
> understanding in the matter, so as to be uniformity in action among the Bishops.
>   The reply was, That though Prest. Young had never council'd parties being
> held in Meeting Houses, yet by his permission, they had been.[36]

Brigham recommended that the bishops take a hand in getting rid of unde-
sirable elements and businesses in the city. "In reference to these drinking
saloons and hurdy gurdies," he said, "if the Bishops were only wide awake to
their duties, they would pour in their petitions to the City Council, until
something was done to rid them from our midst. . . ."[37]

Brigham continued to offer advice to family members about the course
of their lives. To a son who was thinking about marriage, he wrote:

> With regard to your reflections about getting married and choosing from
> amongst the daughters of the East you must be aware of the risk that you run if
> you take into yourself a wife who does not believe the Gospel, and whom you

have no idea will make a good Mormon, one who probably would oppose you in faith and feeling all the days of your life and teach your children to despise the religion of their father. Perhaps in other things she might be as good as many of our Western girls, the course of some of whom I cannot commend. Gen. Sherman has some daughters who might not say *no* to you were your inclinations to run in that direction. But I have never taken a wife since I received the Gospel from amongst any but the people of God, neither, as yet have any of my sons, nor am I anxious that they should do so. Still, further, I have no objections at all to your coming home and taking a wife whenever it pleases you. You have my entire sanction in so doing, and if you wished to take her back and have her stay with you wherever you are stationed it would be entirely agreeable to my feelings for you to do so.[38]

Like Lord Chesterfield's advice to his son, Brigham's counsel to his children was not always adhered to. But several of his children later expressed appreciation for his fatherly concern. Having a large family did not mean ignoring or abandoning those he cherished.

O N the first of November, 1876, Brigham left Salt Lake City for his last trip to St. George, arriving on November 9. Almost immediately—the day after his arrival—he went to the temple to see how it was progressing, visiting every part of the building and checking on the work. His rheumatism troubled him and his health was poor during most of December and January.[39] Nevertheless, he spoke at several Sunday meetings.

New Year's Day, 1877, was a special occasion. The St. George Temple was far enough completed that the lower story could be dedicated. The ceremonies began at noon, with Wilford Woodruff offering the dedicatory prayer. Although Brigham had to be carried from room to room in a chair supported by two men, he addressed the congregation:

> Now we have a temple which will be completely finished in a few days. I want the tongue of seven thunders to awaken the people to action. They can now come here, do the work for the dead and bid the prisoners go free.[40]

In the course of his address at this temple dedication, Brigham became so wrought up at the wrongheadedness of some of the people that he pounded the newly constructed rostrum with his hickory cane and left marks that were still to be seen one hundred years later. "I will never cease my preaching," he shouted, "until Satan and his hosts are overcome and driven from the earth."[41]

During the rest of the winter, Brigham continued to spend much time at the temple. On January 9, still suffering (probably from rheumatism) to the point of having to use a crutch to get around, he witnessed the first baptism there.

General church administrative business still had to be dealt with. For this purpose Brigham had a small office built onto the east wing of his St. George house. The work was coordinated by Brigham and his counselors and clerks in Salt Lake City. Daniel H. Wells and the Salt Lake clerks handled a great deal of the routine work—missionary calls, items relating to the Malad, Idaho, Indian farm, church work projects, settling marital disputes, and the like. Still, most of it was to some extent under Brigham's direction. Letters went back and forth. Wells wrote Brigham, for example, "I have not forgotten your instructions with regard to raising means to pay for the flour sent to the Little Colorado [Arizona] settlements, and we expect to deposit the same to your credit at Z.C.M.I. within a few days as you directed."[42]

The southern missions were much on Brigham's mind. In January he sent a letter of instruction to Daniel W. Jones and the other men involved in the Arizona mission, cautioning them to attend to their prayers, "omit boisterous actions," prohibit vulgar and obscene language, and be careful about choosing sites on which to settle. He also urged them to pattern their settlements on United Order principles. "If your union does not exceed that of the inhabitants of the county where you locate, what better are you than they? You carry the Gospel of Jesus to a benighted people. See to it, that your righteousness exceeds theirs."[43]

Brigham gave similar advice and encouragement to the Saints experimenting with the settlement at Orderville. At this time he especially urged patience:

> We say to you and the brethren with you, be patient, do not suffer yourselves to become unduly exercised by the encroachments that may be made upon you. Keep right on steadily with your business working every department to the best advantage, and by and by, those that oppose will want to either sell out to you, or join you. Make it your business to have something to pay when they desire to sell. Instead of contending with them, all the time have something to pay them, when they come to the place where they want to sell. Their land will piece by piece fall into your hands. Don't be in a hurry. You can afford to wait.[44]

Although he had not served officially as Indian agent since 1858, he continued to be interested in this people that, according to Mormon doctrine, had a great role to fill in God's eternal plan. When the Mormons sold their land in Thistle Valley to the Indians, Brigham encouraged them to make sure the proper transfers were made with the U.S. Land Office so that the Indians' rights would be secured. "It is our duty," he said, "to afford them every reasonable encouragement to acquire the habits of a peaceful productive life and in this the Lord will bless us and them. There is room enough for us all."[45]

Brigham, as always, had many questions come to him from church members about a variety of matters. A Relief Society secretary in Monroe wondered how children should be dressed when buried and to whom children will in certain circumstances belong in the hereafter. Brigham answered such questions

when he could. To her fifth question—women having had two or three husbands, none living their religion, what is the best course for her to pursue?—
he gave a short answer: "Live *her* religion."[46]

Brigham's thoughts even turned to the necessity for a usable church history. He wrote to his counselors in Salt Lake:

> As soon as we can we must have someone of our brethren take hold of the
> matter of getting out a History of the Church in a condensed form. Though we
> have very much published history of the rise and progress of the Church in sundry
> books and publications, we are yet without a History to place in the hands of
> our own people or of the enquirer out in the world.[47]

The high point of Brigham Young's final winter was the annual general
conference of the church held at St. George in April of 1877. He addressed the
congregation at five of the six meetings of the conference, urging the Saints
to live the United Order, to become as unified in temporal things as spiritual,
and to stop buying "needless adornments" and the "importations of Babylon."[48] He also presented a vision of the expanding settlements of the Saints,
filling more and more valleys each year. "As to my health," he said, "I feel
many times that I could not live an hour longer, but I mean to live just as
long as I can. I know not how soon the messenger will call for me, but I
calculate to die in the harness."[49]

The five conference talks did not exhaust the supply of advice and counsel.
Before leaving St. George, Brigham left detailed instructions with the stake
president. The president should pay close attention to Sunday and day schools,
encourage young people's auxiliaries and the Relief Society, provide a decent
library for the citizens, and form associations of mechanics and laborers. He
even gave farming advice: plant raisin grapes instead of wine grapes, raise
tobacco for export, encourage the raising of cotton, fruit, and sheep, but do
not run after outsiders to sell to them. Each family head should spend at least
ten minutes a day in reading or teaching the word of God to his family, keep
the Word of Wisdom, pray, pay tithing, be clean and chaste, and avoid debt,
faultfinding, and stealing. The community must establish factories and industries, plant timber, establish commission houses or depots, and continue to
learn the principles of the United Order.[50] Brigham gave his final talk at St.
George on Sunday, April 15. "I have this to say to those present and those of
this stake of Zion," he said, "you have done an excellent work."[51]

The next day he left for Salt Lake City. All did not go well on the return
trip. A guard of about twenty-five young men accompanied the president's
party through Beaver County. Since the execution of John D. Lee had taken
place only a few weeks before, there was some concern about threats said to
have been made against Brigham's life by Lee's sons.[52] According to M. R.
Werner, as the procession rolled through Ephraim,

Ole Petersen, a Scandinavian convert who claimed that he had been cheated of his land by Brigham Young and sent on a mission that he might be robbed the more easily, waited for Brigham Young's carriage, shook his fist at the Prophet, and shouted in a strident voice: "Oh, you Cheat! Oh, Church Fraud! You coward to forsake your tools! You are the man that they should have hung instead of Lee!" The carriages rolled by, but it was observed that Brigham Young's hard, thin mouth tightened, and his hands clenched the seat of his coach.[53]

On April 25 Brigham stopped and dedicated a site for a temple at Manti, and within three weeks he had done the same in Logan. He instructed that both temples be completed as speedily as possible.[54]

T H E last three months of Brigham Young's life were spent for the most part in Salt Lake City. "The present year," he wrote to one correspondent,

. . . is one that thus far has been unparalleled in the history of the Church of Jesus Christ of Latter-day Saints. In fact, as far as I am acquainted with the records of the Church of God in the various dispensations of His Providence, I do not know of its parallel since the days of Adam, the great father of us all. Within a period of less than six months, one Temple has been completed and dedicated, and the site for two others consecrated to the Lord our God and the work of construction commenced thereon, whilst another (the one in this City) is being pushed forward with greater zeal and energy than has before been manifested since its commencement.[55]

The assurance that the Lord "has accepted our offering of the House built to His name," he wrote his son Willard, "adds to my happiness and inspires me to fresh efforts."[56] He also continued to push the work on the Salt Lake Temple.

Brigham gave Wilford Woodruff instructions for sealings being done in St. George, explaining that children born after their parents were sealed need not be sealed to the parents. He distinguished between the ordinances of adoption and sealing, saying that children sealed to parents who forsook the gospel "might desire to be adopted into some other family, and if so permitted by the priesthood, the ordinance of adoption not of sealing, would have to be attended to."[57] He also explained the procedure for rebaptizing people into the United Order. Only the basic words need be spoken, he said, "but if you want to put in anything else, you can do so."[58]

Brigham continued feeling responsible for seeing to it that temple ordinances were performed for his own deceased family members. Following his seventy-sixth birthday dinner on June 1, he spoke with his brothers Joseph, Phinehas, and Lorenzo and told them that "he had neither time nor strength to complete the Temple and the genealogical work for their ancestors and with solemn words and profound conviction he charged his brothers with the responsibility of carrying that work forward for the Young family line."[59]

Completing the St. George Temple set Brigham on fire about another large-scale project, one that gave him new life just long enough to complete it. To make the earthly priesthood match more perfectly the heavenly, he proceeded to revitalize priesthood operations. Too well he knew how continued church growth had created a myriad of "loose ends" organizationally— stakes not properly staffed, units too large, too few quorums and bishops, apostles presiding over stakes, and other problems. There was an acute need for tightening up.

To achieve this purpose he directed the Twelve to visit every stake, hold special conferences, and make thoroughgoing changes. When the reorganizing dust settled, seven new stakes had been added to thirteen existing ones, 140 new wards added to 101 existing ones, and 53 new stake presidency members called (of 160 total). Hundreds of men were called to bishoprics, stake presidencies, high councils, and quorum presidencies. Youths were ordained to do priesthood work for the first time. The reorganization took place in two stages: stakes were reordered first, and then wards and quorums. Brigham expected the better organizations to produce "a radical change, a reformation, in the midst of this people." Many Saints were rebaptized as part of the reorganizing.[60]

On July 11, 1877, the First Presidency issued a historic epistle containing a long, detailed blueprint of changes and tightenings proposed.[61] Coming in Brigham's seventy-seventh year, it was the most important policy statement on priesthood work since the days of Joseph Smith. The impact of Brigham's last major project was lauded by his assistant counselor, George Q. Cannon:

> He set the Priesthood in order as it has never before been since the first organization of the Church upon earth. He defined the duties of the apostles . . . Seventies . . . High Priests . . . Elders . . . lesser Priesthood, with plainness and distinction and power—the power of God—in a way that is left on record in such unmistakable language that no one need err who has the spirit of God resting down upon him.[62]

Brigham's own perception of the program, as explained in a contemporary letter to his son Willard, was that he had undertaken it "to give greater compactness to the labors of the priesthood, to unite the Saints, to care for the scattering sheep of Israel in these mountains who acknowledge no particular fold, to be in a position to understand the standing of every one calling himself a Latter-day Saint, and to consolidate the interests, feelings and lives of the members of the Church."[63]

He prodded individuals to "put their lives in order." He checked with the bishops to see if they themselves paid their fast offerings and monthly donations. Cannon reported to the bishops that "it was President Young's wish for the Sacrament to be administered to the Sunday School Children by the Bishops and their Counselors." Brigham was also concerned about the noticeable absence of children at services in the tabernacle. Cannon passed on the direction that "President Young would like to apportion a suitable place in the Tabernacle for them to occupy. He thought it would have a good effect on the minds of the children, besides keeping them from roaming around the City."[64]

In July Brigham traveled to Ogden and there, on the nineteenth, organized in Weber Stake the first stake Relief Society—the only one to be organized by Brigham Young himself. His last address to a public church meeting was on August 19 at Brigham City, where he went to organize the Box Elder Stake.[65]

L E S S than a week before his death and on the very eve of his final illness, at the bishops' meeting of August 23 he discussed the duties of the Presiding Bishop and council and then instructed the bishops in their duties, particularly their responsibility "to look after every member in their wards, and not retain in fellowship those who utterly refuse to attend to their prayers, tithing, and other duties." He said it was the duty of the priests and teachers to visit each home weekly. When a bishop's counselor asked if that wasn't too much to expect, Brigham said that these could be very short visits—just enough to "note the various changes of comers and goers that take place as fast as they occur . . . but every member of each ward should be well and thoroughly visited at least once a month."[66]

He appointed a new mission president over the church in California, giving him explicit and detailed instructions concerning land purchases and manufacturing enterprises as well as missionary work. He cautioned the missionaries in Mexico to be very careful in their acquisition of land. He gave direction to immigrant groups from Arkansas, Alabama, and Georgia, helping them find the best locations in which to settle. He encouraged the men who were opening up missionary work in Finland.[67] In the last week of his life, he directed the plans for settling in Castle Valley those residents who had sold their land in Thistle Valley to the Indians. He told the stake president:

> We should like to have, at least, fifty families locate in Castle Valley this fall; but if some of the brethren cannot take their families this Year, it would be well for them to go themselves, secure their locations and commence work. In making your selection choose good, energetic, God-fearing young men, whether single or with families, and others who can be spared without interfering with the interests of the settlements in which they now reside, such ones as will be a strength to the new settlement, and an aid to its growth in all that we, as Latter-day Saints, desire to see increase upon the earth.[68]

Brigham warned his people to remain apart from the nonmembers in their midst. This was especially a problem in the mining areas like Beaver County, where there were many Gentiles. To the bishop there, who was trying to build bridges with the non-Mormons, Brigham said, "The disposition to mix with our enemies, to be hail-fellow-well-met with the wicked, is not of the Lord."[69] Writing to another Beaver resident, he deplored the "disposition to mix so much with the Gentiles in your place. This is wrong, and cannot fail to lead to bad results. It is contrary to the spirit of Zion; and those who give way to it will lose the spirit unless they repent. Steps will be taken to correct this tendency if possible. And you will probably hear something about it upon the visit of the Apostles to organize the Stake."[70] To the apostles in charge of the area he wrote:

> Whatever the idea may be, it is a very mistaken policy, and if something be not done to correct and change this there is danger of that place getting into the same condition as Tooele County. . . . There is too much mixing of the hairs with the butter for the good of the butter. We feel that these things should be stopped and an entire change of policy be adopted. It will not do for Latter-day Saints to mix with the world, and hope thereby to gain their favor and friendship. Oil and water will not mix.[71]

Brigham upbraided the bishop: "We hear you had a celebration on the 4th of July at your City, and that you had a Methodist minister as Chaplain, and an apostate as Orator, and other enemies acting in other positions, and that you have been mixing up with the outside element in a manner to grieve the humble and faithful Latter-day Saints. . . . The Lord is not pleased with his people when they bow to the Gentiles and give them honor, and partake of their spirit. Israel is the head and should take the lead."[72]

On a related issue, Brigham pointed out the necessity of being economically independent of non-Mormon merchants by building up home manufactures. He showed how one snag in the national economy could disrupt the flow of supplies to Utah.

> The present trouble may amount to but little, but it will come. This outbreak of striking workmen has impressed some of the saints, whose hearts are dull, far more than the words of God's servants have done. They can now see some of the ways in which Babylon can be brought to its fall. They can also see how we can be cut off from our supplies, as long as we trust to the artificers and merchants of Babylon.[73]

Brigham was not so intolerant as to consider all non-Mormons evil or dismiss them entirely. At a meeting one bishop was asked to explain and justify his employing a non-Mormon schoolteacher. The bishop replied that the man was well qualified and had friendly feelings toward the Saints. Brigham supported this position. "All outsiders are not necessarily gentiles," he explained, "but those who belong to the rebellious blood are gentile. There are tens of thousands of the blood of Israel who will not embrace the Gospel, neither will they seek to destroy this people, but speak a good word for them, and do good to them whenever they have opportunity. He wished to impress this upon the minds of the elders."[74]

Brigham's eye was everywhere. He instructed local authorities at Beaver to stop the traffic in quick divorces. "To me the idea is horrible, and the amount of misery that men may inflict upon innocent persons by such a practice is terrible to contemplate."[75] On July 24 he deeded to Brigham Young College a tract of land consisting of 9,642 acres south of Logan. He promoted the adoption of a new alphabet. The Deseret Alphabet experience of the 1850s and 1860s had apparently not discouraged him. At a bishops' meeting in July,

> President B. Young said, it was his particular desire that the Bishops, who are the representatives of the Saints, should use their influence, and be interested in the use of the New Alphabet and improved orthography of the English Language. He was fully satisfied, that it would be of incalculable benefit to Foreign Emigrants in learning the English Language after their arrival here from the Old Country.[76]

A committee formed to select the characters for a new alphabet reported back in favor of Pitman's Phonetic Alphabet. Brigham's comments were summarized by a clerk:

> Pres. B. Young said, this subject had occupied much reflection for many years, and the Pitman Phonetic Alphabet beng more simple than the English Alphabet, they had concluded to adopt it. He was very anxious that we should lay aside the old and mysterious way of spelling the English language, as we have laid aside the mystery in the religious dogmas of the day.
>
> We will continue to improve in the whole science of Truth; for that is our business; our religion circumscribes all things, and we should be prepared to take hold of whatever will be a benefit and blessing to us.[77]

Although he was interested in promoting reading, Brigham continued his dislike of novels. The week before his death he advised one of his sons that reading novels was not a wise way of increasing the desire to read. "I should be very foolish if, because I had a poor appetite I took to making my meals of poisonous herbs or berries, because they tasted sweet or were otherwise palatable. It would be better for my appetite to remain poor than that I should destroy my vitality. Novel reading appears to me to be very much the same as swallowing poisonous herbs. It is a remedy that is worse than the complaint." He urged his son to read the revelations of God and historical and scientific works instead, to sell his Dickens and get Josephus or Mosheim or a work on geology. In answer to the claim that novel reading provides "insight into the ways of the world, its life and society," he said that such views of life are often strained or false. Besides, he added, "every Elder in the Church of Jesus Christ, who performs his duty, will have enough experience in the vicissitudes of real life to satisfy him by the time he grows old."[78]

Some of Brigham's many activities were listed in a letter to a son:

Since my return the duties of my calling have kept me actively engaged. What with the Councils of the priesthood, the meetings of the City Council and of the Board of Directors of Z.C.M.I., of the Deseret Bank, of the Street Railroad Co., of the Gas Co., of the Utah Southern Railroad, the Deseret Telegraph Co., &c &c, I find my time most completely engaged.[79]

As always, right up to the final days of his life, Brigham entertained an almost constant stream of visitors. Despite the difficulties, he felt that on balance such an expenditure of time was well worth it.

The constant calls of visitors at the office, all of whom have to be chatted with more or less, are quite a tax on my time and strength yet I am satisfied that such visits are, as a rule, productive of good results. Many a one who comes to Utah filled with all kinds of outrageous ideas with regard to the Mormons in general and Brigham Young in particular, after having visited our City, seen its objects of interest and called at the office, go away with feelings greatly modified, and often afterwards have a kind word for the people of Utah when they hear them assailed, and occasionally will smooth the way of any of our missionaries whom they may chance to meet. This interviewing, then, though sometimes disagreeable is too valuable a means of correcting false ideas, and removing prejudice to be discontinued.[80]

AT first, upon his return to Salt Lake City, Brigham seemed to recover quickly from his illness and rheumatism of the winter. He reported his health as excellent:

I have not for years endured the labor of speaking at Conference and public meetings as well as I have done during this last Conference and of late. I have spoken at each meeting in the New Tabernacle the last two Sundays with no bad effects to myself. The pain which I have so frequently suffered from in my stomach after speaking to large congregations, has troubled me but very little of late.[81]

Within a few weeks, however, he recognized that he had "somewhat overtaxed my strength." Right up to his final illness he continued to feel good. He told his daughter also that his health was excellent, and that he had just been to Black Rock beach and bathed in the Great Salt Lake "for the first time in many years and enjoyed it exceedingly."[82]

On Thursday, August 23, following his meeting with the bishops in the Council House, Brigham fell ill with violent cramps, vomiting, and purging. Despite the efforts of four physicians, he died less than a week later, on August 29. A medical historian who has carefully considered the notes kept by his doctors suggests that what they called "cholera morbus" was, in reality, the as yet unidentified condition of appendicitis. Brigham expired from the infection produced by a ruptured appendix.[83] Although he experienced excruciating pains in the stomach, which came spasmodically, he continued to make occasional "humorous remarks."[84] Throughout his illness, he had been repeatedly administered to by the laying on of hands and had managed a "hearty" amen at the close of each prayer. Nevertheless, he continued to decline. His daughter Zina, who was present during the last days of illness, described the events of August 29:

> It was with sinking hearts that we learned from the doctor that he feared father's illness was going to be fatal. He suffered much pain. His physician administered opiates to relieve the pain and which caused him to sleep during his last hours. He seemed so restless that Dr. Seymour B. Young, his nephew, thought it best to . . . place him before the open window where he would get the air and where his beloved ones could be around him.

Present were his brother Joseph, several of his wives, his son John W., and many of his other children.

"When he was placed upon the bed in front of the window," Zina wrote, her father seemed to partially revive, "and opening his eyes, he gazed upward, exclaiming: 'Joseph! Joseph! Joseph!' and the divine look in his face seemed to indicate that he was communicating with his beloved friend, Joseph Smith, the Prophet. This name was the last word he uttered." Zina's report continued:

> As we saw his life ebbing rapidly, we all knelt down around the bed and Uncle Joseph [Young] offered a fervent prayer to God that his going should be in peace and not in distress. I knelt where I had full view of his countenance, and in the middle of the prayer I was impelled to open my eyes, and father's face was radiant with inward glory. It seemed that a cloud of light surrounded him. . . . As the prayer was finished, the Doctor said, "He is gone." . . . The husband, the father, the leader, the chosen prophet of God, lay sleeping before our eyes never more on earth to give his words of counsel, of wisdom.[85]

T H E body was taken from the Lion House to the tabernacle on Saturday morning, September 1. Until noon the following day, long lines of people came to take a last look at their leader. It was estimated that during the day more than twenty-five thousand people visited the tabernacle.[86]

Four years earlier, at the time he made out his will, Brigham left explicit instructions regarding his funeral services and the disposition of his remains:

> I, Brigham Young, wish my funeral services to be conducted after the following manner:
> When I breathe my last I wish my friends to put my body in as clean and wholesome state as can conveniently be done, and preserve the same for one, two, three or four days, or as long as my body can be preserved in a good condition.
> I want my coffin made of plump 1¼ inch redwood boards, not scrimped in

length, but two inches longer than I would measure, and from two to three inches wider than is commonly made for a person of my breadth and size, and deep enough to place me on a little comfortable cotton bed with a good suitable pillow in size and quality. My body dressed in my Temple clothing and laid nicely into my coffin, and the coffin to have the appearance that if I wanted to turn a little to the right or left I should have plenty of room to do so; the lid can be made crowning.

At my interment I wish all of my family present that can be conveniently, and the male members to wear no crepe on their hats or their coats; the females to buy no black bonnets, nor black dresses, nor black veils; but if they have them they are at liberty to wear them.

The services may be permitted, as singing and a prayer offered, and if any of my friends wish to say a few words, and really desire, do so.

And when they have closed their services, take my remains on a bier and repair to the little burying ground which I have reserved on my lot east of the White House on the hill, and in the southeast corner of this lot have a vault built of mason work large enough to receive my coffin, and that may be placed in a box if they choose, made of the same material as the coffin—redwood. Then place flat rocks over the vault sufficiently large to cover it, that the earth may be placed over it—nice, fine, dry earth—to cover it until the walls of the little cemetery are reared, which will leave me in the southeast corner.

This vault ought to be roofed over with some kind of a temporary roof. There let my earthly house or tabernacle rest in peace and have a good sleep until the morning of the first resurrection; no crying nor mourning with any one, that I have done my work faithfully and in good faith.

I wish this to be read at the funeral, provided that if I should die anywhere in the mountains, I desire the above directions respecting my place of burial to be observed. But if I should live to go back with the Church in Jackson County, I wish to be buried there.

BRIGHAM YOUNG.[87]

The doors of the tabernacle were opened at ten o'clock on Sunday, September 2. By noon the building was "entirely filled, as were the aisles and doorways, and every available standing place." The congregation numbered about twelve thousand, perhaps as many as have ever been in that building at one time. At precisely noon, George Q. Cannon called the congregation to order. Joseph J. Daynes, the tabernacle organist, played the "Dead March" from *Saul,* Mendelssohn's "Funeral March," and a Brigham Young Funeral March that Daynes had composed. The 225-voice Tabernacle Choir, under the direction of George Careless, sang "Hark, from Afar a Funeral Knell," "Thou Dost not Weep to Weep Alone," and "Rest," the latter the director's own composition. Eulogies were delivered by Daniel H. Wells, Wilford Woodruff, Erastus Snow, John Taylor, and George Q. Cannon. Cannon expressed most succinctly, perhaps, what was on the minds of those present:

He [Brigham] has been the brain, the eye, the ear, the mouth and hand for the entire people of the Church. . . . From the greatest problems connected with the organization of this Church down to the smallest minutiae connected with the work, he has left upon it the impress of his great mind—from the organization of the Church, the construction of Temples, the building of Tabernacles, the creation of a Provisional State government, the Territorial government, down to the small matter of directing the shape of these seats upon which we sit this day. Upon all these things, as well as upon all the settlements of the Territory, the impress of his genius is apparent. Nothing was too small for his mind; nothing was too large.[88]

After the ceremonies some four thousand persons, none of whom, at his request, was dressed in black, marched eight abreast to the grave, which was in the "small private cemetery on the hill"—on what is now First Avenue, about two blocks east of the tabernacle. Mary Ann Angell, "Mother Young," who was now seventy-four, leaned on the arm of Amelia Folsom, who was not only a favorite of Brigham but of Mary Ann as well. Brigham was buried in a wooden casket placed in a stone vault with a simple inscription.[89]

Epilogue ✤

Beyond Eulogy:
The Legacy of Brigham Young

I have never particularly desired any man to testify publicly that I am a Prophet; nevertheless, if any man feels joy in doing this, he shall be blest in it. I have never said that I am not a Prophet; but, if I am not, one thing is certain, I have been very profitable to this people. In the providence of God he has placed me to take charge of his flock, and they have been abundantly blessed under my administration.[1]

THE funeral would have gratified some of Brigham Young's profoundest values: the expression of a seemingly united people, enough reaffirmation of religious principles to be emotionally satisfying, enough pageantry to be aesthetically pleasing. Although the settlement of his estate (described in Appendix D) dragged on through two years and violated his fiercely held principles of order, decorum, and family propriety, he would have been pleased with the heritage he left to his people.

Brigham's most obvious achievements were the product of his ever-present and practical decision-making. He instituted the pattern of church government through the Quorum of Twelve Apostles that persists to this day. In leading the Saints across Iowa he issued instructions about wagons and oxen, modes of travel, times of departure, and types of recreation that were followed by the hundreds of companies that crossed the Plains to the Salt Lake Valley in 1847 and succeeding years. In the Great Basin he directed the organization of several hundred Latter-day Saint settlements; took contracts to build the transcontinental telegraph and Pacific Railroad; set up several hundred cooperative retail, wholesale, and manufacturing enterprises; established colleges and universities; and initiated the construction of meetinghouses, tabernacles, and temples. And while doing all of this he carried on a running battle with the United States government in order to preserve the unique Mormon way of life.

Even more important, Brigham kept reminding the Saints that they were the Camp of Israel, the Chosen People in these latter days, God's partners in building a Zionic society. They had made a new and everlasting covenant to participate in preparing for the return of the Savior. Theirs was a divine purpose; what they were doing was part of the eternal plan. God would temper the winds, step up the rainfall, pacify the Indians, and heal the sick in order to assure the survival of their holy kingdom. They were not just settlers on the frontier; they were Saints of the Most High. They were not just struggling against drought, grasshoppers, and early snowfall; they were preparing for the final culmination of this last dispensation. Their affiliation with Mormonism did not simply mean belonging to a new church; they were being molded into Latter-day Saints who would be pleasing in the sight of God. Traveling to their Promised Land and living there under the direction of this nineteenth-century Moses was, as Jan Shipps has reminded us, a transformative experience. Englishmen, Welshmen, Scandinavians, Yankees, and Southerners were "corporately transmuted from their miscellaneousness and variableness into an ethnic body whose shared heritage was a wilderness journey and lives lived out in Zion." This new ethnicity "set the Saints apart, permitting—perhaps mandating—the creation of an LDS culture that would not only survive the death of Brigham Young, but the demise of the practice of plural marriage and the disappearance of Mormon political and economic hegemony."[2]

One of Brigham's legacies, then, was the continuity of his relatively self-sufficient and egalitarian commonwealth of Saints. He had spared no effort to render Mormon society as independent as possible of Gentiles—in business, government, education, and recreation. He had tried to protect "the Kingdom" against inroads of federal troops, "outside" businessmen, the fashions of "Babylon," and the higher learning of agnostics. He was, of course, not successful in maintaining a completely self-contained society; but his efforts to achieve it, assisted by the isolation imposed by their Great Basin refuge, had the effect of creating over the years, however partially and temporarily, a self-conscious and distinctive subculture—a near-nation.[3] It is not without reason that The Harvard Encyclopedia of American Ethnic Groups includes a long essay on "Mormons" as a group constituting the equivalent of an ethnic society.[4]

A second legacy was the tenacious tradition of Mormon cooperative institutions. It was Brigham who organized the "covenant" by which Mormon families in Missouri agreed to place all of their teams, wagons, provisions, cash, and other property at the disposal of a central committee charged with seeing to the care and transportation of all poor and destitute Saints. A similar covenant was made at the time of the expulsion from Nauvoo, with the result that men, supplies, and monies were commandeered to assure that all who needed help were transported to Winter Quarters, Nebraska, and ultimately to the Zion in the Far West. When the movement from Illinois had been essentially completed, Brigham next directed his attention to the thousands of

Saints in the East and in Europe. For this purpose he founded the Perpetual Emigrating Fund Company, which established what Katherine Coman called "the best system of regulated immigration in United States history."[5] Colonization was also facilitated by the system of organized cooperation that saw the laying out of agricultural villages and the appointment of groups to carry out the primary tasks of fencing, digging ditches, erecting dwellings, and herding the livestock. For Mormons on the frontier, life was hard but it was a shared struggle in which there was a mutual sharing of labor and other resources and jointly produced goods and services. This cooperative spirit, so urgently fostered by Brigham, continued well into the twentieth century. Professor Edward C. Banfield of Harvard University is one of many who has commented on the manner in which Mormon settlers in rural villages, through mutual aid and self-government, have maintained a highly organized society that successfully coped with the problems of the Great Depression of the 1930s and other natural and manmade disasters.[6]

Brigham's third legacy was the infusion into Mormon doctrine and practice of the necessity of "working out one's salvation," by making the earth green and productive and by building better homes and communities. Without abandoning religious ordinances, worship, and acts of charity, he recognized the equal, perhaps prior, importance of temporal salvation. On Sunday morning, October 5, 1856, Brigham stood before several thousand Saints seated in the leaf-covered bowery on Temple Square, and delivered the opening address of the semiannual general conference:

> I will now give this people the subject and the text for the Elders who may speak today and during the Conference. It is this. . . . Many of our brethren and sisters are on the Plains with handcarts, and probably many are now seven hundred miles from this place. They must be brought here, we must send assistance to them. The text will be—to get them here! I want the brethren who may speak to understand that their text is the people on the Plains. And the subject matter for this community is to send for them and bring them in before the winter sets in. That is my religion; that is the dictation of the Holy Ghost that I possess. It is to save the people. . . . This is the salvation I am now seeking for, to save our brethren that would be apt to perish, or suffer extremely, if we do not send them assistance. . . .
>
> I will tell you all that your faith, religion, and profession of religion, will never save one soul of you in the celestial kingdom of our God, unless you carry out just such principles as I am now teaching you. Go and bring in those people now on the Plains, and attend strictly to those things which we call temporal, . . . otherwise your faith will be in vain. . . . You will sink to hell unless you attend to the things we tell you. . . . These brethren and sisters [on the Plains] are doing all they can do [for their salvation], and the Lord has done all that is required of Him to do, and has given us the power to bring them in from the Plains, and teach them the further things of the kingdom of God.[7]

During the conference twenty-seven young men with 16 four-mule teams set out to rescue the incoming Saints. By the end of the month 250 teams were on the trail carrying the vegetables, fruit, flour, clothing, quilts, and blankets that were desperately needed by the westering companies delayed by the early snowfall. "My mission," concluded Brigham, "is to teach them [the people] with regard to their everyday lives."[8]

A fourth legacy of Brigham's to his people was an attitude or mind-set that held Mormonism to be synonymous with truth, incorporating scientific and philosophical as well as doctrinal truth. As far as he was concerned, anything that was true had to be part of Mormonism:

> Were you to ask me how it was that I embraced "Mormonism," I should answer, for the simple reason that it embraces all truth in heaven and on earth, in the earth, under the earth, and in hell, if there be any truth there. There is not truth outside of it; there is no virtue outside of it; there is nothing holy and honorable outside of it; for, wherever these principles are found among all the creations of God, the Gospel of Jesus Christ, and his order and Priesthood, embrace them.[9]

> Not only does the religion of Jesus Christ make the people acquainted with the things of God, and develop within them moral excellence and purity, but it holds out every encouragement and inducement possible, for them to increase in knowledge and intelligence, in every branch of mechanism [engineering] or in the arts and sciences, for all wisdom, and all the arts and sciences in the world are from God, and are designed for the good of His people.[10]

This concept—first expressed by Joseph Smith but consolidated into Mormon doctrine by Young—rejected a narrow sectarianism, encouraged Mormons to seek higher education in eastern colleges and universities, and ultimately led to the flowering of church-supported higher education in Utah.

Finally, Brigham Young left the indelible stamp and memory of his powerful personality on his followers and their descendants. President of his church for thirty years, political leader, businessman, colonizer, head of a large and influential family, persuasive speaker, ever-present counselor, he could hardly be forgotten; a considerable body of folklore was left in his wake. Whenever his name is mentioned, as it may be in any gathering in Utah or an adjacent state, someone always has a story to tell about him or a favorite quotation to offer from one of his eight hundred recorded sermons. Very often the stories are hand-me-downs from grandparents or great-grandparents who knew him personally. Some of them are favorable to his memory, some not, but all suggest that the folk appreciated his common-sense approach to life's problems. To pick out a random example, a family tells of an ancestor who "had words" with Brigham; afterward, the ancestor quit going to church. Later, Brigham was speaking in a local meetinghouse when this man walked in. Brigham stopped his sermon, stared at the person, and shouted, "There is the man that owes me $2,000." The man shouted back, "That's a damn lie and you know it." The truth of the story is doubtful—there is no evidence of any transaction between the two in Brigham's financial records—but it illustrates the propensity of pioneer descendants to perpetuate an image of Brigham as a straight-talker who sometimes resorted to public denunciation.

Perhaps one reason for the preoccupation of modern Utahans with their first governor is the continued puzzlement over his character. He could be harsh and outspoken in his censure; he occasionally showed contempt for intellectuality; he indulged at times in exaggeration and hyperbole; and he could be insensitive to the feelings of those close to him. Having paid his "dues" through his own pain and sacrifice, he expected others to do the same, and was a demanding leader.[11] He was also unduly suspicious of the motives of political figures who might be in a position to undermine Mormon institutions and sometimes spoke contemptuously of national leaders like James Buchanan.[12]

Imperfect as he may have been in these respects, he was also human in other ways that caused thousands to love him, admire him, imitate him, and seek his advice. He cried when he saw the suffering of helpless people. His compassion for orphans caused him to invite dozens into his household. He was hard on men who neglected their wives or cheated widows; he was patient with violators of church standards (e.g., men who chewed tobacco); he was a good listener, had a sense of humor, enjoyed theatrical performances and dances, and in the quiet of many homes prayed for the sick to be healed. His understanding of human limitations is illustrated by his refusal on occasion to sanction the excommunication of people who had committed some outrage or dereliction. When the bishop in Ogden, Utah, wrote him inquiring whether a man who had engaged in wrongdoing should be "cut off," Brigham replied, "Men have the liberty of serving God, serving themselves, or serving the devil, just as they please. But do not withdraw fellowship from them."[13] People followed him out of conviction, out of the confidence stimulated by his strength and firmness, rather than out of compulsion. They quoted him because they took delight in his picturesque, if sometimes abrasive, language. In short, Young was a successful leader because of qualities that we assess today as being both positive and negative.

A short-legged man with powerful shoulders and a massive chest whose forceful voice urged a whole generation of Saints to build the Kingdom of God in a desolate and inhospitable region, Brigham gave the appearance of being a hard man—one who did not hesitate to call a spade a spade, one whose tongue cut down hypocrites, betrayers, malingerers. Upon his departure from Missouri, according to a diary entry made by one who had heard him address some friends, he cursed the Missourians:

> Bro. Brigham arose and [made] some pointed and appropriate remarks. He called upon the Lord to bless this place for the good of the Saints, and curse every

Gentile who should attempt to settle here with sickness, rottenness, and death. Also to curse the land of Missouri, that it might cease to bring forth grain or fruit of any kind to its inhabitants, and that they might be cursed [with] sickness, rottenness and death, that their flesh might consume away on their bones, and their blood be turned into maggots and that their torments never cease.[14]

In his sermons he sometimes used strong metaphors; he would whip out his bowie knife to figuratively fight evil, he would scatter the enemy across lots, he would drive in the sword of righteousness to its hilt. And yet, it is possible that these violent expressions were only a cover for Brigham's basically nonviolent feelings, for he was basically a nonviolent person. As he said: "Never, in the days of my life, have I hurt a man with the palm of my hand. I never have hurt any person any other way except with this unruly member, my tongue."[15] Perhaps Brigham's verbal ferocity masked a tender, softhearted person who was ashamed to admit his compassion out of fear that people would think him weak or cowardly. His caustic criticism of others may well have been an external projection of his discontent with his own ambivalence.

Those who immerse themselves in his diaries, letters, and sermons may be pardoned if their perplexity continues. Was he a kindly, benevolent, tenderhearted father figure or the sarcastic, hate-spouting chief of the Danites? As he systematically dressed down some people, even close associates, was he really chastising them, or was he, by chance, talking to himself? Was his criticism of Orson Pratt the result of a considered judgment that Orson's doctrines were wrong? Or was it, instead, a manifestation of confidence that his own doctrinal insight, untutored as it was, was nevertheless a more accurate reflection of the divine nature than the systematically thought-out speculations of the educated scholar? Should he be considered a generous man because he put dozens of children not his own through school, or a skinflint because he adamantly refused to raise the wages of some young men he had employed to survey for the transcontinental railroad? Should he be thought of as a financial wizard because he was one of the most successful businessmen in western America, or as a failure because so many of his enterprises foundered? Some of the fascination with Brigham is that one can know a great deal about him yet never fully understand; his personality was full of ambiguities and complexities.

Nevertheless, certain conclusions are warranted. As a father and husband Brigham was neither dictatorial nor permissive. He set goals, tried to achieve them through persuasion, and resisted the contemporary disposition to break the wills of children. His letters to his children show him to have been affectionate, supportive, and anxious to see them develop their talents.

As a political leader, he was astute. His correspondence with presidents, cabinet members, chairmen of congressional committees, and Thomas L. Kane reveal sagacity and discernment. He was also a person of strong determination, resolute and unwavering—some said intractable. A confident and decisive administrator, he seldom backed down in a test of wills. Not a dictator in the modern sense, he was like the driver of a coach over a perilous mountain road who would encourage the horses here, direct them there, nudge them along, and, when appropriate, apply the whip. Brigham's own description of his mission was expressed in a letter to his nephew in Boston, dispatched from Winter Quarters, Nebraska, just prior to his first departure for the Rocky Mountains. Using biblical imagery, he wrote:

> I feel like a father with a great family of children around me, in a winter storm, and I am looking with calmness, confidence and patience, for the clouds to break and the sun to shine, so that I can run out and plant and sow and gather in the corn and wheat and say, Children, come home, winter is approaching again and I have homes and wood and flour and meal and meat and potatoes and squashes and onions and cabbages and all things in abundance, and I am ready to kill the fatted calf and make a joyful feast to all who will come and partake.[16]

As a businessman, Brigham was scrupulously honest—he would hunt down creditors until they were paid. But like many people who have grown up in poverty, he was seldom generous in a strictly business deal. His employees had to toe the mark, his debtors must keep the money coming, and his prospective purchasers were not to expect any extraordinary discounts.

As a church leader, Brigham showed his spiritual side—he prayed, a few times he was impelled to speak in tongues, he enjoyed the ceremonies of the endowment house and temple, and he is known to have exercised his faith and priesthood authority in healing the sick. As a religious leader he was undeniably sincere—and as president he was so confident of his own abilities that he was loath to delegate responsibility or authority.

Perhaps the single characteristic or quality that Brigham was most proud of was one that he himself cited just one week after he had learned that five thousand federal troops and hangers-on were on their way to occupy Utah. After mentioning some acquaintances who hesitated to lead out, who were diffident, timid, or reluctant, Brigham thanked God that, despite his many weaknesses and shortcomings, his conversion to Mormonism had awakened him to both his privileges and his responsibilities. "When I think of myself," he said, "I think just this—I have the grit in me, and I will do my duty anyhow." Without training as a youth, his education, he said, came along with Mormonism. Early missionary work, participation in the march from Ohio to Missouri known as Zion's Camp, direction of the apostles in England, supervision of many activities of the church in Nauvoo—all these prepared him for the position he would occupy when he succeeded to the position of prophet, led the Camp of Israel to the Salt Lake Valley, and became their political, economic, and spiritual leader for three decades. Brigham Young did not do it, he would have said: it was God. But in exercising his divinely appointed stewardship, he declared, "I was so gritty that I always tried [to do] my best."[17]

Those closest to him agreed. In a letter to the editor of the New York *Herald*, Jedediah M. Grant, who had been one of Brigham's counselors, expressed the Utah consensus in a memorable statement that can serve as a concluding balance-sheet on Young's character:

> I can't undertake to explain Brigham Young to your Atlantic citizens, or expect you to put him at his value. Your great men Eastward are to me like your ivory and pearl handled table knives, balance handles, more shiny than the inside of my watch case; but, with only edge enough to slice bread and cheese or help spoon victuals, and all alike by the dozen one with another. Brigham is the article that sells out West with us—between a Roman cutlass and a beef butcher knife, the thing to cut up a deer or cut down an enemy, and that will save your life or carve your dinner every bit as well, though the handpiece is buck horn and the case a hogskin hanging in the breech of your pantaloons. You, that judge men by the handle and sheath, how can I make you know a good *Blade?*[18]

Appendixes
Notes and References
Bibliographical Essay
Index

APPENDIX A
CHRONOLOGY OF EVENTS
IN THE LIFE OF BRIGHAM YOUNG

1801	June 1	Born in Whitingham, Vermont.
1804		Family moves to Sherburne, New York.
1813		Family moves to Auburn, New York.
1815	June 11	Mother dies of tuberculosis.
1823		Joins Methodist Reformed Church.
1824	October 8	Marries Miriam Works in Aurelius, New York. Employed as carpenter, joiner, painter, glazier.
1829		Moves to Mendon, New York.
1830	Spring	First sees the Book of Mormon.
1831	Fall	Converted to Mormonism.
1832	April 14	Baptized by Eleazer Miller at Mendon, New York. Ordained an elder.
	September 8	Wife, Miriam Works Young, dies of tuberculosis.
	Sept.–Oct.	Travels to Kirtland, Ohio, to meet Joseph Smith.
	December	Leaves on mission to Canada with brother, Joseph Young.
1833	February	Returns to Mendon.
	April–August	Second mission to Canada.
	September	Moves family from Mendon, New York, to Kirtland, Ohio.
1834	February 18	Marries Mary Ann Angell.
	May–July	Travels from Kirtland to Missouri and back with Zion's Camp.
	Summer–Fall	Labors on construction of Kirtland Temple, printing office, etc.
1835	February	Appointed to Quorum of Twelve Apostles.
	May–September	Mission to eastern states with Twelve.
	Fall	Attends Hebrew school in Kirtland.
1836	March 27	Attends Kirtland Temple dedication.
	Summer	Mission to eastern states and New England.
1837	March–June	Business mission to eastern states with Willard Richards.
	June–August	Mission to New York and Massachusetts.
	Fall	Failure of Kirtland Bank.
	December 22	Forced to leave Kirtland, Ohio, for safety.
1838	March 14	Arrives at Far West, Missouri.
	Fall	Organizes Mormon evacuation of Missouri.
1839	January 26	Organizes committee to remove Saints from Missouri.
	February	Moves family to Quincy, Illinois.
	April	Goes with Council of the Twelve to Far West.
	May	Moves family again to Montrose, Iowa.
	September 14	Leaves for mission to England—he and family all very sick.
	October 12	Death of father, John Young.
1840	March 9	Leaves New York for mission to England.
	April 6	Arrival in England.
	April 14	Succeeds to presidency of Quorum of the Twelve.

1841	April 21	Sails from England to return home.
	July 1	Arrives in Nauvoo.
	July 9	Commanded in a revelation to send the "word" abroad and care for his family.
	September	Elected to Nauvoo City Council.
	November 8	Offers dedicatory prayer for baptismal font.
1842	May 4	Receives washings, anointings, and endowments from Joseph Smith.
	May 18	Appointed to committee to aid immigrants.
	Nov.–Dec.	Serious illness—skin peels off.
1843	July–October	Travels in eastern states to raise money for temple and Nauvoo House.
1844	May 21	Trip to East to promote Joseph Smith as presidential candidate.
	June 27	Death of Joseph Smith and Hyrum Smith in Carthage Jail.
	August 6	Arrives in Nauvoo.
	August 8	Claims right of church leadership for the Twelve, is upheld by the congregation.
	August 31	Elected lieutenant general of the Nauvoo Legion. Organizes many Seventies' quorums.
	May 24	Lays capstone of Nauvoo Temple.
	October 5	Dedicates Nauvoo Temple.
	December	Spends much time in temple.
1846	February 15	Departs from Nauvoo, begins Mormon exodus west.
	July	Directs formation of Mormon Battalion.
	Fall	Establishes Winter Quarters.
1847	April 14	Leaves Winter Quarters with first pioneer company.
	July 24	Arrives in Great Salt Lake Valley.
	July 28	Selects site for temple, directs laying out of grid for the city.
	August 8	Begins return trip to Winter Quarters.
	December 5	Ordained as church president at Kanesville.
1848	May 26	Leaves Winter Quarters for Salt Lake again.
	September 20	Arrives in Salt Lake City.
1849		Directs settlement of Utah Valley, Sanpete Valley, Tooele Valley.
	January	Directs first typesetting and printing of currency in the valley.
	February 14	Divides Salt Lake City into wards.
	March 12	Elected governor of provisional State of Deseret.
1850	June	*Deseret News* begins publication.
	July	Appointed as census enumerator for Utah.
	August 28–31	Chooses site for city of Ogden.
	September 15	Named president of Perpetual Emigrating Fund Company.
1851	January 9	Salt Lake City incorporated.
	January 20–28	Visits settlements in north—Davis and Weber counties. Organizes Weber Stake.
	March 17–26	Visits Utah County. Organizes Utah Stake.
	March 24	Sends colonizers to settle San Bernardino.
	April 22–May 24	Organizes settlements in south, visits Parowan, explores Sevier Valley.
	July 21	Organizes three Indian agencies in Utah.
	August 8	Organizes Utah into three judicial districts.
	Oct. 21–Nov. 7	Trip south. Locates territorial capital at Fillmore on October 29.
1852	April 22–May 21	Exploration trip in southern Utah, visits Indians.
	August 28–29	Plural marriage publicly announced.

1853	February 14	Breaks ground for Salt Lake Temple construction.
	April 6	Lays cornerstone for temple.
	July 18	Beginning of Walker Indian war.
	October 26	Indians kill John W. Gunnison and party in southern Utah.
1854	May 4–30	Trip south. Signs treaty with Chief Walker ending war.
1855	May 8–27	Leaves to visit southern settlements.
	June 18–25	Trip to visit northern settlements.
	December	Travels to Fillmore for session of territorial legislature.
1856	January	Returns to Salt Lake City.
	Fall	Reformation and rededication spreads through settlements.
	November	Organizes efforts to relieve handcart companies stranded on plains.
1857	April 24–May 26	Trip to Salmon River settlements.
	July 24	Learns of approaching federal army.
	September 11	Mountain Meadows Massacre in southern Utah.
	September 15	Declares martial law in the territory, forbids entrance of federal troops.
1858	March 21	Directs evacuation of northern Utah settlements.
	April	Moves family to Provo.
	April 12	Greets Alfred Cumming, his successor as governor.
	June 11	Meets with federal peace commissioners, work out agreement.
	June 26	Johnston's army comes through Salt Lake, moves on to Cedar Valley.
	July	Family and other inhabitants return to Salt Lake City.
1859	February	Deseret Alphabet introduced.
	March	Rumors of attempts to arrest Brigham Young.
1860		Makes contract for overland telegraph line of 500 miles.
	June	Visits settlements in Cache Valley.
1861	May 15–June 8	Visits settlements in southern Utah.
	August	Meets with Richard F. Burton during his visit to Salt Lake.
	October 18	Sends first telegram over new overland telegraph.
1862	March 6	Dedicates Salt Lake Theater.
	July 8	Federal antibigamy law signed.
	September 1–25	Visit to settlements in southern Utah.
	October	Visits northern settlements.
	October 20	Colonel Patrick E. Connor and California Volunteers arrive in Salt Lake City.
1863	March 10	Arrested for bigamy and placed under bond.
	April 20–May 19	Visits southern Utah settlements.
	September 7	His woolen factory begins operations.
1864	May 16–26	Visits settlements in Bear Lake Valley for first time.
	September 1–29	Visits settlements in southern Utah.
1865	April	Beginning of Black Hawk Indian war.
	April 10	Plans to build telegraph line throughout Utah settlements.
	May 3–11	Visits Cache Valley settlements.
	July 7–19	Visits Sanpete County settlements.
	August 1–10	Visits Cache Valley.
	September 4–29	Visits settlements in southern Utah.
	November 9	Asks church leaders to assist in building telegraph line.
1866	January 1	*Juvenile Instructor* begins publication.
		Communities disbanded because of Indian problems.
	December 1	Deseret Telegraph line opened.
1867	March 21	Named president of Deseret Telegraph Company.

	April	Abandonment of more settlements in southern Utah.
	April 22–May 15	Visits settlements in southern Utah.
	Fall	Reorganizes Relief Society organization for women.
	October	Tabernacle completed—first conference held there.
	December	Reorganizes School of the Prophets.
1868	May 21	Takes contract for Union Pacific Railroad construction in Utah.
	Summer	Visits settlements.
	September 20	Organizes stake in Nephi.
	October	Elected president of ZCMI.
1869	March 8	Appointed president of Utah Central Railroad.
	May 10	Completion of transcontinental railroad.
	May 17	Breaks ground for Utah Central Railroad—Ogden to Salt Lake.
	June 1	Named president of Provo Woolen Mills.
	June 20	Organizes Bear Lake Stake.
	November	Organizes Young Ladies Cooperative Retrenchment Association.
	December	Godbeite movement takes shape.
1870	January 10	Completion of Utah Central line—drives last spike.
	February 24–April 16	Visits southern Utah and Arizona settlements.
	April 27	Death of oldest brother, John Young.
	Aug. 27–Sept. 24	Trip to southern Utah. Organizes town and ward at Kanab.
	November 25	Leaves to spend winter at St. George.
1871	February 10	Returns to Salt Lake.
	May 1	Groundbreaking for Utah Southern Railroad.
	June 26–July	Visits northern settlements.
	October 2	Arrested on cohabitation charges, confined to his home.
	November 9	Dedicates St. George Temple site.
	December 26	Returns to Salt Lake for trial.
1872	January 2	Appears in court, case continued, remains under custody in his home.
	April 25	Released from custody by writ of habeas corpus.
	August	Visits Cache Valley.
	December	Travels to St. George with Thomas L. Kane.
1873	February 27	Returns to Salt Lake City.
	April 6	Appoints five additional counselors to First Presidency.
	November 28	Leaves for St. George. Organizes United Order in southern Utah settlements.
1874	April 20	Returns to Salt Lake City.
	May	Organizes United Order in Salt Lake City wards.
	June 23	Poland Bill (anti-Mormon legislation) approved.
	October	Ill. Leaves for St. George.
1875	February	Returns to Salt Lake City.
		Ann Eliza Webb sues for divorce.
	Spring	Young Men's Mutual Improvement Association organized in Salt Lake City. Organizes Brigham Young Academy at Provo.
	July 17	Rebaptized at Ephraim.
	August 6	Death of eldest son, Joseph A. Young.
	September 1	Death of first counselor George A. Smith.
	October 3	Visits with President Ulysses S. Grant.
	October 29	Arrested on contempt charges in Ann Eliza case.
	October 30	Deeds land to Brigham Young Academy at Provo.
1876	March	Directs colonization of the Little Colorado in Arizona.
	May 1–July 1	Visits St. George.

	November 1	Leaves for St. George.
1877	April 6	Directs massive organization of stakes throughout the territory.
		Dedicates St. George temple.
	April 25	Dedicates site for temple at Manti.
	April 27	Returns to Salt Lake City.
	July 24	Deeds land to Brigham Young College at Logan.
	August 29	Dies at home in Salt Lake City.

APPENDIX B
THE JOHN AND ABIGAIL YOUNG FAMILY

Name	Birthdate/Place	Married/ Spouse/(No. Children)	Death Date/Place
John Young	7 March 1763 Hopkinton, Mass.	1. 1785 Abigail Howe (11)	12 October 1839 Quincy, Ill.
		2. 1817 Hannah Brown (3)	
Abigail Howe	1766 Shrewsbury, Mass.	1. 1785 John Young (11)	11 June 1815 Cayuga Co., N.Y.
Nancy	6 August 1786 Hopkinton, Mass.	1. 1803 Daniel Kent (8)	22 September 1860 Salt Lake City
Fanny	8 November 1787 Hopkinton, Mass.	1. 1803 Robert Carr	11 June 1859 Salt Lake City
		2. February 1832 Roswell Murray	
Rhoda	10 September 1789 Platauva Dist., N.Y.	1. 11 February 1813 John P. Greene (7)	18 January 1841 Commerce, Ill.
John, Jr.	22 May 1791 Hopkinton, Mass.	1. 1813 Theodosia Kimball (5)	27 April 1870 Salt Lake City
		2. ? Mary Ann Cleveland	
		3. 9 November 1853 Sarah McCleave (3)	
Nabby	23 April 1793 Hopkinton, Mass.	———	1807 Smyrna, N.Y.
Susannah	7 June 1795 Hopkinton, Mass.	1. 1814 James Little (4)	5 May 1852 Salt Lake City
		2. 1829 William Stilson (3)	
Joseph	7 April 1797 Hopkinton, Mass.	1. 18 February 1834 Jane A. Bicknell (11)	16 July 1881 Salt Lake City
		2. July 1845 Lydia C. H. Fleming (3)	

Name	Birthdate/Place	Married/ Spouse/(No. Children)	Death Date/Place
		3. Jan. or Feb. 1846 Lucinda Allen (5)	
		4. ? Mary Ann Huntley (2)	
		5. ? Sarah Jane Snow (1)	
Phinehas Howe	16 February 1799 Hopkinton, Mass.	1. 18 January 1818 Clarissa Hamilton (5)	10 October 1879 Salt Lake City
		2. 1836 Lucy Pearce Cowdery	
		3. November 1853 Phebe Clark (9)	
		4. 1854 Elinor Maria James (5)	
Brigham	1 June 1801 Whitingham, Vt.	1. 5 October 1824 Miriam Works (2)	August 1877 Salt Lake City
		2. February 1834 Mary Ann Angell (6)	
		Other wives listed in Appendix C	
Louisa	25 September 1804 Sherburne, N.Y.	1. 6 October 1824 Joel Sanford (4)	1833 Independence, Mo.
Lorenzo Dow	19 October 1807 Sherburne, N.Y.	1. 6 June 1825 Persis Goodall (10)	1895 Salt Lake City
		2. 9 March 1843 Harriet P. Wheeler (2)	
		3. 29 April 1856 Hannah I. Hewitt (5)	
		4. 25 November 1856 Eleanor Jones (4)	
		5. 18 April 1863 Joanna (Ann) Larson (3)	

APPENDIX C
BRIGHAM YOUNG'S FAMILY

Listed here are the wives by whom Brigham Young had children; date of marriage to each wife is in parentheses.

MIRIAM WORKS, 1806–1832 (1824)
Elizabeth, 1825–1903
Vilate, 1830–1902

MARY ANN ANGELL, 1803–1882 (1834)
Joseph A., 1834–1875
Brigham, Jr., 1836–1903
Mary Ann, 1836–1843
Alice (Emma), 1839–1874
Luna, 1842–1922
John W., 1844–1924

LUCY ANN DECKER, 1822–1890 (1842)
Brigham Heber, 1845–1928
Fanny Caroline, 1849–1892
Ernest Irving, 1851–1879
Shemira, 1853–1915
Arta De Christa, 1855–1916
Feramorz Little, 1858–1881
Clarissa Hamilton, 1860–1939

HARRIETT E. COOK, 1824–1898 (1843)
Oscar Brigham, 1846–1910

CLARISSA DECKER, 1828–1889 (1844)
Jeannette, 1849–1930
Nabbie, 1852–1894
Jedediah Grant, 1855?–1856
Albert Jeddie, 1858–1864?
Charlotte, 1861–1892

CLARISSA ROSS, 1814–1858 (1844)
Mary Eliza, 1847–1871
Clarissa Maria, 1849–1935
Willard, 1852–1936
Phebe Louisa, 1854–1931

EMILY DOW PARTRIDGE, 1824–1899 (1844)
Edward Partridge, 1845–1852
Emily Augusta, 1849–1926
Caroline, 1851–1903
Joseph Don Carlos, 1855–1938
Miriam, 1857–1919

Josephine, 1860–1912
Lura, 1862–1862

LOUISA BEAMAN, 1815–1850 (1846)
Joseph, 1846–1846?
Hyrum, 1846–1846?
Moroni, 1847–1847
Alvah, 1848–1848
Alma, 1848–1848

MARGARET MARIA ALLEY, 1825–1852 (1846)
Evelyn Louisa, 1850–1917
Mahonri Moriancumer, 1852–1884

EMMELINE FREE, 1826–1875 (1846)
Ella Elizabeth, 1847–1890
Marinda Hyde, 1849–1926
Hyrum Smith, 1851–1925
Emmeline Amanda, 1853–1895
Louise Nelle, 1854–1908
Lorenzo Dow, 1856–1905
Alonzo, 1858–1918
Ruth, 1861–1944
Daniel Wells, 1863–1863
Ardelle Elwin, 1864–1900

MARGARET PIERCE, 1823–1907 (1846)
Brigham Morris, 1854–1931

ZINA D. HUNTINGTON, 1821–1901 (1846)
Zina Prescinda, 1850–1931

LUCY BIGELOW, 1830–1905 (1847)
Eudora Lovina, 1852–1922
Susa Amelia, 1856–1933
Rhoda Mabel, 1863–1950

ELIZA BURGESS, 1827–1915 (1852)
Alfales, 1853–1920

HARRIET BARNEY, 1830–1911 (1856)
Phineas Howe, 1862–1903

MARY VAN COTT, 1844–1884 (1865)
Fannie, 1870–1950

WIVES OF BRIGHAM YOUNG BY
WHOM HE DID NOT HAVE CHILDREN

Included in this list are women Brigham Young held out to be wives, in the sense that he cared for them in a temporal way as a husband would. He provided them with a home, listed them in his will, and provided for their children by earlier marriages. One supposes that all or most of these were not connubial marriages. The list does not include the names of some thirty women who were "sealed" to Brigham Young "for eternity only," with no intention that he would share earthly life with them or their children, if any, by earlier marriages. The names below are given in the order of marriage or sealing.*

AUGUSTA ADAMS (COBB) 1802–1886 (1843)
SUSANNAH SNIVELY 1815–1892 (1844)
ELIZA R. SNOW (SMITH) 1804–1887 (1844)
MARTHA BOWKER 1822–1890 (1846)
ELLEN A. ROCKWOOD 1829–1866 (1846)
NAMAH K. J. CARTER (TWISS) 1821–1909 (1846)
MARY JANE BIGELOW 1827–1868 (1847) Divorced 1851
HARRIET AMELIA FOLSOM 1838–1910 (1863)
ANN ELIZA WEBB 1844–? (1868) Divorced 1876

* Two plural wives of Joseph Smith to whom Young was sealed during the winter of 1845–46 died shortly thereafter; they might have been on this list if they had lived longer. They were Olive Grey Frost, 1816–1845, and Maria Lawrence, 1823–1847.

APPENDIX D
THE SETTLEMENT OF THE BRIGHAM YOUNG
ESTATE, 1877–1879

The settlement of Brigham Young's estate during the months after his burial is an important aspect of his history because it illustrates Young's conception of the interrelation of church and private enterprise. With his approval, church and private funds were almost inextricably intermingled. The events surrounding the settlement also contribute to an understanding of some of the problems faced by Brigham in administering economic and religious affairs during the thirty years of his stewardship as leader of the Latter-day Saints (1847–77). In particular, the settlement of the estate revealed how he had attempted to circumvent the kind of confiscatory federal legislation that would have prevented him from carrying out his self-imposed mission to build up Zion. Above all, we can be sure that the long and complicated procedure involved in the settlement would have been highly distasteful to him. It was a matter dealt with by a small group, including one that Brigham despised—lawyers. It fostered disunity in his family. And it forced a separation of private and public affairs that violated the seamless unity that had been his objective ever since he attached himself to the Mormon movement in 1832.[1]

Much of the difficulty was caused by the 1862 passage of the Morrill Anti-Bigamy Act, which, in the process of outlawing polygamy, disincorporated the church and limited its real estate to $50,000.[2] All property in excess of this limitation was forfeit to the United States. Although the act specified that "existing vested rights in real estate shall not be impaired by the provisions of this section," the church technically held no such rights. The United States government, which had acquired from Mexico the territory that included Utah by the Treaty of Guadalupe Hidalgo in 1848, did not grant land titles to Mormon settlers until 1869; thus they were only squatters on the public domain when the act was passed. When Utahans were entitled to enter their tracts in the federal land office, any entries made in the name of the church or its agents would be forfeit if the combined values exceeded $50,000, regardless of how long the lands had been in church possession.

The purpose of the act, said Senator James A. Bayard of Delaware, one of its sponsors, was to prevent the accumulation of property in the hands of "theocratic institutions inconsistent with our form of government." In the absence of the property limitation, he said, "the ecclesiastical institutions which prevail [in Utah Territory] will ultimately become the owners in perpetuity of all the valuable land in that Territory, and so afford a nucleus for the permanence of their general institutions unless a stop be put to it by act of Congress."[3]

The act was generally regarded as unconstitutional, and little attempt was made to enforce it until after Brigham's death. But because of the ever-present threat of stronger anti-Mormon legislation—the Wade bill of 1866, the Cragin bill of 1867–69, the Ashley and Cullom bills of 1869–70, and the Frelinghuysen bill of 1872–73—Brigham and his associates decided to feign compliance rather than engage in open violation.[4] Church property was simply held in the name of Brigham Young or some other trustee. As Brigham stated in a sermon in the Salt Lake Tabernacle: "That is how the government binds us up [alluding to the property limitation imposed by the act]. Never mind, we can build temples, pay our tithing and our free will offerings; we can raise our bread, hire our school teachers and teach our children without help."[5]

That all his associates did not necessarily agree with Brigham's free-wheeling use of church income and wealth in this manner is suggested by a January 1878 notation in the diary of George Q. Cannon: "Some of my brethren . . . did have feelings concerning his [Brigham's] course. . . . In a few words, the feeling seems to be that he transcended the bounds of the authority which he legitimately held. I have been greatly surprised to find so much dissatisfaction in such quarters. It is felt that the funds of the Church have been used with a freedom not warranted by the authority which he held."[6] In a later, more guarded, public statement, Cannon explained:

It is well known that the Church property and his own [President Young's] private property were for years before his death intimately interwoven. He well understood the weighty reasons there were for this. His surviving associates and his Executors were also well acquainted with these reasons. But though this was the case, he was not satisfied to have things remain so. Upon several different occasions he seriously discussed plans by which he could safely transfer the bulk of the estate that stood in his name to the Church.[7]

In 1873, with the help of General Thomas L. Kane, who was visiting Utah, Brigham prepared his will, a lengthy, carefully drawn document designed to stand up in court without costly and embarrassing litigation.[8] The will was part of a general legal settlement of church accounts that followed the opening of the Salt Lake Land Office. On November 21, 1871, Daniel H. Wells as mayor of Salt Lake City had entered the lands within his jurisdiction under the Town-Site Act and in turn began conveying these properties to private individuals and groups. Since the church was involved in some of these grants of property, Brigham resigned the position of trustee-in-trust of the church in April 1873, a first step in clarifying its position in matters of property rights. His counselor, George A. Smith, was appointed trustee-in-trust in his stead, with twelve assistant trustees-in-trust, some of whom were clerks in the office of the church president, others of whom administered tithing funds or managed church enterprises. Young could now unburden himself of "secular cares and responsibilities . . . leaving the minutiae to younger men."[9] The "young men" included Joseph F. Smith, Lorenzo Snow, Brigham Young, Jr., Albert Carrington, John W. Young, and George Q. Cannon.

Within a few months, and probably by November when the will was ready to sign, Brigham made out deeds of church property to this trustee-in-trust successor.[10] These properties included Temple Square, containing the Mormon Tabernacle, the Assembly Hall, the Endowment House, and the partially completed Salt Lake Temple; the Tithing Office grounds east of Temple Square, used for the church mint, the General Tithing Office, the tithing store with its adjacent facilities for animals, and the *Deseret News* building; the Council House lot on part of a block just south of Temple Square, now (1984) occupied by Utah Firstbank and the Union Pacific building; and the Church Farm in south Salt Lake Valley. All had been considered church property since the original Salt Lake City survey of 1848 but had been conveyed to Brigham by Mayor Wells in 1872. Brigham was holding in his own name more church property than these four tracts of land; but because of the federal escheatment threat he conveyed only the most valuable and indisputable pieces to George A. Smith, the new trustee.

Brigham fell back on a second device to avoid complications while divesting himself of church properties. Other private individuals had also held such properties in trust; this policy seems to have been accelerated in 1873. Because of the posture of secrecy, sorting out the exact transactions is difficult. They seem to have included capital stock in the Deseret Telegraph Company, Zion's Savings Bank and Trust Company, the Salt Lake Theater, and title to the *Deseret News* properties, the Church Historian's Office, and the Big Cottonwood Canyon quarry that furnished granite for the Salt Lake Temple.

As an additional step toward simplifying the complicated business affairs of the church, George A. Smith urged its general authorities to settle their own accounts with the trustee-in-trust.[11] The latter had served as the private banker for general authorities at a time when banking was almost completely nonexistent in Utah. Brigham and other authorities had drawn on the tithing resources of the church, repaying all or part of this obligation in money, property, or services. These transactions were apparently interest-free. To the extent that the borrowings represented a form of compensation in lieu of salary for time and labor expended on the church's behalf, the borrower was not required to repay the advances.

The rationale for such transactions seems to have been twofold: first, Brigham and associated general authorities were consecrating their time and fortunes to the church and were therefore entitled to draw from the church treasury on occasion. Second, the projects financed by these borrowed funds were, for the most part, generally beneficial to the community—the construction of railroads, theaters, woolen mills, canals, and gas works.

But there were also substantial private benefits. Brigham's ability to use church funds almost at will was one of the reasons for his worldly success. To a lesser extent, this system also operated to the advantage of other general authorities. George Q. Cannon obtained $27,489 in credits from the trustee-in-trust during the first thirteen years he was an apostle. In 1873, when settlements were being made with George A. Smith, Cannon's account was "balanced" by crediting him with the same amount for "services rendered." Ten years later, Cannon repaid the church by giving his magnificent house on South Temple Street to the trustee-in-trust.[12] That the Bank of Deseret and Zion's Savings Bank were established at approximately the same time these accounts were settled suggests that the trustee-in-trust wanted general authorities in the future to draw on these semiprivate banks rather than on the tithing resources of the church.

When George A. Smith died on September 1, 1875, the resolution of accounts still incomplete, the position of trustee-in-trust reverted to Brigham and remained there until his death in 1877. Brigham transferred some property to endow academies in Provo and Logan. Other local property, such as the tithing grounds at various "old" settlements, had been occupied so long by local church authorities that they held possessory titles. Thus these properties escaped being drawn into the litigation whirlpool that developed after Brigham's death.

Brigham's will was read on September 3, 1877, in the presence of seventeen wives, sixteen sons, twenty-eight daughters, and a few friends.[13] The sons plus a few close friends (Daniel H. Wells, LeGrand Young, George Q. Cannon, Albert Carrington, and James Jack) constituted a committee to go to Brigham's safe and see if there was a will. The committee made a search of the safe and returned with the will. After it was read, Cannon and LeGrand Young explained probate to the family. John W. Young moved that the executors probate the will at once, and after this motion carried unanimously the meeting was dismissed by Cannon.[14]

Control over Young's affairs was now beginning to shift from family members to associates. Although Brigham Young, Jr., acted as one of the executors, Cannon, the principal executor, played a major role in the settlement of his close friend's estate.

The will was filed for probate on September 4, 1877, in the Salt Lake court. Named as executors were Cannon, the oldest son, Brigham Young, Jr., and Albert Carrington. All three were members of the Council of Twelve Apostles.

One reason Brigham had named apostles as executors was to assure that the church received all the properties due it. "The last time he conversed with me upon the subject of his Will," said Cannon a few months later, "he proposed to change it and to give each of his heirs ten thousand dollars apiece and the remainder to the Church." To this end the executors should have "ample powers . . . to fully settle everything of a trust character, so that the interests of the Church should be fully protected."[15] In his private journal, Cannon amplified the "reasons" that prevented Brigham from carrying out his intent: "He and I had conversations a number of times about his property. He was desirous to leave a portion to the Church, but the great difficulty that constantly presented itself to him was the risk of it escheating to the government. . . . After it [the will] was drawn up he frequently expressed the wish that he could leave his property some way to the Church and had a law of Congress not threatened the Church with the confiscation of all over $50,000 I have no doubt that he would have left it a considerable portion of his estate."[16]

With respect to the property legitimately his own, Brigham's will attempted an equitable division among his heirs, designating specific properties each was to receive and acknowledging properties he had transferred to them before his death. Generally, each family inherited the home in which it was living. Until all of the wives died or until the youngest child came of age—and the youngest was then approaching eight years of age—the income from the undistributed properties was to go into a trust to be divided among the various mothers for the support of their children.

Besides the provisions for payment of debts, commissions for executors, property and living allowances for his heirs, and other financial matters, the will also reveals something of Brigham's values and the customs of his society. While it provided that any widow or child who married would lose the right to a share of rents and incomes, it also authorized the payment of $100 to a mother and $500 to a child upon their marriage. (A $500 payment was also allotted to any son going into business after reaching the age of twenty-one.) The will was careful to specify what was meant by "married" or "marriage," including three possibilities: "by ceremony before a lawful magistrate or according to the order of the Church of Jesus Christ of Latter-day Saints, or by their cohabitation in conformity to our custom."[17]

The will gave authority to the mothers to determine the fitness of their children to share in the proceeds of the estate. The mother, along with the trustees and executors, could decide if any child should be allowed the right of residence in the homestead. She could remove a child for "disobedience," "vicious conduct," or "bad habits" and could assign the share of any child judged "wasteful" or "unworthy" to that child's children or to others of her own children or grand-children.[18]

Although the will was carefully drawn to try to make sure that all heirs were treated fairly, difficulties were bound to arise. A twenty-two-year-old son claimed that his father before his death had "openly expressed" his intention to deed to him a certain parcel of land and furnish it with house, barn, livestock, and implements; he wished the executors to carry out that wish.[19] One of the older widows said she could not live on the allowance provided—she needed a little more income and asked the executors to help her pay $100 in outstanding debts.[20] An older son, a speculator, wanted to be sure that some of his business debts his father had taken over shortly before his death would not be deducted from his (the son's) portion of the estate.[21]

The first problem the executors faced was determining the size and value of the estate, and it was a somewhat chilling discovery to realize that the popular impression of its value was much too high. The estate was generally believed to be between $2 million and $2.5 million.[22] Ann Eliza Young's lawyers had estimated Brigham's wealth at $8 million, and Brigham, in replying to her brief, asserted that his fortune did not exceed $600,000.[23] As it turned out, all of them, including Brigham himself, had overestimated. The legal right or title to the Young estate was worth only $1,626,000.[24] But when his debts and the church properties held in trust were sub-tracted, the value of the estate was $361,170. After settlement, with the debts, executors' fees, and other deductions made, the amount finally available to the heirs was $224,242—still a sizable sum but so much less than the heirs had expected that the trustee-in-trust and the executors were forced into court to defend their settlement.[25]

It was not only that family members were disappointed; some federal officials and anti-Mormons were determined to wrest as much property as possible from the church. A court battle was probably inevitable. For its part, the church was determined to protect its property. John Taylor, as president of the Twelve, had assumed leadership of the church upon Brigham's death and succeeded him as both president and as trustee-in-trust.[26] He stated at the general conference in October 1877 that he had been aware for some time of his predecessor's tendency "to transfer certain public properties in his own name." While he agreed that this measure was necessary "to preserve them from the rapacity and spoliation of unprincipled men who sought to rob and despoil" the Saints, Taylor appointed Wilford Woodruff as chairman of a committee to audit all church accounts, including those of Brigham Young.[27]

Taylor's concern about the church holdings included in the Young estate is reflected in the revelation he recorded on November 19, 1877:

I have been asking the Lord to show me how to adjust the property of the Church, held in the name of the late President Brigham Young, so as to do justice to his estate and yet not wrong the Church, and have received the following answer:

You have asked of me, and others of the Twelve have asked of me, that wisdom might be given to you to adjust these property matters of the Church. Thus saith the Lord: Be one, be united, be honest, act upon the principles of justice and righteousness to the living and to the dead and to my Church, and I, the Lord, will sustain you and will acknowledge your labors. Amen.[28]

The auditing committee, it turned out, found it necessary "to go back to the commencement of accounts" in the Salt Lake Valley—November 6, 1848—to separate Brigham's accounts from those of the church.[29] A preliminary survey showed these accounts to be "strictly correct" with "very slight exceptions." The committee produced vouchers authenticating the settlements of President Young to demonstrate "the accuracy of his accounts" as "supervised and adjusted" by his clerical staff.[30]

About a month after the auditing committee began its work, it produced a draft for a proposed basis of settlement. The committee proposed that all church real estate known to be trust property, and all bonds, stocks, and other personal property held by Young in trust be turned over to the trustee-in-trust. Suggesting that a "liberal allowance" be given for Brigham's services and for contingent expenses incurred by him, the committee said it did not want to be "too scrupulous or exacting" in investigating minor matters but wanted to arrive at a "just, equitable and honorable adjustment."[31]

The Council of the Twelve decided that the auditing committee should prepare its final report. After this report was considered by the executors, it would be turned over to the council, whose decision was to be "final."[32]

But arriving at a "just, equitable, and honorable" settlement was more easily stated as a goal than achieved. Soon the auditing committee found itself in the thicket of specific decisions. The frustration of one member of the committee was expressed in a note:

Prest Young has gone behind the veil, he is not before our counsels, we cannot judge him, we must leave him with the Lord and we must also leave his acts there. The Lord is his judge, not us; but we have to do with his accounts, and he has empowered his Executors to settle them, even all trust claims. He did this while living, he had the property to do it with, and evidently *calculated* that these affairs should be adjusted.

We will concede that the President of the Church has the right under certain circumstances to control the people and their properties, and to dictate what they shall do, and how manage their affairs, also appropriate their property to the interests of the Church, and building up of the Kingdom of God on the earth. But has he a right to take property thus dictated and appropriate that to his own use, and for the benefit of his heirs?[33]

The surviving papers of the committee show many reluctant disallowances of estate credits in the trustee-in-trust books.[34] The committee also found shortages or discrepancies in the accounts of some family members with the church.[35]

On April 10, 1878, after six months of study and deliberation, after numerous joint conferences and joint investigations between the auditing committee and the executors, a settlement was concluded and approved by the Twelve. "This is a very important day in the history of my life and the Church," Wilford Woodruff noted in his diary. "After six months of hard labor we have effected a settlement with the executors of the estate, George Q. Cannon, Brigham Young and Albert Carrington, who have done all in their power to settle the business in equity and righteousness."[36]

Five days later, the settlement was taken to the probate court. The heirs petitioned for a quick winding-up of affairs, selected a committee to appraise and divide the property, and signed documents agreeing to accept the settlement.[37] The probate court approved the arrangements and on May 30 John Taylor as trustee-in-trust signed a statement of release accepting the settlement on behalf of the church.[38]

The settlement consisted of three parts. Class I properties were defined as portions of the estate in Brigham Young's name that undeniably belonged to the church. Some of these properties were those that Brigham had conveyed to George A. Smith during his term as trustee-in-trust in 1873 but that had reverted to Brigham after Smith's death in 1875. Since he was clearly holding them only in his capacity as trustee-in-trust, they were conveyed to the new trustee-in-trust, John Taylor. A second type of Class I properties consisted of those that had never been transferred to Smith, although a study of their acquisition and use showed that they belonged to the church, not Brigham himself. These properties were likewise transferred to John Taylor by the executors.

The second part of the settlement dealt with properties Brigham claimed as his own and in which the church agreed it had no interest, or properties that had once belonged to the church but to which Young had acquired legal title. They included the Salt Lake Theater and its grounds, and a sizable acreage of land in the Red Butte area east of the city from which the church had planned to quarry red sandstone for the Salt Lake Temple. Before 1877 all of these properties had been conveyed to Brigham Young, private person, by Brigham Young, trustee-in-trust. Long held in his own name were such properties as the Social Hall and lot, and the Gardo House and its grounds, located on the corner of South Temple and State (now occupied by the Bank of Utah). Brigham had acquired that lot in 1872 from Mayor Wells to build an official residence for the church president to entertain distinguished guests. In his will, he left a life interest in the Gardo House to Mary Ann Angell Young and Amelia Folsom Young. The building was not finished in his lifetime; and shortly before his death, "Mother" Young and Amelia, for unknown reasons, indicated a wish not to live in the house. Accordingly, on September 1, 1876, Brigham executed a ninety-nine-year lease to himself as trustee-in-trust at the nominal rate of $1 per year. Clearly, this arrangement was a legal declaration that he was holding the property in trust for the church. Nevertheless, at the settlement, the house was credited to the heirs. In fact, all properties mentioned in this second part of the settlement were allotted to the estate, except for the consideration of debts that the estate owed to the church, as explained below.

The third part of the settlement divided Brigham's personal property, especially the stocks, bonds, and notes. Tracing the acquisition, use, and ownership of some of the real estate was relatively simple compared with unraveling the transactions that had led to the establishment of Zion's Cooperative Mercantile Institution, the construction of the Utah Southern Railroad, and the formation of other business enterprises.

The auditing committee found countless cross-borrowings and repayments of Brigham Young and the trustee-in-trust since 1848. To everyone's surprise it was discovered that Brigham's clerks had not "settled" his accounts with the church annually, as he had asked others to do, and that his account with the church showed a debit balance of $999,633. George Q. Cannon wrote in his journal that Brigham had once "said to me that he would like to turn his property into the Church and I remarked that I thought he had done sufficient for the Church. I was then under the impression which I entertained until some time after his death that the Church was owing him. Familiar as I was with him and his business I had never seen his account with the Church and had not heard how he stood."[39] Some of these debts were unreimbursed drawings, while others were property held in trust. It was sometimes difficult to determine whether he had drawn on funds as trustee-in-trust or whether entries represented church expenditures made in his own private capacity. For Brigham's purposes, of course, it all amounted to the same thing. As Cannon explained, "When there was a surplus of Church funds, it was customary to invest them that they might accumulate, and in some cases the title was in the name of Brigham Young."[40] Closer investigation revealed that many enterprises bearing Brigham's name as principal stockholder or officer were in fact church enterprises—or at least were financed partly or entirely with church funds. In many of these enterprises, Young had held his stock in part or entirely in trust for the church.[41]

These adjustments did not take into account Brigham's entitlement to an allowance for himself and family during his thirty years as church president. In fairness to his heirs, therefore, the church granted the estate a credit of $300,000—the equivalent of $10,000 a year as a kind of accounting "allowance." Subtracting this credit from his estate's debt to the church left $699,633 worth of personal property in the form of stocks, bonds, and notes—or equivalent real property. In the settlement agreed upon, the church received properties that all understood had belonged to the church anyway: the Gardo House and lot, the Salt Lake Theater and lot, the Social Hall and lot, the LDS Museum and lot, the Council House lot, the office of the President of the church, the Empire Flour Mill and the lands adjacent thereto, notes of the Rio Virgen Manufacturing Company (which operated the Washington, Utah, cotton factory), 1,180 shares of stock in ZCMI, 893 shares of stock in the Provo Manufacturing Company, which operated the Provo Woolen Mills, 2,165 shares of stock in the Salt Lake Street Railroad Company, 800 shares of stock in the Salt Lake Gas Company, and 20 bonds of the Utah Southern Railroad Company.[42]

Since Brigham held a large part of his property in trust for the use and benefit of the church, much of the property the church received in compensation for his debt to the church was really its own property. But the uncertainty of ownership of each specific item made it impossible to divide the estate in any other way.

Brigham's heirs were awarded his holdings in the Deseret National Bank, Utah Northern Railroad, and Utah Western Railroad, and part of his holdings in the Utah Southern Railroad, Provo Woolen Mills, and ZCMI. The properties that went to the church were those in which the church or community had a predominant interest (for example, the Salt Lake Theater, the Social Hall, the LDS Museum, the Constitution Building and Council House, and the office of the President of the church); and those in which the funds came from the church on Brigham's open account that he had directly invested as trustee-in-trust (e.g., the Empire Flour Mill, the Washington Cotton Factory, ZCMI, Provo Woolen Mills, Salt Lake Street Railroad, Salt Lake City Gas Works, and the Utah Southern Railroad). Since they were assigned to the church in the settlement, they obviously were regarded as properties that had received financial and organizational assistance from the church.

Despite the laboriousness and confusion of separating Brigham's private accounts from the church's, everything could have been settled within a year of his death if a small minority of heirs had not objected. As it turned out, the "final" agreement of April 10, 1878, was merely the end of the legal battle's first round, a battle in which the judge of the district court used every legal means available to deprive the church of properties that the executors had assigned to it.[43]

John Taylor moved quickly when he learned that complaints had been filed. A letter to the Young heirs, signed by him and nine apostles, including Brigham Young, Jr., and Albert Carrington, reviewed Brigham's role as trustee-in-trust for the previous thirty years, the effect of the 1862 law limiting church properties to $50,000, and the transfer of church property to his private account. It also described additional steps necessitated by the threat of the federal government to examine the books of the church.[44]

The letter went on to describe how Brigham had made an earlier will in 1871 that left half of his estate to the church, but later changed it "wisely and carefully," so that all debts and claims would be paid out of his estate, thus assuring that the church would receive the property rightfully belonging to it. It ended with a justification of the course of action taken by the executors and a plea to the heirs to all hang together against the outside world and not become pawns of unscrupulous interests that would try to discredit their husband and father:

> In pursuance of this design of our late honored President, the Executors as well as the other apostles have been especially anxious to effect an honorable adjustment of these affairs without parading these old matters before the world which belong only to the Saints and should remain as they hitherto have been locked in the bosoms of the tried friends of President Young. And if it appears to those less informed than ourselves that too much secrecy has been observed in our efforts we would say to all such, that it has been because some of the heirs, who were not fully posted, seemed to be unwittingly

playing into the hands of lawyers and courts, who have no common interest with us, and are generally unscrupulous and vindictive against the Saints, and though unintentionally, the heirs would thus be made the medium of sullying the reputation of their revered father and casting a blighting odium on the surviving family and friends.

To the bereaved family and all Saints we say your safety and honor require union of purpose and confidence in each other, and may we each and all be ever found battling not against each other, but against the common foe.[45]

This was followed by a meeting of church officials with the family in which, as Wilford Woodruff noted, "The 12 Apostles met with the family . . . and plainly talked over the matter of the settlement. . . . Most of the family seemed to be satisfied."[46] Taylor also enlisted the aid of others to visit the heirs and explain the matter fully. The results of these efforts were described in a lengthy letter to the absent George Q. Cannon a week or two later as "gratifying." "There is now a general feeling in the family shared in by all who rightly understand matters that our settlement was just and generous."[47] The heirs signed a paper expressing themselves satisfied with the settlement, based on what they considered to be their father's will and desire. Because of their respect and honor for him, they were willing to trust the executors' judgment.

. . . believing firmly and implicitly in the high sense of honor and perfect knowledge of him for whom we mourn. . . . We confirm the great confidence reposed in you by his action in leaving you as his only legal representatives, to that honored judgment which selected you as Executors we yield our loyal obedience as we would to that beloved one personally had it been God's will to preserve upon the Earth the life we so greatly need to council [sic] and guide us.[48]

Nevertheless, a year later some of the previous claimants, along with some new ones, decided to take the case to the Third District Court, possibly, as indirect evidence shows, with the encouragement of the district judge. The names signed to the suit were Emeline A. Young, Vilate Y. Decker, Elizabeth Y. Ellsworth, Ernest I. Young, Louisa W. Y. Ferguson, Dora Young, and Marinda H. Y. Conrad. (Vilate and Elizabeth later stated that they had been led to sign under false pretenses.) According to President Taylor's court statement, Emeline A. Young, the chief plaintiff, was in California at the time of the agreement but had received her full share of the estate—$21,000—through her agent and had signed receipts and releases that technically barred her from pressing such suits.[49] In the hearing, which consumed June and July 1879, the plaintiffs charged the executors with having unlawfully transferred portions of the estate to the church.[50] Witnesses and defendants were questioned about a number of issues during the hearings.[51]

Considering his long history of promoting anti-Mormon causes, it was no surprise to the church and the executors that on July 12, 1879, Judge Jacob S. Boreman adjudged the executors and John Taylor in contempt of court.[52] Taylor posted bonds for $200,000 and was released from the contempt order, but the three executors were imprisoned in the Utah Penitentiary August 4–28, 1879. The non-Mormon territorial governor, George W. Emery, expressed his "astonishment" at Boreman's decision, "thought it a great outrage," and said that the respectable non-Mormons shared in this feeling.[53] Upon appeal, the territorial supreme court reversed the decision of the district court.[54] This led to an out-of-court settlement on October 4, 1879, in which the church agreed to pay the litigant heirs a combined sum of $75,000 in exchange for terminating the suit.[55] The receivers were discharged, and all properties were returned to the church according to the original settlement.[56]

The suit had been vexatious, but not ruinous. The $75,000 granted to the dissatisfied heirs was accepted by the other heirs, the trustees, and the executors because the cost of litigation threatened to far exceed that sum if the case was continued in the courts. After the decree of the court was made public, John Taylor presented the settlement before the semiannual conference of the church "and the settlement was endorsed by a unanimous vote."[57]

This legal quarrel, however distasteful it would have been to Brigham, shows in unmistakable ways the fruit of his values. When he decided to adopt Mormonism in 1832, he said, he expected "we should be one family, each seeking to do his neighbor good, . . . every man and every woman would assist by actually laboring with their hands in planting, building up, and beautifying this earth to make it like the Garden of Eden."[58] "I laid aside my old account books," he said. "Had I had millions of wealth, and had I devoted it all to the building up of this people, and . . . left myself pennyless, would it have been a sacrifice? No, not to my feelings."[59] Keeping accounts was not important—all, including the Prophet, should contribute labor, means, and talents for the common good. All would benefit as improvements were made, resources developed, and wealth multiplied. The reports of his fabulous wealth stemmed, in most part, from the confusion between his personal activities and those of the church he headed—a confusion the Anti-Bigamy Act of 1862 helped to perpetuate. Brigham's contributions to the cultural and economic development of the Mormon West were as president and trustee-in-trust of the church, rather than as a personally ambitious businessman.[60] He himself tried to be an exemplar of his frequently expressed admonition to his people that all should unite and put their "pile" into building a cooperative Kingdom. "Trusting in God," he said, "and exercising those energies with which he has endowed us, let us continue to found new settlements, build new towns and cities, make roads, construct canals and water ditches, . . . and contribute with our means and strength to every improvement which will extend the area of civilization, enhance the fertility, beauty, and greatness of our State, and add to the comfort, convenience, and happiness of our fellow citizens and the stranger who may visit us."[61]

In referring to the manuscripts, publications, and archives that are the sources for Brigham Young and the Mormons, the following abbreviations or symbols are used in the notes and references.

BY   Brigham Young
BYHD   Brigham Young Holograph Diaries, HDC
BYJ   Brigham Young Journals (Brigham Young Diaries, not holograph)
BYMH   Brigham Young Manuscript History, HDC. When the material is clearly of a diary character, I have sometimes referred to it as Brigham's dictated diary or journal.
BYOJ   Brigham Young Office Journals, HDC
BYP   Brigham Young Papers, HDC
BYTB   Brigham Young Telegram Books, HDC
BYUL   Brigham Young University Library, Provo, Utah
HC   B. H. Roberts, ed., History of The Church of Jesus Christ of Latter-day Saints. Period I. History of Joseph Smith, the Prophet, 2nd ed., 6 vols. (Salt Lake City, 1946 ff.), and Period II, for the "Apostolic Interregnum" (1844–47), vol. 7 (Salt Lake City, 1932).
HDC   Library-Archives of the Historical Department of the Church of Jesus Christ of Latter-day Saints, Church Office Building, Salt Lake City, Utah
HOJ   Historian's Office Journal, HDC
JD   Journal of Discourses, 26 vols. (Liverpool, 1854–86)
JH   Journal History of the Church of Jesus Christ of Latter-day Saints, HDC
JS   Joseph Smith
MHBY   Elden J. Watson, ed., Manuscript History of Brigham Young, 1801–1844 (Salt Lake City, 1968), and 1846–1847 (Salt Lake City, 1971).
USA   Utah State Archives, Salt Lake City, Utah
USHS   Library and Archives of the Utah State Historical Society, Salt Lake City, Utah
UUL   University of Utah Library, Salt Lake City, Utah

In quoting from the many manuscript sources mentioned in the bibliography, I have followed policies similar to those of Julian Boyd and the scholarly editors of the Washington, Jefferson, Adams, and Franklin papers. The result, I hope, is fair both to the original writer and to modern readers who want to draw their impressions directly from the original writing without having it "improved" by well-meaning editorial intervention. For scholars checking fine points or specific passages, the original holograph manuscript will remain the ultimate authority. I have, of course, preserved the wording and spelling of the original, except in the case of a few slips of the pen where I have exercised my own judgment. Inadvertent repetitions of words have been corrected; ampersands are usually printed as "and"; all sentences begin with capital letters; and all personal and geographical names are capitalized. I have also capitalized such words as God, Everlasting Covenant, Bible, Book of Mormon, and similar words that are capitalized today. Sometimes uneducated writers used lowercase and capital letters in random fashion, and I have not felt it necessary to reproduce all of these variations in writing style. Many times it is uncertain whether the writer meant a capital or lowercase letter, and so modern usage has been followed. Every sentence ends with a period, and dashes or commas obviously meant to be terminal marks are converted to periods. Minimum punctuation for clarity is supplied, and I have provided para-graphing when this would assist the reader. I have joined together parts of words that belong together but were separated by the writer, such as "today," "tonight," and "together." I have also separated words that, in writing, were inadvertently joined together. Despite these adjustments, the reader should have no difficulty catching the spirit and flavor of the nineteenth-century originals.

A special problem is presented by quotations from the minute books. There are extant minutes kept by Brigham Young's secretaries of literally thousands of meetings at which Young presided. Some of these minutes have been transcribed and are in "finished" form; others, especially those kept by Thomas Bullock during the years 1844 to 1856, are usually in his own type of briefhand. Examples of Bullock's briefhand are: u for you, r for are, wd for would, B for Brigham Young, J C for Jesus Christ, K for the Kingdom of God, 12 for Council of the Twelve Apostles, b and s for brothers and sisters. It would be excessively pedantic to reproduce these in the form originally recorded by the harried clerk. I have, instead, presented them in the form in which Bullock himself would have transcribed them if he had taken the time to do so.

The following is an example of how I have treated, or would have treated, a given manuscript notation. On October 1, 1848, Brigham Young, among others, spoke to a group of pioneers in the bowery (wood-covered shelter) on Temple Square in Salt Lake City, about the plan to build a Council House that would provide offices for leaders and a place where meetings of small groups could be held. Here is a selection from the notes made by clerk Thomas Bullock on that occasion (they can be found in Thomas Bullock Minutes, Loose Papers, 1848–56, Church Archives, Salt Lake City):

B. Y. is more satisfied that the ppl will do it by tithing, & be satisfied—there r scores of men & women who wo^d ra^r pay their 10 from this time forth & for ever & will lie down & sleep as sweet ag^n bec they av p^d their tithing—they then can say ⅒ of their time is set apart for the service of the L^d & s^d bro & sis is it your feelings to pay tithing—signify it by raising the ri^t hand—(all up)

That literal text I have transcribed as follows:

Brigham Young is more satisfied that the people will do it [build the Council House] by tithing, and be satisfied. There are scores of men and women who would rather pay their tenth from this time forth and forever and will lie down and sleep as sweet angels because they have paid their tithing. They then can say one-tenth of their time is set apart for the service of the Lord. And [he] said, "Brothers and sisters, is it your feelings to pay tithing? Signify it by raising the right hand." All [hands] up.

Where the use of any manuscript source requires different treatment from that described above, such as resort to paraphrase when the complexity of the original wording requires it, I have clearly indicated this in the citation.

Anyone using extensive manuscript materials of public figures is confronted with the problem of the authorship of the documents attributed to him. Were all the letters that were signed by Brigham Young dictated by him word for word? Or did he indicate in a general way the substance and tone of a response and was the letter then composed by a clerk? Or were many of his letters composed by clerks and associates and simply presented to him for his signature? In the case of Brigham Young, the extant correspondence is so extensive—there are letterpress copies of about twenty thousand of his letters in the LDS Church Archives alone—that one suspects there are examples of all three. While there are a few "form letters," my associates and I in the Historical Department of the Church have concluded that virtually all of the letters signed by Brigham Young involved some input on his part and that nearly all of the "significant" letters—those cited in this biography—were dictated rather precisely by the Mormon leader. There are undoubted "Brigham Young-isms" in at least 90 percent of the letters he signed. More than four hundred of the letters were written partly or entirely in his unmistakable hand, with his own phonetic spelling and with his characteristic trenchant expressions and sometimes awkward grammar.

As to the remainder, a careful study of Young's principal clerks and their own letters shows variations from the style used in the Brigham Young letters. The only valid course, I have concluded, is to regard Brigham Young as the author of all the letters attributed to him with the exception of specific ones that are designated herein as probably authored by someone else, with the indicated author suggested. Thus, in the case of the few formal reports and epistles that show in their composition the probable influence of Willard Richards, Daniel H. Wells, Albert Carrington, and/or George Q. Cannon, I have so indicated in the text or endnotes.

In a similar manner, can we rely on the published version of his sermons? To what extent were they "doctored up" to present the leader in a more favorable light than the delivered sermon would have done? There are verbatim texts of about four hundred sermons or "discourses," of which three hundred were published shortly after they were delivered. There are extant stenographic notes of about one hundred of the four hundred; and manuscript copies, with contemporary renderings or transcriptions by the clerk, of about another hundred. The Mormon History Trust Fund, a non-profit agency not connected with the LDS Church, has employed trained stenographers to decipher some of those still available in shorthand, and comparisons have been made with the published and existing transcribed versions. While there are a few differences, I am able to say with confidence that the published versions of his talks are authentically Brigham Young. I have been able to make similar comparisons of stenographic notes of some of his dictated letters with the letters as eventually mailed out. Again, while there are some corrections of grammar, the manuscript letters unquestionably are faithful to Brigham Young's thought and language, if not his spelling. In instances where the language in the shorthand version is different from that in the subsequent published version, I have called this to the reader's attention in the text or endnotes.

I regret to say that a few of the documents available during the preparation of this biography have since been closed to researchers, and it will not be possible for readers of this book to check out every source I have used.

PROLOGUE
"A PORTLY, FRANK, GOOD-NATURED . . . MAN"

[1] JH, 23 August and 13 September 1859.
[2] Daniel J. Boorstin, *The Image, or What Happened to the American Dream* (New York, 1962), p. 15.
[3] Greeley's dispatch, which appeared first in his New York *Tribune* for 20 August 1859, is in *An Overland Journey from New York to San Francisco in the Summer of 1859* (New York, 1863). There are also careful notes by Mormon apostle Wilford Woodruff in his diary, HDC.
[4] Fitz Hugh Ludlow, *The Heart of the Continent* (Cambridge, Mass., 1870), pp. 369–70; Justin McCarthy, *Reminiscences*, 2 vols. (New York, 1899), 2:258–59. Impressions of travelers are given in Edwina Snow, "Singular Saints: The Image of the Mormons in Book-Length Travel Accounts, 1847–1857" (Master's thesis, George Washington University, 1972).
[5] Minutes, 24 April 1859; By sermon, 26 July 1857, JD 5:77.

CHAPTER I:
BOYHOOD IN VERMONT AND NEW YORK

In preparing this chapter I have used the diaries and "histories" of Brigham Young's brothers and sisters, Brigham Young's own published and manuscript "histories," family letters, autobiographical statements by Brigham Young in later sermons and "discourses," and various articles and books that deal with his early life and times. Not all these sources agree, even on such basic points as dates of births or moves. I have incorporated what seems to me to be the most reasonable reading of the historical evidence.

The most valuable secondary treatments are Richard F. Palmer and Karl D. Butler, *Brigham Young: The New York Years* (Provo, Utah, 1982); S. Dilworth Young, *"Here Is Brigham"*: *Brigham Young—the Years to 1844* (Salt Lake City, 1964), pp. 13–49; and Eugene England, "Young Brigham," in *Brother Brigham* (Salt Lake City, 1980), pp. 1–33. The Palmer-Butler work replaces Mary Van Sickle Wait, *Brigham Young in Cayuga County, 1813–1829* (Ithaca, N.Y., 1964), and represents a careful study of the Young family's movements in New York and of Brigham's apprenticeship and work as a carpenter and builder.

The Revolutionary War experience and early life of John Young and his marriage to Nabby Howe are admirably treated in Gene A. Sessions, "John Young: Soldier of the Revolution," in *Latter-day Patriots: Nine Mormon Families and Their Revolutionary War Heritage* (Salt Lake City, 1975), pp. 20–41. See also M. Hamlin Cannon, "A Pension Office Note on Brigham Young's Father," *American Historical Review* 50 (October 1944): 82–90.

Early Whitingham is described in A. Augustine Butterfield, *Some Facts About the Early History of Whitingham, Vermont* (Brattleboro, Vt., 1916), pp. 14–50; Hamilton Child, comp., *Gazeteer & Business Directory of Windham County, Vermont, 1729–1884* (Syracuse, N.Y., 1884), pp. 22–70; Clark Jillson, *Green Leaves from Whitingham, Vermont: A History of the Town* (Worcester, Mass., 1894), pp. 38, 46, 51; and Leonard Brown, *History of Whitingham from Its Organization* to the Present Time (Whitingham, Vt., 1886), p. 9. A local New York history with background is Elliot G. Storke, History of Cayuga County, New York, 1789–1879 (Philadelphia, 1879).

The experiences of Brigham and his parents and brothers and sisters in Whitingham are described in S. Dilworth Young, Young Brigham Young (Salt Lake City, 1962), a book with charming illustrations by the author. This work is partly fictionalized, but is based on available manuscript and published sources and authentic family lore.

Brigham Young's life in Mendon, in the years just before his conversion to Mormonism, is better understoood as the result of the six-year archaeological dig of J. Sheldon Fisher at the site of the Brigham Young Mill described in J. Sheldon Fisher, "Brigham Young as a Mendon Craftsman: A Study in Historical Archeology," New York History 61 (October 1980): 431–47.

[1] Sermon of Brigham Young, delivered in the Mormon Tabernacle in Salt Lake City, 8 August 1869, JD 14:103.

[2] John Haven, speech at meeting of the Young and Haven families in Nauvoo, Illinois, 8 January 1845, Minutes in Brigham Young Collection, HDC; S. Dilworth Young, "Here Is Brigham": Brigham Young—the Years to 1844 (Salt Lake City, 1964), p. 14.

[3] Journal of Franklin Wheeler Young, p. 5, HDC.

[4] Letter of Susannah Brigham Howe, 5 August 1827, published in Susa Young Gates, "Mother of the Latter-day Prophets: Abigail Howe Young," The Juvenile Instructor (Salt Lake City) 59 (January 1924): 6.

[5] Genealogical letter written by Fanny Young to Phinehas Young, 1 January 1845, microfilm copy in Genealogical Department Archives, LDS Church, Salt Lake City.

[6] Whitingham Deeds, p. 675, recorded 18 November 1800, as cited in Richard F. Palmer and Karl D. Butler, Brigham Young: The New York Years (Provo, Utah, 1982), pp. 2, 88.

[7] S. Dilworth Young, "Here Is Brigham", pp. 18–20.

[8] Some of the information about living conditions is based on background histories of the region and times, and not specifically from Brigham Young sources.

[9] See especially S. Dilworth Young, Young Brigham Young (Salt Lake City, 1962), pp. 21–41.

[10] These details are told in James A. Little, "Historical Items on the Life of Brigham Young," notes and research materials collected by Little, Brigham's first cousin, for a biography of BY, James A. Little Collection, HDC; Susa Young Gates, "Family Memories" and draft for chapter on "Ancestry" of BY, in Gates Collection, USHS; and in Franklin Wheeler Young, Young Family Genealogy, p. 13, HDC. This portion of his diary is in the form of a "history" by Joseph Young, Brigham's older brother.

[11] Whitingham Deeds, p. 821, shows the property deeded by John to Joseph Mosely on 24 December 1802. Query: Did John arrange with Mosely to remain another year after his tentative decision to leave? Or did John simply sell the land back to Mosely early in order to get back $50, or whatever was the sale price, to live on? See Palmer and Butler, Brigham Young, pp. 2, 88.

[12] In this and the following paragraphs, I have followed S. Dilworth Young, Young Brigham Young, pp. 41–53. Apparently the family moved to Sherburne, but in 1808 the town was divided and the place they lived on became part of Smyrna. Frank B. Hough, Gazeteer of the State of New York (Albany, 1872), p. 224, cited in Palmer and Butler, Brigham Young, p. 3.

[13] Palmer and Butler, Brigham Young, pp. 2–3.

[14] Sermon of 2 August 1857, JD 5:97. Also JD 4:312; JD 14:103; Minutes, 22 October 1848, General Minutes Collection, HDC.

[15] Sermon of 8 October 1868 in Salt Lake Tabernacle, JD 12:287.

[16] James A. Little, "Historical Items," pp. 2–3, HDC.

[17] Sermon of 2 August 1857, JD 5:97.

[18] Franklin W. Young Journal, p. 14.

[19] Little, "Historical Items," p. 3. See also History of Tioga, Chemung, Tompkins and Schuyler Counties (Philadelphia, 1879), p. 680.

20 James A. Little, "Biography of Lorenzo Dow Young," *Utah Historical Quarterly* 14 (1946): 130. On the Tyrone adventures, see also Diary of Lorenzo Dow Young, HDC.

21 Sermons of Brigham Young, 25 May 1862, JD 9:294; 2 August 1857, 5:97.

22 Sermon of 6 November 1864, JD 10:360.

23 Little, "Biography of Lorenzo Dow Young."

24 JD 10:360.

25 Sermon of 31 August 1875, JD 18:76. See also Biographical Sketch of Brigham Young, HDC. For much of this material, I have relied on Palmer and Butler, *Brigham Young*, chapter 2.

26 Palmer and Butler, *Brigham Young*, chapter 2. The Arts and Sites Division of the Church of Jesus Christ of Latter-day Saints has acquired a number of these Brigham Young mantelpieces, chairs, and desks for the purpose of exhibition in the Church Museum on West Temple Street in Salt Lake City.

27 JD 10:360.

28 David M. Dunning in *Auburn Advertising-Journal*, 13 January 1917.

29 The information on the Littles is in Palmer and Butler, *Brigham Young*, pp. 11 and 23, and is based on Harriet F. Little, *Descendants of William Little, Jr., and Allied Families* (Provo, Utah, 1958), pp. 21–22.

30 Brigham's Bucksville or Port Byron adventures are described briefly in an article by William Hayden published in the *Deseret News* for 20 December 1913.

31 Young, *"Here Is Brigham"*, p. 41; William Hayden in *Syracuse Sunday Herald*, 21 February 1904.

32 Young, *"Here Is Brigham"*, p. 41.

33 Ibid., p. 42.

34 Hayden, loc. cit.

35 Ibid. There are problems with Hayden's statements. I have tried to be selective in the use of his "recollections."

36 Susa Young Gates, with Leah D. Widtsoe, *The Life Story of Brigham Young* (New York, 1930), p. 19. Also see William Hayden, "In the Days of Long Ago," *Auburn* (N.Y.) *Bulletin*, 17 February 1904.

37 *Cayuga Patriot*, 3 November 1824, cited in Palmer and Butler, *Brigham Young*, p. 19. It is a curious coincidence that Gilbert Weed was a great-grandfather of Ann Eliza Webb, a plural wife of Brigham Young in later years. See Elizabeth Churchill Webb to *Auburn* (N.Y.) *Bulletin*, 11 September 1877, and Ann Eliza Webb, *Wife No. 19* (Hartford, Conn., 1875), pp. 468–69.

38 William Hayden, "In the Days of Long Ago," *Syracuse Sunday Herald*, 21 February 1904, and *Port Byron Chronicle*, 5 March 1904. For corroboration on the favorable image of Brigham in Port Byron, see also David B. Smith to BY, 8 February 1853, HDC.

39 Hiram McKee to BY, 4 April 1860, BYP; BY to Elder Hiram McKee, 3 May 1860, BYP.

40 It is to be noted that the 1830 census also lists Brigham living in Canandaigua, No. 9.

41 John Fowler, *Journal of a Tour in the State of New York in the Year 1830* (London, 1831), p. 97.

42 Heber C. Kimball, "History," manuscript, book 94-B, Heber C. Kimball Papers, HDC.

43 Gates with Widtsoe, *Life Story of Brigham Young*, p. 5.

44 Undated newspaper clippings from *Ontario Republican Times*, Canandaigua, New York, letter of unnamed correspondent dated 7 September 1857, HDC.

45 Heber C. Kimball, sermon of 7 June 1862, JD 9:329.

46 Undated clippings, *Ontario Republican Times*. Other evidence of Brigham's work in Mendon is reviewed in Palmer and Butler, *Brigham Young*, passim.

47 Rev. J. Willard Webb, "A Memorial Sermon—the Life and Character of George Hickox," undated newspaper clipping, HDC. See also George Hickox to BY, 7 February 1876, and BY to George Hickox, 19 February 1876, BYP.

48 George Washington Allen, "Brigham Young and Mormonism," original in possession of J. Sheldon Fisher, Valentown Museum, Fishers, New York. Also M. Joyce Hutchinson, "An Excerpt

from the Life of Brigham Young" (May 1940 history class paper in possession of Dr. Robert Skabelund, Logan, Utah), p. 7.
[49] J. Sheldon Fisher, "Brigham Young as a Mendon Craftsman: A Study in Historical Archeology," *New York History* 61 (October 1980): 435–46.
[50] Ibid., pp. 440–43.
[51] Ibid., pp. 444–45.
[52] Sermon of 2 August 1857, JD 5:97.

C H A P T E R   2 :
C O N V E R S I O N   A N D   C O M M I T M E N T

Brigham Young's introduction to Mormonism is described in S. Dilworth Young, *"Here Is Brigham": Brigham Young—the Years to 1844* (Salt Lake City, 1964), pp. 50–76; Richard F. Palmer and Karl D. Butler, *Brigham Young: The New York Years* (Provo, Utah, 1982), chapter 5; Rebecca Cornwall and Richard F. Palmer, "The Religious and Family Background of Brigham Young," *Brigham Young University Studies (BYU Studies)* 18 (Spring 1978): 286–310; Ronald K. Esplin, "The Emergence of Brigham Young and the Twelve to Mormon Leadership, 1830–1841" (Ph.D. diss., Brigham Young University, 1981), esp. pp. 36–89; and Eugene England, *Brother Brigham* (Salt Lake City, 1980), pp. 1–33. The conversion of the Young family is described in Leonard J. Arrington and JoAnn Jolley, "The Faithful Young Family: The Parents, Brothers, and Sisters of Brigham," *The Ensign* 10 (August 1980): 52–57.

On the religious and cultural setting in America as background to the founding and early success of Mormonism, I have benefited from reading Gordon S. Wood, "Evangelical America and Early Mormonism," *New York History* 61 (October 1980): 359–86; Timothy L. Smith, "The Book of Mormon in a Biblical Culture," *Journal of Mormon History* 7 (1980): 3–21; and R. Laurence Moore, "Insiders and Outsiders in American Historical Narrative and American History," *American Historical Review* 87 (April 1982): 390–412. See also Leonard J. Arrington, "Mormonism: From Its New York Beginnings," *New York History* 61 (October 1980): 387–410.

The Young family's own story is told in Journal of Franklin Wheeler Young, holograph, HDC; MHBY; Miriam Maxfield, "A Compiled History of Phinehas Howe Young," typescript, HDC; and James A. Little, "Biography of Lorenzo Dow Young," *Utah Historical Quarterly* 14 (1946): 25–171.

The richest source for Brigham's religious feelings and experiences before he became a Mormon are the reminiscences incorporated in his sermons. These have been best collected and summarized in Ronald W. Walker and Ronald K. Esplin, "Brigham Himself: An Autobiographical Recollection," *Journal of Mormon History* 4 (1977): 19–34. I have made extensive use of this splendid article with their full permission.

[1] Sermon of Brigham Young, 8 August 1852, JD 3:91.
[2] MHBY, pp. xviii–xix. Smith also left a copy with Brigham's sister Rhoda and her husband John P. Greene, an account of which is told in HC 7:217–18. Phinehas's story about his copy was first published in Brigham Young's "History," *Deseret News*, 3 February 1858, p. 377.
[3] BY sermon of 8 August 1852, JD 3:91.
[4] Sermon of 6 April 1860, JD 8:38. Mormon scholars are not agreed on whether Brigham read Phinehas's book or the Greene book. Brigham merely noted that the first Book of Mormon he saw was Phinehas's copy (MHBY, p. 1). B. H. Roberts thought it was the Greene copy (HC 7:218n). Preston Nibley, *Brigham Young, the Man and His Work* (Salt Lake City, 1937), p. 5, was sure it was Phinehas's copy.
[5] Leonard J. Arrington and JoAnn Jolley, "The Faithful Young Family: The Parents, Brothers, and Sisters of Brigham," *The Ensign* 10 (August 1980).
[6] Little, "Biography of Lorenzo Dow Young," *Utah Historical Quarterly* 14 (1946): 28.

7 "Family Memories," Susa Young Gates Collection, USHS.

8 Journal of Franklin Wheeler Young, holograph, HDC. p. 10.

9 Esplin, "The Emergence of Brigham Young and the Twelve," p. 49.

10 James A. Little,"Historical Items on the Life of Brigham Young," notes and research materials collected by Little for a biography of Brigham Young, James A. Little Collection, HDC. See also Rebecca Cornwall and Richard F. Palmer, "The Religious and Family Background of Brigham Young," BYU Studies 18 (Spring 1978): 294–99.

11 Mrs. Edwin P. Smith, comp., "Records of Discontinued Churches of Northern Chenango County," vol. 3, typescript, 1969, pp. 60ff., LDS Genealogical Department Archives, Salt Lake City. Cited in Cornwall and Palmer, pp. 301–2.

12 Journal of Franklin Wheeler Young, p. 10.

13 MHBY, p. xi.

14 MHBY, p. xvii.

15 Miriam Maxfield, "A Compiled History of Phinehas Howe Young," typescript, pp. 1–2, HDC.

16 Little, "Biography of Lorenzo Dow Young," p. 26.

17 Little, "Historical Items."

18 Thomas Bullock Minutes, 23 September 1849, HDC; Minutes of Family Meeting, 8 January 1845, BYP.

19 MHBY, p. 62.

20 Ronald W. Walker and Ronald K. Esplin, "Brigham Himself: An Autobiographical Recollection," Journal of Mormon History 4 (1977): 24.

21 Maxfield, "A Compiled History," pp. 3–6. On Solomon Chamberlain's role in early Mormonism, see Larry C. Porter, "A Study of the Origins of the Church of Jesus Christ of Latter-day Saints in the States of New York and Pennsylvania, 1816–1831" (Ph.D. diss., Brigham Young University, 1971), esp. pp. 277–85.

22 Ibid.

23 Heber C. Kimball, "History," Deseret News, 31 March 1858, p. 25; and manuscript, book 94-B, Heber C. Kimball Papers, HDC.

24 Ibid.

25 Eunice E. Curtis, The Ancestors and Descendants of Enos Curtis and Ruth Franklin—Utah Pioneers, 1783–1964, and Related Families (Salt Lake City, n.d.), p. 13.

26 Kimball, "History," manuscript, book 94-B, Kimball Papers, HDC. Phinehas later said that at the end of 1831 or beginning of 1832 he and Brigham "both became more interested in the subject of Mormonism" and got Kimball to join them in traveling to Pennsylvania. In his "History," published as a part of Brigham's, he says they left about 20 January 1832. Phinehas Young to BY, 11 August 1845, BYP; and BY, "History," Deseret News, 3 February 1853, p. 377. This is another indication that Brigham Young had little to do with Mormons until after he had passed judgment on the Book of Mormon. Nor is there any evidence that Young ever met with any of the Smith family in the Palmyra area, even though they resided less than fifteen miles from Mendon for perhaps nine months after he first examined the Book of Mormon.

27 BY, "History," manuscript no. 2, Historian's Office Papers, HDC. Apparently the wives had as much interest in observing the Saints as did their husbands, or they would not have braved the 250-mile round-trip winter journey. We can surmise that Vilate Kimball remained behind to care for the children of the Kimballs and Youngs.

28 Joseph Young, fragment of an autobiography in Franklin Wheeler Young Papers, HDC; Millennial Star 25 (4 July 1863): 424.

29 Minutes of Family Meeting, 8 January 1845, BYP.

30 MHBY, pp. 2–3; also JD 9:219.

CHAPTER 3 :
ARDENT DISCIPLE, 1832–1834

The most valuable secondary works on Brigham's activities in these years are Ronald K. Esplin, "The Emergence of Brigham Young and the Twelve to Mormon Leadership, 1830–1841" (Ph.D. diss., Brigham Young University, 1981), chapter 3; Richard F. Palmer and Karl D. Butler, *Brigham Young: The New York Years* (Provo, Utah, 1982), chapter 6; Eugene England, *Brother Brigham* (Salt Lake City, 1980), chapters 1 and 3; Susa Young Gates, "Brigham Young's Missionary Experiences," *The Juvenile Instructor* 63 (May 1928): 240–44; Eugene England, "Brigham Young as a Missionary," *The New Era* 7 (November 1977): 30–37; S. Dilworth Young, *"Here Is Brigham": Brigham Young—the Years to 1844* (Salt Lake City, 1964), pp. 60–132; and Stanley B. Kimball, *Heber C. Kimball: Mormon Patriarch and Pioneer* (Urbana, Illinois, 1981).

The key primary source is Brigham Young's first holograph diary, April 1832–September 1836, HDC. Other important sources are the Brigham Young "History" in various drafts and the diaries of Heber C. Kimball and of Wilford Woodruff.

The situation in the early days in Kirtland is clarified in several recent studies, including: Milton V. Backman, Jr., *The Heavens Resound: A History of the Latter-day Saints in Ohio, 1830–1838* (Salt Lake City, 1983); Max H. Parkin on "The Nature and Cause of Internal and External Conflict of the Mormons in Ohio between 1830 and 1838" (Master's thesis, Brigham Young University, 1966); and idem, "Kirtland: A Stronghold for the Kingdom," in F. Mark McKiernan et al., *The Restoration Movement: Essays in Mormon History* (Lawrence, Kansas, 1973), pp. 63–98. Also Marvin S. Hill, C. Keith Rooker, and Larry T. Wimmer, "The Kirtland Economy Revisited: A Market Critique of Sectarian Economics," *BYU Studies* 17 (Summer 1977): 386–476; Marvin S. Hill, "Cultural Crisis in the Mormon Kingdom: A Reconsideration of the Causes of Kirtland Dissent," *Church History* 49 (September 1980): 286–97; D. Michael Quinn, "Echoes and Foreshadowings: The Distinctiveness of the Mormon Community," *Sunstone* 3 (March–April 1978): 12–17; Robert L. Layton, "Kirtland: A Perspective on Time and Place," *BYU Studies* 11 (Spring 1971): 423–38; and Davis Bitton, "Kirtland as a Center of Missionary Activity, 1830–1838," *BYU Studies* 11 (Spring 1971): 497–516.

On Zion's Camp, the best analytical treatments are Peter Crawley and Richard L. Anderson, "The Political and Social Realities of Zion's Camp," *BYU Studies* 14 (Summer 1974): 406–20; Warren A. Jennings, "The Army of Israel Marches into Missouri," *Missouri Historical Review* 62 (January 1968): 107–35; and Wilburn D. Talbot, "Zion's Camp" (Master's thesis, Brigham Young University, 1973). Primary sources include the diaries and recollections of Brigham Young, Heber C. Kimball, Levi W. Hancock, and George A. Smith. See also Andrew Jenson, "Zion's Camp," *Historical Record* 7 (June 1888): 577–91.

[1] JD 1:313–14.
[2] JD 13:211.
[3] JD 5:97.
[4] JD 4:21.
[5] BY, "History," manuscript no. 2, Historian's Office Papers, HDC.
[6] S. Dilworth Young, *"Here Is Brigham": Brigham Young—the Years to 1844* (Salt Lake City, 1964), pp. 61–62.
[7] *Millennial Star* 25 (11 July 1863): 438.
[8] BYHD, p. 1.
[9] *Millennial Star* 25 (11 July 1863): 438.
[10] J. Sheldon Fisher, "Brigham Young as a Mendon Craftsman: A Study in Historical Archeology," *New York History* 61 (October 1980): 435–46.
[11] *Millennial Star* 25 (11 July 1863): 439; Joseph Young to Lewis Harvey, 16 November 1880, BYUL.
[12] BYHD, 1832.

[13] *Millennial Star* 25 (11 July 1863): 439.

[14] MHBY, p. 4.

[15] Joseph Young to Lewis Harvey, 16 November 1880, BYUL.

[16] MHBY, p. 4. According to later testimony, Joseph Smith added, "The time will come when Brother Brigham Young will preside over this church." If, indeed, this declaration was made, Brigham does not record it in his diary, nor did he mention it to anyone, although several years later, just before the death of the Prophet, he heard of the declaration from others. Brigham later said that Joseph Smith had told him in 1843 that he was the only person who could handle the job of directing the church. Discourse of 8 October 1866, unpublished, HDC. There is no evidence, however, that Young had any expectation of presiding over the church until after the death of Joseph Smith. See also Joseph Young to Lewis Harvey, 16 November 1880, BYUL.

[17] Acts 2:4.

[18] Glossolalia is rare among Mormons. See Scott Dunn, "Glossolalia: Evolution of a Religious Phenomenon in Mormonism" (Paper presented at the Sunstone Symposium in Salt Lake City, August 1981, copy in possession of the writer). Also Bruce R. McConkie, "Tongues," in *Mormon Doctrine* (Salt Lake City, 1958), pp. 722–23.

[19] There are a few later instances in which Brigham Young exercised the gift. See MHBY, 6 December 1839, p. 60; Wilford Woodruff Diary, 29 December 1846, 15 February 1858, HDC; JH, 3 January 1847; MHBY 10 January 1847.

[20] Joseph Young to Lewis Harvey, 16 November 1880, BYUL.

[21] BY, "History," manuscripts no. 1, 3, Minutes of Family Meeting, 8 January 1845, Historian's Office Papers, HDC.

[22] MHBY, p. 5.

[23] Woodruff Diary, 15 February 1858. See also BY to Joseph Young, 7 February 1855.

[24] BYHD, entries for 1, 6, 14, 15 July 1833.

[25] BY sermon, 3 February 1867, JD 11:294–95; George A. Smith later referred to hearing the same charge, see Sermon of George A. Smith, 29 December 1867, JD 12:150.

[26] JD 12:59.

[27] John Young Revolutionary War Pension File #W,11908 BLWT 101. 305-160-55, National Archives, Washington, D.C.; Monroe County Deeds, Liber 28, p. 23; *Millennial Star* 25 (9 May 1863): 295; James A. Little, "Biography of Lorenzo Dow Young," *Utah Historical Quarterly* 14 (1946): 42.

[28] JD 11:295.

[29] The peak number of LDS residents in the Kirtland area was reached in 1837 when there were 1,200 in Kirtland and 200 in the environs.

[30] Emmeline B. Wells, "Biography of Mary Ann Angell Young," *The Juvenile Instructor* 26 (1 January 1891): 17–18.

[31] MHBY.

[32] JD 11:295; also JD 2:128. Recently, a BY overcoat with a plausible lineage was acquired by the Arts and Sites Division of the Church of Jesus Christ of Latter-day Saints. It was apparently left behind by Brigham in Mendon, lending some credence to his later claiming that he had given away part of his meager possessions before moving. Although the coat is plain, it is warm, well made, and very serviceable—well worth taking along, especially for a frugal, poor man. One suspects there may have been special reasons for leaving it—perhaps a gift to someone more needy than he. Apparently Brigham arrived in Kirtland with no coat and simply borrowed an old and worn one for a time.

[33] JD 11:295, 2:128; *Millennial Star* 25 (11 July 1863): 440; BY, "History," *Deseret News*, 10 February 1858.

[34] The difficulties in Missouri are related in Warren Jennings, "Zion Is Fled: The Expulsion of the Mormons from Jackson County, Missouri" (Ph.D. diss., University of Florida, 1962); Richard L. Anderson, "Jackson County in Early Mormon Descriptions," *Missouri Historical Review* 65 (April 1971): 270–93; Richard Bushman, "Mormon Persecutions in Missouri, 1833," *BYU Studies*

3 (Autumn 1960): 17–20. A brief description is found in James B. Allen and Glen M. Leonard, *The Story of the Latter-day Saints* (Salt Lake City, 1976), pp. 81–93.

35 MHBY, p. 8.

36 Wells, "Biography of Mary Ann Angell Young," p. 18; Young, "*Here Is Brigham*", pp. 90–93.

37 Two of Heber C. Kimball's journals in HDC, covering the years 1838–48, are now catalogued as the Heber C. Kimball Autobiography and are in the handwriting of various church clerks. The extract given is in Autobiography, p. 21.

38 HC 2:183–85.

39 BY sermon, 28 September 1856, JD 4:101–2.

40 BY sermon, 16 November 1856, JD 4:92.

41 *Deseret News*, 12 October 1865.

42 Kimball, Autobiography, p. 21.

43 Jerena East Giffen, " 'Add a Pinch and a Lump': Missouri Women in the 1820s," *Missouri Historical Review* 65 (July 1971): 261–78.

44 *Deseret News*, 13 October 1934, in JH that date. See also George A. Smith Diary, 1834, BYUL, and "Memoirs of George A. Smith," p. 12, typescript of original at BYUL.

45 "History of George Albert Smith, Zion's Camp," p. 1, BYUL.

46 Observation by George D. Watt, reporting the October 12, 1865, Zion's Camp reunion in the *Deseret News*. Also Levi Hancock in ibid., 19 October 1865.

47 HC 2:186.

48 George A. Smith, "Historical Discourse," 15 November 1864, JD 11:7.

49 HC 2:67.

50 George A. Smith, "Memoirs," pp. 19–20.

51 "Extract from the Journal of Elder Heber C. Kimball," *Times and Seasons* 6:773. Italics in original.

52 George A. Smith, "Memoirs," p. 25. My italics.

53 JD 10:20; recollection of Joseph B. Noble, *Salt Lake Herald*, 26 March 1892.

54 For a detailed account of the exchanges between leaders of the church and government officials in Missouri, see Smith, HC, 2:84–99; also pp. 107, 113–15, 117–34.

55 Kimball, Autobiography, p. 33.

56 Lyman O. Littlefield, "The Prophet Joseph Smith in Zion's Camp," *The Juvenile Instructor* 27 (1 March 1892): 145–46. Littlefield accompanied the camp as a youth of thirteen.

57 Levi Hancock, Diary of Levi W. Hancock, p. 81, typescript, BYUL.

58 Nathan Bennett Baldwin, recording his reminiscences of Zion's Camp as apparently requested by Wilford Woodruff. Written from Fillmore City, September 1882. Copy of typewritten note, HDC.

59 Kimball, Autobiography, pp. 3–4.

60 Ibid., p. 34.

61 "Extract from the Journal of Heber C. Kimball," *Times and Seasons* 6:790; HC 2:105.

62 Kimball, Autobiography, p. 35.

63 Ibid., p. 36.

64 Ibid.

65 Doctrine and Covenants 105.

66 HC 2:112.

67 Ibid.

68 Kimball, Autobiography, p. 40.

69 Journal of Joseph B. Noble, p. 14, microfilm of original handwritten document, BYUL.

70 Kimball, Autobiography, p. 43.

71 Ibid., p. 42.

72 Ibid.

73 Kimball, "History," *Times and Seasons* 6:839.

74 MHBY, p. 9.

[75] Salt Lake High Council Record, 1869–72, pp. 83–84, HDC.
[76] Ibid. Italics mine.
[77] JD 10:20.
[78] JD 2:10.

C H A P T E R 4 :
APOSTLE

The primary sources of Brigham's activity as an early apostle are BYHD, 1832–40; Record Book of the Twelve, 1835, HDC; Heber C. Kimball, "History," manuscript, book 94-B, Heber C. Kimball Papers, HDC; and Joseph Smith Diary, 1835–36, HDC.

Secondary sources include: S. Dilworth Young, *"Here Is Brigham": Brigham Young—the Years to 1844* (Salt Lake City, 1964) pp. 112–259; Ronald K. Esplin, "The Emergence of Brigham Young and the Twelve to Mormon Leadership, 1830–1841" (Ph.D. diss., Brigham Young University, 1981), chapters 2 and 3; Susa Young Gates, "Brigham Young's Missionary Experiences," *The Juvenile Instructor* 63 (May 1928): 240–44; Eugene England, "Brigham Young as a Missionary," *The New Era* 7 (November 1977): 30–37; Richard F. Palmer and Karl D. Butler, *Brigham Young: The New York Years* (Provo, Utah, 1982), chapters 9 and 10; Leonard J. Arrington and Ronald K. Esplin, "The Role of the Quorum of the Twelve during Brigham Young's Presidency of the Church . . . ," *Task Papers in LDS History*, no. 31 (Salt Lake City, 1979).

The Missouri difficulties are covered in Max H. Parkin, "A History of the Latter-day Saints in Clay County, Missouri, from 1833 to 1837" (Ph.D. diss., Brigham Young University, 1976); and Leland H. Gentry, "A History of the Latter-day Saints in Northern Missouri from 1836 to 1839" (Ph.D. diss., Brigham Young University, 1965).

The Kirtland difficulties are discussed in Milton V. Backman, Jr., *The Heavens Resound: A History of the Latter-day Saints in Ohio, 1830–1838* (Salt Lake City, 1983); R. Kent Fielding, "The Growth of the Mormon Church in Kirtland, Ohio" (Ph.D. diss., Indiana University, 1957); D. Michael Quinn, "Echoes and Foreshadowings: The Distinctiveness of the Mormon Community," *Sunstone* 3 (March–April 1978): 12–17; and Max H. Parkin, "The Nature and Cause of Internal and External Conflict among the Mormons in Ohio between 1830 and 1838" (Master's thesis, Brigham Young University, 1966); and "Kirtland: A Stronghold for the Kingdom," in F. Mark McKiernan et al., *The Restoration Movement: Essays in Mormon History* (Lawrence, Kansas, 1973), pp. 63–98.

A brief overview of the organization and early development of the Quorum of the Twelve is Wilburn D. Talbot's "The Duties and Responsibilities of the Apostles of the Church of Jesus Christ of Latter-day Saints, 1835–1945" (Ph.D. diss., Brigham Young University, 1978), chapter 3. See also D. Michael Quinn's "Organizational Development and Social Origins of the Mormon Hierarchy, 1832–1932: A Prosopographical Study" (Master's thesis, University of Utah, 1973). Particularly valuable for this chapter is the Esplin dissertation, mentioned above, which is detailed and analytical. I am grateful for his willingness to allow me to use his material.

[1] JD 8:173.
[2] MHBY, p. 10. See also B. C. Fowles, "About Mormons," manuscript in the Western Reserve Historical Society Library, Cleveland, Ohio.
[3] Fowles, "About Mormons"; Minutes of the 10 October 1865 Reunion of Zion's Camp Veterans, BYP, HDC.
[4] Joseph Young, *History of the Organization of the Seventies* (Salt Lake City, 1878), p. 102. Also, Minutes of the 10 October 1864 Reunion of Zion's Camp Veterans, BYP.
[5] See Doctrine and Covenants 18.
[6] Heber C. Kimball, "History," *Times and Seasons* 6:668. The original minutes for this meeting are in the Kirtland Record Book, p. 147, HDC. The printing of those minutes in HC 2:181–82,

185–89, will be followed here unless otherwise indicated. See also Kimball, "History," manuscript, book 94-B, Heber C. Kimball Papers, HDC.

7 HC 2:186–89. The first appointees to the Quorum of the Twelve were listed by age. Later appointees were seated and ranked by order of ordination.

8 HC 2:188–89.

9 Unpublished sermon of 8 October 1866, BYP.

10 HC 2:193–98.

11 Kirtland Council Minute Book, p. 88, HDC; HC 2:198–200; Record Book of the Twelve, 27 February 1835. Organizing meetings of the Twelve were held 14, 21, 27 February and 12, 28 March 1835.

12 Doctrine and Covenants 107.

13 BY, "History," *Deseret News*, 10 February 1858, p. 386.

14 MHBY, 2 May 1835.

15 See Matt. 10:14, Mark 6:11, Luke 9:5.

16 Joseph Millett Journal, Appendix, HDC, as cited in Eugene England, "Brigham Young as a Missionary," *The New Era* 7 (November 1977): 30–37.

17 Minutes, 2 May 1835, Record Book of the Twelve.

18 JD 7:229 and 2:18.

19 Jonathan Crosby reminiscence, HDC. Crosby says that Brigham Young later mentioned the incident many times, but to his knowledge the others never did. Perhaps it was this experience that Young related in 1860 "a time in his past history, when he was so poor he did not know where to get bread for his family." President's Office Journal, 18 January 1860, BYP.

20 JS Diary, 24 February 1836, HDC.

21 Ibid., 5 October 1835.

22 Ibid., 12 November 1835.

23 Ibid., 13–16 January 1836; Kirtland Council Record Book, pp. 200ff., 233ff., HDC.

24 Minutes, 30 November 1847, BYP. Or, as another version of the minutes reads, only "true servants . . . are to get the power—and if they would become great and think themselves great, then they aint fit for power."

25 JS Diary, 16 January, 12 February, 3 March 1836.

26 Ibid., 17 January 1836.

27 Ibid., 22–23 January 1836.

28 Ibid., 12 November 1835. Also BY sermons in JD 4:287–88, 371–72.

29 JS Diary, 27 March 1835.

30 BY, "History," *Deseret News*, 10 February 1858, p. 386.

31 Stephen Post Diary, 30 March 1836, HDC. Also see Emmeline B. Wells, "Biography of Mary Ann Angell Young," *The Juvenile Instructor* 26 (1 January 1891): 18, for mention of a heavenly manifestation in the temple that Brigham described to Mary Ann the same night, after his return home.

32 JS Diary, 30 March 1836.

33 JD 2:31.

34 Wilford Woodruff Diary, 23 February 1859.

35 JS Diary, 3 April 1836; Doctrine and Covenants 110.

36 Ronald K. Esplin, "The Emergence of Brigham Young and the Twelve to Mormon Leadership, 1830–1841" (Ph.D. diss., Brigham Young University, 1981), p. 221, note 128.

37 JD 2:19.

38 BY to Mary Ann Young, 3 June 1836, Philip Blair Collection, UUL.

39 BY to Mary Ann Young, 21 July 1836, Blair Collection, UUL.

40 BYHD, 23 July 1836, unpaged.

41 Minutes of Family Meeting, 8 January 1845, BYP.

42 JD 4:305.

43 BY sermons, 31 August 1856, JD 4:34–35, and 5 April 1857, JD 4:305.

⁴⁴ BY, "History," *Deseret News*, 10 February 1858, p. 386, and Willard Richards, "History," *Deseret News*, 23 June 1858. See also HC 2:469–70 footnote where B. H. Roberts says that Richards first got the Book of Mormon as a result of Young's 1835 mission. Joseph Young reports visiting the Richards family in the 1836 tour as well, and it is clear that Willard and his brother made their way to Kirtland soon after.

⁴⁵ Warren A. Cowdery reminiscing about the year before in *Messenger and Advocate* (Kirtland, Ohio) 3 (June 1837): 520–21.

⁴⁶ Woodruff Diary, 26 November 1836, in Dean C. Jessee, "The Kirtland Diary of Wilford Woodruff," *BYU Studies* 12 (Summer 1972): 371.

⁴⁷ Brigham Young, now an "old-timer" in the community, saw the population of Kirtland almost double during his years there. See estimate in Marvin S. Hill, C. Keith Rooker, and Larry T. Wimmer, "The Kirtland Economy Revisited: A Market Critique of Sectarian Economics," *BYU Studies* 17 (Summer 1977): 387–475.

⁴⁸ Willard Richards to Hepsibah Richards, 20 January 1837, Willard Richards Papers, HDC. Also see *Painesville Telegraph* for 18 November 1836 as cited in Max H. Parkin, "The Nature and Cause of Internal and External Conflict of the Mormons in Ohio Between 1830 and 1838" (Master's thesis, Brigham Young University, 1966), p. 203.

⁴⁹ Hill, Rooker, and Wimmer, "Kirtland Economy Revisited," pp. 431–32, 459–60; D. Paul Sampson and Larry T. Wimmer, "The Kirtland Safety Society: The Stock Ledger Book and the Bank Failure," *BYU Studies* 12 (Summer 1972): 430; Dale W. Adams, "Chartering the Kirtland Bank," *BYU Studies* 23 (Fall 1983): 467–82. Brigham's lack of understanding of banking operations is indicated by the story that he deposited marked currency in the Kirtland Bank and was surprised to receive some of it back in a subsequent sale of land. Thinking that banks should preserve all deposits, he was convinced that "roguery" was afoot; he was even more suspicious of the motives of the dissenters. See Andrew Jenson, "Joseph Smith, The Prophet," *Historical Record* (Salt Lake City) 7 (January 1888): 433–34.

⁵⁰ The best discussion of noneconomic causes of dissent in Kirtland is Marvin S. Hill's "Cultural Crisis in the Mormon Kingdom: A Reconsideration of the Causes of Kirtland Dissent," *Church History* 49 (September 1980): 286–97.

⁵¹ Woodruff Diary, 10 January 1837.

⁵² Unpublished sermon of 8 October 1866, HDC.

⁵³ *Deseret News*, 10 February 1858, p. 386.

⁵⁴ BY, "History," ibid.

⁵⁵ Woodruff, "History," *Deseret News*, 14 July 1858, p. 86. Woodruff Diary, 19 February 1837, in Jessee, "The Kirtland Diary of Wilford Woodruff," p. 385; BY, "History," *Deseret News*, 10 February 1858, p. 386.

⁵⁶ BY sermon, 11 September 1853, JD 1:74; Richards Diary, 13–14 March and 11 June 1837, HDC. For details of their travels (not their business), see the diary of Richards or a summary drawn from that diary and published in *Deseret News*, 28 June 1858, p. 73. Apparently because this was a business mission and not a proselyting one, Young made no diary entries himself.

⁵⁷ BY to Mary Ann Young, 24 March 1837, Blair Collection, UUL.

⁵⁸ JD 1:74–75. There is some evidence that an additional cause of uneasiness was the inkling that the Prophet was considering the introduction of plural marriage. Joseph Smith and Oliver Cowdery apparently began considering doctrinal justifications for the practice in 1831, while working through the Book of Genesis. One study suggests that Smith may have taken a plural wife during the Kirtland years. See Danel W. Bachman, "A Study of the Mormon Practice of Plural Marriage before the Death of Joseph Smith" (Master's thesis, Purdue University, 1975), pp. 73–77 and 86–88. See also Bachman's "New Light on an Old Hypothesis: The Ohio Origins of the Revelation on Eternal Marriage," *Journal of Mormon History* 5 (1978): 28–32.

⁵⁹ Woodruff Diary, 13 April 1837; Kirtland Record Book, 11 May 1837.

⁶⁰ JD 10:363–64.

⁶¹ Marvin Hill, in "Cultural Crisis in the Mormon Kingdom," p. 296, concluded that "the degree

of control to be possessed by the church and its leaders, the degree of consolidation in the kingdom," was the basic issue. Dissenters wanted a more open society, closer to the values and traditions of evangelical Protestantism. Also Esplin, "The Emergence of Brigham Young and the Twelve," p. 243.

[62] JD 4:297.
[63] JD 1:215, 3:120–21.
[64] BY to David B. Smith, 1 June 1853.
[65] JD 4:297.
[66] Heber Kimball's printed account of his call and his mission can be found in Heber C. Kimball, *President Heber C. Kimball's Journal*, Faith Promoting Series, no. 7 (Salt Lake City, 1882; reprinted from a Nauvoo edition prepared by Robert B. Thompson). In addition, information about the call appears in Heber C. Kimball, "History," *Deseret News*, 14 April 1858, p. 33, and in manuscript, book 94-B, Heber C. Kimball Papers, HDC; and in Willard Richards Diary, 11 June 1837.
[67] Woodruff Diary, 25 June 1857.
[68] BY, "History," *Deseret News*, 10 February 1858, and HC 2:602.
[69] *Deseret News*, 17 February 1858, p. 393.
[70] Kirtland Record Book, 3 September 1837.
[71] Minutes, 10 September 1837, Kirtland Record Book.
[72] *Elders Journal* 1 (July 1838): 36.
[73] Minutes, 30 November 1837, Kirtland Record Book or HC 2:526–27. According to Ebenezer Robinson, who left Kirtland in early spring 1837, Roger Orton, one of the Seventy, was among those who in the winter and spring of 1837 "objected to the course being pursued by brother Joseph Smith, Jr. and the church." See *The Return*, August 1889, p. 116.
[74] See Thomas Marsh, in *Elders Journal* 1 (July 1838): 37.
[75] JD 2:18; BY, "History," *Deseret News*, 17 February 1858, p. 393.
[76] Wells, "Biography of Mary Ann Angell Young," pp. 18–19.

CHAPTER 5 :
THE MISSOURI INTERLUDE

Primary sources on Brigham Young in Missouri include Brigham's "History" and diary and Heber C. Kimball's "History." Secondary accounts include Ronald K. Esplin, "The Emergence of Brigham Young and the Twelve to Mormon Leadership, 1830–1841" (Ph.D. diss., Brigham Young University, 1981), and S. Dilworth Young, *"Here Is Brigham": Brigham Young—the Years to 1844* (Salt Lake City, 1964).

Serious studies of "the Missouri Interlude" include Leland H. Gentry, "A History of the Latter-day Saints in Northern Missouri from 1836 to 1839" (Ph.D. diss., Brigham Young University, 1965); Max H. Parkin, "A History of the Latter-day Saints in Clay County, Missouri, from 1833 to 1837" (Ph.D. diss., Brigham Young University, 1976); and Clark V. Johnson, "The Missouri Redress Petitions: New Evidence of the Mormon Side of the Missouri Conflict in 1834 and 1838," typescript generously furnished by the author.

[1] Missouri Conference Minutes, 29 January 1839, HDC.
[2] BY, "History," *Deseret News*, 17 February 1858, p. 393; HC 3:2.
[3] Joseph Smith to the Kirtland Presidency, 29 March 1838, Joseph Smith Papers, HDC.
[4] BY sermon, 24 July 1854, JD 2:18, and BY, "History," *Deseret News*, 17 February 1858, p. 393. Brigham Young told a congregation that he left behind property in Kirtland worth $5,000. More accurately, he wrote to an acquaintance of his youth that he left behind property worth "$3 or 4000." See BY to David B. Smith, 1 June 1853, BYP.
[5] Emmeline B. Wells, "Biography of Mary Ann Angell Young," *The Juvenile Instructor* 26 (1

January 1891): 19; BY, "History," *Deseret News*, 17 February 1858, p. 393. The revelation can be found in HC 3:23.

[6] BY sermon, 17 February 1862, JD 3:209.

[7] JD 4:41; HOJ, 2 December 1847, HDC.

[8] JD 3:209.

[9] Far West Record, HDC. Also in *Elders Journal* 1 (July 1838): 46–47.

[10] Doctrine and Covenants 117, 119, 120.

[11] BYHD; Doctrine and Covenants 118.

[12] Heber C. Kimball, *President Heber C. Kimball's Journal*, Faith Promoting Series, no. 7 (Salt Lake City, 1882), pp. 52–53, and Orson Hyde, "History," *Deseret News*, 12 May 1858, p. 49.

[13] BY, "History," *Deseret News*, 17 February 1858, p. 393. Also BY sermon, 11 July 1852, JD 1:41: "To my certain knowledge," he says twice here, that occurred and he could name names.

[14] James A. Little, "Biography of Lorenzo Dow Young," *Utah Historical Quarterly* 14 (1946): 52–53. For a consideration of the Missouri Danites see Leland H. Gentry, "A History of the Latter-day Saints in Northern Missouri from 1836 to 1839" (Ph.D. diss., Brigham Young University, 1965), pp. 213–44.

[15] JD 5:207.

[16] Thomas Marsh, "History," *Deseret News*, 24 March 1858, p. 18, and sermon of Marsh, 6 September 1857, JD 5:207. One of the tensions between Marsh and Joseph Smith may have been over Missouri lands. Marsh was one of several who controlled much of the land in Far West and may have rebelled against Smith's handling of land sales and distribution. See Lyndon W. Cook, "Thomas B. Marsh Returns to the Church," *BYU Studies* 20 (Summer 1980): 389–400.

[17] Sermon of Heber C. Kimball, 12 July 1857, JD 5:28–29.

[18] G. Homer Durham, ed., *The Gospel Kingdom* (Salt Lake City, 1944), p. 187. Also HC 3:165 and *Deseret News*, 24 March 1858, p. 18.

[19] See Walter Litchfield, "Thomas B. Marsh, Physician to the Church" (Master's thesis, Brigham Young University, 1956), pp. 117–35, for a comprehensive review of his return to the church in 1857. See also Cook, "Thomas B. Marsh," pp. 396–400. "I left the Church in Missouri in 1838. I never wrote against the Church nor persecuted the people. I did nothing to disturb or hinder its progress. I just left it and kept myself away from it, and have been silent." Journal of Wandell Mace as quoted in Walter Litchfield, "Thomas B. Marsh," p. 117.

[20] HC 3:175. Emphasis deleted.

[21] As given in his sermon of 13 August 1871, JD 14:206.

[22] See Parley P. Pratt's "A History, of the Persecution, of the Church of Jesus Christ of Latter Day Saints in Missouri," *Times and Seasons* 1 (June 1840): 115–16. This series ran serially beginning in number two of the volume and running to the conclusion of the volume in October. BY, "History," *Deseret News*, 17 February 1858, p. 393. Consult Gentry, "A History of the Latter-day Saints in Northern Missouri," pp. 312–51, for the siege of Far West and its aftermath. See also HC 3:182–208 and a version by JS in *Time and Seasons* 1 (November 1839): 5.

[23] Was this a dishonorable betrayal by traitors in their own ranks and a violation of a flag of truce, as the Mormons saw it, or a delivering up of prisoners to prevent the destruction of Far West, as the militia viewed it? For the point of view of General Samuel D. Lucas, see HC 3:195–99. Gentry reviews the evidence in "A History of the Latter-day Saints in Northern Missouri," pp. 342–45.

[24] *Deseret News*, 17 February 1858, p. 393.

[25] Ibid., p. 394; Kimball, *Journal*, pp. 60, 64, 65.

[26] HC 3:202–4, emphasis deleted. Both Heber and Brigham include the speech in their histories: BY, "History," *Deseret News*, 17 February 1858, p. 393, and Kimball, *Journal*, pp. 60–62.

[27] Sidney Rigdon, JS, Hyrum Smith to Kimball and Young, 16 January 1839, Joseph Smith Papers, HDC. Another manuscript copy has been preserved in Kimball Family Papers, HDC.

[28] Ibid.

[29] Heber C. Kimball, "History," *Deseret News*, 28 April 1858, p. 41.

[30] See account in *Times and Seasons* 1 (September 1840): 165.

[31] HC 4:247.

[32] Minutes, 29 January 1839, HDC; HC 3:250–51. Copies of the covenant with signatures are filed with General Minutes Collection, HDC.

[33] See minutes for February, March, and April, General Minutes Collection, HDC. See also Kimball, *Journal*, pp. 11–74.

[34] See Helen Mar Kimball Whitney's "Early Reminiscences," *The Woman's Exponent* 9 (1 June 1880): 5–6, and Heber C. Kimball, *Journal*, pp. 67–68. A manuscript version of Young's history has this sentence lined out: "The persecution became so bitter against me (and my life was so diligently sought for) that I was compelled to flee." The context provided for the story in Susa Young Gates with Leah D. Widtsoe, *The Life Story of Brigham Young* (New York, 1930), pp. 20–21, is flawed but the event may well have occurred. Emmeline B. Wells, "Biography of Mary Ann Angell Young," p. 19, says that "Mrs. Young informed me that her husband would take her and her little ones a short distance, and with such help as he could get he would return and gather up the poorer and more destitute of the brethren and sisters, the widows and helpless orphans of those who had fallen victims at the hands of the mob, and help them forward upon their journey."

[35] JS and others to Edward Partridge and the church, 25 March 1839, *Times and Seasons* 1 (May 1840): 100–3; JS to Mrs. Norman Buell, 15 March 1839, HC 4:286.

[36] JS and others to Partridge, 25 March 1839, *Times and Seasons* 1 (May 1840): 102, and *Times and Seasons* 1 (July 1840): 131–32.

[37] Woodruff Diary 17, 18, 20 March and 8 April 1839.

[38] Orson Hyde to BY, 30 March 1839, BYP; Hyde, "History," *Deseret News*, 12 May 1858, p. 49.

[39] Woodruff Diary, 17 April 1839.

[40] BY, "History," manuscript no. 3, BYP. For a reminiscent account of this meeting, see sermon of Wilford Woodruff, 12 December 1869, JD 13:159.

[41] MHBY, 21 April 1839, p. 36; BY, "History," manuscript no. 3.

[42] Kimball, *Journal*, p. 74.

[43] Minutes, 26 April 1839, in General Minutes Collection, HDC, and in Woodruff's diary. See also Kimball, *Journal*, p. 75.

[44] Kimball, *Journal*, p. 75, and HC 4:339–40; George A. Smith, "History," HDC.

[45] BY, "History," *Deseret News*, 17 February 1858, p. 394.

[46] See Woodruff Diary (entered after 29 May entry) for minutes of the 4–5 May meetings. Minutes of 6 May conference can be found in General Minutes Collection, HDC. All three days are reprinted in HC 4:344–47.

[47] Woodruff Diary, 2 July 1839. My italics.

[48] Woodruff Diary and Joseph Smith Diary.

[49] BY, "History," *Deseret News*, 24 February 1858, p. 401.

[50] Woodruff Diary, 25 July 1839; Woodruff in JD 13:159–60.

[51] Kimball, *Journal*, p. 83; Joseph Smith Diary, 5 August 1839.

[52] Leonora Taylor to John Taylor, 9 September 1839, as published in Ronald K. Esplin, "Sickness and Faith, Nauvoo Letters," *BYU Studies* 15 (Summer 1975): 427–31.

[53] MHBY, 14 September 1839, p. 50.

[54] JD 13:211.

[55] MHBY, 6 December 1839, p. 61.

[56] Heber C. Kimball to Vilate Kimball, 19 September 1840, Heber C. Kimball Papers, HDC. Compare this with the insistence of John E. Page, who did not go, that poverty and a sick wife were adequate reasons for not being at his post: Page to BY, 12 April 1844, BYP.

[57] BY to Mary Ann Young, 15 September 1839, Philip Blair Collection, UUL.

[58] For Brigham and Heber's journey, see BY, "History," *Deseret News*, 24 February 1858, pp. 401–2, and 3 March 1858, p. 409. Also Kimball, *Journal*, pp. 85–97.

[59] BYHD, October 1839.

[60] Kimball, *Journal*, p. 88, and Heber Kimball to Vilate Kimball, 24 October 1839, Kimball Papers, HDC.

[61] George A.'s account can be found in George A. Smith, "History," manuscript, HDC.

[62] MHBY, 11 October 1839, p. 52.

[63] MHBY, 4 October 1839, p. 53.

[64] MHBY, 7 January 1840, p. 64.

[65] Heber Kimball to Vilate Kimball, 24 October 1839, Kimball Papers, HDC: "The brethren toock the team and went on and left. . . ."

[66] HOJ, 16 February 1859. For detailed retellings of this experience see BY, "History," *Deseret News*, 24 February 1858, p. 402, and Kimball, *Journal*, pp. 90–92.

[67] Kimball, *Journal*, p. 92.

[68] HOJ, 16 February 1859, my italics; and President's Office Journal, 18 January 1860. See also Minutes, 18 January 1873, General Minutes Collection, HDC.

[69] BYHD, 4 November 1839.

[70] BYHD, 26 November 1839; MHBY, 22 November 1839, pp. 58–59.

[71] MHBY, 6 December 1839, p. 60.

[72] BY, "History," *Deseret News*, 24 February 1858, p. 402.

[73] MHBY, 2 February 1840, p. 67.

[74] Minutes, 10 October 1865, General Minutes Collection, HDC. Compare this with what Smith told all the Twelve in 1835: ". . . and you each have the same authority in other nations that I have in this nation." Minutes, 7 February 1835, Record Book of the Twelve, HDC.

[75] BY, "History," *Deseret News*, 3 March 1858, p. 409; BY sermon, 17 July 1840, JD 13:211–12; MHBY, 5, 6 April 1840, p. 69.

CHAPTER 6:
THE BRITISH MISSION

Primary sources on the British mission of the Twelve include: BYHD; Woodruff Diary; Record Book of the Twelve, 1839–41; and *Times and Seasons* and the *Millennial Star*, 1840–42. Studies on the British mission of the Twelve include: James B. Allen and Malcolm R. Thorp, "The Mission of the Twelve to England, 1840–41: Mormon Apostles and the Working Classes," *BYU Studies* 15 (Summer 1975): 499–526; Eugene England, *Brother Brigham* (Salt Lake City, 1980), pp. 34–61; and Ronald K. Esplin, "The Emergence of Brigham Young and the Twelve to Mormon Leadership, 1830–1841" (Ph.D. diss., Brigham Young University, 1981), chapter 10, pp. 427–98.

The setting of Britain in the early 1840s is described in: John W. Dodds, *The Age of Paradox: A Biography of England 1841–1851* (London, 1953), esp. pp. 3–101 (he discusses the Mormon missionaries on pp. 28–29); Asa Briggs, *The Age of Improvement 1783–1867* (London, 1959); John F. C. Harrison, *The Early Victorians* (New York, 1971); Frederick Engels, *The Condition of the Working Class in England in 1844*, trans. and ed. W. O. Henderson and W. H. Chaloner (New York, 1973); W. W. Rostow, *British Economy of the Nineteenth Century* (New York, 1948); William R. Ward, *Religion and Society in England, 1790–1850* (London, 1972); and Arthur L. Bowley, *Wages in the United Kingdom in the Nineteenth Century* (Cambridge, 1900).

Other useful studies include: Ronald W. Walker, ed., "The Willard Richards and Brigham Young 5 September 1840 Letter from England to Nauvoo," *BYU Studies* 18 (Spring 1978): 466–75; Norman Hill, "The Trumpet of Zion: Mormon Conversion and Emigration in Britain," *Tangents* 3 (Provo, Utah) (Spring 1975): 56–69; Phillip A. M. Taylor, *Expectations Westward: The Mormons and the Emigration of Their British Converts in the Nineteenth Century* (Edinburgh and London, 1965); John E. Thompson, "A History of the British Mission of the Latter Day Saints (1837–1841)," in *Restoration Studies*, ed. Maurice L. Draper (Independence, Mo., 1980), 1: 42–57; Susa Young Gates, "Brigham Young's Missionary Experiences," *The Juvenile Instructor* 63 (May 1928): 306–11, 368–73, 422–27; S. Dilworth Young, *"Here Is Brigham": Brigham*

Young—the Years to 1844 (Salt Lake City, 1964), esp. pp. 231–87; Robert L. Lively, Jr., "The Catholic Apostolic Church and the Church of Jesus Christ of Latter-day Saints: A Comparative Study of Two Minority Millenarian Groups in Nineteenth-century England" (Ph.D. diss., University of Oxford, 1977), esp. pp. 175–97; James B. Allen and Thomas G. Alexander, eds., *Manchester Mormons: The Journal of William Clayton, 1840 to 1842* (Santa Barbara and Salt Lake City, 1974); Malcolm R. Thorp, "The Religious Backgrounds of Mormon Converts in Britain, 1837–52," *Journal of Mormon History* 4 (1977): 51–65; Ronald K. Esplin, "Inside Brigham Young: Abrahamic Tests as Preparation for Leadership," *BYU Studies* 20 (Spring 1980): 300–10; Richard L. Evans, *A Century of Mormonism in Great Britain* (Salt Lake City, 1937); and Stanley B. Kimball, "Second Mission to England," in *Heber C. Kimball: Mormon Patriarch and Pioneer* (Urbana, Illinois, 1981), pp. 70–80.

[1] BY and Willard Richards to First Presidency, from Manchester, England, 5 September 1840, *BYU Studies* 18 (Spring 1978): 472–73.

[2] BY, "History," *Deseret News*, 2 March 1858, p. 409.

[3] Joseph Fielding Diary, 9 April 1840, typescript, HDC.

[4] Heber C. Kimball and Joseph Fielding to the editors of the *Times and Seasons*, 6 May 1840, in *Times and Seasons* 1 (July 1840): 138–39.

[5] Minutes, 14 April 1840, BYP; Willard Richards Diary, 14 April 1840.

[6] Woodruff Diary, 15 April 1840; Minutes, 16 April 1840, BYP. Brigham later said that "Parley P. Pratt craved the privilege of editing it, and we granted him the privilege." See BY sermon, 31 August 1856, JD 4:35.

[7] The report and minutes were published in *Times and Seasons* 1 (June 1840): 119–22 and also in HC 4:114–20. See also William Clayton Diary, 17 April 1840, in James B. Allen and Thomas G. Alexander, eds., *Manchester Mormons: The Journal of William Clayton, 1840 to 1842* (Santa Barbara, Calif., and Salt Lake City, 1974), p. 141.

[8] MHBY, pp. 71–72. Also James B. Allen and Malcolm R. Thorp, "The Mission of the Twelve to England, 1840–41: Mormon Apostles and the Working Classes," *BYU Studies* 15 (Summer 1975): 506.

[9] *Millennial Star* 1 (July 1840): 72; Woodruff Diary, 21–23 April 1840.

[10] Woodruff Diary, 17–18 April 1840; BY, "History," *Deseret News*, 3 March 1858, p. 409.

[11] BY to George A. Smith, 4 May 1840, BYP.

[12] BY to JS, 7 May 1840, Joseph Smith Papers, HDC.

[13] See his diary for later April and May 1840, for notation of his travels, preaching, baptizing.

[14] Woodruff Diary, 17 May 1840.

[15] Woodruff Diary, 18 May 1840. For a brief account of Woodruff's Herefordshire experience from the beginning in March, see Woodruff to the *Millennial Star*, 9 July 1840, published in *Millennial Star* 1 (July 1840): 71–72, and *Millennial Star* 1 (August 1840); 81–84. Another version covering the beginnings of the work but continuing the story further is Wilford Woodruff to the *Times and Seasons*, 7 October 1840, *Times and Seasons* 2 (15 February 1841): 311–14.

[16] Woodruff Diary, 3 June 1840.

[17] Woodruff Diary, 14, 21, 22 June 1840. See also the account in Wilford Woodruff to Phebe Woodruff, 8 July 1840, in *Times and Seasons* 1 (September 1840): 168.

[18] *Millennial Star* 25 (14 November 1863): 727.

[19] See BY to George A. Smith, 4 May 1840, BYP; also JD 4:35.

[20] *The Athenaeum*, 3 April 1841, p. 252.

[21] See financial papers relating to publishing in Brigham Young Miscellaneous Papers, BYP. These accounts and notations evidence Young's personal concern and involvement with the publishing, especially of the Book of Mormon. He carried these papers to Nauvoo, presumably for review by Joseph Smith, and then kept them among his own papers. BY to Richards and Woodruff, 24 May 1840, and BY to Willard Richards, 10 June and 17 June 1840, BYP, details some of the printing arrangements and comments on other of Young's activities.

[22] John W. Dodds, *The Age of Paradox: A Biography of England 1841–1851* (London, 1953), pp. 11–12, 27, 160–62. All this is substantiated in Heber Kimball's letter to Vilate, written from Manchester 27 May 1840. See also the Joseph Fielding Diary, 14 July 1840; Woodruff Diary, 20 January 1840.

[23] BYHD, 30 May through June 1840, BY, "History," *Deseret News*, 3 March 1858, p. 410; BY to Willard Richards, 17 June 1840, BYP.

[24] BY to Richards, 17 June 1840, BYP.

[25] Heber C. Kimball to Vilate Kimball, 27 May 1840, Kimball Family Letters, HDC.

[26] BYHD, 3–4 June 1840, and BY to Willard Richards, 10 June 1840.

[27] BY to Mary Ann Young, 2 June 1840, Philip Blair Collection, UUL.

[28] For Young's earlier assistance, see Vilate Kimball to Heber C. Kimball, 6 June 1840, Heber C. Kimball Papers, HDC. BY to Mary Ann Young, 15 January 1841, Blair Collection, UUL. Hyrum Smith to Parley Pratt, 22 December 1839, Joseph Smith Letterbook, Joseph Smith Papers, HDC.

[29] From Emmeline B. Wells, "Biography of Mary Ann Angell Young," *The Juvenile Instructor* 26 (1 January 1891): 56–57.

[30] Leonora Taylor to John Taylor, 13 April 1840, in *Millennial Star* 1 (July 1840): 63–65. Similarly, Phebe Woodruff to Wilford Woodruff, 4 May 1840 in *Millennial Star* 1 (August 1840): 89–90, where Phebe reports all the wives well but Leonora Taylor.

[31] BYHD, 11 June 1840.

[32] BY to Mary Ann Young, 12 June 1840, Blair Collection, UUL.

[33] Ibid., 20, 24 June 1840, Blair Collection, UUL. See also BY and Willard Richards to First Presidency, 5 September 1840, Joseph Smith Papers, HDC.

[34] BY to Willard Richards, 17 June 1840, BYP.

[35] Joseph Fielding Diary, 6 July 1840, typescript, HDC. I have changed the past tense to present.

[36] BY and Willard Richards to First Presidency, 5 September 1840, JS Papers, HDC. See also the treatment in Allen and Thorp, "Mission of the Twelve," pp. 511–15.

[37] BYHD, 5–10 September 1840, and William Clayton Diary, 8 September 1840, in Allen and Alexander, *Manchester Mormons*, pp. 172–73. The group arrived in Nauvoo 24 November 1840 after a journey of eleven weeks.

[38] Notes, 6 October 1840, Miscellaneous Papers, BYP.

[39] Woodruff Diary, 6 October 1840; Minutes, 6 October 1840, *Millennial Star* 1 (October 1840): 165–68.

[40] BY to George A. Smith, 30 December 1840; Woodruff Diary, 8 January 1841; Woodruff Diary, 8 February 1841. BY to George A. Smith, 11 February 1841; BY to Kimball and Smith, 5 March 1841, BYP. Handbinding a 5,000-copy edition was no small task. Nor did Young's responsibility end with publication. Some part of the edition was finished with a special binding and gilded pages. When some copies of the special edition proved defective, Young followed through to see them corrected. See BY to Willard Richards, 1, 5, 8 March 1841, BYP.

[41] BY to Mary Ann Young, 16, 20, 30 October 1840, Blair Collection, UUL.

[42] BY, "History," *Deseret News*, 3 March 1859, p. 410.

[43] Vilate Kimball to Heber C. Kimball, 6 June 1840, Heber C. Kimball Papers, HDC.

[44] See BYHD for December and January and also BY, "History," *Deseret News*, 3 March 1858, p. 410, and 10 March 1858, p. 1. BY to Willard Richards and Levi Richards, 5 December 1840, BYP.

[45] George A. Smith Diary, 17 September 1840; Heber Kimball to Vilate Kimball, 19 September 1840, Heber C. Kimball Papers, HDC. See also Kimball to the *Times and Seasons*, 4 August 1841, in *Times and Seasons* 2 (16 August 1841): 507–11. Kimball, Woodruff, and Smith reported their August–September mission in a 12 October 1840 letter to the *Times and Seasons* printed in *Times and Seasons* 2 (15 December 1840): 250–52. See *Times and Seasons* 2 (15 September 1841): 535–38, for "the word of the Lord to the citizens of London . . . ," a proclamation issued by Kimball and Woodruff. See also Woodruff to the *Millennial Star*, 20 February 1841, in *Millennial Star* 1 (March 1841): 281–83, and Heber C. Kimball Diary, last week of December 1840 to 25 February 1841, HDC.

[46] Woodruff to the editors, 7 October 1840, *Times and Seasons* 2 (15 February 1841): 330.

[47] Kimball, Woodruff, and George A. Smith to Ebenezer Robinson and D. C. Smith, 12 October 1840, in HC 4:220–24.

[48] BY to Mary Ann Young, 16 October, 12 November 1840, 15 January 1841, Blair Collection, UUL.

[49] BY to Mary Ann Young, 15 January 1841, Blair Collection, UUL.

[50] Woodruff Diary, 18 January 1841, HDC. BY to George A. Smith, 11 February 1841, BYP.

[51] *Times and Seasons* 2 (1 January 1841): 58–64, and *Times and Seasons* 2 (15 January 1848): 273–76; *Millennial Star* 2 (March 1841): 265–74.

[52] Part of Young's 16 October 1840 letter to Mary Ann Young, Blair Collection, UUL.

[53] For a chronology of these months, see BYHD and *Deseret News*, 10 March 1858, p. 1. The latter source gives names of ships and number sailing.

[54] BY to George A. Smith, 11 February 1841, BYP; Minutes, 11 February 1841, BYP.

[55] BY to George A. Smith, 13 February 1841, BYP.

[56] George A. Smith, "History," 17–18 February 1841, HDC. BY to Levi Richards, 13 March 1841, BYP.

[57] Article on Family Prayer in *Millennial Star* 1 (March 1841): 286–87.

[58] Woodruff Diary, 5 April 1841.

[59] These totals are from the representations in the minutes published in the *Millennial Star*, figures that Young and others included in their published histories.

[60] Printed minutes in *Millennial Star* 1 (April 1841): 301–5.

[61] HC 4:347–48; *Millennial Star* 1 (April 1841): 304–5.

[62] JD 13:212.

[63] Woodruff Diary, 19 April 1841.

[64] BY, "History," *Deseret News*, 10 March 1858.

[65] BYHD entries before and after 5 May 1841.

[66] BYHD, 1840–41, no dates given.

[67] Manuscript copies of this revelation are in the JS and BYP Collections. A slightly edited version is published in Doctrine and Covenants 126.

CHAPTER 7 :

NAUVOO

Primary sources include the BY Diary, Minutes of Nauvoo High Council, Minutes of Nauvoo City Council, Record Book of the Twelve, and MHBY, all in HDC.

Scholarly studies include: Robert B. Flanders, *Nauvoo: Kingdom on the Mississippi* (Urbana, Illinois, 1965); Kenneth W. Godfrey, "Causes of Mormon–Non-Mormon Conflict in Hancock County, Illinois, 1839–1846" (Ph.D. diss., Brigham Young University, 1967); T. Edgar Lyon, "Nauvoo and the Council of the Twelve," in F. Mark McKiernan et al., *The Restoration Movement: Essays in Mormon History* (Lawrence, Kansas, 1973), pp. 167–205; Robert B. Flanders, "The Kingdom of God in Illinois; Politics in Utopia," *Dialogue* 5 (Spring 1970): 26–36; Leonard J. Arrington and Jon Haupt, "The Missouri and Illinois Mormons in Ante Bellum Fiction," *Dialogue* 5 (Spring 1970): 37–50; David E. Miller and Della S. Miller, *Nauvoo: The City of Joseph* (Santa Barbara, Calif., and Salt Lake City, 1974); E. Cecil McGavin, *Nauvoo the Beautiful* (Salt Lake City, 1946); Stanley B. Kimball, *Heber C. Kimball: Mormon Patriarch and Pioneer* (Urbana, Illinois, 1981); Leonard J. Arrington, *Charles C. Rich: Mormon General and Western Frontiersman* (Provo, 1974); idem, *From Quaker to Latter-day Saint: Bishop Edwin D. Woolley* (Salt Lake City, 1976); various articles in the *Journal of the Illinois State Historical Society* 64 (Spring 1971); various articles in *BYU Studies* 15 (Summer 1979); Ronald K. Esplin, "The Emergence of Brigham Young and the Twelve to Mormon Leadership, 1830–1841" (Ph.D. diss., Brigham Young University, 1981); Samuel W. Taylor, *The Kingdom of God or Nothing: The Life of John Taylor,*

Militant Mormon (New York, 1976); D. Michael Quinn, "The Council of Fifty and Its Members, 1844–1945," *BYU Studies* 20 (Winter 1980): 163–97; Lawrence Foster, *Religion and Sexuality: Three American Communal Experiments of the Nineteenth Century* (New York, 1981); Danel W. Bachman, "A Study of the Mormon Practice of Plural Marriage before the Death of Joseph Smith" (Master's thesis, Purdue University, 1975); Richard P. Howard, "The Changing RLDS Response to Mormon Polygamy: A Preliminary Analysis," *The John Whitmer Historical Association Journal* 3 (1983): 14–29.

[1] BY Diary no. 3, 31 May 1843.
[2] MHBY, p. 109.
[3] MHBY, pp. 109–10.
[4] MHBY, p. 106.
[5] Minutes, 16 August 1841, General Minutes Collection, HDC; BY, "History," *Deseret News*, 10 March 1858, p. 2.
[6] Willard Richards Diary, 16 August 1841, HDC.
[7] There is no evidence that Brigham continued his Masonic affiliation after 1844, except one photograph taken about 1852 that shows a Masonic pin on his shirt. Although the charter of the Nauvoo lodges was canceled by the Grand Lodge in 1843, some Mormons continued to participate in Masonic meetings until 1845, when Brigham suggested that they put all their emphasis on church work. Kenneth W. Godfrey, "Joseph Smith and the Masons," *Journal of the Illinois State Historical Society* 64 (Spring 1971): 79–90; Mervin B. Hogan, "Mormonism and Freemasonry: The Illinois Episode," *Little Masonic Library* 2 (1977): 267–326. Appended to the latter article is a list of Hogan's other writings, a substantial scholarly output, on the subject of Mormonism and Masonry. A short valuable recent article by Hogan is "Mormon Interfaces with Masonry in Illinois and Iowa Between 1841 and 1844," *BYU Studies*, forthcoming.
[8] *Deseret News*, 17 September 1856, p. 219.
[9] MHBY, p. 111.
[10] JD 3:266.
[11] B. H. Roberts, *The Life of John Taylor* (Salt Lake City, 1892), p. 101.
[12] MHBY, pp. 134–36.
[13] A sheaf of documents relating to Lucy's history is in the possession of Jeffrey Johnson, cataloguer in HDC, photocopies generously furnished to the writer.
[14] MHBY, p. 116.
[15] MHBY, p. 129.
[16] See D. Michael Quinn, "Latter-day Saint Prayer Circles," *BYU Studies* 19 (Fall 1978): 79–105.
[17] MHBY, pp. 122–24.
[18] MHBY, pp. 124–25.
[19] Lester E. Bush, Jr., "Brigham Young in Life and Death: A Medical Overview," *Journal of Mormon History* 5 (1978): 79–103.
[20] MHBY, pp. 126, 149; BY to Mary Ann Angell, 17 August 1843, Yale University Library.
[21] MHBY, p. 130.
[22] See *The Brigham Young Site and Residence, 1840–1846*, pamphlet distributed at the home by Nauvoo Restoration, Inc. After the Mormons left Nauvoo in 1846, the home was sold at public auction for $600.
[23] Emmeline B. Wells, "Biography of Mary Ann Angell Young," *The Juvenile Instructor* 26 (1 January 1891): 16–20, 56–58.
[24] Remarks at general conference, 6 April 1843, HC 5:329–30.
[25] HC 5:322, 6 April 1843.
[26] Ibid.
[27] HC 5:414; also Woodruff Diary, 14 June 1843.
[28] MHBY, p. 111.
[29] MHBY, p. 132.

[30] MHBY, p. 138.

[31] MHBY, pp. 147–48.

[32] MHBY, p. 148.

[33] MHBY, pp. 144–45.

[34] MHBY, p. 146.

[35] MHBY, pp. 150–51. See also Davis Bitton and Gary L. Bunker, "Phrenology Among the Mormons," *Dialogue* 9 (Spring 1974): 43–61.

[36] MHBY, pp. 138–39.

[37] MHBY, pp. 161–63.

[38] Mary Ann Young to BY, 16 and 17 August 1843, HDC.

[39] "Record of Deaths in the City of Nauvoo," HDC.

[40] BY to Mary Ann Young, 17 August 1843, Yale University Library.

[41] See George U. Hubbard, "Abraham Lincoln as Seen by the Mormons," *Utah Historical Quarterly* 31 (Spring 1963): 91–108.

[42] Joseph Fielding Smith, *Essentials in Church History*, 22d ed. (Salt Lake City, 1973), p. 291.

[43] BYD No. 3, 13 March 1844.

[44] MHBY, p. 164. The Council of Fifty is well researched. See Hyrum L. Andrus, *Joseph Smith and World Government* (Salt Lake City, 1958); Klaus J. Hansen, *Quest for Empire: The Political Kingdom of God and the Council of Fifty in Mormon History* (East Lansing, Mich., 1967); D. Michael Quinn, "The Council of Fifty and Its Members, 1844 to 1945," *BYU Studies* 20 (Winter 1980): 163–97; and Andrew F. Ehat, " 'It Seems Like Heaven Began on Earth': Joseph Smith and the Constitution of the Kingdom of God," *BYU Studies* 20 (Spring 1980): 253–79.

[45] From an undated draft of a statement about this experience (probably late in 1844) in BYP. See also Woodruff statement of 21 September 1883, Woodruff Papers; Orson Hyde to Ebenezer Robinson, 19 September 1844, in Robinson's publication, *The Return*, April 1890, p. 253.

[46] Orson Hyde to Ebenezer Robinson, 19 September 1844, in Robinson's publication, *The Return*, April 1890, p. 253. See also Parley P. Pratt, "Proclamation. To the Church of Jesus Christ of Latter-day Saints," *Millennial Star* 5 (March 1845): 149–53.

[47] BY to Mary Ann Young, 12 June 1844, original in possession of Dr. Wade Stephens, Bradenton, Florida. Quoted in Dean C. Jessee, "Brigham Young's Family, Part I 1824–1845," *BYU Studies* 18 (Spring 1978): 326.

[48] See treatments in Donna Hill, *Joseph Smith, the First Mormon* (Garden City, N.Y., 1977); Dallin H. Oaks and Marvin S. Hill, *Carthage Conspiracy: The Trial of the Accused Assassins of Joseph Smith* (Urbana, Ill., 1975); B. H. Roberts, *A Comprehensive History of the Church of Jesus Christ of Latter-day Saints: Century I*, 6 vols. (Salt Lake City, 1930); Keith Huntress, ed., *Murder of an American Prophet* (San Francisco, 1960); and Dean C. Jessee, "Return to Carthage: Writing the History of Joseph Smith's Martyrdom," *Journal of Mormon History* 8 (1981): 3–20. I have also benefited from using the interpretive summary of early Mormon history in Marvin S. Hill, "The Rise of the Mormon Kingdom of God," in *Utah's History*, ed. Richard D. Poll (Provo, Utah, 1978), pp. 97–112.

[49] MHBY, p. 171.

[50] Mary Ann Young to BY, 30 June 1844, HDC.

[51] MHBY, p. 171.

[52] BY to Vilate Young, 11 August 1844, HDC. For a time Brigham believed that Joseph had been inspired to go west to avoid imprisonment in Carthage and that he was coaxed into surrendering by Saints who feared that the mob would lay siege to Nauvoo if he escaped. Recently discovered documents have demonstrated that the decision to return from Iowa and give himself up was Smith's own decision. See *A Series of Instructions and Remarks by President Young at a Special Council, Tabernacle, March 21, 1858* (Salt Lake City, 1858), HDC; Jessee, "Return to Carthage," pp. 3–19.

CHAPTER 8 :
CITY OF JOSEPH

On Nauvoo, I have made use of the references given in the notes for Chapter 7. The succession crisis is discussed in: Ronald K. Esplin, "Joseph, Brigham and the Twelve: A Succession of Continuity," *BYU Studies* 21 (Summer 1981): 301–41; BYHD, entries for 1844–46; Andrew F. Ehat, " 'It Seems Like Heaven Began on Earth': Joseph Smith and the Constitution of the Kingdom of God," *BYU Studies* 20 (Spring 1980): 253–79; Andrew Jenson, "Succession in the Church," *The Historical Record*, 4 vols. (Salt Lake City, 1884–92), 7: 785–92; D. Michael Quinn, "The Mormon Succession Crisis of 1844," *BYU Studies* 16 (Winter 1976): 187–233; Douglas W. Larche, "The Mantle of the Prophet: A Rhetorical Analysis of the Quest for Mormon Post-Martyrdom Leadership 1844–1860" (Ph.D. diss., Indiana University, 1977), esp. chapter 3, "Brigham Young: Lion of the Lord," pp. 53–91.

Other aspects of Brigham's life in Nauvoo are discussed in: S. Dilworth Young, "*Here Is Brigham*": *Brigham Young—the Years to 1844* (Salt Lake City, 1964), 1801–44; Leonard J. Arrington and Ronald K. Esplin, "The Role of the Quorum of the Twelve during Brigham Young's Presidency of the Church . . . ," *Task Papers in LDS History*, no. 31 (Salt Lake City, 1979); Dean C. Jessee, "Brigham Young's Family: The Wilderness Years," *BYU Studies* 19 (Summer 1979): 474–500; Maureen Ursenbach Beecher, " 'All Things Move in Order in the City': The Nauvoo Diary of Zina Diantha Huntington Jacobs," *BYU Studies* 19 (Spring 1979): 285–320; James L. Kimball, Jr., "The Nauvoo Charter: A Reinterpretation," *Journal of the Illinois State Historical Society* 64 (Spring 1971): 66–78; and Leonard J. Arrington, " 'In Honorable Remembrance': Thomas L. Kane's Services to the Mormons," *BYU Studies* 21 (Fall 1981): 389–402.

The decision to relocate in the Great Basin was influenced by John C. Frémont, *The Exploring Expedition to the Rocky Mountains and to Oregon and North California* (Washington, D.C., 1845); and Lansford W. Hastings, *The Emigrants' Guide to Oregon and California* (St. Louis, 1845); and many articles in the St. Louis and other newspapers. Also Reverend Samuel Parker, *Journal of an Exploring Tour beyond the Rocky Mountains* (Ithaca, New York, 1840).

The most complete account of choosing the location of eventual settlement in the West is Richard H. Jackson, "Myth and Reality: Environmental Perception of the Mormons, 1840–1865, an Historical Geosophy" (Ph.D. diss., Clark University, 1970), esp. pp. 87–122. See also Lewis Clark Christian, "Mormon Foreknowledge of the West," *BYU Studies* 21 (Fall 1981): 403–15; and Ronald K. Esplin, " 'A Place Prepared': Joseph, Brigham, and the Quest for Promised Refuge in the West," *Journal of Mormon History* 9 (1982): 34–58.

Treatments of the trip across Iowa and temporary locations in Iowa and Nebraska include Richard E. Bennett, "Mormons at the Missouri" (Ph.D. diss., Wayne State University, 1984); William J. Petersen, "The Mormon Trail of 1846," *The Palimpsest* 37 (November 1956): 513–27; and E. Widtsoe Shumway, "History of Winter Quarters, Nebraska, 1846–1848" (Master's thesis, Brigham Young University, 1953); and several articles in *BYU Studies* 21 (Fall 1981). They are: Stanley B. Kimball, "The Mormon Trail Network in Iowa 1838–1863: A New Look," pp. 417–30; Susan W. Easton, "Suffering and Death on the Plains of Iowa," pp. 431–39; Leland H. Gentry, "The Mormon Way Stations: Garden Grove and Mt. Pisgah," pp. 445–61; Reed C. Durham, Jr., "The Iowa Experience: A Blessing in Disguise," pp. 463–74; John F. Yurtinus, " 'Here Is One Man Who Will Not Go, Dam'um': Recruiting the Mormon Battalion in Iowa Territory," pp. 475–87; Lawrence Coates, "Refugees Meet: The Mormons and Indians in Iowa," pp. 491–514.

[1] BY, in a talk to the Saints of Nauvoo, 8 August 1844, HC 7:233.
[2] Woodruff Diary, 7 August 1844.
[3] HC 7:229; Andrew Jenson, "Succession in the Church," *The Historical Record*, 4 vols. (Salt Lake City, 1884–92), 7:789.
[4] HC 7:230.
[5] Jenson, *Historical Record*, 7:789.

[6] BYHD, 8 August 1844.

[7] There is some confusion in Latter-day Saint literature about the timing of the "mantle of the Prophet" episode. Most published accounts have it occurring during the afternoon meeting, but my reading of Brigham Young's own diary, entry made on August 8, and the recollections of others who were there have persuaded me that it must have occurred when Brigham made his brief talk after Rigdon's speech in the morning.

[8] Benjamin F. Johnson, *My Life's Review* (Independence, Mo., 1928), pp. 103–4.

[9] "Life Story of Mosiah Lyman Hancock," BYU Special Collections, 1965, p. 23.

[10] George Q. Cannon, *The Juvenile Instructor* 22 (29 October 1870): 174–75.

[11] *Deseret News*, 15 March 1892.

[12] *Times and Seasons* 5 (15 October 1844): 675.

[13] JD 5:57–58.

[14] Brigham's talk is found in HC 7:231–36.

[15] HC 7:240; Woodruff Diary, 8 August 1844; Heber C. Kimball Diary, 8 August 1844; William Clayton Diary, 8 August 1844, HDC.

[16] HC 7:240–42.

[17] Staines Diary as quoted in HC 7:236n; "History of William Adams," p. 15, BYUL.

[18] BYD No. 2, 8 August 1844.

[19] BYHD, 1 September 1844. See also F. Mark McKiernan, *The Voice of One Crying in the Wilderness: Sidney Rigdon, Religious Reformer, 1793–1876* (Lawrence, Kansas, 1971).

[20] A colleague takes me to task for saying this. In the first place, we cannot be absolutely sure he didn't visit Emma. While there is a lack of evidence that he did, that is not conclusive. Second, this colleague thinks that the "fault" was mutual—that the basic controversy was over the continued practice of plural marriage, which Emma opposed. If Brigham didn't visit Emma, my friend contends, it was because he knew what was in store between them rather than because he was socially insensitive or otherwise preoccupied.

[21] Unpublished sermon of BY, 7 October 1866, BYP.

[22] The evidence that this was a viable alternative is given in D. Michael Quinn, "The Mormon Succession Crisis of 1844," *BYU Studies* 16 (Winter 1976): 187–233.

[23] The best treatment is Valeen Tippetts Avery and Linda King Newell, "The Lion and the Lady: Brigham Young and Emma Smith," *Utah Historical Quarterly* 48 (Winter 1980): 81–97. See also idem, *Mormon Enigma: Emma Hale Smith* (Garden City, N.Y., 1984).

[24] For an account of Brigham's death, see Susa Young Gates, with Leah D. Widtsoe, *The Life Story of Brigham Young* (New York, 1930), p. 362. Emma's death is described in Alexander Hale Smith, *Zion's Ensign*, a contemporary periodical of the Reorganized Church of Jesus Christ of Latter Day Saints, 31 December, 1903.

[25] The considerable literature on Strang includes Milo M. Quaife, *The Kingdom of St. James: A Narrative of the Mormons* (New Haven, Conn., 1930); Mark A. Strang, ed., *The Diary of James J. Strang* (Lansing, Mich., 1961); Robert P. Weeks, *King Strang* (Ann Arbor, Mich., 1971); Klaus J. Hansen, "The Making of King Strang: A Re-examination," *Michigan History* 46 (September 1962): 201–19; Robert P. Weeks, "A Utopian Kingdom in the American Grain," *Wisconsin Magazine of History* 61 (Autumn 1977): 3–30; and William D. Russell, "King James Strang: Joseph Smith's Successor?" in F. Mark McKiernan et al., *The Restoration Movement: Essays in Mormon History* (Lawrence, Kansas, 1973), pp. 231–56.

[26] HC 7:431.

[27] See Deut. 25:5; Matt. 22:24; Gen. 38:8.

[28] Susa Young Gates Papers, box 12, folder 2 USHS, Salt Lake City. Stanley P. Hirshson, in *The Lion of the Lord: A Biography of Brigham Young* (New York, 1969), suggests, on the basis of an 1870 article in the New York *World*, that Brigham tried to marry Emma Smith (p. 225). I have gone carefully through all the diaries, letters, comments, and other materials left by contemporaries of both Brigham and Emma and can find no evidence that he discussed marriage with her. Brigham was certainly realistic enough to appreciate the futility of such a proposal.

[29] Thomas Gregg, *History of Hancock County, Illinois* (Chicago, 1880), p. 372.

[30] Flanders, *Kingdom on the Mississippi*, p. 307; also Kimball, "The Nauvoo Charter."

[31] HC 7:399.

[32] Flanders, *Kingdom on the Mississippi*, p. 326.

[33] HC 7:397–98.

[34] Richard H. Jackson, "Myth and Reality: Environmental Perception of the Mormons, 1840–1865, an Historical Geosophy" (Ph.D. diss., Clark University, 1970), p. 99.

[35] *Nauvoo Neighbor*, 19 March 1845.

[36] Ibid., 13 August 1845.

[37] Ibid., 17 September 1845.

[38] HC 7:440.

[39] HC 7:443, 445.

[40] T. Edgar Lyon, "Nauvoo and the Council of Twelve," p. 199, and HC 7:447–53; *Nauvoo Neighbor*, 29 October 1845.

[41] Leonard J. Arrington, "Mississippi Saints," *The Ensign* 7 (June 1977): 46–51.

[42] HC 7:454.

[43] HC 7:465. Brigham's diary, entry for 13 September 1845, notes that he told Heber and Andrew Perkins that all those going on the expedition west "must expect to come upon the apostles doctrine: no man say ought that he has is his own but all things are the Lord's and we his stewards."

[44] HC 7:479.

[45] HC 7:479–80.

[46] This story is told by Brigham in JD 14:218–19.

[47] JH, 28 June 1846. See also John D. Lee Diary, 7 August 1846, HDC; and MHBY 2, 7 August 1846, pp. 298–99.

[48] JH, 9 August 1846; Jackson, "Myth and Reality," p. 97n.

[49] On the Mormon Battalion see B. H. Roberts, *A Comprehensive History of the Church of Jesus Christ of Latter-day Saints: Century I*, 6 vols. (Salt Lake City, 1930), 3:60–121; James B. Allen and Glen M. Leonard, *The Story of the Latter-day Saints* (Salt Lake City, 1976), pp. 225–33; John F. Yurtinus, "A Ram in the Thicket: A History of Mormon Battalion in the Mexican War" (Ph.D. diss., Brigham Young University, 1975); Ray Luce, "The Mormon Battalion: An Historical Accident," unpublished paper in possession of the writer.

[50] JH, 11 September 1846.

[51] Hiram M. Chittenden and Alfred T. Richardson, *Life, Letters and Travels of Father Pierre-Jean De Smet, S.J.* (New York, 1905), 4:1402–7.

[52] MHBY 2, 6 March 1847, p. 111.

CHAPTER 9:
THE PIONEER TREK TO THE GREAT BASIN

The finest scholarly account of the 1847 and 1848 crossings is in Stanley B. Kimball, *Heber C. Kimball: Mormon Patriarch and Pioneer* (Urbana, Illinois, 1981). Kimball has a superb treatment of the trail. Also of value in the preparation of this chapter were Leland H. Creer, *The Founding of an Empire: The Exploration and Colonization of Utah, 1776–1856* (Salt Lake City, 1947); Andrew Love Neff, *History of Utah, 1847 to 1869*, ed. Leland H. Creer (Salt Lake City, 1940); B. H. Roberts, *A Comprehensive History of the Church of Jesus Christ of Latter-day Saints: Century I*, 6 vols. (Salt Lake City, 1930), esp. vol. 3; Leonard J. Arrington, *Great Basin Kingdom: An Economic History of The Latter-day Saints, 1830–1900* (Cambridge, Mass., 1958), chapters 2–3; Preston Nibley, *Exodus to Greatness: The Story of the Mormon Migration* (Salt Lake City, 1947); Eugene E. Campbell, "The Mormon Migrations to Utah," in *Utah's History*, ed. Richard D. Poll (Provo, Utah, 1978), pp. 113–32; and Richard H. Jackson, "The Overland Journey to Zion," in *The Mormon Role in the Settlement of the West*, ed. Richard H. Jackson (Provo, Utah, 1978), pp. 1–28.

Primary sources include Thomas Bullock Minutes, HDC; Heber C. Kimball Journal; Andrew Jenson, "Pioneers of 1847," typescript, HDC; Moroni Snow, ed., "From Nauvoo to Salt Lake in the Van of the Pioneers: The Original Diary of Erastus Snow," published serially in *Improvement Era* 14 and 15 (1911–12); *William Clayton's Journal* (Salt Lake City, 1921); and the diaries of other participants.

[1] Brigham Young, remarks at a meeting held 8 March 1847 at Winter Quarters; recorded by Thomas Bullock. Typescript of minutes on file in HDC.
[2] James A. Little, "Biography of Lorenzo Dow Young," *Utah Historical Quarterly* 14 (1946): 79.
[3] BY, remarks at 8 March 1847 meeting.
[4] Little, "Biography of Lorenzo Dow Young," p. 80.
[5] BY, remarks made at general conference, Winter Quarters, 6 April 1847, minutes recorded by Thomas Bullock, HDC.
[6] Woodruff Diary, 13 April 1847.
[7] Thomas Bullock Pioneer Journal, 14 April 1847, typescript, HDC.
[8] Norton Jacob's Record, 16 April 1847, HDC.
[9] Woodruff Diary, 17 April 1847.
[10] Horace K. Whitney Journal, 18 April 1847, bound typescript, HDC.
[11] Bullock Journal, 18 April 1847.
[12] *William Clayton's Journal* (Salt Lake City, 1921), entry for 19 April 1847, p. 83.
[13] Ibid. A full description of the odometer and of its invention is given in Norman E. Wright, "The Pioneer Odometer," *The Ensign* 11 (August 1981): 30–31.
[14] Woodruff Diary, 18 April 1847.
[15] Heber C. Kimball Journal, 21 April 1847, holograph, HDC.
[16] BY to Mary Ann Angell, 20 April 1847, HDC.
[17] Erastus Snow Diary, 21 April 1847, in *Improvement Era* (July 1911): 818.
[18] Ibid.
[19] Woodruff Diary, 23 April 1847.
[20] Kimball Journal, 23 April 1847.
[21] Bullock Journal, 25 April 1847.
[22] Erastus Snow Diary, 25 April 1847, in *Improvement Era* 14 (July 1911): 819.
[23] Bullock Journal, 25 April 1847.
[24] Ibid. Under date of 26 April 1847 Norton Jacob carried the point still further: "Yesterday President Young . . . said he had scolded some for which he would now ask pardon of Col. Wright, for he was the only man that had a legal right to find fault and murmur; whoever, therefore, who had any grumbling to do must call on Col. Wright for permission, and he was then formally elected to the office of grumbler. This Col. Wright is no other than Henry G. Sherwood, one of the High Council who assumed the cognoman of Col. Wright last summer, when returning from the Camp of Israel to get his family for the purpose of traveling without being known by the mob. Well, this arrangement of making him chief grumbler for the camp had an excellent effect in putting a check upon some fractious persons, especially one . . . who had all the time been quarreling with his team or some one else, but after this he was tolerably decent." Cited in Andrew Jenson, "Pioneers of 1847," typescript, HDC.
[25] Bullock Journal, 26 April 1847.
[26] Clayton, *Journal*, entry for 26 April 1847, p. 111.
[27] Ibid., entry for 30 April 1847, p. 115.
[28] Luke Johnson Diary, 20 May 1847, holograph, HDC.
[29] Little, "Biography of Lorenzo Dow Young," p. 83.
[30] Clayton, *Journal*, entry for 1 May 1847, p. 124.
[31] George A. Smith Diary, 1 May 1847, HDC.

[32] Ibid., 2 May 1847.

[33] Woodruff Diary, 6 May 1847.

[34] Bullock Journal, 5 May 1847.

[35] BY to Mary Ann Angell, 20 April/4 May 1847, typescript of holograph, HDC.

[36] Appleton M. Harmon Journal, 7 May 1847, holograph, HDC.

[37] Whitney Journal, 7 May 1847.

[38] Bullock Journal, 7 May 1847. The Young-Snow incident is treated with some detail in Andrew Karl Larson, *Erastus Snow: The Life of a Missionary and Pioneer for the Early Mormon Church* (Salt Lake City, 1971), pp. 138–39.

[39] Woodruff Diary, 11 May 1847.

[40] Bullock Journal, 10 May 1847.

[41] Woodruff Diary, 29 May 1847.

[42] Kimball Journal, 29 May 1847.

[43] Ibid.

[44] Clayton, *Journal*, entry for 1 June 1847, p. 207.

[45] The gentleman's name is spelled variously: Bordeaux, Bourdreau, Boudeaux, Bedeau, Bondeau, Birdoe.

[46] Wilford Woodruff, "Pioneer Incidents," typescript, HDC.

[47] Orson Pratt Diary, 9 June 1847.

[48] Harmon Journal, 8 June 1847.

[49] Little, "Biography of Lorenzo Dow Young," pp. 89–90.

[50] Woodruff Diary, 17 June 1847.

[51] Bullock Journal, 16 June 1847.

[52] Woodruff Diary, 19 June 1847.

[53] Kimball Journal, 19 June 1847.

[54] Clayton, *Journal*, entry for 20 June 1847, pp. 246–47.

[55] Whitney Journal, 21 June 1847.

[56] Ibid., 23 June 1847.

[57] Little, "Biography of Lorenzo Dow Young," p. 91.

[58] Woodruff Diary, 29 June 1847. See also Richard H. Jackson, "The Overland Journey to Zion," in *The Mormon Role in the Settlement of the West*, ed. Richard H. Jackson (Provo, Utah, 1978), pp. 1–27; and idem, "Utah's Harsh Lands, Hearth of Greatness," *Utah Historical Quarterly* 49 (Winter 1981): 4–25, esp. p. 11.

[59] Howard Egan Journal, 28 June 1847, HDC.

[60] Woodruff Diary, 28 June 1847.

[61] MHBY, 30 June 1847, p. 561.

[62] Egan Journal, 30 June 1847.

[63] Orson Pratt Diary, 5 July 1847.

[64] Jacob Journal, 4 July 1847.

[65] MHBY, 4 July 1847, p. 561.

[66] Clayton, *Journal*, entry for 6 July 1847, p. 285.

[67] Ibid., 10 July 1847, p. 289.

[68] Bullock Journal, 10 July 1847.

[69] Whitney Journal, 11 July 1847.

[70] Lester E. Bush, Jr., "Brigham Young in Life and Death: A Medical Overview," *Journal of Mormon History* 5 (1978): 85–86. See also MHBY, pp. 562–64; Preston Nibley, *Brigham Young, the Man and His Work* (Salt Lake City, 1937), pp. 97–99, 102; Clayton, *Journal*, 12–14 July 1847, pp. 291–94; Andrew Jenson, "The Pioneers of 1847," *The Historical Record* 9 (April 1890): 79; and recollections of Susan Noble Grant in Gene A. Sessions, *Mormon Thunder: A Documentary History of Jedediah Morgan Grant* (Urbana, Illinois, 1982), p. 65.

[71] Whitney Journal, 15 July 1847.

[72] Pratt, 16 July 1847.

73 Whitney Journal, 19 July 1847.

74 Pratt, Diary, 20 July 1847.

75 Ibid., 21 July 1847.

76 Cited in Jenson, from holograph on file in HDC.

77 Bullock Journal, 22 July 1847.

78 Ibid.

79 Ibid.

80 Ibid., 23 July 1847.

81 MHBY, p. 564. Also JH, 24 July 1847. Note: Brigham's "This is the place" statement has been ascribed to a number of different places and circumstances, though it is likely that if he actually spoke these famous words, he did so on this occasion. The following account is related by Gilbert Belnap, whose wife was the sister-in-law of Andrew S. Gibbons, a member of the pioneer camp (from "An Autobiography of Gilbert Belnap," typescript, HDC):

> She [Belnap's wife] stated that Brigham Young had been ill from mountain fever and was lying in a bed prepared for him in a covered wagon. In a vision, he had seen the Great Salt Lake Valley and as the party entered the valley, he asked to be lifted up and looking out over the valley, he exclaimed, "This is the Place." He was assisted out of the wagon by members of the party and placing his cane on the ground he said three times, "This is the place; this is the place; this is the place." She was very emphatic in her statement (meaning my wife), saying that her brother-in-law had told her all about it, himself.

82 Little, "Biography of Lorenzo Dow Young," p. 98.

83 Lorenzo Young Diary, 24 July 1847.

84 MHBY, p. 564.

85 Woodruff Diary, 25 July 1847.

86 Ibid., 28 July 1847.

87 Bullock Journal, 23 August 1847; Clara Decker, "A Woman's Experience with the Pioneer Band," p. 8, Ms., Bancroft Library, Berkeley, Calif.

88 Whitney Journal, 3 August 1847.

89 Bullock Journal, 27 July 1847.

90 Thomas Bullock, Minutes of Sacrament Meeting, 8 August 1847.

91 Bullock Journal, 22 August 1847.

92 Whitney Journal, 31 July 1847.

93 Bullock Journal, 17 September 1847.

94 Ibid., 7 September 1847.

95 BY to Clara Decker Young, 8, 9 September 1847, HDC.

96 JH, 9 September 1847.

97 Clayton, Journal, entry for 14 September 1847, p. 362.

98 Bullock Journal, 24 September 1847.

99 Ibid.

100 Bullock Journal, 29–30 September 1847.

101 Ibid., 8 October 1847.

102 Ibid., 13 October 1847.

103 Whitney Journal, 8 October 1847.

104 Ibid., 4 October 1847.

105 Ibid.

106 Bullock Journal, 16 October 1847.

107 Whitney Journal, 18 October 1847.

108 Ibid., 25 October 1847.

109 Ibid., 29 October 1847.

110 Ibid., 30 October 1847.

[111] BY, 30 October 1847, HC 7:616.
[112] Ibid., 31 October 1847, HC 7:616–17.

CHAPTER IO:
TO ZION, 1848

See the references mentioned for chapter 9.

[1] *Millennial Star* 10 (15 March 1848): 81–88.
[2] The minutes of these November–December 1847 meetings are in BYP.
[3] Contemporary records contain no hint that the failure to organize a Presidency in 1844 was due to any lack of unity within the quorum, or to any fear that a Presidency would be less effective with the people than the familiar Twelve.
[4] See Minutes for 5 December 1847 and 12 February 1849, HDC.
[5] Brigham did not agree with Orson Pratt that organizing the Presidency would divide the Twelve. The Twelve would not lose their standing: "If one man is taken as President and his two councillors, I understand the Twelve stands as now. . . . When all Twelve sit together they [would] sit as now." Minutes for 5 December 1847.
[6] The case prompting the discussion was the September chastisement of Parley P. Pratt and John Taylor before the pioneer camp for having reorganized their companies with complete disregard for the detailed preparations already completed by Brigham and the rest of the Twelve. Orson Pratt, who raised the question, readily admitted that "uprooting the councils of this Church" was wrong and required action, but he wanted it handled in private. Brigham agreed that many things should be handled privately, but "when things are done wrong publicly in the Kingdom of God, I have a right to deal with them publicly. I was right when I spoke of Parley and Taylor."
[7] Minutes for 16 November 1847. "It is the right of one man to chastize this Church," Brigham maintained. "Any man who wants to stand where I am must be a Lion." Later he said that perhaps the reason the Lord had called him to his position was that he was not afraid to speak his mind. He viewed it his calling not to coddle but to prod the Saints, not to praise them but to warn, instruct, move them to greater effort. As he once wrote to a local leader: "You may think this very severe chastisement, and it is, but receive it kindly and it will do you good."
[8] Ibid. Brigham presented a motion that "this Counsel shall dictate what I shall say and do," and Heber immediately countered with a motion "that you be dictated to by the Holy Ghost and speak as you are led to."
[9] Ibid.
[10] Ibid.
[11] Ibid. Brigham recognized that his tendency to use vigorous and graphic language was not always appropriate. Although normally he used his hyperbole and color for calculated effect, he admitted he occasionally spoke what he should not have. "I have but one unruly member of my body," he confessed on one occasion, "my tongue."
[12] Minutes, 27 December 1847; BY to Orson Spencer, 23 January 1848; and Woodruff Diary, 27 December 1847.
[13] See Norton Jacob's Record, HDC, and BY to Orson Spencer, 23 January 1848.
[14] *Millennial Star* 10 (15 March 1848): 81–88.
[15] Ibid.
[16] Robert Glass Cleland and Juanita Brooks, eds., *A Mormon Chronicle: The Diaries of John D. Lee, 1848–1876*, 2 vols. (San Marino, Calif., 1955), 1:28 (entry for 16 May 1848).
[17] Thomas Bullock Journal, May 1848–September 1848, entry for 24 May, typescript, HDC.
[18] Ibid., 16 June 1848. According to B. H. Roberts, *A Comprehensive History of the Church of Jesus Christ of Latter-day Saints: Century I*, 6 vols. (Salt Lake City, 1930), 3:319, the camp was composed of two major divisions, one headed by Brigham and the other by Heber Kimball, with

Young presiding over the entire body. The totals of both divisions were 623 wagons, 1,891 souls, 131 horses, 44 mules, 2,012 oxen, 983 cows, 334 loose cattle, 654 sheep, 237 pigs, 904 chickens, 54 cats, 134 dogs, 3 goats, 10 geese, 5 beehives, 11 doves, 1 squirrel, and 5 ducks. Roberts neglected to itemize the crow.

19 BYMH, 1848, p. 35. Also Cleland and Brooks, *Mormon Chronicle*, p. 30 (entry for 26 May 1848).

20 Bullock Journal, 31 May 1848.

21 Based on "A History of Ralph Frost, Great Grandson of Elisha and Lucy Groves," holograph, Brigham Young University Women's History Archives.

22 *Young Woman's Journal* 6 (July 1895): 467.

23 Bullock Journal, 6 June 1848.

24 Cleland and Brooks, *Mormon Chronicle*, p. 39 (entry for 15 June 1848).

25 Ibid. (entry for 16 June 1848).

26 Oliver Boardman Huntington, Diary, p. 28, typescript, USHS.

27 Louisa Barnes Pratt Journal, p. 146, holograph, HDC.

28 Cleland and Brooks, *Mormon Chronicle*, pp. 41–42 (entry for 18 June 1848). I have placed Brigham's remarks, as recorded by John D. Lee, in present tense and have corrected Lee's spelling.

29 Juanita Brooks, ed., *On the Mormon Frontier: The Diary of Hosea Stout* (Salt Lake City, 1964), 1:316 (entries for 19, 22 June 1848).

30 Ibid., p. 317 (entries for 30 June–1 July 1848); Bullock Journal, 29 June 1848.

31 Louisa Pratt Journal, p. 147.

32 Brooks, *Mormon Frontier*, 1:317 (entry for 4 July 1848).

33 Bullock Journal, 4 July 1848.

34 Ibid., 8 July 1848.

35 Huntington Diary, p. 31.

36 Bullock Journal, 10, 12 July 1848; Huntington Diary, p. 32; Brooks, *Mormon Frontier*, 1:318 (entry for 12 July 1848).

37 Bullock Journal, 16, 17 July 1848.

38 Cleland and Brooks, *Mormon Chronicle*, p. 57 (entry for 14 July 1848).

39 JD 2:283; Cleland and Brooks, *Mormon Chronicle*, p. 63 (entry for 20 July 1848).

40 Kate B. Carter, ed., *Heart Throbs of the West*, 12 vols. (Salt Lake City, 1950), 11:162.

41 Brooks, *Mormon Frontier*, 1:319 (entry for 20 July 1848); Bullock Journal, 22 July 1848.

42 Huntington Diary, p. 35.

43 Cleland and Brooks, *Mormon Chronicle*, p. 65 (entry for 23 July 1848).

44 Bullock Journal, 30 July 1848.

45 Ibid., 2 August 1848.

46 Ibid., 4, 5, 16 August 1848.

47 Ibid., 5, 10, 11 August 1848; Brooks, *Mormon Frontier*, 1:322 (entries for 8–12 August 1848).

48 Huntington Diary, p. 38.

49 Brooks, *Mormon Frontier*, 1:323 (entry for 17 August 1848); Bullock Journal, 28, 30 August 1848.

50 Huntington Diary, p. 38.

51 Cleland and Brooks, *Mormon Chronicle*, p. 75 (entry for 1 September 1848); Bullock Journal, 1–2 September 1848.

52 Bullock Journal, 3 September 1848.

53 Ibid., 13 September 1848; Brooks, *Mormon Frontier*, 1:325 (entry for 14 September 1848).

54 John Pulsipher, "A Short Sketch of the History of John Pulsipher," p. 28, typescript, HDC. Also Brooks, *Mormon Frontier*, 1:326 (entry for 18 September 1848).

55 Pulsipher, "History," p. 29; Bullock Journal, 18–20 September 1848; Brooks, *Mormon Frontier*, 1:326 (entry for 21 September 1848).

56 Mary Isabella Horne, "Home Life in the Pioneer Fort," in *Our Pioneer Heritage*, comp. Kate B. Carter, 20 vols. (Salt Lake City, 1958–77), 9:111.

[57] Brooks, *Mormon Frontier*, 1:327 (entry for 24 September 1848).
[58] Bullock Journal, no date.
[59] Brooks, *Mormon Frontier*, 1:327 (entry for 24 September 1848).

CHAPTER 11:
THE COLONIZER PRESIDENT

The physical setting and the early years in the Salt Lake Valley are discussed in Milton R. Hunter, *Brigham Young the Colonizer* (Independence, Mo., 1945); John S. McCormick, *Salt Lake City, the Gathering Place* (Salt Lake City and Woodland Hills, Calif., 1980); Preston Nibley, *Brigham Young, the Man and His Work* (Salt Lake City, 1936); Leland H. Creer, *The Founding of an Empire: The Exploration and Colonization of Utah, 1776–1856* (Salt Lake City, 1947); Richard H. Jackson, "Myth and Reality: Environmental Perception of the Mormons, 1840–1865, an Historical Geosophy" (Ph.D. diss., Clark University, 1970), esp. pp. 213–41; Andrew Love Neff, *History of Utah, 1847 to 1869*, ed. Leland H. Creer (Salt Lake City, 1940): Joel E. Ricks, *Forms and Methods of Early Mormon Settlement . . .* (Logan, Utah, 1964); and Leonard J. Arrington, "Colonizing the Great Basin," *The Ensign* 10 (February 1980): 18–22.

Brigham's family life is discussed in Clarissa Young Spencer and Mabel Harmer, *Brigham Young at Home* (Salt Lake City, 1947); and Susa Young Gates, with Leah D. Widtsoe, *The Life Story of Brigham Young* (New York, 1930).

On tithing, see D. Gene Pace, "The LDS Presiding Bishopric, 1851–1888: An Administrative Study" (Master's thesis, Brigham Young University, 1978); Leonard Arrington, "The Mormon Tithing House: A Frontier Business Institution," *Business History Review* 28 (March 1954): 24–58; and idem, "The Six Pillars of Utah's Pioneer Economy," *Encyclia: Journal of the Utah Academy of Sciences, Arts, and Letters* 54 (1977 Part 1): 9–24.

[1] JD 4:32.
[2] This description is similar to the one I have used in *Great Basin Kingdom: An Economic History of the Latter-day Saints, 1830–1900* (Cambridge, Mass., 1958, 1967), pp. 43–44.
[3] Sermon quoted in James S. Brown, *Life of a Pioneer* (Salt Lake City, 1900), pp. 121–22.
[4] The 1980 population of the Salt Lake Valley approached five hundred thousand, of whom more than 70 percent were Mormons. The Salt Lake Oasis includes nearby valleys.
[5] Feramorz Young Fox, "The Mormon Land System: A Study of the Settlement and Utilization of Land under the Direction of the Mormon Church" (Ph.D. diss., Northwestern University, 1932), p. 41.
[6] *William Clayton's Journal* (Salt Lake City, 1921), p. 326, entry for 28 July 1847; Wilford Woodruff Diary, 25 July 1847; "Norton Jacob's Record," 25 July 1847; JH, 9 September 1847. I have changed two verbs to present tense.
[7] Remarks of 28 July 1847, as reported in "Norton Jacob's Record," p. 74.
[8] See Clarissa Young Spencer and Mabel Harmer, *Brigham Young at Home* (Salt Lake City, 1947); Susa Young Gates, with Leah D. Widtsoe, *The Life Story of Brigham Young* (New York, 1930); Catherine V. Waite, *The Mormon Prophet and His Harem . . .* (Cambridge, Mass., 1866); and Cornelia Ferris, *The Mormons at Home* (New York, 1856).
[9] The list is in BYP. Also Salt Lake County Clerk's Office.
[10] [Emmeline B. Wells], "A Distinguished Woman: Zina D. H. Young," *The Woman's Exponent* 10 (15 November; 10, 15 December 1881; 1 January 1882): 91, 99, 107, 115; David Henry Jacobs, "Some Insights on the Life of Zina Diantha Huntington Jacobs, Smith, Young," typescript, 1977, 33 pp.
[11] "Norton Jacob's Record," p. 25.

[12] Zina D. H. Young to Emmeline Free Young [in Fillmore, Utah], January 1856, HDC.

[13] Susa Gates Papers, USHS.

[14] Joel E. Ricks, ed., *The History of a Valley: Cache Valley, Utah–Idaho* (Logan, Utah, 1956), p. 30.

[15] JD 4:325, talk given 31 May 1857.

[16] JD 4:325–26.

[17] Richard H. Jackson, "Myth and Reality: Environmental Perception of the Mormons, 1840–1865, an Historical Geosophy" (Ph.D. diss., Clark University, 1970), p. 222.

[18] Ibid., pp. 215–16.

[19] JD 10:25–26.

[20] BY to Parley P. Pratt, 29 January 1855, Letterbook 1:843–45.

[21] JH, 5 January 1852.

[22] BY to Rufus C. Allen, 29 August 1855, Letterbook 2:317–18. See also BY to Silas Smith, 31 January 1856, Letterbook 2:555–57.

[23] BY to Brigham Young, Jr., 18 October 1865, Letterbook 7:776–84.

[24] BY to Orson Pratt, 29 May 1857, Letterbook C:579–82.

[25] See Ricks, ed., *History of a Valley*, pp. 32–86.

[26] BY to John D. Lee, 22 November 1851, Letterbook 1:2.

[27] BY to Bro. John Rees and the other Brethren whose names are on the list, 6 September 1858, Letterbook 4:362.

[28] BY to Joseph Horn, 23 January 1858, Letterbook 4:33–35.

[29] BY to John Rees et al., 6 September 1858, Letterbook 4:362.

[30] BY to Geo. M. Wilkin, 30 August 1865, Letterbook 7:724.

[31] BY to Bp. Thos. Callister, 31 October 1867, Letterbook 10:455.

[32] BY to Bp. Hancock, 2 January 1857, Letterbook C:605.

[33] BY to the Bishops and Brethren in Utah County, 25 August 1861, Letterbook 5:875–76.

[34] BY to Orson Hyde, 29 August 1861, Letterbook 5:877–78.

[35] BY to Edwin Bryant, Edmund Marchant, Thomas Gibbons, and eighteen others, 18 August 1866, Letterbook 9:130–31.

[36] Report of Daniel MackIntosh, clerk, in Brigham Young Financial Papers, Miscellaneous Papers, President's Office.

[37] JD 1:52.

[38] JD 2:306–7.

[39] JD 8:317.

[40] JD 8:201–2.

[41] JD 1:341; 10:210, 270.

[42] JH, 4 March 1860.

[43] "Eleventh General Epistle of the Presidency," 10 April 1854, *Deseret News*, 13 April 1854.

[44] JD 4:32.

[45] JH, 8 July 1849.

[46] JH, 8 April 1850.

[47] JH, 26 May 1850.

[48] See Eugene E. Campbell, "The Mormon Gold-Mining Mission of 1849," *BYU Studies* 1–2 (Autumn 1959–Winter 1960): 19–31.

[49] Arrington, *Great Basin Kingdom*, chapter 3.

[50] Ibid., pp. 116–29.

[51] Governor's Message, 2 December 1850, *Utah Historical Quarterly* 8 (1940): 193.

[52] JH, 10 April 1853.

[53] BYMH, 1855, p. 70.

[54] *Deseret News*, 10 December 1856.

[55] B. H. Roberts, *A Comprehensive History of the Church of Jesus Christ of Latter-day Saints:*

Century I, 6 vols. (Salt Lake City, 1930), 3:399–491; Philip De La Mare, "History of the Deseret Manufacturing Company," ms., HDC; Fred G. Taylor, *A Saga of Sugar* (Salt Lake City, 1944), p. 50.

[56] JH, 14 October 1849.

[57] JH, 24 February 1851.

[58] Malicent C. Wells, "History of John Murray Murdoch," typescript in possession of Mrs. Cleone Baird Arrington, Twin Falls, Idaho.

[59] According to the record book of the company, Southern Utah State College Library, Cedar City, Utah.

[60] "Sixth General Epistle . . . ," 22 September 1851, *Millennial Star* 14 (1852): 20. Also JH, 30 June 1851, 24 February 1852.

[61] A report on their activities is found under the title "Manufacture of Iron in Utah," *Millennial Star* 17 (1855): 2.

[62] "Minute Book of the Deseret Iron Company," ms., in Southern Utah State College Library, Cedar City, Utah. Extracts from the minutes are found in John G. Crook, "The Development of Early Industry and Trade in Utah" (Master's thesis, University of Utah, 1926), pp. 39ff.

[63] Copies of the acts approved 27 December 1852, and 5, 17 January 1853, are in *Deseret News*, 22 January 1853, and *Acts, Resolutions and Memorials* (Salt Lake City, 1855), pp. 235–37.

[64] *Millennial Star* 17 (1855): 3.

[65] Journal of Isaac C. Haight, Part 2, typescript, Library of Congress (Utah, W.P.A. Collection), p. 13. Under date of 8 October 1853, Haight wrote: "I had much rather have stayed here [Salt Lake City], but am willing to obey the counsel of my Brethren."

[66] Matthias F. Cowley, ed., *Wilford Woodruff, . . . : History of His Life and Labors as Recorded in His Daily Journals* (Salt Lake City, 1909), p. 346.

[67] The shares of Utah Territory were purchased by a transferral to the Perpetual Emigrating Fund Company in Salt Lake, which, in turn, issued a warrant in favor of the iron company. The church paid for its two shares by transferring to the iron company accounts from the local tithing offices, as follows: from the Cedar City Tithing Office, $2,897.20; from Harmony Tithing Office, $105.57; from Parowan Tithing Office, $1,837.25. The company then drew a general assortment of goods from these offices. "Records of the Deseret Iron Company," Crook, pp. 49, 58.

[68] *Millennial Star* 18 (1856): 14, 251.

[69] Journal of Isaac C. Haight, p. 21 (entry for September 1857).

[70] Ibid., p. 25.

[71] Heber C. Kimball to William H. Kimball, 29 February 1856, *Millennial Star* 18 (1856): 397; Andrew Jenson, ed., "History of Las Vegas Mission," *Nevada State Historical Papers* 5 (Reno, Nev., 1926): 270.

[72] Jenson, "History of Las Vegas Mission," p. 271. In anticipation of immediate results from the mission, the church public works cast five lead molds; see JH, 3 July 1856. Soon afterward, several teams were requested to go to Vegas to pick up lead and lead ore.

[73] JD 2:282.

[74] Sermon of 16 March 1862, *Deseret News*, 28 May 1862. Wells's sermon is in *Deseret News*, 4 June 1862. Similar remarks were made by Brigham on 7 April 1861, recorded in *Deseret News*, 22 May 1861.

CHAPTER 12:
PRESIDENT OF THE CHURCH

The history of the Mormon church in the Salt Lake Valley is best covered in James B. Allen and Glen M. Leonard, *The Story of the Latter-day Saints* (Salt Lake City, 1976). The relationship of Brigham to his adviser-friends is told in some detail in Leonard J. Arrington and Ronald K. Esplin, "The Role of the Quorum of the Twelve during Brigham Young's Presidency of the Church . . . ," *Task Papers in LDS History*, no. 31 (Salt Lake City, 1979). Brigham's sermons are published in JD and *Deseret News*; unpublished sermons are in HDC. Studies of Brigham Young as a speaker include Chester J. Myers, "A Critical Analysis and Appraisal of the Work of Brigham Young as a Public Speaker" (Ph.D. diss., University of Southern California, 1940).

Brigham Young's theology is discussed in Davis Bitton, "The Sovereignty of God in John Calvin and Brigham Young," *Sunstone* 5 (September–October, 1980): 26–30; Carl J. Furr, "The Religious Philosophy of Brigham Young" (Ph.D. diss., University of Chicago, 1937); Gary James Bergera, "The Orson Pratt–Brigham Young Controversies: Conflict within the Quorums, 1853 to 1868," *Dialogue* 13 (Summer 1980): 7–58; Robert Miller, "Understanding Brigham Young: The Role of His Cosmology," unpublished paper, 1981; and Davis Bitton, "Brigham Young as Homo Religiosus," unpublished paper, 1981.

[1] JD 8:124–25.

[2] Stanley B. Kimball, *Heber C. Kimball: Mormon Patriarch and Pioneer* (Urbana, Illinois, 1981).

[3] Claire Noall, *Intimate Disciple* (Salt Lake City, 1957), somewhat fictionalized.

[4] Gene A. Sessions, *Mormon Thunder: A Documentary History of Jedediah Morgan Grant* (Urbana, Illinois, 1982).

[5] Bryant S. Hinckley, *Daniel Hanmer Wells and Events of His Time* (Salt Lake City, 1942).

[6] C. Kent Dunford, "The Contributions of George A. Smith to the Establishment of the Mormon Society in the Territory of Utah" (Ph.D. diss., Brigham Young University, 1970).

[7] William E. Hunter, *Edward Hunter: Faithful Steward*, ed. Janath R. Cannon (Salt Lake City, 1970).

[8] Joseph Young, *History of the Organization of the Seventies* (Salt Lake City, 1878); Andrew Jenson, *Latter-day Saint Biographical Encyclopedia*, 4 vols. (Salt Lake City, 1901–36), 1:187–88.

[9] Eliza R. Snow, "A Sketch of My Life, 1885," ms., Bancroft Library, Berkeley, California; Maureen U. Beecher, "The Eliza Enigma," *Dialogue* 11 (Spring 1978): 30–43.

[10] Albert L. Zobell, Jr., *Sentinel in the East: A Biography of Thomas L. Kane* (Salt Lake City, 1965); Leonard J. Arrington, " 'In Honorable Remembrance': Thomas L. Kane's Services to the Mormons," *BYU Studies* 21 (Fall 1981): 389–402.

[11] Gwynn W. Barrett, "John M. Bernhisel: Mormon Elder in Congress" (Ph.D. diss., Brigham Young University, 1968); Stanford O. Cazier, "The Life of William Henry Hooper: Merchant Statesman" (Master's thesis, University of Utah, 1956).

[12] Leonard J. Arrington and Ronald K. Esplin, "The Role of the Quorum of the Twelve during Brigham Young's Presidency of the Church . . . ," *Task Papers in LDS History*, no. 31 (Salt Lake City, 1979).

[13] Hugh Nibley, "Educating the Saints: A Brigham Young Mosaic," *BYU Studies* 11 (Autumn 1970): 61–87; Leonard J. Arrington, "The Latter-day Saints and Public Education," *Southwestern Journal of Social Education* 7 (Spring–Summer 1977): 9–25.

[14] William J. McNiff, *Heaven on Earth: A Planned Mormon Society* (Oxford, Ohio, 1940); Joseph Heinerman, "Early Utah Pioneer Cultural Societies," *Utah Historical Quarterly* 47 (Winter 1979): 70–89.

[15] Diary of Levi Savage, HDC; Levi Peterson, "A Mormon and Wilderness: The Saga of the Savages," *Sunstone* 4 (December 1979): 69–72.

[16] Juanita Brooks, ed., *On the Mormon Frontier: The Diary of Hosea Stout* (Salt Lake City, 1964) 2:456–98, entries for 20 October 1852 to 8 December 1853.

[17] Woodruff Diary, 24 October 1851.

[18] JD 13:175. Also JD 14:113; 13:214; 13:175; 14:135, 280; 2 Peter 2:16.

[19] Unpublished sermons, 8 October 1854. These are stenographic notes, of which I have made a "free-flowing" transcription.

[20] This story was told me on 21 August 1947 by the aged but alert William R. Wallace, son of Utah pioneers and noted Utah irrigation engineer, who said that as a boy he was a personal witness to the episode.

[21] BY to L. B. Hutching, 15 October 1859, Letterbook, 5:276–77.

22 BY to B. H. Watts, 11 June 1867, Letterbook 10:216.

23 BY to Benj. F. Johnson, 20 March 1865, Letterbook 7:517.

24 BYOJ 1857–60, 18 August 1858, p. 45, HDC.

25 BY to Elizabeth Green, clerk's draft penned on letter of Elizabeth Green to BY, 28 December 1851, BY Secretary's Drafts, HDC.

26 BY to [name deleted because confidential communication], 19 April 1858, Letterbook 4:134.

27 BY to [name deleted because confidential communication], 20 March 1865, Letterbook 7:517.

28 JD 3:324.

29 Leonard J. Arrington, *From Quaker to Latter-day Saint: Bishop Edwin D. Woolley* (Salt Lake City, 1976), p. 391.

30 Ibid., p. 449.

31 Leonard J. Arrington and Davis Bitton, *Saints without Halos: The Human Side of Mormon History* (Salt Lake City, 1976), p. 61.

32 JH, 28 July 1847.

33 For a discussion of Brigham's dependence on Joseph Smith's thought, see Ronald K. Esplin, "Brigham Young and Priesthood Denial to the Blacks: An Alternate View," *BYU Studies* 19 (Spring 1979): 394–402.

34 BY to Daniel H. Wells and Brigham Young, Jr., 19 October 1864, Letterbook 7:298–305.

35 Sterling M. McMurrin, *The Theological Foundations of the Mormon Religion* (Salt Lake City, 1965); Lowell L. Bennion, *The Religion of the Latter-day Saints* (Salt Lake City, 1940).

36 See Sterling M. McMurrin, *The Philosophical Foundations of Mormon Theology* (Salt Lake City, 1959), pp. 23–24.

37 Brigham Young, like most conservative Christians of his era, accepted the historicity of Adam and Eve. Essentially, the Mormon position has continued to be characterized by a persistent literalness. However, the notion of pre-Adamites was circulating among some Mormons in Young's lifetime, and many educated modern Mormons have subscribed to some form of Christian evolutionism.

38 See also Heber C. Kimball Diary, 28 December 1845; BY unpublished sermon, 8 October 1854.

39 The Adam-God doctrine, it should be emphasized, is not Mormon doctrine, and Brigham cautioned his followers not to delve too deeply into the "mysteries." See Van Hale, "What About the Adam-God Theory?" *Mormon Miscellaneous Response Series* (Salt Lake City, 1982); Culley K. Christensen, *The Adam-God Maze* (Scottsdale, Arizona, 1981); David John Buerger, "The Adam-God Doctrine," *Dialogue* 15 (Spring 1982): 14–58; Gary James Bergera, "The Orson Pratt–Brigham Young Controversies: Conflict within the Quorums, 1853 to 1868," *Dialogue* 13 (Summer 1980): 7–58; and Carl Broderick, Jr., "Another Look at Adam-God," *Dialogue* 16 (Summer 1983): 4–7.

40 James R. Clark, comp., *Messages of the First Presidency*, 6 vols. (Salt Lake City, 1865–75): 1:331.

41 What follows is based upon Bergera, "The Orson Pratt–Brigham Young Controversies"; and T. Edgar Lyon, "Orson Pratt, Early Mormon Leader" (Master's thesis, University of Chicago, 1932).

42 Pratt to BY, 4 November 1853, BYP.

43 "Minutes of a Meeting of the Presidency and Twelve . . . ," Woodruff Diary, 27 January 1860.

44 Ibid.

45 BYOJ, 31 January 1860.

46 BY Secretary's Journal, 1 October 1860.

47 Pratt to BY, 1 July 1868, BYP.

CHAPTER 1 3 :
INDIANS: FRIENDSHIP AND CAUTION

Some general discussions of Brigham's relationships with Indians can be found in Nels Anderson, *Desert Saints* (Chicago, 1942); Andrew Love Neff, *History of Utah, 1847 to 1869*, ed. Leland H. Creer (Salt Lake City, 1940), chapter 18; Leonard J. Arrington and Davis Bitton, *The Mormon Experience: A History of the Latter-day Saints* (New York, 1979), chapter 8; Leonard J. Arrington, "The Mormons and the Indians: A Review and Evaluation," *The Record*, Washington State University, 1970, pp. 5–30; and Gustive O. Larson, "Brigham Young and the Indians," *Seminar on Brigham Young, May 12, 1962* (Provo, Utah, 1963). An excellent and carefully detailed and documented study of the period of Brigham Young's superintendency is Dale L. Morgan, "The Administration of Indian Affairs in Utah, 1851–1858," *Pacific Historical Review* 17 (1948): 383–409. A more limited account is Floyd O'Neil and Stanford Layton, "Of Pride and Politics: Brigham Young as Indian Superintendent," *Utah Historical Quarterly* 46 (Summer 1978): 236–51.

BYMH contains day-by-day accounts of relations with Indians, Indian attacks, meetings, and peace efforts, military orders, letters and epistles, directions to Indian agents, reports on Indian missions, excerpts from speeches, etc. Additional speeches and comments by Brigham about Indians are in JD.

Brigham's outgoing correspondence is in his Letterbooks nos. 1, 2, C, and 4, the Miscellaneous Letterbook and the Governor's Office Letterbook. BYP contains incoming and outgoing correspondence with Indians, correspondence with commissioners of Indian affairs and other government officials, claims and losses in Indian uprisings, correspondence with Indian agents Armstrong, Bedell, Holeman, Hurt, and Ross, their vouchers and accounts, other miscellaneous papers concerning them, and various licenses, permits, vouchers, and accounts of the superintendent.

Territorial papers at the Utah State Archives containing material related to Young's Indian superintendency are the Utah Territorial Executive Papers for the period and two books of Executive Proceedings—Book A, 1850–54, and Book B, 1852–71. They include proclamations relating to Indian difficulties, Indian reports, affidavits, and military directions. A few such items are also included in United States State Department, Territorial Papers—Utah Series—in the National Archives (on microfilm at the USHS and elsewhere), reel 1, 30 April 1853 to 24 December 1859.

In the records of the United States Bureau of Indian Affairs in the National Archives are collections of letters received by the Office of Indian Affairs (OIA). Those concerned with Utah during the 1850s are in Record Group (RG) 75, microcopy 234, reels 897 and 898. They include letters from the superintendent and agents, from other government officials and departments, and from private individuals. A collection of government documents and correspondence concerning the Shoshoni Indians is in Dale Morgan, ed., "A Selection of Documents from the Records of the Utah Superintendency of Indian Affairs," *Annals of Wyoming* 25 and 26 (July 1953–July 1954).

Information on Brigham's relationships with Indians previous to his superintendency can be found in Howard Christy, "Open Hand and Mailed Fist: Mormon-Indian Relations in Utah, 1847–1852," *Utah Historical Quarterly* 46 (Spring 1978): 216–35; and Lawrence G. Coates, "Brigham Young and Mormon Indian Policies: The Formative Period, 1836–1851," *BYU Studies* 18 (Spring 1978): 428–52. Beverly P. Smaby, "The Mormons and the Indians: Conflicting Ecological Systems in the Great Basin," *American Studies* 16 (Spring 1975): 35–48, describes both the Mormon and the Indian values and culture and recounts the conflict over land and resources.

A detailed collection of Indian depredations in Utah is in Peter Gottfredson, ed., *History of Indian Depredations in Utah* (Salt Lake City, 1919). William J. Snow, "Utah Indians and Spanish Slave Trade," *Utah Historical Quarterly* 2 (July 1929): 68–90, gives an overview and many documents relating to this subject.

The activities of Chief Walker are described in Conway B. Sonne, *World of Wakara* (San Antonio, Texas, 1962); and Gustive O. Larson, "Walkara's Half Century," *Western Humanities*

Review 6 (Summer 1952): 235–59. The Walker War is treated in Howard A. Christy, "The Walker War: Defense and Conciliation as Strategy," *Utah Historical Quarterly* 47 (Fall 1979): 395–420.

Beverly Beeton, "Teach Them to Till the Soil: An Experiment with Indian Farms, 1850–1862," *American Indian Quarterly* 3 (Winter 1977–78): 299–319, is a good account of the farm projects under Brigham Young, Garland Hurt, and Jacob Forney. A collection of letters concerning Young's attempts to induce Washakie to take up farming is in Rhett S. James, ed., "Brigham Young—Chief Washakie Indian Farm Negotiations, 1854–1857," *Annals of Wyoming*, October 1967, pp. 245–56.

Lawrence G. Coates, "A History of Indian Education by the Mormons, 1830–1900" (Ed.D. diss., Ball State University, 1969), deals with Mormon attempts to help Indians in agriculture, literacy, and morality as well as the spiritual aims of the missionary program. Juanita Brooks, "Indian Relations on the Mormon Frontier," *Utah Historical Quarterly* 12 (January–April 1944): 1–48, describes the economic and social relations of Mormons and Indians, especially intermarriage, adoption, and other aspects of Indian acculturation to Mormon society. Eugene E. Campbell, "Brigham Young's Outer Cordon—A Reappraisal," *Utah Historical Quarterly* 41 (Summer 1973): 220–53, argues that the Mormon outpost settlements were basically Indian missionary projects rather than posts for colonizing or control of routes into the territory. Norman F. Furniss, *The Mormon Conflict, 1850–1859* (New Haven, Conn., 1960), includes much information on Mormon–Indian–American relations during the Utah War period as well as information about various Indian agents.

Recent articles on the pioneer Mormon program for giving tithing produce, livestock, and other supplies to Indian peoples include Leonard J. Arrington, "The Mormon Tithing House: A Frontier Business Institution," *Business History Review* 28 (March 1954): esp. 44–46; idem, "How the Saints Fed the Indians," *The Improvement Era* 57 (November 1954): 800ff.; and Richard L. Jensen, "Clothing the Indians and Strengthening the Saints," *Task Papers in LDS History*, no. 27 (Salt Lake City, 1979).

[1] BYMH, 1 January 1850.

[2] Lawrence G. Coates, "A History of Indian Education by the Mormons, 1830–1900" (Ed.D. diss., Ball State University, 1969), p. 436, and sources quoted by him; Susa Young Gates, with Leah D. Widtsoe, *The Life Story of Brigham Young* (New York, 1930), p. 136; *Memoirs of John R. Young* (Salt Lake City 1920), pp. 62–63.

[3] JD 2:143, 3 December 1854. The Book of Mormon published by the Mormons (Kirtland, Ohio, 1837) uses the phrase "pure and delightsome." Brigham probably used the term "white and delightsome" in this sense. See Book of Mormon, 2 Nephi 30:6.

[4] BY to George Manypenny, 31 March 1856, Governor's Office Letterbook, pp. 442–51.

[5] BY to Wm. Bringhurst, 31 July 1855, Letterbook 2:275–77.

[6] JD 1:105, 8 May 1853.

[7] BYMH, 16 January 1853, p. 6.

[8] BY to George W. Bradley, 13 June 1854, Letterbook 1:552–54.

[9] *William Clayton's Journal* (Salt Lake City, 1921), pp. 327–30, 335, cited in Lawrence G. Coates, "Brigham Young and Mormon Indian Policies: The Formative Period, 1836–1851," *BYU Studies* 18 (Spring 1978): 435. Howard Christy, "Open Hand and Mailed Fist: Mormon-Indian Relations in Utah, 1847–1852," *Utah Historical Quarterly* 46 (Spring 1978): 219, has this being said by Heber C. Kimball, speaking for BY, who was ill.

[10] BY to Luke Lea, 13 August 1851, BYP, reel 91, box 58, folder 6. Also BY to Bernhisel, 27 May 1856, Letterbook 2:772–76.

[11] Minutes of meeting at Walker's tent, Utah Valley, 22 May 1850, BYP, reel 92, box 58, folder 14.

[12] BY to Luke Lea, 29 September 1852, "Letters Received by the Office of Indian Affairs," National Archives, Record Group (RG) 75, microcopy 234.

[13] Statement of E. B. Ryan, 26 November 1853, BYP, reel 92, box 58, folder 14.

14 BY to Lorin Farr, 11 July 1851, Brigham Young Collection, microfilm reel 31, box 12, folder 15, cited in Howard Christy, "Open Hand and Mailed Fist," p. 231.

15 BY to Bernhisel, 20 November 1850, BYP.

16 JD 11:264, 28 July 1866 in Springville.

17 JD 1:105, 8 May 1853.

18 Ibid., p. 106.

19 Holeman to Luke Lea, 29 April 1853 and 21 May 1853, Office of Indian Affairs (OIA), RG 75.

20 BYMH, 21 July 1853, p. 112.

21 Daniel H. Wells to Major Nelson Higgins, 31 July 1853, Letterbook 1:150–52.

22 JD 1:168, 31 July 1853.

23 BYMH, 19 August 1853, p. 116; BY to Capt. H. Standage et al., 24 August 1853, Letterbook 1:182, 183, 184, 230, 231.

24 JD 1:168, 31 July 1853.

25 BY to Samuel W. Richards, 31 August 1853, Letterbook 1:212–14.

26 BY to Edward Martin, 30 November 1853, Letterbook 1:344–45; Andrew Love Neff, *History of Utah, 1847 to 1869*, ed. Leland H. Creer (Salt Lake City, 1940), p. 370.

27 Reports of G. W. Bean, 24 June 1854, BYP, reel 92, box 58, folder 14.

28 Minutes of meeting held 4 September 1852, Brigham Young Collection, 1848–54, HDC.

29 BY to Walker, 22 January 1855, Letterbook 3:197–98.

30 BYMH, 13 January 1853, p. 6.

31 Daniel H. Wells to Major David Moore, 1 September 1853, Letterbook 1:228–29.

32 Alex. Williams to BY, 22 September 1854, BYP, reel 91, box 58, folder 3.

33 BY to Alex. Williams, 23 September 1854, Letterbook 1:689–90. See also BY to P. W. Conover, 18 June 1854, Letterbook 1:555–56; BY to Geo. W. Bradley and the brethren at Nephi, 18 June 1854, Letterbook 1:557–58.

34 Minutes of meeting at Walker's tent, 22 May 1850, BYP, reel 92, box 58, folder 14.

35 BY to Luke Lea, 8 June 1852, BYP, reel 92, box 58, folder 6.

36 BY to Kane, 31 January 1854, Letterbook 1:407–13.

37 BY to Wm. D. Huntington & Company, 9 October 1854, Letterbook 1:706–8.

38 BY to Hurt, 23 November 1855, Governor's Office Letterbook, pp. 389–91.

39 BY to Rufus Allen, 2 March 1855, Letterbook 2:11–13.

40 Hurt to commissioner of Indian affairs, 2 May 1855, OIA, RG 75.

41 BY to Lorin Farr, 25 June 1855, Letterbook 2:234.

42 BY to Thomas S. Smith and brethren of the Bannock and Flathead Mission, 12 September 1855, Letterbook 2:364–65.

43 BY to William Bringhurst, 30 October 1855, Letterbook 2:244–47.

44 BY to Saml. Thompson, 4 February 1857, Letterbook C:363.

45 BY to Rose, 10 February 1854, Governor's Office Letterbook, pp. 53–54.

46 BY to the Presidents, Bishop, and brethren at Fillmore City, 13 March 1854, Letterbook 1:465–66.

47 Arapeen's name is also spelled Arapene, Arrapeen, Arrapene, and Arropeen.

48 BYMH, 10 September 1851, p. 67.

49 BY to Sow-i-et, White Eye, Pe-teet-neet, Arapeen, Tee-shar-rar-shee-geeg, 3 December 1853, Governor's Office Letterbook, pp. 30–31.

50 BY to Isaac C. Haight and brethren of the southern settlements in Iron County, 18 August 1854, Letterbook 1:631.

51 BY to Bishop John Browning, 5 August 1856, Governor's Office Letterbook, p. 520.

52 BY to Wm. D. Huntington & Company, 9 October 1854, Letterbook 1:706–8.

53 BYMH, 8 September 1856, p. 629.

54 BY to Hurt, 11 February 1857, Governor's Office Letterbook, pp. 588–89.

55 BY to Manypenny, 30 June 1855, Governor's Office Letterbook, pp. 281–89.

[56] BY to Arapeen, 13 January 1857, Letterbook C:279.

[57] BYMH, 12 May 1851, p. 46.

[58] BY, to Major David Moore, 27 November 1854, Letterbook 1:756–57.

[59] BY to Manypenny, 31 March 1855, Governor's Office Letterbook, pp. 230–39.

[60] JD 14:86–87, 9 April 1871.

CHAPTER 14:
GOVERNOR OF UTAH

Brief general discussions of the politics and main events of Brigham Young's governorship are in Edward W. Tullidge, *History of Salt Lake City and Its Founders* (Salt Lake City, c. 1886); H. H. Bancroft, *History of Utah, 1540–1886* (San Francisco, 1889); Nels Anderson, *Desert Saints: The Mormon Frontier in Utah* (Chicago, 1942); and Andrew Love Neff, *History of Utah, 1847 to 1869* (Salt Lake City, 1940). More detailed accounts that include the texts of several documents can be found in B. H. Roberts, *A Comprehensive History of the Church of Jesus Christ of Latter-day Saints: Century I*, 6 vols. (Salt Lake City, 1930), vols. 3 and 4; and Orson F. Whitney, *History of Utah*, 4 vols. (Salt Lake City, 1892–1904), vol. 1.

BYMH provides a day-to-day account of many of Brigham's activities as governor as well as president of the church. It includes reports of meetings—both public and private—and of Brigham's statements. It also quotes from letters or includes them in full. Many speeches and sermons of Brigham are included in volumes of JD. His outgoing correspondence for the period is contained mostly in Letterbooks 1, 2, C, and 4; the Governor's Office Letterbook; and the Miscellaneous Letterbook, volume 2 (1851–62).

Territorial papers pertaining to Brigham's governorship are at USA. The boxes of Utah Territorial Executive Papers contain correspondence, petitions, reports, and so forth as well as election papers. Two books of Executive Proceedings—Book A, 1850–54, and Book B, 1852–71—deal with the time period of Brigham's term as governor and include some of the same material as the collection of Executive Papers plus other correspondence, pardons, oaths, commissions, proclamations, messages, etc. Additional territorial papers are collected in United States State Department, Territorial Papers—Utah Series in the National Archives (on microfilm at the USHS and elsewhere). Reel 1—30 April 1853 to 24 December 1859—covers most of the period of Brigham's governorship.

The BYP contain reports and letters to the president of the United States, petitions, pardons, certificates, and licenses to and from the governor's office, memorials and resolutions, certificates of presence, financial estimates, correspondence with various federal departments (treasury, war, state), election returns, census papers, commissions and applications along with many routine letters acknowledging the receipt or the sending of various documents and numerous territorial financial papers.

Brigham's conflict with Perry E. Brocchus is treated in Leland H. Gentry, "The Brocchus-Young Speech Controversy of 1851" (Master's thesis, University of Utah, 1958). BYMH contains detailed synopses of the speeches. Brigham's correspondence with Brocchus and other papers concerning Brocchus are in BYP, as are letters and papers concerning Broughton D. Harris. A detailed collection of letters and reports dealing with the ensuing controversy is found in Daniel Webster, *Report from the Secretary of State*, in the Appendix to the *Congressional Globe*, 9 January 1852, U.S. Congress 32nd, 1st session, House.

Brigham's annual Governor's Messages to the Legislature are collected in a typed volume at USHS and BYP.

Brigham's political attitudes are discussed in J. Keith Melville, "The Political Ideas of Brigham Young" (Ph.D. diss., University of Utah, 1956). Klaus J. Hansen, *Quest for Empire: The Political Kingdom of God and the Council of Fifty in Mormon History* (East Lansing, Mich., 1967), gives information about Brigham's attitudes toward the United States government and how Brigham viewed his kingdom and his role.

The voluminous correspondence of BY and John Bernhisel is in BYP as well as in the Letterbooks.

A good treatment of the Utah War period (and all of the 1850s, in fact) is Norman F. Furniss, *The Mormon Conflict, 1850–1859* (New Haven, Conn., 1960). B. H. Roberts also gives an extensive account in volume 4 of his *Comprehensive History*. Brigham's diary for much of the year 1857 is in the Brigham Young Collection, Special Collections, at UUL. Most of Brigham's correspondence as commander-in-chief of the military is contained in the Nauvoo Legion Letterbook in HDC.

Brigham's correspondence with Alexander and Johnston is in the United States State Department, Territorial Papers—Utah Series, National Archives (on microfilm at USHS).

Correspondence between Brigham and Alfred Cumming can be found in the Brigham Young Collection at USHS, the Brigham Young Collection in the Special Collections division, UUL, and BYP. Letters and additional Cumming papers from Duke University are on microfilm at USHS.

[1] JD 1:187, 19 June 1853.
[2] BYMH, 1849, pp. 26–27, 38.
[3] Andrew Love Neff, *History of Utah, 1847 to 1869*, ed. Leland H. Creer (Salt Lake City, 1940), pp. 121–22.
[4] BYMH, 8 July 1849, p. 99.
[5] BYMH, 26 August 1849, p. 122.
[6] BYMH, 1850, pp. 1, 35.
[7] Orson F. Whitney, *History of Utah*, 4 vols. (Salt Lake City, 1892–1904), 1:455–57.
[8] BYMH, 1850, p. 4.
[9] Leland H. Creer, *Utah and the Nation* (Seattle, 1929), pp. 74–75. See also idem, *The Founding of an Empire: The Exploration and Colonization of Utah, 1776–1856* (Salt Lake City, 1947), p. 317; and Howard R. Lamar, *The Far Southwest, 1846–1912: A Territorial History* (New Haven, Conn., and London, 1966), esp. pp. 305–411.
[10] Creer, *Utah and the Nation*, p. 74.
[11] Wilford Woodruff Diary, 26 November 1849.
[12] BYMH, 6 September 1849, p. 128.
[13] Bernhisel to BY, 7 September 1850, BYP.
[14] "Fourth General Epistle of the First Presidency," 12 September 1850.
[15] BYMH, 26 November 1849, pp. 161–63.
[16] Bernhisel to BY, 7 September 1850, BYP.
[17] Bernhisel to BY, 12 September 1850, BYP.
[18] Fanny Young Murray to Nancy Young Kent, addition dated 29 January to letter dated 27 January 1851, HDC.
[19] Neff, *History of Utah*, p. 168; MHBY, 1851, pp. 6–7.
[20] Report of Messrs. Brandebury, Brocchus, and Harris to the president of the United States, Appendix to the *Congressional Globe*, 9 January 1852, U.S. Congress 32nd, 1st session, House, p. 86.
[21] Ibid.
[22] Ibid., p. 87.
[23] Ibid.
[24] Ibid.
[25] BY to Millard Fillmore, BYMH, 29 September 1851, p. 99.
[26] JD, 1:186–87, 19 June 1853.
[27] JD 3:259, 16 March 1856.
[28] BYMH, 1852, pp. 11–13.
[29] Message of President James Buchanan, BYMH, 8 December 1857, p. 831.

[30] Report of Messrs. Brandebury . . . , p. 88.

[31] BYMH, 1851, p. 48.

[32] JD 1:188, 19 June 1853. Italics in original.

[33] JD 2:320, 17 June 1855.

[34] BY to John C. L. Smith, Letterbook 1:102–3.

[35] BY to Thomas Kane, 30 October 1854, Letterbook 1:722–27.

[36] JD 5:228.

[37] *Sacramento Daily Union*, 19 December 1857.

[38] JD 1:217–18, 9 October 1852.

[39] BYMH, 1852, p. 80.

[40] JD 2:188, 18 February 1855. On another occasion Brigham noted that a man with the priesthood "should be far better qualified to wisely and righteously administer in any civil office, and in this manner the channel of true intelligence would be opened, and light and truth flow freely into every avenue of social life." JD 2:322–23, 17 June 1855.

[41] BY to Bernhisel, 31 October 1853, Letterbook 1:332–33.

[42] Neff, *History of Utah*, p. 177.

[43] BYMH, 8 July 1855, p. 73.

[44] Sermon at Fillmore, BYMH, 13 January 1855, p. 62.

[45] BY to Orson Hyde, 1 September 1856, Letterbook C:47–50.

[46] BY to Bernhisel, 29 October 1856, Letterbook C:149–52.

[47] BY to Bernhisel, 28 February 1854, Letterbook 1:440–43, 445–49.

[48] JD 1:110, 8 May 1853.

[49] BYMH, 1850, p. 132.

[50] BYMH, 23 July 1851, p. 56.

[51] JD 1:359, 1 August 1852.

[52] BY to Bernhisel, 28 December 1853, Miscellaneous Letterbook, vol. 2, 1853, pp. 125–26.

[53] BY to Bernhisel, 31 January 1854, Letterbook 1:398–406.

[54] BYMH, 18 December 1856, pp. 1245–46. See also Utah Territorial Papers, Executive Proceedings, box 2, #651–56, USA—Babbitt to BY, 26, 27 October 1854; BY to Babbitt, 27 October 1854.

[55] BY to Bernhisel, 31 January 1854, Letterbook 1:398–406.

[56] BY to Elisha Whittlesey, 31 January 1852, Utah Territorial Papers, Executive Proceedings, Book A, p. 46, USA.

[57] Elisha Whittlesey to BY, 11 November 1851, plus other correspondence, BYP.

[58] BY to Bernhisel, 1 May 1854, Governor's Office Letterbook; BY to Bernhisel, 1 October 1855, Letterbook 1:412–13.

[59] BY to Bernhisel, 30 September 1854, Governor's Office Letterbook.

[60] BY to Bernhisel, 17 July 1856, Letterbook 2:867–77.

[61] BY to Jefferson Davis, 30 September 1853, Letterbook 1:263; Auditor's Office to BY, 6 February 1854, BYP.

[62] BY to Bernhisel, 27 May 1856, Letterbook 2:772–76.

[63] See for example BY to John Taylor, 8 September 1855, Letterbook 2:346–52.

[64] BY to Kane, 14 April 1856, Letterbook 2:693–97.

[65] BY to Richards, 11 April 1856, Letterbook 2:704–11.

[66] BY to Bernhisel, 30 June 1856, Letterbook 2:809–15.

[67] BY to John Taylor, 30 June 1856, Letterbook 2:827–34.

[68] BY to Bernhisel, 17 July 1856, Letterbook 2:867–77.

[69] JD 5:98–99, 2 August 1857.

[70] Floris Olsen, "Early Nineteenth Century Shorthand Systems and the Deseret Alphabet" (Master's thesis, Brigham Young University, 1952).

[71] BY to Chas. W. Humphrey, 24 May 1852, Letterbook 1:54.

[72] BY to Kane, 31 January 1854, Letterbook 1:407–13; BY to President Pierce, 30 January 1854, Governor's Office Letterbook.

[73] Thomas Ellerbeck Diary, 16 December 1852, Church Archives.

[74] BYMH, 21 January 1853, p. 7.

[75] BY to "Brother Morley," 23 November 1853, Letterbook 1:342; BY to Madison D. Hamilton, 23 November 1853, Governor's Office Letterbook.

[76] BY to the legislature, 4 January 1854, Governor's Office Letterbook.

[77] Utah Territorial Papers, Executive Proceedings, Book A, p. 35, USA.

[78] Governor's Message, 15 December 1857.

[79] BYMH, account of remarks to legislature, 5 January 1852, pp. 1–2.

[80] Governor's Message, 13 December 1852, JH.

[81] BY to Lea, 8 June 1852, BYP, reel 92, box 58, folder 6.

[82] BY to Lea, 20 October 1851, BYP, reel 91, box 58, folder 6.

[83] BY to Manypenny, 26 June 1855, Letterbook 2:221–33.

[84] BY to Bernhisel, 28 February 1854, Letterbook 1:440–49.

[85] BY to Manypenny, 31 March 1856, Governor's Office Letterbook, pp 442–51.

[86] BY to Denver, 12 September 1857, Governor's Office Letterbook, pp. 647, 652.

[87] BY to Manypenny, 31 December 1853, Governor's Office Letterbook, pp. 39–43.

[88] BY to Hurt, 20 February 1855, Governor's Office Letterbook, pp. 215–16.

[89] BY to Walker, 13 June 1854, Letterbook 1:549–51.

[90] BY to Manypenny, 31 March 1854, Governor's Office Letterbook 1:66–69.

[91] BY to Armstrong, 19 February 1856, Governor's Office Letterbook, p. 428. The actual account books, however, show very few farm implements being given to Indians during these years, according to Beverly P. Smaby, "The Mormons and the Indians: Comflicting Ecological Systems in the Great Basin," *American Studies* 16 (Spring 1975): 48, ftnt. 47.

[92] BY to Armstrong, 14 March 1857, Governor's Office Letterbook, pp. 597–98.

[93] BY to "Brother" (possibly Bernhisel), 30 November 1853, Governor's Office Letterbook, pp. 22–29; David H. Miller, "The Impact of the Gunnison Massacre on Mormon-federal Relations: Colonel Edward Jenner Steptoe's Command in Utah Territory, 1854–1855" (Master's thesis, University of Utah, 1968).

[94] BY to Mrs. J. W. Gunnison, 30 November 1853, Letterbook 1:356–58.

[95] BYMH, 21 February 1856, p. 136.

[96] BY to "Inhabitants of the Territory of Utah," 22 February 1856, Governor's Office Letterbook, p. 429.

[97] BY to Bernhisel, 29 February 1856, Letterbook 2:591–95.

[98] BY to P. W. Conover, 7 March 1856, Letterbook 2:635–36.

[99] BYMH, 28 June 1856, pp. 363–64.

[100] BY to Gideon D. Wood, 22 February 1855, Letterbook 1:944; BY to Drummond, 11 February 1856, Letterbook 2:569–72.

[101] Susa Young Gates, "Brigham Young, Patriot, Pioneer, Prophet," radio address, station KSL, 1 June 1929, HDC.

[102] JD 1:362, 1 August 1852.

[103] Bernhisel to Willard Richards, 24 December 1851, quoted in Neff, *History of Utah*, p. 175; Bernhisel to BY, 7 January 1852, BYP.

[104] BY to Orson Hyde, 28 February 1852, Miscellaneous Letterbook, vol. 2, pp. 37–38; BY to Bernhisel, 27 May 1852, ibid., pp. 66–69.

[105] JD 1:110, 8 May 1853, and JD 1:187, 19 June 1853.

[106] JD 1:187, 19 June 1853.

[107] JD 2:183, 18 February 1855. Italics in original.

[108] Bernhisel to BY, 12 December 1853, BYP.

[109] BY to Bernhisel, 28 February 1854, Letterbook 1:440–43, 445–49.

[110] BYMH, 15 December 1854, p. 111.

[111] Bernhisel to BY, 14 December 1854, BYP.

[112] BY to John Taylor, 6 February 1855, and BY to Bernhisel, 31 January 1855 and 7 February 1855, Letterbook 1:855–58, 908–12, and 918–21.

[113] Bernhisel to BY, 18 January 1855, BYP.

[114] JD 2:187–88, 18 February 1855.

[115] BY to Bernhisel, 7 February 1855, Letterbook 1:918–21.

[116] BY to Erastus Snow, 28 February 1855, Letterbook 2:2–4.

[117] BY to Bernhisel, 1 April 1855, Letterbook 2:74–76.

[118] JD 2:319, 17 June 1855.

[119] BY to Taylor, 31 May 1855, Letterbook 2:171–80.

[120] JD 4:41, 31 August 1856.

[121] Ibid.

[122] Bernhisel to BY, 19 October 1855, BYP.

[123] BY to Rich, 31 January 1856, Letterbook 2:551–54.

[124] BY to Kane, 7 January 1856, Letterbook C: 273–77.

[125] BY to Phineas A. Young, 20 January 1856, and BY to E. T. Benson, 26 January 1857, Letterbook C:308–11, 317–20.

[126] Bernhisel to BY, 17 March 1857, BYP.

[127] BY Diary, 28 June 1857, Brigham Young Collection, UUL.

[128] BYMH, 29 June 1857, p. 357.

CHAPTER 15:
THE "INVASION" OF UTAH

The most complete treatment of Utah history during the years 1856–58 is B. H. Roberts, *A Comprehensive History of the Church of Jesus Christ of Latter-day Saints: Century I,* 6 vols. (Salt Lake City, 1930), 4:181–471. Based primarily on the documentation in the "History of Brigham Young," the narrative and analysis is replete with citations and annotations from other sources. With some exceptions, the approach is detached and scholarly. A documentary account is LeRoy R. Hafen and Ann W. Hafen, *The Utah Expedition, 1857–1858* (Glendale, Calif., 1958). Other general accounts include Edward W. Tullidge, *History of Salt Lake City and Its Founders* (Salt Lake City, c. 1886); Orson F. Whitney, *History of Utah,* 4 vols. (Salt Lake City, 1892–1904), vol. 1; and Eugene E. Campbell, "Governmental Beginnings," in *Utah's History,* ed. Richard D. Poll (Provo, Utah, 1978), pp. 153–73.

Three excellent monographs on the period are Leland H. Creer, *Utah and the Nation* (Seattle, 1929); and Richard D. Poll, "The Mormon Question, 1850–1865: A Study in Politics and Public Opinion" (Ph.D. diss., University of California, Berkeley, 1948). The latter presents the Mormon question in relation to the national political scene. A remarkably useful monograph is Norman F. Furniss, *The Mormon Conflict, 1850–1859* (New Haven, 1960). The events of the period, as reflected in the pages of the *Deseret News,* are also treated in A. R. Mortensen, "A Local Paper Reports on the Utah War," *Utah Historical Quarterly* 25 (1957): 297–318.

A contemporary running commentary on the Mormon War and on Utah affairs in general is found, among other places, in successive issues of *Harper's Weekly* 1–2 (1857–58); and *Daily National Intelligencer* (1857–58). The best Mormon commentary, which includes many documents not elsewhere available, is in successive issues of the *Millennial Star* 20 (1858). The crosscurrents of emotion are also captured in Juanita Brooks, *The Mountain Meadows Massacre* (Stanford, Calif., 1950). In the present work heavy reliance is placed on BYMH.

The most complete discussion of the activities of the Brigham Young Express and Carrying Company is in Leonard J. Arrington, *Great Basin Kingdom: An Economic History of the Latter-day Saints, 1830–1900* (Cambridge Mass., 1958, 1967), pp. 162–69.

The best available monograph on the Utah War is Everett L. Cooley, "The Utah War" (Master's thesis, University of Utah, 1947). M. Hamlin Cannon's study, "The Mormon War: A Study in Territorial Rebellion" (Master's thesis, George Washington University, 1938), is brief and relies almost entirely on federal sources. The most disappointing attempt is E. Cecil McGavin, *U.S. Soldiers Invade Utah* (Boston, 1937), which uses much primary material but lacks documentation, perspective, and depth. A fast-moving brief account is Paul Bailey, "Holy Smoke: A Dissertation on the Utah War," in *The Westerners Brand Book* (Los Angeles, 1948), pp. 101–20.

The Utah Expedition has been the subject of a number of monographs, the earliest being [Albert G. Browne, Jr.], "The Utah Expedition," *Atlantic Monthly* 3 (1859): 361–75, 474–95, 570–84, which was written by a correspondent with Johnston's army. These articles also contain useful descriptions of contemporary Mormon social and economic institutions. A military account is W. R. Hamilton, "History of the Mormon Rebellion of 1856–57," *The United Service* (Philadelphia), new series, 4 and 5 (1890–91), serialized. The lieutenant, who pours out his vitriol on Mormons and scheming politicians alike, relies heavily on William Prescott Johnston's *The Life of Gen. Albert Sidney Johnston . . .* (New York, 1878), who in turn relies heavily on T. B. H. Stenhouse, *Rocky Mountain Saints* (New York, 1873). A later study is Nils Henderson Lago, "The Utah Expedition, 1857–1858" (Master's thesis, University of Oklahoma, 1939). The supply operations of Russell, Majors, and Waddell are described in Raymond W. Settle and Mary Lund Settle, *Empire on Wheels* (Stanford, Calif., 1949), esp. pp. 17–32.

Contemporary personal accounts include Jesse A. Gove, *The Utah Expedition, 1857–1858*, ed. Otis G. Hammond (Cleveland, 1928); "The Utah War: Journal of Albert Tracy, 1858–1860," *Utah Historical Quarterly* 13 (1945): 1–128; Cornelius Conway, *The Utah Expedition . . .* (Cincinnati, 1858), which is an account by "a Wagonmaster of the Expedition"; "The Echo Canyon War," *The Contributor* 3 and 4 (1881–83), serialized, which gives Mormon accounts; and Hamilton Gardner, ed., "A Teritorial Militiaman in the Utah War: Journal of Newton Tuttle," *Utah Historical Quarterly* 22 (1954): 297–320. The activities of one division of the Nauvoo Legion are recorded in "Record of Orders, Returns and Courts Martial &c of 2nd Brigade, 1st Division, Nauvoo Legion, Headquarters 14th Ward, Great Salt Lake City [1857–68]," typescript, BYU. One phase of the call back to Zion in 1857 is told in Dale Morgan, *The Humboldt, Highroad of the West* (New York, 1943), pp. 234–47. Much of the political history of the times can be reconstructed from letterbooks in the Utah Territorial Papers, National Archives.

Much interesting social history in connection with the Move South is published in Kate B. Carter, ed., *Heart Throbs of the West*, 12 vols. (Salt Lake City, 1936–51), 10:233–68.

[1] "Citizens of Utah," broadside proclamation, 5 August 1857, HDC.

[2] Smoot's recollections are in Edward W. Tullidge, *History of Salt Lake City and Its Founders* (Salt Lake City, c. 1886), pp. 156–57.

[3] The best single account is Norman F. Furniss, *The Mormon Conflict, 1850–1859* (New Haven, 1960).

[4] This history and its significance to the Mormons is given in Richard D. Poll, "The Mormon Question, 1850–1865: A Study in Politics and Public Opinion" (Ph.D. diss., University of California, Berkeley, 1948).

[5] Eugene E. Cambell, "Governmental Beginnings," in *Utah's History*, ed. Richard D. Poll (Provo, Utah, 1978), p. 165.

[6] The background for Buchanan's action is given in Furniss, *The Mormon Conflict;* Leland H. Creer, *Utah and the Nation* (Seattle, 1929); and Campbell, "Governmental Beginnings," pp. 165–70. Although some Mormon writers have emphasized Secretary Floyd's cupidity, implying that he wanted opportunities for large contracts and expenditures, and was later indicted for fraud, I am inclined to minimize this as a cause of Buchanan's decision to send the expedition.

[7] John Bassett Moore, ed., *The Works of James Buchanan* (Philadelphia, 1910), 10:152; also 12:212–18.

[8] JD 5:95.

[9] See Gary L. Bunker and Davis Bitton, *Mormon Graphic Image, 1834–1914* (Salt Lake City, 1983); and Stanley Kimball, *Heber C. Kimball: Mormon Patriarch and Pioneer* (Urbana, Illinois, 1981), p. 218, note 22.

[10] *Deseret News*, 17 June 1857.

[11] JD 5:77–78.

[12] "Citizens of Utah," broadside proclamation, 5 August 1857, HDC.

[13] BY Diary, 11 August 1857, Brigham Young Collection, UUL. Also BY to Eldredge, 7 August 1857, BYP, box B 93–1, folder 3, pp. 24–25, USHS.

[14] Leonard J. Arrington, *Great Basin Kingdom: An Economic History of the Latter-day Saints, 1830–1900* (Cambridge, Mass., 1958, 1967), p. 175.

[15] Campbell, "Governmental Beginnings," p. 167.

[16] JH, 15 September 1857.

[17] These orders were found on Major Joseph Taylor when captured by government troops. See R. B. Marcy, *Thirty Years of Army Life on the Border* (New York, 1866), pp. 270–71; and in *House Exec. Doc. No. 71*, U.S. Congress 35th, 1st session, 10:56–57.

[18] *House Exec. Doc. No. 71*, 10:63.

[19] BY to Alexander, 14 October 1857, U.S. State Department, Territorial Papers—Utah Series, National Archives (microfilm, USHS).

[20] BY to Alexander, 16 October 1857, ibid.

[21] JD 5:338, 18 October 1857.

[22] BY to Alexander, 16 October 1857, U.S. State Department, Territorial Papers—Utah Series, National Archives.

[23] BYMH, 8 December 1857, pp. 834–35.

[24] Hurt to commissioners, 2 May 1855, Office of Indian Affairs, Record Group 75, National Archives.

[25] BY to Manypenny, 28 June 1853, BYP, reel 92, box 58, folder 7.

[26] George W. Bradley to Daniel H. Wells, 10 June 1854, BYP, reel 92, box 58, folder 14.

[27] BY to Denver, 12 September 1857, Governor's Office Letterbook, pp. 647–52.

[28] BYMH, 23 March 1858, pp. 273–74; 9 April 1858, p. 340; Arapeen to BY, 28 February 1858, BYP, reel 92, box 58, folder 1. Although Furniss says there is no evidence to substantiate any of these accusations, Mormon leaders thought they had proof.

[29] BY to Wash-e-keek, 2 November 1857, Letterbook C: 914–15; BY to Ben Simons, 2 March 1858, Letterbook 4: 101–2.

[30] BY to Nathaniel V. Jones, 4 August 1857, Letterbook C: 762–64. Also BY to William Felshaw, 4 August 1857, Letterbook C: 759–60, 955.

[31] BY to Hamblin, 4 August 1857, in Furniss, *The Mormon Conflict*, p. 163.

[32] BY to Jeter Clinton, 12 September 1857, Letterbook C: 839–43.

[33] Letterbook 3:827–28.

[34] "The Lee Trials," *Deseret News*, 16 September 1876, p. 544.

[35] BY to Denver, 6 January 1858, Governor's Office Letterbook, pp. 691–94.

[36] BYMH, 8 November 1857, pp. 776–77.

[37] BY to John Sharp, 28 September 1857, Nauvoo Legion Letterbook, p. 115, HDC.

[38] BY to Daniel H. Wells, John Taylor, and George A. Smith, 17 October 1857, Nauvoo Legion Letterbook, pp. 137–40.

[39] Ibid.

[40] Arrington, *Great Basin Kingdom*, p. 177.

[41] Ibid. As indicated earlier, some of these colonies were found to be untenable by early 1857, and the approach of the Utah Expedition offered a convenient excuse for abandonment. See Eugene Campbell, "Brigham Young's Outer Cordon—A Reappraisal," *Utah Historical Quarterly* 41 (Summer 1973): 220–53.

[42] BYMH, 7 October 1857, p. 659.

[43] Ibid., 21 December 1857, pp. 913–15.

[44] Frederick Kesler Diary, 28 November 1857, Kesler Papers, Special Collections, UUL.

[45] Orson Pratt and E. T. Benson to Asa Calkins, BYMH, 23 December 1857, p. 920.

[46] These letters are published in Albert L. Zobell, Jr., *Sentinel in the East: A Biography of Thomas L. Kane* (Salt Lake City, 1965), pp. 104–6.

[47] Ibid., pp. 110–15.

[48] Ibid., p. 119.

[49] Ibid., p. 120.

[50] BYMH, 9 April 1858, pp. 341–42.

[51] BYMH, 11 April 1858, p. 349.

[52] Cumming to Johnston, 14, 21 April 1858 in John B. Floyd, *Report of the Secretary of War* (Washington, D.C., 1858).

[53] Diary of Thomas L. Kane, BYU Library. Also Oscar O. Winther, ed., *The Private Papers and Diary of Thomas Leiper Kane: A Friend of the Mormons* (San Francisco, 1937), p. ix.

[54] Zobell, *Sentinel in the East*, p. 172.

[55] Wilford Woodruff to Thomas L. Kane, 1859, in Zobell, *Sentinel in the East*, p. 213.

[56] Letterbook 4:153–56.

[57] BY Letterbook 4:169–88.

[58] BYMH, 1858, p. 4.

[59] Justin McCarthy, *A History of Our Own Times . . .* , 11th ed. in 4 vols. (London, 1879), 2:339–40; also Diary of Hosea Stout, 4, 9 July 1855, USHS.

[60] BYMH, 21 March 1858.

[61] *A Series of Instructions and Remarks by President Brigham Young, at a Special Council, Tabernacle, March 21, 1858 . . .* (Salt Lake City, [1858]), p. 5, copy in HDC and in the Yale Library. The reference to Sebastopol is on page 11.

[62] BY to Thomas L. Kane, 22 March 1858, Kane Collection, HDC.

[63] "Instructions," of BY, 28 March 1858, *Deseret News*, 14 April 1858.

[64] [James H. Martineau?], "Seeking a Refuge in the Desert," *The Contributor* 11 (1890): 249.

[65] BYMH, 1858, pp. 27–29; *Memoirs of John R. Young* (Salt Lake City, 1920), pp. 105, 110, 114–15.

[66] I am grateful to Harvard University Press for permission to use some sentences from *Great Basin Kingdom*, pp. 185–87.

[67] BYMH, 1858, p. 20; JH, 12 June 1858.

[68] BYMH, 28 April 1858, p. 466.

[69] BY to Bernhisel, 6 May 1858, Letterbook 4:143–49.

[70] BYMH, 10 May 1858, pp. 501–2.

[71] Ibid., pp. 511–12.

[72] W. Medill to John Appleton, 10 December 1858, U.S. State Department, Territorial Papers—Utah Series, National Archives (microfilm, USHS).

[73] JD 2:322, 17 June 1855.

[74] JD 11:324, 10 February 1867.

[75] BY to Commissioner of Indian Affairs, 30 June 1858, OIA, RG 75.

[76] Forney to BY, 9 July 1858, BYP, reel 91, box 58, folder 3.

[77] BY to Bernhisel, 5 February 1862, Letterbook 6:128–31.

[78] BYMH, 17 June 1855, p. 67.

[79] BY to Kane, 29 June 1854, Letterbook 1:570–72.

[80] BY to Manypenny, 26 June 1855, Letterbook 2:221–33.

[81] BY to Hurt, 1 September 1855, Governor's Office Letterbook, pp. 372–73.

[82] BY to Bernhisel, 31 January 1855, Letterbook 1:855–58.

[83] BY to P. Clayton, Second Auditor, 7 February 1855, Governor's Office Letterbook, pp. 210–13.

[84] JD 5:236, 13 September 1857.

[85] Nels Anderson, *Desert Saints: The Mormon Frontier in Utah* (Chicago, 1942), pp. 206–7; B. H. Roberts, *A Comprehensive History of the Church of Jesus Christ of Latter-day Saints: Century I*, 6 vols. (Salt Lake City, 1930), 4:520.

⁸⁶ Juanita Brooks, "Indian Relations on the Mormon Frontier," *Utah Historical Quarterly* 12 (January–April 1944): 24–25.
⁸⁷ Rhett S. James, ed., "Brigham Young–Chief Washakie Indian Farm Negotiations, 1854–1857," *Annals of Wyoming*, October 1967, p. 12.
⁸⁸ Irish to Commissioner of Indian Affairs, 9 June 1865, *House Exec. Doc. No. 1*, U.S. Congress 39th, 1st session, 2:318, in Dale L. Morgan, "The Administration of Indian Affairs in Utah, 1851–1858," *Pacific Historical Review* 17 (1948): 409.

CHAPTER 16:
BABYLON WARS: ZION GROWS

Helpful studies on the army "occupation" of Utah include Norman F. Furniss, *The Mormon Conflict, 1850–1859* (New Haven, 1960), esp. pp. 168–234; Davis Bitton, "The Cradlebaugh Court (1859): A Study in Early Mormon-Gentile Misunderstanding," American West Center, University of Utah, *Occasional Papers*, 1975, pp. 71–97; Charles S. Peterson, "A Historical Analysis of Territorial Government in Utah Under Alfred Cumming, 1857–1861" (Master's thesis, Brigham Young University, 1958); and B. H. Roberts, *A Comprehensive History of the Church of Jesus Christ of Latter-day Saints, Century I*, 6 vols. (Salt Lake City, 1930), vol. 4.

Further on the Mountain Meadows Massacre is in Juanita Brooks, *The Mountain Meadows Massacre* (Stanford, Calif., 1950); and *John Doyle Lee: Zealot, Pioneer Builder, Scapegoat* (Glendale, Calif., 1961). A good analysis of the factors that caused the massacre and the extent to which Brigham and George A. Smith deliberately suppressed the facts of the tragedy to protect the church is in C. Kent Dunford, "The Contributions of George A. Smith to the Establishment of the Mormon Society in the Territory of Utah" (Ph.D. diss., Brigham Young University, 1970), pp. 178–208; and Merlo J. Pusey, "Explosion at Mountain Meadows," in *Builders of the Kingdom: George A. Smith, John Henry Smith, George Albert Smith* (Provo, Utah, 1981), pp. 101–9.

On the Civil War and its impact, I have used Gustive O. Larson, "Utah and the Civil War," *Utah Historical Quarterly* 33 (Winter 1965): 55–77; E. B. Long, *The Saints and the Union: Utah Territory During the Civil War* (Urbana, Illinois, 1981); Richard D. Poll, "The Mormon Question, 1850–1865: A Study in Politics and Public Opinion" (Ph.D. diss., University of California, Berkeley, 1948); and George U. Hubbard, "Abraham Lincoln as Seen by the Mormons," *Utah Historical Quarterly* 31 (Spring 1963): 91–108.

On the Salt Lake Theater the best studies are Roberta Reese Asahina, "Brigham Young and the Salt Lake Theater, 1862–1877" (Ph.D. diss., Tufts University, 1980); and Francis Therald Todd, "The Operation of the Salt Lake Theater, 1862–1875" (Ph.D. diss., University of Oregon, 1973). Reminiscent accounts include John Lindsay, *The Mormons and the Theatre* (Salt Lake City, 1905); Alfred Lambourne, *A Playhouse* (Salt Lake City, n.d.); George D. Pyper, *The Romance of an Old Playhouse* (Salt Lake City, 1928); Clarissa Young Spencer with Mabel Harmer, "The Theatre," in *Brigham Young at Home* (Salt Lake City, 1947), pp. 139–61; and Annie Adams Kiskadden, eight articles entitled "Maude Adams and Her Mother," in *The Green Book Magazine*, June to December 1914 and January 1915. Also of value is William J. McNiff, *Heaven on Earth: A Planned Mormon Society* (Oxford, Ohio, 1940), esp. pp. 130–55.

Useful economic studies have included Leonard J. Arrington, "Brigham Young and the Transcontinental Telegraph Line," *Improvement Era* 54 (July 1951): 510–11, 529; idem, "The Mormon Cotton Mission in Southern Utah," *Pacific Historical Review* 25 (August 1956): 221–38; and idem, *Great Basin Kingdom: An Economic History of the Latter-day Saints, 1830–1900* (Cambridge, Mass., 1958, 1967) pp. 195–234.

¹ BY to Amasa Lyman and George Q. Cannon, 15 November 1861, Letterbook 6:33–36.
² Wilford Woodruff Diary, 13 June 1858.
³ Secretary's minutes, 17 June 1858.

[4] *Deseret News*, 23 June 1858.

[5] BY to Cumming, 18 June 1858, Letterbook 4:249–50.

[6] BYMH, 26 June 1858, pp. 735–36; "The Utah War: Journal of Captain Albert Tracy, 1858–1860," *Utah Historical Quarterly* 13 (1945): 27–28; Norman F. Furniss, *The Mormon Conflict, 1850–1859* (New Haven, 1960), pp. 201–2.

[7] BY to Cumming, 1 July 1858, Letterbook 4:285.

[8] Furniss, *The Mormon Conflict*, p. 97.

[9] Cass instructions to Cumming, 30 July 1857, in "Utah Affairs," U.S. State Department, Territorial Papers—Utah Territory, vol. 1, National Archives (microfilm, USHS).

[10] Furniss, *The Mormon Conflict*, p. 98.

[11] Ibid.

[12] Johnston to Cumming, 22 March 1859, *Senate Exec. Doc. No. 2*, U.S. Congress 36th, 1st session, 2:151–52.

[13] Davis Bitton, "The Cradlebaugh Court (1859): A Study in Early Mormon-Gentile Misunderstanding," American West Center, University of Utah, *Occasional Papers*, 1975, p. 81.

[14] Ibid., pp. 81–82; JH, 11 March 1859.

[15] Ibid.; Furniss, *The Mormon Conflict*.

[16] Proclamation, 27 March 1859, U.S. State Department, Territorial Papers—Utah Series, National Archives; JH, 30 March 1859.

[17] JH, 22, 24, 29 March 1859.

[18] JH, 26, 30 March 1859.

[19] BY to George A. Smith, 10 March 1859, JH; JH, 24 March 1859.

[20] BY to George A. Smith, 15 March 1859, JH.

[21] Black to Cradlebaugh and Sinclair, 17 March 1859, *Senate Exec. Doc. No. 32*, U.S. Congress 36th, 1st session, 1860. Past tense changed to present tense in some instances.

[22] Floyd to Johnston, 6 May 1859, *Senate Exec. Doc. No. 2*, U.S. Congress 36th, 1st session, vol. 2.

[23] See especially Cradlebaugh's "Utah and the Mormons" (Speech delivered in Congress on the proposed admission of Utah as a state, Washington, D.C., 1863).

[24] As late as 23 December 1866, Brigham delivered a sermon in which he declared that there were "some things he could not think of . . . he could not think of the Mountain Massacre. He [earlier] supposed they were massacred by savages, but he did not think before that they were as brutal as that." Woodruff Diary, 23 December 1866. Brigham's nephew, John R. Young, stated that Brigham did not know the full extent of LDS involvement until 1865, at which time he withdrew the hand of fellowship from John D. Lee, saying, "John, what made you lie to me about that Mountain Meadow Massacre?" Although Lee was removed from his position as bishop, Brigham continued to assist Lee in his family and other affairs and did not excommunicate him until 1870. See John R. Young to W. S. Erekson, February 1928, d 1253, box 3, HDC.

[25] B. H. Roberts, *A Comprehensive History of the Church of Jesus Christ of Latter-day Saints: Century I*, 6 vols. (Salt Lake City, 1930), 4:166–67; JH, 18 June 1858; Juanita Brooks, *The Mountain Meadows Massacre* (Stanford, Calif., 1950), pp. 120–21.

[26] Court Record, Lee's second trial, testimony of Hamblin, ms., Huntington Library.

[27] From James A. Little, ed., *Jacob Hamblin: A Narrative of His Personal Experience as a Frontiersman, Missionary to the Indians, and Explorer* (Salt Lake City, 1881), pp. 56–57. When BY was asked in the Lee trial why he had not, as governor, instituted proceedings to investigate that massacre and bring the guilty authors thereof to justice, Brigham responded:

> Because another governor had been appointed by the president of the United States, and was then on the way to take my place, and I did know how soon he might arrive, and because the United States judges were not in the territory. Soon after Governor Cumming arrived, I asked him to take Judge Cradlebaugh, who belonged to the southern district, with him and I would accompany them with sufficient aid to investigate the matter and bring the offenders to Justice.

Cited in Roberts, *Comprehensive History*, 4:168.

[28] George A. Smith to BY, 17 August 1858, Historian's Office Letterbook, pp. 885–91; George A. Smith to T. B. H. [Stenhouse], 2 June 1859, ibid., p. 75; General Minutes, 24 April 1859, HDC.

[29] HOJ 25 May 1859. Past tense changed to present.

[30] Sermon of 8 March 1863, JD 10:110. See also George A. Smith, "Account of Mountain Meadows Massacre sent to Mr. Clair," in Historian's Office Letterbook, vol. 2, ca. 25 November 1869. "There has never been a time when President Brigham Young and his brethren were not ready to give every aid in their power to discover and bring to Justice the participators in this Massacre," said Smith. Other evidences of Brigham's attempts to induce Governor Cumming to investigate the massacre include: Telegram, David O. Calder to John W. Young, 31 July 1877, box 16, folder 21, HDC; BY to William W. Belknap, Secretary of War, 21 May 1872, Letterbook 13:80–84; BY Office Journal C, 2 September 1859.

[31] Furniss, *The Mormon Conflict*, pp. 212–22.

[32] BY Office Journal C, 27 August 1859.

[33] BY to Wm. W. Belknap, Letterbook 13:80–84. The non-Mormon superintendent of Indian affairs, Jacob Forney, who recovered the surviving children after the massacre and sought to determine the "real facts" of the tragedy, stated that many of the federals were more anxious to connect the church with the massacre than to find the actual perpetrators. *Senate Document*, U.S. Congress 36th, 1st session, vol. 11, no. 2, p. 86.

[34] Juanita Brooks, *John Doyle Lee: Zealot, Pioneer Builder, Scapegoat* (Glendale Calif., 1961), pp. 288–89, 293–96.

[35] BY to [name deleted because confidential communication], 16 February 1869, Letterbook 11:362–63.

[36] Woodruff Diary, 25 May 1861.

[37] BY et al. to Orson Hyde, 16 October 1849, JH.

[38] BY to John Brown, 1 January 1868, Letterbook 10:571–74.

[39] BY et al., "Fourth General Epistle of the First Presidency," 27 September 1850, JH.

[40] BY et al., "Sixth General Epistle of the First Presidency," 22 September 1851, JH.

[41] BY to John Taylor, 28 July 1856, Letterbook 2:890–96.

[42] BY et al., "Fourteenth General Epistle of the First Presidency," 10 December 1856, JH.

[43] BY to Orson Pratt, 27 January 1857, Letterbook C:325–28.

[44] Remarks at conference, 8 September 1850, General Minutes, BYP.

[45] List of property, 31 August 1855, Letterbook 2:334–36.

[46] See BY to George Q. Cannon, 11 October 1862, Letterbook 6:402–6.

[47] BY to Asa Calkin, 10 September 1858, Letterbook 4:368–73.

[48] BY to Hooper, 20 December 1867, Letterbook 10:559–62.

[49] BY to Nathaniel V. Jones and Jacob Gates, 20 December 1860, Letterbook 5:650–51.

[50] BY to Amasa Lyman, 15 November 1861, Letterbook 6:33–36.

[51] JH, 9 April 1871.

[52] Emilia McMahon to BY, 7 February 1866, BYP.

[53] BY to Mrs. E. McMahon, 4 May 1866, Letterbook 8:375–76.

[54] Mrs. E. McMahon to BY, 8 April, 3 May 1866; to BY, undated letter received 5 August 1866, BYP; 7 January 1869, Letterbook 11:282.

[55] BY to Asa Calkin, 10 September 1858, Letterbook 4:368–73.

[56] BY, Circular to Presidents and Bishops, September 1855, in James R. Clark, comp., *Messages of the First Presidency*, 6 vols. (Salt Lake City, 1965–75), 2:174–76.

[57] BY to editor, *The Religio-Philosophical Journal*, 7 January 1869, Letterbook 11:283–86. See also Richard L. Jensen, "Brigham Young and the Immigrants," unpublished paper generously furnished the writer.

[58] Milton R. Hunter, *Brigham Young the Colonizer* (Independence, Mo., 1945), esp. pp. 362–64.

[59] Council Meeting, 23 August 1863, Minutes, Brigham Young Collection, 1855–77, pp. 176–80.

[60] BYP.

[61] BYP.

[62] JH, 15 December 1861.

[63] JH, 16 August 1861.

[64] Visitor descriptions of the theater include William Hepworth Dixon, *The New America*, 2 vols. (London, 1867), pp. 122–24; Fitz Hugh Ludlow, "Among the Mormons," *Atlantic Monthly* 13 (April 1864): 290 ff.

[65] Fitz Hugh Ludlow, *The Heart of a Continent* (Cambridge, Mass., 1870), pp. 370–71.

[66] Annie Adams Kiskadden, "Maude Adams and Her Mother," *The Green Book Magazine*, June 1914, pp. 893–94; John Lindsay, *The Mormons and the Theatre* (Salt Lake City, 1905), p. 23; Leonard J. Arrington, *Great Basin Kingdom: An Economic History of the Latter-day Saints, 1830–1900* (Cambridge, Mass., 1958, 1967), p. 199; also Hiram Clawson, "Theatricals in Utah," Minute Book 2, 23 January 1870, Daughters of Utah Pioneers Museum, Salt Lake City; BY to Elders Clawson, Calder, and Caine, 18 July 1861, Letterbook 5:833.

[67] Clarissa Young Spencer and Mabel Harmer, *Brigham Young at Home* (Salt Lake City, 1947), p. 140.

[68] JD 6:70.

[69] JD 9:243.

[70] JD 1:30.

[71] JD 9:244.

[72] JD 9:245.

[73] Ibid.

[74] *Daily Telegraph*, 11 January 1865.

[75] Alfred Lambourne, *A Playhouse* (Salt Lake City, n.d.), p. 40.

[76] Spencer and Harmer, *Brigham Young at Home*, p. 147. This story is corroborated in George D. Pyper, *The Romance of an Old Playhouse* (Salt Lake City, 1928), p. 230.

[77] Pyper, p. 231.

[78] *Utah: A Guide to the State* (New York, 1945), p. 178.

[79] Kiskadden, *The Green Book Magazine*, July 1914, p. 5.

[80] Ibid., pp. 8–12.

[81] Roberta Reese Asahina, "Brigham Young and the Salt Lake Theater, 1862–1877" (Ph.D. diss., Tufts University, 1980), pp. 145–46.

[82] Pyper, pp. 231–32.

[83] Lindsay, p. 82.

[84] Asahina, pp. 171–73; Francis Therald Todd, "Operation of the Salt Lake Theater, 1862–1875" (Ph.D. diss., University of Oregon, 1973), pp. 283–87; Kiskadden, *The Green Book Magazine*, August 1914, pp. 211–12.

[85] Asahina, pp. 30–31.

[86] BY to Hooper, 20 December 1860, Beinecke Library, Harvard University; also Coe Collection, Yale University Library.

[87] Roberts, *Comprehensive History*, 5:2; Hooper to Cannon, 16 December 1860, *Millennial Star* 23 (5 January 1861): 29–30.

[88] BYTB, 18 October 1861.

[89] JD 10:111, 8 March 1863.

[90] BY to Orson Hyde, 13 October 1861, BYP.

[91] *Deseret News*, 1 October 1862.

[92] Gustive O. Larson, "Utah and the Civil War," *Utah Historical Quarterly* 33 (Winter 1965): 59.

[93] *Deseret News*, 30 April 1862.

[94] A splendid biographical sketch is Charles S. Peterson, "A Portrait of Lot Smith—Mormon Frontiersmen," *Western Historical Quarterly* 1 (October 1970): 393–414.

[95] Richard D. Poll, "The Mormon Question, 1850–1865: A Study in Politics and Public Opinion" (Ph.D. diss., University of California, Berkeley, 1948).

⁹⁶ E. B. Long, *The Saints and the Union: Utah Territory during the Civil War* (Urbana, Illinois, 1981), p. 101.
⁹⁷ Minutes, Brigham Young Collection, 1855–77, p. 170.
⁹⁸ Leonard J. Arrington, "Agricultural Price Control in Pioneer Utah," *Agricultural History* 30 (July 1956): 104–13.
⁹⁹ Long, *The Saints and the Union*, p. 113.
¹⁰⁰ Ibid., p. 162.
¹⁰¹ T. B. H. Stenhouse, *The Rocky Mountain Saints* (New York, 1872), p. 604.
¹⁰² Long, *The Saints and the Union*, p. 165.
¹⁰³ Fred B. Rogers, *Soldiers of the Overland . . .* (San Francisco, 1938), p. 112.
¹⁰⁴ Ibid., pp. 111–17; Richard H. Orton, comp., *Records of California Men in the War of the Rebellion, 1861–1867* (Sacramento, 1890), pp. 505–10.
¹⁰⁵ Connor to R. C. Drum, Assistant Adjutant General, U.S. Army, 21 July 1864, cited in *Tullidge's Quarterly Magazine* 1 (January 1881): 185.
¹⁰⁶ Woodruff Diary as cited in Arrington, *Great Basin Kingdom*, p. 202.
¹⁰⁷ For example, *Deseret News*, 22, 29 June, 8 August, 30 November 1864; 4 January, 14 June 1865; 3 May, 6 September 1866; 6 March, 17 December 1867; 21 March 1868.
¹⁰⁸ JH, 9 April 1868.
¹⁰⁹ Cited in Arrington, *Great Basin Kingdom*, p. 203.
¹¹⁰ Connor to General Halleck, 15 February 1865, in Orton, comp., *Records of California Men*, p. 516.
¹¹¹ BY to Charles S. Kimball, 31 December 1864, Letterbook 7:414–16.

CHAPTER 17:
GOVERNOR AND COUNSELOR

The principal sources for this chapter were the BY Letterbooks, Record Book of the Twelve, Minutes of the School of the Prophets, and Minutes of the Women's Relief Society, all in HDC.

On Brigham Young's medical advice, I have used Linda P. Wilcox, "The Imperfect Science: Brigham Young on Medical Doctors," *Dialogue* 12 (Fall 1979): 26–36; Robert T. Divett, *Medicine and the Mormons* (Bountiful, Utah, 1981), esp. pp. 135–43; Leonard J. Arrington, "An Economic Interpretation of the Word of Wisdom," *BYU Studies* 1 (Winter 1959): 37–49; and essays by Lester Bush, Robert McCue, and Thomas Alexander in *Dialogue* 14 (Autumn 1981): 46–88.

I am especially grateful to Linda Wilcox, who undertook a study of Brigham Young as a domestic counselor and generously shared her findings with me.

¹ JD 12:204.
² D. Michael Quinn, "Latter-day Saint Prayer Circles," *BYU Studies* 19 (Fall 1978): 79–105.
³ Record Book of the Twelve, p. 113; Leonard J. Arrington and Ronald K. Esplin, "The Role of the Quorum of the Twelve during Brigham Young's Presidency of the Church . . .," *Task Papers in LDS History*, no. 31 (Salt Lake City, 1979), pp. 46–47.
⁴ Wilford Woodruff Diary, 4 April 1860; Miscellaneous Minutes, 4 April 1860, BYP.
⁵ Record Book of the Twelve, p. 40.
⁶ Woodruff Diary, 4 April 1860.
⁷ Miscellaneous Minutes, 5 April 1860, BYP.
⁸ Ibid.; Woodruff Diary, 5 April 1860; HOJ, 5 April 1860.
⁹ HOJ, 5 April 1860; Woodruff Diary, 23 September 1860.
¹⁰ Leonard J. Arrington, *Great Basin Kingdom: An Economic History of the Latter-day Saints, 1830–1900* (Cambridge, Mass., 1958, 1967), pp. 245–54.
¹¹ Minutes of the Salt Lake School of the Prophets, 1867–72; Minutes of Grantsville, Parowan, Tooele, Utah Valley Schools of the Prophets, HDC.

[12] In what follows, see Gordon Irving, "Encouraging the Saints: Brigham Young's Annual Tours of the Mormon Settlements," *Utah Historical Quarterly* 45 (Summer 1977): 233–51.

[13] Woodruff Diary, 27 May 1861.

[14] Charles R. Savage, "A Trip South with President Young in 1870," *Improvement Era* 3 (1899–1900): 367, 295, 298.

[15] Elizabeth Wood Kane, *Twelve Mormon Homes, Visited in Succession on a Journey through Utah to Arizona* (Philadelphia, 1874), pp. 113–14.

[16] Solomon F. Kimball; "President Brigham Young's First Trip to Bear Lake Valley," *Improvement Era* 10 (February 1907): 296–303.

[17] Story told by Mrs. Ken Rogerson, granddaughter of Anson Call, in an oral history interview, 30 January 1978, HDC.

[18] Solomon F. Kimball, "President Brigham Young's Excursion Party," *Improvement Era* 14 (January 1911): 189–201; (February 1911): 311–21; (March 1911): 415–21; (April 1911): 507–12.

[19] Robert G. Cleland and Juanita Brooks, eds., *A Mormon Chronicle: The Diaries of John D. Lee, 1848–1876*, 2 vols. (San Marino, Calif., 1955) 1:315; Woodruff Diary, 8 May 1869, 14 June 1870.

[20] Notes of BY's medical lecture to the Board of Health at Great Salt Lake City, December 1851, Woodruff Diary; unpublished sermon of 16 January 1861, HDC.

[21] JD 13:142, 11 July 1869.

[22] *Deseret News*, 13 December 1851.

[23] JD 4:109.

[24] Chris Rigby Arrington, "Pioneer Midwives," in *Mormon Sisters: Women in Early Utah*, ed. Claudia L. Bushman (Cambridge, Mass., 1976), pp. 43–65. "Pioneer Midwives," in *Our Pioneer Heritage*, ed. Kate B. Carter, 20 vols. (Salt Lake City, 1958–77), 6:361–560, gives many examples of women called by Brigham to become midwives.

[25] Daniel Tyler, *A Concise History of the Mormon Battalion in the Mexican War, 1846–1847* (n.p, 1881), p. 146.

[26] BY et al., "Seventh General Epistle of the First Presidency," JH, 18 April 1852.

[27] JD 4:24.

[28] JD 8:361–62.

[29] *Deseret News*, 11 May 1870.

[30] This paragraph is put together from items given in Minutes, Brigham Young Collection, 1855–77, HDC, entries for 25, 28 October 1860; and BY, Secretary's Journals, 1857–63, entries for 2 March 1857; 26 March, 23 April 1861; 25, 31 March, 28 April, 7, 12 May 1862. The story of the plug of tobacco in the hip pocket is told in several places. See Susa Young Gates Papers, USHS. The upper plate of these gold-plated dentures is in the possession of Ted Kimball of Salt Lake City, a great-grandson of Brigham.

[31] BY, Secretary's Journals, 1857–63, 7 July 1861.

[32] BY to Thomas Hollis, 20 October 1853, Letterbook 1:311.

[33] BY to Volney King, 13 June 1871, Letterbook 12:721.

[34] BY to Bishop Bronson, 6 July 1857, Letterbook C: 702–3.

[35] BY to Br. Henry Standish and family, 17 December 1860, Letterbook 5:648–49.

[36] BY to Edwin H. Thomas, 23 June 1867, Letterbook 10:246.

[37] BY to Charles D. Evans, 25 April 1865, Letterbook 7:601.

[38] BY to Heman Hyde, 8 May 1860, Letterbook 5:501.

[39] BY to John M. Higbee, 28 October 1865, and BY to John S. Higbee, 29 October 1865, Letterbook 7:794, 797.

[40] BY to Samuel Mulliner, 6 June 1867, Letterbook 10:185.

[41] BY to Miss A. B. C., 9 April 1862, Letterbook 6:196.

[42] BY to Warren S. Snow, 11 May 1860, Letterbook 5:506.

[43] BY to Thomas Jaques, 23 February 1868, Letterbook 10:666.

[44] BY to Bp. John Brown, 27 November 1875, Letterbook 14:28–29.

[45] BY to Jacob Hamblin, 1 April 1857, Letterbook C:516.

46 BY to [name deleted], 13 February 1860, Letterbook 5:378.

47 BY to Thomas R. King, 8 July 1861, Letterbook 5:826.

48 BY to John Van Cott et al., 6 January 1863, Letterbook 6:450–51.

49 BY to Wm. I. Appleby, 13 April 1855, Letterbook 2:98.

50 BY to S. A. Baker, 27 August 1868, Letterbook 11:1–2, 4.

51 BY to Charles H. Hales, 18 August 1869, Letterbook 11:733–35.

52 BY to Agnes Hoagland, 19 August 1859, Letterbook 5:215.

53 BY to Bp. A. Johnson, 21 June 1866, Letterbook 9:3.

54 BY to Lydia Williams, 4 September 1854, Letterbook 1:670.

55 BYOJ, 1857–60, 19 April 1858, p. 21.

56 BY to J. M. Raymond, Esq., 18 July 1870, Letterbook 12:242–41 [sic].

57 BY to Wm. H. Dame, 8 August 1867, Letterbook 10:340.

58 BY to Lydia Williams, 4 September 1854, Letterbook 1:670.

59 BY to John Van Cott, his first wife, and Mary Ann, the wife of James Cobb, 6 January 1863, Letterbook 6:450–51.

60 BY to Bishop Bronson, 15 July 1857, Letterbook C:719.

61 BY to Bp. McCullough, 4 April 1857, Letterbook C:542.

62 BY to Melissa M. Wallace, 29 March 1859, Letterbook 5:95.

63 BY to Lorin Farr, 7 August 1855, Letterbook 2:294.

64 BY to Bp. C. W. West, 21 August 1865, Letterbook 7:719.

65 BY to Bp. John Stoker, 15 March 1865, Letterbook 7:511 A.

66 BY to Bp. J. G. Bigler, 29 March 1871, Letterbook 12:626.

67 BY to Elias Smith, 13 June 1877, Letterbook 14:915.

68 BY to Mary Ann Jolley, 26 October 1865, Letterbook 7:786.

69 BY to Mrs. Susan Damron, 30 June 1865, Letterbook 7:885.

70 JD 16:161; JD 12:124.

CHAPTER 18:
PUBLIC IMAGE AND PRIVATE REALITY

Visitors' impressions of Brigham Young have been discussed in Edwina Snow, "Singular Saints: The Image of the Mormons in Book-Length Travel Accounts, 1847–1857" (Master's thesis, George Washington University, 1972); and in Rebecca Cornwall and Leonard J. Arrington, "Men and Women of Letters Encounter Brigham Young," BYU Studies, in press.

Treatments of the Brigham Young family include Clarissa Young Spencer and Mabel Harmer, Brigham Young at Home (Salt Lake City, 1947); Mrs. Catherine V. Waite, "Brigham as Lord of the Harem," and "The Wives of Brigham Young," in The Mormon Prophet and His Harem: An Authentic History of Brigham Young, His Numerous Wives and Children, 3rd ed. (Cambridge, Mass., 1867), pp. 177–214; Susa Young Gates, with Leah D. Widtsoe, The Life Story of Brigham Young (New York, 1930); Susa Young Gates, "How Brigham Young Brought Up His 56 Children," Physical Culture, February 1925, pp. 29–31, 138–44; idem, "Family Life among the Mormons," The North American Review 150 (March 1890): 339–50; Dean C. Jessee, ed., Letters of Brigham Young to His Sons (Salt Lake City, 1974), and idem, "Brigham Young's Family," BYU Studies 18 (Spring 1978): 311–27; and 19 (Summer 1979): 474–500.

1 BY, "For the Perusal of My Family," 2 April 1866, BYP.

2 Andrew Love Neff, History of Utah, 1847 to 1869, ed. Leland H. Creer (Salt Lake City, 1940), pp. 555–63.

3 The Morrill Anti-Bigamy Act of 1862 provided penalties against plural marriage and also contained provisions to curb the economic power of the Mormon church. When it proved to be ineffective and possibly unconstitutional, subsequent bills designed to affect only Utah were

proposed to abolish trial by jury, to provide for the federal appointment of county judges, to prohibit officers of the church from solemnizing marriages, to place the selection of jurors in the hands of the United States attorney, to deprive wives of immunity as witnesses in cases involving their husbands, and to punish "cohabitation." Other proposed legislation would have dismembered Utah by transferring large slices of it to Nevada, Wyoming, and Colorado. None of these provisions was enacted during Brigham's lifetime, though they were a constant threat.

[4] See Edwina Snow, "Singular Saints: The Image of the Mormons in Book-Length Travel Accounts, 1847–1857" (Master's thesis, George Washington University, 1972).

[5] Jules Remy and Julius Brenchley, *A Journey to Great-Salt-Lake City*, 2 vols. (London, 1861), reviewed by Elisee Reclus, "Le Mormonisme et Les Etats-Unis," in *Revue Des Deux Mondes* 32 (April 1861), series 8, p. 882.

[6] Remy and Brenchley 1:201–11, 302–3, 496; 2:57.

[7] Ibid.

[8] Ibid.

[9] Daniel J. Boorstin, *The Image, or What Happened to the American Dream* (New York, 1962), p. 15. Also Horace Greeley, "Two Hours with Brigham Young," *New York Tribune*, 20 August 1859. The interview is reprinted in Charles T. Duncan, ed., *An Overland Journey from New York to San Francisco in the Summer of 1859 by Horace Greeley* (New York, 1964), pp. 177–83.

[10] Greeley, *Overland Journey*, pp. 183–84.

[11] Ibid., p. 182.

[12] JH, 3, 11, 13, 18 September 1860.

[13] Richard F. Burton, *The City of the Saints* (New York, 1862), pp. 239–40.

[14] Ibid., p. 263.

[15] See Ivan Benson, *Mark Twain's Western Years* (Stanford, Calif., 1938); Effie Mona Mack, *Mark Twain in Nevada* (New York, 1947); Frederick Anderson, ed., *Mark Twain's Notebooks and Journals*, 2 vols. (Berkeley, 1975), vol. 1 (1855–73); and Twain himself in *Roughing It* (Hartford, 1872), pp. 19–20.

[16] BY, Secretary's Journals, 1857–63, 7 August 1861.

[17] Twain, *Roughing It*, pp. 107, 112.

[18] Ibid., p. 113.

[19] Ibid., p. 136.

[20] Fitz Hugh Ludlow, "Among the Mormons," *Atlantic Monthly* 13 (April 1864): 479–95; idem, *The Heart of the Continent* (Cambridge, Mass., 1870). We have had access only to a review of Ludlow's *Golden Era* articles by the *San Francisco Hebrew* of 27 March 1864 as cited in JH for that date.

[21] Ludlow, *Heart of the Continent*, p. 364; BY, Secretary's Journals, 3 July 1863.

[22] Ludlow, *Heart of the Continent*, pp. 368–69.

[23] Ludlow, "Among the Mormons," p. 485.

[24] Ludlow, *Heart of the Continent*, p. 373.

[25] Ludlow, "Among the Mormons," pp. 485, 487.

[26] See *The Complete Works of Artemus Ward* (London, 1922).

[27] E. P. Hingston was Ward's manager and companion from 1864 until Ward's death in 1869. See Hingston, ed., *Artemus Ward: His Travels among the Mormons* (London, 1865) and idem, *The Genial Showman, Being Reminiscences of the Life of Artemus Ward* (London, 1870).

[28] Hingston, *The Genial Showman*.

[29] Hingston, ed., *Artemus Ward: His Travels among the Mormons*, pp. 78, 52.

[30] Ibid., p. 60.

[31] Ibid., p. 56.

[32] JH, 20 April 1864.

[33] William Hepworth Dixon, *The New America*, 2 vols. (London, 1867); idem, *Spiritual Wives*, 2 vols. (London, 1868).

[34] Charles Wentworth Dilke, *Greater Britain: A Record of Travel in English-speaking Countries During 1866 and 1867*, 2d ed. in 2 vols. (London, 1869).

[35] Dixon is referring to the Shaker movement as well as Mormonism in his preface to *New America.*

[36] Paraphrased slightly from Dixon's account in *New America*, 1:210.

[37] Ibid., 1:252–3.

[38] Ibid., pp. 222, 265, 284, 299, 348.

[39] Dilke, *Greater Britain*, p. 148.

[40] Ibid., p. 149.

[41] JH, 5 December 1874, quoting from *Salt Lake Herald.*

[42] Justin McCarthy, *Reminiscences*, 2 vols. (New York, 1899), 2:262.

[43] John H. Beadle, *Life in Utah; or the Mysteries and Crimes of Mormonism* (Philadelphia, 1870), pp. 7, 9, 296, 400.

[44] Clarissa Young Spencer and Mabel Harmer, *Brigham Young at Home* (Salt Lake City, 1947).

[45] William H. Knight, "Interviewing Brigham Young in 1859," *Journal of American History*, 1927, pp. 113–17.

[46] Spencer and Harmer, *Brigham Young at Home*, pp. 71–72. According to his daughter Clarissa, Brigham's recipe for composition tea—sometimes referred to as "the Mormon highball"—was: 4 ounces each of ground bayberry, poplar bark, and hemlock; 2 ounces each of ground ginger, cloves, and cinnamon; and 1 ounce of cayenne pepper. Take a small bit on the end of a spoon, fill the cup with hot water, and use plenty of cream and sugar.

[47] Ibid., p. 21.

[48] Ibid., p. 37.

[49] Ibid., p. 21.

[50] Ibid., p. 32.

[51] Ibid., p. 34.

[52] Susa Young Gates, "Family Life among the Mormons," *The North American Review* 150 (March 1890): 343.

[53] Susa Young Gates Papers, USHS, box 1, file 5, p. 20.

[54] JD 11:117.

[55] JD 10:361. Also JD 12:174; 9:196; 19:221.

[56] JD 19:69–70.

[57] Cited in Dean C. Jessee, ed., *Letters of Brigham Young to His Sons* (Salt Lake City, 1974), p. xxiv. See also JD 9:196; Woodruff Diary, 21 August 1858.

[58] Susa Young Gates Papers, USHS; Susa Young Gates, "President Brigham Young: Anecdotes of the Great Pioneer and Leader," *Improvement Era* 8 (June 1905): 562.

[59] Spencer and Harmer, *Brigham Young at Home*, pp. 73–74.

[60] Eliza J. Webb to BY, BYP, reel 58, box 30, folder 5; BY to Eliza J. Webb, 6 December 1865, Letterbook 7:843; BY to Judge Elias Smith, 9 December 1865, Letterbook 7:850.

[61] Eugene Traughber, "The Prophet's Courtship: President Young's Favorite Wife, Amelia, Talks," *Salt Lake Tribune*, 4 March 1894.

[62] Woodruff Diary, 21 August 1858.

[63] BY to W. H. Hooper, 29 November 1860, Letterbook 5:639–41.

[64] BY to H. B. Clawson, 16 May 1868, Letterbook 10:842–44.

[65] BY to George Q. Cannon, 29 November 1861, Letterbook 6:50–53.

[66] BY to Brigham Young, Jr., 24 June 1863, Letterbook 6:622–24.

[67] Greeley, *Overland Journey*, p. 180.

[68] B. F. Grant, "The Kindness of Brigham Young," a memo in the Heber J. Grant General Correspondence, box 112, folder 2, HDC.

[69] Ellis Shipp Musser, ed., *The Early Autobiography and Diary of Ellis Reynolds Shipp, M.D.* (Salt Lake City, 1962).

[70] JD 13:61, 18 July 1869.

[71] BY to "the Brethren at work in Big Cottonwood Kanyon," 18 June 1855, Letterbook 2:210.

[72] BY to Feramorz Little, 23 April 1855, Letterbook 2:108–9.

[73] BY to John T. Conk, 8 November 1867, Letterbook 10:459.

[74] BY to Arthur Smith, 22 April 1865, Letterbook 7:596.

[75] BY to Jared Porter, 9 February 1857, Letterbook C:341.

[76] BY to Frederick Perris and Brother Slaugh, 13 July 1864, Letterbook 7:235–36.

[77] Although I have heard this remark from members of the Young family, this is taken from an oral interview of Francis G. Bennett by Ronald W. Walker, 6 August 1981, HDC.

CHAPTER 19:
PROTECTING THE KINGDOM

On the economic and political differences between Mormons and non-Mormons in the 1860s, I have followed the themes that are expressed in Leonard J. Arrington, *Great Basin Kingdom: An Economic History of the Latter-day Saints, 1830–1900* (Cambridge, Mass., 1958, 1967), pp. 235–322; and E. B. Long, *The Saints and the Union: Utah Territory During the Civil War* (Urbana, Illinois, 1981). The cooperative construction and operation of the Deseret Telegraph is discussed in Leonard J. Arrington, "The Deseret Telegraph—A Church-owned Public Utility," *Journal of Economic History* 11 (Spring 1951): 117–39. The impact of the coming of the railroad on Brigham's policies is examined in Leonard J. Arrington, "The Transcontinental Railroad and Mormon Economic Policy," *Pacific Historical Review* 20 (May 1951): 143–57. Brigham's attempt to mobilize women behind his policies is discussed in Leonard J. Arrington, "The Economic Role of Pioneer Mormon Women," *Western Humanities Review* 9 (Spring 1955): 145–64. On the Young Women's Retrenchment Society, studies include Susa Young Gates, *History of the Young Ladies' Mutual Improvement Association [1869–1910]* (Salt Lake City, 1911), esp. pp. 1–13; and Marba C. Josephson, *History of the YWMIA* (Salt Lake City, 1955), esp. pp. 1–22. The account of the first meeting comes from Bathsheba W. Smith (Mrs. George A.), the only woman present who was not a member of Brigham's family.

The history of the University of Deseret is detailed in Ralph V. Chamberlin, *The University of Utah: A History of Its First Hundred Years, 1850 to 1950* (Salt Lake City, 1960), pp. 55–85.

The Godbeite schism is discussed in several works, contemporary and recent. They include Ronald W. Walker, "The Commencement of the Godbeite Protest: Another View," *Utah Historical Quarterly* 42 (Summer 1974): 216–44; T. B. H. Stenhouse, *The Rocky Mountain Saints* (New York, 1872), pp. 622–45; *The Utah Magazine*, 3 vols., weekly (Salt Lake City, 1868–69); The *Mormon Tribune* and *Salt Lake Tribune*, 2 vols., weekly (Salt Lake City, 1870–71); and Edward W. Tullidge, "The Reformation in Utah," *Harper's New Monthly Magazine* 43 (1871): 602–10.

[1] JD 12:54.

[2] BY to Brigham Young, Jr., and Daniel H. Wells, 15 May 1865, BY Letterbook 7:619–25.

[3] HOJ, 14 June 1865.

[4] JD 11:119–28; Samuel Bowles, *Across the Continent* . . . (Springfield, Mass., 1865), pp. 118–21. Richard F. Burton, who had listened to some of Brigham's sermons five years earlier, mentioned his use of such colloquialisms as "he become" and "for you and I." *The City of the Saints* (New York, 1862), p. 261.

[5] Bowles, *Across the Continent*, p. 95.

[6] BY to Daniel H. Wells, as cited in JH, 20 June 1865.

[7] *War of the Rebellion: Official Records of the Union and Confederate Armies* (Washington, D.C., 1880–1900), series I, vol. L., pt. 2, p. 1186.

[8] Bowles, *Across the Continent*, p. 113.

[9] A transcript of the meeting on the issue discussed below is found in Minutes, 1855–77, p. 149–61, HDC (hereafter cited as Transcript). These quotations are from pp. 152, 154. The transcript

itself is undated, but the Potter-Young meeting is summarized in JH, 8 May 1866, and is copied from the BYMH, 1866, p. 404.

[10] Great Salt Lake City, City Ordinances & Resolutions, Book B, 1860–67, microfilm, HDC, 2 February, 20 June 1865.

[11] Transcript, p. 150.

[12] Ibid., p. 161.

[13] Ibid., p. 151.

[14] Ibid., p. 159.

[15] The boycott is discussed in Andrew Love Neff, *History of Utah, 1847 to 1869*, ed. Leland H. Creer (Salt Lake City, 1940), pp. 815–22.

[16] JD 12:270.

[17] Neff, *History of Utah*, pp. 819–20.

[18] Ibid., p. 822.

[19] This is evident from an examination of Tithing Office Ledgers, Trustee-in-Trust Collection, HDC.

[20] Heber C. Kimball to David and Charles Kimball, November 1862, HO Letterpress Copybook, 2:286.

[21] See especially Leonard J. Arrington, "Brigham Young and the Transcontinental Telegraph Line," *Improvement Era* 54 (July 1951):510 ff; and idem, "The Deseret Telegraph—A Church-owned Public Utility," *Journal of Economic History* 11 (Spring 1951): 117–39.

[22] JH, 18 February 1867.

[23] First telegram in BYTB no. 1, HDC.

[24] Chauncey W. West to John Donnellon, JH, 21 November 1865.

[25] E. B. Long, *The Saints and the Union: Utah Territory during the Civil War* (Urbana, Illinois, 1981), pp. 268–69.

[26] Ibid., p. 270.

[27] Dean L. May, "Towards a Dependent Commonwealth," in *Utah's History*, ed. Richard D. Poll (Provo, Utah, 1978), p. 217.

[28] A complete account of the ceremonies is in *Deseret News*, 11 January 1870.

[29] See Leonard J. Arrington, *Great Basin Kingdom: An Economic History of the Latter-day Saints, 1830–1900* (Cambridge, Mass., 1958, 1967), pp. 270–89.

[30] Arden Beal Olsen, "The History of Mormon Mercantile Cooperation in Utah" (Ph.D. diss., University of California, Berkeley, 1935), p. 80.

[31] Arrington, *Great Basin Kingdom*, pp. 300–1.

[32] Olsen, "Mormon Mercantile Cooperation," pp. 130–33.

[33] Arrington, *Great Basin Kingdom*, pp. 303–6.

[34] Ibid., pp. 306–7.

[35] *Deseret News*, 6 December 1867.

[36] Arrington, *Great Basin Kingdom*, pp. 251 ff.

[37] Leonard J. Arrington, "The Economic Role of Pioneer Mormon Women," *Western Humanities Review* 9 (Spring 1955): 148; BY to Albert Carrington, JH, 13 April 1869.

[38] BY family manuscript record of talk for 28 November 1869.

[39] See Susa Young Gates, *History of the Young Ladies' Mutual Improvement Association* [1869–1910] (Salt Lake City, 1911), p. 12.

[40] Ibid.

[41] See especially Ralph V. Chamberlin, *The University of Utah: A History of Its First Hundred Years, 1850 to 1950* (Salt Lake City, 1960), pp. 55–85.

[42] Ibid., p. 95.

[43] Ibid., p. 97.

[44] JD 8:40.

[45] S. S. Ivins, "Free Schools Come to Utah," *Utah Historical Quarterly* 22 (October 1954): 321–

23; and Frederick S. Buchanan, "Education among the Mormons: Brigham Young and the Schools of Utah," typescript, 1981, copy generously supplied by the author.

[46] *Salt Lake Tribune*, 9 April 1873.

[47] In what follows, I have used Edward W. Tullidge, "The Godbeite Movement," *The Utah Magazine*, 3 vols., weekly (Salt Lake City, 1868–69); *Tullidge's Quarterly Magazine* 1 (1880): 14–64; T. B. H. Stenhouse, *The Rocky Mountain Saints* (New York, 1872), pp. 622–45; Arrington, *Great Basin Kingdom*, pp. 243–44; Ronald W. Walker, "The Commencement of the Godbeite Protest: Another View," *Utah Historical Quarterly* 42 (Summer 1974); Edward W. Tullidge, "The Reformation of Utah," *Harper's New Monthly Magazine* 43 (1871): 602–10.

[48] Stenhouse, *Rocky Mountain Saints*, p. 632.

[49] Walker, "Godbeite Protest," p. 225.

[50] Stenhouse, *Rocky Mountain Saints*, p. 637.

[51] Woodruff Diary, 17, 18 October 1869.

[52] Stenhouse, *Rocky Mountain Saints*, p. 639.

[53] The proceedings that took place on 25 October 1869, pursuant to Cannon's charge dated two days earlier, are in the Minute Book of the Salt Lake Stake High Council, HDC. The following is based on that record. See also Cannon's recapitulation in *Deseret Evening News*, 1 November 1869.

[54] Minutes of the School of the Prophets, Salt Lake City, 29 January 1870.

[55] BY to Brigham Heber Young, 16 February 1870.

[56] In the municipal election of 14 February 1870, a total of 2,004 votes were cast for the church-designated candidates, and only 297 for the opposition. If one subtracts the Gentile votes, there were surely not more than a few dozen Godbeite voters. See Dean C. Jessee, ed., *Letters of Brigham Young to His Sons* (Salt Lake City, 1974), pp. 139–40.

CHAPTER 20:
RESPONDING TO THE CHALLENGES OF THE 1870S

In recent years there has been an outpouring of research on the history of women in pioneer Utah. Books include Claudia Bushman, ed., *Mormon Sisters: Women in Early Utah* (Cambridge, Mass., 1976); Vicky Burgess-Olson, ed., *Sister Saints* (Provo, Utah, 1978); and Kenneth W. Godfrey, Audrey M. Godfrey, and Jill Mulvay Derr, *Women's Voices: An Untold History of the Latter-day Saints, 1830–1900* (Salt Lake City, 1982). Significant articles and papers include Leonard J. Arrington, "Blessed Damozels: Women in Mormon History," *Dialogue* 6 (Summer 1971): 22–31; idem, "Persons for All Seasons: Women in Mormon History," *BYU Studies* 20 (Fall 1979): 39–58; Maureen Ursenbach Beecher, "Under the Sunbonnets: Mormon Women with Faces," *BYU Studies* 16 (Summer 1976): 471–84; Beverly Beeton, "Woman Suffrage in Territorial Utah," *Utah Historical Quarterly* 46 (Spring 1978): 100–20; Thomas G. Alexander, "An Experiment in Progressive Legislation: The Granting of Woman Suffrage in Utah in 1870," *Utah Historical Quarterly* 39 (January 1970): 20–30; Lawrence Foster, "From Frontier Activism to Neo-Victorian Domesticity: Mormon Women in the Nineteenth and Twentieth Centuries," *Journal of Mormon History* 6 (1979): 3–21; and three unpublished papers by Maureen Ursenbach Beecher, "Eddies in the Mainstream: Mormon Women and American Society," "The Undercurrent: Female Networks in Nineteenth Century Mormon Utah," and "Women's Work on the Mormon Frontier." Copies of the latter three generously furnished to the writer by the author.

Brigham Young's role in the educational development of Utah is told in Leonard J. Arrington, "The Latter-day Saints and Public Education," *Southwestern Journal of Social Education* 7 (Spring–Summer 1977): 9–25; Hugh Nibley, "Educating the Saints: A Brigham Young Mosaic," *BYU Studies* 11 (Autumn 1970): 61–87; Ernest L. Wilkinson, ed., *Brigham Young University: The First One Hundred Years*, 4 vols. (Provo, Utah, 1975–76); James R. Clark, "Church and State Relationships in Education in Utah" (Ph.D. diss., Utah State University, 1958); D. Michael Quinn, "The Brief Career of Young University at Salt Lake City," *Utah Historical Quarterly* 41 (Winter 1973): 69–89; and Milton Lynn Bennion, *Mormonism and Education* (Salt Lake City, 1939). Unpublished papers include Robert D. Lewis, "Banner of Crimson: The Brigham Young College in Logan"; and Frederick S. Buchanan, "The History of Education in Utah: From Rhetoric to Reality." The latter two generously furnished the writer by the authors.

The role of women in medicine in Utah is described in Keith Terry, "The Contribution of Medical Women During the First Fifty Years in Utah" (Master's thesis, Brigham Young University, 1964); Clair Noall, *Guardians of the Hearth: Utah's Pioneer Midwives and Women Doctors* (Bountiful, Utah, 1974); and Christine Croft Waters, "Pioneer Physicians of Utah, 1847–1900" (Master's thesis, University of Utah, 1976).

Political developments of the 1870s are reviewed in Orson F. Whitney, *History of Utah*, 4 vols. (Salt Lake City, 1892–1904); and in Gustive O. Larson, *The "Americanization" of Utah for Statehood* (San Marino, Calif., 1977).

The United Order is treated in Leonard J. Arrington, Feramorz Y. Fox, and Dean L. May, *Building the City of God: Community and Cooperation Among the Mormons* (Salt Lake City, 1976).

[1] JD 16:170.

[2] Wyoming passed the first female suffrage act in December 1869, enfranchising some fifteen hundred women. Utah passed a similar act in February 1870 giving the franchise to some forty-three thousand women. Utah women voted in February 1870, however, while Wyoming women were not able to exercise their franchise until October 1870. See Thomas G. Alexander, "Experiment in Progressive Legislation: The Granting of Woman Suffrage in Utah in 1870," *Utah Historical Quarterly* 39 (January 1970): 20–30; and T. A. Larson, "Emancipating the West's Dolls, Vassals, and Hapless Drudges: The Origins of Women's Suffrage in the West," in *Essays in Western History in Honor of T. A. Larson*, ed. Roger Daniels (Laramie, Wyoming, 1971), pp. 1–16. See also Ralph L. Jack, "Woman Suffrage in Utah as an Issue in the Mormon and non-Mormon Press of the Territory, 1870–1887" (Master's thesis, Brigham Young University, 1954).

[3] BY to Hooper, 4 January 1868, BY Letterbook, 10:579–81.

[4] As he predicted in a letter to F. D. Richards, 7 January 1868, BY Letterbook 10:582–85.

[5] B. H. Roberts, *A Comprehensive History of the Church of Jesus Christ of Latter-day Saints: Century I*, 6 vols. (Salt Lake City, 1930), 5:232.

[6] BY to Hooper, 11 January 1870, Letterbook 11:949–52.

[7] Minutes of Women's Mass Indignation Meeting, *Deseret News*, 19 January 1870.

[8] Beverly Beeton, "Woman Suffrage in Territorial Utah," *Utah Historical Quarterly* 46 (Spring 1978): 118.

[9] Her daughter Charlotte, who had been adopted by Brigham and reared as one of his children, had later married William Godbe, but remained faithful to Mormonism after her husband's apostasy.

[10] Beeton, "Woman Suffrage"; Alexander, "Experiment in Progressive Legislation." The governor, S. A. Dawson, was in the East and apparently Mann knew that he was opposed—it would only add more votes to the Mormon majorities. Mann was not sure he favored it and not sure that he dared exercise the authority. But the women apparently persuaded him on both counts.

[11] *Deseret News*, 15 February 1870. Despite assertions to the contrary, the act was not intended to assure Mormon political control. Utah Territory was not in danger of being overrun by outsiders. In 1870 the territory's population was eighty-seven thousand, less than forty-five hundred of whom were non-Mormons. In the years 1871 to 1896, Mormon male voters outnumbered non-Mormon voters by four to one. Obviously, it was not necessary to double the Mormon electorate by giving women the vote.

[12] Beeton, "Woman Suffrage," p. 118.

[13] Diary of Mary Jane Mount Tanner, 28 January 1878, HDC.

¹⁴ See General Epistle, January–February 1868, manuscript, p. 26, BY Circular Letters, HDC; JD 13:61.

¹⁵ Arrington, "Louisa Lula Greene Richards: Woman Journalist of the Early West," *Improvement Era* 72 (May 1969): 28–31.

¹⁶ Linda P. Wilcox, "The Imperfect Science: Brigham Young on Medical Doctors," *Dialogue* 12 (Fall 1979): 26–36; *Harper's Weekly* 13 (2 October 1869): 30; "Seventh General Epistle of the First Presidency," 18 April 1852; Robert O. Divett, *Medicine and the Mormons* (Bountiful, Utah, 1981), pp. 135–43.

¹⁷ Dean C. Jessee, ed., *Letters of Brigham Young to His Sons* (Salt Lake City, 1974); Charles S. Peterson, "A New Community: Mormon Teachers and the Separation of Church and State to Utah's Territorial Schools," *Utah Historical Quarterly* 48 (Summer 1980): 295.

¹⁸ JD 16:19.

¹⁹ A. N. Sorensen, "Brigham Young College," in *The History of a Valley: Cache Valley, Utah–Idaho*, ed. Joel E. Ricks (Logan, Utah, 1956), pp. 349–69.

²⁰ Emmeline B. Wells, "The Grain Question," *Relief Society Bulletin* 1 (September 1915): 1.

²¹ *Deseret News*, 11 August 1869.

²² Junius F. Wells, "Historic Sketch of the Y.M.M.I.A.," *Improvement Era* 28 (June 1925): 715. See also Edward H. Anderson, "The Past of Mutual Improvement," *Improvement Era* 1 (November 1897): 2–3.

²³ The story is told in Heber J. Grant and Rachel Grant Taylor, "When Brigham Young Watched a Waltz," *Improvement Era* 44 (1941): 654, 678.

²⁴ McKean to Judge Louis Dent, brother-in-law of Ulysses S. Grant, quoted in Edward W. Tullidge, *Life of Brigham Young; or, Utah and Her Founders* (New York, 1876), pp. 420–21.

²⁵ *Deseret News*, 18 October 1871.

²⁶ Nels Anderson, *Desert Saints: The Mormon Frontier in Utah* (Chicago, 1942), p. 269.

²⁷ Quoted from the *Salt Lake Tribune* in ibid., pp. 269–70.

²⁸ Anderson, *Desert Saints*, p. 271; and James B. Allen and Glen M. Leonard, *The Story of the Latter-day Saints* (Salt Lake City, 1976), pp. 246–47.

²⁹ See Roberts, *Comprehensive History* 5:442–54; Anderson, *Desert Saints*, p. 291.

³⁰ Anderson, *Desert Saints*, p. 292.

³¹ Roberts, *Comprehensive History* 5:504–5; *Deseret News Weekly*, 6 October 1875; Edward W. Tullidge, *History of Salt Lake City and Its Founders* (Salt Lake City, c. 1886), chapter 73; Orson F. Whitney, *History of Utah*, 4 vols. (Salt Lake City, 1892–1904), 2:778, 3:116n; *Tullidge's Quarterly Magazine*, July 1881, pp. 662–63.

³² On Taylor, see B. H. Roberts, *The Life of John Taylor . . .* (Salt Lake City, 1892); and Samuel W. Taylor, *The Kingdom or Nothing: The Life of John Taylor, Militant Mormon* (New York and London, 1976).

³³ Whitney, *History of Utah* 2:334.

³⁴ See especially Schuyler Colfax, *The Mormon Question. Being a speech of Vice-president Schuyler Colfax, at Salt Lake City. A reply thereto by Elder John Taylor . . .* (Salt Lake City, 1870).

³⁵ Ibid.; Roberts, *Life of John Taylor*, pp. 302–5.

³⁶ Roberts, pp. 309–10.

³⁷ See John Taylor, *Succession of the Presidency* (Salt Lake City, 1882), pp. 2, 16–17; Reed C. Durham, Jr., and Steven H. Heath, *Succession in the Church* (Salt Lake City, 1970), pp. 73–77; George Q. Cannon, JD 23:365; also JD 19:234–35.

³⁸ JD 18:260.

³⁹ Gen. 5:24; Pearl of Great Price (a Mormon scripture), Book of Moses 7:69.

⁴⁰ JH, 2 January 1870.

⁴¹ The following is based on Leonard J. Arrington, "Cooperative Community in the North: Brigham City, Utah," *Utah Historical Quarterly* 33 (Summer 1965): 198–217.

⁴² *Tullidge's Quarterly Magazine* 2 (January 1883): 400.

⁴³ Leonard J. Arrington, *Great Basin Kingdom: An Economic History of the Latter-day Saints,*

1830–1900 (Cambridge, Mass., 1958, 1967), p. 326; Lorenzo Snow received a specially inscribed copy of *Looking Backward* after its publication.

⁴⁴ JD 15:220–29.

⁴⁵ The following is based upon Leonard J. Arrington, Feramorz Y. Fox, and Dean L. May, *Building the City of God: Community and Cooperation among the Mormons* (Salt Lake City, 1976), pp. 155–75.

⁴⁶ The Office of the County Recorder of Washington County, Utah, contains the articles of incorporation of the United Order of St. George. See also the Manuscript History of St. George Stake and the St. George Historical Record, HDC.

⁴⁷ This precise wording is found on an untitled slip of paper in the United Order file, HDC.

⁴⁸ See Arrington, Fox, and May, *Building the City of God*, pp. 203–24.

⁴⁹ See Leonard J. Arrington, *Orderville, Utah: A Pioneer Mormon Experiment in Economic Organization* (Logan, Utah, 1954).

⁵⁰ Arrington, Fox, and May, *Building the City of God*, pp. 311–12.

CHAPTER 21:
THE LAST YEAR

The most important primary sources used were the Brigham Young Letterbooks 14, 15, and 16 for the years 1876 and 1877, and the Minutes of Bishops' Meetings, 1871–79, HDC. Secondary sources include the Young biographies by Anderson, Werner, Gates, and Nibley; Francis Gibbons, *Brigham Young, Modern Moses/Prophet of God* (Salt Lake City, 1981); Orson F. Whitney, *History of Utah*, 4 vols. (Salt Lake City, 1892–1904); Ray B. West, Jr., *Kingdom of the Saints: The Story of Brigham Young and the Mormons* (New York, 1957); and Dale Glen Wood, "Brigham Young's Activities in St. George During the Later Years of his Life" (Master's thesis, Brigham Young University, 1963).

Other sources include Lester E. Bush, Jr., "Brigham Young in Life and Death: A Medical Overview," *Journal of Mormon History* 5 (1978): 79–103; *Circular of the First Presidency*, July 11, 1877 (Salt Lake City, 1877); and William G. Hartley, "The Priesthood Reorganization of 1877: Brigham Young's Last Achievement," *BYU Studies* 20 (Fall 1979): 3–36.

¹ *New York Times*, 2 June 1877.

² BY to William C. Staines, 11 January 1876, Letterbook 14:124–26. See also BY to George Q. Cannon, 7 January 1876, Letterbook 14:105–8.

³ Bishops' Meetings 1871–79, 22 January 1876, p. 547.

⁴ Bishops' Meetings 1871–79, 29 January 1876, pp. 549–50.

⁵ BY to Lot Smith and other Presidents of Fifties, 18 March 1876, Letterbook 14:246–48.

⁶ BY to Alma L. Smith, 22 April 1876, Letterbook 14:314–16.

⁷ BY to Daniel W. Jones, 22 January 1876, Letterbook 14:148–51.

⁸ George Reynolds to William C. Staines, 21 January 1876, Letterbook 14:145–46.

⁹ BY to George Q. Cannon, 24 January 1876, Letterbook 14:152–55.

¹⁰ BY to Albert Carrington, 24 February 1876, Letterbook 14:218–22.

¹¹ Dale Glen Wood, "Brigham Young's Activities in St. George during the Later Years of his Life" (Master's thesis, Brigham Young University, 1963), p. 54.

¹² Preston Nibley, *Brigham Young, the Man and His Work* (Salt Lake City, 1936), p. 523; Wood, "Brigham Young's Activities," p. 54.

¹³ Susa Young Gates, "From Impulsive Girl to Patient Wife: Lucy Bigelow Young," *Utah Historical Quarterly* 45 (Summer 1977): 286.

¹⁴ A. Karl Larson and Katharine Miles Larson, eds., *Diary of Charles Lowell Walker*, 2 vols. (Logan, Utah, 1980), 1:424–26, entries for 27 May through 1 June 1876.

¹⁵ Ibid., p. 427, entry for 11 June 1876. Some changes in capitalization and quotation marks supplied.

[16] See Robert G. Cleland and Juanita Brooks, eds., *A Mormon Chronicle: The Diaries of John D. Lee, 1848–1876*, 2 vols. (San Marino, Calif., 1955), 2:377–78, 16 October 1875.

[17] See Leonard J. Arrington, "Crusade against Theocracy: The Reminiscences of Judge Jacob Smith Boreman of Utah, 1872–1877," *Huntington Library Quarterly* 24 (November 1960): 1–45, esp. p. 63, note 60. See also Juanita Brooks, *John Doyle Lee: Zealot, Pioneer Builder, Scapegoat* (Glendale, Calif., 1961).

[18] There are many treatments of the massacre, but the most complete and dependable are in B. H. Roberts, *A Comprehensive History of the Church of Jesus Christ of Latter-day Saints, Century I*, 6 vols. (Salt Lake City, 1930), 4:139–80; and Juanita Brooks, *The Mountain Meadows Massacre* (Stanford, Calif., 1950). Both Roberts and Brooks are thorough in their research and relentless in following the evidence where it leads. Brooks's most valuable insight has to do with the fact that the Mormons in southern Utah had come to perceive the Fancher Train as criminals and enemies, that a war psychology had been whipped up by the approach of a body of twenty-five hundred federal troops, and that once a series of events was set in motion it became impossible to reverse it. The possibility of Brigham Young's complicity is one that Roberts and Mrs. Brooks considered; they concluded that he could not be blamed for the crime in the sense of having ordered it. A recent work by William Wise, *Massacre at Mountain Meadows: An American Legend and a Monumental Crime* (New York, 1976), is widely inaccurate in its statements of "fact" and in its interpretations. Written without the use of the unpublished trial records, reports, letters, and diaries in the Henry E. Huntington Library & Art Gallery in San Marino, California; the Brigham Young University Library; and the LDS Archives in Salt Lake City, it is a slanted, poorly researched work.

[19] Affidavit of Collins R. Hakes, 6 May 1916, in Mountain Meadows Massacre file, HDC.

[20] BY to Elders Smith, Lake, Ballenger, Allen, and the Brethren encamped on the Little Colorado, 15 July 1876, Letterbook 14:384–88.

[21] BY to Lot Smith, 29 July 1876, Letterbook 14:401–4.

[22] BY to George Lake, 4 September 1876, Letterbook 14:452–54.

[23] BY to the Bishops, etc., 16 September 1876, Letterbook 14:502–3.

[24] BY to Dan W. Jones, 19 September 1876, Letterbook 14:510–12; BY to Lot Smith, etc., September 1876, Letterbook 14:505–9.

[25] BY to Albert Carrington, 14 July 1876, Letterbook 14:348–83.

[26] Bishops' Meetings 1871–79, 7 September 1876, p. 573.

[27] Bishops' Meetings 1871–79, 19 October 1876, p. 582; Bishops' Meetings 1871–79, 1 September 1876, pp. 575–76; BY to the president and members of the Relief Societies . . . , 4 October 1876, Letterbook 14:533–34.

[28] BY to Isaac Groo, 8 September 1876, Letterbook 14:466–73.

[29] BY to James Lewis, 16 October 1876, Letterbook 14:567–68.

[30] Bishops' Meetings 1871–79, 21 September 1876, p. 577.

[31] BY to James A. Little, 14 August 1876, Letterbook 14:429–31.

[32] BY to Alfales Young, 17 August 1876, Letterbook 14:435–37.

[33] BY to Willard Young, 19 October 1876, Letterbook 14:578–83.

[34] BY to Alfales Young, 26 October 1876, Letterbook 14:601–4.

[35] Bishops' Meetings 1871–79, 5 October 1876, p. 581.

[36] Bishops' Meetings 1871–79, 16 November 1876, p. 587.

[37] Bishops' Meetings 1871–79, 21 September 1876, p. 576.

[38] BY to Willard Young, 19 October 1876, Letterbook 14:578–83.

[39] Daniel H. Wells to A. M. Musser, 22 December 1876, Letterbook 14:663–68.

[40] Hazel Bradshaw, ed., *Under Dixie Sun* (Panguitch, Utah, 1950), p. 342.

[41] Larson and Larson, eds., *Diary of Charles Walker*, p. 433, entry for 1 January 1877. Converted to present tense.

[42] Daniel H. Wells to BY, 5 February 1877, Letterbook 14:721–25.

[43] BY to Daniel W. Jones, etc., 16 January 1877, Letterbook 16:4–8.

44 BY to Bp. Howard O. Spencer, 5 March 1877, Letterbook 16:73, 72.

45 BY to Bp. W. S. Seeley, 26 February 1877, Letterbook 16:61–62.

46 BY to Eliza Cooper, 9 March 1877, Letterbook 16:82–83.

47 BY to Presidents John W. Young and D. H. Wells, 13 February 1877, Letterbook 16:26–29.

48 Orson F. Whitney, *History of Utah*, 4 vols. (Salt Lake City, 1892–1904), 2:843.

49 JD 18:353–57, 6 April 1877.

50 BY to J. D. T. McAllister, 18 April 1877, Letterbook 16:113–25.

51 Stake records, 15 April 1877, in Wood, "Brigham Young's Activities," p. 60.

52 Whitney, *History of Utah* 2:843.

53 M. R. Werner, *Brigham Young* (New York, 1925), p. 452.

54 Whitney, *History of Utah* 2:843.

55 BY to Ward E. Pack, 23 May 1877, Letterbook 14:851–54.

56 BY to Willard Young, 23 May 1877, Letterbook 14:840–43.

57 BY to Wilford Woodruff, 12 June 1877, Letterbook 14:916–21.

58 BY to W. C. Allen, 12 July 1877, Letterbook 14:978–81.

59 Susa Young Gates, with Leah D. Widtsoe, *The Life Story of Brigham Young* (New York, 1930), p. 360.

60 William G. Hartley, "The Priesthood Reorganization of 1877: Brigham Young's Last Achievement," *BYU Studies* 20 (Fall 1979): 3–36.

61 *Circular of the First Presidency, July 11, 1877* (Salt Lake City, 1877).

62 *Deseret News Weekly*, 3 September 1877.

63 BY to Willard Young, 23 May 1877, Letterbook 14:840–43.

64 Bishops' Meetings 1871–79, 31 May, 14 June 1877, pp. 610–11.

65 Whitney, *History of Utah*, 2: 837–38, 844–45.

66 Bishops' Meetings 1871–79, 23 August 1877, p. 622. Also George Q. Cannon in Bishops' Meetings 1871–79, 6 September 1877, p. 624.

67 BY to Job Smith, 6 June 1877, Letterbook 14:875–78; BY to Helaman Pratt, 13 July 1877, Letterbook 15:5–7; BY to N. P. Beebe, 18 July 1877, Letterbook 15:47–50; BY to O. N. Liljenquist, 27 July 1877, Letterbook 15:65–68.

68 BY to Pres. Canute Peterson, 22 August 1877, Letterbook 15:157–58.

69 BY to Richard S. Horne, 17 July 1877, Letterbook 15:16–17.

70 BY to Daniel Tyler, 17 July 1877, Letterbook 15:18–19.

71 BY to Wilford Woodruff and Erastus Snow, 16 July 1877, Letterbook 15:22–25.

72 BY to Bp. John R. Murdock, 17 July 1877, Letterbook 15:31–33.

73 BY to J. D. T. McAllister, 25 July 1877, Letterbook 15:52–54.

74 Bishops' Meetings 1871–79, 26 July 1877, p. 619.

75 BY to Daniel Tyler, 17 July 1877, Letterbook 15:18–19.

76 Bishops' Meetings 1871–79, 12 July 1877, p. 616.

77 Bishops' Meetings 1871–79, 26 July 1877, pp. 619–20.

78 BY to Fera Young, 23 August 1877, Letterbook 15:170–74.

79 BY to Willard Young, 23 May 1877, Letterbook 14:840–43.

80 BY to Wilford Woodruff, 12 June 1877, Letterbook 14:916–21.

81 BY to William C. Staines, 11 May 1877, Letterbook 14:808–13.

82 BY to Wilford Woodruff, 12 June 1877, Letterbook 14:916–21; BY to Susa Dunford, 13 August 1877, Letterbook 15:144–46.

83 Lester E. Bush, Jr., "Brigham Young in Life and Death: A Medical Overview," *Journal of Mormon History* 5 (1978): 92–103.

84 Gates, *Brigham Young*, p. 361.

85 Quoted in Gates, *Brigham Young*, pp. 361–63. See also the diary of Richard Young, 29 August 1877, HDC, which describes the final passing with no mention, however, of the dying exclamation attributed to him by Zina.

86 Werner, *Brigham Young*, pp. 459–60; Nibley, *Brigham Young*, pp. 534–35.

[87] From *Deseret News*, 5 September 1877, p. 493. See also the anonymous *Death of President Young* (Salt Lake City, 1877).

[88] In Gates, *Brigham Young*, pp. 363–64; *Death of President Young*.

[89] Werner, *Brigham Young*, p. 461; Whitney, *History of Utah* 2:846–47; Gates, *Brigham Young*, p. 364; Nibley, *Brigham Young*, pp. 534–38.

EPILOGUE:
BEYOND EULOGY: THE LEGACY OF BRIGHAM YOUNG

Every biography of Brigham Young, of course, has summary statements about his life and accomplishments. Many American historians have also included a brief appraisal in their general and monographic histories and in biographies of persons with whom Young had dealings. Allan Nevins wrote that Brigham was "the most commanding single figure of the [American] West," in *The Emergence of Lincoln*, 2 vols. (New York, 1950), 1:315. Herbert Bolton compared him with other American colonizers and concluded that none "so completely molded his people and their institutions as Brigham Young molded the Mormons." See his article, "The Mormons in the Opening of the Great West," in the *Utah Genealogical and Historical Magazine* 44 (1926): 64. Favorable appraisals of him by Mormon scholars include: Milton R. Hunter, *Brigham Young the Colonizer*, 3d ed. (Independence, Missouri, 1945), esp. pp. 8–16; and Eugene England, *Brother Brigham* (Salt Lake City, 1980). A less favorable view by a non-Mormon scholar is Stanley P. Hirshson, *The Lion of the Lord: A Biography of Brigham Young* (New York, 1969).

Article-length assessments of Young include P. A. M. Taylor, "The Life of Brigham Young—A Biography Which Will Not Be Written," *Dialogue* 1 (Autumn 1966): 101–10; and Leonard J. Arrington and Ronald K. Esplin, "Building a Commonwealth: The Secular Leadership of Brigham Young," *Utah Historical Quarterly* 45 (Summer 1977): 216–32.

As I was finishing the basic text of this biography I was pleased to read Jan Shipps, "Brigham Young and His Times: A Continuing Force in Mormonism," *Journal of the West* 23 (January 1984): 48–54. An insightful essay, Dr. Shipps's paper points to Brigham's role as a gifted practical administrator, as a religious leader and spiritual counselor, and as a charismatic figure who "created a cohesive self-conscious body of Latter-day Saints whose primary identity was Mormon and whose understanding of Mormonism paralleled his own" (p. 51).

[1] JD 10:339. Sermon of 7 October 1864.

[2] Jan Shipps, "Brigham Young and His Times: A Continuing Force in Mormonism," *Journal of the West* 23 (January 1984): 53.

[3] It is true that Brigham welcomed the telegraph, the railroad, and the new medicine. But many scholars place the beginning of the long process of accommodation that resulted in what has been called "The Americanization of Mormon Utah" at a time more than ten years after Brigham's death. See "Church and Kingdom: Creative Adjustment and Reinvigoration," Ch. 13 in Leonard J. Arrington and Davis Bitton, *The Mormon Experience: A History of the Latter-day Saints* (New York, 1979), pp. 243–61; and Gustive O. Larson, *The "Americanization" of Utah for Statehood* (San Marino, Calif., 1971).

[4] Dean L. May, "Mormons," in *The Harvard Encyclopedia of American Ethnic Groups*, ed. Stephen Thernstrom (Cambridge, Mass., 1980).

[5] Katherine Coman, *Economic Beginnings of the Far West*, 2 vols. (New York, 1912), 2:184.

[6] Edward C. Banfield, *The Moral Basis of a Backward Society* (Glencoe, Illinois, 1958), pp. 7–19, 37. This is also a central theme of Thomas F. O'Dea, *The Mormons* (Chicago, 1957), and Bruce D. Blumell, "The Latter-day Saint Response to the Teton, Idaho, Flood, 1976," *Task Papers in LDS History*, no. 16 (Salt Lake City, 1976).

[7] JD 4:113. I have slightly modified the sentencing. This quotation also appears in LeRoy R. Hafen and Ann W. Hafen, *Handcarts to Zion, 1856–1860* (Glendale, California, 1960), pp. 120–21; and

in P. A. M. Taylor, "The Life of Brigham Young: A Biography Which Will Not Be Written," *Dialogue* 1 (Autumn 1966): 101–2.

[8] JD 12:228.

[9] JD 11:213.

[10] JD 13:147.

[11] An article suggesting that Brigham had "paid his dues" and therefore felt justified in asking seemingly unconscionable sacrifices of others is Ronald K. Esplin, "Inside Brigham Young: Abrahamic Tests as Preparation for Leadership," *BYU Studies* 20 (Spring 1980): 300–10.

[12] In a private conversation Brigham let down his guard and revealed his true feelings about Buchanan's decision to send federal troops to Utah in 1857–58 (Minutes, 1855–77, BYP, 24 May 1858):

> A more pusillanimus government never was upon the face of the earth. James Buchanan might have better hired a little boy to have been his adviser than to have done as he has done. The people might say we knew he was a dam'd old fool and we did not know of any use for him so we stuck him up in the President's chair to get rid of him and we are going to hire a little boy to rule our nation. He manifests more sense when the ladies visit him and he asks them his three stereotyped questions, "Have you been to Washington before? Have you seen the Capitol? Have you been to the Smithsonian Institute? I would advise you to visit them." He exhibits better sense in this than in anything else he does.

[13] BYTB, 9 December 1866. In 1868 Brigham demonstrated his understanding of human proclivities:

> I am ready to acknowledge that the Latter-day Saints are the best people, and the most willing people to do right that I know anything about. . . . But were they to be counseled, for instance, to go to the gold mines, many of them would obey with alacrity. If they were to be counseled to chew or smoke tobacco, many would lift up both hands for this, and shout for joy. If the sisters . . . were counseled to continue the use of tea and coffee they would sit up all night to bless you. When we are counseled to do that which pleases us, then are we willing to obey counsel. JD, 12:192.

[14] Mary Haskin Parker Richards Diary, 14 May 1848, HDC. Spelling corrected.

[15] JD 1:108.

[16] BY to Jesse C. Little, 26 February 1847, BYP.

[17] JD 5:97.

[18] "Letter II" to the New York *Herald*, 8 April 1852, in Jedediah M. Grant, *Three Letters to the New York Herald* (New York, 1852), p. 27. I have made a slight modification in punctuation. In writing these letters, Grant is said to have had the help of Thomas L. Kane. See Gene A. Sessions, *Mormon Thunder: A Documentary History of Jedediah Morgan Grant* (Urbana, Ill., 1982), pp. 100–10.

APPENDIXES A, B, C, D

The sources for Appendix A include Andrew Jenson, *Church Chronology*, 2d ed. (Salt Lake City, 1899); Appendix A in *Letters of Brigham Young to His Sons*, ed. Dean C. Jessee (Salt Lake City, 1974), pp. 352–56; and notes from my own examination of the Brigham Young Papers in HDC and elsewhere.

Appendix B was compiled from genealogical sheets in the LDS Genealogical Archives, Salt Lake City; S. Dilworth Young, *"Here Is Brigham": Brigham Young—the Years to 1844* (Salt Lake City, 1964); papers in the Susa Young Gates Collection, USHS; and Leonard J. Arrington and

JoAnn Jolley, "The Faithful Young Family: The Parents, Brothers, and Sisters of Brigham," *The Ensign* 10 (August 1980): 52–57.

Appendix C was compiled from Jessee, *Letters of Brigham Young to His Sons*, pp. 357–59; and from papers furnished me by Dean C. Jessee, Jeff Johnson, Carol Madsen, and Maureen Beecher.

Appendix D is based partly upon Leonard J. Arrington, "The Settlement of the Brigham Young Estate, 1877–79," *Pacific Historical Review* 21 (February 1952): 1–20. More recently, my assistant Linda Wilcox and I have gone through an extensive body of papers not accessible in 1952. Among the Brigham Young Papers in the LDS Church Archives are four boxes that contain estate papers (boxes 146–49). Included in these materials is information about the heirs—lists of all heirs, lists of wives to be supported, lists of property allotted to provide for them. Two folders contain extensive reports and papers of the auditing committee, including minutes of meetings.

Court papers include items from the probate court and the district court dealing with the settlement of the estate and the complaints brought against the executors, transcripts of the hearings held in the summer of 1879, exhibits prepared by the executors and the church for the court hearing, and the findings of the territorial supreme court on the appeal.

There are several folders of executors' papers, including lists of property, financial accounts, correspondence, official appointments as "special administrators" and then as executors, property appraisals, deeds of conveyance of property, inventories, and financial reports. Ledgers and rent receipt books are also included in these materials as well as records of the accounts of the executors with the estate.

Executive Book "H" (1877–82) at the Utah State Archives (USA) contains transcripts of supposedly all the court documents involved in the settlement of the estate. Included are Brigham Young's will and codicils, the petition for the probate of the will, special letters of administration for the executors, the appointment of the executors, appraisers, and valuers, petitions of sureties asking for release, petitions of heirs asking executors to wind up the estate, and estimates of the assets of the estate. There are also property descriptions, releases by heirs, petitions for portions of the estate, lists of trust real estate conveyed to the trustee-in-trust, lists and descriptions of property sold by the executors, transcripts of the hearing on petition of the executors for discharge, the report of the executors of their distribution of property, and appointments of successor trustees.

Also at the state archives are two large boxes of vouchers labeled "Brigham Young 4858." These include receipts from widows of payments of living allowances both before and after the estate settlement; payments to doctors, engineers, craftsmen, laborers, merchants, etc. for services and goods provided either for the heirs or for estate property; payments for debts of Brigham Young; court fees, advertising expenses, and other expenses of the estate; and financial reports (some of which are also in the Church Archives).

Relevant outgoing correspondence of John Taylor on estate matters is in the First Presidency letterpress copybook for the years 1877–79 (vols. 1–3). Incoming letters to him are in the John Taylor Collection (both in the Church Archives).

[1] On the background of the properties involved in the settlement of the Brigham Young estate see Leonard J. Arrington, *Great Basin Kingdom: An Economic History of the Latter-day Saints, 1830–1900* (Cambridge, Mass., 1958).

[2] 12 Stat. L. 501 (1862), entitled "An Act to Punish and Prevent the Practice of Polygamy in the Territories of the United States, and Other Places, and Disapproving and Annulling Certain Acts of the Legislative Assembly of the Territory of Utah."

[3] Cited in Edward W. Tullidge, *History of Salt Lake City and Its Founders* (Salt Lake City, 1888), p. 263.

[4] These bills are summarized and their history reviewed in Orson F. Whitney, *History of Utah*, 4 vols. (Salt Lake City, 1892–1904), vol. 2.

[5] JH, 6 April 1871.

[6] Quoted in Joseph J. Cannon, "George Q. Cannon," *The Instructor*, June 1945, p. 259.

[7] *Deseret News*, 5 August 1879.

[8] Complete text of the will can be found in *Heart Throbs of the West*, ed. Kate B. Carter, 12 vols. (Salt Lake City, 1936–51), 7:338–52.

[9] JH, 8 April 1873; BY to the *New York Herald*, JH, 10 April 1873.

[10] *Deseret News*, 30 June 1879; findings of the Utah Supreme Court as reproduced in the *Deseret News*, 9 Ocotober 1888, and 136 J.S. 1, 10ff.

[11] Cannon, "George Q. Cannon," p. 309.

[12] Ibid., pp. 308–9.

[13] *Salt Lake Herald*, 5 September 1877.

[14] BYP, box 146, folder 1, HDC.

[15] *Deseret News*, 5 August 1878.

[16] Cannon, "George Q. Cannon," pp. 259–60.

[17] Executive Book "H," Sections 24, 30, 36, pp. 11–19, USA.

[18] Ibid., Section 35, p. 18.

[19] 24 September 1877, BYP, box 146, folder 14.

[20] Williams and Young to executors, 28 October 1878, BYP, box 147, folder 2. The estate also paid other extra expenses for her, such as bills at ZCMI to the amount of $1,425. Voucher no. 139, 27 February 1886, USA—box labeled "Brigham Young 4858."

[21] 20, 28 November 1877, BYP, box 146, folder 14; Williams and Young to executors, 18 February 1878, BYP, box 147, folder 1; John W. Young to executors, 21 March 1878, BYP, box 147, folder 1. This claim was allowed and approved 5 April 1878.

[22] *Salt Lake Herald*, 5 September 1877; Roberts, *A Comprehensive History of the Church of Jesus Christ of Latter-day Saints: Century I*, 6 vols. (Salt Lake City, 1930), 5:525.

[23] M. R. Werner, *Brigham Young* (New York, 1925), p. 331.

[24] Court document reproduced in the *Deseret News*, 30 June 1879.

[25] Statement of George Q. Cannon, *Deseret News*, 5 August 1879.

[26] This is discussed in Roberts, *Comprehensive History*, 5:521, and John Taylor, *Succession in the Priesthood* (Salt Lake City, 1881), pp. 16–17.

[27] *Millennial Star* 40 (1878): 677.

[28] BYP, box 146, folder 3.

[29] *Millennial Star* 14 (1852): 323.

[30] Ibid., 40 (1878): 679.

[31] "Draft for proposed basis of settlement," First Presidency letterpress copybook, vol. 1, p. 209, 27 November 1877.

[32] Minutes, 27 November 1877, BYP, box 146, folder 4.

[33] BYP, box 146, folder 13, n.d.

[34] BYP, box 146, folder 4, possibly December 1877 (falls between two items dated in December).

[35] Joseph F. Smith to John Taylor, 30 March 1878, First Presidency letterpress copybook, vol. 1, p. 469.

[36] JH, 10 April 1878.

[37] According to the *Millennial Star* 40 (1878): 679, all heirs signed the receipts except "three or four."

[38] *Deseret News*, 30 June 1879.

[39] Cannon, "George Q. Cannon," p. 259. See also BYP, box 146, folder 2. There is a discrepancy of $200. The committee uses the figure of $999,633, but the subtotals add up to $999,433.

[40] *Deseret News*, 20 October 1891.

[41] Ibid.

[42] JH, 19, 20 April 1878.

[43] BYP, box 146, folder 7; JH, 3, 21, 24 May 1880.

[44] 13 April 1878, BYP, box 147, folder 1.

[45] Ibid.

[46] Woodruff Diary, 19, 20 April 1878.

[47] John Taylor to George Q. Cannon, 23 April 1878, First Presidency letterpress copybook, vol. 1, pp. 518–20.

[48] BYP, box 147, folder 1. See also George Q. Cannon to John Taylor, 30 April 1878, John Taylor Collection, box 1, folder 16.

[49] Case reviewed by the territorial supreme court in Emeline A. Young et al. v. George Q. Cannon et al., 2 Utah 560 (1879). See also *Deseret News Weekly*, 18 June 1879.

[50] As soon as the complaint was filed, the other heirs made it plain that they were not involved in the suit. More than forty-five of them signed a statement on 19 June 1879 saying that they declined to join the suit as plaintiffs. But even after the suit had been settled, many of the uninvolved heirs felt it necessary to make the record clear and issued a public statement that was printed in the *Deseret News*. In it they emphasized that they had "no sympathy, in any way, with the plaintiffs in said suit; and a document was signed by us to this effect last June, immediately after the inauguration of the suit, repudiating any connection therewith." That statement, they went on to say, was supposed to have been published but never got into print. They wished everyone to know that they did not sympathize with the plaintiffs. On the contrary, they had aided the executors and observed the terms of the original settlement. This statement was signed by twenty-seven heirs and endorsed as being "correct, to the best of our knowledge," by John Taylor on behalf of himself, the Council of the Twelve, and the executors. BYP, box 146, folders 2, 10.

[51] BYP, box 146, folders 9, 12. Folder 12 is apparently a court transcript.

[52] On Judge Boreman, see Leonard J. Arrington, "Crusade against Theocracy: The Reminiscences of Judge Jacob Smith Boreman of Utah, 1872–1877," *Huntington Library Quarterly* 24 (November 1960):1–45.

[53] Cannon, "George Q. Cannon," pp. 346–51.

[54] Emeline A. Young et al. v. George Q. Cannon et al., 2 Utah 560 (1879). See also JH, 1, 2, 4, 28 August 1879.

[55] JH, 5 August, 4 October 1879.

[56] JH, 3, 4 May 1880.

[57] Roberts, *Comprehensive History* 5:531.

[58] JD 1:314, 20 February 1853; JD 18:260, 8 October 1876.

[59] JD 1:313–14.

[60] The charge that Brigham's wealth was obtained by the ruthless exploitation of a poverty-stricken community is made, among other places, in T. B. H. Stenhouse, *The Rocky Mountain Saints* (New York, 1872), pp. 665–68.

[61] Governor's Message, State of Deseret, 21 January 1866, JH.

MANUSCRIPT COLLECTIONS: LDS CHURCH ARCHIVES

The most extensive collection of manuscript and printed sources for the life of Brigham Young, the history of the Mormons, and the history of the states and territories in which Brigham Young lived and traveled is in the Library-Archives of the Historical Department of the Church of Jesus Christ of Latter-day Saints, Salt Lake City, Utah. The Church Archives, as this depository is called, with the assistance of professional historians then connected with the Historical Department and now forming the staff of the Joseph Fielding Smith Institute for Church History at Brigham Young University, completed in 1980 the cataloguing of the massive primary materials for Brigham Young's life. In addition to a near-complete collection of books, periodicals, and newspapers published by and about Latter-day Saints, from 1830 to the present, the manuscript holdings of particular relevance to Brigham Young include:

1. Brigham Young Diaries and Office Journals, 1832–63. Three volumes of holograph diaries cover the following periods: April 9 [14], 1832, to September 9, 1836, 68 pages of holograph writing describing 6 short missionary journeys; July 27, 1837, to April 14, 1845, 116 pages of holograph with some gaps in the narrative; and October 2, 1840, to August 1, 1844, 130 pages of faded holograph with an interrupted narrative. Nine additional volumes kept by clerks or Young's private secretaries cover the years 1844 to 1863 and add details about his routine, personal habits, and demanding responsibilities. Because of different clerks, there is some overlapping. Some of the volumes give the name of the clerk and add the phrase "indited by Brigham Young," which suggests that Young dictated or approved most or all of the entries. The office journals cover the following periods:

September 28, 1844, to February 3, 1846. This is a first-person Brigham Young account in the handwritings of William Clayton, Evan Greene, John D. Lee, and Willard Richards.

April 28, 1850 to July 6, 1852
August 16, 1852 to March 25, 1853
March 25, 1853 to July 12, 1853
November 8, 1855 to December 20, 1856
December 20, 1856 to December 24, 1857
January 1, 1857 to May 26, 1857
December 5, 1857 to January 15, 1860
August 8, 1858 to September 30, 1863

One other journal has surfaced, covering the period May 27, 1857 to September 21, 1857. Part of it is in the third person, written by Thomas D. Brown; most of it is in Brigham's first person and in the handwriting of Brigham's son, Joseph A. Housed in the Western Americana Collection at the University of Utah, the journal was recently published as *Diary of Brigham Young, 1857*, ed. Everett L. Cooley (Salt Lake City, 1980). This is the only journal that has been published and made generally available to scholars.

2. "History of Brigham Young" Manuscripts, 1801–44. In 1856 Wilford Woodruff, Assistant LDS Church Historian, began compiling, with the close association and supervision of Brigham Young, Young's autobiographical history, containing information on Brigham Young's family

and a lengthy autobiography of Young from birth to 1844. Most of the material is organized in chronological order under date captions. Three drafts of this "History," found in the Historian's Office Papers, preceded its publication. These are referred to as no. 1, no. 2, and no. 3, in order of preparation. There is evidence that Young not only assisted in the preparation of each of the three versions but that he also approved the "final" manuscript. This "History" was originally published as the "History of Brigham Young" in the *Deseret News*, 27 January–24 March 1858; it was republished in England by the *Latter-day Saints' Millennial Star* (Liverpool) 25 (9 May 1863) to 26 (4 June 1864). It can also be consulted in a modern printing: Elden J. Watson, ed., *Manuscript History of Brigham Young, 1801–1844* (Salt Lake City, 1968).

3. The Manuscript History of Brigham Young, 1801–77. In forty-seven hand-written volumes—about one thousand pages per volume—this history was commenced under the direction of George A. Smith and Wilford Woodruff in 1856. The bound volumes in which the history appears contain the legend "Documentary History." For that reason the collection was once referred to as the Documentary History of the Church. The commonly used title for the collection today, Manuscript History of Brigham Young, serves to distinguish manuscript volumes from the printed "History of Brigham Young," described above. The first portion was published in Elden J. Watson, ed., *Manuscript History of Brigham Young, 1801–1844* (Salt Lake City, 1968). The period from August 9, 1844, to February 28, 1846, with some additional excerpts to 1848, was published in B. H. Roberts, ed., *History of the Church: Apostolic Interregnum* (Salt Lake City, 1932), pp. 247–603. The portion from January 1, 1846, to July 31, 1847, was published in Elden J. Watson, ed., *Manuscript History of Brigham Young, 1846–1847* (Salt Lake City, 1971).

4. The Journal History of the Church, 1830–1981. Most of the Manuscript History of Brigham Young is copied into the Journal History of the Church, a collection of readily available, chronologically arranged scrapbook volumes that have typescript entries and printed documents for each day from the organization of the Mormon church, April 6, 1830, to the present. The Journal History, as it is usually called, was compiled under the direction of Andrew Jenson, beginning in the 1880s, and is well indexed. An even 100 volumes cover the period from August 1844, when Brigham Young assumed leadership of the Mormons, until his death in August 1877. Thirty-one additional volumes cover the years from the organization of the church in 1830 to 1844 and 1877 to 1879, when the Brigham Young estate was settled. Each of these volumes averages approximately two hundred legal-size pages. The principal sources for the materials included in the 100 Brigham Young–era volumes are excerpts from the Brigham Young Manuscript History, usually denoted Doc. Hist. or HBY; clippings from the *Deseret Evening News*, denoted DEN; *Latter-day Saints' Millennial Star*, denoted MS; *Salt Lake Herald* and other local Utah newspapers; occasional typescripts of letters and memoranda written and received at church headquarters; and excerpts from diaries describing events of a given day. There are also occasional entries from the Church Historian's Office Journal, denoted HOJ. (The abbreviations in the present work are not necessarily the same as those used in the BYMH.)

5. Brigham Young Letterbooks. These twenty-one volumes of about one thousand pages each contain letterpress copies of letters hand-written by Brigham Young or his staff from 1844 through 1877. These are the richest single sources of Brigham Young's thoughts, attitudes, motives, policies, and procedures. One selection of these letters has been published in Dean C. Jessee, ed., *Letters of Brigham Young to His Sons* (Salt Lake City, 1974).

6. Brigham Young Incoming Correspondence. Twenty-eight archival boxes, with perhaps one thousand leaves per box, house the letters that Brigham Young received, 1844–77.

7. Brigham Young Telegram Books. Four bound volumes and one archival box of loose telegrams contain copies of approximately twelve hundred telegrams sent or received by Young's office, 1861–77.

8. Brigham Young Papers. Fifteen archival boxes contain his speeches, minutes of meetings, rough draft copies of letters, certificates, miscellaneous papers, sermons, and papers connected with the settlement of the Brigham Young estate. About eight hundred of Brigham Young's sermons and "discourses," all of which were delivered extemporaneously or impromptu, were

recorded, about half in verbatim form. About half of the latter were published, mostly in the *Journal of Discourses*, 26 vols. (Liverpool, 1854–86). Some of these were published also in the *Deseret News* and reprinted in the *Latter-day Saints' Millennial Star* and in other contemporary Mormon periodicals.

9. Brigham Young's Political and Indian Affairs Papers. Eleven archival boxes document Young's activities as governor of the Territory of Utah and superintendent of Indian affairs, 1851–58.

10. Brigham Young Business Records and Office Papers. Seventy-six archival boxes contain the documentation of Young's extensive business affairs and office operations. Memoranda books, account books, legal papers, drafts, notes, and receipts are all represented.

11. Historian's Office Journal, 1845–1961. Thirty volumes of this valuable source cover the Brigham Young era.

12. First Presidency Papers, 1833–1969, of which one box contains Brigham Young material. Particularly helpful is James R. Clark, comp., *Messages of the First Presidency*, 6 vols. (Salt Lake City, 1965–75), esp. 1:231–363 and 2:25–295.

13. Council of Twelve Papers, 1847–1969, of which one box contains Brigham Young material.

14. Brigham Young–related collections. This category includes the hundreds of account books in the "Trustee-in-Trust" collection, detailing the operation of public works and other church-related enterprises that Young oversaw. Young's activities in directing Mormon emigration can be studied in the "Emigration Papers" collection. The "Utah Territory" collection provides additional documentation of his political activities.

15. Diaries and Papers of Brigham Young's Close Associates. These include diaries and/or papers of Heber C. Kimball, Willard Richards, Daniel H. Wells, George A. Smith, Orson Pratt, Wilford Woodruff, Orson Hyde, Erastus Snow, Horace Eldredge, Thomas B. Marsh, William H. Hooper, Parley P. Pratt, John Bernhisel, Jedediah M. Grant, and Lorenzo Snow. Also found here are journals and papers of his clerks (Thomas Bullock and William Clayton); three of his wives (Eliza R. Snow, Emily D. Partridge, and Zina D. Huntington); four of his children (Susa, John W., Brigham, Jr., and Willard); and several of his brothers, sisters, nieces, and nephews. There are also several hundred original diaries of contemporaries of Brigham Young, including missionary companions; ward, stake, mission, and general church leaders; and colonizers and business associates. The task of making the most effective use of these was facilitated by using Davis Bitton, *Guide to Mormon Diaries and Autobiographies* (Provo, Utah, 1977).

16. There are several hundred boxes of minute books, account books, and papers of virtually all the enterprises with which Brigham Young was connected, such as banks, railroads, manufactories, wholesale and retail establishments, and farms and irrigation enterprises.

17. Journal histories, often called manuscript histories, of the stakes and missions of the church, one or more volumes for each stake and mission. These are chronologically arranged documentary histories of the various settlements and ecclesiastical units of the Latter-day Saints, made up to resemble the Journal History of the Church. They include relevant typescripts of diaries, letters, reports, minutes of meetings, sermons, and newspaper clippings pertaining to the locality concerned. An abbreviated summary compilation is Andrew Jenson, *Encyclopedic History of the Church of Jesus Christ of Latter-day Saints* (Salt Lake City, 1941).

18. Original journals, account books, minute books, and other records of immigration and colonizing parties, of ecclesiastical organizations, and of associations, corporations, and other business enterprises with which the church and its officers have been associated.

19. Economic Records (Tithing, Trustee-in-Trust, and other Financial Accounts). These include dated entries of contributions to the church in the form of labor, commodities, livestock, handicrafts, and cash; transactions of individuals and businesses with the church tithinghouses, involving both withdrawals and receipts; church appropriations for the construction of buildings and other public works; properties acquired and disposed of; and other financial records. Several hundred ledgers and account books are extant, testifying to the careful recording of all transactions, most of which involved noncash exchanges during the Brigham Young era.

20. Three other sources known to exist in the vault of the First Presidency of the church but

not made available to me for this study are the diaries of George Q. Cannon and Francis M. Lyman, and the "Book of the Law of the Lord." The latter contains manuscript revelations, blessings, names of contributors to the Nauvoo Temple, names of tithepayers, and names of those who consecrated their properties to the church. I wish to acknowledge also my failure to locate the diaries of John Taylor, Brigham Young's successor, which are known to have existed in the Church Archives in the 1920s but which are not there now.

OTHER ARCHIVAL COLLECTIONS

The Utah State Historical Society, Salt Lake City, in its library and archives division has primary source material not available in the LDS Church Library-Archives, including Utah territorial documents and the great mass of materials accumulated and typed by the Utah Works Progress Administration. The Salt Lake Public Library is a valuable source for early Utah newspapers and periodicals, both Mormon and non-Mormon. The libraries of the University of Utah, Utah State University, and Brigham Young University each have extensive holdings of printed and manuscript materials dealing with Brigham Young, Utah, the Mormons, and the West. Each has prepared a bibliography of such holdings. The Daughters of Utah Pioneers, in their Pioneer Memorial Building, Salt Lake City, have collected a large number of manuscripts and ephemera, which are not generally available, but some of which have been reproduced, under the editorship of Kate B. Carter, in *Heart Throbs of the West*, 12 vols. (Salt Lake City, 1936–51); *Treasures of Pioneer History*, 6 vols. (Salt Lake City, 1952–57); *Our Pioneer Heritage*, 20 vols. (Salt Lake City, 1958–77); and *An Enduring Legacy*, 5 vols. (Salt Lake City, 1978–82).

Outside of Utah, important collections are found in the Henry E. Huntington Library & Art Gallery, San Marino, California; Bancroft Library, University of California, Berkeley, California; and in the Coe Collection, Yale University, New Haven, Connecticut. The Bancroft collection is described in S. George Ellsworth, "A Guide to the Manuscripts in the Bancroft Library Relating to the History of Utah," *Utah Historical Quarterly* 22 *(1954):* 197–247. The Yale holdings are described in Mary C. Withington, comp., *A Catalogue of Manuscripts in the Collection of Western Americana Founded by William Robertson Coe, Yale University Library* (New Haven, 1952). The Huntington collection, which features a large number of diaries and journals, is briefly described in Peter Crawley, "Mormon Americana at the Huntington Library," *Dialogue: A Journal of Mormon Thought* 6 (Autumn–Winter 1971): 138–40. A valuable part of the Bancroft holdings is a 550-page manuscript excerpt from the Manuscript History of Brigham Young that was copied by clerks in the Church Historian's Office and sent to H. H. Bancroft at the time he was writing his *History of Utah* in the 1880s. This material is bound into three volumes entitled "Early Records of Utah [1847–51]," "Incidents in Utah History [1852–54]," and "Utah Historical Incidents [1855–67]."

The National Archives, Washington, D.C., contains a wealth of documents pertaining to Brigham Young and Utah territorial history; and the Library of Congress and New York Public Library have extensive printed holdings. The Library of Congress also has the large collection of typescripts of Mormon diaries and journals prepared by Works Progress Administration. The Houghton Library, Harvard University, has a large Mormon pamphlet collection, while the New York Public Library is particularly rich in early Mormoniana. The list of items in the Berrian Collection of the latter is an excellent beginning bibliography and is available in the *New York Public Library Bulletin* for March 1909. A list of museums, which frequently contain manuscripts, is published in the *Utah Historical Quarterly* 21 (1953): 43–56.

GENERAL WORKS ON UTAH,
THE MORMONS, AND THE WEST

General histories on Utah, the Mormons, and the West that have been particularly helpful in tracing and interpreting the life of Brigham Young include: H. H. Bancroft, *History of Utah, 1540–1886* (San Francisco, 1889); Edward W. Tullidge, *History of Salt Lake City and Its Founders* (Salt Lake City, c. 1886); Orson F. Whitney, *History of Utah*, 4 vols. (Salt Lake City, 1892–1904); S. George Ellsworth, *Utah's Heritage* (Salt Lake City, 1972); and Richard D. Poll, ed., *Utah's History* (Provo, Utah, 1978). Nels Anderson's penetrating and instructive *Desert Saints: The Mormon Frontier in Utah* (Chicago, 1942), is as much a history of Utah to 1900 as it is a study of the Mormons and their social system. A social and economic history covering the Brigham Young period is Leonard J. Arrington, *Great Basin Kingdom: An Economic History of the Latter-day Saints, 1830–1900* (Cambridge, Mass., 1958, 1967).

Biographical sources include: Andrew Jenson, *Latter-day Saint Biographical Encyclopedia*, 4 vols. (Salt Lake City, 1901–36), which gives biographies of prominent Mormons; Frank W. Esshom, *Pioneers and Prominent Men of Utah* (Salt Lake City, 1913); and biographical sections in the Tullidge and Whitney volumes mentioned above.

The most important contemporary newspaper in pioneer Utah was the *Deseret News* (Salt Lake City), published by the Latter-day Saints' church. Founded in 1850, it had a weekly edition until 1922, and a daily edition from 1867 to date. Microfilm copies have been made available to libraries by the Church Historian's Office. It is a veritable mine of information on all aspects of Utah history. Good introductions to it are provided in Wendell J. Ashton, *Voice in the West: Biography of a Pioneer Newspaper* (New York, 1950); A. R. Mortensen, "The *Deseret News* and Utah, 1850–1867" (Ph.D. diss., University of California, Los Angeles, 1949); and Monte B. McLaws, *Spokesman for the Kingdom: Early Mormon Journalism and the Deseret News, 1830–1898* (Provo, Utah, 1977). Also valuable are *The Herald* (Salt Lake City), published daily from 1870 to 1909, during most of its life a Mormon, but not church-owned, paper; and the *Salt Lake Tribune*, a non-Mormon paper published daily from 1871 to date.

The *Utah Historical Quarterly*, published by the Utah State Historical Society since 1932, has printed hundreds of useful documents and annotated articles on phases of Utah history during the Brigham Young period.

Most of the published contemporary travel accounts deal chiefly with the geography, conditions of travel, and the peculiarities of the Mormon religion. The best bibliography of such accounts is in Henry R. Wagner, *The Plains and the Rockies: A Bibliography of Original Narratives of Travel and Adventure, 1800–1865*, 3d ed., revised by Charles L. Camp (Columbus, Ohio, 1953). The most useful will be mentioned in connection with specific chapters. There is an exciting volume of Utah and Mormon commentaries: William Mulder and A. Russell Mortensen, eds., *Among the Mormons: Historic Accounts by Contemporary Observers* (New York, 1958).

Two recent histories of the Mormons that incorporate current research and interpretation are James B. Allen and Glen M. Leonard, *The Story of the Latter-day Saints* (Salt Lake City, 1976), a well-written narrative history, with an excellent bibliography, and Leonard J. Arrington and Davis Bitton, *The Mormon Experience: A History of the Latter-day Saints* (New York, 1979), topical and analytical approach. An earlier, authoritative official history of the church is B. H. Roberts, *A Comprehensive History of the Church of Jesus Christ of Latter-day Saints: Century I*, 6 vols. (Salt Lake City, 1930). A contemporary document of value is George A. Smith, *The Rise, Progress and Travels of the Church* (Salt Lake City, 1869, 1872, 1873).

Primary sources of Mormon doctrine, the knowledge of which is basic to an understanding of Brigham Young's policies and practices, are the so-called "standard works"—The Bible, the Book of Mormon, the Pearl of Great Price, and especially the Doctrine and Covenants of the Church of Jesus Christ of Latter-day Saints, containing revelations given to Joseph Smith and his successors (Salt Lake City, many editions). Explanation and elaboration are found in the compiled sermons and writings of the prophets of the church, of whom Joseph Smith, John Taylor, Wilford Woodruff, Lorenzo Snow, and Joseph F. Smith were contemporaries of Brigham Young. Complete texts of the sermons of nineteenth-century prophets and other general church authorities were published periodically in the *Journal of Discourses*, 26 vols. (Liverpool, 1854–86). The variety of subjects covered in these addresses reflects official interest and church participation in all phases of pioneer life. Official textbooks on church doctrine include James E. Talmage, *A Study of the Articles of Faith*, 19th ed. (Salt Lake City, 1940); and Lowell L. Bennion, *The Religion of the Latter-day Saints* (Salt Lake City, 1940).

The earliest general interpretation of Mormon social history is E. E. Ericksen, *The Psychological and Ethical Aspects of Mormon Group Life* (Chicago, 1923), in which particular attention is paid to "the genetic development of Mormon group consciousness." A more recent work by a sociologist with a deep understanding of Mormon social philosophy is Thomas F. O'Dea, "Mormon Values: The Significance of a Religious Outlook for Social Action" (Ph.D. dissertation, Harvard University, 1953). Part of this brilliant work is now available as *The Mormons* (Chicago, 1957).

Other interpretive studies are Gustive O. Larson, *The "Americanization" of Utah for Statehood* (San Marino, Calif., 1971); Therald N. Jensen, "Mormon Theory of Church and State" (Ph.D. dissertation, University of Chicago, 1938); S. George Ellsworth, "A History of Mormon Missions in the United States and Canada, 1830–1860" (Ph.D. dissertation, University of California, Berkeley, 1951); G. Homer Durham, "Political Interpretation of Mormon History," *Pacific Historical Review* 13 (1944): 136–50; and Gaylon L. Caldwell, "Mormon Conceptions of Individual Rights and Political Obligation" (Ph.D. dissertation, Stanford University, 1952). A skillful short interpretation, with emphasis on the gathering, is William Mulder, *The Mormons in American History* (Salt Lake City, 1957), which was the 1957 Reynolds Lecture at the University of Utah. Professor Mulder carries out the same theme at greater length in his highly readable *Homeward to Zion: The Mormon Migration from Scandinavia* (Minneapolis, 1957). A brief study of Mormon economic organization is P. A. M. Taylor and Leonard J. Arrington, "Religion and Planning in the Far West: The First Generation of Mormons in Utah," *Economic History Review* 11 (July 1958): 71–86.

For many persons the best introduction to "the Mormon way" will be found in the accurate and charming essays of Wallace Stegner in *Mormon Country* (New York, 1942). Also of interest is Austin Fife and Alta Fife, *Saints of Sage & Saddle: Folklore among the Mormons* (Bloomington, Indiana, 1956). A study of the negative visual stereotyping of Mormons, including a considerable discussion of Brigham Young and his era, is Gary L. Bunker and Davis Bitton, *Mormon Graphic Image, 1834–1914* (Salt Lake City, 1983).

The Latter-day Saints' Millennial Star, published monthly in Manchester, England, from 1840 to 1842; monthly in Liverpool, 1842 to 1845; semimonthly from 1845 to 1851; and weekly, in Liverpool, January 1, 1852 to December 31, 1970, is of tremendous value because of its reports of general conferences in Salt Lake City, its letters from church authorities to agents in England describing events in the Great Basin, and its extensive coverage of the church picture in the West. Also of value are *The Contributor* (Salt Lake City), published monthly by the church from 1879 to 1896; and its successor, *The Improvement Era* (Salt Lake City), published monthly from 1897 to 1970. Occasionally there have been articles of historical value in *The Juvenile Instructor* (Salt Lake City), published semimonthly by the church 1866–88, monthly 1889–1929, and monthly as *The Instructor* from 1930 to 1970.

WORKS ON BRIGHAM YOUNG: BOOKS, ARTICLES, AND THESES

Many nineteenth-century political and literary figures traveled to Zion as a part of their tour of the Great American West and wrote books telling their experiences and impressions of Brigham Young. Among the most helpful of those written in the 1850s are: J. W. Gunnison, *The Mormons*, *or Latter-day Saints* . . . (London, 1857); S. N. Carvalho, *Incidents of Travel and Adventure in the Far West* (New York, 1858); Jules Remy and Julius Brenchley, *A Journey to Great-Salt-Lake City*, 2 vols. (London, 1861); Richard F. Burton, *The City of the Saints* . . . (New York, 1862); John Hyde, Jr., *Mormonism: Its Leaders and Designs* (New York, 1857); Benjamin G. Ferris, *Utah and the Mormons* (New York, 1854); and Horace Greeley, *An Overland Journey from New York to San Francisco in the Summer of 1859* (New York, 1863).

Accounts of the 1860s and 1870s include: Samuel Bowles, *Across the Continent* . . . (Springfield, Mass., 1865) and *Our New West* (Hartford, Conn., 1867); Charles Wentworth Dilke, *Greater Britain: A Record of Travel in English-speaking Countries during 1866 and 1867*, 2d ed. in 2 vols. (London, 1869); [William Elkanah Waters], *Life among the Mormons, and a March to their Zion* (1868); Fitz Hugh Ludlow, *The Heart of the Continent* . . . (London, 1870); James F. Rusling, *Across America: Or, the Great West and the Pacific Coast* (New York, 1874), esp. pp. 157–222; John W. Clampitt, *Echoes from the Rocky Mountains* [in Utah 1866–69] (Chicago, 1889), esp. pp. 253–428; James Bonwick, *The Mormons and the Silver Mines* (London, 1872), particularly pp. 164–75; John Codman, *The Mormon Country* . . . (New York, 1874); John Todd, *The Sunset Land* . . . (Boston, 1870), esp. 161–212; Miriam F. Leslie, *California: A Pleasure Trip from Gotham to the Golden State* (New York, 1877), esp. pp. 70–103; and the sympathetic account of the wife of Thomas L. Kane, published as Elizabeth Wood Kane, *Twelve Mormon Homes Visited in Succession on a Journey through Utah to Arizona* (Philadelphia, 1874). Also helpful are two significant articles: Charles Marshall, "Salt Lake City and the Valley Settlements," *Fraser's Magazine* (London), n.s., 4 (1871): 97–108; and R. H. Seeley, "The Mormons and Their Religion," *Scribner's Monthly* (later *The Century*) 3 (1872): 396–408. The earliest of these travel accounts have been discussed in Edwina Snow, "Singular Saints: The Image of the Mormons in Book-Length Travel Accounts, 1847–1857" (Master's thesis, George Washington University, 1972); and in Rebecca Cornwall and Leonard J. Arrington, "Men and Women of Letters Encounter Brigham Young," *BYU Studies*, in press.

A year before Brigham Young's death, Edward W. Tullidge published a eulogistic *Life of Brigham Young; or, Utah and Her Founders* (New York, 1876). Other biographies include: Edward Henry Anderson, *The Life of Brigham Young* (Salt Lake City, 1893); Frank J. Cannon and George L. Knapp, *Brigham Young and His Mormon Empire* (New York, 1913); Eugene England, *Brother Brigham* (Salt Lake City, 1980); Susa Young Gates, in collaboration with Leah D. Widtsoe, *The Life Story of Brigham Young* (New York, 1930); Stanley P. Hirshson, *The Lion of the Lord: A Biography of Brigham Young* (New York, 1969); Preston Nibley, *Brigham Young, the Man and His Work* (Salt Lake City, 1936; 5th ed., 1965), an outgrowth of a series of articles in the Church Section of the *Deseret News* during the years 1934 and 1935; Clarissa Young Spencer and Mabel Harmer, *Brigham Young at Home* (Salt Lake City, 1947), originally published as *One Who Was Valiant* (Caldwell, Idaho, 1940); Mrs. Catherine Waite, *The Mormon Prophet and His Harem; or, An Authentic History of Brigham Young, His Numerous Wives and Children* (Cambridge, Mass., 1866); M. R. Werner, *Brigham Young* (New York, 1925), which had appeared as a series in *The Ladies' Home Journal* (1924–25); Ray B. West, Jr., *Kingdom of the Saints: The Story of Brigham Young and the Mormons* (New York, 1957); Leah D. Widtsoe, *Brigham Young, the Man of the Hour* (Salt Lake City, 1947). Works that portray part of his life are cited in chapters that deal with those phases.

Additional articles are cited in the notes to particular chapters. Particularly helpful are:

Arrington, Leonard J. "The Settlement of the Brigham Young Estate, 1877–79." *Pacific Historical Review* 21 (February 1952): 1–20; and "Willard Young: The Prophet's Son at West Point." *Dialogue* 4 (Winter 1969): 37–46.

Arrington, Leonard J., and Esplin, Ronald K. "Building a Commonwealth: The Secular Leadership of Brigham Young." *Utah Historical Quarterly* 45 (Summer 1977): 216–32.

Bennion, Glynn. "Brigham Young and Jim Bridger." *The Improvement Era* 44 (July 1941): 400ff.

Bitton, Davis. "George Francis Train and Brigham Young." *BYU Studies* 18 (Spring 1978): 410–27.

Bolino, August C. "Brigham Young as Entrepreneur." *American Journal of Economics and Sociology* 18 (January 1959): 181–92.

Bruce, Donald M. "Brigham Young and Horace S. Eldredge." *The Improvement Era* 45 (April 1942): 214, 215.

Bush, Lester E., Jr. "Brigham Young in Life and Death: A Medical Overview." *Journal of Mormon History* 5 (1978): 79–103.

Campbell, Eugene E. "Brigham Young's Outer Cordon—A Reappraisal." *Utah Historical Quarterly* 41 (Summer 1973): 220–53.

Clark, Bruce B. *Brigham Young on Education.* Provo, Utah, 1970.

Cluff, W. W. "An Incident in the Life of President Brigham Young." *The Improvement Era* 4 (June 1901): 570–72.

Coates, Larry G., ed. "George Catlin, Brigham Young and the Plains Indians." *BYU Studies* 17 (Autumn 1976): 114–18.

Cornwall, Rebecca, and Palmer, Richard F. "The Religious and Family Background of Brigham Young." *BYU Studies* 18 (Spring 1978): 286–310.

Croft, David James. "The Private Business Activities of Brigham Young, 1847–1877." *Journal of the West* 16 (October 1977): 36–51.

D'Arc, James V. "Saints on Celluloid: The Making of the Movie 'Brigham Young.' " *Sunstone* 1 (Fall 1976): 11–28.

Derr, Jill Mulvay. "Woman's Place in Brigham Young's World." *BYU Studies* 18 (Spring 1978): 377–95.

England, Eugene. "Brigham Young as a Missionary." *The New Era* 7 (November 1977): 30–37; "Brigham and Joseph." *The New Era* 7 (December 1977): 43–50; and "Brigham's Gospel Kingdom." *BYU Studies* 18 (Spring 1978): 328–76.

Esplin, Ronald K. "Brigham Young and the Priesthood Denial to the Blacks: An Alternate View." *BYU Studies* 19 (Spring 1979): 394–402; and "From the Rumors to the Records: Historians and the Sources for Brigham Young." *BYU Studies* 18 (Spring 1978): 453–65.

Esplin, Ronald K., ed. "The Willard Richards and Brigham Young 5 September 1840 Letter from England to Nauvoo." *BYU Studies* 18 (Spring 1978): 466–75.

Felt, Alma Elizabeth Miner. "As a Pioneer Girl Remembers Brigham Young." *The Improvement Era* 42 (July 1939): 412.

Gates, Susa Young. "From Impulsive Girl to Patient Wife: Lucy Bigelow Young." *Utah Historical Quarterly* 45 (Summer 1977): 270–88. Edited by Miriam B. Murphy; and "Family Life among the Mormons by a Daughter of Brigham Young." *The North American Review* 150 (1890): 239–350.

Hicks, Michael. "Notes on Brigham Young's Aesthetics." *Dialogue* 16 (Winter 1983): 124–30.

Hinckley, Bryant S. "Brigham Young as I Knew Him." *The Instructor* 90 (June 1956): 163–72.

Hunter, Milton, R. "Brigham Young, Colonizer." *Pacific Historical Review* (December 1937): 341–60.

Irving, Gordon. "Encouraging the Saints: Brigham Young's Annual Tours of Mormon Settlements." *Utah Historical Quarterly* 45 (Summer 1977): 233–51.

James, Rhett S., ed. "Brigham Young–Chief Washakie, Indian Farm Negotiations." *Annals of Wyoming* 39 (October 1967): 245–56.

Jessee, Dean C. "Brigham Young's Family, Part I, 1824–1845." *BYU Studies* 18 (Spring 1978): 311–27; "Brigham Young's Family: The Wilderness Years." *BYU Studies* 19 (Summer 1979): 474–500; "The Prophet's [Brigham Young] Letters to His Sons." *The Ensign* 4 (March and April 1974): 63–69; and "The Writings of Brigham Young." *The Western Historical Quarterly* 4 (July 1973): 273–94.

Kimball, Solomon F. "President Brigham Young's Excursion Party." *The Improvement Era* 14 (January–March 1911): 189–210, 311–21, 415–21, 507–12; and "President Brigham Young's First Trip to Bear Lake Valley." *The Improvement Era* 10 (February 1907): 296ff.

Kimball, Stanley B. "Brigham and Heber." *BYU Studies* 18 (Spring 1978): 396–409.

Knight, William H. "Interviewing Brigham Young in 1859." *Journal of American History* 2: 112–17.

Lambourne, Alfred. "Meeting a Great Man." *The Improvement Era* 21 (June 1918): 661–67.

Lyon, T. Edgar. "Nauvoo and the Council of the Twelve." In *The Restoration Movement: Essays in Mormon History.* Edited by F. Mark McKiernan et al. Lawrence, Kansas, 1973, pp. 167–205.

Madsen, Truman G. "Notes on the Succession of Brigham Young." *Seminar on Brigham Young, 1962.* Provo, Utah, 1963, pp. 3–12.

Melville, J. Keith. "Brigham Young's Ideal Society: The Kingdom of God." *BYU Studies* 5 (Autumn 1962): 3–18; and "Brigham Young on Politics and Priesthood." *BYU Studies* 10 (Summer 1970): 488–90; and "Theory and Practice of Church and State During the Brigham Young Era." *BYU Studies* 3 (Autumn 1960): 33–55.

Moorman, Donald R. "Shadows of Brigham Young as Seen by His Biographers." *Utah Historical Quarterly* 45 (Summer 1977): 252–64.

Morgan, Dale L. "The Administration of Indian Affairs in Utah, 1851–1858." *Pacific Historical Review* 17 (November 1948): 383–409.

Munro, Wilford A. "Among the Mormons in the Days of Brigham Young." *Proceedings of the American Antiquarian Society*, New Series, 36 (1926): 214–30.

Myers, Chester J. "Brigham Young as a Public Speaker." *The Improvement Era* 44 (June 1941): 333, 377–78.

Nibley, Hugh. "Brigham Young and the Enemy." *The Young Democrat.* Provo, Utah, n.d.; "Brigham Young on the Environment." In *To the Glory of God: Mormon Essays on the Great Issues.* Edited by Truman G. Madsen and Charles Tate. Salt Lake City, 1972, pp. 3–29; and "Educating the Saints—a Brigham Young Mosaic." *BYU Studies* 11 (Autumn 1970): 61–87.

Nibley, Preston. "Brigham Young in Nauvoo." *The Improvement Era* 73 (November 1970): 54–57 [appeared originally in 29 (December 1925): 95–107].

O'Neil, Floyd A. "Of Pride and Politics: Brigham Young as Indian Superintendent." *Utah Historical Quarterly* 46 (Summer 1978): 236–50.

Quinn, D. Michael. "Brigham Young, Man of the Spirit." *The Ensign* 7 (August 1977): 34–37; and "The Mormon Succession Crisis of 1844." *BYU Studies* 16 (Winter 1976): 187–233.

Roberts, B. H. "Brigham Young—a Character Sketch." *The Improvement Era* 6 (June 1903): 561–74.

Savage, C. R. "A Trip South with President Brigham Young in 1870." *The Improvement Era* 3 (February, March, April 1900): 293–99, 363–69, 431–36.

Searle, Howard C. "Authorship of the History of Brigham Young: A Review Essay." *BYU Studies* 22 (Summer 1982): 367–74.

Taylor, P. A. M. "Early Mormon Loyalty and the Leadership of Brigham Young." *Utah Historical Quarterly* 30 (1961): 102–32; and "The Life of Brigham Young—a Biography Which Will Not Be Written." *Dialogue* 1 (Autumn 1966): 101–10.

Walker, Ronald W., and Esplin, Ronald K. "Brigham Himself: An Autobiographical Recollection." *Journal of Mormon History* 4 (1977): 19–34.

Watt, Ronald G. "Calligraphy in Brigham Young's Office." *Utah Historical Quarterly* 45 (Summer 1977): 265–70.

Wells, Junius F. "President Young's Northern Trip—1870." *Utah Genealogical and Historical Magazine* 14 (April 1923): 49–61.

Widtsoe, Leah D. "Remember Brigham Young." *The Improvement Era* 64 (June 1961): 384–85, 449.

Wilcox, Linda P. "The Imperfect Science: Brigham Young on Medical Doctors." *Dialogue* 12 (Autumn 1979): 26–36.

Theses and dissertations on Brigham Young include:

Bollinger, David Lawrence. "An Historical Investigation of the Recreational Philosophy, Views, Practices and Activities of Brigham Young." Master's thesis, Brigham Young University, 1972.

Esplin, Ronald K. "The Emergence of Brigham Young and the Twelve to Mormon Leadership, 1830–1841." Ph.D. dissertation, Brigham Young University, 1981.

Furr, Carl J. "The Religious Philosophy of Brigham Young." Ph.D. dissertation, University of Chicago, 1937.

Gowans, Frederick R. "A History of Brigham Young's Indian Superintendency (1851–1857), Problems and Accomplishments." Master's thesis, Brigham Young University, 1963.

Hunter, Milton R. "Brigham Young the Colonizer." Ph.D. dissertation, University of California, Berkeley, 1936.

Johnston, William James. "The Educational Views and Practices of Brigham Young." Master's thesis, Brigham Young University, 1968.

Larche, Douglas Wayne. "The Mantle of the Prophet: A Rhetorical Analysis of the Quest for Mormon Post-Martyrdom Leadership, 1844–1860." Ph.D. dissertation, Indiana University, 1977.

Lees, Georgiana Taylor. "The Cultural Aspects, particularly as they relate to Speech and Theatre, of the Descendants of Four Families of Brigham Young." Master's thesis, University of Utah, 1952.

Lloyd, Wesley P. "An Analysis of the Social Philosophies of Brigham Young and John Calvin with Special Reference to Their Similarities as They Were Expressed through the Utah and Geneva Theocracies." Master's thesis, Brigham Young University, 1934.

Marlow, H. Carleton. "Brigham Young's Philosophy of History." Master's thesis, Brigham Young University, 1959.

Melville, J. Keith. "The Political Philosophy of Brigham Young." Master's thesis, University of California, Berkeley, 1949; and "The Political Ideas of Brigham Young." Ph.D. dissertation, University of Utah, 1956.

Myers, Chester James. "A Critical Analysis and Appraisal of the Work of Brigham Young as a Public Speaker." Ph.D. dissertation, University of Southern California, 1940.

Searle, Howard C. "Early Mormon Historiography: Writing the History of the Mormons, 1830–1858." Ph.D. dissertation, University of California, Los Angeles, 1979, chapter 7, pp. 337–57, "The History of Brigham Young."

Stevens, Thomas M. "The Union Pacific Railroad and the Mormon Church, 1868–1871: An In-depth Study of the Financial Aspects of Brigham Young's Grading Contract and Its Ultimate Settlement." Master's thesis, Brigham Young University, 1972.

Wood, Dale Glen. "Brigham Young's Activities in St. George during the Later Years of His Life." Master's thesis, Brigham Young University, 1963.

INDEX

Young, Vilate, daughter, 16, 33, 54, 87, 90, 105, 108, 110, 112, 127, 334, 420

Young, Willard, son, 367, 393–4

Young, Zina, daughter, 171, 399, 420; *see also* Williams, Zina Young

Young, Zina D. H. Jacobs, plural wife, 120–1, 171, 338–9

Young Ladies' Mutual Improvement Association (YLMIA), 353, 370

Young Ladies' Retrenchment Association, 352–3, 370

Young Men's Mutual Improvement Association (YMMIA), 370–1

Y. X. Company, *see* Brigham Young Express and Carrying Company

Zion (City of God), 37, 205–6, 403

Zion's Camp, 38–46, 47–8, 52, 72, 127

Zion's Cooperative Mercantile Institution (ZCMI), 350–1, 391, 398, 428

Zion's Savings Bank & Trust Company, 423–4

A NOTE ABOUT THE AUTHOR

Leonard J. Arrington was born in Twin Falls, Idaho, in 1917. Educated at the universities of Idaho and North Carolina, he is the author of several books on the history of the Mormons and the American West, among them *Great Basin Kingdom: An Economic History of the Latter-day Saints, 1830–1900* (1958) and *The Mormon Experience: A History of the Latter-day Saints* (1979), co-authored with Davis Bitton. He is also a regular contributor to many scholarly journals and has received a number of awards, including the 1984 Western History Association Special Award for Distinguished Writing in Western History. Prof. Arrington has taught at North Carolina State, UCLA, and Utah State University and since 1972 has been Lemuel Redd Professor of Western History at Brigham Young University. He is the former Director of the History Division of the Church of Jesus Christ of Latter-day Saints.

Mormon History from the
University of Illinois Press

MORMONISM IN
TRANSITION
The Latter-day Saints and Their
Church, 1890-1930
THOMAS G. ALEXANDER

JOSEPH SMITH AND THE BE-
GINNINGS OF MORMONISM
RICHARD L. BUSHMAN

NAUVOO
Kingdom on the Mississippi
ROBERT BRUCE FLANDERS

RELIGION AND SEXUALITY
The Shakers, the Mormons, and
the Oneida Community
LAWRENCE FOSTER

HEBER C. KIMBALL
Mormon Patriarch and Pioneer
STANLEY B. KIMBALL

THE SAINTS AND
THE UNION
The Utah Territory during the
Civil War
E. B. LONG

POLITICAL DELIVERANCE
The Mormon Quest for Utah
Statehood
EDWARD LEO LYMAN

CARTHAGE CONSPIRACY
The Trial of the Accused Assas-
sins of Joseph Smith
DALLIN H. OAKS AND MARVIN S.
HILL

STUDIES OF THE BOOK
OF MORMON
B. H. ROBERTS

MORMON THUNDER
A Documentary History of Jede-
diah Morgan Grant
GENE A. SESSIONS

MORMONISM
The Story of a New Religious
Tradition
JAN SHIPPS

759

LINCOLN CHRISTIAN COLLEGE

289.332
.Y689 A